CONSTITUTION MAKING DURING STATE BUILDING

How can fragmented and divided societies that are not immediately compatible with centralized statehood best adjust to state structures? This book argues that the answer to this question rests in part on the role that constitution making can play in state building. This book is an exercise in both comparative constitutional law and comparative politics, as it proposes the idea of a constituent process, whereby public participation in constitution making plays a positive role in state building. Public participation can help to foster a sense of political community and to produce a constitution that enhances the legitimacy and efectiveness of state institutions, because a liberal-local hybrid can emerge to balance international liberal practices with local customary ones. This book represents a sustained attempt to examine the role that public participation has played during state building and the consequences it has had for the performance of the state. It is also the first attempt to conduct a detailed empirical study of the role played by the liberal-local hybrid approach in state building.

Joanne Wallis is a lecturer in the School of International, Political and Strategic Studies at the Australian National University. She has previously taught at the University of Cambridge, the University of Melbourne, and Swinburne University. She completed her PhD in politics and international studies at the University of Cambridge in 2011. From January 2009 to January 2012, she was an honorary fellow of the School of Social and Political Sciences at the University of Melbourne. In 2006, she was a Fulbright Scholar at the Walker Institute of International and Area Studies at the University of South Carolina. She has also worked as a lawyer and has conducted research consultancies for Australian and international NGOs. Her research considers the role that constitution making plays in building states and nations in postconflict societies, with a particular emphasis on the opportunities for engagement between liberal and local approaches to law, governance, and development.

Constitution Making during State Building

JOANNE WALLIS

Australian National University

CAMBRIDGE
UNIVERSITY PRESS

University Printing House, Cambridge CB2 8BS, United Kingdom

Cambridge University Press is part of the University of Cambridge.

It furthers the University's mission by disseminating knowledge in the pursuit of education, learning and research at the highest international levels of excellence.

www.cambridge.org
Information on this title: www.cambridge.org/9781107666658

© Joanne Wallis 2014

This publication is in copyright. Subject to statutory exception
and to the provisions of relevant collective licensing agreements,
no reproduction of any part may take place without the written
permission of Cambridge University Press.

First published 2014
First paperback edition 2016

A catalogue record for this publication is available from the British Library

Library of Congress Cataloguing in Publication data
Wallis, Joanne, author.
Constitution making during state building / Joanne Wallis.
    pages   cm
ISBN 978-1-107-06471-3 (Hardback)
1. Constitutional law–Timor-Leste–Interpretation and construction. 2. Constitutional law–Papua New Guinea–Bougainville Island–Interpretation and construction.   3. Political participation–Timor-Leste.   4. Political participation–Papua New Guinea–Bougainville Island.   5. Constituent power–Timor-Leste.   6. Constituent power–Papua New Guinea–Bougainville Island.   7. Representative government and representation–Timor-Leste.   8. Representative government and representation–Papua New Guinea–Bougainville Island.   I. Title.
KNC539.W35 2014
342.598702′9–dc23   2014014327

ISBN 978-1-107-06471-3 Hardback
ISBN 978-1-107-66665-8 Paperback

Cambridge University Press has no responsibility for the persistence or accuracy of URLs for external or third-party internet websites referred to in this publication, and does not guarantee that any content on such websites is, or will remain, accurate or appropriate.

For my parents,
LORRAINE AND GREGORY WALLIS

Contents

List of maps	page ix
List of tables	x
Acknowledgments	xi
List of acronyms	xv
Introduction	1
PART I NORMATIVE JUSTIFICATION FOR A CONSTITUENT PROCESS	15
1 The normative justification	17
2 A constituent process	40
PART II MINIMAL PARTICIPATION IN TIMOR-LESTE	73
3 State building and constitution making in Timor-Leste	75
4 Constituent power in Timor-Leste	109
5 Constituted power in Timor-Leste	148
PART III EXTENSIVE PARTICIPATION IN BOUGAINVILLE	193
6 State building and constitution making in Bougainville	195
7 Constituent power in Bougainville	229
8 Constituted power in Bougainville	261

PART IV COMPARING THE TWO CASES AND CONCLUSIONS 301

9 Comparing the constitution-making processes 303

10 The role of a constituent process in state building 315

Conclusion 345
Bibliography 351
Index 395

Maps

1 Melanesia　　　*page* xiii
2 Timor-Leste　　　xiii
3 Bougainville　　　xiv

Tables

1 Timor-Leste development indicators *page* 170
2 Bougainville development indicators 281

Acknowledgments

This book has grown from my PhD research, and I gratefully acknowledge my PhD supervisor at the University of Cambridge, James Mayall. In one of our last supervisions, James observed that I had undergone an "intellectual transformation" during my time in Cambridge. To the extent that I did, it was in large part due to the confidence and inspiration that I gained from his supervision and friendship. I was fortunate to have my PhD examined by leading scholars in the fields of liberal-local hybridity, Oliver Richmond, and constitution making, Barbara Metzger. The advice and encouragement that they gave me greatly contributed to the development of my PhD research into this book.

During my PhD, I received generous financial support from the Cambridge Commonwealth Trust via a Poynton Cambridge Australia Scholarship and travel and fieldwork funding. I also received financial support from Wolfson College via a Wolfson College Commonwealth Studentship and travel funding. My studies were facilitated by the Overseas Research Studentship I received from the University of Cambridge, and my fieldwork was supported by grants from the Mary Euphrasia Morely, Sir Bartle Frere, and Worts Travel Funds and the Smuts Memorial Fund.

Many people gave their time to assist me during my fieldwork. I am grateful to the Timorese and Bougainvilleans who so graciously and patiently helped me to understand their experiences and aspirations, particularly my Timorese research assistant, Detaviana Madalena Guterres Freitas, who worked with me in 2013. I hope that the admiration that I have for the courage, generosity, and resilience of ordinary Timorese and Bougainvilleans is evident throughout this book.

After finishing my PhD, I was fortunate to take up a position as a lecturer in the Strategic and Defence Studies Centre in the School of International, Political and Strategic Studies at the Australian National University in Canberra.

I gratefully acknowledge the support and encouragement of the head of the center, Brendan Taylor; the school research director, Joan Beaumont; and the school education director, Ian Hall. I also thank my colleagues in the center, particularly for their comments during our Work In Progress seminar, including John Blaxland, Richard Brabin-Smith, Emma Campbell, Andrew Carr, Paul Dibb, Russell Glenn, Daniel Marston, Charles Miller, and Garth Pratten. I also thank my colleagues in the Asian Security Reading Group for their feedback, particularly David Envall, Luke Glanville, Evelyn Goh, Andy Kennedy, Amy King, and Yongwook Ryu. I gratefully acknowledge the financial support provided by the center and by the Research School of Asia and the Pacific at the university for my additional fieldwork.

On moving to Canberra, I was also fortunate to meet my partner, Ross, whom I thank for his love, understanding, and support while I finalized this book. Most importantly, I thank my parents, Lorraine and Greg, and my brother, Mark. Everything I am and have done is due to their love, encouragement, and support.

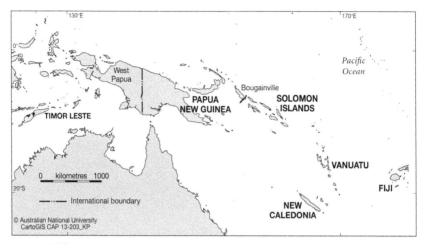

MAP 1 – Melanesia

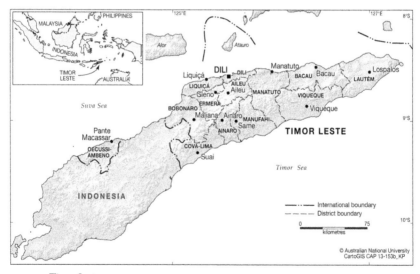

MAP 2 – Timor-Leste

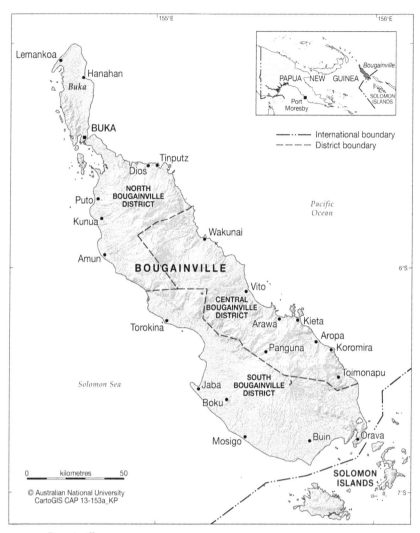

MAP 3 – Bougainville

Acronyms

ABG	– Autonomous Bougainville Government
AMP	– Aliança da Maioria Parlamentar (Alliance of the Parliamentary Majority)
APODETI	– Associação Popular Democratica Timorense (Timorese Popular Democratic Association)
ASDT	– Associação Social Democrata Timorense (Timorese Social Democratic Association)
BCC	– Bougainville Constitutional Commission
BCL	– Bougainville Copper Limited
BFF	– Bougainville Freedom Fighters
BGK	– Bloku Governu Koligasaun (Government Coalition Block)
BIG	– Bougainville Interim Government
BIPG	– Bougainville Interim Provincial Government
BPC	– Bougainville People's Congress
BPS	– Bougainville Police Service
BRA	– Bougainville Revolutionary Army
BRF	– Bougainville Resistance Forces
BTG	– Bougainville Transitional Government
CAPS	– Community Auxiliary Police Service
CAVR	– Comissão de Acolhimento, Verdade e Reconciliaçao (Commission for Reception, Truth and Reconciliation)
CNRT	– Congresso Nacional de Reconstrução de Timor-Leste (National Congress for the Reconstruction of Timor-Leste)
(The) CNRT	– Conselho Nacional da Resistencia Timorense (The National Council of Timorese Resistance)
CPD-RDTL	– Council for the Popular Defence of the Democratic Republic of Timor-Leste
CTF	– Truth and Friendship Commission (Indonesia–Timor-Leste)

ETPA	– East Timor Public Administration
ETTA	– East Timor Transitional Administration
FALINTIL	– Forças Armadas de Libertação Nacional de Timor-Leste (Armed Forces for the National Liberation of East Timor)
F-FDTL	– FALINTIL-Forças de Defesa de Timor Leste (FALINTIL-Defence Force of Timor-Leste)
FRELIMO	– Frente de Libertação de Moçambique (Liberation Front of Mozambique)
FRETILIN	– Frente Revolucionaria de Timor Leste Independente (Revolutionary Front for an Independent Timor)
GDP	– gross domestic product
IDPs	– internally displaced persons
InterFET	– International Force for East Timor
JSB	– Joint Supervisory Body
KOTA	– Klibur Oan Timor Aswain (Association of Timorese Warrior Sons)
LPV	– limited preferential voting
MDF	– Me'ekamui Defence Force
MGU	– Me'ekamui Government of Unity
MHRs	– members of the House of Representatives (Bougainville)
MP	– member of Parliament
NSPG	– North Solomons Provincial Government
OMG	– Original Me'ekamui Government
PD	– Partido Democratica (Democratic Party)
PDL	– Programa Dezenvolvimentu Lokal (Decentralized Development Program)
PMG	– Peace Monitoring Group
PNGDF	– Papua New Guinea Defence Force
PNTL	– Policia Nacional de Timor-Leste (National Police of Timor-Leste)
POLRI	– Polisi Republik Indonesia (Indonesian National Police)
PPT	– Partido do Povo de Timor (People's Party of Timor)
PSD	– Partido Socialista Democratica (Social Democrat Party)
PST	– Partido Socialista de Timor (Socialist Party of Timor)
RPNGC	– Royal Papua New Guinea Constabulary
TMG	– Truce Monitoring Group
UDT	– União Democratica Timorense (Timorese Democratic Union)
UN	– United Nations
UNDP	– United Nations Development Programme

UNMISET	– United Nations Mission of Support in East Timor
UNMIT	– United Nations Integrated Mission in Timor-Leste
UNOMB	– United Nations Observer Mission in Bougainville
UNTAET	– United Nations Transitional Administration in East Timor
UNTAS	– Uni Timor Aswain (Union on Timorese Heroes)
WILMO	– Wisai Liberation Movement

Introduction

Since the end of the Cold War, the international community has engaged in a series of state-building operations in new and postconflict states. State building is supposed to help states achieve control over their territories, gain the loyalty of their populations, and build durable, centralized institutions that hold a monopoly over the legitimate use of physical force.[1] Many of these operations have been guided by the "liberal peace,"[2] which is based on the theory that liberal democratic states are more inclined to respect the rights of their citizens and less likely to go to war with democratic neighbors.[3] These operations have consequently aimed at institutionalizing the main tenets of the liberal peace – democratization, the rule of law, human rights, and free-market economies – often via the new constitution.[4]

The results of many liberal peace state-building operations have not been promising, as states have remained weak, or in some cases have lapsed into

---

[1] The distinction between state building and nation building is addressed in Chapter 1.
[2] High Level Panel on Threats, Challenges and Change, *Report of the Secretary-General's High Level Panel on Threats, Challenges and Change*, UN Doc. A/59/565, December 1, 2004; ICISS, *The Responsibility to Protect: Report of the International Commission on Intervention and State Sovereignty* (Ottawa: International Development Research Centre, 2001).
[3] M. Doyle, "Three Pillars of the Liberal Peace," *American Political Science Review* 99:3 (2005): 463–466.
[4] O. P. Richmond, "The Problem of Peace: Understanding the 'Liberal Peace,'" *Conflict, Security & Development* 6:3 (2006): 291–314. Note that Mac Ginty identifies the "risk of overestimating the power and coherence of the liberal peace," with liberal peace state building "so fraught with contradictions that it is not even consistent in its own support of liberal goals." R. Mac Ginty, "Hybrid Peace: The Interaction Between Top-Down and Bottom-Up Peace," *Security Dialogue* 41:4 (2010): 395, 406. Moreover, Chandler questions whether institutionalizing the tenets of the liberal peace is actually the goal of many recent international interventions, and argues that many have instead aimed for "*status quo* aspirations" of stability and security. D. Chandler, "The Uncritical Critique of 'Liberal Peace,'" *Review of International Studies* 36:1 (2010): 148.

conflict again. These effects have been most obvious in Afghanistan, Iraq, and parts of Asia, the Balkans, and Africa, where state institutions have struggled to achieve control over, or the loyalty of, their fragmented and divided societies. While liberal democratic institutions evolved gradually in most states that are considered to be consolidated liberal democracies, in new and postconflict states they are frequently delivered before the transition "from feudalism to landlordism and from landlordism to modern democracy"[5] has occurred. As a result, the capacity of these institutions is often poor and local sociopolitical institutions remain resilient, which means that state institutions are not necessarily embedded in society. How, then, can fragmented and divided societies that are not immediately compatible with centralized statehood best be accommodated and adjust to state structures?

THE ARGUMENT

This book argues that the answer to this question rests in part on the role that constitution making can play in state building. Constitution making can play a central role in state building because a constitution can represent a tangible manifestation of the social contract that creates state institutions, provides a legal framework for the exercise of state power, and establishes the relationship between the people and their government. Therefore, constitution making is an "inherently political,"[6] "distinctive object of positive analysis,"[7] because constitutions perform not only the technical role of providing the "operating system" that establishes state institutions and regulates state power,[8] but also a foundational role by defining the political bond between the people and embedding state institutions in society.[9] This suggests that the process of constitution making should be viewed not only as a technical exercise conducted by constitutional lawyers, but also as an important political process for political scientists and a practical one for practitioners.

---

[5] I. Jennings, *The Approach to Self-Government* (Cambridge: Cambridge University Press, 1956), 3.
[6] V. Hart, "Constitution Making and the Right to Take Part in a Public Affair," in *Framing the State in Times of Transition: Case Studies in Constitution Making*, ed. L. E. Miller (Washington: U.S. Institute of Peace Press, 2010), 20.
[7] J. Elster, "Ways of Constitution-Making," in *Democracy's Victory and Crisis: Nobel Symposium No. 93*, ed. A. Hadenius (Cambridge: Cambridge University Press, 1997), 123.
[8] S. F. Kreimer, "Invidious Comparisons: Some Cautionary Remarks on the Process of Constitutional Borrowing," *University of Pennsylvania Journal of Constitutional Law* 1 (1999): 640.
[9] B. Kissane and N. Sitter, "National Identity and Constitutionalism in Europe: Introduction," *Nations and Nationalism* 16:1 (2010): 1–5; H. Lerner, *Making Constitutions in Deeply Divided Societies* (Cambridge: Cambridge University Press, 2011).

As the liberal principle of popular sovereignty holds that ultimate political authority resides in the political will or consent of the people,[10] this implies that, at least in states that aspire to be liberal democracies, people should be given the opportunity to participate in making their state's constitution.[11] Despite this, a study of 194 cases of constitution making since 1975 found that only one-third involved some form of public participation.[12] Instead, constitutions have tended to be made by political elites and/or international state builders with little public participation, partly because liberal theorists understand the principle of popular sovereignty in hypothetical terms, as what individuals would agree to if they were acting rationally, rather than as requiring their actual consent.

In new states, the assumptions on which liberal democracy are based require a "shift in the popular sovereignty stories we find plausible."[13] Inviting the people to participate in constitution making reflects the original intent of the principle of popular sovereignty by recognizing that the state cannot be legitimate without the voices of all of its people being involved in a discussion about its purpose. This book argues that public participation[14] in constitution making can play a particularly important role in state building because it can provide fragmented and divided societies with the opportunity to resolve their grievances, agree upon common values and norms, and work out how they are going to be best accommodated and adjust to the transition to statehood.

Despite the important role that constitution making can play in state building, scholars and practitioners have lamented that there is not enough research on the impact of constitution-making processes. Scholarship in comparative constitutional law and comparative politics has "deemphasized

[10] J. J. Rousseau, *The Social Contract and Other Later Political Writings*, ed. V. Gourevitch (Cambridge: Cambridge University Press, 1997).
[11] F. Michelman, "Is the Constitution a Contract for Legitimacy?," *Review of Constitutional Studies* 8 (2003): 101–128.
[12] In just over 30 percent, more than one technique for soliciting views was used, and in 25 percent, consultation efforts extended to remote as well as urban locations. J. A. Widner, "Constitution Writing and Conflict Resolution Project," Princeton University, accessed March 6, 2010, www.princeton.edu/~pcwcr/; J. A. Widner, "Constitution Writing and Conflict Resolution," *The Round Table* 94:381 (2005): 503–518.
[13] S. Chambers, "Democracy, Popular Sovereignty, and Constitutional Legitimacy," *Constellations* 11:2 (2004): 153.
[14] The term "public" is used to describe popular participation, rather than to denote a distinction between participation that occurs in what are often characterized as the "public" (that is, formal) and "private" (informal) spheres of social life. It would be false to draw such a distinction, given that the line between the two spheres is often blurred and that much participation occurs in what is often considered the informal sphere.

the constitution-making process itself as an object of study."[15] As a result, our knowledge of constitution-making processes and their consequences is "cloudy at best."[16] This is surprising given that a study of every independent state between 1789 and 2005 identified 935 different constitutional systems,[17] which suggests that constitutionalism has become a "globally shared mode of organising socio-political formations."[18]

Our knowledge of the role that public participation can play in constitution making is even cloudier. The literature has not progressed far beyond speculation about what benefits public participation in constitution making may offer, and there have been few empirical studies of the benefits of public participation both during the constitution-making process and in its aftermath.[19] Scholars and practitioners have lamented that "there is too little research on the impact of public consultation in constitution-making processes."[20] Accordingly, this book represents a sustained attempt to examine the role that public participation has played during state building and the consequences it has had for the performance of the state.

The emerging emphasis on popular sovereignty as requiring actual, rather than hypothetical, participation has also generated a growing literature that critiques the liberal peace project and the elite-led state-building operations undertaken in its name. These critiques converge on the emerging consensus that the principle of popular sovereignty requires state builders to engage in "unscripted conversations"[21] about the design of the state with individuals and communities in the everyday spaces where they live.[22] The critical literature posits that holding these conversations will result in a "post-liberal peace" or "liberal-local" approach.[23]

---

[15] D. Landau, "The Importance of Constitution-Making," *Denver University Law Review* 89:3 (2012): 612; M. Brandt et al., *Constitution-Making and Reform: Options for the Process* (Switzerland: Interpeace, 2011).

[16] J. Blount, Z. Elkins, and T. Ginsburg, "Does the Process of Constitution-Making Matter?" in *Comparative Constitutional Design*, ed. T. Ginsburg (New York: Cambridge University Press, 2012), 31.

[17] Z. Elkins, T. Ginsburg, and J. Melton, *The Endurance of National Constitutions* (New York: Cambridge University Press, 2009).

[18] J. Go, "A Globalizing Constitutionalism? Views from the Postcolony, 1945–2000," in *Constitutionalism and Political Reconstruction*, ed. S. A. Arjomand (Leiden: Brill, 2007), 90; B. Ackerman, "The Rise of World Constitutionalism," *Virginia Law Review* 83 (1997): 771–802.

[19] This literature is reviewed in Chapter 1.   [20] Brandt et al., *Constitution-Making and Reform*.

[21] M. Duffield, *Development, Security and Unending War* (London: Polity, 2007), 234.

[22] M. de Certeau, *The Practice of Everyday Life* (Berkeley: University of California Press, 1984); O. P. Richmond, "Resistance and the Post-liberal Peace," *Millennium* 38:3 (2010): 665–692.

[23] O. P. Richmond, "A Post-liberal Peace: Eirenism and the Everyday," *Review of International Studies* 35:3 (2009): 557–580. Much of the literature on the liberal-local approach aims to achieve "peace-building," as articulated in Boutros Boutros-Ghali's *An Agenda for Peace*, which describes operations that look beyond building state institutions and seek to engage in a

This approach recognizes the "hybridity"[24] of diverse and competing liberal and local sociopolitical institutions and practices that "co-exist, overlap, interact, and intertwine."[25] Rather than viewing local institutions and practices as spoilers or hurdles to overcome in building a liberal state, this literature focuses on their strength and resilience. From this perspective, it is possible to construct alternative methods of liberal state building that recognize local political agency and work with embedded local sociopolitical practices.

There have been few sustained attempts within the literature on a liberal-local hybrid approach to state building to understand the empirical "dynamics of the relationship between the liberal and the local, and of the interface between the two in terms of everyday life for local communities and actors, as well as for more abstract institutional frameworks" involved in state building.[26] Although the connection has not yet been made in the literature, given that much of the state's apparatus is contained in the constitution, this book argues that the constitution-making process provides one of the most important opportunities for a liberal-local hybrid approach to state building to occur. This book represents the first attempt to understand how a liberal-local hybrid approach can emerge during constitution making, and one of the first attempts to conduct a detailed empirical study of the role played by the liberal-local hybrid approach in state building.

Therefore, this book is an exercise in both comparative constitutional law and comparative politics, as it synthesizes the literature on constitution making and a liberal-local approach to state building to provide a normative justification for public participation in constitution making and a liberal-local hybrid approach to state building. Based on this synthesis, this book proposes the idea of a constituent process, whereby public participation in constitution making plays a positive role in state building by fostering a sense of political community, which is necessary for people to exercise their popular sovereignty, and by producing a constitution that enhances the legitimacy and effectiveness of the state institutions it creates by achieving liberal-local hybridity.

---

    range of political, social, economic, and developmental tasks at both the state and local levels in order to address the multidimensional and multilevel causes of conflict. For the sake of simplicity, and to reflect the involvement of both external and internal agencies and the combination of liberal and local approaches in the case studies, this book uses the term "state building" to refer to all operations in which the institutions of a state are built, regardless of whom they are conducted by and the political ideology that guides them.

[24] H. Bhabha, *The Location of Culture* (London: Routledge, 1994).
[25] V. Boege et al., "Hybrid Political Orders, Not Fragile States," *Peace Review* 21 (2009): 17.
[26] Richmond, "A Post-liberal Peace," 576.

WHY GENERATE A CONSTITUENT PROCESS?

This book tests this normative justification on the cases of Timor-Leste[27] and Bougainville[28] to demonstrate why a constituent process should be generated, in order to identify insights for theory and practice in states and societies facing comparable challenges.

In May 2002, after twenty-four years of Indonesian occupation and almost three years of United Nations (UN) transitional administration, world leaders gathered to celebrate Timor-Leste's independence and declare it a success story of post-Cold War state building. Yet almost four years later, in April and May 2006, Timor-Leste's stability was challenged by a major security crisis that originated between (and within) the police and military but quickly engulfed the wider population. During the crisis, more than one-tenth of the population was internally displaced, many houses and buildings were burned, and thirty-eight people were killed. Although a vastly expanded UN mission and an Australian-led International Stabilization Force were required to restore stability, low-level violence continued and culminated in attempts to assassinate the president and prime minister in February 2008.

Just over three thousand kilometers to the east of Timor-Leste, the Bougainville region of Papua New Guinea signed a peace agreement with the Papua New Guinea government in August 2001 that ended a civil war that had raged since 1989. The war had been partly a secessionist struggle and partly a conflict between Bougainvilleans. The peace agreement gave the region significant autonomy and the right to vote on its political future between 2015 and 2020. With minimal external intervention, between 2001 and 2005 Bougainvilleans built their autonomous government. Since then, they have engaged in extensive reconciliation and have avoided a recurrence of major conflict.

The Timor-Leste and Bougainville cases highlight the challenges and opportunities that arise when new and postconflict states engage in state building. The Timor-Leste state-building operation was chosen for exploration in this book because it was in many ways a paradigmatic example of

---

[27] See Map 2. Timor-Leste is the Portuguese name of the state, which is also referred to in English as East Timor and in Tetum (the local *lingua franca*) as Timor Loro S'ae. Although many English publications use the term "East Timor," as the country is officially designated as the Democratic Republic of Timor-Leste and since the term is now widely used by Timorese people, this book uses the term "Timor-Leste."

[28] See Map 3. Bougainville is officially designated in both the Bougainville and Papua New Guinea Constitutions as the "Autonomous Region of Bougainville." It was also previously known as the "North Solomons Province of Papua New Guinea." This book will use the term "Bougainville" since it is now in common usage within the region.

liberal peace state building,[29] from which lessons could be learned for other state-building operations, such as those in Afghanistan and Iraq. Liberal peace state-building operations had previously been attempted in Cambodia and Liberia and were ongoing in Bosnia and Kosovo at the time that the operation began in Timor-Leste in 1999. However, the Timor-Leste statebuilding operation was the "most expansive assertion of sovereignty" ever assumed by the UN.[30] Therefore, in 1999 Timor-Leste arguably constituted the best case in which a liberal peace state-building operation could be expected to succeed.

Bougainville was chosen for consideration as, for the reasons given below, it shares a number of similarities with Timor-Leste, making it an especially suitable comparator. Bougainville is also one of the first instances of a complex self-determination dispute being successfully settled. Lessons learned from the Bougainville settlement have been applied to other, similar disputes, most notably in Kosovo and South Sudan, and are increasingly being considered elsewhere in the Balkans, Caucus, Africa, and Southeast Asia. Bougainville is also a comparatively rare case of relatively successful state building in a new and postconflict state. Although Bougainville is an autonomous region rather than a sovereign state, it can be characterized as having engaged in state building because it has been given powers that verge on full sovereignty, as well as the option to vote on becoming independent between 2015 and 2020.[31] Along with Somaliland, Bougainville also offers one of the first examples of a liberal-local hybrid state-building operation, where local political and legal pluralism was brought into a critical dialogue with liberalism from the outset.[32] Therefore, the Bougainville case offers guidance concerning how the liberal-local hybrid approach functions in practice and how it may be developed and applied to state building in the future.

Based on its comparative study, this book concludes that the higher the level of public participation involved in constitution making, the more likely it is to generate a constituent process, and consequently to play a positive role in state building. In Bougainville, there was extensive public participation in constitution making, which generated a constituent process that built a

---

[29] J. Wallis, "A Local-Liberal Peace Project in Action? The Increasing Engagement between the Local and Liberal in East Timor," *Review of International Studies* 38:4 (2012): 735–761.
[30] S. Chesterman, "East Timor," in *United Nations Interventionism, 1991–2004*, ed. M. Berdal and S. Economides (Cambridge: Cambridge University Press, 2007), 199.
[31] J. Wallis, "Ten Years of Peace: Assessing Bougainville's Progress and Prospects," *The Round Table* 101:1 (2012): 29–40.
[32] J. Wallis, "Building a Liberal-Local Hybrid Peace and State in Bougainville," *Pacific Review* 25:5 (2012): 613–635.

relatively strong political community by creating a sense of common identity and by reconciling the most severe divisions between societal groups.[33] In contrast, there was minimal public participation in Timor-Leste, which did not generate a constituent process and consequently did not create a unified political community, and certain societal divisions remain unreconciled, while others have become salient. The constituent process generated in the Bougainville process also produced a constitution and state institutions that make sense to Bougainvilleans, as it achieved liberal-local hybridity. In contrast, the Timor-Leste process produced a liberal peace constitution and state institutions that did not recognize the local practices that regulated most Timorese people's lives, which has challenged their legitimacy. It is hoped that these findings contribute not only to the theoretical literature but also at a practical level. The experiences of Timor-Leste and Bougainville as new, postconflict states are not unique and provide lessons for future constitution-making and state-building processes.

TESTING THE ROLE OF A CONSTITUENT PROCESS

In order to test the role played by a constituent process in state building, this book conducts a comparative case study and adopts the "most similar systems" research design.[34] The advantage of conducting a comparative study is that it allows rich qualitative data to be compiled in order to construct a relatively thorough narrative. This can help to clarify the causal link between the level of participation involved in constitution making and the outcomes for state building in more detail than could be achieved by a quantitative analysis. Accordingly, field research, including semistructured interviews with political elites and local leaders and ethnographic observation of local sociopolitical processes, was conducted in Timor-Leste in 2009, 2010, and 2013 and in Bougainville in 2011.[35] This book also constructs a strong normative framework against which to test the comparison so that suggestive generalizations can be drawn. Moreover, the aspects of constitution making in Timor-Leste and Bougainville relevant to this study are sufficiently similar to the rest of the population of constitution-making processes that inferences relating to both theory and practice can be drawn from its findings.

---

[33] However, there are exceptions, as described in Chapter 7.
[34] A. M. Przeworski and H. Teune, *The Logic of Comparative Social Inquiry* (New York: John Wiley, 1970).
[35] For brevity, references to specific field observations are not individually cited. As Timor-Leste and Bougainville are post-conflict societies, all interviews were anonymous to protect interviewees.

Timor-Leste and Bougainville were selected as they differ with respect to the independent variable (the level of participation involved in constitution making), but broadly match across other potentially explanatory variables. In Timor-Leste, the constitution-making process took one year[36] and involved minimal opportunities for public participation. In contrast, in Bougainville, the constitution-making process took over two years[37] and involved an extensive program of public participation. Therefore, differences in the outcomes of these state-building processes can be partly explained by differences in the levels of public participation in their constitution-making processes, and consequently whether a constituent process emerged.

Both Timor-Leste and Bougainville fall within Melanesia, one of three geographical and cultural areas in the South Pacific region.[38] Consequently, both exhibit similar broad cultural and socioeconomic characteristics. Both have relatively small, primarily rural, subsistence populations. They have similar geography, as they consist of islands divided by mountains and rivers, which makes transport and communication difficult. This has created natural barriers that have kept their populations fragmented into small political and linguistic communities. Despite this, their societies are connected via marriage, trade, and – at least in the past – warfare networks.

The territories of Timor-Leste and Bougainville were demarcated by arbitrary European colonial borders. In the sixteenth century, Timor Island was carved in two, with the Dutch claiming the western half[39] and the Portuguese the eastern half (which later became independent Timor-Leste). In 1914, a determination of the Permanent Court of Arbitration formalized this arrangement. In 1960, the UN General Assembly declared that Portuguese Timor was a "non-self-governing" territory. In the nineteenth century, the islands that constitute the contemporary Papua New Guinea and Solomon Islands were annexed by Germany and Britain (which later transferred its colony to Australia). In 1889, Germany ceded all islands in the Solomon archipelago to Britain, apart from Bougainville, which was incorporated into German New Guinea. In exchange, the British transferred sovereignty over Western Samoa to Germany. Australia seized German New Guinea at the beginning of the

---

[36] This is a generous interpretation because it includes preparatory activities. As described in Chapter 3, the drafting process itself took only six months.
[37] If the peace process is included, the process took seven years.
[38] See Map 1. This classification is contested, but the term "Melanesia" is commonly used. The inclusion of Timor-Leste in Melanesia is controversial, although it is becoming more common in academic and policy practice.
[39] With the exception of the small enclave of Oecussi, which was retained by the Portuguese as it was the place they first landed on Timor Island.

First World War and was allocated a "C" Class League of Nations Mandate over it in 1921. After the Second World War, Australia merged the former British and German territories and the UN approved the creation of the combined "non-self governing" Territory of Papua and New Guinea in 1947.

In both cases, the colonial administrations exercised little real control beyond their fortifications until the early twentieth century. Instead, they relied on systems of indirect rule, which allowed indigenous sociopolitical structures to continue relatively undisturbed. Therefore, while colonial penetration disrupted local sociopolitical practices, it did not displace them. Consequently, in both cases state-level institutions are a recent import. However, Portuguese colonizers did attempt limited assimilation by socializing part of the Timorese population to Lusophone culture and language and via intermarriage with local women. While Australia sought to educate Bougainvilleans and to propagate the English language, it was less concerned with acculturation.

After European and Australian decolonization, large portions of the population of both attempted self-determination. However, in 1975 Timor-Leste was occupied by Indonesia and Bougainville was incorporated into Papua New Guinea. Both were then engaged in long – and bloody – struggles, in which their populations sought to exercise their right to self-determination, sometimes in cooperation with each other. There are estimates that at least 10 percent of the Timorese population were killed during the Indonesian occupation, while many more were internally displaced.[40] Similarly, there are estimates that several thousand Bougainvilleans (from a population of 160,000 people) died as a result of the struggle, while up to 40 percent were internally displaced.[41]

These self-determination struggles concluded in 1999 in Timor-Leste and in 2001 in Bougainville, both of which then underwent state-building operations. The Timor-Leste operation was directed by an extensive UN intervention and transitional administration. In Bougainville, the operation was locally led and international intervention was light. In both cases, when these operations began, there were no formal state-level institutions, although

---

[40] CAVR, *Chega! The Report of the Commission for Reception, Truth and Reconciliation in Timor-Leste: Executive Summary* (Dili: Commission for Reception, Truth, and Reconciliation Timor-Leste, 2005).
[41] V. Boege and L. Garasu, "Papua New Guinea: A Success Story of Postconflict Peacebuilding in Bougainville," in *Searching for Peace in Asia Pacific: An Overview of Conflict Prevention and Peacebuilding Activities*, ed. A. Heijmans, N. Simmonds, and H. va de Veen (Boulder: Lynne Rienner, 2004); A. J. Regan, *Light Intervention: Lessons from Bougainville* (Washington: U.S. Institute of Peace Press, 2010).

neither was a political *tabula rasa*, as there were local political institutions and organizations.

Although there are many similarities between the two cases, extraneous variables may affect the conduct and outcome of constitution-making processes, including the nature of any conflict or societal division, culture, languages, geography, history, leadership, resources, and degree of external interest. The size of the relevant state may also be influential. The populations of both Timor-Leste and Bougainville are small, with Timor-Leste's population approximately 1.1 million people and Bougainville's estimated at 300,000. This raises the question of whether generalizations drawn based on these two cases are applicable to states with larger populations, such as those making new constitutions in North Africa and the Middle East in the aftermath of the "Arab Spring." However, Timor-Leste and Bougainville can act as petri dishes in which hypotheses can be tested and developed on a small, relatively manageable scale before they are exposed to the rigors of a larger context. Moreover, as the two cases are small, it is easier to hold the independent variable constant and to limit the effect of extraneous variables, which enhances the validity of the findings.

CHAPTER OUTLINE

In Part I of this book, Chapter 1 outlines the normative justification for public participation in constitution making and a liberal-local hybrid approach to state building. This justification is based on the liberal principle of popular sovereignty, which implies that people should consent to the manner in which their political unit is governed by participating in making their constitution and by deciding the extent to which that constitution – and the state institutions it creates – reflects liberal and local principles. This argument implies that the people exercise their popular sovereignty, or constituent power, to make a constitution, with the constitution then codifying the institutionalization of the people's will in a government, converting their sovereign power into constituted power. This chapter considers the challenges posed by identifying who "the people" are in order to exercise their constituent power and concludes that a process of nation building may be required in order to knit fragmented or divided populations together. It then explores the ways in which state institutions exercise the people's constituted power and outlines the challenge posed to liberal peace state building by the liberal-local hybrid approach. This chapter concludes by proposing the idea of a constituent process.

Chapter 2 examines the idea of a constituent process in more detail. It begins by identifying the main steps involved in most constitution-making processes. It then turns to the literature relating to public participation in constitution making, which has its intellectual foundations in the literature on the benefits of political participation, which in turn has its roots in the literature on deliberative democracy. It identifies five claimed benefits of public participation in constitution making, which can generate a constituent process: first, it can have positive effects on the constitution-making process; second, it may assist people to unite to exercise their constituent power; third, it may encourage reconciliation and the resolution of grievances; fourth, it can encourage individuals to become citizens who recognize the legitimacy of their constitution and the state institutions it creates to exercise their constituted power; and fifth, it can result in a liberal-local hybrid constitution and state institutions that better reflect public understandings and views. Based on this discussion, this chapter identifies indicators that can be used to assess whether a constituent process has occurred and what role it has played in state building.

Part II (Chapters 3–5) applies this normative justification to the case of Timor-Leste, using the indicators identified to assess whether a constituent process occurred and what role it has played in state building. Chapter 3 begins by outlining a brief historical background of Timor-Leste and provides a contextual description of the state-building project. It finds that there was minimal public participation in the constitution-making process.

Chapter 4 assesses whether the minimal public participation affected the creation of constituent power in Timor-Leste. It finds that it did, and consequently that a constituent process was not generated, as there were few opportunities for Timorese to reconcile or to negotiate a unifying sense of national identity to bind together a political community. Instead, the national narrative enshrined in the constitution has actually proved divisive and societal divisions have challenged the state.

Chapter 5 assesses whether the minimal public participation affected the creation of state institutions to exercise the Timorese people's constituted power. It again finds that it did, as a constituent process was not generated and there are consequently questions about the legitimacy and functioning of state institutions, particularly their ability to exercise the Timorese people's constituted power. Most significantly, minimal participation meant that Timorese were not able to advocate the recognition of their local sociopolitical practices, resulting in a gap between them and state institutions. After independence, this gap became evident, and the state has consequently made efforts to engage with the Timorese via the decentralization of political, administrative, and law and order functions. This chapter concludes that, had Timorese been given the opportunity to engage in extensive participation during constitution making, it is likely they would have ensured that their local practices were formally recognized and incorporated into their new state. This might have helped the constitution to create state institutions that were perceived to legitimately exercise their constituted power.

By way of comparison, Part III (Chapters 6–8) applies the normative justification and the indicators identified to the case of Bougainville. Chapter 6 begins by outlining a brief historical background of Bougainville and provides a contextual description of the peace process that led to Bougainville being granted autonomy. It finds that there was extensive public participation in the constitution-making process.

Chapter 7 assesses whether the extensive public participation has created relatively unified constituent power in Bougainville. It finds that it has and attributes this largely to the fact that it generated a constituent process in which different groups negotiated a widely resonant understanding of common identity and resolved their grievances. This chapter concludes that while challenges remain, the constituent process that emerged in Bougainville facilitated extensive reconciliation and helped knit together its divided society and allowed the people to exercise their constituent power.

Chapter 8 assesses whether the extensive public participation played a role in creating state institutions to exercise the Bougainvillean people's constituted power. It finds that institutions have been created and are functioning relatively well. Most significantly, because there was extensive public participation, the constitution provides for decentralization of political, administrative, and law and order functions to local sociopolitical leaders and institutions. Consequently, it has created liberal-local hybrid institutions that make sense to the people whose constituted power they exercise. This has enhanced the legitimacy of both the constitution and the institutions it creates, which has assisted their operation and effectiveness.

Part IV (Chapters 9 and 10) compares the two cases and considers the role that a constituent process can play in state building, so that generalizable conclusions can be drawn relating to the literature and lessons can be learned for future constitution-making processes. Chapter 9 identifies the main points of difference between the two processes as being their time frames, the type of body that drafted their constitutions, the method by which constitution drafters where selected, the manner in which their constitutions were drafted, the levels of publicity and secrecy involved, the opportunities for and role of public participation, the degree of international involvement, and the manner in which their constitutions were adopted. This chapter finds that the constitution-making process in Bougainville better reflects the recommendations made in the literature and that it was in many ways an ideal type of extensive public participation in constitution making. In contrast, the minimal public participation in Timor-Leste meant that it was an elite-led constitution-making process.

Chapter 10 finds that the relatively strong sense of unified political community evident in Bougainville suggests that extensive participation in constitution making will generate a constituent process that assists in building a sense of united constituent power. The minimal participation in Timor-Leste has generated contrary results. In relation to constituted power, it finds that the minimal participation in Timor-Leste saw the creation of state institutions heavily influenced by the liberal peace approach. As the gap between the constitution and the society it sought to govern became obvious, a liberal-local hybrid approach has slowly emerged. In contrast, in Bougainville, the constituent process saw immediate engagement between the liberal and the local, so that liberal-local hybridity was achieved. This suggests that the higher the level of participation involved in constitution making, the more likely it is that the resulting constitution and the institutions it creates will make sense to the society they seek to govern.

PART I
NORMATIVE JUSTIFICATION FOR A CONSTITUENT PROCESS

1

The normative justification

This chapter provides a normative justification for a constituent process. Since building a state is the goal of state building, this chapter begins by defining what a state is. It finds that states are generally considered to require an effective and legitimate government, with the liberal principle of popular sovereignty holding that legitimacy should be drawn from the people's consent, which they express by entering into the social contract. As the constitution is often regarded as the tangible manifestation of the social contract, this implies that the people should exercise their popular sovereignty, or constituent power, to make a constitution, with the constitution then codifying the institutionalization of the people's will in a government, converting their sovereign power into constituted power. This chapter considers the challenges posed by identifying who "the people" are in order to exercise their constituent power and concludes that a process of nation building may be required in order to knit fragmented or divided populations together. It then outlines the ways in which state institutions exercise the people's constituted power and notes that the liberal idea that popular sovereignty can legitimately be exercised only by state institutions through democratic means has guided liberal peace state building. It outlines the challenge posed to liberal peace state building by the liberal-local hybrid approach, which seeks to recognize the ongoing legitimacy and influence of local sociopolitical institutions and practices. This chapter concludes by proposing the idea of a constituent process, whereby public participation in constitution making plays a positive role in state building by fostering a sense of political community and by producing a constitution that enhances the legitimacy and effectiveness of the state institutions it creates by achieving liberal-local hybridity.

WHAT IS A STATE?

In order to provide a normative justification for a constituent process, it is first necessary to define a "state." According to international law, a state has four characteristics: a defined territory, a permanent population, an effective government, and the capacity to enter into formal relations with other states.[1] When an entity is recognized as possessing these characteristics, it is acknowledged as a state and is afforded the right to sovereignty.[2]

There is no particular test of whether a government is effective. The dominant approach owes its origins to Max Weber, who defined an effective government as one "that (successfully) claims the *monopoly of the legitimate use of physical force* within a given territory."[3] Neo-Weberian approaches have expanded this definition to include the government's institutional capacity to deliver public goods and services.[4] However, an effective government also appears to require legitimate authority in order to motivate (or mandate) its citizenry (or subjects) to act as an organized, effective entity. Consequently, a government's institutional capacity and its legitimacy[5] are "mutually constitutive."[6] Therefore, to assess how effectively the governments of Timor-Leste and Bougainville are functioning, Chapters 5 and 8 consider three questions: Have state institutions been created, and are they functioning effectively? Are the state institutions delivering public goods and services? And, are law and order enforced and is the rule of law observed?

THE SOCIAL CONTRACT

According to the liberal principle of popular sovereignty, the legitimacy of a government is drawn from the people's consent, which they express by entering into the social contract. Early analyses of the social contract were

---

[1] Montevideo Convention on Rights and Duties of States, 1933, art. 1.
[2] Charter of the United Nations, 1949, art. 2.
[3] M. Weber, "Science as a Vocation," in *From Max Weber: Essays in Sociology*, ed. H. H. Gerth and C. Wright Mills (New York: Oxford University Press, 1958), 78.
[4] M. Mann, "The Autonomous Power of the State: Its Origins, Mechanisms and Results," in *States in History*, ed. J. A. Hall (Oxford: Basil Blackwell, 1986); R. I. Rotberg, "Failed States, Collapsed States, Weak States: Causes and Indicators," in *State Failure and State Weakness in a Time of Terror*, ed. R. I. Rotberg (Cambridge: Brookings Institution Press, 2003).
[5] Legitimacy is taken to mean the "normative belief by an actor that a rule or institution ought to be obeyed. It is a subjective quality, relational between actor and institution, and defined by the actor's perception of the institution." I. Hurd, "Legitimacy and Authority in International Relations," *International Organization* 53:2 (1999): 381.
[6] N. Lemay-Hébert, "Statebuilding without Nation-Building? Legitimacy, State Failure and the Limits of the Institutionalist Approach," *Journal of Intervention and Statebuilding* 3:1 (2009): 28.

concerned with the contract between the ruler and the ruled.[7] Although the feudal reality of the day meant that this contract was fictitious, "fictions can be powerful, and the idea was to be repeated again and again in the course of European history."[8] In the early sixteenth century, the concept of "political community" emerged, characterized as a partnership among individuals, created by a contract among them.[9] This shifted the understanding of the social contract to one between individuals to create a political community that would establish rule.[10] When accompanied by the emerging belief that all individuals are inherently free and equal, this gave rise to the idea that all legitimate rule is constituted by those who are to be ruled simultaneously agreeing to act in unity and to be bound by that rule.[11]

However, theorists continued to treat the social contract as a fiction because popular sovereignty was understood hypothetically. This was partly because the idea of "the people" was itself a fiction, since in reality the people are not a corporate body capable of speaking in one voice. To navigate past the impracticality of individuals governing themselves by themselves, theorists conceived of the idea of the "general will" to identify what the people would want if they were acting reasonably.[12] This was expanded in the twentieth century to recognize that individuals may have conflicting – as well as common – interests. It was argued that individuals were likely to enter into a social contract only once they had agreed that they would each be offered the protection of basic principles of justice.[13]

THE CONSTITUTION AS SOCIAL CONTRACT

The social contract is "an exercise of the imagination," and no political theorist claims it to be a "historical event."[14] Instead, liberal theorists often regard the constitution as its tangible manifestation, with Thomas Paine

---

[7] The founder of social contract analysis is commonly identified as an Alsatian monk, Manegold of Lautenbach, who lived in the late eleventh century. His ideas were taken up by St. Thomas Aquinas in the mid-thirteenth century and Engelbert of Volkersdorf, the abbot of an Austrian monastery, in the early fourteenth century.

[8] M. Lessnoff, "Introduction: Social Contract," in *Social Contract Theory*, ed. M. Lessnoff (Oxford: Basil Blackwell Ltd, 1990): 6.

[9] This was proposed by Mario Salamonio, a Roman jurist, in *De Principatu* (1511–13).

[10] S. Pufendorf, *On the Law of Nature and Nations, Eight Books*, bk. VIII, ch. i, para. 5.

[11] M. Forsyth, "Hobbe's Contractarianism: A Comparative Analysis," in *The Social Contract from Hobbes to Rawls*, ed. D. Boucher and P. Kelly (London: Routledge, 1994).

[12] Rousseau, *The Social Contract*.

[13] J. A. Rawls, *A Theory of Justice* (Cambridge: The Bellnap Press of Harvard University Press, 1971).

[14] M. Loughlin and N. Walker, "Introduction," in *The Paradox of Constitutionalism: Constituent Power and Constitutional Form*, ed. M. Loughlin and N. Walker (Oxford: Oxford University Press, 2007), 2.

observing that "the constitution of a country is not the act of its government, but of the people constituting its government."[15] This idea was relatively uncontroversial when applied to the early written constitutions adopted in Western states in the late eighteenth century. It was thought possible, following the influence of Abbé de Sieyès, to identify the people's hypothetical general will, according to which they would exercise their popular sovereignty, or constituent power (*pouvoir constituant*), to make a constitution.[16] The constitution then codified the institutionalization of the people's will in a government, converting their sovereign power into constituted power (*pouvoir constitué*).[17] Consequently, constitutions give rise to a paradox: they are established by the people exercising their sovereign power, yet they impose limits and rules on that power. This led Joseph de Maistre to lament that the people "are a sovereign that cannot exercise sovereignty."[18] However, liberal theory argues that it is necessary to impose rules on the people's sovereign power, as there must be self-imposed limits on majority decision making in order for all people to exercise their popular sovereignty equally.[19] This is commonly referred to as the principle of constitutionalism, which holds that limitations should be imposed on the powers of government, the rule of law should be observed, and fundamental human rights should be protected.[20] Therefore, the principle of constitutionalism requires more than a state having a written constitution.[21]

In what has become a widely cited typology, Daniel Elazar has identified five models of constitution. This typology reveals how constitutions have evolved from being unwritten and based on ancient and continuing constitutional traditions, to acting as loose frameworks for governments and guarantors of rights, to representing revolutionary manifestos, then becoming detailed

---

[15] T. Paine, *The Rights of Man*, 1779.
[16] U. K. Preuss, "Constitution-Making and Nation-Building: Reflections on Political Transformations in East and Western Europe," *European Journal of Philosophy* 1:1 (1993): 81–92.
[17] U. K. Preuss, "Constitutional Powermaking for the New Polity: Some Deliberations on the Relations between Constituent Power and the Constitution," *Cardozo Law Review* 14 (1992): 639–660; E. J. Sieyès, *What Is the Third Estate?* ed. S. E. Finer and trans. M. Blondel (New York: Praeger, 1963).
[18] J. de Maistre, *Against Rousseau: "On the State of Nature" and "On the Sovereignty of the People,"* ed. and trans. R. A. Lebrun (Montreal: McGill-Queen's University Press, 1996), 45.
[19] R. A. Dahl, *Democracy and Its Critics* (New Haven: Yale University Press, 1989).
[20] T. Paine, *Common Sense and the Rights of Man*, ed. T. Benn (London: Phoenix Press, 2000); M. Rosenfeld, *Constitutionalism, Identity, Difference, and Legitimacy: Theoretical Perspectives* (Durham: Duke University Press, 1994).
[21] Indeed, some states do not have written constitutions, including the United Kingdom, New Zealand, and Israel.

codes and, finally, long documents that express a political ideal about what citizens believe the state should be.[22] This evolution may be due to decolonization and secessionism, which have seen the creation of states with fragmented or divided societies, and globalization, which has seen the emergence of new political actors.[23] Constitution makers may have decided that a more detailed constitution would create a stronger social contract to unite their populations and to legitimate state institutions in these challenging circumstances.

CONSTITUENT POWER

When written constitutions were being made in well-established Western states, it appeared relatively uncontroversial to argue that the people's hypothetical general will could be identified, even if it generally represented a convenient rhetorical device more than a reflection of actual societal harmony. However, answering the question of who "the people" are, and consequently what their general will would be, is much more difficult in the fragmented and divided societies that populate many new states that have emerged since the latter half of the twentieth century. These new states have developed within an international legal regime dominated by the principle of self-determination. This principle is based on the premise that a people should be able to determine the territorial extent of their sovereign jurisdiction. It received quasi-official recognition at the 1919 Paris Peace Conference. As articulated by Woodrow Wilson, the principle held that a people should be able to self-determine their future political status as they should be "dominated and governed only by their own consent."[24] Yet, as Ivor Jennings points out, this idea is "ridiculous," as "the people cannot decide until somebody decides who are the people."[25]

Despite this inherent paradox, after the Second World War the ideal of self-determination as a categorical right of all colonial peoples was asserted in a number of UN General Assembly resolutions[26] and enshrined in

---

[22] D. J. Elazar, "Constitution-Making: The Pre-eminently Political Act," in *Redesigning the State: The Politics of Constitutional Change*, ed. K. G. Banting and R. Simeon (Toronto: University of Toronto Press, 1985).
[23] K. G. Banting and R. Simeon, "Introduction: The Politics of Constitutional Change," in Banting and Simeon, *Redesigning the State*.
[24] W. Wilson, "Address on War Aims," delivered at a Joint Session of the Two Houses of Congress, Washington, February 18, 1918.
[25] Jennings, *The Approach to Self-Government*, 56.
[26] United Nations General Assembly, A/Res/421, *Draft International Covenant on Humans Rights and Measures of Implementation: Future Work of the Commission on Human Rights*, December 4, 1950; A/Res/637, *The Right of Peoples and Nations to Self-determination*,

international law.[27] In 1960, the application of the principle was effectively limited to situations in which the territorial integrity of a state would not be disrupted. Accordingly, in 1963 the Organisation of African Unity revived the international legal principle of *uti possidetis juris*,[28] which holds that existing boundaries are the preemptive basis for determining territorial jurisdictions in the absence of affected state parties mutually agreeing otherwise.[29] As a result, respect for existing – including artificial colonial – borders was enshrined in international law[30] and the "political map of the world became frozen."[31] This changed the definition of the collective "self," which was no longer determined by a people based on race, ethnicity, religion, or other distinguishing characteristics, but was instead understood to indicate the entire population of a given territory.[32] Therefore, while it has been claimed that "it is for the people to determine the destiny of the territory and not the territory the destiny of the people,"[33] in reality, "the territorial issue *does* come first."[34] Consequently, the process of decolonization was effectively divorced from the idea of popular sovereignty, and a number of new states have emerged that are made up of fragmented or divided societies that do not necessarily share a general will.

This fact has largely been overlooked, and there have been few analyses of the notion of "the people" in recent political theory.[35] This is partly because liberal political theorists assume that all individuals are inherently free and equal to form their own opinion and pursue their particular interests.

December 16, 1952; A/Res/1188, *Recommendations Concerning International Respect for the Right of Peoples and Nations to Self-determination*, December 11, 1957.

[27] United Nations General Assembly, A/Res/1514, *Declaration on the Granting of Independence to Colonial Countries and Peoples*, December 14, 1960; A/Res/2621, *Programme of Action for the Full Implementation of the Declaration on the Granting of Independence to Colonial Countries and Peoples*, October 12, 1970.

[28] This principle was also enshrined in the 1975 Helsinki Final Act. It was reiterated in the 1990 Charter of Paris for a New Europe and was the basis for the 1995 Dayton Agreement.

[29] *Burkina Faso v. Mali Frontier Dispute, Merits*, ICJ Reports (1986), p. 564; *Guinea-Bissau v. Senegal, Arbitral Award*, RGDIP (1990), p. 240; S. R. Ratner, "Drawing a Better Line: Uti Possidetis and the Borders of New States," *American Journal of International Law* 90:4 (1996): 590–624.

[30] In *Opinion No. 2 of the Badinter Arbitration Commission* (1992), 31 ILM 1497.

[31] R. Jackson, *Sovereignty: Evolution of an Idea* (Cambridge: Polity Press, 2007), 107.

[32] R. Jackson, *Quasi-States: Sovereignty, International Relations, and the Third World* (Cambridge: Cambridge University Press, 1990), 77.

[33] J. Dillard, *Western Sahara, Advisory Opinion*, ICJ Reports (1975), 12.

[34] R. Higgins, *Problems and Process: International Law and How We Use It* (Oxford: Clarendon Press, 1994), 127.

[35] M. Canovan, "The People," in *The Oxford Handbook of Political Theory*, ed. J. S. Dryzek, B. Honig, and A. Phillips (Oxford: Oxford University Press, 2006).

As liberalism assumes that individuals are motivated mostly by self-interest, it sees them as the best judges of what this interest requires. In this context, it is claimed that individuals can constitute a political community around a constitution that establishes a neutral set of rules to reconcile and aggregate their individual interests. On this reading, the people are the "demos" rather than the "ethnos," and the "character of the individuals who in fact composed the people" is assumed to be irrelevant.[36] However, this "presupposes the idea of a demotic entity of individuals."[37] Indeed, liberal political theorists generally take for granted that the individuals who constitute "the people" share sufficiently strong normative bonds that it is possible to identify their general will.[38]

Similarly, republican theorists argue that a civic identity,[39] whereby a population makes the rational decision to unify around the state's democratic constitution, can generate sufficient solidarity to constitute people into a political community by generating "constitutional patriotism"[40] or "republican citizenship."[41] They argue that this can be achieved through active citizenship, civic virtue, and the pursuit of public values.[42] Accordingly, republicans advocate enumerating the duties and obligations of citizens in the constitution, since they see each citizen as owing a "debt of responsibility to the society in which he or she lives."[43]

The adoption of purportedly liberal or republican constitutions during the second wave of decolonization, and in most state-building operations since the end of the Cold War, has challenged the assumptions on which liberalism and republicanism are based. In many of these societies, there is little sense of a statewide political community able to "knit together" fragmented,

---

[36] Preuss, "Constitution-Making," 85.   [37] Preuss, "Constitutional Powermaking," 647.
[38] C. Calhoun, *Nations Matter: Culture, History, and the Cosmopolitan Dream* (London: Routledge, 2007); M. Canovan, "Sleeping Dogs, Prowling Cats, and Soaring Doves: Three Paradoxes in the Political Theory of Nationhood," *Political Studies* 49 (2001): 203–215.
[39] J. Habermas, *Between Facts and Norms: Contributions to a Discourse Theory of Law and Democracy*, trans. W. Rehg (Cambridge: MIT Press, 1996), 500.
[40] J. Habermas, "The European Nation State: On the Past and Future of Sovereignty and Citizenship," in *The Inclusion of the Other: Studies in Political Theory*, ed. C. Cronin and P. De Greiff (Cambridge: Polity Press, 1999).
[41] M. Viroli, *For Love of Country: An Essay on Patriotism and Nationalism* (New York: Clarendon Press, 1995).
[42] J. Habermas, *The New Conservatism: Cultural Criticism and the Historians' Debate*, ed. and trans. S. Weber Nicholsen (Cambridge: MIT Press, 1989); P. Pettit, *Republicanism: A Theory of Freedom and Government* (Oxford: Oxford University Press, 1997).
[43] J. Elster, C. Offe, and U. K. Preuss, *Institutional Design in Post-communist Societies: Rebuilding the Ship at Sea*, (Cambridge: Cambridge University Press, 1998), 91; R. Bellamy, *Political Constitutionalism: A Republican Defence of the Constitutionality of Democracy* (Cambridge: Cambridge University Press, 2007).

localized social groups to exercise constituent power.[44] This reveals the fact that the liberal and republican models take for granted the preexistence of a unified people, since "a polity needs to be strong and well integrated to be able to manifest" the democratic values around which a political community is expected to coalesce.[45] Therefore, liberal constitutionalism appears to rest on a "false assumption that the liberal democratic state is neutral in cultural or societal terms."[46] Instead, when one looks more deeply, "all liberal democracies have acted as nationalising agencies for specific cultural particularisms."[47] Similarly, republicans presuppose that "only a national consciousness…makes subjects into citizens of a single political community" capable of sustaining a democratic government.[48] Indeed, de Sieyès conceived constituent power as a "return to the state of nature," in which the "nation" was the source of political authority.[49] Therefore, although both liberals and republicans advocate decoupling culture from politics, they "neglect the importance of other nationalist imaginaries to the nurturance of democratic politics."[50]

The failure of constitutions adopted during the second wave of decolonization to entrench liberal democratic governance led to a new focus on how to design constitutions to manage a lack of societal consensus due to fragmentation and division. The radical method is for the constitution to provide a right of secession, whereby a people can politically separate from the existing state, usually as the result of an act of self-determination, to create "a new state upon territory forming part of an existing one."[51] However, as the right

---

[44] S. Dinnen, *The Twin Processes of Nation-Building and State-Building: State, Society and Governance in Melanesia Briefing Note*, No. 1/2007 (Canberra: Australian National University, 2007).
[45] M. Canovan, "Patriotism Is Not Enough," *British Journal of Political Science* 30:3 (2000): 422.
[46] S. Tierney, *Constitutional Law and National Pluralism* (Oxford: Oxford University Press, 2004), 10.
[47] F. Requejo, "Introduction," in *Democracy and National Pluralism*, ed. F. Requejo (London: Routledge, 2001), 4.
[48] Habermas, "The European Nation State," 113; Canovan, "Sleeping Dogs, Prowling Cats"; F. Requejo, "Democratic Legitimacy and National Pluralism," in *Democracy and National Pluralism*, ed. F. Requejo (London: Routledge, 2001).
[49] C. Klein and A. Sajó, "Constitution-Making: Process and Substance," in *The Oxford Handbook of Comparative Constitutional Law*, ed. M. Rosenfeld and A. Sajó (Oxford: Oxford University Press, 2012), 427.
[50] C. Calhoun, "Imagining Solidarity: Cosmopolitanism, Constitutional Patriotism, and the Public Sphere," *Public Culture* 14:1 (2002): 151.
[51] S. Mancini, "Secession and Self-Determination," in *The Oxford Handbook of Comparative Constitutional Law*, ed. M. Rosenfeld and A. Sajó (Oxford: Oxford University Press, 2012), 481–482; P. Radan, "Secession: A Word in Search of a Meaning," in *On the Way to Statehood: Secession and Globalisation*, ed. A. Pavkovic and P. Radan (Aldershot: Ashgate, 2008).

to self-determination has been limited by international law, secession is usually difficult, with Bangladesh the only case of successful secession prior to the end of the Cold War. While the collapse of Yugoslavia and the USSR saw a number of new states emerge, territories such as Kosovo, Chechnya, Somaliland, Puntland, South Ossetia, Abkhazia, and Transnistria have all attempted secession with limited success. This suggests that methods to manage fragmentation and division within existing states will be most common for some time. Four main methods of institutional engineering have been proposed to achieve this goal: first, consociational techniques, such as governmental power-sharing, proportionality of parliamentary representation, equitable bureaucratic appointments and state financial benefits, and agreements on the transfer of economic resources;[52] second, integrative power-sharing, which involves electoral formulas that reward candidates for moderation and cross-communalism;[53] third, compromise constitutional settlements that utilize autonomous or federal structures;[54] and fourth, the granting of minority rights, guaranteed parliamentary representation, and veto rights for minorities.[55] However, these techniques rely on people exhibiting at least a minimal commitment to constitutionalism if the arrangements are to be respected and differences between societal groups resolved through constitutional mechanisms. Yet the challenge in many new states is that the people lack a commitment to constitutionalism, and even to the state as a mode of political organization. This is partly because the new constitutions, and the state institutions that they create, are "too young to be proven to be good" and consequently are not perceived as deserving "loyalty and sacrifice."[56] It is also partly because relying on loyalty to the constitution and state institutions seems "too thin, too emptied of any cultural content of any kind" to provide the "we" feeling that would generate sufficient social solidarity to enable a people to exercise their constituent power.[57]

---

[52] A. Lijphart, *Thinking about Democracy: Power Sharing and Majority Rule in Theory and Practice* (London: Routledge, 2007).
[53] D. Horowitz, *Ethnic Groups in Conflict* (Berkeley: University of California Press, 1985); T. Sisk, *Power Sharing and International Mediation in Ethnic Conflict* (Washington: United States Institute of Peace Press, 1996).
[54] M. Weller, *Escaping the Self-determination Trap* (Dordrecht: Martinus Nijhoff, 2008).
[55] W. Kymlicka, *Multicultural Citizenship: A Liberal Theory of Minority Rights* (Oxford: Oxford University Press, 1995).
[56] J. Spinner-Halev, "Democracy, Solidarity and Post-nationalism," *Political Studies* 56 (2008): 609; Habermas, "The European Nation-State."
[57] R. Eckersley, "From Cosmopolitan Nationalism to Cosmopolitan Democracy," *Review of International Studies* 33 (2007): 688; Calhoun, "Imagining Solidarity"; W. Connor, *Ethno-Nationalism: The Quest for Understanding* (Princeton: Princeton University Press, 1994).

Instead, "something stronger than pure rationality is needed to bind complex communities together."[58]

This raises the challenge of how to motivate people in fragmented or divided societies to feel sufficient unity to enable them to constitute a political community that exercises constituent power and to recognize as legitimate the state institutions created to exercise their constituted power. This challenge is often met by nationalism, which holds that only the tie of national identity is likely to generate a feeling of "collective unity" that could bind people with the kind of long-term political solidarity that can create a political community capable of exercising constituent power.[59] A sense of solidarity is important if a people is to exercise their constituted power, as they need to reach a "societal consensus" on an "agreement to disagree," based on the assumption that other citizens have a right to different views and that constitutional institutions are a legitimate forum for resolving disputes.[60] Although nationalism and liberalism are often assumed to be in conflict because liberalism advocates universality while nationalism emphasizes difference, attempts have been made to reconcile them,[61] and a constitution can constrain the more destructive essentialist elements of nationalism.[62] A sense of solidarity is particularly important for liberal democracies if people are to have "sufficient unity and organisational structure to generate representatives"[63] without descending into conflict and the mobilization of communal sentiments to attract votes.[64] Nationalism differs from other communal sentiments, such as ethnicity, because it is a "theory of political legitimacy" that links the cultural and the political.[65] Therefore, nationalism argues that the state cannot afford to be neutral about

---

[58] M. Howard, "Ethnic Conflict and International Security," in *Nationalism: Critical Concepts in Political Science, Vol. V*, ed. J. Hutchinson and A. D. Smith (London: Routledge, 2000), 1637.

[59] Calhoun, *Nations Matter*, 78; M. Canovan, *Nationhood and Political Theory* (Cheltenham: Edward Elgar, 1996); D. Miller, *On Nationality* (Oxford: Oxford University Press, 1995); B. Yack, "Popular Sovereignty and Nationalism," *Political Theory* 29:4 (2001): 517–536.

[60] D. P. Franklin and M. J. Baun, "Introduction: Political Culture and Constitutionalism," in *Political Culture and Constitutionalism: A Comparative Approach*, ed. D. P. Franklin and M. J. Baun (New York: M. E. Sharpe, 1995), 6–7; M. Lind, "In Defence of Liberal Nationalism," *Foreign Affairs* 1:23 (1994): 87–99.

[61] Y. Tamir, *Liberal Nationalism* (Princeton: Princeton University Press, 1995).

[62] Kissane and Sitter, "National Identity and Constitutionalism in Europe," 2.

[63] M. Moore, "Normative Justifications for Liberal Nationalism: Justice, Democracy, and National Identity," *Nations and Nationalism* 7:1 (2001): 8; Miller, *On Nationality*.

[64] E. D. Mansfield and J. Snyder, "Democratization and the Danger of War," *International Security* 20:1 (1995): 5–38; J. Snyder, *Transitions to Democracy and the Rise of Nationalist Conflict* (Israel: Leonard Davis Institute, 2000).

[65] E. Gellner, *Nations and Nationalism* (Oxford: Basil Blackwell, 1983), 1; E. Kedourie, *Nationalism* (London: Hutchinson, 1960); J. S. Mill, *"On Liberty" and Other Writings*, ed. S. Collini (Cambridge: Cambridge University Press, 1989).

national identity "if various substantive values (social mobility, democracy, and so forth) are to be advanced."[66] This is why, in nearly all liberal democracies, the "nation" comes to possess an additional sense of collective identity apart from the state.[67]

This raises the challenge of identifying the nation. Some theorists presume that there is a "nation in waiting." Bernard Yack argues that the nation is "the prepolitical basis of political community," as the idea of popular sovereignty means that a sovereign people must exist prior to the government in order to decide the institutions it will have.[68] Charles Taylor agrees, arguing that "a sovereign people, in order to have the unity needed for collective agency, had already to have an antecedent unity or culture, history or (more often in Europe) language."[69] However, in new and postconflict states, there may be little sense of preexisting national identity capable of generating sufficient unity to support the collective action of exercising constituent power. Consequently, it falls to the constitution and the state institutions it creates to "do much of the work to create the nation."[70] With this in mind, the idea of nation building recognizes that the nation may have to be "built."[71] Anthony Smith argues that this is "still the orthodoxy about both state-making and nation-building." Yet, the "forces that impel people to seek to belong to 'nations' rather than any other type of unit" are elusive.[72] In this regard, Craig Calhoun's argument that nationhood should be taken as something that is discursively produced on an ongoing basis is relevant. Indeed, all modern constitutions and state institutions "in order to survive, strive to create national allegiances to their own measure."[73]

How the task of nation building occurs depends on the definition of "nationalism" that is adopted. Modernist theory argues that nationalism is "the general imposition of a high culture on society...in place of a previous

---

[66] A. Patten, "Beyond the Dichotomy of Universalism and Difference: Four Responses to Cultural Diversity," in *Constitutional Design for Divided Societies: Integration or Accommodation?*, ed. S. Choudhry (New York: Oxford University Press, 2008), 96.
[67] Spinner-Halev, "Democracy, Solidarity"; Canovan, *Nationhood and Political Theory*.
[68] Yack, "Popular Sovereignty and Nationalism," 524.
[69] C. Taylor, "Democratic Exclusion (and Its Remedies?)," in *Multiculturalism, Liberalism and Democracy*, ed. A. K. B. Rajeev Bhargava and R. Sudarshan (New Delhi: Oxford University Press, 1999), 141.
[70] Spinner-Halev, "Democracy, Solidarity," 607.
[71] K. W. Deutsch and W. Foltz, ed., *Nation-Building* (New York: Atherton Press, 1966).
[72] A. D. Smith, "State-Making and Nation-Building," in *The State: Critical Concepts Vol. II*, ed. J. A. Hall (London: Routledge, 1994), 61.
[73] C. Calhoun, "Constitutional Patriotism and the Public Sphere: Interests, Identity, and Solidarity in the Integration of Europe" in *Global Justice and Transnational Politics*, ed. P. de Greiff and C. Cronin (Cambridge: MIT Press, 2002), 280.

complex structure of local groups."[74] This high culture is disseminated through the development of an educated, literate, and mobile labor force necessitated by the shift in the mode of production from agriculture to industrialization. While modernist theories focus on a range of socioeconomic,[75] sociopolitical,[76] cultural,[77] and ideological approaches,[78] the most influential approach has focused on the socially constructed character of the nation. Constructionists argue that the development of print capitalism cultivated the emergence of an "imagined community" of people who did not know each other directly.[79] They see nationalism mainly as a form of discourse that imagines the political community as finite, sovereign, and horizontally cross-class.[80] This national narrative is propagated via national symbols, education, language, religion, and military service. Therefore, nation building is an ongoing discursive practice that is often the product of "banal practices," "imaginative construction," and "political ideology."[81]

The constructionist approach dominated the first wave of anthropological scholarship on Melanesian nationalism. This literature focused on the "invention of tradition" by the elites of decolonizing states and was concerned about the "authenticity" and potential for manipulation of national identities defined and propagated by elites.[82] However, attempts to disseminate "invented" national identities utilizing constructionist methods largely failed, since Melanesia's fragmented subsistence populations did not have access to the technologies of education and bureaucracy that modernists say are required to inculcate nationalism.[83]

---

[74] Gellner, *Nations and Nationalism*, 57.
[75] M. Hechter, *Internal Colonialism: The Celtic Fringe in British National Development, 1536–1966* (London: Routledge and Kegan Paul, 1975); T. Nairn, *The Break-up of Britain: Crisis and Neo-Nationalism* (London: Verso, 1977).
[76] J. Breuilly, *Nationalism and the State* (Manchester: Manchester University Press, 1993); A. Giddens, *The Nation-State and Violence* (Cambridge: Polity Press, 1985).
[77] J. Hutchinson, *Modern Nationalism* (London: Fontana, 1994).   [78] Kedourie, *Nationalism*.
[79] B. Anderson, *Imagined Communities: Reflections on the Origins and Spread of Nationalism* (London: Verso, 1991).
[80] E. Hobsbawm and T. Ranger, ed., *The Invention of Tradition* (Cambridge: Cambridge University Press, 1983).
[81] Calhoun, *Nations Matter*; M. Billig, *Banal Nationalism* (London: Sage, 1997).
[82] M. Jolly and N. Thomas, ed., *Oceania Special Issue: The Politics of Tradition in the Pacific*, 62 (1992); R. M. Keesing and R. Tonkinson, ed., *Mankind Special Issue, Reinventing Traditional Culture: The Politics of Kastom in Island Melanesia*, 13:4 (1982).
[83] R. J. Foster, ed., *Nation Making: Emergent Identities in Postcolonial Melanesia* (Ann Arbor: University of Michigan Press, 1995); T. Otto and N. Thomas, ed., *Narratives of Nation in the South Pacific* (Amsterdam: Harwood Academic Publishers, 1997).

The other main branches of nationalism theory, perennialism and primordialism, share the common belief that nations are in some sense "natural," that they are a potent focus of human loyalty, and that some are long-standing.[84] Primordialists go further to argue that national identities are based on organic characteristics that originate from biological[85] or cultural factors,[86] psychological and kinship ties,[87] or the instrumental use of these factors,[88] which make national identity and *ethnies* (that is, ethnic origins) largely immutable.[89] The relevance of primordialist theories to Melanesia is questionable, as there is debate over whether the concept of ethnicity resonates in Melanesian societies.[90] Even if a loose definition is applied, the phenomenon is relatively new, and any perceptions of ethnicity that do exist are based on historical and cultural circumstances.[91] Yet they may become more relevant because elites are increasingly using ethnic identities instrumentally to generate political support.

Primordialism has acquired pejorative connotations of "fixity, essentialism and naturalism."[92] Ethno-symbolist theory has emerged to avoid these connotations and is concerned with the analysis of social and cultural patterns over the long term, in order to reveal "the complex relationships between past, present and future and the place of *ethnies* and nations in history."[93] As a result of this analysis, ethno-symbolism emphasizes the cultivation of myths, symbols, traditions, and memories of one or more culture communities (especially *ethnies*). This common heritage can then be used to develop a uniform public culture (common customs and laws) that can be disseminated to and observed by all members of the community. Ethno-symbolists admit that in fragmented societies the development of a national identity will require *"vernacular mobilization,"* whereby an intelligentsia educates

---

[84] A. Hastings, *The Construction of Nationhood: Ethnicity, Religion and Nationalism* (Cambridge: Cambridge University Press, 1997); H. Seton-Watson, *Nations and States* (London: Methuen, 1977).

[85] P. van den Berghe, "Does Race Matter?," *Nations and Nationalism* 1:3 (1995): 357–368.

[86] C. Geertz, *The Interpretation of Cultures* (London: Fontana, 1973); E. Shils, "Primordial, Personal, Sacred and Civil Ties," *British Journal of Sociology* 8:2 (1957): 130–147.

[87] Connor, *Ethno-Nationalism*; S. Grosby, "Religion and Nationality in Antiquity," *European Journal of Sociology* 32:2 (1991): 229–265.

[88] P. Brass, *Ethnicity and Nationalism* (London: Sage, 1991); Breuilly, *Nationalism and the State*.

[89] Geertz, *The Interpretation of Cultures*.

[90] J. Linnekin and L. Poyer, ed., *Cultural Identity and Ethnicity in the Pacific* (Honolulu: University of Hawaii Press, 1990).

[91] Otto and Thomas, *Narratives of Nation*.

[92] A. D. Smith, *Nationalism: Theory, Ideology, History* (Cambridge: Polity Press, 2001), 54.

[93] A. D. Smith, *The Antiquity of Nations* (Cambridge: Polity Press, 2004), 19; J. Armstrong, *Nations before Nationalism* (Chapel Hill: University of North Carolina Press, 1982).

"the people" in selected national "myths, symbols, traditions and memories, and in their vernacular codes and customs."[94] In contrast to the modernists' narrow focus on elites, ethno-symbolists argue that while a high culture may be imagined or invented, it needs to consist of "myths, symbols and memories...[that] resonate among large sections of the population...if people are to feel a sense of collective belonging and engage in common action."[95]

The second – and current – wave of anthropological scholarship on Melanesian nationalism adopts the ethno-symbolist approach. It utilizes the idea of "nation making" to focus on the production and dissemination of national narratives and identities that resonate with local culture and customs.[96] This approach has particular utility in Melanesia, as the often-divisive recent histories of its population mean that nation builders have to look back in time to find memories that can support a unifying national narrative.

Constitutions can play a role in nation building by recognizing and organizing the popular sovereignty of the people; establishing binding, reciprocal relationships among them; and serving as an expression of their self-determination.[97] In so doing, they often identify shared characteristics, values, aspirations, symbols, and principles that build a sense of national identity capable of constituting a political community.[98] This role is usually performed in the preamble, often through the inclusion of "directive principles"[99] and in the definitions of a "national" (that is, the legal bond of affiliation of an individual to a particular state) and a "citizen" (that is, who belongs to "the people" and is capable of acting as a competent member of the political community).[100] However, it must be noted that when there is insufficient public participation in constitution making, these efforts can also entrench a potentially divisive, exclusionary, and destabilizing view of the state and its people's identity, as occurred in Iraq.[101] Despite this important implication, relatively little theoretical or comparative scholarly attention has been paid to

---

[94] Smith, *The Antiquity of Nations*, 22.   [95] Smith, *Nationalism. Theory*, 128–129.
[96] Foster, *Nation Making*; Otto and Thomas, *Narratives of Nation*.
[97] Lerner, *Making Constitutions*.
[98] V. Hart and S. C. Stimson, "Introduction," in *Writing a National Identity: Political, Economic, and Cultural Perspectives on the Written Constitution*, ed. V. Hart and S. C. Stimson (Manchester: Manchester University Press, 1993); N. R. L. Haysom, "Constitution Making and Nation Building," in *Federalism in a Changing World – Learning from Each Other*, ed. R. Blindenbacher and A. Koller (Montreal: McGill-Queen's University Press, 2003).
[99] G. J. Jacobsohn, "Constitutional Values and Principles," in Rosenfeld and Sajó, *Comparative Constitutional Law*.
[100] D. S. Lutz, *Principles of Constitutional Design* (New York: Cambridge University Press, 2006).
[101] A. S. Weiner, "Constitutions as Peace Treaties: A Cautionary Tale for the Arab Spring," *Stanford Law Review Online* 64:8 (2011): 8–15.

the political and sociological role that constitutions play in constituting "the people."[102] While there have been some studies that consider how constitutions represent "the people" in plural societies, they tend to focus on existing constitutional arrangements rather than the process of constitution making.[103] The literature on pluralism and multiculturalism has a similar focus and consequently leaves the same gap.[104] This book addresses this gap with its consideration of the role that public participation in constitution making can play in nation building. Accordingly, the first question considered in Chapters 4 and 7 is, does the constitution enumerate a unifying national identity?

Constitutions also create their own sense of "constitutional identity," whereby the constitution represents a "mutually enforceable fundamental charter that unifies a collectivity of strangers"[105] and links "the constitution, its environment, and those who launched it as well as those for whom it was intended."[106] Michel Rosenfeld argues that while this constitutional identity will draw on national identity, it must be "distinct from national identity and from all other relevant pre-constitutional and extra-constitutional identities." This is because "the 'we' who gives itself a constitution must project beyond itself and even agree to become bound against (part of) what previously made it into a self" when making a constitution.[107] While this may be true in well-established states with existing national identities, this assertion highlights an element of Eurocentrism in Rosenfeld's work, as his discussion focuses on North American and European examples.[108] The need to distinguish between constitutional identity and national identity is less evident in fragmented or divided new and postconflict states in Africa, Asia, and the Pacific, where the constitution itself may be required to establish that national identity, and therefore where constitutional and national identity may be one and the same.

---

[102] Notable contributions include B. Breslin, *The Communitarian Constitution* (Baltimore: Johns Hopkins University Press, 2004); Chambers, "Democracy, Popular Sovereignty"; G. Jacobsohn, *Constitutional Identity* (Cambridge: Harvard University Press, 2010); and Lerner, *Making Constitutions*.

[103] For example, see Choudhry, *Constitutional Design*; Tierney, *Constitutional Law*; J. Tully and A. G. Gagnon, ed., *Multinational Democracies* (Cambridge: Cambridge University Press, 2001).

[104] For example, see Kymlicka, *Multicultural Citizenship*; and J. Tully, *Strange Multiplicity: Constitutionalism in an Age of Diversity* (Cambridge: Cambridge University Press, 1995).

[105] M. Rosenfeld, *The Identity of the Constitutional Subject: Selfhood, Citizenship, Culture, and Community* (Abingdon: Routledge, 2010), 18; Jacobsohn, *Constitutional Identity*.

[106] M. Rosenfeld, "Constitutional Identity," in Rosenfeld and Sajó, *Comparative Constitutional Law*, 760.

[107] Rosenfeld, *The Identity of the Constitutional Subject*, 10.

[108] M. Tushnet, "How Do Constitutions Constitute Constitutional Identity?," *International Journal of Constitutional Law* 8:3 (2010): 671–676.

Moreover, as Gary Jacobsohn cautions, constitutional identity "emerges *dialogically*" through the everyday "practices and culture of the body politic," which may or may not necessarily resonate with the written text.[109]

CONSTITUTED POWER

In liberal democracies, constitutions create state institutions to exercise the people's constituted power and provide a legal framework for the limitation and future exercise of that power. The liberal idea that popular sovereignty can legitimately be exercised only by state institutions through democratic means has become almost universal at the international level[110] and has guided liberal peace state building. Liberal scholars say that democracy provides a mechanism to recognize the "intrinsic equality" and "personal autonomy" of individuals, who are treated as though they are the best judge of their own interest and good.[111] It may also promote "social well-being" by "increasing the likelihood that government will act in the interest of the citizenry, rather than the other way around,"[112] because democracy "gives a regime's population collective power to determine its own fate."[113]

State institutions typically include a legislature, executive, and judiciary. Liberal constitutions generally separate powers and provide a system for checks and balances between them. The power of the legislature, compared to that of the executive, determines how the system is structured. In liberal democracies, the legislature usually consists of elected representatives and acts as the main forum in which the people's popular sovereignty is exercised. The executive may be either elected or appointed and exercises an administrative or managerial role. An executive may be overseen by a prime minister (appointed by a majority of the legislature in a parliamentary system) or a president (directly elected in a presidential system). The judiciary enforces the liberal principle of the rule of law, which is based on the idea that the law must be universally and consistently applied – including to the government – by a formal regulatory system in which there is a clear hierarchy

---

[109] G. Jacobsohn, "The Formation of Constitutional Identities," in *Comparative Constitutional Law*, ed. T. Ginsburg and R. Dixon (Cheltenham: Edward Elgar, 2011), 129, 131.
[110] Universal Declaration on Human Rights, 1948, art. 21(3); T. M. Franck, "The Emerging Right to Democratic Governance," *The American Journal of International Law* 86 (1992): 46–91.
[111] Dahl, *Democracy and Its Critics*, 86.
[112] C. R. Sunstein, *Designing Democracy: What Constitutions Do* (New York: Oxford University Press, 2001), 6.
[113] C. Tilly, *Democracy* (Cambridge: Cambridge University Press, 2007), 6.

of law.[114] While this essentially breaches the democratic ideal of majority rule,[115] this "quasi guardianship" is seen as necessary in order for all people to exercise their popular sovereignty equally.[116] In addition, as there is a tension between untrammelled majority rule and the liberal requirement that individuals are free and equal, liberal constitutions often protect individual human rights, which are usually enforced via the courts. Since liberals assume that individuals are for the most part motivated by self-interest, they hold that material interests are best realized through exchange in a market economy, with politics interfering only when interests cannot be met to mutual benefit.

LIBERAL-LOCAL HYBRID APPROACH TO STATE BUILDING

As noted, many constitutions adopted since the end of the Cold War have been influenced by the liberal peace project. However, the liberal assumption that individuals are abstract and self-interested does not reflect the reality that individuals in fragmented or divided non-Western societies are often influenced by social attachments to their community. It also provides little space for recognizing local group-oriented practices, and liberal peace constitutions have consequently been "viewed with suspicion in more communal societies."[117] Therefore, liberal peace constitutions do not necessarily build "a social contract on the ground through which to develop...local legitimacy."[118] Instead, they facilitate "low intensity constitutional democratization," which has provided "the legal and political basis of a new phase of Western imperialism."[119] This has generated substantial criticism from communitarian[120]

---

[114] B. Z. Tamanaha, *On the Rule of Law: History, Politics, Theory* (Cambridge: Cambridge University Press, 2004).
[115] Since it limits ordinary political power by effectively giving the courts the power to substitute their judgment for that of the people. D. Dyzenhaus, "The Politics of the Question of Constituent Power," in *The Paradox of Constitutionalism*, ed. M. Loughlin and N. Walker (Oxford: Oxford University Press, 2007).
[116] Dahl, *Democracy and Its Critics*, 188.
[117] K. Lidén, R. Mac Ginty, and O. P. Richmond, "Introduction: Beyond Northern Epistemologies of Peace: Peacebuilding Reconstructed?," *International Peacekeeping* 16:5 (2009): 587–598, 587; T. Fleiner et al., "Federalism, Decentralisation and Conflict Management in Multicultural Societies," in *Federalism in a Changing World – Learning from Each Other*, ed. R. Blindenbacher and A. Koller (Montreal: McGill-Queen's University Press, 2003).
[118] O. P. Richmond, "The Romanticisation of the Local: Welfare, Culture and Peacebuilding," *The International Spectator* 44:1 (2009): 153.
[119] J. Tully, "The Imperialism of Modern Constitutional Democracy," in Loughlin and Walker, *Paradox of Constitutionalism*, 333.
[120] For an overview, see M. Sandel, *Liberalism and the Limits of Justice* (Cambridge: Cambridge University Press, 1982); C. Taylor, *Sources of the Self* (Cambridge: Cambridge University Press, 1989); M. Walzer, *Spheres of Justice* (Oxford: Basil Blackwell, 1983).

and pluralist[121] thinkers, who argue that liberalism – and the constitutions it shapes – should take account of societal difference. At one extreme, these criticisms essentially agree that the liberal peace should be institutionalized but are critical of the methods by which state-building operations have sought to achieve this.[122] At the other extreme, they are critical both of the liberal peace project (particularly of its imperialist and capitalist motivations) and its state-building methodology.[123] Lying in between are critiques that take a reflexive view of the project and its state-building methodology by seeking to ensure that both reflect the particularities of the societies in question.[124]

Liberalism has begun to grapple with questions of moral universalism and cultural difference.[125] Theorists have attempted to reconcile liberalism and pluralism by arguing that the liberal principles of freedom, equality, and autonomy can provide space for the recognition of difference.[126] Yet this reconciliation is complicated by the fact that liberty and individualism trump diversity and group interest in liberal society. While no pluralist argues that the liberal state should be replaced with group sovereignty, several argue for "*shared* sovereignty," according to which groups are given "political liberty and autonomy to practice diverse moral beliefs, and the limited sovereignty to

---

[121] For an overview, see G. Deleuze and F. Guattari, *Anti-Oedipus: Capitalism and Schizophrenia* (Minneapolis: University of Minnesota Press, 1983); C. Mouffe, "Democracy, Power, and the 'Political,'" in *Democracy and Difference: Contesting the Boundaries of the Political*. ed. S. Benhabib (Princeton: Princeton University Press, 1996).

[122] R. Paris, *At War's End: Building Peace after Civil Conflict* (Cambridge: Cambridge University Press, 2004).

[123] D. Chandler, *Empire in Denial: The Politics of State-Building* (London: Pluto Press, 2006); Duffield, *Development, Security*; M. Pugh, "The Political Economy of Peacebuilding: A Critical Theory Perspective," *International Journal of Peace Studies* 10:2 (2005): 23–42; M. Pugh et al., "Conclusion: The Political Economy of Peacebuilding – Whose Peace? Where Next?," in *Whose Peace? Critical Perspectives on the Political Economy of Peacebuilding*, ed. M. Pugh et al. (London: Palgrave, 2008).

[124] R. Mac Ginty, "Indigenous Peace-Making Versus the Liberal Peace," *Cooperation and Conflict* 43:2 (2008): 139–163; R. Mac Ginty and O. P. Richmond, "Myth or Reality: The Liberal Peace and Post-Conflict Reconstruction," *Global Society* 21:4 (2007): 491–497; Richmond, "The Romanticisation of the Local."

[125] R. Euben, *Enemy in the Mirror: Islamic Fundamentalism and the Limits of Modern Rationalism* (Princeton: Princeton University Press, 1999); B. Honig, *Democracy and the Foreigner* (Princeton: Princeton University Press, 2001); B. Parekh, *Rethinking Multiculturalism: Cultural Diversity and Political Theory* (London: Palgrave, 2000).

[126] G. Crowder, "From Value Pluralism to Liberalism," in *Pluralism and Liberal Neutrality*, ed. R. Bellamy and M. Hollis (London: Frank Cass, 1999); M. Deveaux, *Cultural Pluralism and Dilemmas of Justice* (Ithaca: Cornell University Press, 2000); W. Galston, *Liberal Pluralism: The Implications of Value Pluralism for Political Theory and Practice* (Cambridge: Cambridge University Press, 2002).

make that liberty meaningful."[127] Others have identified the potential for a "mediated state"[128] in situations where groups exercise a sometimes high degree of autonomy.

When applied to state building, the pluralist-liberal engagement has crystallized in a call for a liberal-local hybrid approach. This approach implicitly recognizes that local populations did not reside in "Hobbesian anarchy" before the "liberal" state arrived.[129] Indeed, despite the extent of its hegemony, Western constitutional democracy has not entirely displaced local sociopolitical practices, which continue to dominate the day-to-day lives of millions of people.[130] Liberal peace state builders have tended to use Orientalist[131] assumptions to "misrecognise" and "delegitimate" these practices by describing them as "'mere' customs, uncivilized, savage, the lawless state of nature, *terra nullius*."[132] However, these practices are "not simply dead forms inherited from the past" but are instead collectively created "social achievements."[133] Rather than viewing local practices as hurdles to state building, the liberal-local hybrid approach focuses on their "strength and resilience."[134] From this perspective, it argues that existing political and legal pluralism should be neither rejected as uncivilized nor accepted uncritically, but brought into critical dialogues concerning the future design of the state during the constitution-making process.[135] In particular, while liberal peace state building has focused on institutionalizing the liberal emphasis on individualism by protecting individual human rights and encouraging the development of market economies, a liberal-local hybrid approach provides space to recognize that communalism, custom, needs, and welfare are valued aspects of everyday life in many societies.[136] The liberal-local hybrid approach also engages with

---

[127] D. Schlosberg, "The Pluralist Imagination," in *The Oxford Handbook of Political Theory*, ed. J. S. Dryzek, B. Honig, and A. Phillips (Oxford: Oxford University Press, 2006), 157.
[128] K. Menkhaus, "Governance without Government in Somalia," *International Security* 31: 3 (2006/07): 74–106.
[129] V. Boege et al., *On Hybrid Political Orders and Emerging States: State Formation in the Context of "Fragility"* (Berlin: Berghof Research Center for Constructive Conflict Management, 2008), 6; R. Mac Ginty, *International Peacebuilding and Local Resistance: Hybrid Forms of Peace* (Basingstoke: Palgrave Macmillan, 2012).
[130] L. Benton, *Law and Colonial Cultures 1400–1900* (Cambridge: Cambridge University Press, 2001); B. De Sousa Santos, *Toward a New Legal Common Sense* (Cambridge: Cambridge University Press, 2004).
[131] E. Said, *Orientalism* (New York: Vintage Books, 1978).
[132] Tully, "Imperialism of Modern Constitutional Democracy," 336.
[133] Calhoun, *Nations Matter*, 20.   [134] Boege et al., "Hybrid Political Orders," 13–14.
[135] B. De Sousa Santos, *The World Social Forum: A User's Manual*, 2005, accessed February 14, 2011, www.ces.uc.pt/bss/documentos/fsm_eng.pdf.
[136] Richmond, "Resistance and the Post-liberal Peace."

"legal pluralism," whereby "two or more legal systems coexist in the same social field."[137] Legal pluralism challenges the liberal principle of the rule of law, since it can result in inconsistent decision making if different laws are applied by different justice mechanisms. However, legal pluralism also recognizes that in many regions the state does not hold a monopoly over the legitimate use of physical force, but that instead "it is nonstate-informal authorities that are primarily responsible for the distribution of public goods such as security and justice."[138]

In this context, "local" is taken to mean sociopolitical practices such as "customary law, traditional societal structures (extended families, clans, tribes, religious brotherhoods, village communities) and traditional authorities (such as village elders, headmen, clan chiefs, healers, *bigmen*, religious leaders)" that determine "the everyday social reality of large parts of the population in developing countries…particularly in rural and remote peripheral areas."[139] These practices are local as "they operate in a geographically and politically defined sub-national and sub-regional space" and "enforce the prevailing order of that locality."[140] There is some debate about whether the "local" and "everyday" can be elided. Wiuff Moe argues that "the concept of the 'everyday' transcends description of the 'local' (as distinct territorially bound places) and instead refers to empirical, but not territorially fixed, relational sites of contestation, repulsion, reshaping and accommodation between international, liberal, state-based agencies and local agencies, customs and practices."[141] However, it should be recognized that local practices are not immutable relics of the "pre-contact" past but have instead been transformed as a result of colonization, globalization, and intervention.[142]

The word "hybrid" is used to emphasize that, while useful for the purposes of analysis, it is an oversimplification to juxtapose the liberal and the local and to view them as being in a "competitive rather than a co-constitutive

---

[137] S. E. Merry, "Legal Pluralism: Review Essay," *Law and Society Review* 22:5 (1988): 870; J. Griffiths, "What Is Legal Pluralism?," *Journal of Legal Pluralism and Unofficial Law* 24 (1986): 1–55.
[138] B. Baker, "Justice and Security Architecture in Africa: The Plans, the Bricks, the Purse and the Builder," *Journal of Legal Pluralism* 63 (2011): 34.
[139] V. Boege et al., "On Hybrid Political Orders and Emerging States: What is Failing? States in the Global South or Research and Politics in the West?" in *Building Peace in the Absence of States: Challenging the Discourse of State Failure*, ed. M. Fisher and B. Schmelzle (Berlin: Berghof Research Centre, 2009), 20.
[140] Baker, "Justice and Security Architecture," 29.
[141] L. Wiuff Moe, "Hybrid and 'Everyday' Political Ordering: Constructing and Contesting Legitimacy in Somaliland," *Journal of Legal Pluralism and Unofficial Law* 63 (2011): 150.
[142] Boege et al., "Hybrid Political Orders," 15.

relationship."[143] The liberal peace is by necessity a "hybrid social formation" as it adapts to, and is adopted by, the context in which it is being implemented.[144] Similarly, local sociopolitical practices are "not static," since the cultures in which they exist are living organisms that are constantly "evolving."[145] Although local practices may not necessarily have been "pervasively altered or shaped" by external contact,[146] the extensive nature of this contact suggests that there is no clear line between the exogenous "modern" and the endogenous "customary."[147] In fact, many local practices and institutions partner with the state and other actors or "integrate seemingly antagonistic political systems, world views and powers" in order to manage problems or advance their interests.[148] Similarly, state practices and institutions have adopted, and adapted to, local practices and institutions, such that "neither exists in a pure form."[149] Therefore, this book describes these practices, customs, and institutions as "local," as this "expose[s] specific local indigenous characteristics that distinguish them from introduced institutions that belong to the realm of the state and civil society."[150]

Despite this, the liberal-local hybrid approach has been criticized for reifying the binary between the "liberal" and the "local" as the root cause of the failure of liberal peace state building. By attributing the determinants of the success of state building to the local level, this approach is said to overlook broader structural problems that may also challenge state building.[151] Similar critiques are made with respect to the tendency of the hybrid approach to focus its analysis on ideational issues and institutions and to overlook the material issues of social welfare and human security.[152] The hybrid approach

---

[143] J. Heathershaw, "Towards Better Theories of Peacebuilding: Beyond the Liberal Peace Debate," *Peacebuilding* 1:2 (2013): 280.
[144] M. Laffey and S. Nadarajah, "The Hybridity of Liberal Peace: States, Diasporas and Insecurity," *Security Dialogue* 43:5 (2012): 406.
[145] M. A. Brown, "Security, Development and the Nation-Building Agenda – East Timor," *Conflict, Security and Development* 9:2 (2009): 155.
[146] N. Thomas, *In Oceania: Visions, Artefacts, Histories* (Durham: Duke University Press, 1997), 13.
[147] A. Rumsey, "The Articulation of Indigenous and Exogenous Orders in Highland New Guinea and Beyond," *The Australian Journal of Anthropology* 17:1 (2006): 47–69.
[148] M. Renders and U. Terlinden, "Negotiating Statehood in a Hybrid Political Order: The Case of Somaliland," *Development and Change* 41:4 (2010): 726; K. Menkhaus, "State Failure and Ungoverned Space," *Adelphi Series* 50:412–413 (2010): 171–188.
[149] P. Larmour, "Political Institutions," in *Tides of History: The Pacific Islands in the Twentieth Century*, ed. K. R. Howe et al. (Honolulu: University of Hawaii Press, 1994), 384.
[150] Boege et al., "Hybrid Political Orders," 15.
[151] D. Chandler, "Peacebuilding and the Politics of Non-linearity: Rethinking 'Hidden' Agency and 'Resistance,'" *Peacebuilding* 1:1 (2013): 17–32.
[152] E. Newman, "A Human Security Peace-Building Agenda," *Third World Quarterly* 32:10 (2011): 1737–1756.

has also been criticized for "fail[ing] to offer a way forward, beyond problematising and deconstructing liberal peace-building."[153] In addition, the concept of hybridity has been faulted for potentially essentializing groups and obscuring issues of injustice and differential power relationships. However, it also offers a powerful tool for engaging people in conversations during constitution making and consequently for potentially revealing alternative approaches to state building.[154]

CONSTITUENT PROCESS

This chapter has described how a people exercise their popular sovereignty, or constituent power, to make a constitution, with the constitution then codifying the institutionalization of the people's general will in a government, converting their sovereign power into constituted power. As noted, it was thought possible to identify the people's hypothetical general will when the early written constitutions were adopted in Western states in the late eighteenth century, which allowed the constitution to be made with relatively little popular participation. However, in the fragmented and divided societies that populate many new states that have emerged since the latter half of the twentieth century, identifying this general will is much more difficult. This has led to calls for a "process-based view of popular sovereignty" in which the "people get to speak" during the constitution-making process, so that they may negotiate and agree about their general will.[155] Indeed, the principle of popular sovereignty implies that the people's sovereign will must "occup[y] centre stage in the process of producing a legitimate, credible and enduring constitution."[156] That is, the people should be given voice through invitations to participate in constitution making. The people will speak with many voices – some of which will contradict each other – but "what is important is that citizens feel that they were heard, that they were part of the process, and that their opinions, interests, concerns, and claims counted for something."[157]

---

[153] Ibid., 1747.
[154] J. H. Peterson, "A Conceptual Unpacking of Hybridity: Accounting for Notions of Power, Politics and Progress in Analyses of Aid-Driven Interfaces," *Journal of Peacebuilding & Development* 7:2 (2012): 9–22.
[155] Chambers, "Democracy, Popular Sovereignty," 161, 158.
[156] J. Hatchard, M. Ndulo, and P. Slinn, *Comparative Constitutionalism and Good Governance in the Commonwealth: An Eastern and Southern African Perspective* (Cambridge: Cambridge University Press, 2004), 3; Elazar, "Constitution-Making."
[157] Chambers, "Democracy, Popular Sovereignty," 158; S. Benhabib, "Toward a Deliberative Model of Democratic Legitimacy," in *Democracy and Difference: Contesting the Boundaries of the Political*, ed. S. Benhabib (Princeton: Princeton University Press, 1996).

If the people are given the opportunity to exercise their popular sovereignty through a constituent process, this can "de-imperialise" constitution making[158] by engaging with "the local voices which are supposed to be part of the social contract upon which the liberal state is built."[159] This approach reinserts popular sovereignty into state building by arguing that it should take account of and engage with local voices and differences by conducting "unscripted conversations"[160] between state builders and the local population about the design of their state. This fits with the pluralist emphasis on trying to understand "the standards of others."[161] These agonistic encounters can generate mutual respect and recognition that will "enhance a critical attitude to one's own culture and a tolerant and critical attitude towards others."[162] Constitution making can provide a forum for agonistic encounters between state builders and the local population, which can minimize the likelihood that disagreements will spill over into open conflict or generate intolerance.[163] The literature posits that such agonistic encounters can lead to the hybridity of liberal and local sociopolitical institutions being recognized.[164] Using a participatory constitution-making process to achieve such recognition would enable people to truly exercise their popular sovereignty to self-determine the way in which their local agency will be translated into the state.

Accordingly, when there is significant public participation in constitution making, which fosters a sense of political community and produces a constitution that enhances the legitimacy and effectiveness of the state institutions that it creates by accommodating both the liberal and local, this can be described as a constituent process. The concept of a constituent process is examined in more detail in the next chapter.

---

[158] Tully, "Imperialism of Modern Constitutional Democracy," 333.
[159] O. P. Richmond, "Becoming Liberal, Unbecoming Liberalism: Liberal-Local Hybridity via the Everyday as a Response to the Paradoxes of Liberal Peacebuilding," *Journal of Intervention and Statebuilding* 3:3 (2009): 333.
[160] Duffield, *Development, Security*, 254.
[161] I. Berlin, *Four Essays on Liberty* (Oxford: Oxford University Press, 1969), 103.
[162] Tully, *Strange Multiplicity*, 207; W. Connolly, *The Ethos of Pluralization* (Minneapolis: University of Minnesota Press, 1995); B. Honig, *Political Theory and the Displacement of Politics* (Ithaca: Cornell University Press, 1993).
[163] M. Deveaux, "Agonism and Pluralism," *Philosophy and Social Criticism* 25:4 (1999): 1–22; Sunstein, *Designing Democracy*.
[164] M. Barcham, *Conflict, Violence and Development in the Southwest Pacific: Taking the Indigenous Context Seriously*, Centre for Indigenous Governance and Development Working Paper Series, Working Paper Number 4/2005 (Palmerston North: Massey University, 2005).

2

A constituent process

This chapter examines the concept of a constituent process and the role it can play in state building. It begins by identifying the main steps involved in most constitution-making processes. It then turns specifically to the literature relating to participation in constitution making, which has its intellectual foundations in the literature on the benefits of political participation, which in turn has its roots in the literature on deliberative democracy. This chapter identifies five claimed benefits of participatory constitution making: first, it can have positive effects on the constitution-making process; second, it may assist people to unite to exercise their constituent power; third, it may encourage reconciliation and the resolution of grievances; fourth, it can encourage individuals to become citizens who recognize the legitimacy of their constitution and the state institutions it creates in order to exercise their constituted power; and fifth, it can result in a liberal-local hybrid constitution and state institutions that better reflect public understandings and views. Based on this discussion, the chapter identifies indicators that can be used to assess whether a constituent process has occurred and what role this can play in state building.

CONSTITUTION MAKING

Before considering the role that public participation in constitution making can play in generating a constituent process, it is first necessary to consider the process of constitution making. As constitution making has historically been treated as a technical process, the literature relating to comparative constitution making, or even to the process of constitution making from a normative perspective, is relatively thin. Historically, the academic literature has typically seen constitutions as a contract between the ruler and the elite. This contract was made by unelected elites, internally imposed by a sovereign lawmaker, externally imposed by a foreign power, or made by internal constitution makers acting under external constraints.[1] Since the Second World War, as the right to political participation has grown in prominence, constitution making has slowly been democratized. There has also been a shift toward separating out deliberation and drafting from the adoption of the constitution.[2]

The most significant attempt to theorize constitution making has been made by Jon Elster.[3] More recently, Jennifer Widner has considered a number of comparative cases.[4] Other academic studies have utilized case studies of specific constitution-making events,[5] although attempts to survey the theoretical literature are slowly emerging.[6] Much of the recent literature on constitution making has come from think tanks.[7] As the literature on constitution making is relatively young, it does not yet represent a bounded canon. Despite this, there is sufficient consensus concerning several aspects of the constitution-making process that the literature can be taken as providing guidance for the present discussion.

The literature notes that when there is no existing constitution to guide the process, a framework should be adopted. In postconflict settings, such frameworks are often contained in peace agreements or cease-fires, but they may also be developed at a roundtable of key actors, established by interim authorities, set out in legislation, or outlined in an international agreement or treaty.

---

[1] Elster, "Ways of Constitution-Making."
[2] Elkins, Ginsburg, and Melton, *Endurance of National Constitutions*.
[3] J. Elster, "Constitution-Making in Eastern Europe: Rebuilding the Boat in the Open Sea," *Public Administration* 71:1–2 (1993): 169–217; J. Elster, "Forces and Mechanisms in the Constitution-Making Process," *Duke Law Journal* 45:2 (1995): 364–396.
[4] Widner, "Constitution Writing"; J. A. Widner, "Constitution Writing in Post-Conflict Settings: An Overview," *William and Mary Law Review* 49 (2007): 1513–1537.
[5] For example: A. Arato, *Constitution Making under Occupation: The Politics of Imposed Revolution Iraq* (New York: Columbia University Press, 2009); A. E. D. Howard, ed., *Constitution Making in Eastern Europe* (Washington: Woodrow Wilson Center Press, 1993); G. Hyden and D. Venter, *Constitution-Making and Democratization in Africa* (Pretoria: Institute of South Africa, 2001); D. C. Moehler, *Distrusting Democrats: Outcomes of Participatory Constitution Making* (Ann Arbor: University of Michigan Press, 2008).
[6] J. Blount, "Participation in Constitutional Design," in *Comparative Constitutional Law*, ed. T. Ginsburg and R. Dixon (Cheltenham: Edward Elgar, 2011); J. Carey, "Does It Matter How a Constitution Is Created?" in *Is Democracy Exportable?*, ed. Z. Barany and R. G. Moser (New York: Cambridge University Press, 2009).
[7] The most important contributions are: Brandt et al., *Constitution-Making and Reform*; IDEA, *Constitution Building after Conflict: External Support to a Sovereign Process* (Stockholm: International Institute for Democracy and Electoral Assistance, 2011); Miller, *Framing the State*; *Proceedings, Workshop on Constitution Building Processes*, Bobst Center for Peace and Justice, Princeton University, in conjunction with Interpeace and International IDEA, May 17–20, 2007; K. Samuels, *Constitution Building Processes and Democratization: A Discussion of Twelve Case Studies* (Stockholm: International Institute for Democracy and Electoral Assistance, 2006).

Frameworks are seen as advantageous as they can identify key actors, provide guidance on the process, minimize procedural disputes, and indicate the resources needed for the process. Frameworks may also contain guiding principles concerning how the process will be conducted and what the content of the constitution will be. Guiding principles can "provide a shared vision of a better future" and protect minorities, both of which may be beneficial in preventing the resumption of violence in postconflict environments. A framework might also provide guidance concerning transitional arrangements, including an interim constitution, to administer or govern the state while the constitution is being made.[8] Caution has been expressed that frameworks, particularly those contained in peace agreements or cease-fires, can disproportionately empower certain political actors (particularly those with weapons) and limit opportunities for public participation.[9] Frameworks might also generate "unsatisfactory consequences" in the long term, exemplified by the Dayton Peace Accords, which resulted in the Bosnia-Herzegovina constitution entrenching ethnic divisions and a weak central government.[10]

While deadlines can be useful for maintaining momentum and controlling costs, the literature generally concludes that an unhurried time frame is preferable. A short time frame may be favorable in cases where there is a risk of a return to conflict or a coup, but it is claimed that a rushed process may fail or result in a defective constitution.[11] A short time frame might also limit opportunities for public participation and "give the impression of the process being manipulated."[12] Indeed, internal forces can rush the process in order to entrench their own interest, which was an issue in Timor-Leste and also arose in Venezuela and Namibia.[13] The Timor-Leste, Cambodia, and Iraq cases

---

[8] Brandt et al., *Constitution-Making and Reform*, 61; A. Arato, "Redeeming the Still Redeemable: Post Sovereign Constitution Making," *International Journal of Politics, Culture, and Society* 22 (2009): 427–443.

[9] S. Choudhry, "Civil War, Ceasefire, Constitution: Some Preliminary Notes," *Cardozo Law Review* 33 (2011–2012): 1917.

[10] C. Saunders, "Constitution Making in the 21st Century," *Melbourne Legal Studies Research Paper No. 630* (Melbourne: University of Melbourne, 2012).

[11] Elster, Offe, and Preuss, *Institutional Design*; Brandt et al., *Constitution-Making and Reform*.

[12] Y. P. Ghai, *The Role of Constituent Assemblies in Constitution Making*, Institute for Democracy and Electoral Assistance Research Paper, unpublished, 2006.

[13] See N. Kritz, "Constitution-Making Process: Lessons for Iraq," testimony before a joint hearing of the Senate Committee on the Judiciary, Subcommittee on the Constitution, Civil Rights, and Property Rights, and the Senate Committee on Foreign Relations, Subcommittee on Near Eastern and South Asian Affairs, June 25, 2003; L. E. Miller, "Designing Constitution-Making Processes: Lessons from the Past, Questions for the Future," in *Framing the State in Times of Transition: Case Studies in Constitution Making* (Washington: U.S. Institute of Peace Press, 2010).

suggest that short time frames are particularly likely in situations of international occupation.[14] In contrast, in Bougainville, Poland, and South Africa, unhurried processes allowed time for constitution makers to reflect on lessons learned along the way, build consensus, undertake public consultation and for civil society to develop.[15] If the drafting body is also acting as the legislature, an unhurried timetable may provide sufficient time for it to perform both roles. However, there is some utility in imposing time limits, as they prevent groups from using delaying tactics to get their way.[16] For example, in Hungary, the process was so drawn-out that the window of opportunity to draft a completely new constitution was missed.[17] In addition, an extended time frame creates space for new interests to emerge and new opposition to form, so that consensus can become more difficult.[18] Overall, there appears to be some merit in providing a deadline, but it should be flexible and not overly rushed. Therefore, the first element of constitution making considered in Chapters 3 and 6 is the time frame given for the process.

The nature of the body making the constitution can affect the process. Jon Elster identifies four types of constitution-making bodies: constitutional conventions, which are "elected for the sole purpose of adopting the constitution"; mandated constituent legislatures, which are elected with the "double task of adopting a constitution and performing the task of an ordinary legislature"; self-created constituent legislatures, which are elected as ordinary parliaments but then turn themselves into constituent assemblies; and self-created legislating assemblies, which are elected as constitutional conventions but then assume legislative powers.[19] If the constitution is made by an elected convention or assembly, political leaders may be encouraged to buy in, which was relevant in Timor-Leste. An elected constitution-making body may also be perceived as legitimate, since its members are selected to speak on behalf of their constituents and members of the public are given an opportunity to

---

[14] Ghai, *Role of Constituent Assemblies*; Miller, "Designing Constitution-Making Processes."
[15] L. Garlicki and Z. A. Garlicka, "Constitution Making, Peace Building, and National Reconciliation: The Experience of Poland," in Miller, *Framing the State*; Hatchard, Ndulo, and Slinn, *Comparative Constitutionalism*; Miller, "Designing Constitution-Making Processes"; C. Murray and R. Simeon, "Recognition without Empowerment: Minorities in a Democratic South Africa," in Choudhry, *Constitutional Design*.
[16] Elster, "Ways of Constitution-Making."
[17] A. Arato and Z. Miklósi, "Constitution Making and Transitional Politics in Hungary," in Miller, *Framing the State*.
[18] *Proceedings, Workshop on Constitution Building Processes*.
[19] J. Elster, "The Optimal Design of a Constituent Assembly," in *Collective Wisdom: Principles and Mechanisms*, ed. H. Landemore and J. Elster (New York: Cambridge University Press, 2012), 152.

communicate their interests to candidates during the election campaign.[20] However, electing constitution makers "is no guarantee of a representative, inclusive body," particularly if it "becomes an exercise in majoritarianism."[21] In addition, if minority groups or potential spoilers fail to gain seats in the body, they may seek to challenge the legitimacy of the process and the resulting constitution. In order to be participatory, a constitution-making process should also be inclusive of all societal groups. As a result, there has been an increasing tendency to reserve seats for underrepresented or disadvantaged groups, such as women, as occurred in Bougainville.[22] Accordingly, the second element of constitution making considered in Chapters 3 and 6 is the type of institution that was designated to draft the constitution.

If a constitution is made or adopted by an elected body, the timing of elections can affect the process. As the Timor-Leste, Afghanistan, and Iraq cases illustrate, the international community tends to push for early elections when it is involved in state-building operations, which often reflects strong popular demand for political participation and representation. Indeed, until elections are held, transitional governments or administrations run by the international community or appointed local elites may face serious legitimacy problems. However, the literature cautions that elections should not be held "prematurely," as there is a danger that without a period to promote inclusion and public participation, they can be seen as "winner-takes-all." One suggested method is to delay elections according to a transparent, agreed-upon timetable.[23]

Much of the literature contends that when an election is held, constitution-making bodies should be elected via a proportional, rather than majoritarian, system. This is seen as the best way to ensure broad representation, by providing small parties with the greatest opportunity of being elected,[24] as occurred in Colombia.[25] However, proportional representation does not guarantee a representative assembly, since the design of the electoral system will

---

[20] Ibid. [21] Blount, "Participation in Constitutional Design," 42–43.
[22] H. Irving, "Drafting, Design and Gender," in Ginsburg and Dixon, *Comparative Constitutional Law*.
[23] K. Papagianni, "Participation and Legitimation," in *Building States to Build Peace*, ed. C. T. Call and V. Wyeth (Boulder: Lynne Rienner, 2008).
[24] J. I. Colon-Rios, "Notes on Democracy and Constitution-Making," *New Zealand Journal of Public and International Law* 9 (2011): 32; Elster, "Ways of Constitution-Making"; Miller, "Designing Constitution-Making Processes"; *Proceedings, Workshop on Constitution Building Processes*; K. Samuels, *State-Building and Constitutional Design after Conflict* (New York: International Peace Academy, 2006).
[25] R. Segura and A. M. Bejarano, "¡Ni una asamblea más sin nosotros! Exclusion, Inclusion, and the Politics of Constitution-Making in the Andes," *Constellations* 11:2 (2004): 217–236.

involve choices about which groups are to be represented. In addition, electing constitution makers does not necessarily guarantee effective representation, particularly if there are no mechanisms to hold them accountable,[26] as occurred in Venezuela and Bolivia.[27]

If the constitution is made by an elected assembly that is already functioning as an ordinary legislature (which has been the most frequently utilized approach since the Second World War),[28] or if the assembly will convert into a legislature after the constitution is adopted, "institutional self-interest" may shape both the process and the resulting constitution.[29] In particular, a constituent legislature may feel little motivation to bind itself and an overwhelming inclination to limit the power of other branches of government.[30] However, a recent study found little support for this hypothesis, and in fact found that constituent assemblies were more likely to empower future legislatures.[31] Moreover, a constituent legislature may be appropriate if there are insufficient competent candidates to fill both a legislature and a drafting body. It may also be inefficient in terms of human and economic resources to have two bodies running concurrently, and there is a risk of competition and conflict between them.[32]

Capacity permitting, the literature generally concludes that it is preferable for constitutions to be drafted by specially convened conventions. These are said to be "more likely to embody the process value of free and unconstrained deliberation" and consequently more likely to "promote the predominance of *reason* over *interest*."[33] In this context, reason refers not only to "impartial ends" but also to "informed beliefs," and interest may become acceptable if all parties are allowed to appeal to their own self-interest.[34] Specially convened bodies may also be better placed to negotiate "great compromises" without the "noise" created by regular politics and the temptation to engage in logrolling.

---

[26] Hart, "Constitution Making and the Right to Take Part."
[27] D. Landau, "Constitution-Making Gone Wrong," *Alabama Law Review*, forthcoming.
[28] Elster, "Ways of Constitution-Making."
[29] Elster, Offe, and Preuss, *Institutional Design*, 79.
[30] J. Elster, "Legislatures as Constituent Assemblies," in *The Least Examined Branch: The Role of Legislatures in the Constitutional State*, ed. R. W. Bauman and T. Kahana (New York: Cambridge University Press, 2006). Yet it should be noted that a recent study found little empirical support for this claim. See T. Ginsburg, Z. Elkins, and J. Blount, "Does the Process of Constitution Making Matter?," *Annual Review of Law and Social Science* 5 (2009): 201–223.
[31] Blount, Elkins, and Ginsburg, "Does the Process of Constitution-Making Matter?"
[32] Elster, "Legislatures as Constituent Assemblies"; Ghai, *Role of Constituent Assemblies*.
[33] Elster, "Legislatures as Constituent Assemblies," 185.
[34] J. Elster, "Clearing and Strengthening the Channels of Constitution Making," in Ginsburg, *Comparative Constitutional Design*, 15.

Moreover, if a body's members are not directly involved in day-to-day politics, there is less likelihood that their judgment will be clouded by political interests.[35] The danger of political interests (and differences) influencing the constitution-making process was evident at times in Venezuela, where the process was influenced by immediate political events.[36] This suggests that it is better to appoint, rather than elect, such a body, since elections may induce political parties to engage in politicking and create an assembly in which majoritarian interests hold sway.[37] In contrast, if the convention is appointed in a broadly representative manner, as occurred in Bougainville and Afghanistan, it stands a greater chance of drafting a constitution that satisfies all societal groups.[38] However, the background of the constitution drafters may be influential, as those who have experience in other states or of previous constitutional models (including those of former colonizers) may be influenced by them.[39] There may also be a need to offer constitution makers educational assistance on topics such as rules of procedure and substantive constitutional issues to prepare them for their role.[40] Accordingly, the third element of constitution making considered in Chapters 3 and 6 is the method by which the constitution drafters were selected and how representative they were.

The rules of procedure, speaking rules, and manner in which the body drafting the constitution makes decisions are also seen as influential. This issue is particularly relevant to difficult decisions, which are commonly made by a majority vote.[41] This can raise problems regarding what constitutes a majority vote (with options being a majority of those present, of those present and voting, or of the total membership), particularly when the body is elected and divided according to party lines. The Timor-Leste case illustrates

---

[35] R. Gavison, "Legislatures and the Phases and Components of Constitutionalism," in *The Least Examined Branch: The Role of Legislatures in the Constitutional State*, ed. R. W. Bauman and T. Kahana (New York: Cambridge University Press, 2006), 206; Elster, "Legislatures as Constituent Assemblies."

[36] M. Kornblith, "The Politics of Constitution-Making: Constitutions and Democracy in Venezuela," *Journal of Latin American Studies* 23:1 (1991): 61–89.

[37] J. Benomar, "Constitution-Making after Conflict: Lessons for Iraq," *Journal of Democracy* 15:2 (2004): 81–95; Miller, "Designing Constitution-Making Processes"; *Proceedings, Workshop on Constitution Building Processes*.

[38] D. Horowitz, "Conciliatory Institutions and Constitutional Processes in Post-Conflict States," *William and Mary Law Review* 49:4 (2008): 1213–1248; J. A. Thier, "Big Tent, Small Tent: The Making of a Constitution in Afghanistan," in Miller, *Framing the State*.

[39] Arato, *Constitution Making*; Elster, Offe, and Preuss, *Institutional Design*; Horowitz, "Conciliatory Institutions."

[40] Brandt et al., *Constitution-Making and Reform*.

[41] Ibid.; *Proceedings, Workshop on Constitution Building Processes*.

that decision making by majority vote may allow one party (or coalition) to dictate all decisions, thereby calling into question the representativeness of the resulting constitution.[42] The manner of voting may also be influential, with secret ballots seen as a way of avoiding intimidation in Afghanistan and Nepal but as antidemocratic in Kenya.[43] Alternatively, decisions can be made by consensus, with deadlocks broken by achieving "sufficient" – rather than absolute – consensus, which was the approach adopted in South Africa.[44] It might also be feasible to defer particularly difficult decisions by providing that they will be addressed by later law or decided by referendum.[45] Therefore, the fourth element of constitution making considered in Chapters 3 and 6 is the manner in which the designated institution drafted the constitution.

One of the most debated issues concerns how to achieve a balance between the competing interests of publicity and secrecy, particularly concerning whether the constitution-making body's hearings should be open to the public and what role the media should play. In favor of publicity, it is argued that framers are generally more careful to (or at least to appear to) offer impartial arguments framed in terms of the common good or public interest when they are under scrutiny from the public, a process described as the *"civilizing force of hypocrisy."*[46] Publicity can also help minimize opportunities for partisan interests and logrolling to hold sway.[47] However, there is skepticism about whether publicity encourages appeals to public reason, as it may actually "privilege appeals to private interest."[48] Publicity can also have negative effects, as it can increase the opportunity for strategic precommitment and encourage the irreversibility of publicly stated positions.[49] Publicity can encourage "grandstanding and rhetorical overbidding."[50] In turn, secrecy may facilitate compromise and provide space for constitution makers to think clearly and draft carefully.[51] This suggests that the process should involve elements of both secrecy (perhaps in the form of closed committee

---

[42] Ibid.; Benomar, "Constitution-Making after Conflict"; Ghai, *Role of Constituent Assemblies*.
[43] Brandt et al., *Constitution-Making and Reform*.
[44] Haysom, "Constitution Making and Nation Building."
[45] *Proceedings, Workshop on Constitution Building Processes*.
[46] Elster, Offe, and Preuss, *Institutional Design*, 78.
[47] Elster, "Ways of Constitution-Making"; Elster, "Legislatures as Constituent Assemblies."
[48] N. J. Brown, "Reason, Interest, Rationality, and Passion in Constitution Drafting," *Perspectives on Politics* 6:4 (2008): 679.
[49] Elster, Offe, and Preuss, *Institutional Design*.
[50] Elster, "Ways of Constitution-Making," 138; *Proceedings, Workshop on Constitution Building Processes*.
[51] Elster, "Legislatures as Constituent Assemblies"; Horowitz, "Conciliatory Institutions."

discussions of difficult issues) and publicity (open plenary discussions).[52] Elster recommends an "hourglass-shaped" process, whereby public consultations are held at the beginning of the process regarding the main constitutional issues, secrecy is maintained during the drafting process, and then the constitution is ratified via a referendum.[53] Consequently, the fifth element of constitution making considered in Chapters 3 and 6 is the levels of publicity and secrecy involved in the process.

The level of publicity involved in a constitution-making process can play an important role in determining the degree of public participation. Examples of opportunities for public participation include providing means for the people to elect a constituent assembly to draft and/or ratify the constitution or to ratify the constitution directly at a referendum.[54] However, the extensive public participation involved in several recent constitution-making processes has seen the idea develop well beyond this. For example, in Eritrea, civic education reached more than 500,000 citizens, and more than 22,000 citizens participated in constitutional consultations. In Rwanda, an extensive program of public education and debate was conducted as part of the process, and in South Africa, there was a massive campaign of public education and consultation.[55] Participation now includes civic educational programs, which, while not constituting direct participation, are often a necessary precondition for equipping citizens to be able to effectively participate when they are consulted. Civic education can take place through television and radio information campaigns, billboards, newspapers, magazines, internet sites, cultural and sporting events, games and competitions, mobile messaging services, and social media and workshops.[56] Public participation also includes consultations with political parties, which may be useful in generating a political consensus.[57] However, this approach elevates party elites and may not be sufficiently representative if parties do not represent all groups in society. Including civil society groups in consultations may be more inclusive and less elitist.[58] Public

---

[52] J. Elster, "Deliberation and Constitution-Making," in *Deliberative Democracy*, ed. J. Elster (Cambridge: Cambridge University Press, 1998); Ghai, *Role of Constituent Assemblies*; Miller, "Designing Constitution-Making Processes."
[53] Elster, "Optimal Design."   [54] Widner, "Constitution Writing."
[55] Chambers, "Democracy, Popular Sovereignty"; H. Deegan, "A Critical Examination of the Democratic Transition in South Africa: The Question of Public Participation," *Commonwealth and Comparative Politics* 40:1 (2002): 43–60; B. H. Selassie, "Constitution Making in Eritrea: A Process-Driven Approach," in Miller, *Framing the State*.
[56] Benomar, "Constitution-Making after Conflict"; Brandt et al., *Constitution-Making and Reform*; Ghai, *Role of Constituent Assemblies*; Hart, "Constitution Making and the Right to Take Part."
[57] Moehler, *Distrusting Democrats*.
[58] Hart, "Constitution Making and the Right to Take Part."

debates, focus groups, and open meetings convened by constitution makers, the government, or the civil society are another example, as occurred in Uganda and Mali.[59] Written submissions from the public are yet another example; these were utilized in South Africa, where the first round of consultation elicited approximately 11,000 substantive submissions, along with 2 million signatures on petitions.[60] Public participation also includes broadcasting constitutional deliberations and publicity in the media and via materials produced by constitution makers, such as drafts of the constitution, explanatory materials, or newsletters. In societies with low literacy rates or poor communications and transport infrastructure, such materials may have to be particularly creative. For example, in Eritrea, the 80 percent illiteracy rate necessitated that the Constitutional Commission organize songs, poetry, short stories, a comic book, mobile theater groups, concerts, and radio programs dealing with constitutional themes.[61] More recently, in Ecuador, constitution makers used a blog,[62] and in Iceland, constitution makers utilized technology such as social media, email, and websites to achieve an extremely high level of public participation.[63] Questions have been raised concerning whether "translating the proposed written constitution into some other form inevitably alters its meaning," potentially in substantive and controversial ways.[64]

If a constitution-making process includes opportunities for public participation, the timing of that participation is likely to affect what kind of public feedback is gathered. Participation that takes place before a draft is prepared is likely to focus on how the process should occur, as well as on broad-based proposals for what issues should be covered in the resulting constitution. Once the process begins, consultations may be held before a draft constitution is prepared in order to ensure that the draft focuses on issues of concern to the public. Consultations may also be held on draft(s) of the constitution to garner feedback, particularly on potentially divisive issues.[65]

---

[59] Ghai, *Role of Constituent Assemblies*; Moehler, *Distrusting Democrats*; A. M. Tripp, "The Politics of Constitution Making in Uganda," in Miller, *Framing the State*.

[60] Benomar, "Constitution-Making after Conflict"; Deegan, "A Critical Examination of the Democratic Transition in South Africa"; J. Hatchard and P. Slinn, "The Path towards a New Order in South Africa," *International Relations* 12:4 (1995): 1–26.

[61] Selassie, "Constitution Making in Eritrea."

[62] Colon-Rios, "Notes on Democracy and Constitution-Making," 33.

[63] R. Bater, "Hope from Below: Composing the Commons in Iceland," December 1, 2011, accessed August 14, 2013, www.opendemocracy.net/richard-bater/hope-from-below-composing-commons-in-iceland.

[64] M. Tushnet, "Constitution-Making: An Introduction," *Texas Law Review* 91 (2013): 1998.

[65] Brandt et al., *Constitution-Making and Reform*.

Whether public participation is legally mandated is also likely to affect its role in and influence on the process and resulting constitution. How that mandate is constructed will be important, as while constitution-making bodies may be required to conduct consultations, there may be no specification of their length or depth and no requirement for the bodies to take account of the public's views. For example, in Timor-Leste, the Constituent Assembly was not required to take account of the public feedback gathered at extensive UN-run consultations, and it consequently had negligible impact on the resulting constitution. In contrast, in Bougainville, the Constitutional Commission was mandated to use public feedback as the basis of its drafting, and it subsequently had a significant impact on shaping the constitution. Mandates to consult the public were also evident in Afghanistan, during Kenya's 2001 constitutional review, and during Uganda's constitution-making process, although only Uganda adopted a similar approach to that of Bougainville and required constitution makers to reflect the public's feedback in the resulting draft.[66]

The way in which public feedback is collected and analyzed will also affect its role in the process. Constitution makers may receive thousands of written submissions, draft constitutions, survey responses, oral testimonies, and reports of public meetings. For example, Afghan constitution makers received over 100,000 submissions. How thoroughly that feedback is reviewed and analyzed will determine whether (and what type of) public feedback influences the resulting constitutions. The most common ways of analyzing public feedback are via summary reports and matrices or by statistical studies that identify the main themes expressed by participants, consider data on specific potentially controversial issues, outline options for responding to these issues, and detect variations across social groups. The task often overwhelms the capacity of constitution makers, leading to cases such as Rwanda, where only 7 percent of the responses to 50,000 public questionnaires were analyzed, or Iraq, where the results of thousands of public questionnaires were never considered. This can undermine the emergence of a constituent process and call the resulting constitution into question. A common way of mitigating these effects is for constitution makers to prepare reports on their work, including how they used and responded to public feedback, as occurred in Bougainville and Uganda.[67] Accordingly, the sixth element of constitution making considered in Chapters 3 and 6 is the opportunity for public participation and its role in the process.

External influence may be exercised on the constitution-making process. This influence may be explicit, in the form of direct intervention, or implicit,

---

[66] Ibid.   [67] Ibid.

via the influence of international norms such as human rights and liberal democratic governance.[68] The most common form of external involvement is constitutional advisers, who can play an influential role, particularly as elected constitution makers often lack technical expertise or experience. This role can be valuable if it includes neutral technical and administrative support, although it may be undermined if advisers themselves are inexperienced and lack capacity.[69] The literature cautions that the role of such advisers should be kept to a minimum because experts may "resist the technically flawed and deliberately ambiguous formulations that may be necessary to achieve consensus."[70] If external advisers are perceived to have played a highly influential role in the process, this may also undermine the credibility of the constitution in the eyes of "suspicious citizens."[71] It is important to distinguish between advice and technical assistance, on the one hand, and interference, on the other.[72] This is particularly relevant as it relates to the tendency of international organizations to make "normative recommendations about what 'should' be included in a constitution" without being sufficiently aware of "the intensely local political considerations 'on the ground.'"[73] It also relates to the tendency for foreign governments to seek to promote their own interests, which is said to have occurred in both Afghanistan and Iraq,[74] or to favor one political party over others,[75] an issue that arose in Timor-Leste. However, international actors have played a crucial role in ensuring that a good process is adopted, mediating differences, and sponsoring constitutional negotiations. This was evident in Kosovo, where international actors mediated negotiations between Serb and Kosovar Albanian leaders.[76] Cheryl Saunders has proposed

---

[68] Z. Al-Ali, "Constitutional Drafting and External Influence," in Ginsburg and Dixon, *Comparative Constitutional Law*; T. Ginsburg, S. Chernykh, and Z. Elkins, "Commitment and Diffusion: How and Why National Constitution Incorporate International Law," *University of Illinois Law Review* (2008): 201–237.

[69] Brandt et al., *Constitution-Making and Reform*; Ghai, *Role of Constituent Assemblies*; Kritz, "Constitution-Making Process."

[70] Elster, "Ways of Constitution-Making," 138.

[71] M. Tushnet, "Some Skepticism about Normative Constitutional Advice," *William and Mary Law Review* 49:4 (2008): 1480.

[72] Y. Ghai and G. Galli, *Constitution Building Processes and Democratization* (Stockholm: International Institute for Democracy and Electoral Assistance, 2006); Miller, "Designing Constitution-Making Processes."

[73] Tushnet, "Some Skepticism," 1474; Elster, "Ways of Constitution-Making"; IDEA, *Constitution Building after Conflict*.

[74] J. Morrow, "Deconstituting Mesopotamia: Cutting a Deal on the Regionalization of Iraq," in Miller, *Framing the State*; Thier, "Big Tent, Small Tent."

[75] Kritz, "Constitution-Making Process."

[76] Miller, "Designing Constitution-Making Processes"; Tushnet, "Some Skepticism."

that "the solution lies in the use of experts with comparative insights and in crafting a role for experts that makes their knowledge and skills available in a form that is as helpful as possible without pre-empting either local direction or choice."[77] In this regard, the international community can be too stinting in their involvement, especially if they have an eye to ending an occupation or transitional administration, as arguably occurred in Timor-Leste and Cambodia.[78] Therefore, the seventh element of constitution making considered in Chapters 3 and 6 is the degree of international involvement.

The manner in which the constitution is adopted is significant, since it will determine the credentials of the document as an exercise of the people's constituent power. To that end, an elected legislature could be given a place in ratifying the constitution,[79] or it could be ratified by popular referendum,[80] which is an increasingly frequent occurrence.[81] A referendum can generate significant publicity and promote societal debate. It can also help to legitimize a constitution since it provides a definitive opportunity for the people to exercise their constituent power.[82] Yet, it must be acknowledged that a referendum constitutes "mass consent" rather than the public engaging in deliberation whereby they arrive at considered judgments after weighing competing arguments.[83] The Polish case suggests that knowing the draft will be put to referendum can also check constitution makers, since they are forced to anticipate what the public will find acceptable.[84] This knowledge can "hamstring" leaders when it comes to making constitutional compromises,[85] particularly if they are forced to bow to majoritarian pressures at the cost of making a constitution that satisfies all groups. Moreover, referendums merely offer citizens a yes or no vote, and not the chance to provide substantive reasons why they do or do not approve the constitution.[86] Referendums

---

[77] Saunders, "Constitution Making in the 21st Century," 4.
[78] S. P. Marks, "The Process of Creating a New Constitution in Cambodia," in Miller, *Framing the State*.
[79] Kritz, "Constitution-Making Process."
[80] Elster, "Deliberation and Constitution Making." In her study, Jennifer Widner found that referendums on final constitutional texts were held in 41.5 percent of the 194 cases of modern constitution making. See Widner, "Conflict Writing and Conflict Resolution Project."
[81] Blount, Elkins, and Ginsburg, "Does the Process of Constitution-Making Matter?"
[82] Ibid.; Ghai, *Role of Constituent Assemblies*.
[83] J. S. Fishkin, "Deliberative Democracy and Constitutions," in *What Should Constitutions Do?*, ed. E. Frankel Paul, F. D. Miller, and J. Pail (New York: Cambridge University Press, 2011), 243.
[84] Garlicki and Garlicka, "Constitution Making, Peace Building"; Hatchard, Ndulo, and Slinn, *Comparative Constitutionalism*.
[85] Ginsburg, Elkins, and Blount, "Does the Process of Constitution Making Matter?," 6.
[86] Q. Oliver, "Developing Public Capacities for Participation in Peacemaking," in *Owning the Process: Public Participation in Peacemaking*, ed. C. Barnes (London: Conciliation Resources, 2002).

can also be divisive as, depending on their outcome, they can create the impression of "a 'we the people who won' versus a 'we the people who lost,'"[87] particularly if political parties become involved.[88] The way in which the referendum vote is structured, its timing, its turnout and voter thresholds, and the amount of funding devoted to it may also affect the legitimacy of the outcome. However, these problems can be partly mitigated by the referendum being preceded by consultation and education. This occurred in Rwanda, where the referendum was preceded by a two-year program of education and discussion.[89] Accordingly, the eighth element of constitution making considered in Chapters 3 and 6 is the manner in which the constitution was adopted.

The literature often advocates adopting a constitution on an interim basis. This sees a temporary constitution operate during the constitution-making process[90] or the coming into effect of a new constitution delayed for a set period after it has been adopted, "so as to reduce the impact of short-term partisan motives."[91] Indeed, Simone Chambers proposes a continuous process in which constitution making is viewed as an ongoing "conversation" rather than a contractual moment.[92] However, as new constitutions are usually required to fill a political vacuum or to mediate a crisis, this option is unlikely in most situations. An extended delay can also be dangerous when there are high expectations of the process and a risk that an uncertain political vacuum may develop.[93] Another option is to include a "sunset clause," whereby the constitution must be reviewed after a set period of time or at intervals to "return to the well of contemporary popular sovereignty."[94] This procedure can be used to give parties to a conflict time to adjust, such as by offering reserved seats in the new legislature, with that arrangement to be reviewed after a set period.[95] Balanced against this must be the fact that frequent reviews of the constitution may undermine its fundamental nature and its ability to inculcate habits of obedience.[96] Constitution makers also sometimes elect to

---

[87] S. Chambers, "Contract or Conversation? Theoretical Lessons from the Canadian Constitutional Crisis," *Politics & Society* 26:1 (1998): 159.
[88] Tushnet, "Constitution-Making: An Introduction."
[89] Hart, "Constitution Making and the Right to Take Part."
[90] V. C. Jackson, "What's in a Name? Reflections on Timing, Naming, and Constitution-Making," *William and Mary Law Review* 49:4 (2008): 1249–1305.
[91] Elster, "Ways of Constitution-Making," 138; Elster, "Deliberation and Constitution Making."
[92] Chambers, "Contract or Conversation?"; V. Hart, "Constitution-Making and the Transformation of Conflict," *Peace & Change* 26:2 (2001): 153–176.
[93] *Proceedings, Workshop on Constitution Building Processes.*
[94] Elkins, Ginsburg, and Melton, *Endurance of National Constitutions*, 14.
[95] *Proceedings, Workshop on Constitution Building Processes.*
[96] Elkins, Ginsburg, and Melton, *Endurance of National Constitutions.*

defer (often controversial or procedural) issues to the future rather than include them in the constitution. For example, the South African constitution deferred issues such as the abolition of the death penalty to the future Constitutional Court.[97] It is also common to defer procedural issues such as electoral laws, which would "require greater detail than is often achievable in the constitution-making process."[98] Often, constitution makers specify that these important procedural issues will be resolved in "organic laws" to be adopted by the future legislature.[99] Therefore, the ninth element of constitution making considered in Chapters 3 and 6 is whether the constitution was adopted on an interim basis or included a "sunset" clause.

An under-researched element of the constitution-making process is implementation of the resulting constitution.[100] Whether a constitution is implemented will depend on whether actions are taken to give it effect, such as passing laws and creating institutions, and whether an "ethos of constitutionalism" is inculcated, whereby people recognize that it is "their constitution" and feel bound by its provisions and the state institutions it creates.[101] Recently, more focus has been devoted to implementation, exemplified by the case of the Kenyan constitution, which contains schedules identifying the legislation that needs to be passed, the timelines set to pass these laws, and sanctions imposed for failures to do so.[102] Accordingly, this book considers the implementation of the Timor-Leste constitution (Chapters 4 and 5) and the Bougainville constitution (Chapters 7 and 8) to assess whether there is a gap between their written text and the reality of their implementation.

CONSTITUENT PROCESS

In addition to the normative justification for a constituent process discussed in Chapter 1, practitioners are increasingly recognizing the role that public participation can play in constitution making.[103] The Commonwealth Human

---

[97] P. N. Bouckaert, "Shutting down the Death Factory: The Abolition of Capital Punishment in South Africa," *Stanford Journal of International Law* 32 (1996): 287–326.
[98] Tushnet, "Constitution-Making: An Introduction," 2008.
[99] Organic laws "fall between ordinary legislation and constitutional provisions on the scale of difficulty of adoption, amendment, and repeal" and typically require qualified, or super, majorities for their adoption. Ibid., 2009.
[100] Saunders, "Constitution Making in the 21st Century."
[101] Hatchard, Ndulo, and Slinn, *Comparative Constitutionalism*, 28–29.
[102] A. Waki and W. Gituro, "The New Constitution of Kenya: The Process of Implementation," accessed August 14, 2013, www.coulsonharney.com/News-Blog/Blog/The-new-constitution-Implementation.
[103] CHRI/M. Daruwala, *Civil Society Involvement in Constitutional Review: A Letter from Maja Daruwala, Director of Commonwealth Human Rights Initiative (CHRI) to Justice M. N.*

Rights Initiative has argued that the "process of constitution making is, and is seen to be, as important as the substance of the constitution itself."[104] Jennifer Widner has undertaken a study of 194 cases of constitution making since 1975 and concluded that "our instincts tell us that process makes a difference."[105] The International Institute for Democracy and Electoral Assistance has conducted a study of twelve cases. It concluded that "a participatory process can...play a reconciliation and healing role through societal dialogue, and can support sustainable peace by forging a consensus vision of the future of the state."[106] The United States Institute of Peace and United Nations Development Programme (UNDP) conducted a study of eighteen processes and concluded that "participatory constitution making is today a fact of constitutional life as well as a good in itself."[107] More recently, the institute conducted a study of nineteen cases, from which it concluded that there is "increasing regard for process in the public and academic discourses on constitution making."[108] It also expressed the cautious note that "the extent to which participation *actually* produces legitimacy and ownership is difficult to assess."[109]

At present, the international law relating to public participation in constitution making appears inconclusive. Vivien Hart has proposed an emerging human right to public participation, based on a combination of international law and practice[110] with the emerging "right to democratic governance" identified by Thomas Franck.[111] Franck, writing with Arun Thiruvengadam, is more skeptical, drawing on universal procedural norms relating to self-determination, nondiscrimination, and democratization to conclude that

---

Venkatachelliah, Chairman of the National Commission for Reviewing the Constitution and Chief Justice of India, 2001; Citizen's Forum for Constitutional Reform, *Background*, www.cdd.org.uk/cfcf/bkg.htm, 1999, accessed March 6, 2010.

[104] CHRI, "Background Paper to Accompany CHRI's Recommendations to CHOGM '99" and "Recommendations to Commonwealth Heads of Government" in *Promoting a Culture of Constitutionalism and Democracy in Commonwealth Africa*, ed. H. Ebrahim, K. Fayemi, and S. Loomis (Pretoria: Commonwealth Human Rights Initiative, 1999).

[105] Widner, "Constitution Writing in Post-Conflict Settings," 1514.

[106] Samuels, *Constitution Building Processes and Democratization*, 4.

[107] V. Hart, *Democratic Constitution Making, U.S. Institute of Peace Special Report 107* (Washington: U.S. Institute of Peace, 2003), 2.

[108] Miller, "Designing Constitution-Making Processes," 602.   [109] Ibid., 637.

[110] These include the right "to take part in the conduct of public affairs" granted by the International Convention on Civil and Politics Rights, art. 25, and Universal Declaration of Human Rights, art. 21, combined with regional conventions, the jurisprudence of international and regional organizations, and state practice. Hart, "Constitution Making and the Right to Take Part."

[111] Franck, "The Emerging Right," 46.

there may be "growing evidence" that constitution-making processes should provide opportunities for public participation.[112]

The developing literature on public participation in constitution making has its intellectual foundations in the literature relating to the benefits of political participation, which has its roots in the literature on deliberative democracy. Deliberative democracy emerged in the early 1990s to challenge the established liberal models that regard politics as the aggregation of preferences defined mostly in the private realm.[113] Instead, deliberative democrats argue that reflection upon – and consequently transformation of – preferences in a public forum is essential.[114] Definitions of deliberative democracy vary. For example, Susan Stokes defines deliberation by its outcome: "the endogenous change of preferences resulting from communication."[115] Diego Gambetta defines it by features of the process: "a conversation whereby individuals speak and listen sequentially before making a collective decision."[116] And, Joshua Cohen advocates the more ambitious idea of "free and public reasoning among equals."[117] Despite this, all theorists agree that deliberative democracy includes public collective decision making by discussion between all free and equal citizens who will be affected by the decision (or their representatives).[118] During this discussion, people bargain and weigh competing arguments on their merits based on the values of rationality and impartiality.[119] The only normatively acceptable decisions are those that meet the

---

[112] This argument is based on a reading of International Convention on Civil and Political Rights, arts. 1(1), 2(1), 3, 25, 26, and 27, combined with jurisprudence from international and regional organizations and evidence of state practice. T. M. Franck and A. K. Thiruvengadam, "Norms of International Law Relating to the Constitution-Making process," in Miller, *Framing the State*.

[113] J. Cohen, "Deliberation and Democratic Legitimacy," in *The Good Polity: Normative Analysis of the State*, ed. A. Hamlin and P. Pettit (Oxford: Basil Blackwell, 1989).

[114] J. S. Dryzek, *Discursive Democracy: Politics, Policy, and Political Science* (New York: Cambridge University Press, 1990); M. R. James, *Deliberative Democracy and the Plural Polity* (Lawrence: University of Kansas, 2004).

[115] S. C. Stokes, "Pathologies of Deliberation," in Elster, *Deliberative Democracy*, 123.

[116] D. Gambetta, "'Claro!': An Essay on Deliberative Machismo," in Elster, *Deliberative Democracy*, 19.

[117] J. Cohen, "Democracy and Liberty," in Elster, *Deliberative Democracy*, 186.

[118] Benhabib, "Toward a Deliberative Model"; Cohen, "Deliberation and Democratic Legitimacy"; J. Elster, "Introduction," in Elster, *Deliberative Democracy*; A. Gutmann and D. Thompson, *Democracy and Disagreement* (Cambridge, MA: Belknap Press of Harvard University Press, 1996).

[119] Elster, "Introduction," in Elster, *Deliberative Democracy*; J. Fishkin and C. Farrar, "Deliberative Polling: From Experiment to Community Resource," in *The Deliberative Democracy Handbook: Strategies for Effective Civic Engagement in the Twenty-First Century*, ed. J. Gastil and P. Levine (San Francisco: Jossey-Bass, 2005).

agreement of affected parties[120] and that are made on terms acceptable to all, even when they disagree with the details of the decision.[121] However, as the definition of deliberative democracy is relatively narrow and idealized, scholars have proposed a wider idea of "discursive participation" that places less strict requirements on the quality and conditions of public discourse. Discursive participation involves discourse between citizens that occurs both within, and outside, the formal institutions and processes of civic and political life. This discourse can occur face-to-face, but also through a variety of media.[122]

For the sake of brevity, the arguments drawn from the literature on deliberation, discursive participation, and public participation in constitution making are considered together to identify the role that a constituent process can play in state building. Again, although these arguments have not yet reached canonical status, there is sufficient consensus about them in the literature that they can be treated as providing guidance for the present discussion.

First, public participation can have positive effects on the constitution-making process. It can improve the accountability of constitution makers if participants are given opportunities to challenge them for being incompetent, corrupt, or inattentive.[123] It can also broaden the minds of constitution makers by exposing them to more information and ideas,[124] particularly relating to the need to engage with local sociopolitical practices and institutions. It may even lead to the emergence of a liberal-local hybrid approach to constitution making. There is also evidence that the public *wants* to participate and will enthusiastically take up the opportunity.[125] Indeed, the growing number of participatory constitution-making processes has created a demonstration effect, whereby there is an emerging expectation that future processes will involve a degree of participation.[126] For example, members of Timorese civil society frequently referred to the highly participatory nature of the

---

[120] J. Habermas, *The Structural Transformation of the Public Sphere* (Cambridge: MIT Press, 1989).

[121] Cohen, "Democracy and Liberty"; I. O'Flynn, *Deliberative Democracy and Divided Societies* (Edinburgh: Edinburgh University Press, 2006).

[122] M. X. Delli Carpini et al., "Public Deliberation, Discursive Participation, and Citizen Engagement: A Review of the Empirical Literature," *American Review of Political Science* 7 (2004): 315–344.

[123] Moehler, *Distrusting Democrats*.

[124] *Proceedings, Workshop on Constitution Building Processes*.

[125] For example, in South Africa, over 2 million public submissions were made. Miller, "Designing Constitution-Making Processes."

[126] Ibid., 638.

South African process when protesting the level of participation offered to them.[127] For these factors to be realized, scholars caution that participation must be perceived to be genuine and not just a "cosmetic pretence."[128] For example, there was an extensive program of public consultation in Zimbabwe, but as President Mugabe was not obliged to accept the public's recommendations, he rejected a number of them. Consequently, the government was perceived to have disingenuously consulted the public while actually ensuring its own control over the process.[129]

Second, participation in constitution making may assist in building a sense of political community so that the people unite to exercise their constituent power.[130] As constitutions should be made in moments of "higher lawmaking," during which people put aside their private interests,[131] deliberation or discursive participation during constitution making requires individuals to provide reasons for their proposals[132] and to negotiate about issues of mutual concern.[133] These deliberations need not necessarily be rational; they may engage with passions and interests so that the resulting constitution reflects a "plurality of interests."[134] To achieve this, it must be acknowledged that participants will be susceptible to "vanity and *amour-propre*" and that the best standard that their collective decision making will achieve will be "*impure procedural justice.*"[135] Achieving even this imperfect standard may result in the population agreeing to common societal values, aspirations, and shared

---

[127] NGO Forum, *Letter from East Timor NGO Forum to Members of the Security Council United Nations*, March 17, 2001, accessed January 15, 2010, available from www.etan.org/news/2001a/03ngoconst.htm.

[128] Ghai and Galli, *Constitution Building Processes*; Haysom, "Constitution Making and Nation Building."

[129] M. Ndulo, "Zimbabwe's Unfulfilled Struggle for a Legitimate Constitutional Order," in Miller, *Framing the State*.

[130] Elster, "Introduction," in Elster, *Deliberative Democracy*; J. D. Fearon, "Deliberation as Discussion," in Elster, *Deliberative Democracy*. This argument is also made by republican theorists, who argue that participation can help people arrive at shared conceptions of the common good. See Pettit, *Republicanism*. On the role that participation in constitution making can play in building a sense of political community, see Ghai, *Role of Constituent Assemblies*; Ghai and Galli, *Constitution Building Processes*; Proceedings, *Workshop on Constitution Building Processes*.

[131] B. Ackerman, *We the People: Foundations* (Cambridge: Belknap Press of Harvard University Press, 1991), 6.

[132] Cohen, "Democracy and Liberty"; O'Flynn, *Deliberative Democracy*.

[133] B. Ackerman and J. Fishkin, *Deliberation Day* (New Haven: Yale University Press, 2004); S. Chambers, *Reasonable Democracy* (Ithaca: Cornell University Press, 1996); Fearon, "Deliberation as Discussion."

[134] Brown, "Reason, Interest, Rationality," 685.

[135] Elster, "Clearing and Strengthening the Channels," 17.

symbols that can generate a sense of identity and solidarity.[136] In particular, as this book argues that a sense of national identity may be required to generate sufficient solidarity to unify a political community, constitutions can play a role in nation building if these values, aspirations, and symbols resonate widely.[137] Accordingly, when considering whether a unified political community is present in Timor-Leste and Bougainville in Chapters 4 and 7, this book considers the following question: Does the constitution enumerate a unifying national identity?

Third, if public participation provides a forum in which grievances can be addressed without resorting to violence, involvement in constitution making can assist parties to a conflict to mediate their differences, refine their aspirations, and facilitate the making of "big compromises."[138] This may in turn encourage the resolution of grievances and reconciliation.[139] Reconciliation involves achieving "negative peace," defined by Joseph Galtung as the cessation of violence and the (re)establishment of relationships that permit the coexistence of formerly hostile individuals or groups.[140] It also aims to achieve "positive peace," whereby it addresses "conflictual and fractured relationships" in order to build and heal relationships.[141] Reconciliation may take place at the interpersonal level, whereby relationships are restored between the perpetrators and victims of nonpolitical harm, or at the political level, to address wrongs committed by agents of the state, members of the opposition, separatist movements, militias, or warring factions in the name of the organization or

---

[136] A. Arato, "Iraq and Its Aftermath," *Dissent*, 51:2 (2004): 21–28; Benomar, "Constitution-Making after Conflict"; Citizen's Forum for Constitutional Reform, *Background*; Daruwala, *Civil Society Involvement in Constitutional Review*; L. J. Diamond, "Lessons from Iraq," *Journal of Democracy*, 16:1 (2005): 9–23; Ghai, *Role of Constituent Assemblies*; Hart, *Democratic Constitution Making*; Haysom, "Constitution Making and Nation Building"; Kritz, "Constitution-Making Process"; Widner, "Constitution Writing."

[137] B. Breslin, *From Words to Worlds: Exploring Constitutional Functionality* (Baltimore: Johns Hopkins University Press, 2009); A. B. Inbal and H. Lerner, "Constitutional Design, Identity, and Legitimacy in Post-Conflict Reconstruction," in *Governance in Post-Conflict Societies: Rebuilding Fragile States*, ed. D. W. Brinkerhoff (London: Routledge, 2007); W. F. Murphy, "Constitutions, Constitutionalism, and Democracy," in *Constitutionalism and Democracy: Transitions in the Contemporary World*, ed. D. Greenberg et al. (New York: Oxford University Press, 1993).

[138] Tierney, *Constitutional Law*, 202.

[139] Ghai, *Role of Constituent Assemblies*; *Proceedings, Workshop on Constitution Building Processes*; K. Samuels, "Post-Conflict Peace-Building and Constitution-Making," *Chicago Journal of International Law*, 6:2 (2006): 663–682.

[140] J. Galtung, "Cultural Violence," *Journal of Peace Research* 27:3 (1990): 291–305.

[141] B. Hamber and G. Kelly, *A Working Definition of Reconciliation* (Belfast: Democratic Dialogue, 2004), 3; J. P. Lederach, *Building Peace: Sustainable Reconciliation in Divided Societies* (Washington: U.S. Institute of Peace Press, 1997).

cause with which they are affiliated, in order to establish societal and political processes that prevent a reversion to conflict.[142] It is possible to achieve interpersonal reconciliation without political reconciliation and vice versa, and the two may actually happen at the expense of each other. However, they are interconnected, as rebuilding interpersonal relationships is often the key to facilitating broader political reconciliation between opposing individuals and groups. As unresolved resentments, underlying tensions, and simmering hostilities have the potential to generate further conflict,[143] reconciliation can act not only as a panacea for past wrongs but as a form of social inoculation against a future return to violence.[144]

There is evidence that a participatory approach to constitution making can facilitate reconciliation; Jennifer Widner has found that in cases where constitution makers were democratically elected representatives, violence decreased in 42 percent of cases in the five years after the constitution was ratified and remained the same in 35 percent of cases.[145] As the "passage from negative to positive peace runs through justice," reconciliation can also be facilitated if constitution making is accompanied by a combination of international or domestic criminal trials, truth commissions,[146] reparations, rehabilitation, and indigenous peace initiatives.[147] In this regard, constitution making has increasingly been utilized in conflict resolution.[148] At the same time, a constitution-making process can prolong or restart a conflict if it perpetuates the political dynamics that gave rise to the conflict, as occurred in Bosnia,[149]

---

[142] D. Philpott, *The Politics of Past Evil: Religion, Reconciliation, and Transitional Justice* (Notre Dame: University of Notre Dame Press, 2006).

[143] N. Biggar, "Making Peace or Doing Justice: Must We Choose?" in *Burying the Past: Making Peace and Doing Justice After Civil Conflict*, ed. N. Biggar (Washington: Georgetown University Press, 2003); P. Collier and A. Hoeffler, "Greed and Grievance in Civil War," *Oxford Economic Papers*, 56 (2004): 563–595.

[144] W. Long and P. Brecke, *War and Reconciliation: Reason and Emotion in Conflict Resolution* (Cambridge: MIT Press, 2003), 13.

[145] Widner, "Constitution Writing."

[146] Whereby wrongdoings committed during a conflict are publicly admitted and accompanied by some acknowledgement of responsibility by the wrongdoers and a measure of reparation for the victims.

[147] O. Ramsbotham, T. Woodhouse, and H. Miall, *Contemporary Conflict Resolution* (Cambridge: Polity Press, 2011), 251; R. Teitel, "Transitional Justice and the Transformation of Constitutionalism," in Ginsburg and Dixon, *Comparative Constitutional Law*.

[148] S. A. Arjomand, "Constitutional Development and Political Reconstruction from Nation-Building to New Constitutionalism," in Arjomand, *Constitutionalism and Political Reconstruction*; USIP, *Iraq's Constitutional Process: Shaping a Vision for the Country's Future*, Special Report 132 (Washington: U.S. Institute of Peace, 2005).

[149] J. C. O'Brien, "The Dayton Constitution of Bosnia and Herzegovina," in Miller, *Framing the State; Proceedings, Workshop on Constitution Building Processes*.

or if it fails to achieve genuine consensus, as arguably occurred in Iraq.[150] Therefore, when considering whether a unified political community is present in Timor-Leste and Bougainville in Chapters 4 and 7, this book considers the following questions: Has reconciliation been achieved? And, are there divisions within society?

Fourth, if participation involves the distribution of information and the provision of education, it can play a role in the process of "citizenization," whereby individuals "become 'citizens'" who are educated about their rights and responsibilities, become interested in government, and seek out future opportunities for participation in public life.[151] In this regard, it may help to inculcate an ethos of constitutionalism, whereby the people see the constitution and the state institutions and legal system that it creates as legitimate or "respect-worthy"[152] and have "faith that the system will remain sufficiently acceptable to them to enjoy the goods of union, or...that things will actually get better in the future."[153] Indeed, based on a study of all constitutions made between 1789 and 2005, Zachary Elkins and his collaborators find that public participation during the constitution-making process positively correlated with the endurance of the resulting constitution.[154] After a detailed study of the Ugandan constitution-making process, Devra Moehler concluded that participation created "distrusting democrats," who have higher democratic expectations of their government and a greater awareness of existing democratic deficits. While this has the positive effect of creating an educated citizenry with "new tools with which to evaluate critically the performance of their government institutions," Moehler also warned that these citizens may become disillusioned quickly if the government fails to perform.[155] An ethos of constitutionalism may enhance the legitimacy of the state institutions created by the constitution, most significantly by encouraging citizens to channel their grievances through these institutions rather than resorting to open conflict.[156] It may also inspire the emergence of an active public

---

[150] Morrow, "Deconstituting Mesopotamia"; J. Morrow, *Iraq's Constitutional Process II: An Opportunity Lost, Special Report 155* (Washington: U.S. Institute of Peace, 2005).

[151] J. Tully, "The Unfreedom of the Moderns in Relation to Their Ideals of Constitutionalism and Democracy," *Modern Law Review* 65 (2002): 210–211; J. Mansbridge, *Does Participation Make Better Citizens?*, 1995, accessed March 6, 2010, www.cpn.org/sections/new_citizenship/theory/mansbridgeI.html.

[152] Michelman, "Is the Constitution a Contract for Legitimacy?," 105.

[153] J. M. Balkin, "Respect-Worthy: Frank Michelman and the Legitimate Constitution," *Tulsa Law Review*, 39 (2003–2004): 494–495.

[154] Elkins, Ginsburg, and Melton, *Endurance of National Constitutions*.

[155] Moehler, *Distrusting Democrats*, 2.

[156] *Proceedings, Workshop on Constitution Building Processes*.

sphere[157] in which the media and civil society facilitate citizens' engagement with the constitution and the state institutions it creates by providing them with information and empowering them to engage in political participation.[158] In this regard, the literature posits that participation will see the constitution include more opportunities for public participation in politics.[159] Consequently, when considering whether a unified political community is present in Timor-Leste and Bougainville in Chapters 4 and 7, this book considers the following questions: Does the community exhibit evidence of citizenization? And, is there a strong public sphere?

Fifth, participation can affect the contents of the constitution so that it becomes "an autobiography of the nation"[160] that is "built upon the culture, knowledge, and experiences of the people who will breathe life into...[it] and make...[it a] living document... that truly *matter[s]* in the lives of those whom...[it] will govern."[161] The resulting state institutions may therefore "emerge out of existing social forces" and "represent real interests,"[162] potentially via liberal-local hybridity. While there is room for skepticism concerning how many public submissions are actually incorporated into final constitutions, there is some positive evidence. Examples from the Asia-Pacific suggest that participation can result in constitutions that recognize local sociopolitical practices, institutions, and customary law as people exercise their constituent power to create institutions that reflect their society rather than being unquestioningly based on liberal peace assumptions. It has also seen constitutions provide for a system of devolution or decentralization of state functions and powers to locally legitimate institutions.[163] The literature is also optimistic that participation will see the constitution include more provisions to protect human rights and civil liberties. Indeed, based on a study of twelve

---

[157] In this context, the "public sphere" is defined as an arena of association that is concerned with state affairs, but which is not part of the formal state structure. Habermas, *Between Facts and Norms*.
[158] R. Eyben and S. Ladbury, *Building Effective States: Taking a Citizen's Perspective* (Brighton: Centre for Citizenship, Participation and Accountability, 2006); Habermas, *The Inclusion of the Other*.
[159] Ginsburg, Elkins, and Blount, "Does the Process of Constitution Making Matter?"; Samuels, *Constitution Building Processes and Democratisation*.
[160] M. Ndulo, "The Democratic State in Africa: The Challenges for Institution Building," *National Black Law Journal* 16:1 (1998–2000): 83.
[161] R. Gordon, "Growing Constitutions," *University of Pennsylvania Journal of Constitutional Law* 1:3 (1999): 582.
[162] D. Chandler, "Introduction: Peace without Politics?" *International Peacekeeping* 12:3 (2005): 309; Hart, "Constitution Making and the Right to Take Part."
[163] G. Hassall and C. Saunders, *Asia-Pacific Constitutional Systems* (Cambridge: Cambridge University Press, 2002).

constitution-making processes, the International Institute for Democracy and Electoral Assistance found that more participatory processes result in more progressive rights provisions.[164] Tom Ginsburg and his collaborators also found that constitution-making processes that involved a referendum on the final constitution were more likely to create constitutions that include extensive human rights protections, universal suffrage, referendum processes in ordinary governance, and a public role in approving constitutional amendments.[165] Conversely, based on a study of 195 constitution-making processes between 1975 and 2002, Jennifer Widner found that "the level of public participation does not correlate with stronger rights protection."[166] Therefore, when considering how the governments of Timor-Leste and Bougainville are functioning in Chapters 5 and 8, this book considers the following questions: To what extent are state institutions perceived to be legitimate? And, are human rights and civil liberties protected?

When public participation in constitution making achieves the benefits described above and plays a positive role in state building, it can be described as a constituent process. The extent to which a constitution-making process can be described as a constituent process will depend upon the level of public participation involved. Minimal participation is unlikely to achieve a constituent process; moderate participation[167] is likely to achieve some (but not all) of the benefits of participatory constitution making; and extensive participation is likely to achieve most (if not all) of the benefits of a constituent process. Consequently, the higher the level of public participation in constitution making, the more likely it is that a constituent process will emerge and play a positive role in state building.

QUESTIONS ABOUT A CONSTITUENT PROCESS

Despite these claimed benefits of a constituent process, critics are skeptical about the potential role that public participation can play in constitution making. First, elitist accounts question whether ordinary people possess sufficient knowledge and expertise to judge what is in their collective interests.[168]

---

[164] Samuels, *Constitution Building Processes and Democratisation*.
[165] Ginsburg, Elkins, and Blount, "Does the Process of Constitution Making Matter?"
[166] Widner, "Constitution Writing in Post-Conflict Settings," 1532; *Proceedings, Workshop on Constitution Building Processes*.
[167] G. A. Almond and S. Verba, *The Civic Culture: Political Attitudes and Democracy in Five Nations* (Princeton: Princeton University Press, 1963), 360.
[168] R. A. Dahl, "Further Reflections on the Elitist Theory of Democracy," *American Political Science Review* 60:2 (1966): 296–305; C. Pateman, *Participation and Democratic Theory*

These accounts warn that if they do not, they are likely to either become disillusioned or targets of manipulation, deception, and extremism.[169] Therefore, deliberation may induce people to hold beliefs that are inaccurate, biased, or not in their best interest.[170] However, this overlooks the fact that participation provides a forum for challenging such beliefs in the "marketplace of ideas"[171] rather than allowing them to fester in the private sphere and potentially destabilize the state. Scholars also argue that several long-standing constitutions, such as those of Australia, Canada, and the United States, were made by elites without public participation or an overt exercise of constituent power, yet they have acquired legitimacy. Similar arguments have been made about more recent constitutions adopted in post-Communist Europe, which have "established strong systems of constitutional review without using popular mechanisms to draft and ratify their constitutions."[172] Vicki Jackson notes that constitutions negotiated by elites may "create bonds of legitimacy between a constitutional instrument and a majority of the polity to which it applies."[173] Moreover, numerous constitutions made recently that involved a high degree of public participation have failed to achieve legitimacy, most notably in Fiji, Eritrea, Ethiopia, and Thailand.[174] However, this overlooks the fact that most of the long-standing constitutions were made in states in which "state and nation emerge *pari passu*."[175] In fragmented societies, the constitution has to do much more than merely record a societal consensus among an existing political community; it has to constitute both that consensus and that community.

Second, participation may conceal existing power relations and "mask...biases in interests and needs based on, for example, age, class, caste, ethnicity, religion and gender."[176] This highlights the highly political nature

---

(Cambridge: Cambridge University Press, 1970); J. L. Walker, "A Critique of the Elitist Theory of Democracy," *American Political Science Review* 15:3 (1966): 285–295.

[169] J. Fearon and D. Laitin, "Violence and the Social Construction of Ethnic Identity," *International Organization* 54:4 (2000): 845–877; Ghai and Galli, *Constitution Building Processes*; J. Snyder and K. Ballentine, "Nationalism and the Marketplace of Ideas," *International Security* 21:2 (1996): 5–40.

[170] Przeworski, "Deliberation and Ideological Domination"; Stokes, "Pathologies of Deliberation."

[171] Mill, *"On Liberty" and Other Writings*.

[172] W. Partlett, "The Dangers of Popular Constitution-Making," *Brooklyn Journal of International Law* 38:1 (2012): 195.

[173] Jackson, "What's in a Name?," 1293–1294; Ghai and Galli, *Constitution Building Processes*.

[174] Blount, Elkins, and Ginsburg, "Does the Process of Constitution-Making Matter?"; Ghai and Galli, *Constitution Building Processes*.

[175] Smith, "State-Making and Nation-Building," 67.

[176] B. Cooke and U. Kothari, "The Case for Participation as Tyranny," in *Participation: The New Tyranny?*, ed. B. Cooke and U. Kothari (London: Zed Books, 2001), 6.

of the design of a constitution-making process, including decisions about who can participate, how they participate, and at what point in the process their participation occurs. Moreover, participation through face-to-face interaction can generate unintended consequences, particularly in hierarchical societies. If participation is conducted in groups (the most common form), it can see participants make collective decisions that are riskier than decisions they would have made individually; they can also second-guess what other participants want, self-censor, and provide space for the manipulation of the groups' decision making for ideological or other beliefs.[177] However, if the "ways in which participation relates to existing power structure and political systems" are understood, it may be possible to ameliorate these effects and empower marginalized groups.[178]

If participation is solicited through high-level institutions that are alien to the population, this may reduce political trust.[179] This suggests that the trustworthiness and representativeness of the body or bodies involved in constitution making will be relevant.[180] In addition, in fragmented or divided societies, people will often have different ideas of what constitutes good reasons for a political decision. Therefore, even in ideal deliberative conditions in which reasons are given and understood, it may still be difficult to find reasons on which all agree, particularly when there is fragmentation and division.[181] This is particularly likely in situations of scarce resources, incompatible values, and incomplete understanding. In this regard, material inequalities among participants are almost inevitable,[182] which may disadvantage the inarticulate or those who may not have access to sophisticated

---

[177] B. Cooke, "The Social Psychological Limits of Participation," in Cooke and Kothari, *Participation: The New Tyranny?*
[178] S. Hickey and G. Mohan, "Towards Participation as Transformation: Critical Themes and Challenges," in *Participation: From Tyranny to Transformation?*, ed. S. Hickey and G. Mohan (London: Zed Books, 2004), 5.
[179] J. Gaventa, "Towards Participatory Governance: Assessing the Transformative Possibilities," in Hickey and Mohan, *Participation*; S. M. Lipset, "Some Social Requisites of Democracy: Economic Development and Political Legitimacy," *American Political Science Review* 53:1 (1959): 69–105; D. Narayan, *Voices of the Poor: Can Anyone Hear Us?* (New York: Oxford University Press, 2000).
[180] B. Radcliff and E. Wingenbach, "Preference Aggregation, Functional Pathologies, and Democracy: A Social Choice Defence of Participatory Democracy," *Journal of Politics* 62:4 (2000): 977–998.
[181] T. McCarthy, "Legitimacy and Diversity: Dialectical Reflections on Analytical Distinctions," in *Habermas on Law and Democracy: Critical Exchanges*, ed. M. Rosenfeld and A. Arato (Berkeley: University of California Press, 1998).
[182] W. E. Scheuerman, "Critical Theory beyond Habermas," in Dryzek, Honig, and Phillips, *Handbook of Political Theory*.

political vocabulary.[183] However, as these challenges are likely to persist after the state has been built, public participation in constitution making seems to offer a good way to address them and negotiate compromises rather than imposing a constitution with minimal participation that may satisfy no one, or only those who made it.

Third, instrumentalists argue that people are self-interested and participate only in order to access resources or power. If they do not succeed, they may become alienated, particularly if resources are scarce and competition to obtain them is fierce.[184] Factions may then develop, and when deliberation cannot dissolve disagreement, there is a danger of "group polarisation," with constitutional debates ending in bitterness, frustration, and deadlock.[185] Therefore, in fragmented or divided societies, it may be difficult to achieve the level of trust or mutual understanding required for deliberation.[186] Skeptics also question whether people are likely to transcend their own particular interests and consider the common good, noting that constitutional politics "turns out to be remarkably similar to normal politics."[187] Indeed, they caution that since the stakes are high and the institutions to mediate conflict are not yet in place, participation is likely to foster conflict, polarize populations, and slide into populism,[188] as occurred in Venezuela and Bolivia.[189] In particular, elections can "foment polarization and civil strife,"[190] as occurred in Iraq[191] and Chad.[192] Therefore, it is vital to create "stable institutions"[193] and "find rules and principles that will restrain the ability of powerful individual figures, minorities, or temporary majorities from imposing their own desired

---

[183] Ghai and Galli, *Constitution Building Processes*; C. Mouffe, *The Deliberative Paradox* (London: Verso, 2000); L. Sanders, "Against Deliberation," *Political Theory* 25:3 (1997): 347–376; I. M. Young, "Communication and the Other: Beyond Deliberative Democracy," in Benhabib, *Democracy and Difference*.
[184] N. Bermeo, *Ordinary People in Extraordinary Times: The Citizenry and the Breakdown of Democracy* (Princeton: Princeton University Press, 2003); J. J. Linz and A. C. Stepan, *The Breakdown of Democratic Regimes: Crisis, Breakdown, and Reequilibration*, Vol. I (Baltimore: Johns Hopkins University Press, 1978).
[185] Sunstein, *Designing Democracy*, 8; R. A. Dahl, "The City in the Future of Democracy," *American Political Science Review* 61 (1967): 953–969.
[186] J. Johnson, "Arguing for Deliberation: Some Skeptical Considerations," in Elster, *Deliberative Democracy*; O'Flynn, *Deliberative Democracy*; Young, "Communication and the Other."
[187] Bellamy, *Political Constitutionalism*, 133.
[188] Arato, "Iraq and Its Aftermath"; Horowitz, "Conciliatory Institutions"; Partlett, "The Dangers of Popular Constitution-Making."
[189] Landau, "Constitution-Making Gone Wrong."
[190] Blount, "Participation in Constitutional Design," 44.
[191] Ghai and Galli, *Constitution Building Processes and Democratization*.
[192] Widner, "Constitution Writing."
[193] Partlett, "The Dangers of Popular Constitution-Making," 234.

constitution."[194] Participation can also raise expectations to an extent that cannot be satisfied, leading to disillusionment with the new constitution and the state institutions it creates.[195] These risks are real, but participation in constitution making can provide a space for agonistic encounters between groups to take place and for compromises to be reached. Indeed, it has been argued that "the problem is not too much passion and interest but too little attempt to engage them" during constitution making.[196] If passions and interests are engaged with, they can be incorporated into the process to "help make a constitution more just and durable."[197]

Fourth, scholars are concerned about the expense and institutional capacity required to facilitate large groups of people deliberating on a constitution.[198] While this suggests that representatives could instead engage in deliberation, it raises the questions of how representatives are chosen and whether they should deliberate based on reasons that they find compelling or reasons that appeal to their constituents. In addition, if representatives are members of political parties, the question of whether they are accountable to their constituents or the supporters of their party comes into play,[199] which was an issue that haunted the Timor-Leste process. Compounding these concerns, in developing societies, constitution-making bodies are unlikely to be able to afford to devote sufficient resources to this task. Critics caution that if the demand for participation overwhelms capacity, this may give rise to instability and disorder, particularly if it spills outside institutional channels into open conflict.[200] They also caution that participation is time-consuming and can prolong transitional rule, entrench the regime overseeing the process, and distract attention from other development issues.[201] Too much publicity and information sharing may also be difficult to achieve, given that constitution making often involves sensitive negotiations that may require secrecy.[202] These risks are real, particularly in postconflict societies where a single

---

[194] Landau, "The Importance of Constitution-Making," 631.
[195] Ghai and Galli, *Constitution Building Processes*.
[196] Brown, "Reason, Interest, Rationality," 675.   [197] Ibid., 683.
[198] A. L. Bannon, "Designing a Constitution-Drafting Process: Lessons from Kenya," *Yale Law Journal* 116 (2007): 1824–1872.
[199] Gutmann and Thompson, *Democracy and Disagreement*.
[200] S. P. Huntington, *Political Order in Changing Societies* (New Haven: Yale University Press, 1968).
[201] W. H. Riker, "The Experience of Creating Institutions: The Framing of the United States Constitution," in *Explaining Social Institutions*, ed. J. Knight and I. Sened (Ann Arbor: University of Michigan Press, 1995).
[202] Gutmann and Thompson, *Democracy and Disagreement*; Horowitz, "Conciliatory Institutions."

liberation movement may view itself as having "won" and as having the right to control the constitution-making process. This suggests that the international community may be required to play a role to ensure that all parties are able to participate and that open conflict is discouraged.

Fifth, critics challenge the meaning of "participation," noting that it is a "relatively vague and abstract" concept, as compared with the clarity of elections.[203] This leads them to question whether much participation is superficial if it means just "showing up" at public meetings,[204] particularly if literacy levels are low, the process is conducted in a largely unfamiliar language, or civil society is weak and unable to promote clear agendas. While it is true that participation is likely to be most beneficial when participants are well informed and their involvement is meaningful, particularly when civil society is robust and pluralistic,[205] the Bougainville case illustrates that benefits can still be achieved in less ideal conditions. Moreover, skeptics caution that in difficult conditions, individual contributions to collective decisions are so likely to be small that the rational citizen would not invest the time required to become informed about the issues.[206] However, the Timor-Leste and Bougainville cases illustrate that even when constitution making is conducted in difficult conditions, the levels of participation can be high. (For example, in Timor-Leste, it was estimated that 25 percent of the electorate participated in civic education and 10 percent in constitutional consultations.)

Alternatively, if participation requires more meaningful expressions of views on a constitutional issue or, even more demandingly, for those views to be recorded and transmitted into the draft constitution, this could place unrealistic expectations on citizens, since it can be time-consuming and requires a "vast increase" in the level of political participation. Indeed, deliberation requires patience, a willingness to hear others out, and the careful evaluation of information.[207] In this regard, scholars have begun to consider the role of people and groups "who do not participate (or do so minimally) in public political and civic processes."[208] This nonparticipation can be distinguished

---

[203] H. J. Steiner, "Political Participation as a Human Right," *Harvard Human Rights Yearbook* 1 (1988): 77–78.
[204] Miller, "Designing Constitution-Making Processes," 636. [205] Ibid.
[206] Horowitz, "Conciliatory Institutions."
[207] Scheuerman, "Critical Theory beyond Habermas," 96; C. Offe, "Micro-aspects of Democratic Theory: What Makes for the Deliberative Competence of Citizens?," in Hadenius, *Democracy's Victory*.
[208] R. Mac Ginty, "Between Resistance and Compliance: Non-participation and the Liberal Peace," *Journal of Intervention and Statebuilding* 6:2 (2012): 172.

from passivity and "does not preclude consciousness, social and cultural engagement with others, and economic activity."[209] Scholars note that many liberals assume that people are enabled to participate in public processes such as constitution making,[210] and indeed have a duty to participate,[211] with nonparticipation regarded as "somehow irresponsible or feckless."[212] As a result, liberal state builders fail to recognize that there are often structural barriers to participation, and that participation in liberal peace state building often involves accepting "Western bureaucratic norms" and processes designed by external actors.[213] Nonparticipation may be voluntary, which "denotes some form of agency and autonomy."[214] It may also be involuntary, as it is prevented by structural barriers such as discriminatory laws, lack of opportunity, or an unstable security situation. Finally, nonparticipation might be a consequence of the circumstances, as many people may not be conscious of the constitution-making process because they are preoccupied with their survival. Indeed, in developing countries, subsistence lifestyles mean that peoples' daily lives are occupied by more immediate concerns, with onerous expectations of participation giving rise to potential "tyranny."[215] Most citizens of established Western democracies played no role in making their constitutions and engage in little ongoing political participation beyond voting at elections. However, citizens in Western democracies engage in "latent" participation, whereby they know where and how to make complaints and are able to address them to functioning institutions. This participation is aided by active civil societies and established media. In contrast, in new states, the avenues of latent participation are often less clear, and active participation, including during constitution making, can play a valuable role in achieving citizenization. In addition, in situations where the population has fought a long struggle for self-determination, it may be difficult to deny people the opportunity to participate.

If a wide definition of participation is used and participants make significant contributions to the constitutional debate, critics question how seriously constitution drafters should be expected to deliberate on these contributions in order for participation to "serve plausible normative or instrumental

---

[209] Ibid. [210] Rawls, *A Theory of Justice*.
[211] P. Starr, *Freedom's Power: The History and Promise of Liberalism* (New York: Basic Books, 2007).
[212] Mac Ginty, "Between Resistance and Compliance," 170; C. J. Pattie, P. Seyd, and P. Whiteley, *Citizenship in Britain: Values, Participation and Democracy* (Cambridge: Cambridge University Press, 2001).
[213] Mac Ginty, "Between Resistance and Compliance," 171. [214] Ibid., 173.
[215] Cooke and Kothari, "The Case for Participation as Tyranny," 3.

purposes."[216] In this regard, Angela Banks argues that inclusion in participatory constitution making requires "not only that individuals are physically present in the decision-making forums" but that they have an "effective opportunity to influence the thinking of others."[217] Related to this, skeptics question how public input should be treated and what weight should be accorded to submissions by individuals, as opposed to civil society and interest groups. This is particularly salient when access to the process may be uneven and when the constitution drafters are themselves democratically elected. For example, in South Africa, a disproportionate share of submissions appeared to come from the well educated, the middle class, former politicians, academics, professionals, and political activists.[218] This highlights the challenge of identifying which members of the population should be involved in constitution making: local elites; political, social, economic, or customary actors; members of civil society; or ordinary citizens.[219] Indeed, it is likely that public submissions from these different actors will vary – and perhaps contradict one another.[220] In this regard, it is most common for public submissions and the findings of public consultations to be digested for review by constitution drafters, who then exercise their own discretion.[221] However, they may also be subjected to statistical analysis, with the majority view holding sway. This was the approach adopted in Uganda, where constitution makers could not agree on ten issues and used the results of the public consultations to decide their ultimate fate.[222] Skeptics question whether this results in more than "cosmetic changes to the proposed constitution,"[223] although the Bougainville case highlights how public feedback can be used as the basis for the draft. Conversely, skeptics also argue that if extensive public consultation does result in significant changes, this can lead to an incoherent, cumbersome, and inconsistent constitution if the drafters are unable to channel the public's input into a rational framework.[224] This occurred in Brazil, where an extensive

---

[216] Miller, "Designing Constitution-Making Processes," 636.
[217] A. M. Banks, "Expanding Participation in Constitution Making: Challenges and Opportunities," *William and Mary Law Review* 49:4 (2008): 1043–1069, 1044.
[218] S. Gloppen, *South Africa: The Battle over the Constitution* (Brookfield: Ashgate, 1997).
[219] O. P. Richmond, "Beyond Local Ownership in the Architecture of International Peacebuilding," *Ethnopolitics* 11:4 (2012): 354–375.
[220] Hatchard, Ndulo, and Slinn, *Comparative Constitutionalism*.
[221] Miller, "Designing Constitution-Making Processes."
[222] *Proceedings, Workshop on Constitution Building Processes*.
[223] Tushnet, "Some Skepticism," 1492.
[224] Elster, "Constitution-Making in Eastern Europe"; S. Voigt, "The Consequences of Popular Participation in Constitutional Choice – Toward a Comparative Analysis," in *Deliberation and Decision*, ed. A. van Aaken et al. (Aldershot: Ashgate, 2003).

popular consultation saw over 122 popular amendments submitted to the Constituent Assembly.[225] Conversely, widespread participation might also "lead to more specific and detailed constitutional documents," and there is presently little empirical evidence to link participation to poor drafting.[226] Indeed, although there was extensive public participation in Bougainville, the detailed – but coherent – constitution has functioned relatively well in a difficult environment.

Overall, levels of public participation in constitution making can be measured along a continuum. At one extreme, public participation is minimal, with the constitution made by local elites or imposed by an external force, or where there are opportunities for participation but the outcomes of this participation are largely ignored by constitution makers and have little impact on the resulting constitution. At the other extreme, there is extensive public participation, in which there is broad consultation of the affected population and genuine opportunities for public feedback to shape the future constitution. Lying in between are cases of moderate participation, where the affected population is given some opportunity to influence the constitution-making process, but this influence translates into few real changes to the resulting document.

While acknowledging the skepticism about the role of public participation, this book argues that extensive public participation in constitution making is most likely to achieve the benefits of a constituent process, while moderate participation is likely to achieve some benefits and minimal participation is unlikely to achieve many – if any – benefits. As it is argued that a constituent process can play an important role in state building by fostering a sense of political community and producing a constitution that enhances the legitimacy and effectiveness of the state institutions that it creates by accommodating both the liberal and local, the level of public participation in constitution making is therefore likely to affect state building. However, it is acknowledged that "many of the assumptions of proponents of participation remain untested,"[227] and it may be that "the content of the institutions embodied in a constitution is...more important for the democratic future of a state."[228] Accordingly, using the indicators identified above, Parts II and III assess whether constitution making in Timor-Leste and Bougainville involved a constituent process and what role this played in state building.

---

[225] K. S. Rosenn, "Conflict Resolution and Constitutionalism: The Making of the Brazilian Constitution of 1988," in Miller, *Framing the State*.
[226] Blount, Elkins, and Ginsburg, "Does the Process of Constitution-Making Matter?," 50.
[227] Ginsburg, Elkins, and Blount, "Does the Process of Constitution-Making Matter?," 219.
[228] Horowitz, "Conciliatory Institutions," 1232.

PART II
MINIMAL PARTICIPATION IN TIMOR-LESTE

3

State building and constitution making in Timor-Leste

This chapter begins by outlining a brief historical background of Timor-Leste, which is necessary to understand contemporary constitutional developments. It then provides a contextual description of the state-building project in Timor-Leste, of which the constitution-making process formed a part. The main elements of constitution making identified in Chapter 2 are then used to examine the constitution-making process.

BRIEF HISTORICAL BACKGROUND OF TIMOR-LESTE

Prior to European colonization, Timor Island was fragmented into small settlements, which exhibited great social, political, and linguistic-cultural heterogeneity. Each settlement was part of a hierarchical tribal group or "house" (*uma lulik*), which was in turn part of a traditional kingdom (*rais*). Society was divided into three classes: chiefs and nobles (*liurai* and *dato*), commoners (*reino*), and slaves (*atan*). The kingdoms were linked by alliances between the *liurais*, which were renewed by ritual exchange and marriage.[1]

Although the Portuguese arrived in the sixteenth century, they did not exert any real control beyond their fortifications until the early twentieth century. Even after Portugal incorporated its half of Timor Island into the Portuguese state in 1951, most Timorese had only infrequent direct contact with the colonial administration and continued to live in rural areas "within the confines of the realms of the traditional rulers."[2] However, Portugal did invest in education, and by the late 1960s, young, educated Timorese began to move into administrative positions or were recruited into the Portuguese army. They

---

[1] D. Kammen, "Master-Slave, Traitor-Nationalist, Opportunist-Oppressed: Political Metaphors in East Timor," *Indonesia* 76 (2003): 69–85.
[2] J. Dunn, *East Timor: A Rough Passage to Independence* (Double Bay: Longueville Books, 2003), 4.

soon became "frustrated and resentful over the lack of opportunities."[3] Consequently, in the early 1970s, an incipient nationalist movement began to take shape.

After the April 1974 Revolução do Cravos in Portugal, the Timorese were granted the right to establish political associations. Four main associations emerged. One was the União Democratica Timorense (UDT), a center-right association that advocated "progressive autonomy" – that is, a period of continuing affiliation with Portugal as a means of achieving independence. A second was the Associação Social Democrata Timorense (ASDT), a left-leaning association that also sought progressive autonomy. In September 1974, ASDT changed its name to Frente Revolucionaria de Timor Leste Independente (FRETILIN), after which it moved further to the left and demanded immediate independence. A third was Associação Popular Democratica Timorense (APODETI), which advocated transitional autonomy within Indonesia. Finally, there was Klibur Oan Timor Aswain (KOTA), a small association seeking to reinvigorate traditional social organization.[4]

In late 1974, the Indonesian military began a covert disinformation campaign that convinced UDT that FRETILIN intended to seize power and impose a communist regime. Consequently, UDT withdrew from the coalition it had formed with FRETILIN and on August 11, 1975, staged a coup. The Portuguese administration withdrew to Atauro Island. Many members of UDT and KOTA fled to Indonesian West Timor, along with approximately 40,000 refugees. An estimated 1,500 to 3,000 people died in the resulting civil war between FRETILIN and UDT. However, the war was short, as Timorese members of the Portuguese army overwhelmingly supported FRETILIN. On August 20, 1975, these soldiers formed the Forças Armadas de Libertação Nacional de Timor-Leste (FALINTIL). FRETILIN/FALINTIL controlled all of the territory by late September 1975, and on November 28, 1975, FRETILIN leader Xavier do Amaral made a unilateral declaration of independence.

On November 30, 1975, APODETI and (certain) UDT leaders signed the Balibo Declaration, which declared the territory's integration into Indonesia. Indonesia used this to justify a full-scale invasion on December 7, 1975. By the end of December 1975, Indonesia had up to 20,000 troops in the territory,

---

[3] J. Ramos-Horta, *Funu: The Unfinished Saga of East Timor* (Trenton, NJ: The Red Sea Press, 1987), 26; X. Gusmão, *To Resist Is to Win! The Autobiography of Xanana Gusmão*, ed. S. Niner (Richmond: Aurora Books, 2000).

[4] J. Taylor, *Indonesia's Forgotten War: The Hidden History of East Timor* (New York: Zed Books, 1994).

the savagery of whom "greatly stiffened the resolve of the resistance and provided FRETILIN with a degree of popular support greater than it might otherwise have enjoyed."[5] Yet other Timorese began to collaborate with Indonesia, persuaded by threats, violence, and bribery. By the end of the 1970s, FALINTIL could no longer sustain conventional military resistance and instead emerged as a guerrilla force, supported by an extensive civilian "clandestine resistance."[6]

Before the invasion, a small delegation of FRETILIN leaders, headed by Mari Alkatiri and José Ramos-Horta, had fled to Mozambique. Ramos-Horta soon moved to Australia to lead efforts to pursue the Timorese cause at the UN. Under the influence of the Frente de Libertação de Moçambique (FRELIMO), those remaining in Mozambique were radicalized, embraced Marxist ideology, and proclaimed themselves the exclusive representatives of the Timorese people.[7] Within the territory, Kay Rala Xanana Gusmão emerged to lead FALINTIL. Although Gusmão was a member of FRETILIN, he recognized the importance of forging unity and cooperation among the resistance. He also managed to negotiate a cease-fire with the Indonesian military in 1983. FRETILIN loyalists opposed these negotiations, and after the cease-fire broke down, they attempted a coup to displace Gusmão. Although they were unsuccessful, the coup attempt instigated a split between Gusmão and FRETILIN. Gusmão then continued his efforts to widen the resistance by reaching out to UDT and other political groups. In 1987, he established The Conselho Nacional da Resistencia Timorense (The CNRT) to unify the resistance, resigned from FRETILIN, and declared that FALINTIL was a nonpartisan "national army." Gusmão then emerged as a strident critic of FRETILIN, which he claimed exhibited "political infantilism," "senseless radicalism," and a "sectarian mentality" that worked against the unification of the resistance.[8] Consequently, FRETILIN leaders took until 1989 to join The CNRT. Following this, Ramos-Horta distanced himself from FRETILIN and aligned himself with Gusmão, officially becoming The CNRT's overseas representative in 1990.

In May 1998, economic collapse forced Indonesian president Suharto to resign. His replacement sought to resolve the "East Timor question" quickly by agreeing that a "popular consultation" would be held in the territory in August 1999, in which Timorese would be given the option of "special

---

[5] Dunn, *East Timor*, 253.   [6] CAVR, *Chega*.
[7] H. Hill, *Stirrings of Nationalism in East Timor: FRETLIN 1974–1978* (Otford: Otford Press, 2002); Ramos-Horta, *Funu*.
[8] In speeches reproduced in Gusmão, *To Resist Is to Win!*, 131–132, 214.

autonomy" within Indonesia. If special autonomy was rejected, the UN would hold authority and "initiate the procedure enabling East Timor to begin a process of transition towards independence."[9] The popular consultation was held on August 30, 1999, and 98 percent of those who registered voted, with 21.5 percent of voters supporting the proposal for autonomy and 78.5 percent rejecting it.

After this result was announced on September 4, 1999, the Indonesian military and their supporting Timorese militias engaged in a "scorched earth" campaign, systematically destroying infrastructure and up to 74 percent of houses and buildings.[10] On September 15, 1999, the UN Security Council authorized the International Force for East Timor (InterFET) "to take all necessary measures" to restore peace and security; it deployed on September 20.[11]

CONTEXTUAL DESCRIPTION OF THE STATE-BUILDING PROJECT

On October 25, 1999, InterFET was replaced by the UN Transitional Administration in East Timor (UNTAET). UNTAET was mandated to build the new state by temporarily assuming sovereign powers.[12] The power to exercise "all legislative and executive authority, including the administration of justice" was concentrated in the special representative of the UN secretary-general, the "transitional administrator," Sergio Vieira de Mello.[13] Very little direction was provided concerning how state building should occur, which

---

[9] UN, *Report of the Secretary-General: Question of East Timor*, attaching Annex I, *A Constitutional Framework for a Special Autonomy for East Timor and Agreement between the Republic of Indonesia and the Portuguese Republic on the Question of East Timor*; Annex II, *Agreement Relating to the Modalities of the Popular Consultation of East Timorese through a Direct Ballot*; and Annex III, *East Timor Popular Consultation*, UN Doc. A/53/951-S/1999/513, May 5, 1999. These agreements were endorsed by the UN Security Council. S/Res/1236, *On the Situation in East Timor*, May 7, 1999.

[10] J. Dunn, *Crimes against Humanity in East Timor, January to October 1999: Their Nature and Causes* (Dili: UNTAET, February 14, 2001); UN, *Report of the Security Council Mission to Jakarta and Dili, 8 To 12 September 1999*, UN Doc. S/1999/976, September 14, 1999; UNOHCHR, *Report of the International Commission of Inquiry on East Timor to the Secretary-General*, UN Doc. A/54/726, S/2000/59, January 31, 2000.

[11] S/Res/1264, *On the Situation in East Timor*, September 15, 1999.

[12] S/Res/1272, *On the Situation in East Timor*, October 25, 1999. UNTAET's mandate was later extended by S/Res/1319, *On the Situation in East Timor*, September 20, 2000; S/Res/1338, *On the Situation in East Timor*, January 31, 2001; and S/Res/1392, *On the Situation in East Timor*, January 31, 2002.

[13] S/Res/1272, para. 1. See also UNTAET Regulation No. 1999/1, *On the Authority of the Transitional Administration in East Timor*, UN Doc. UNTAET/REG/1991/1, November 27, 1999.

led de Mello to complain that "there was no instruction manual attached to the mandate."[14]

While UNTAET was active in the capital, Dili, during its early stages, it did little to penetrate the rural areas in which almost 90 percent of the population lived.[15] Consequently, people fell back on their local sociopolitical practices.[16] UNTAET overlooked these local practices and instead "tended to treat the Timorese political system as a *tabula rasa.*"[17]

As UNTAET was mandated to "consult and cooperate closely with the East Timorese people,"[18] on December 2, 1999, the transitional administrator created the unelected part-Timorese National Consultative Council to advise him.[19] As this body was "mostly closed," it generated frustration among the Timorese.[20] Recognizing this, in July 2000 the transitional administrator created an East Timor Transitional Administration (ETTA) to govern and administer the territory. The transitional administrator and the heads of the eight (later nine) ETTA departments then formed the cabinet of the Transitional Government.[21] The National Consultative Council was replaced in October 2000 by the all-Timorese National Council. The National Council had the power to initiate, modify, and recommend draft UNTAET regulations and to question cabinet members.[22] Members of the National Council and

---

[14] Quoted in G. Robinson, "With UNAMET in East Timor: A Historian's Personal View," in *Bitter Flowers, Sweet Flowers: East Timor, Indonesia and the World Economy*, ed. R. Tanter, M. Selden, and S. Shalom (Oxford: Rowman and Littlefield, 2000), 70.

[15] J. Federer, *The UN in East Timor: Building Timor Leste, a Fragile State* (Darwin: Charles Darwin University Press, 2005); World Bank, *Report of the Joint Assessment Mission to East Timor* (Washington: World Bank, 1999).

[16] S. Ospina and T. Hohe, *Traditional Power Structures and Local Governance in East Timor*, Études Courtes no. 5 (Geneva: Graduate Institute of Development Studies, 2002).

[17] Chesterman, "East Timor," 199.   [18] S/Res/1272, para. 8.

[19] The National Council had fifteen members, including representatives of UNTAET, one representative of the Catholic Church, seven The CNRT members, and three members of political groupings outside of The CNRT (that is, pro-integrationists). This division was more or less proportional to the results of the 1999 popular consultation. UNTAET Regulation No. 1999/2, *On the Establishment of a National Consultative Council*, UN Doc. UNTAET/REG/1992/2, December 2, 1999.

[20] J. Della-Giacoma, "Results over Process, Analysis of the Creation of the East Timor Constituent Assembly," unpublished paper, undated.

[21] Of the eight initial portfolios, four were assigned to Timorese and four to UNTAET staff. A fifth Timorese portfolio was created in October 2000 when José Ramos-Horta was appointed cabinet member for foreign affairs. UNTAET Regulation No. 2000/23, *On the Establishment of the Cabinet of the Transitional Government in East Timor*, UN Doc. UNTAET/REG/2000/23, July 14, 2000.

[22] The National Council consisted of thirty-three (later thirty-six) members who were all Timorese. The National Council included seven The CNRT members, three non-The CNRT party members, and representatives from the districts, NGOs, women's groups, labor, students,

ETTA were selected primarily from The CNRT, which had remained relatively united and had held several congresses relating to the transition to independence. However, by mid-2000, tensions within The CNRT had become evident. FRETILIN withdrew in August 2000, and in June 2001, The CNRT was dissolved in favor of creating political parties. The CNRT's dissolution highlighted the internal divisions within the Timorese leadership, particularly between Gusmão and FRETILIN. On the one hand, Gusmão believed that he was "of the people" and therefore contested the privileged status that had been afforded to FRETILIN. On the other hand, FRETILIN Secretary-General Alkatiri believed that FRETILIN had "always been the 'true representative' of the Timorese people," and therefore he afforded other political leaders, parties, or organizations "little status."[23]

MAIN ELEMENTS OF THE CONSTITUTION-MAKING PROCESS

In late 2000, UNTAET turned its attention to making a constitution for the new state.

The time frame given for the process

From the outset, the time frame available for the constitution-making process was relatively clear, as the UN secretary-general envisaged that the transition to independence would take two to three years. As predicted in the constitution-making literature, rather than being based on a judgment of what needed to take place, this was largely driven by the major contributors' budgets and the Security Council's patience. While The CNRT had initially envisaged the transition lasting eleven to thirteen years, based on the scale of state building required, it progressively shortened its time frame because of growing dissatisfaction with the opportunities for Timorese participation.[24] Indeed, in November 2000, The CNRT proposed a political calendar under which the constitution would be debated, drafted, and adopted in ninety days, by December 15, 2001, with the UN to withdraw by the end of 2001. On

---

business, the Catholic and Protestant Churches, and Muslims. UNTAET Regulation No. 2000/24, *On the Establishment of a National Council*, UN Doc. UNTAET/REG/2000/24, July 14, 2000.

[23] S. Niner, "Martyrs, Heroes and Warriors: The Leadership of East Timor," in *East Timor: Beyond Independence*, ed. D. Kingsbury and M. Leach (Clayton: Monash University Press, 2007), 122.

[24] A. Goldstone, "UNTAET with Hindsight: The Peculiarities of Politics in an Incomplete State," *Global Governance* 10:1 (2004): 83–98.

December 12, 2000, Gusmão presented this calendar to the National Council.[25] It was rejected on the grounds of lack of information. Gusmão threatened to resign unless the calendar was adopted, but he relented after the council agreed to hold public hearings to generate recommendations.

The National Council held its public hearings from January 18 to 24, 2001. Twenty-two representatives of civil society and political parties not represented on the council gave oral testimony and made written submissions. APODETI and UDT approved the proposed calendar, while civil society groups and the Catholic Church expressed concern about its shortness.[26] However, few recommendations were incorporated into the calendar, and it was approved by the council in February 2001. FRETILIN representatives on the National Council pushed this approval as they "essentially viewed themselves as having won, and they wanted to take over power quickly."[27] As has been cautioned in the literature, FRETILIN appears to have sought to rush the process in order to seize the opportunity of entrenching its own leadership of the new state. However, there was also concern that if debate was not minimized and independence was not achieved quickly, this might generate instability, which Indonesia could use to justify reoccupying the territory.

In February 2001, several Timorese civil society groups presented a draft regulation proposing a nine-month calendar.[28] After this proposal was rejected by the National Council, these groups wrote to the UN Security Council to express their "serious concerns" about the shortness of the calendar, which they argued provided insufficient time for civic education and consultation.[29] These concerns reflected those of the literature, particularly the fact that a short time frame could limit opportunities for Timorese participation.

Despite these objections, the calendar was formally adopted on March 16, 2001, in the UNTAET regulation relating to the constitution-making process. This regulation provided that between the promulgation of the relevant

---

[25] The CNRT, *Broad Timeline for the Process Leading to East Timor's Declaration of Independence*, presented to the National Council by The CNRT/National Council president Xanana Gusmão, December 12, 2000 (Dili: The CNRT, 2000).

[26] Committee on Political Affairs, *Report on the Political Transitional Calendar* (Dili: National Council, February 22, 2001).

[27] A. J. Regan, "Constitution Making in East Timor: Missed Opportunities?," in *Elections and Constitution Making in East Timor*, ed. D. de Costa Babo Soares et al. (Canberra: Australian National University, 2003), 37–38.

[28] East Timor International Support Centre, *A Gradual Path to Full Sovereignty in East Timor* (Dili: East Timor International Support Centre, 2001).

[29] A. de Jesus Soares, "For an Interim Constitution," *La'o Hamutuk Bulletin*, 2:5 (2001); interview with a former member of the Constituent Assembly and government official, February 2, 2010; NGO Forum, *Letter from East Timor NGO Forum*.

legislation in March 2001 and the Constituent Assembly elections scheduled for August 30, 2001, the following had to be completed: a UNTAET civic education program, public consultations via Constitutional Commission hearings, registration for the Constituent Assembly elections, and the Constituent Assembly election.[30] The timetable then provided the Constituent Assembly with ninety days to produce a constitution. Independence would occur on May 20, 2002. Setting this date in advance excluded the possibility of extending the calendar if required.

The type of institution that was designated to draft the constitution

It was left to the National Council to decide the nature of the body that would draft the constitution. There was broad agreement that the process should be "popular" and "democratic."[31] The CNRT initially agreed that an appointed constitution convention, comprising all social and political groups, should draft the constitution and ensure full public consultation and participation. The draft would then be submitted to an elected constituent assembly for debate and adoption.[32] This proposal reflected the literature, which suggests that a specially convened convention is more likely to negotiate compromises, achieve consensus, and avoid distraction by everyday politics. However, the director of the UNTAET Political Affairs Department and the transitional administrator hijacked The CNRT's debate by announcing that an elected constituent assembly should draft, debate, and adopt a constitution.[33]

This issue was discussed at the National Council's public hearings in January 2001. Most speakers preferred that an appointed convention draft the constitution, with an elected assembly then adopting it, and several civil society groups submitted a draft regulation to this effect.[34] The draft regulation

---

[30] UNTAET Regulation No. 2001/2, *On the Election of a Constituent Assembly to Prepare a Constitution for an Independent and Democratic East Timor*, UN Doc. UNTAET/REG/2001/2, March 16, 2001.

[31] S. V. de Mello quoted in J. Morrow and R. White, "The United Nations in Transitional East Timor: International Standards and the Reality of Governance," *Australian Year Book of International Law* 22 (2002): 35.

[32] The CNRT, *Outcomes of the CNRT National Congress 21–30 August 2000* (Dili: The CNRT, August 2000); CNRT, *Reconstructing East Timor: Analysis of the Past and Perspectives for the Future Conference, Final Report (Tibar Document)* (Tibar: The CNRT, May 29–June 2, 2000).

[33] P. Galbraith, speaking at the Conference on Reconstructing East Timor: Analysis of the Past and Perspectives for the Future, Tibar, May 29, 2000; UNTAET, "Transcript of the Address of SRSG Sergio Vieira de Mello, at the 1st CNRT Congress," UNTAET press briefing media note, August 21, 2000.

[34] A. Gutierrez, proposed UNTAET regulation, presented to the National Council in January 2001.

was supported by civil society groups, the Catholic Church, and some Timorese leaders. In contrast, the UNTAET Political Affairs Department repeated its claim that an elected assembly should both make and adopt the constitution, given the important decisions involved and to ensure that the process was perceived to be Timorese-owned rather than excessively influenced by the UN.[35] This argument reflects the claim in the literature that an elected assembly may be perceived as a more legitimate forum to deal with state-building decisions. It might also reflect the calculation that an elected assembly could encourage political leaders – particularly FRETILIN – to buy in. However, given that FRETILIN had emerged as a dominant political actor, this suggests that UNTAET should have exercised caution relating to the potential for politicking and majoritarianism in an elected assembly.

The issue became one of the most contentious of the constitution-making process, given that smaller political parties and civil society recognized that FRETILIN would be advantaged in an elected constituent assembly. In particular, Gusmão changed his mind and supported the civil society draft regulation. However, it was unpopular among most members of the National Council, particularly those representing FRETILIN. Accordingly, on March 16, 2001, the council formally reached a decision in favor of electing the Constituent Assembly.[36]

The method by which the constitution drafters were selected, and how representative they were

After the National Council decided to elect the Constituent Assembly, it adopted a regulation to govern the election. The council decided on a hybrid electoral system. Voters would elect a district representative (one from each of the thirteen districts) through districtwide plurality, which was seen as "offering the advantage of the personalization of the candidates and assuring their accountability before the electorate."[37] Voters would also elect seventy-five national representatives on a closed party list system, whereby people voted for a single party, with the party choosing the order of candidate priority. This proportional system was seen as offering the "advantage of placing all voters on an equal footing and encouraging plurality."[38] There was also some

---

[35] Interview with an international academic and observer of the Constituent Assembly, January 5, 2010.
[36] UNTAET Regulation No. 2001/2.
[37] L. Aucion and M. Brandt, "East Timor's Constitutional Passage to Independence," in Miller, *Framing the State*, 256.
[38] Ibid.

suggestion that UNTAET advocated this system because it could dilute FRETILIN's influence,[39] as much of the literature agrees that proportional electoral systems encourage broad representation. However, it also meant that the national representatives would not be accountable to or obliged to consult with specific constituencies. It also empowered political parties and forced individuals and groups to work through them, as while people could stand independently, the time and expense involved in campaigning on a national scale were prohibitive.[40]

On February 16 and 17, 2001, the National Council conducted public hearings concerning the registration of political parties and invited heads of political parties and representatives of civil society to appear. The most contentious issue was the council's proposal that parties submit their platforms as a condition of registration. The council also wanted to prevent the registration of parties with pro-Indonesia leanings, as there was fear that the election might revive the tensions that arose during the popular consultation. UNTAET was concerned that this might constitute an unacceptable breach of political freedom and association. Eventually, a compromise was reached whereby parties and candidates were required to agree that they were registering for the election of the Constituent Assembly, which would "prepare a constitution for an independent and democratic East Timor."[41] They also had to declare that their officers would reside in the territory for at least three months prior to the election, which was designed to ensure that pro-integration forces based in West Timor could not frustrate the election. While UNTAET deferred to the council on this issue, it was careful to specify that any restrictions on participation in the election would not affect the right of a party or group, whether registered or not, to exercise its right to freedom of speech, opinion, and peaceful assembly.[42]

The National Council also disagreed about whether parties should be required to field female candidates, as proposed by the UNTAET Gender Affairs Unit and Timorese women's leaders.[43] UNTAET Political Affairs officials opposed this proposal on the basis that it would undermine the

---

[39] Interview with a member of Timorese civil society (a), May 14, 2010.
[40] In order to stand independently at the district level, applicants had to secure 100 signatures of support; at the national level, 500 signatures were required. UNTAET Regulation No. 2001/2, s. 34.
[41] Ibid., s. 1.
[42] UNTAET, *Political Activity, a Fundamental Right*, Public Statement (Dili: UNTAET, November 1, 2000).
[43] M. Pires, "East Timor and the Debate on Quotas," 2000, accessed February 25, 2010, www.quotaproject.org/fr/CS/CS_East_Timor.pdf.

legitimacy of the elections by forcing parties to propose women who might not be their preferred candidates. In the January 2001 public hearings, the idea was taken up in the council by the new center-right party, Partido Socialista Democratica (PSD). After a debate on March 13, 2001, the council voted against the proposal. Women's groups lobbied the transitional administrator to override this decision, and eventually de Mello introduced measures intended to "accomplish the spirit" of the proposals.[44] In any event, 268 women registered as candidates for the election, and 23 were elected (representing 27 percent of the Constituent Assembly seats).

Overall, sixteen political parties and 1,138 party and independent candidates registered for the election. To minimize conflict between parties, a "Pact of National Unity" was signed on July 8, 2001, by all but two of the registered parties. In this pact, the parties agreed to eschew violence and to accept the results of the popular consultation and election.[45]

As many members of the National Council planned to run for election, it was formally dissolved on July 14, 2001. In the interim period before the Constituent Assembly was created, the transitional administrator continued to promulgate essential regulations.

In order to prepare people for the Constituent Assembly election and constitution-making process, UNTAET conducted a civic education program, which was intended to "provide the foundation for an informed public engagement" in the process.[46] This reflects the literature, which identifies the importance of the distribution of information and the provision of education for citizenization.

The civic education program commenced in May 2001 in some areas and as late as July 2001 in others. In each of the thirteen districts, civic education teams were composed of four Timorese and two international staff. When designing the program, UNTAET had difficulty finding a model on which the Timorese leadership and civil society groups could agree.[47] Indeed, a coalition of Timorese civil society groups rejected its first iteration on the basis that there had been inadequate consultation and because the majority of the budget was to be spent on international staff. This delayed the start of the

---

[44] Quoted in UNTAET, "First Democratic Elections in East Timor to Be Held on 30 August 2001," UNTAET press briefing media note, March 16, 2001.

[45] *Pact of National Unity*, Dili, July 8, 2001, accessed February 24, 2011, members.pcug.org.au/~wildwood/01augnup.htm.

[46] UNTAET, "Dili Conference: 'Timorization' Needs to Be Strengthened," UNTAET press briefing media note, March 29, 2001.

[47] UN, *Interim Report of the Secretary-General on the United Nations Transitional Administration in East Timor*, UN Security Council, UN Doc. S/2001/436, May 2, 2001.

program and encouraged UNTAET to develop "a proposal that essentially excluded these groups."[48] Despite this, Timorese enthusiastically embraced the program, with hundreds of people attending its meetings, with estimates that more than 100,000 people (from a population of 800,000) participated overall.[49] A 2002 survey revealed that almost two-thirds of Timorese voters reported exposure to at least one form of civic education prior to the Constituent Assembly election.[50]

While it had a wide-ranging reach, the conventional wisdom is that the civic education program "came too late and delivered too little."[51] Due to its short time frame, the program focused mostly on the technical process of voting and encouraging people to vote[52] and was "less successful in conveying civic education more broadly."[53] Consequently, many Timorese remained confused about the concept of democracy. For example, a survey conducted in January 2002 found that only 17 percent of respondents could describe any characteristics of democracy.[54] While the program had intended to cover constitutional themes using "concrete narratives showing how these themes impact on village life,"[55] there were problems translating liberal ideas to the local environment. For example, "democracy" was translated as *nahe biti* (stretching the mat), which refers to a woven mat where traditional chiefs and the community gather to discuss community interests and resolve

---

[48] Goldstone, "UNTAET with Hindsight," 95.
[49] UNTAET, "Civic Education Events Draw Thousands," UNTAET press briefing media note, August 20, 2001.
[50] Sixty-two percent of respondents participated in civic education or election-related discussions; 60 percent received information via a brochure or pamphlet, 59 percent from an Independent Electoral Commission information session, 53 percent from newspapers, and 24 percent from a video CD. Asia Foundation, *Timor Lorosa'e National Survey of Citizen Knowledge* (Dili: Asia Foundation, 2002), 19.
[51] Goldstone, "UNTAET with Hindsight," 95; Conflict, Security and Development Group, *A Review of Peace Operations: A Case for Change East Timor Study* (London: Kings College London, 2003).
[52] Interview with a member of Timorese civil society (a), May 14, 2010; interview with a member of Timorese civil society (b), May 14, 2010.
[53] Carter Center, *The East Timor Political and Election Observation Project: Final Project Report* (Atlanta: Carter Center, April 2004), 37; A. Baltazar, "An Overview of the Constitution Drafting Process in East Timor," *East Timor Law Journal*, 9 (2004).
[54] Twenty-eight percent of respondents objected to unpopular political parties being allowed to hold local meetings, and 68 percent did not support allowing someone to make a speech critical of a government employee. Asia Foundation, *Timor Lorosa'e National Survey*, 20.
[55] UNTAET Constitutional Affairs Branch, *Draft Constitutional Introduction, Themes and Narratives* (Dili: UNTAET, April 19, 2001, and May 18, 2001); UNTAET Constitutional Affairs Branch, *Civic Education Material* (Dili: UNTAET, undated).

disputes.[56] As *nahe biti* emphasizes consensus decision making, it does not capture the competitive nature of democracy. Confusion over the meaning of key terms led to societal conflict in some instances, with people interpreting democracy to mean that they no longer had to listen to chiefs, which led to "village-level anarchy."[57] There were also claims that many Timorese remained confused about the idea of a competitive party system and that the 1975 civil war "left a profound fear of partisan politics among the population."[58] However, an international observer noted that Timorese were "not politically unsophisticated."[59] Anecdotal evidence also suggests that some Timorese had a high level of political knowledge, with one civic education officer recounting a meeting at which he was surprised when a fourteen-year-old boy asked him about the benefits of Australia's system of compulsory voting.[60]

Despite this, the civic education program appears to have been inadequate, which had implications for public participation in the constitution-making process. After a long period of Portuguese colonization during which most Timorese were disenfranchised, followed by Indonesian occupation during which elections were "stage-managed," Timorese had very limited experience of genuinely democratic elections.[61] Therefore, if they were to be able to make an informed electoral choice in the Constituent Assembly election and a genuine contribution to the public consultation on the constitution, they needed a more thorough program of civic education. This also suggests that the program missed the opportunity of achieving the positive effects of information dissemination and education identified in the literature.

Concerns about the adequacy of the civic education program exacerbated several other factors that cast doubt on the legitimacy of the election and the representativeness of the Constituent Assembly. First, anecdotal evidence from election observers suggests that many voters "seemed unclear" about the purpose of the assembly election.[62] Indeed, a survey conducted before the

---

[56] D. Babo-Soares, "*Nahe Biti*: The Philosophy and Process of Grassroots Reconciliation and Justice in East Timor," *The Asia Pacific Journal of Anthropology* 5:1 (2004): 15–33.

[57] T. Hohe, "The Clash of Paradigms: International Administration and Local Political Legitimacy in East Timor," *Contemporary Southeast Asia* 24:3 (2002): 583; A. K. Molnar, *Timor Leste: Politics, History, and Culture* (Abingdon: Routledge, 2009).

[58] E. Bowles and T. Chopra, "East Timor: Statebuilding Revisited," in *Building States to Build Peace*, ed. C. T. Call (Boulder: Lynne Rienner, 2008), 281.

[59] N. M. Lutz, "Constitutionalism as Public Culture in East Timor," paper presented at the Law and Society Association meeting, Pittsburgh, June 7, 2003.

[60] Personal communication from a former UNTAET civic education officer, July 3, 2009.

[61] Ramos-Horta, *Funu*, 49.

[62] Carter Center, *East Timor Political and Election Observation*, 37; D. Babo Soares, "Election in East Timor: Some Unresolved Issues," in Babo Soares, *Elections and Constitution Making*.

election found that 60 to 70 percent of the rural population did not understand its purpose.[63] Moreover, many did not understand why the election was necessary, believing that they had already voted for The CNRT with Gusmão as president during the 1999 popular consultation.[64] This perception was aided by the fact that The CNRT flag had been used on the popular consultation ballot paper to indicate support for independence.

Second, as the civic education program was inadequate, the proportional electoral system confused many voters. For example, many who voted for FRETILIN were surprised when it was revealed that, because FRETILIN had placed largely unknown members of the diaspora toward the top of its list, they were members of the Constituent Assembly.[65] Other parties put candidates who were familiar to the public at the top of their party list, and after the election swapped these candidates with others. For example, in order to appear "progressive," the Partido Socialista de Timor (PST) put a well-known woman first on its party list. However, when it received only one seat, the woman resigned and was replaced by the party leader.[66] Similarly, the program had not made it clear that the assembly could convert into the first Parliament at independence. This further confused voters as to the purpose of the election and how they should make their electoral choice. It also meant that when the assembly later announced its intention to convert, there was "criticism and widespread public outrage."[67]

Third, the tight time frame raised questions about the preparedness of most political parties. The CNRT dissolved in June 2001, and the Constituent Assembly election campaign period began on July 15, running until August 28, 2001. This left little time for new parties that had come under The CNRT to establish their own profiles or develop and promote their policies. Most parties also had difficulty organizing in rural areas due to a lack of funds and vehicles, although this was partially ameliorated by UNTAET donating air transport and a car to each registered party. While most parties attempted to campaign in rural areas, "some were unofficially discouraged, or given the cold shoulder

---

[63] Asia Foundation, *East Timor National Survey of Voters' Knowledge (Preliminary Findings)* (Dili: Asia Foundation, 2001).

[64] A. K. Molnar, "The First Democratic Elections in East Timor, Asia's Newest Nation: Factors of Social and Political Conditions Surrounding the Election of the First Constitutional Assembly," paper presented at the Brown Bag Lecture series of the Center for Southeast Asian Studies, Northern Illinois University, November 9, 2001.

[65] Bowles and Chopra, "East Timor: Statebuilding Revisited"; interview with a member of Timorese civil society (a), May 14, 2010.

[66] J. Della-Giacoma, "'Ensuring the Well-being of a Nation: Developing a Democratic Culture through Constitution Making in East Timor," paper presented at the Fletcher Conference on Innovative Approaches, Boston, April 1, 2005.

[67] Baltazar, "An Overview"; Regan, "Constitution Making in East Timor."

by village heads."[68] This created a "political vacuum" beyond Dili, and party representatives "were often not aware of party programmes or even the differences between their parties."[69]

To compensate, the transitional administrator and party representatives participated in "open dialogue" sessions around the territory, in which they answered questions about the upcoming election. UNTAET gave each party time on television and newspaper space; however, as the reception of television channels and distribution of newspapers was confined to the Dili area, the effectiveness of these methods was limited. UNTAET also gave parties radio time, which was transmitted more broadly, and distributed wind-up radios to each hamlet. The UNTAET Political Resource Center provided telephone communications, computers and internet access, and photocopying and media liaison services to all parties and independent candidates. However, face-to-face campaigning remained the most important source of information in rural areas. As most parties faced difficulties in achieving this, equality between them was a "fiction."[70]

As a result, it is unclear whether many voters were able to differentiate between parties. This was a particular issue with regard to the ballot papers. As there were low rates of literacy (43 percent in total, but only 37.2 percent in rural areas), the papers showed party symbols, names, and acronyms. However, there was confusion over which symbols represented which party, enhanced by the fact that some parties had similar symbols and some attempted to utilize symbols of the resistance to boost their electoral fortunes. For example, the Partido Democratica (PD) attempted to utilize images of Gusmão and Ramos-Horta, even though neither was formally associated with it. Gusmão also continued to be widely associated with FRETILIN, and there is some suggestion that people voted for FRETILIN on this basis. This conclusion is supported by the fact that many people who voted for FRETILIN also voted for Gusmão, rather than for the FRETILIN-supported candidate, in the later presidential election.

Fourth, the difficulties faced by new parties suggest that FRETILIN may have been disproportionately advantaged. Many voters fell back on FRETILIN because it was the party that represented the resistance. FRETILIN was aware of its advantage and astutely "used potent traditional and resistance

---

[68] D. Y. King, "East Timor's Founding Elections and Emerging Party System," *Asian Survey* 43:5 (2003): 750.

[69] Carter Center, *East Timor Political and Election Observation*, 32.

[70] Interview with a member of Timorese civil society (a), May 14, 2010; interview with a former member of the Constituent Assembly and member of Parliament, September 30, 2010.

symbols to ensure loyalty."[71] FRETILIN was also by far the best organized and financed party and managed to maintain party discipline and formulate a substantial policy platform. From January 2001, it conducted a census of its supporters and held elections for party, youth, and women representatives, which meant that its network covered the territory. This is an example of the danger of premature elections raised by the literature, as rather than promoting inclusion and participation, the election might instead have been perceived as winner – FRETILIN – takes all.

Fifth, there is some evidence that voters were misled and intimidated throughout the election campaign. Some candidates made poor-quality statements to the media. For example, one candidate from the Partido do Povo de Timor (PPT) claimed that he was a relative of Prince Charles and a major shareholder in the World Bank, which would allow him to access huge funds once he was elected – which he was. FRETILIN is also said to have used intimidating language, with its spokespeople talking of *dasa rai* (sweeping the ground clean) to describe what it planned to do to its opponents, which was a phrase associated with the Indonesian military during the 1970s.[72] In response, the Independent Electoral Mediation Panel issued a statement calling the use of *dasa rai* a "disturbing form of apparent verbal harassment."[73] FRETILIN also labeled UDT "nondemocratic," which led to a UDT campaign car becoming the target of a rock-throwing mob. The Council for the Popular Defence of the Democratic Republic of Timor-Leste (CPD-RDTL), an anti-system political group, also engaged in intimidation. It claimed that Timor-Leste had already declared independence in 1975 and consequently refused to acknowledge the validity of the elections or the authority of UNTAET.[74]

Sixth, during the election, 50,000 to 80,000 Timorese who had fled during the 1999 violence remained in "refugee camps" in West Timor.[75] Many had not supported independence, and as there were reports of violence and intimidation against them, they faced obstacles when attempting to return.[76]

---

[71] Niner, "Martyrs, Heroes and Warriors," 122; Babo Soares, "Election in East Timor"; Federer, *The UN in East Timor*.

[72] M. Dodd, "FRETILIN Accused of Threatening Poll Tactics," *Sydney Morning Herald*, August 24, 2001; "Two East Timorese Party Activists Arrested over Campaign Threats," *Agence France-Presse*, August 24, 2001.

[73] Quoted in A. L. Smith, "East Timor: Elections in the World's Newest Nation," *Journal of Democracy* 15:2 (2004): 151.

[74] UN, *Progress Report of the Secretary-General on the United Nations Transitional Administration in East Timor*, UN Security Council, UN Doc. S/2001/719, July 24, 2001; UN Doc. S/2001/436.

[75] UNTAET Human Rights Unit, *UNTAET Human Rights Unit Report* (Dili: UNTAET, March 2001).

[76] UNHCHR, *Report of the High Commissioner for Human Rights on the Situation of Human Rights in East Timor*, February 6, 2001, UN Doc. E/CN.42001/37.

Therefore, they were not able to participate in the election, and consequently up to 10 percent of the population was unrepresented in the constitution-making process.

Turnout for the election was strong, which suggests that the civic education program and election campaign did at least succeed in motivating people to vote. In the election of national representatives, 91.3 percent of those registered actually voted, while in the election of district representatives, 91.1 percent actually voted. The election itself went smoothly and was declared "free and fair" by both the Independent Electoral Commission and international observers.[77] FRETILIN won 57.4 percent of the national vote and twelve of the thirteen district seats (the thirteenth seat of Oecussi went to an independent), giving it fifty-five of the eighty-eight seats in the Constituent Assembly. PD, a youth-oriented party that has its roots in the clandestine resistance, won 8.7 percent and seven seats. PSD, a UDT breakaway party, received 8.2 percent and six seats. The revived ASDT won 7.8 percent and six seats. Eight smaller parties won a seat or two each, and one independent received a seat.

While the literature cautions that a premature election can result in a winner-takes-all outcome, and Alkatiri had predicted that FRETILIN would win 80 to 85 percent of the vote,[78] this did not come to fruition. This might be partly explained by the adoption of the proportional electoral system, which seems to have diluted FRETILIN's influence. It might also be explained by the fact that FRETILIN "probably antagonized many voters with its overconfident expectation of a supermajority."[79] Gusmão had attended rallies of opposition parties and publicly expressed his concern about FRETILIN leaders' aggressive conduct and the negative effects a FRETILIN landslide would have on democracy.[80] New parties and individuals also drew away votes. Therefore, although FRETILIN adopted the same mind-set as other liberation movements by presenting itself as the "true representative" of the Timorese people, the election results suggest that this view was not shared by many of them.

---

[77] Carter Center, *East Timor Political and Election Observation*; Independent Electoral Commission, *Statement of Reasons in Relation to Decision Number 2001-79 of 9 September 2001* (Dili: Independent Electoral Commission, September 9, 2001).

[78] "East Timor Leader Says FRETILIN Confident of Winning Presidential [sic] Election," *Xinhua News Agency*, June 26, 2001; B. Woodley, "The Countdown to Democracy," *The Australian*, August 11, 2001.

[79] Smith, "East Timor: Elections," 151.

[80] Quoted in R. McGurik, "Fretilin Majority Could Be Bad," *Australian Associated Press*, September 1, 2001.

The manner in which the designated institution drafted the constitution

The Constituent Assembly convened on September 15, 2001. It was mandated to produce a constitution within ninety days and to adopt the constitution by a vote of at least sixty of its eighty-eight members.[81] The mandate also provided that if the constitution provided for it, the assembly could transform into the first Parliament at independence.[82] This raised the danger of institutional self-interest identified in the literature, if assembly members were tempted to shape the new constitution to best reflect their interests. Indeed, one adviser noted that "there were clear signs that FRETILIN was adapting its constitution...to meet the institutional and functional needs it felt it required to exercise government."[83]

The Constituent Assembly began with three days of orientation on constitutional issues. It elected a speaker, Francisco "Lu-Olo" Guterres, the president of FRETILIN, by a vote of sixty-eight in favor, one against, seventeen abstentions, and two absentees. This early vote exhibited divisions within the assembly, as FRETILIN combined with ASDT to secure control. KOTA and PST members also tended to vote with FRETILIN. The other parties emerged as an opposition. Therefore, FRETILIN was able to control all decisions and the opportunity for reconciliation and consensus building was lost. Indeed, comments made by Alkatiri about FRETILIN's significant power indicated that he was "more committed to FRETILIN dominance than he was to successful plural politics."[84] This suggests that the decision to create an elected assembly to draft and adopt the constitution "failed to account" for FRETILIN's dominance and meant that the danger of winner-takes-all politics came to fruition.[85] Indeed, there were indications that this perception had developed among the community, with focus group discussions revealing that participants expressed discomfort with assembly members voting along party lines.[86]

The UNTAET regulation that established the Constituent Assembly contained little detail concerning the framework for the constitution-making

---

[81] UNTAET Regulation No. 2001/2, s. 2, para. 2.2.   [82] Ibid., s. 2, para. 2.6.
[83] S. Zifcak, *Making Timor's Constitution*, unpublished memorandum, undated.
[84] D. Kingsbury, "Political Development," in Kingsbury and Leach, *East Timor: Beyond Independence*, 20.
[85] Aucion and Brandt, "East Timor's Constitutional Passage," 253; Regan, "Constitution Making in East Timor."
[86] NDI, *Carrying the People's Aspirations: A Report on Focus Group Discussions in East Timor* (Dili: National Democratic Institute for International Affairs and Faculty of Social and Political Sciences, University of East Timor, 2002).

process or binding principles to shape the new constitution. This was done "in deference to the sovereignty" of the assembly, so that the constitution would be viewed as the "exclusive purview" of the assembly and not as "foreign-imposed."[87] However, it "led to confusion," as the short time frame meant that assembly members had to rush to draft the constitution but "had little or no experience regarding how to go about doing so."[88] This confusion was evident when the assembly debated its rules of procedure. Most assembly members were inexperienced, but because UNTAET had opted for a "hands-off" approach, it "had not prepared options for suggested rules of procedure."[89] After three weeks of debate, on the suggestion of FRETILIN exiles who had returned from Mozambique and Portugal, the assembly adopted rules similar to those governing the 1975 Portuguese Constituent Assembly. The rules of procedure created the Systematization and Harmonization Commission. The commission was charged with analyzing, harmonizing, and compiling reports from thematic committees and with presenting the first draft of the constitution to the full assembly. The commission also deliberated on recommendations and proposals received from the public, government, and civil society. Although the commission had forty members, in practice three of its members with legal training dominated the drafting work.[90]

The Systematization and Harmonization Commission created four thematic committees.[91] The Constituent Assembly president instructed each thematic committee to draft their section of the constitution based on five constitutional texts presented by the political parties. On October 17, 2001, the thematic committees began meeting. They were given ten days to review the drafts, call for expert advice, and provide their recommendations to the committee. As the FRETILIN majority claimed they had a mandate, a FRETILIN draft, based on the 1989 version of the Portuguese constitution (modified to an extent by the 1990 Mozambican constitution), came to dominate debates.[92]

---

[87] M. Brandt, *Constitutional Assistance in Post-Conflict Countries: The UN Experience: Cambodia, East Timor & Afghanistan* (New York: United National Development Programme, 2005), 9.
[88] Aucion and Brandt, "East Timor's Constitutional Passage," 254.
[89] Brandt, *Constitutional Assistance*, 16.
[90] Interview with a former member of the Constituent Assembly and government official, February 2, 2010; interview with a former member of the Constituent Assembly and member of parliament, May 13, 2010.
[91] The committees were (1) Rights, Duties and Liberties; and Defence and National Security; (2) Organisation of the State; and Organisation of Political Power; (3) Economic, Social and Financial Organisation; and (4) Fundamental Principles; Guarantees, Control and Amendment of the Constitution.
[92] FRETILIN, Frente Revolucionaria de Timor-Leste Independente (FRETILIN): Projecto De Constituiçao (Draft Constitution), adopted at the Extraordinary National Conference of

This meant that the committees "cut and pasted" from these constitutions, did not take account of the "local context,"[93] and "occasionally focused on issues that had no relevance" to Timor-Leste.[94] This bore out the prediction in the literature that drafters may be influenced by previous constitutional models of which they have experience. However, FRETILIN had not put its draft before the electorate during the assembly election, even though it had been completed in 1998, which raised questions about its democratic legitimacy.

By November 30, 2001, the Systematization and Harmonization Commission had harmonized the recommendations submitted by the thematic committees, completed the first draft, and distributed copies to Constituent Assembly members. It was basically the FRETILIN draft, to which the commission had made "relatively minor changes."[95] The assembly had from December 3 to 15, 2001, to debate and adopt the draft. This deadline was later extended to January 25, 2002. The debate was conducted under "tremendous pressure" from UNTAET, FRETILIN assembly members, and the FRETILIN-dominated ETTA.[96] This pressure was eased only in late January 2002, when the assembly received a letter from several members of the United States Congress suggesting that the process be extended.[97] The letter had been solicited by several younger assembly members, in cooperation with civil society groups. One assembly member notes that when this letter was read aloud, relieved assembly members from opposition parties greeted it with applause.[98] Consequently, the deadline was further extended to February 28, and later to March 22, 2002.

FRETILIN (Sydney: FRETILIN, August 14–20, 1998) (hereafter FRETILIN draft constitution); interview with a former member of the Constituent Assembly and government official, February 2, 2010; interview with a former member of the Constituent Assembly and member of Parliament, May 13, 2010; interview with an international adviser to the Constituent Assembly, August 31, 2010.

[93] Interview with a former member of the Constituent Assembly and member of Parliament, September 30, 2010.

[94] Aucion and Brandt, "East Timor's Constitutional Passage," 255.

[95] Regan, "Constitution Making in East Timor," 39; Constituent Assembly Systemisation and Harmonisation Commission, *Matrix of Recommendations by the Thematic Committees and the Chair of the Systemisation and Harmonisation Commission* (Dili: Constituent Assembly, December 7, 2001); interview with a former member of the Constituent Assembly and member of Parliament, May 13, 2010.

[96] Regan, "Constitution Making in East Timor," 39; interview with a former member of the Constituent Assembly and government official, February 2, 2010.

[97] D. J. Kucinich et al., *Letter to Mr. Francisco "Lú-olo" Guterres, Speaker, Constituent Assembly*, January 10, 2002, accessed February 25, 2011, available from members.pcug.org.au/~wildwood/02jancongress.htm.

[98] Interview with a former member of the Constituent Assembly and government official, February 2, 2010.

The quality of the Constituent Assembly's debates has been questioned. One adviser remarked that no more than twelve to fourteen members appeared to be "really across the issues" and understand what they were voting on, while the remainder voted according to party lines.[99] This is hardly surprising, given that many had their education disrupted during the Indonesian occupation. Indeed, one assembly member argued that it was a "significant achievement" that they managed to debate and adopt the constitution at all.[100] However, it does suggest that there was some merit to proposals that an expert convention draft the constitution.

The Constituent Assembly's debates were also affected by its rules of procedure. As they were in Portuguese, a precedent was set for the assembly's documents (including drafts of the constitution) to be primarily in Portuguese. This favored the older generation of FRETILIN leaders, who had been educated during colonization and then later in universities in Mozambique and Portugal during their exile. In contrast, the younger generation from the clandestine resistance had attended universities in Indonesia and been educated in Bahasa Indonesia.[101] While funding was provided for translations, some assembly members faced delays before they could access documents.[102] Consequently, they were often forced to vote on documents that they did not fully understand.[103]

The rules of procedure also enshrined majority decision making. While the literature notes that this is the most common way that constitution-making bodies make decisions, it also cautions that it can allow a single party or coalition to dominate decision making. This occurred in the Constituent Assembly and was compounded by FRETILIN's suggestion that voting be conducted by an open show of hands. Assembly members from opposition parties favored voting by secret ballot, as there was concern that open voting would encourage voting on party platforms.[104] While one assembly member described majority decision making as "very democratic,"[105] an adviser

---

[99] Interview with an international adviser to the Constituent Assembly and the CAVR, December 6, 2010; interview with a Timorese intellectual, May 12, 2010.
[100] Interview with a former member of the Constituent Assembly and government official, February 2, 2010.
[101] Bahasa Indonesia is a variety of the Malay language Bahasa Melayu.
[102] Interview with a former member of the Constituent Assembly and government official, February 2, 2010; UNTAET, *Proceedings of the Constituent Assembly Week 7, 29 October – 2 November 2001: Report to the Human Rights Unit* (Dili: UNTAET, 2001).
[103] Interview with an international adviser to the Constituent Assembly and the CAVR, December 6, 2010.
[104] Carter Centre, *East Timor Political and Election Observation*.
[105] Interview with a former member of the Constituent Assembly and member of Parliament, May 13, 2010.

claimed that it allowed FRETILIN to "ram through" its preferences, which were based more on "politics" than on achieving an "impartially conceived" constitution.[106] Two other advisers note that this meant FRETILIN "did not need to build consensus or compromise."[107] Indeed, a FRETILIN assembly member admitted that FRETILIN "did not understand how to get others on board."[108] Therefore, the constitution-making process "proved to be less a process of conflict resolution than a stage for the contest for power."[109]

Despite this, international observers found that the Constituent Assembly's debates were "for the most part open and respectful, with a good representation of alternative political views."[110] However, almost every vote reflected the split between the FRETILIN majority and opposition parties.[111] As a result, many observers and assembly members from minority parties felt that "ultimately the constitution was not the product of genuine legal and intellectual debate but merely the result of consensus among FRETILIN leaders."[112] When minority parties proposed amendments to the draft, they were rarely considered, with "even small or reasonable changes that would not have affected the substance of articles...voted down time and again."[113] Indeed, one FRETILIN assembly member admitted that FRETILIN's conduct was "narrow-minded" and not inclusive.[114] According to observers, "this led to increasing frustration and a sense of futility among many of the smaller parties."[115] However, both an assembly member and an international adviser

---

[106] Interview with an international adviser to the Constituent Assembly and the CAVR, December 6, 2010.

[107] Aucoin and Brandt, "East Timor's Constitutional Passage," 258.

[108] Interview with a former member of the Constituent Assembly and government official, February 2, 2010.

[109] R. Garrison, *The Role of Constitution-Building Processes in Democratisation: Case Study, East Timor* (Stockholm: International IDEA, 2005), 2.

[110] Carter Center, *East Timor Political and Election Observation*, 42.

[111] For example, s. 106 on the dismissal of government was adopted by a vote of sixty-two in favor, one against, and thirteen abstentions; s. 107 on the criminal liability of members of the government was adopted by a vote of sixty-four in favor, four against, and eight abstentions; s. 108 on the competencies of the government was adopted by a vote of sixty-one in favor, four against, and ten abstentions; s. 109 on the competencies of the Council of Ministers was adopted by a vote of fifty-nine in favor, three opposed, and one abstention; s. 115 on the categories of courts was adopted by a vote of sixty-seven in favor, five against, and nine abstentions. Constituent Assembly secretariat, press releases, January 10, 2002; January 11, 2002; and January 14, 2002).

[112] Carter Center, *East Timor Political and Election Observation*, 43.   [113] Ibid.

[114] Interview with a former member of the Constituent Assembly and government official, February 2, 2010.

[115] Carter Center, *East Timor Political and Election Observation*, 43; interview with an international adviser to the Constituent Assembly and the CAVR, December 6, 2010.

noted that opposition parties "were always responding to new FRETILIN drafts" and generally did not submit clear proposals or alternatives when seeking amendments, which made it difficult for them to be debated.[116] On February 9, 2002, the assembly approved the first draft by a vote of sixty-five in favor, with thirteen abstentions and ten absentees. Again, this vote indicated the split within the assembly and raises questions over its representativeness.

In addition to its mandate to prepare and adopt a constitution, the Constituent Assembly replaced the National Council and considered draft regulations submitted by the transitional administrator. A specialized legislative council was created to perform this task. A council of ministers drawn from the assembly and appointed by the transitional administrator replaced the transitional cabinet.[117] FRETILIN Secretary-General Alkatiri was its chief minister. ETTA was also replaced by the East Timor Public Administration (ETPA). Therefore, day-to-day governmental responsibility was held by assembly members. The rationale was that Timorese self-government would "begin under the protective sponsorship of UNTAET, with UNTAET having the reserve authority to correct any serious errors."[118] However, the practical effect was that many of the most competent assembly members were involved in this task rather than in constitution making.[119] In addition, as the period for the draft constitution to be produced was extended to mid-March 2002 and the date for independence had already been set for May 20, 2002, the assembly "had no time to prepare to fill the legislative vacuum," and "a post-independence legislative logjam" resulted.[120]

The levels of publicity and secrecy involved in the process

The literature argues that secrecy can facilitate bargaining and consensus building. However, the Constituent Assembly was dominated by FRETILIN, whose members did not need to engage in either in order to have their draft of the constitution adopted. Instead, since FRETILIN had already made most of its decisions when preparing its draft in the late 1990s, it was relatively comfortable with allowing a high degree of publicity concerning

---

[116] Interview with a former member of the Constituent Assembly and government official, February 2, 2010; interview with an international adviser to the Constituent Assembly and the CAVR, December 6, 2010.
[117] UNTAET Regulation No. 2001/28, *On the Establishment of the Council of Ministers*, UN Doc. UNTAET/REG/2001/28, September 19, 2001.
[118] P. Galbraith, *The Shape of Things to Come: Thoughts on the Post-Election Government of East Timor*, unpublished paper, June 7, 2001.
[119] Zifcak, *Making Timor's Constitution*. [120] Goldstone, "UNTAET with Hindsight," 89.

the Constituent Assembly's work. Therefore, the assembly's plenary sessions and thematic committee hearings were open to the public. However, as most members of the public had little knowledge of the contents of the draft, these sessions were often difficult to understand. The assembly's swearing-in ceremony and first day of sitting were also broadcast on television and radio, and its plenary debates were broadcast on the radio. As these events were often conducted in Portuguese, few members of the public could understand them, given that only 5 percent of the population understood Portuguese.[121]

The media attempted to cover the Constituent Assembly's deliberations. At the time there were two daily newspapers, a free fortnightly UNTAET newspaper, and a few weekly magazines. They faced severe challenges in producing and distributing their publications beyond Dili and in finding qualified journalists to gather and analyze information. It was also difficult to access information about the assembly's work, and after several requests the assembly developed daily press releases and held weekly press conferences.[122] The assembly also prepared a handout on its work and distributed 50,000 copies of a constitutional magazine to explain the draft constitution.[123] However, low adult literacy rates limited the usefulness of all publications.

The opportunities for public participation and its role in the process

The civic education program and Constituent Assembly elections were opportunities for public participation in the constitution-making process. In addition, Constitutional Commission hearings occurred before the assembly election and the assembly itself conducted consultations.

The political calendar provided for a public consultation before the Constituent Assembly election.[124] Despite this, FRETILIN members encouraged the National Council to reject a proposal by both the Committee on Political Affairs of the council and UNTAET to set up the Constitutional Commission to canvas grassroots opinion, on the grounds that they would undermine the assembly's autonomy.[125] Gusmão was so enraged by this decision that he

---

[121] UNDP, *East Timor Human Development Report 2002: Ukun Rasik A'as, the Way Ahead* (Dili: United National Development Programme, 2002).
[122] UNTAET, *Proceedings of the Constituent Assembly Week 6, 22–27 October 2001: Report for the Human Rights Unit* (Dili: UNTAET, 2001).
[123] Constituent Assembly, *Handout on Constitution of East Timor (As Approved by the Constituent Assembly up to 24 December, 2001)* (Dili: Constituent Assembly, 2001).
[124] UNTAET Regulation No. 2001/2, s. 2, para. 2.4.
[125] UNTAET, "National Council Defeats Constitution Committees," UNTAET press briefing media note, March 27, 2001.

resigned as president of the council, complaining that it "no longer reflected the aspirations of the people."[126] The rejection signaled the generally ambivalent attitude of much of the Timorese leadership toward public participation. Indeed, the rejection led UNTAET staff to warn of "worrying authoritarian tendencies" within elements of the Timorese leadership, with one observing, "I have grave doubts that anything democratic will come out of this [process]."[127] Timorese civil society groups were also critical of the decision, with one spokesperson highlighting the "culture of command" that could be traced to the resistance movement.[128]

Consequently, the transitional administrator established the Constitutional Commission via a directive that mandated that the commission "solicit the views of the people...on the future Constitution" and prepare a written report to be submitted to the Constituent Assembly. It was also mandated to "take notice of" and "coordinate with" civil society initiatives.[129] However, on April 18, 2001, the Timorese NGO Forum wrote to UNTAET declining to be involved in the commission. The NGO Forum was aware of the literature on the benefits of participatory constitution making[130] and considered that the commission would "be seriously insufficient both in terms of substance and process."[131]

Despite these criticisms, the Constitutional Commission process went ahead. It began in April 2001 with a public information campaign. An all-Timorese panel then selected the seventy-two Timorese commissioners based on lists submitted by each of the territory's thirteen districts. Commissioners and their administrative staff were trained in constitutional issues and the organization of public hearings.[132] Thirteen groups of between five and seven commissioners then undertook a two-week familiarization tour, during which

---

[126] Quoted in "Xanana Resigns as National Council President," *Suara Timor Lorosae*, March 30, 2001; UNTAET, "National Council Reconvenes After Gusmão's Resignation," UNTAET press briefing media note, March 30, 2001; UN Doc. S/2001/436.

[127] Quoted in S. Chesterman, "East Timor in Transition: Self-Determination, State-Building and the United Nations," *International Peacekeeping* 9:1 (2002): 69.

[128] Quoted in ibid., 70.

[129] UNTAET Directive No. 2001/3, *On the Establishment of Constitutional Commissions for East Timor*, UN Doc. UNTAET/DIR/2001/3, March 31, 2001, ss. 2.1, 2.2, 2.3, and 3.

[130] Interview with a former member of the Constituent Assembly and government official, February 2, 2010.

[131] A. de Jesus Soares (on behalf of NGO Forum's board of directors) and F. B. dos Reis (on behalf of NGO Forum's executive director), letter to Peter Galbraith, Department of Political Affairs and Timor Sea, UNTAET, April 18, 2001, accessed March 7, 2011, www.etan.org/et2001b/may/13–19/14ngo.htm.

[132] Interview with an international adviser to the Constituent Assembly and the CAVR, December 6, 2010; UNTAET Constitutional Affairs Branch, *Training of Trainers Workshop: Constitutional Commissions* (Dili: UNTAET, May 2001).

they visited each of the sixty-five subdistricts to inform the public about the commission's work. They then conducted public hearings in each of the thirteen districts and sixty-five subdistricts between June 18 and July 14, 2001, accompanied by thirteen constitutional advisers who answered technical questions. The commissioners began each hearing by explaining the basic elements of a constitution, and open discussion followed. While the commissioners were given a list of suggested areas for discussion, they were not asked to use a questionnaire to ensure that each hearing covered the same material. Hearings also differed, with some taking the form of a single large discussion group, while others were broken down into smaller groups. People also submitted written reports. A rapporteur recorded the results of the sessions.[133] However, no set procedure was used to ensure that there was accurate recording of people's views.[134]

There was an enthusiastic response to the Constitutional Commission, with a total of 38,000 people (almost 10 percent of the electorate) attending 212 hearings.[135] This exceeded UNTAET's expectations and involved holding more than three times the planned number of hearings.[136] At the hearings, people expressed clear views on a number of topics.[137] The commission hearings appear to have been a relatively good example of public participation, as they involved the distribution of information about constitution making and provided a forum in which Timorese could debate their future constitution. Although they did not adopt systematized methods of covering the same material in each hearing or organizing feedback, each group of commissioners did compile their findings and submit reports to the transitional administrator. Given the high level of attendance at the commission hearings, these reports could be taken as a relatively good indicator of public views. The high attendance also suggests that Timorese wanted to participate in the constitution-making process.

The transitional administrator forwarded the Constitutional Commission's reports to the Constituent Assembly when it convened in September 2001.

---

[133] UNTAET Constitutional Affairs Branch, *A Report of the National Constitutional Consultation in East Timor, June-July 2001* (Dili: UNTAET, 2001).
[134] Aucion and Brandt, "East Timor's Constitutional Passage."
[135] Interview with a former member of the Constituent Assembly and government official, February 2, 2010; UNTAET Constitutional Affairs Branch, *A Report of the National Constitutional Consultation*.
[136] UNTAET Constitutional Affairs Branch, *Constitutional Consultation: Fact Sheet No. 4* (Dili: UNTAET, July 3, 2001).
[137] UNTAET Constitutional Affairs Branch, *Constitutional Commission Public Hearings, Executive Summary* (Dili: UNTAET, September 2001).

While the law creating the assembly did not specify how it should respond to the reports, it did require it to give them "due consideration."[138] Many assembly members interpreted this to mean that they were not legally bound to consider them,[139] so they were "ignored"[140] and "never seen or discussed again."[141] The assembly also rejected requests from the commissioners to present their findings, partly because some assembly members thought that the commissions represented "UNTAET's own views" and that the process had been too short and not genuinely Timorese.[142] Other assembly members argued that "a largely illiterate population had been insufficiently educated to understand the constitutional technicalities at stake."[143] Therefore, despite the strong attendance at the commission hearings and the wide range of public feedback enumerated in the reports, the commission had "little impact on the substance" of the constitution.[144]

The regulation that established the Constituent Assembly did not mandate it to consult the public. Despite this, the thematic committees conducted public hearings in October 2001. Representatives of civil society, international organizations, UNTAET, ETPA, and the Catholic Church testified and made written submissions.[145] While many of these submissions were "useful," they were "rarely referred to" during the committees' deliberations.[146] Similarly, while members of the public made thousands of written submissions, assembly members "failed to consider, or even read, any of them."[147] Moreover, when minority party assembly members proposed sending the draft constitution to civil society groups for comment, this was refused by the FRETILIN majority.[148] Combined, these decisions created a "general perception of a lack

---

[138] UNTAET Regulation No. 2001/2, s. 2, para. 2.4.
[139] Interview with a former member of the Constituent Assembly and government official, February 2, 2010.
[140] Interview with an international adviser to the Constituent Assembly, August 31, 2010.
[141] Interview with an international adviser to the Constituent Assembly and the CAVR, December 6, 2010.
[142] Interview with a former member of the Constituent Assembly and member of parliament, May 13, 2010.
[143] Lutz, "Constitutionalism as Public Culture."
[144] H. Charlesworth, "The Constitution of East Timor, May 20, 2002," *International Journal of Constitutional Law* 1:2 (2003): 328.
[145] UNTAET, *Proceedings of the Constituent Assembly Week*, 6.
[146] Aucion and Brandt, "East Timor's Constitutional Passage," 255.
[147] D. Babo Soares, "The Challenges of Drafting a Constitution," in Babo Soares, *Elections and Constitution Making*, 30.
[148] Interview with a former member of the Constituent Assembly and government official, February 2, 2010.

of transparency in decision-making and the feeling that the opportunity for citizens' input into the process was limited."[149]

This perception was exacerbated by the fact that Constituent Assembly members rarely travelled beyond Dili, other than for the assembly's public consultations. Indeed, in a 2002 survey, only 22 percent of respondents said that assembly members had come to their districts to discuss the constitution.[150] The short time frame and the fact that assembly members were not allocated time to visit their constituents worked against assembly members spending too much time outside Dili. Moreover, because the assembly was not mandated to conduct public consultations, many assembly members did not see it as a priority. Some members also argued that because they had been elected, they already knew the views of their constituents.[151] This was particularly the case with respect to FRETILIN, which had an extensive network throughout the territory and "felt comfortable that it was enshrining the desires of the people in the Constitution."[152] While the thirteen district representatives had been specifically elected to represent their districts, most did not "consult their constituents, visit their districts to give progress reports, or involve their constituencies in any way."[153]

After pressure from Gusmão and the Catholic bishop of Dili, Carlos Belo, the Constituent Assembly conducted its own public consultation.[154] Indeed, a January 2002 survey revealed that 67 percent of respondents wanted to be consulted before the constitution was approved, with 72 percent stating their belief that public participation was very important.[155] The minority parties in the assembly proposed a month-long consultation. The FRETILIN majority imposed a week-long limit, which they saw as a "compromise, in view of their electoral victory."[156] The FRETILIN majority also voted that rather than soliciting comments on the existing draft, the consultation would instead brief attendees on its content.

---

[149] Morrow and White, "The United Nations in Transitional East Timor," 44.
[150] Asia Foundation, *Timor Lorosa'e National Survey*, 28.
[151] Aucion and Brandt, "East Timor's Constitutional Passage"; Carter Center, *East Timor Political and Election Observation*; Della-Giacoma, "Ensuring the Well-Being."
[152] Interview with a member of Parliament, May 11, 2010.
[153] Carter Center, *East Timor Political and Election Observation*, 43; interview with an international academic and observer of the Constituent Assembly, January 5, 2010.
[154] C. X. Belo, *The Road to Freedom: A Collection of Speeches, Pastoral Letters, and Articles from 1997–2001* (Sydney: Caritas Australia, 2001); UNTAET, "Gusmão, Bishop Belo Call For More Constitutional Debate," UNTAET press briefing media note, February 20, 2002.
[155] Asia Foundation, *Timor Lorosa'e National Survey*, 29.
[156] Brandt, *Constitutional Assistance*, 17.

In preparation for the consultation, 25,500 copies of the draft constitution (18,000 in Indonesian, 5,000 in Portuguese, and 2,500 in English) were distributed on February 20, with 35,000 copies in the local *lingua franca*, Tetum, distributed on February 25, only a day before the consultations were scheduled to begin. These drafts were accompanied by a magazine summarizing the process and main articles of the draft. The limited timetable and logistical difficulties meant that documents were often received only on the day of consultation meetings, if at all. Observers noted that "this proved problematic in some areas, as citizens wanted more time to analyse the contents of the constitution."[157] Indeed, it was reported that in some areas, "the public ripped up their copies of the constitution in protest and declared the process a sham because there was no time to read the draft, prepare comments and properly participate."[158] Moreover, while the magazine did contain cartoons illustrating the constitution-making process, little attempt was made to provide information about the draft constitution to the 60 percent of the population who were illiterate. Despite these problems, in many areas schools distributed unofficial copies of the draft, and in most places people were informed of its general content. Radio and television broadcasts of the Constituent Assembly sessions had also kept some citizens informed. As a result, "even illiterate villagers had opinions on construction, and all who participated listened intently during the consultations."[159]

Between February 25 and March 2, 2002, panels of five to seven Constituent Assembly members travelled to the thirteen districts and (some of) the sixty-five subdistricts and held more than eighty public consultation meetings. While the format of the meetings varied, they generally involved assembly members reading parts of the draft constitution, followed by question-and-answer sessions. Some consultation teams spent hours explaining the draft, which left attendees little time to provide comments. As a result, one assembly member described the consultations as "more like information sessions than feedback sessions."[160] This led to some frustration, with participants becoming bored and leaving meetings.[161] Many participants also complained that the consultation process was too short, occurred only late in the drafting process, and was targeted more at local-level leadership

---

[157] Carter Center, *East Timor Political and Election Observation*, 45.
[158] Brandt, *Constitutional Assistance*, 17.
[159] Carter Center, *East Timor Political and Election Observation*, 45.
[160] Interview with a former member of the Constituent Assembly and government official, February 2, 2010; personal communication from a Timorese academic, April 26, 2010.
[161] Aucion and Brandt, "East Timor's Constitutional Passage"; Carter Center, *East Timor Political and Election Observation*.

than the general public.[162] Despite this, the consultations attracted tens of thousands of participants, indicating a high level of public interest.[163] However, this also meant that many meetings "were too crowded for real debate."[164] PD, PSD, and UDT members of the assembly had proposed a scientific formula for collating public feedback, but this was rejected by FRETILIN and ASDT members. Instead, there was no uniform approach and notes were taken on the initiative of individual members of the assembly secretariat.[165] Consequently, "no detailed public records of these meetings were known to have been kept."[166]

Constituent Assembly members individually compiled the recommendations that they had gleaned from the consultation meetings, which were gathered into district-level reports and submitted to the Systematization and Harmonization Commission on March 6, 2002. The commission then met with each of the thirteen consultation teams and recommended amendments, to which all parties had to agree. On March 15, the commission presented a report to the assembly, in which it recommended forty-five amendments to the draft. The commission's report was discussed by the political parties and then bought to the full plenary for discussion and debate. While PD members tried to have as much public feedback as possible discussed, "very few issues were in reality debated."[167] Indeed, only eight amendments proposed by the public and thirteen by civil society organizations were considered by the plenary.

Therefore, the impact of the public consultation on the constitution was "insignificant."[168] One FRETILIN member of Parliament (MP) argued that "the views of the people were clear" and should be conceptualized as a "set of values" rather than as the "minute matters" raised during the consultations.[169] Of the recommended changes outlined in the Systematization and Harmonization Commission's report, only four were adopted by the Constituent Assembly, none of which were based on suggestions made during the public consultations. Two involved removing articles explicitly adopting the

---

[162] UNTAET, "East Timorese Voice Their Views on Draft Constitution," UNTAET press briefing media note, March 1, 2002.
[163] Aucion and Brandt, "East Timor's Constitutional Passage"; interview with a former member of the Constituent Assembly and government official, February 2, 2010.
[164] Bowles and Chopra, "East Timor: Statebuilding Revisited," 280–281.
[165] Baltazar, "An Overview"; Brandt, *Constitutional Assistance*; Lutz, "Constitutionalism as Public Culture."
[166] Della-Giacoma, "Ensuring the Well-Being."
[167] Carter Centre, *East Timor Political and Election Observation*, 45; Regan, "Constitution Making in East Timor."
[168] Della-Giacoma, "Ensuring the Well-Being."
[169] Interview with a member of Parliament, May 11, 2010.

separation of church and state and mentioning divorce, at the request of Bishop Belo. One involved removing an article guaranteeing protection against discrimination on the basis of sexual orientation, again after pressure from the Catholic Church. Finally, while the original draft had provided that only Portuguese would be an official language, this was amended so that both Portuguese and Tetum were designated as official languages and English and Bahasa were recognized as "working" languages. These changes were a concession to the younger generation, who had objected to the privileged status afforded to Portuguese within the assembly.[170]

Overall, the public consultations were "rushed, poorly conceived and executed, peripheral, shallow, and tokenistic."[171] As a result, even though there were high levels of take-up of opportunities for public participation, as the outcomes of this participation had almost no impact on the constitution, there was only minimal public participation in constitution making. While this suggests that certain Constituent Assembly members were uninterested in the public's views, one adviser notes that there was also "deep concern" to avoid instability, particularly given the enduring legacy of the 1975 civil war. Consequently, there was a "tendency to feel a need to keep the lid on debate, to get things moving quickly."[172] While this is understandable, it did mean that "for most Timorese the writing of their constitution was a remote and hidden process."[173] The minimal public participation meant that Timorese appear to have lost the opportunity to achieve the benefits of participation identified in the literature.

The degree of international involvement

The constitution-making literature notes that external advisers can play an influential role, particularly as constitution makers often lack technical expertise. This was the case in Timor-Leste, where the Constituent Assembly secretariat included a technical staff of five international parliamentary experts, four Portuguese and one Canadian. The fact that four of these experts were Portuguese assisted in encouraging the emphasis on the Portuguese constitution that emerged during the assembly's debates. Several international organizations also provided advisers.[174] While the Systematization and

---

[170] A. de Jesus Soares, *Speaking My Language – The Rise and Fall of Linguistic Empires*, New Internationalist Radio, July 8, 2008; interview with a former member of the Constituent Assembly and government official, February 2, 2010.
[171] Della-Giacoma, "Ensuring the Well-Being."
[172] Regan, "Constitution Making in East Timor," 40.
[173] Della-Giacoma, "Ensuring the Well-Being."
[174] The UNDP, the Asia Foundation, and the Inter-Parliamentary Union.

Harmonization Commission is said to have "largely welcomed" their advice, little of it was accepted by the broader assembly.[175] Indeed, international advisers reported that although assembly members from minority parties would seek their advice, it made little difference to the final draft.[176]

While UNTAET provided budgeting and funding for the Constituent Assembly's work, as well as logistical support, security, and photocopying, it initially maintained a distance from the process. This was based on the transitional administrator's belief that the constitution should be locally written and owned.[177] Rather than provide advice, UNTAET officials were assigned to observe assembly meetings and report back to the transitional administrator. However, it soon became common practice for these officials to provide comments on the draft. Indeed, in January 2002, the UN high commissioner for human rights wrote to the Speaker of the assembly, and on February 22, 2002, the transitional administrator wrote to the heads of the political parties represented in the assembly, both conveying concerns about the initial draft. Accordingly, the draft was revised to adhere to international human rights standards by affording basic rights protections to all persons, regardless of their citizenship. However, the assembly reserved other rights only for citizens and ignored a suggestion relating to guaranteeing security of judicial tenure.

Overall, two international advisers concluded that it was "wise" for UNTAET to distance itself from the process. In particular, this meant that no one characterized the resulting constitution "as having been prescribed by UNTAET."[178] However, UNTAET may have been overly hands-off when the process was being established, particularly when the regulation establishing the Constituent Assembly was debated by the National Council. It appears that while UNTAET encouraged the adoption of a proportional electoral system to dilute FRETILIN's influence, it "could have done more" to promote the interests of parties other than FRETILIN at this stage,[179] which might have created an assembly that provided more space for consensus building and public consultation. Indeed, one FRETILIN assembly member

---

[175] Interview with a former member of the Constituent Assembly and government official, February 2, 2010.
[176] Interview with an international adviser to the Constituent Assembly, August 31, 2010; interview with an international adviser to the Constituent Assembly and the CAVR, December 6, 2010.
[177] S. V. de Mello quoted in Morrow and White, "The United Nations in Transitional East Timor," 40.
[178] Aucion and Brandt, "East Timor's Constitutional Passage," 266.
[179] Interview with an international adviser to the Constituent Assembly and the CAVR, December 6, 2010.

noted that, on reflection, UNTAET was wrong to put so much faith in the legitimacy of FRETILIN, particularly given that the electoral results signaled that FRETILIN did not have overwhelming broad-based support.[180]

The manner in which the constitution was adopted

The constitution was adopted on March 22, 2002, by a vote of seventy-two in favor (FRETILIN combined with ASDT, KOTA, and PST), fourteen against, one abstention, and one absentee (due to illness). As sixty votes were required to adopt the constitution, this result was arguably beyond immediate challenge. Moreover, all Constituent Assembly members signed the text "placing national unity above party interest."[181] However, the size of the vote against the constitution was high enough to cause concern. Assembly members who voted against it specified that they thought the process had been "too one-sided, without enough cooperation or compromise within the Assembly or enough input from civil society."[182] Indeed, the literature cautions that the manner in which a constitution is adopted will determine its credentials as an exercise of the people's constituent power. The size of the vote against the constitution also raises the critical distinction between it being *legally* – as compared to *legitimately* – adopted. This suggests that it might have instead been better to seek consensus among assembly members rather than rely on a majoritarian vote. This might have built support for the constitution across political parties, instead of leaving some parties questioning its legitimacy and feeling as though they had "lost."[183]

If any party could be perceived to have "won," it was FRETILIN, which managed to have its draft of the constitution adopted with very few substantive changes. While FRETILIN had a majority in the Constituent Assembly, its actions undermined the representativeness of the process, as well as the opportunity for genuine public participation. Consequently, the process was "haunted by dissatisfaction and protests by opponents of FRETILIN, and claims that FRETILIN unilaterally imposed its will, thus undermining the views of smaller parties."[184]

---

[180] Interview with a former member of the Constituent Assembly and government official, February 2, 2010.
[181] UN, *Report of the Secretary-General on the United Nations Transitional Administration in East Timor*, UN Security Council, UN Doc. S/2002/432, April 27, 2002, para. 4.
[182] Carter Center, *East Timor Political and Election Observation*, 47.
[183] Regan, "Constitution Making in East Timor," 40.
[184] Babo Soares, "The Challenges of Drafting a Constitution," 29.

*Whether the constitution was adopted on an interim basis
or included a "sunset" clause*

As a result of concerns that the constitution was too FRETILIN-centric, minority parties argued that it should be adopted on an interim basis, pending its promulgation after a five-year period of correction and further opportunities for public consultation.[185] While this proposal was overruled by FRETILIN, the literature notes that it may have reduced the impact of FRETILIN's short-term political motives and might have provided the Timorese people with more time to fully exercise their constituent power. The constitution may be revised at any time, but motions to initiate revisions require an almost prohibitive four-fifths majority of Parliament. Amendments require a two-thirds majority of Parliament in order to be adopted, while certain sections can be amended only after a national referendum.[186] As a four-fifths majority would have been extremely difficult for the opposition members of the first Parliament to muster, this ensured that the FRETILIN draft was insulated from review throughout the FRETILIN government's first term.

In early 2001, a Timorese bishop compared a constitution to a "house of our dreams" that "you cannot build…overnight. You need to consult everyone who will live in it so that it is properly designed to suit the interests of everyone. The design takes a long time."[187] The constitution-making process in Timor-Leste did not heed this advice but instead represented a series of lost opportunities. Some opportunities were lost due to decisions made by the UN, which provided a very short time frame for the transition to independence, particularly considering the level of social and material devastation that occurred in 1999. Others were due to the decisions of Timorese elites, most specifically FRETILIN. While FRETILIN undoubtedly played an important role in the independence struggle, its decision to interpret this as providing it with a mandate to control the state-building process meant that it placed partisan interests above those of building consensus and achieving reconciliation. Nowhere was FRETILIN's influence more evident than during the constitution-making process, in which it provided only minimal opportunities for public participation and took almost no account of public feedback, marginalized other political parties, and sidelined civil society. As a result, almost all of the positive benefits of public participation in constitution making identified in the literature were missed. In addition, the Timorese people's opportunity to exercise the popular sovereignty that they had fought for throughout the Indonesian occupation was lost.

---

[185] Ibid.   [186] *Constitution of the Democratic Republic of Timor-Leste* (2002), ss. 154–156.
[187] Quoted in de Jesus Soares, "For an Interim Constitution."

4

Constituent power in Timor-Leste

This chapter begins with a brief contextual description of political developments in Timor-Leste since independence. It then assesses whether the minimal public participation involved in the constitution-making process affected the creation of a political community by considering the following five indicators, which assess the extent to which a unified political community is present:

- Does the constitution enumerate a unifying national identity?
- Has reconciliation been achieved?
- Are there divisions within society?
- Does the community exhibit evidence of citizenization?
- Is there a strong public sphere?

CONTEXTUAL DESCRIPTION OF POLITICAL DEVELOPMENTS SINCE INDEPENDENCE

On April 14, 2002, an election was held for the first president. Two candidates stood: Xanana Gusmão, who ran as an independent (although he was endorsed by eleven parties), and Francisco Xavier do Amaral, from ASDT. Gusmão won, with 82.69 percent of the vote.

Timor-Leste became independent on May 20, 2002. UNTAET was replaced by the UN Mission of Support in East Timor (UNMISET).[1] On

---

[1] UNMISET was mandated to provide assistance to core administrative structures, interim law enforcement, and public security. It started with 5,000 military troops, 1,250 civilian police, and a civilian support group of 100 specialists filling core functions, and then progressively downsized. Its mandate was extended three times. S/Res/1410, *On the Situation in East Timor*, May 17, 2002; S/Res/1480, *On the Situation in Timor-Leste*, May 19, 2003; S/Res/1543, *On the Situation in Timor-Leste*, May 14, 2004; S/Res/1573, *On the Situation in Timor-Leste*, November 16, 2004.

May 20, 2005, UNMISET was replaced by the smaller UN Office in Timor-Leste.[2] On August 25, 2006, an expanded UN Integrated Mission in Timor-Leste (UNMIT) was established in response to the security crisis described below.[3]

The constitution provided that the Constituent Assembly would convert into the first Parliament at independence.[4] This was due partly to the tight political calendar and partly to pressure from UNTAET to avoid the expense of another election. There was also a widespread belief among FRETILIN assembly members that the outcome of another election would reflect that of the first. There was heated debate in the assembly concerning whether there should be fresh elections, as minority parties assumed that their electoral performance would improve because they were more widely known after the constitution-making process. They also argued that the assembly election had not made it clear that constitution drafters could stay on to govern the new state.[5] Support for another election was expressed during the assembly's public consultations[6] and by Gusmão and Bishop Belo.[7] In the Parliament, FRETILIN remained in a coalition with ASDT, and FRETILIN leader Mari Alkatiri became prime minister.

In April and May 2006, Timor-Leste suffered a major security crisis. This was precipitated by tensions within – and between – the army and police forces, which expanded to include veterans of the resistance, youth groups,

---

[2] UNOTIL was a one-year peace-building mission that had only a few dozen advisers and no security force. Its mandate was limited to supporting the capacity development of critical state institutions, particularly the police force. While this mission was scheduled to finish on May 20, 2006, after the April and May 2006 security crisis (described in the following text), its mandate was initially extended for one month, and then twice more, until August 25, 2006. S/Res/1599, *On the Situation in Timor-Leste*, April 28, 2005; S/Res/1677, *On the Situation in Timor-Leste*, May 12, 2006; S/Res/1690, *On the Situation in Timor-Leste*, June 20, 2006; S/Res/1703, *On the Situation in Timor-Leste*, August 18, 2006.

[3] UNMIT was mandated to support the government to consolidate stability, enhance a culture of democratic governance, and achieve national reconciliation. Its mandate was extended six times. S/Res/1704, *On the Situation in Timor-Leste*, August 25, 2006; S/Res/1745, *On the Situation in Timor-Leste*, February 22, 2007; S/Res/1802, *On the Situation in Timor-Leste*, February 25, 2008; S/Res/1867, *On the Situation in Timor-Leste*, February 26, 2009; S/Res/1912, *On the Situation in Timor-Leste*, February 26, 2010; S/Res/1969, *On the Situation in Timor-Leste*, February 24, 2011; S/Res/2037, *On the Situation in Timor-Leste*, February 23, 2012.

[4] Constitution, s. 167(1).

[5] UNTAET, "Assembly Votes to Transform Itself into Legislature," UNTAET press briefing media note, January 31, 2002.

[6] UNTAET, "Public Speaks Out to Assembly Members on Constitution," UNTAET press briefing media note, March 1, 2002.

[7] "East Timorese Constituent Assembly to Become First National Parliament," *Associated Press Newswires*, January 13, 2002.

and, eventually, wider society. In response, the government requested an International Stabilization Force, led by Australia, which deployed on May 26, 2006. On June 20, 2006, President Gusmão requested that Alkatiri resign as prime minister, due to rumors that he had exacerbated the crisis. As law and order had completely collapsed, the FRETILIN government found itself increasingly unable to govern; Alkatiri's position became untenable, and he resigned on June 26, 2006. FRETILIN then proposed three alternative prime ministers. Gusmão selected José Ramos-Horta, who was sworn in on July 8, 2006. Despite Alkatiri's resignation, violence and instability continued.

The first round of the second presidential election was held on April 9, 2007. Eight candidates nominated themselves, from FRETILIN, PD, ASDT, PSD and UDT, as well as three independent candidates, one of whom was Ramos-Horta. Presidential elections are decided on a plurality basis,[8] and as no candidate reached an absolute majority in the first round, a run-off election was held between the two candidates who received the most votes: FRETILIN's Francisco "Lu-Olo" Guterres, with 27.89 percent of the vote, and Ramos-Horta, with 21.81 percent. In the second round, on May 9, 2007, Ramos-Horta received 69.18 percent of the vote and Lu-Olo 30.82 percent. Ramos-Horta was appointed president on May 20, 2007.

The parliamentary election took place on June 30, 2007. Parliamentary elections follow the proportional system utilized for the Constituent Assembly election, with two amendments. First, every third candidate on a party list must be a woman.[9] Second, parties must receive at least 3 percent of the total valid votes in order to receive a seat in Parliament.[10] Gusmão led a new party, Congresso Nacional de Reconstrução de Timor-Leste (CNRT), into the election. In total, twelve parties and two coalitions stood. Seven parties received at least 3 percent of the total valid votes: FRETILIN received 29.02 percent and was allotted twenty-one seats; CNRT 24.1 percent and eighteen seats; the ASDT-PSD coalition 15.73 percent and eleven seats; PD 11.3 percent and eight seats; and three minor parties won two or three seats each. As the thirteen district representative seats had been abolished, there were sixty-five seats in the Parliament,[11] and consequently no single party had an absolute majority. President Ramos-Horta called on FRETILIN, as the party that had received the most votes, to form a coalition government, but its attempts to

---

[8] Law on the Election of the President of the Republic No. 07/2006 (2006) (TL), as amended by Law 05/2007.
[9] Law on the Election of the National Parliament No. 6/2006 (2006) (TL), as amended by Law No. 7/2011, art. 12(3).
[10] Constitution, s. 65; Law on the Election of the National Parliament.
[11] Law on the Election of the National Parliament, art. 10.

negotiate with other parties were rebuffed. Ramos-Horta then attempted to negotiate a "grand coalition" between FRETILIN and CNRT, which also failed. Instead, CNRT successfully invited PD and ASDT-PSD to form a majority coalition, the Aliança da Maioria Parlamentar (AMP – Alliance for a Parliamentary Majority), with thirty-seven seats. The president invited the AMP to form a government on August 6, 2007, and on August 8 appointed Gusmão prime minister.

Although the presidential and parliamentary elections were relatively peaceful, arsonists destroyed about 800 houses.[12] After the formation of the AMP government was announced, gangs burned buildings in Dili and in the second major city of Baucau. The violence reached a crescendo in February 2008, when a small group of army deserters attempted to assassinate Prime Minister Gusmão and President Ramos-Horta. These deserters were shot or captured or surrendered after the attack.

The security situation stabilized after the assassination attacks, and the first round of the third presidential election on March 17, 2012, was peaceful. Thirteen candidates nominated for the election (although one candidate died beforehand). The most notable candidates were then–Parliament Speaker Fernando "Lasama" do Araujo, from PD; FRETILIN's Lu-Olo; Ramos-Horta; and Jose Maria Vasconcelos (known as "Taur Matan Ruak"), the former chief of the army, who stood down from his position in September 2011 to participate in the election. Controversially, CNRT withdrew the tacit support that it had given to Ramos-Horta during the 2007 election and nominated Matan Ruak as its preferred candidate. FRETILIN's Lu-Olo received 28.7 percent of the vote, almost exactly the same amount as he received in the 2007 election, with Matan Ruak in second place with 25.7 percent, reflecting the support he received from CNRT. Ramos-Horta was third with 17.5 percent and Lasama was fourth with 17.3 percent. Consequently, Lu-Olo and Matan Ruak contested the second round on April 16. Matan Ruak decisively won, taking 61.23 percent of the vote to Lu-Olo's 38.77 percent.

The result of the election was widely accepted, and the parliamentary election campaign was generally peaceful. Twenty-one parties registered to compete in the election on July 7, 2012. CNRT increased its vote to 36.66 percent and received thirty seats, as did FRETILIN, which received 29.87 percent and twenty-five seats, while the vote for PD dropped to 10.31 percent

---

[12] Carter Center, *Timor-Leste Election Democratic and Peaceful: Carter Center Preliminary Statement* (Dili: Carter Center, July 3, 2007); EU, *EU Election Observer Mission, Presidential Elections 9 April 2007, Preliminary Statement* (Dili: Delegation of the European Union to East Timor, April 11, 2007).

and eight seats, and Frente-Mudança (a splinter group from FRETILIN) received 3.11 percent and two seats. Seventeen of the parties that contested the election and received less than 3 percent of the vote were ruled out of seats in Parliament. Ramos-Horta again attempted to persuade Gusmão to form a "national unity" government with FRETILIN, which expressed interest in the proposal. CNRT instead engaged in negotiations with PD and Frente-Mudança to form a coalition, Bloku Governu Koligasaun (BGK – Government Coalition Block). After the announcement of the BGK coalition, there were demonstrations and rock-throwing, and cars and houses were burned around Dili, Baucau, and the FRETILIN stronghold of Viqueque. One FRETILIN member died and four policemen were injured in the violence, which was reportedly led by FRETILIN supporters who were angry about allegedly inflammatory comments made about FRETILIN by CNRT leaders.

Apart from this isolated violence, as the elections were relatively peaceful, UNMIT began withdrawing in October 2012 and completed its mission on December 31, 2012. The International Stabilization Force also withdrew in December 2012.

THE ROLE OF PARTICIPATION IN CONSTITUTING THE POLITICAL COMMUNITY

Does the constitution enumerate a unifying national identity?

The Constituent Assembly attempted to articulate a national identity in the constitution that would be disseminated to unite society. To that end, the constitution begins by outlining a number of "national principles" that enumerate an official historical narrative, identify shared national symbols, define future national identity, and classify who qualifies as a Timorese citizen.

Official historical narrative
The official historical narrative adopts a modernist approach to building national identity. As described in Chapter 1, modernist theories typically predict that a high culture will be disseminated via the development of an educated, literate, and mobile labor force necessitated by the shift in the mode of production from agriculture to industrialization, or via the development of print capitalism. As Timor-Leste is primarily a subsistence agricultural society in which there are low levels of literacy, political parties have sought to act as a substitute mechanism of nation building.

The official historical narrative draws on a selective memory of Timorese history to focus on the "Valorisation of Resistance" by the "*Maubere* People."[13] While this resistance was first to Portuguese colonization, the emphasis is strongly on the *funu* (struggle) against Indonesian occupation,[14] which the constitution "sacralises" as the core historical narrative.[15] The narrative focuses heavily on the contribution of the older generation, particularly FRETILIN, as the constitution notes that independence was first declared by FRETILIN in 1975 and that the resistance was initially led by FRETILIN. Moreover, the term "*Maubere*" (which comes from the Mambai language and had been given a derogatory meaning by the Portuguese) is closely associated with FRETILIN, which had "appropriated and broadened" the term to refer to the exploitation of all Timorese.[16] Indeed, the initial FRETILIN draft referred only to the "*Maubere* People"[17] and had to be expanded during the Constituent Assembly's debates to include "all those who fought for national independence."

A non-FRETILIN Constituent Assembly member admitted that the official historical narrative was "controversial."[18] However, a FRETILIN assembly member argued that FRETILIN was a "historical truth" that "could not be denied."[19] To an extent, FRETILIN followed the approach of other liberation movements, which have similarly sought to enshrine themselves as central to their new state. However, as FRETILIN won only 57.4 percent of the vote in the assembly election, it arguably did not have a broad-based mandate to entrench itself as the only historical truth. Moreover, the logic behind emphasizing the role of a political party is questionable. In Timor-Leste, commitment to political parties is often "passionately felt" and based on long-standing historical, familial, and clan allegiances,[20] so emphasizing FRETILIN's role may have "unnecessarily politicised" the constitution.[21] One Timorese intellectual laments that this may have created a perception that allegiance to a "political party is more important than the nation, the national interest or national unity."[22]

---

[13] Constitution, s. 11 and preamble.   [14] Ramos-Horta, *Funu*.
[15] M. Leach, "Valorising the Resistance: National Identity and Collective Memory in East Timor's Constitution," *Social Alternatives* 21:3 (2002): 43.
[16] Ramos-Horta, *Funu*, 37.   [17] FRETILIN draft constitution, art. 11(1).
[18] Interview with a former member of the Constituent Assembly and member of Parliament, May 13, 2010.
[19] Interview with a former member of the Constituent Assembly and government official, February 2, 2010.
[20] S. Niner, *Xanana: Leader of the Struggle for Independent Timor-Leste* (North Melbourne: Australian Scholarly Publishing, 2009): 227.
[21] Interview with a Timorese intellectual, May 12, 2010.
[22] J. Trindade, "Reconciling Conflicting Paradigms: An East Timorese Vision of the Ideal State," in *Democratic Governance in Timor-Leste: Reconciling the Local and the National*, ed. D. Mearns (Darwin: Charles Darwin University Press, 2008), 171.

By focusing on the *funu*, the constitution also prioritizes the role of FALINTIL, which has generated the perception among many FALINTIL veterans that they are a privileged group. This privilege is manifest in the large pension scheme that many benefit from, but also in their increasing political activism.[23] One MP cautiously observed that veterans remain "waiting in the mountains, ready to come back down to Dili and cause problems."[24] Veterans are able to exercise considerable influence within Parliament as several politicians are identified with them, or in some cases are veterans themselves.[25] A political party, Unidade Nacional Democrátia da Resistência Timorense (National Democratic Union of Timorese Resistance), formed to represent veterans and between 2007 and 2012 held two parliamentary seats.

By focusing on FRETILIN and FALINTIL, the constitution largely overlooks the contribution of the younger generation involved in the clandestine resistance. While many in the clandestine resistance were FRETILIN members, it was not perceived as a partisan entity. Therefore, although the official historical narrative mentions the clandestine resistance's role, it fails to "truly valorise...all key participants in the resistance."[26] The logical implication of the narrative is also that those who supported integration with Indonesia have no place in the history of independent Timor-Leste. As many pro-integration supporters have competing memories of the Indonesian invasion and occupation, the narrative has been characterized as creating a sense of "inclusion and exclusion."[27] One descendent of a pro-Indonesia family notes that those who supported integration interpret it as implying that they are "second class to those involved in the resistance."[28]

The official historical narrative also overlooks the role of local tradition and custom. Proposals to draw upon local tradition and custom received little sympathy from FRETILIN in the Constituent Assembly. This reflected FRETILIN's longstanding suspicion of traditional *liurai* "feudalism" and the strong links between many *liurai* and FRETILIN's political opponents in UDT at the time of the 1975 coup.[29] Instead, as the narrative focuses on a political reading of history, it is framed in terms of an anticolonial struggle.

---

[23] J. Wallis, "Victors, Villains and Victims: Capitalizing on Memory in Timor-Leste," *Ethnopolitics* 12:2 (2013): 133–160.

[24] Interview with a member of Parliament, September 30, 2010.   [25] Ibid.

[26] M. Leach, "History Teaching: Challenges and Alternatives," in Kingsbury and Leach, *East Timor: Beyond Independence*, 45.

[27] Interview with an international governance adviser (c), May 10, 2010.

[28] Interview with a Timorese intellectual, May 12, 2010.

[29] D. Fitzpatrick, "Land Claims in East Timor: A Preliminary Assessment," *Australian Journal of Asian Law* 3:2 (2001): 138.

This is despite the fact that, in line with an ethno-symbolist approach to nationalism, many young Timorese emphasize a more "indigenous" historiography that acknowledges their cultural unity with West Timor and offers, "in their view, a truly postcolonial perspective on nationalism."[30] Such a reading is often based on the idea of Timoria, a "pan-Timor identity...based on indigenous cultural conceptualisations of common origins and shared ancestral founders."[31] This identity resonates most strongly in the enclave of Oecussi[32] and in the regions where traditional kingdoms were separated by the colonial border that split Timor Island. Significantly, the Wehali kingdom, which is now located in West Timor, was the "most important centre of precolonial power,"[33] which is one of the reasons why APODETI favored integration in 1975. However, an indigenous historiography too heavily based on Timoria could give rise to irredentist claims and would pose a serious challenge to Timor-Leste's relationship with Indonesia. Indeed, this was one of the reasons put forward by Indonesia to justify its occupation. More recently, this has been the case with the ethno-nationalist Negara Timor Raya (Nation of the Land of Timor) movement located in West Timor, which promotes a vision of greater Timorese unity. This movement has a significant following among West Timorese elites and has gained impetus since Timor-Leste began to access significant oil revenues in 2005.[34] Although the movement has little public support in Timor-Leste, the extensive cross-border links mean that its increased salience cannot be discounted in the future.

The official historical narrative does acknowledge the role of the Catholic Church,[35] reflecting the church's identity as the "bastion of the people" during the occupation, as it sought to protect Timorese from human rights abuses.[36] This was a result of the strong leadership of its bishops and the Vatican's insistence on dealing directly with the Timorese – rather than the Indonesian – diocese. The church also played an important role in incubating Timorese nationalism. Indeed, on a modernist reading, the church has in

---

[30] M. Leach, "History on the Line: East Timorese History after Independence," *History Workshop Journal* 61:1 (2006): 232; interview with a Timorese intellectual, May 12, 2010.

[31] Molnar, *Timor Leste*, 33; interview with an international academic, January 7, 2010.

[32] Interview with an international academic, January 18, 2010; interview with an international academic, December 22, 2009.

[33] Kammen, "Master-Slave, Traitor-Nationalist," 72; T. Therik, *Wehali: The Female Land, Traditions of a Timorese Ritual Centre* (Canberra: Pandanus Books, 2004).

[34] R. Nixon, "Indonesian West Timor: The Political-Economy of Emerging Ethno-Nationalism," *Journal of Contemporary Asia* 34:2 (2004): 163–185.

[35] Constitution, s. 11(2).

[36] Interview with a government official, April 27, 2010; A. Kohen, "The Catholic Church and the Independence of East Timor," in Tanter, Selden, and Shalom, *Bitter Flowers*.

some sense substituted for print capitalism because it refused to adopt Bahasa after Indonesia forced the abandonment of the Portuguese language in 1979.[37] Instead, it conducted services in Tetum-Praça (market Tetum), a common local language that had been adopted and developed by the Portuguese. This helped to spread Tetum, which subsequently emerged as the *lingua franca*. The church's utilization of Tetum also meant that the church offered the only public space not controlled by Indonesia, and consequently there was a "dramatic increase" in conversions, from the estimated 27.8 percent of the population who were professed Catholics in 1973 to 98 percent by the end of the occupation.[38] This was assisted by the church's willingness to syncretize its practices with local religious beliefs, which has allowed Catholicism to be "indigenised."[39]

Despite this, the church was not explicitly mentioned in the official historical narrative in the FRETILIN draft,[40] which reflects the secularism of the FRETILIN leadership. There is also some suggestion that FRETILIN Constituent Assembly members wanted to make a clear statement on the future relationship between the government and the church, the "only political actor…capable of challenging FRETILIN."[41] To that end, the FRETILIN draft also stated that Timor-Leste would be a "secular State" with a "separation between the State and churches."[42] After opposition in the assembly and from the church, these provisions were diluted.[43] However, in light of the extent of popular affiliation with the church, during the assembly's public consultations, many Timorese expressed the view that its historical role should be recognized prominently.[44]

National symbols

The constitution identifies a number of national symbols. There was public debate in the Constitutional Commission hearings concerning whether to

---

[37] B. Anderson, "Imagining East Timor," *Arena Magazine* 4 (1993).
[38] Ramos-Horta, *Funu*, 201; A. Field, "Acknowledging the Past, Shaping the Future: How the Churches and Other Religious Communities are Contributing to Timor-Leste's Development," in Mearns, *Democratic Governance*.
[39] Interview with a government official, April 27, 2010.   [40] FRETILIN draft constitution, art. 11.
[41] D. Kingsbury and M. Leach, "Introduction," in Kingsbury and Leach, *East Timor: Beyond Independence*, 4–5.
[42] FRETILIN draft constitution, art. 12(1).
[43] One was moved to the part on human rights, appearing as "religious denominations are separated from the State." Constitution, s. 45(1). A new clause was also included that specifically requires the state to "recognise and respect the different religious denominations." Constitution, s. 12.
[44] Interview with a former member of the Constituent Assembly and government official, February 2, 2010; NDI, *"Timor Loro Sa'e Is Our Nation": A Report on Focus Group Discussions in East Timor* (Dili: The National Democratic Institute for International Affairs, 2001).

adopt the flag used by FRETILIN when it declared independence in 1975 or the flag used by FALINTIL (and later The CNRT) during the occupation.[45] While the most popular compromise was to incorporate the two flags, the constitution instead adopts the FRETILIN flag.[46] There are claims that FRETILIN Constituent Assembly members saw this as a further way to entrench FRETILIN's symbolic importance,[47] although a non-FRETILIN Timorese government official argued that the flag instead represents "the blood and bone of all those who fought and died for this country."[48]

The name of the new state, República Democrática de Timor-Leste,[49] echoes the name coined by FRETILIN in 1975, although at the time it used the Tetum *Timor Lorosa'e*. Consequently, there was relatively widespread public agreement in the Constitutional Commission hearings in favor of *Timor Lorosa'e*.[50] Despite this, FRETILIN Constituent Assembly members strongly advocated the Portuguese *Timor-Leste*.

The date of independence, November 28, 1975, is the day that FRETILIN declared independence from Portugal.[51] During the Constituent Assembly's public consultations, Timorese expressed concern that this date was too partisan. They had been planning to celebrate independence on May 20, 2002, the date that Timor-Leste would become formally independent.[52] Yet even this date was partisan as it was the anniversary of the establishment of ASDT, FRETILIN's predecessor. Alternatively, August 30 might have performed a more unifying role. Indeed, during the Constitutional Commission hearings, Timorese expressed a desire for general elections to be held on August 30 to commemorate the popular consultation.[53]

To compound the emphasis on FRETILIN, the national anthem is "Patria Patria,"[54] the FRETILIN anthem. Along with the more traditionally oriented "Foho Ramelau," this did receive widespread support in the Constitutional Commission hearings.[55] The constitution also renames the army the FALINTIL-Forças de Defesa de Timor Leste (F-FDTL – FALINTIL-Defence Force of Timor-Leste),[56] which, it has been argued, represents an "attempt to

---

[45] UNTAET Constitutional Affairs Branch, *Constitutional Commission Public Hearings*.
[46] Constitution, s. 15; Law on National Symbols No. 2/2007 (2007) (TL), art. 3.
[47] F. da Costa Guterres, *Elites and Prospects of Democracy in East Timor*, PhD Thesis, Griffith University, January 2006.
[48] Interview with a government official, April 27, 2010.   [49] Constitution, s. 1(1).
[50] UNTAET Constitutional Affairs Branch, *Constitutional Commission Public Hearings*.
[51] Constitution, s. 1(2).   [52] UNTAET, "Public Speaks Out to Assembly Members."
[53] UNTAET Constitutional Affairs Branch, *Constitutional Commission Public Hearings*.
[54] Constitution, s. 166; Law on National Symbols, art. 5.
[55] UNTAET Constitutional Affairs Branch, *Constitutional Commission Public Hearings*.
[56] Constitution, s. 146.

link the future defence force with FRETILIN history and overcome the 1987 withdrawal of FALINTIL from FRETILIN."[57]

Each of these national symbols reflects a FRETILIN-led memory of history. This approach was contested in the Constituent Assembly, with opposition parties arguing that the use of FRETILIN symbols set "a dangerous precedent bespeaking an authoritarian tendency to conflate the ruling party with the state itself."[58] Minority parties instead proposed relatively neutral symbols, such as those that resonate with local traditional identities.[59] Indeed, this was widely favored in the Constitutional Commission hearings, and the public made numerous suggestions for national symbols that emphasized local tradition and custom.[60]

Defining national identity

The constitution seeks to define certain aspects of national identity. It emphasizes that Timor-Leste will maintain "privileged ties" with Lusophone countries.[61] Lusophone culture is said to mark Timor-Leste as a "distinctive grouping" and to signify its cultural difference from Indonesia.[62] This was important during the resistance as it countered Indonesia's attempt to emphasize Timor-Leste's connections to West Timor, and to Malay culture more broadly. References to Lusophone culture also reflect the values of the older, FRETILIN-led generation, who were socialized by the education they received during colonization to value becoming a "good Portuguese" and to cut ties with "barefoot Timorese culture."[63]

Despite this, the emphasis on Lusophone culture suggests the political leadership was disconnected from ordinary Timorese, who largely perceived

---

[57] UN, *Report of the United Nations Independent Special Commission of Inquiry for Timor-Leste*, UN Doc. S/2006/822, October 2, 2006: 18.

[58] Smith, "East Timor: Elections," 153.

[59] Constituent Assembly Thematic Commission IV: Fundamental Principles/Guarantee, Monitoring and Revision of the Constitution/Final and Transitional Provisions, *Report to the Systematization and Harmonization Commission* (Dili: Constituent Assembly, undated).

[60] These included a traditional house; Mount Ramelau (as being the place of ancestors); a traditional sword, spear, or dagger (symbolizing the long struggle for independence); cotton or rice (representing Timor's agricultural heritage); the island of Timor; a crocodile (representing the shape of the island of Timor, as well as images from popular mythology); a dove (representing peace, or the holy spirit delivering news of peace); images of people in traditional dress (representing culture); the Bible or cross (representing the importance of religion); or the sun. UNTAET Constitutional Affairs Branch, *Constitutional Commission Public Hearings*.

[61] Constitution, s. 8(3).

[62] Leach, "Valorising the Resistance," 46; J. Ramos-Horta, quoted in T. Zubrycki (dir.) and S. Browning (prod.), *The Diplomat*, (Lindfield: Film Australia, 2000).

[63] Gusmao, *To Resist Is to Win!*, 5–6.

Portugal as an oppressive colonial regime. Indeed, during the Constitutional Commission hearings, many Timorese expressed a belief that reparations should be sought from Portugal. The emphasis on Lusophone culture also has little relevance to the younger generation, who grew up under Indonesian occupation, which has led to "a distinct and deep divide between the young and old leaders today."[64] This division was exemplified when then-prime minster Alkatiri referred to young Timorese educated in Indonesian universities as *supa mie* (instant noodles), which "insulted them by suggesting that their Indonesian education had little value."[65]

In keeping with the emphasis on Lusophone culture, the constitution declares that Portuguese and Tetum are official languages.[66] Bahasa and English are "working languages," to be used within the public service for "as long as deemed necessary."[67] It also provides that Tetum and other indigenous languages should be "valued and developed."[68] The initial FRETILIN draft had sought to enshrine only Portuguese as an official language, with Tetum a "national" language to be developed to official status in five to ten years.[69] This indicates the dismissive attitude to Tetum among the older generation of political leadership. In contrast, Portuguese was seen as integral to "the uniqueness of East Timor."[70] There was also apparently a belief that adopting Portuguese would "eradicate" Bahasa[71] and strategically align Timor-Leste with the Lusophone world.[72]

While it is common for former colonies to adopt their colonizers' language, at the time the constitution was made, only 5 percent of Timorese actually spoke Portuguese. In contrast, 82 percent spoke Tetum, while as many as 91 percent understood it and as many as 58 percent could read it.[73] This was aided by the fact that Tetum emerged as the language of the clandestine resistance and was adopted by the Catholic Church.[74] During the public consultations, there was overwhelming support for Tetum to be developed into an official language and for Portuguese to be an official language only

---

[64] Niner, "Martyrs, Heroes and Warriors," 114.
[65] A. Wigglesworth, *Becoming Citizens: Civil Society Activism and Social Change in Timor Leste*, PhD Thesis, Victoria University, 2010, 113.
[66] Constitution, s. 13(1).   [67] Ibid., s. 159.   [68] Ibid., s. 13(2).
[69] FRETILIN draft constitution, art. 13.
[70] J. Ramos-Horta quoted in "Forum: East Timor's Jose Ramos Horta," *BBC News*, June 12, 2002.
[71] J. Ramos-Horta quoted in D. Babo Soares, "Challenges for the Future," in *Out of the Ashes: Destruction and Reconstruction of East Timor*, ed. J. J. Fox and D. Babo Soares (Canberra: ANU E-Press, 2003), 271.
[72] Interview with a member of Parliament, May 11, 2010; M. Leach, "Talking Portuguese: China and East Timor," *Arena Magazine*, December 2007.
[73] UNDP, *East Timor Human Development Report 2002*.   [74] Kohen, "The Catholic Church."

until this occurred.[75] Despite this, a young Constituent Assembly member noted that considerable pressure had to be exerted on older FRETILIN assembly members to secure recognition of Tetum.[76] Yet, while the majority of Timorese speak Tetum, many are unable to comfortably read or write in it, which reflects the impact of Indonesia's decision to make Bahasa the language of education and government during the first two decades of occupation. Indeed, at the time the constitution was made, 43 percent of the population spoke Bahasa, and 90 percent of those under the age of thirty-five had been educated in it.[77] The situation had changed little by the 2010 census, which found that 84.9 percent of the population could speak Tetum and 53.4 percent could speak, read, and write it, while 44 percent could speak Bahasa and 36 percent could speak, read, and write it. However, reflecting both the government and Portugal's concerted efforts to promote Portuguese, 29.6 percent identified that they could speak Portuguese, while 23.6 percent could speak, read, and write it.[78]

In light of the generational disparity in language ability, the decision to adopt Portuguese as an official language undermined the emergence of a sense of unified national identity, particularly as the relatively undeveloped nature of formal Tetum means that almost all official documents and laws are published in Portuguese. This is contrary to modernist theory, which argues that common literacy is the main way that a national identity will be disseminated. It has also separated the Portuguese-speaking elite from the majority of non-Portuguese speakers. For example, while debates in Parliament generally take place in Tetum, most draft laws are produced in Portuguese, meaning that many MPs cannot read the laws on which they vote.[79] The choice of Portuguese as an official language feeds into societal divisions because access to political and economic power can be affected by language ability. As a result, many Timorese perceive that "a division based on who speaks which languages" determines access to political power and state resources.[80] The adoption of Portuguese also excluded the younger generation from the "symbolic sources of power and cultural identity."[81] To the younger generation, the

---

[75] UNTAET Constitutional Affairs Branch, *Constitutional Commission Public Hearings*.
[76] Interview with a former member of the Constituent Assembly and government official, February 2, 2010.
[77] UNDP, *East Timor Human Development Report 2002*.
[78] NSD, *Population and Housing Census of Timor-Leste, 2010: Social and Economic Characteristics* (Dili: National Statistics Directorate, 2011), 181, 194.
[79] Interview with an international governance adviser (a), May 10, 2010.
[80] CEPAD, *Timor-Leste: Voices and Paths to Peace* (Dili: Centre of Studies for Peace and Development and Interpeace, 2010), 13.
[81] Leach, "Valorising the Resistance," 46.

"symbolism" of choosing Portuguese "seemed all wrong," as it represented a reversion "to the dominant vehicle for an earlier colonial rule."[82] Therefore, the Constituent Assembly's decision on official languages created "a lost generation, lacking fluency in the only internationally recognisable language of the state."[83] Reflecting this, many younger FRETILIN supporters shifted their support to opposition parties.[84] This decision has also challenged the delivery of education by teachers who are themselves frequently illiterate in Portuguese, which led the World Bank to reflect that "a full cohort of the population may be functionally illiterate."[85] In recognition of this effect, the government has taken steps to promote local languages and has adopted a trial program to teach schoolchildren in their local language.

The Constituent Assembly attempted to balance the emphasis on Lusophone culture and language by including a provision stating that Timor-Leste will maintain "special ties of friendship and cooperation" with its neighboring countries and region.[86] This was not included in the original FRETILIN draft[87] but was added under the influence of younger assembly members. This clause is also problematic, as Indonesia is Timor-Leste's nearest neighbor and maintaining special ties with that state may not sit well with Timorese who endured the brutality of the occupation. Indeed, the pursuit of justice and reconciliation in relation to the occupation has been controversial, as is discussed in Chapter 5.

The Constituent Assembly also incorporated provisions that encourage the state to "assert and value the personality and the cultural heritage of the East Timorese people."[88] The constitution specifies that "everyone has the right to cultural enjoyment and creativity and the duty to preserve, protect and value cultural heritage."[89] These provisions were favored during the public consultations, in which Timorese expressed their desire that customary cultural traditions be preserved.[90] However, the provisions are framed in aspirational terms, which reflects the fact that many FRETILIN assembly members were drawn from the diaspora and tended to see the recognition of local tradition and custom as "bringing back the dark ages."[91] One

---

[82] D. Mearns, "Introduction: Imagining East Timor Again: The Ideas of a 'National Identity' and 'Democratic Governance' in Timor-Leste," in Mearns, *Democratic Governance*, xvi.
[83] Leach, "Valorising the Resistance," 46.
[84] Garrison, *The Role of Constitution-Building Processes*.
[85] Independent Evaluation Group, *Evaluation of the World Bank Group Program, Timor-Leste Country Program Evaluation, 2000–2010* (Washington: The World Bank, 2011), ix.
[86] Constitution, s. 8(4).   [87] FRETILIN draft constitution, art. 9.   [88] Constitution, s. 6(g).
[89] Ibid., s. 59(5).
[90] UNTAET Constitutional Affairs Branch, *Constitutional Commission Public Hearings*.
[91] Interview with a member of Parliament, May 11, 2010.

FRETILIN MP commented that FRETILIN "takes seriously" the word "Revolutionary" in its title and "wants to change society, rather than remain in the past."[92] FRETILIN's approach signaled the "growing gap between elite and popular values" with respect to the role of local tradition and custom.[93] The result is that "people don't see their culture included in the Constitution and nation-state."[94] Gusmão was critical of FRETILIN's approach and argued that the Timorese should not be "ashamed of ourselves...[for] having our own historic and cultural identity that formed the basis of our emancipation."[95]

There appear to be strong elements of commonality between local traditional myths, symbols, and cultural practices, which provide fertile ground in which to cultivate an ethno-symbolist Timorese national identity. Almost all Timorese belong to an *uma lulik*, which is physically represented by a sacred building. And, almost all Timorese recognize the practice of having *sasan lulik* (sacred objects), which are kept within the *uma lulik*.[96] Indeed, since 1999, *uma luliks* have been rebuilt and *sasan luliks* that had been hidden during the Indonesian occupation have resurfaced. Most elders engage in *mamah bua malus* (chewing of betel nut), many rural women manufacture *tais* (traditional cloth), and most communities hold traditional *tebe-tebe* or *kore-metan* dances to commemorate the first anniversary of someone's death.[97] Almost all Timorese recognize the *nahe biti* reconciliation ceremony,[98] the *juramentu* (blood oath) used to create social unity and build relationships,[99] and the *tarabandu*, "an agreement among the community regulating aspects of behaviour and relationships among people, between people and natural resources, and economic life."[100]

Reflecting its approach in the Constituent Assembly, apart from a temporary national *uma lulik* erected in Dili to commemorate independence, the

---

[92] Ibid.
[93] M. Leach, "Surveying East Timorese Tertiary Student Attitudes to National Identity: 2002–2007," *South East Asia Research* 16:3 (2008): 409.
[94] Interview with a Timorese intellectual, May 12, 2010.
[95] X. Gusmão, speech at his inauguration as president of Timor-Leste, Dili, May 19, 2002, reproduced in X. Gusmão, *Timor Lives! Speeches of Freedom and Independence* (Alexandria: Longueville Media, 2005), 4.
[96] A. McWilliam, "Houses of Resistance in East Timor: Structuring Sociality in the New Nation," *Anthropological Forum* 15:1 (2005): 27–44.
[97] Molnar, *Timor Leste*; Trindade, "Reconciling Conflicting Paradigms."
[98] Babo-Soares, "Nahe Biti." [99] Trindade, "Reconciling Conflicting Paradigms."
[100] M. A. Brown and A. F. Gusmao, "Peacebuilding and Political Hybridity in East Timor," *Peace Review* 21 (2009): 67; Belun, *Tara Bandu: Its Role and Use in Community Conflict Prevention in Timor-Leste* (Dili: Belun and Asia Foundation, 2013).

first FRETILIN government did little to engage with local tradition and custom, and when it did, it was "superficial."[101] In the aftermath of the 2006 security crisis, Prime Minister Ramos-Horta recognized the need to change approach. His government held a series of *nahe biti* reconciliation ceremonies, beginning at the village level and culminating in a national ceremony in Dili under a temporary national *uma lulik* in front of the Government Palace. It is claimed that the national ceremony was not conducted in accordance with customary requirements, which undermined its legitimacy.[102] Consequently, it was perceived as an empty "cultural show," leading to a mass brawl erupting afterwards.[103] Despite this, the decision to hold the ceremony signals that some political leaders did recognize the continuing – and unifying – resonance of local tradition and custom.

Under Prime Minister Gusmão's influence, the AMP (and now BGK) government continued this approach. Although this signals a positive recognition of the role of local tradition and custom, it has verged on being disingenuous. Gusmão justifies his conciliatory approach toward Indonesia on the basis that it reflects the local practice of prioritizing *badame* (reconciliation) over justice.[104] Similarly, the minister of petroleum and mineral resources has facilitated the negotiation of a *tarabandu* to limit the sand mining and erosion of the Dili River.[105] It is generally agreed that this *tarabandu* has been successful, as it involved local leaders and was concluded according to local practices.[106] Conversely, the minister also arranged a *tarabandu* to legitimize the state's right to explore natural resources. Critics claim that this *tarabandu* was not conducted in accordance with local practices and did not involve legitimate local leaders.[107] Despite these missteps, the fact that the majority of Timorese continue to follow local tradition and customs suggests that, if utilized, they could play a role in creating a unifying national identity that could assist in constituting the political community.

---

[101] L. Palmer and D. do Amaral de Carvalho, "Nation Building and Resource Management: The Politics of 'Nature' in Timor Leste," *Geoforum* 39:3 (2008): 1330.
[102] Trindade, "Reconciling Conflicting Paradigms."
[103] Interview with a Timorese intellectual, May 12, 2010; interview with an international academic, January 18, 2010.
[104] Gusmão, *Timor Lives!*; interview with a Timorese intellectual, May 12, 2010; interview with an international governance adviser (a), May 10, 2010.
[105] Personal communication a government official, April 29, 2010.
[106] Interview with a member of Timorese civil society (a), May 14, 2010.
[107] Ibid.; interview with a Timorese intellectual, May 12, 2010.

Timorese citizenship

The definition of Timorese citizenship is also important, since it defines who belongs to "the people" and is capable of acting as a member of the Timorese political community. The FRETILIN draft initially proposed a restrictive definition of an original citizen as a person born in Timor-Leste to a Timorese parent or to stateless parents.[108] As this would have excluded some people born in Timor-Leste – mostly of Indonesian origin – it was expanded by the Constituent Assembly to include children of a foreign father or mother who, being over seventeen years old, declares his or her will to become a Timor-Leste national, and people born overseas to a Timorese father or mother.[109]

The FRETILIN draft also failed to include a provision relating to the acquisition of citizenship. This would have had serious implications for people who had not been born in Timor-Leste but who had lived there for a number of years, again mostly people of Indonesian origin. Once it was agreed to provide acquired citizenship, FRETILIN proposed preventing people with acquired citizenship from working in Timor-Leste's foreign affairs, military, or intelligence services. This was controversial, with younger Constituent Assembly members concerned about the provision's discriminatory effect.[110] It was eventually removed. A law relating to acquired citizenship was adopted by the FRETILIN government in 2002. It provides that citizenship can be acquired by the children of Timorese with acquired citizenship, by the adopted children of Timorese citizens, by marriage to a Timorese citizen, and by naturalization (in very limited circumstances).[111] This has resulted in hundreds of people of Indonesian origin becoming stateless, as they do not consider themselves Indonesian because of their long residence in Timor-Leste but are unable to qualify for Timorese citizenship. Almost 300 such people were deported to Indonesia in late 2004.

FRETILIN's relatively restrictive approach to citizenship may be interpreted as an attempt to achieve a degree of commonality, at least in terms of birth, among the Timorese citizenry. According to primordialist theories of nationalism, this may in turn facilitate the formation of a sense of national identity. However, as the restrictions imposed are most likely to affect people of Indonesian origin, it also suggests a lack of openness and tolerance of pluralism among the FRETILIN leadership. The effect of this restrictive

---

[108] FRETILIN draft constitution, art. 3.   [109] Constitution, s. 3.
[110] Interview with a former member of the Constituent Assembly and government official, February 2, 2010.
[111] Law on Citizenship No. 9/2002 (2002) (TL), arts. 9–12

approach is hardened by the facts that only Timorese citizens can own land[112] and certain human rights protections are unavailable to noncitizens.[113]

Overall, the partisan nature of the official historical narrative and national symbols, as well as the gap between the national identity enumerated in the constitution and the reality of local ethno-symbolist Timorese identity, highlight the danger of establishing an elected constituent assembly to make a constitution. In Timor-Leste, this allowed political parties to control the constitution-making process. Utilizing an appointed and broadly representative constitutional convention might have provided a forum in which compromises could have been reached and consensus built concerning Timor-Leste's history and identity. In addition, providing more opportunities for Timorese to participate and taking their feedback seriously might have resulted in a narrative, symbols, and national identity with which all Timorese could identify, and would be more likely to constitute the political community.

Has reconciliation been achieved?

The second indicator of whether a unified political community has been created is whether reconciliation has been achieved. The most obvious conflict that required reconciliation was between pro-independence and pro-integration supporters. Another less obvious – but no less serious – conflict was between political elites.

Between integration and independence supporters

While the majority of Timorese supported independence, a significant minority favored integration with Indonesia. In the aftermath of the popular consultation, Timorese militia supported the Indonesian military during their "scorched earth" campaign. Therefore, the most significant societal division during the constitution-making process was between the pro-autonomy and the pro-independence groups. Many militiamen and other pro-integrationists had fled to West Timor after the result of the popular consultation was announced. Consequently, when UNTAET deployed, there were approximately 250,000 refugees in West Timor, although by the end of 1999 over 125,000 had been repatriated. During 2000 and 2001, UNTAET attempted to return the remaining refugees, partly to ensure that they were able to participate in the Constituent Assembly and presidential elections. However, there were reported cases of intimidation and mistreatment of returning refugees.[114]

---

[112] Constitution, s. 54(4).   [113] Discussed in Chapter 5.
[114] Conflict, Security and Development Group, *A Review of Peace Operations*.

In late 2001, the transitional administrator established a small team to conduct reconciliation between Timorese on both sides of the border. Within Timor-Leste, reconciliation efforts focused on the Comissão de Acolhimento, Verdade e Reconciliação (CAVR – Commission for Reception, Truth and Reconciliation), which was established on June 20, 2001.[115] The CAVR was mandated to establish the truth about human rights violations that took place before, during, and in the aftermath of the Indonesian occupation and to facilitate reconciliation between victims and offenders at the community and national levels. The CAVR's mandate was confirmed in the constitution.[116] However, the CAVR commissioners did not hold their first meeting until February 2002 and did not begin conducting reconciliation hearings until May 2002, which meant that no formal reconciliation was conducted during the constitution-making process.

The CAVR is widely considered to have been a success, as it allowed a range of Timorese to participate in and jointly create a "foundational document of the nation," in the form of its final report. The CAVR's report draws on shared memories of suffering to create a historical narrative that functions as a "generalised history" for all Timorese.[117] Significantly, it takes a nonpartisan approach by finding that human rights abuses were committed by both pro-integration and pro-independence supporters (including FRETILIN/ FALINTIL).[118] Therefore, the report presents a more balanced – and potentially unifying – narrative than the one enshrined in the constitution. The CAVR process also highlights the utility of drawing on local tradition and custom, as its community-based reconciliation hearings used the *nahe biti* ceremony. One adviser observed that this "enhanced the understanding and acceptability of community reconciliation."[119] However, it should be noted that the CAVR was criticized by human rights advocates and some victims for prioritizing reconciliation over justice, failing to handle cases uniformly (due

---

[115] UNTAET Regulation No. 2001/10, *On the Establishment of a Commission for Reception, Truth and Reconciliation in East Timor*, UN Doc. UNTAET/REG/2001/10, July 13, 2001, extended by Law No. 13/2004 and Law No. 11/2005.

[116] Constitution, s. 162.

[117] D. Grenfell, *Reconstituting the Nation: Reconciliation and National Consciousness in Timor-Leste* (Melbourne: RMIT Publishing, 2006), 21; interview with an international adviser to the Constituent Assembly and the CAVR, December 6, 2010.

[118] CAVR, *Chega!*

[119] S. Zifcak, *Restorative Justice in East Timor: An Evaluation of the Community Reconciliation Process of the Constituent Assembly* (New York: Asia Foundation, 2004), 29. See also S. Scheeringa, "Enhancing the Local Legitimacy of Transnational Justice Institutions: Local Embeddedness and Customary Law in Constituent Assembly," in Kingsbury and Leach, *East Timor: Beyond Independence*.

to the localized nature of the *nahe biti* ceremony), and providing minimal trauma counseling or support for victims.[120]

Despite the CAVR's efforts, there are estimates that between 100,000 and 200,000 Timorese remain in West Timor (some having fled again after their initial return).[121] As most are not well integrated into local communities and are landless and unemployed, it is likely that many will eventually return to Timor-Leste. This likelihood has been enhanced by Timor-Leste gaining access to extensive oil revenues, as many Timorese would be eligible for financial benefits. In addition, as the government is debating a new land tenure system, many exiled Timorese could return to exercise their property rights. Their return may reveal the "unsustainability of the uneasy status quo" on issues relating to reconciliation and justice, which highlights the importance of genuine and widespread reconciliation.[122] As the official historical narrative arguably marginalizes pro-integration supporters, this suggests the state will need to do more to construct a unifying national identity with which all Timorese can identify and which can encourage them to reconcile.

Between political elites

As outlined in Chapter 3, the two major Timorese political groups, FRETILIN and UDT, engaged in a civil war in 1975. While there were efforts to reconcile FRETILIN and UDT leaders under the auspices of The CNRT during the occupation, memories persisted of FRETILIN's decision in 1975 to take revenge on UDT and UDT's decision to sign the Balibo Declaration. A second division emerged between the three main pro-independence factions: those who spent the occupation in Australia, led by Ramos-Horta; the FRETILIN "Maputo Group," who spent it in Mozambique and Portugal, led by Alkatiri; and the younger generation of the clandestine resistance, many of whom were educated in Indonesian universities, led by Lasama from PD. However, the most significant division was between FRETILIN and Gusmão.

As noted, because the National Council opted for an elected constituent assembly, partisan interests were encouraged to hold sway during the

---

[120] JSMP, *Unfulfilled Expectations: Community Views on Constituent Assembly's Community Reconciliation Process* (Dili: Judicial System Monitoring Programme, 2004); B. Larke, "'...And the Truth Shall Set You Free': Confessional Trade-Offs and Community Reconciliation in East Timor," *Asian Journal of Social Science* 37 (2009): 646–676; P. Pigou, *Crying without Tears, In Pursuit of Justice and Reconciliation in Timor-Leste: Community Perspectives and Expectations* (Dili: International Center for Transitional Justice, 2003).

[121] The last reliable estimate was made in September 2010. ICG, *Timor-Leste: Reconciliation and Return from Indonesia*, Asia Briefing No. 122 (Dili: International Crisis Group, 2011)

[122] Ibid.

constitution-making process. Therefore, the process did not provide an opportunity to reconcile differences but instead further entrenched them. The decision of FRETILIN Constituent Assembly members to adopt a partisan historical narrative has enshrined competition over the "symbolic 'ownership' of the resistance, and its narrative of national liberation" in the constitution.[123] Consequently, attempts to achieve reconciliation have been largely unsuccessful, and "a lingering bitterness remains."[124]

The split between pro-independence factions also continues, and it is common to identify political elites based on their membership in the Australian, Maputo, or Indonesian groups. This split manifested itself in the Parliament in May 2006, when a moderate reforming faction of FRETILIN called Mudança ("Shift"), primarily made up of people from the Indonesian group, challenged Alkatiri's leadership. This saw FRETILIN solidify into two factions: Maputo and Mudança. The Mudança faction formed a political party, Frente-Mudança; contested the 2007 parliamentary election; and supported Ramos-Horta instead of the FRETILIN candidate in the 2007 presidential election.

Similarly, the split between FRETILIN and Gusmão has not been resolved. Indeed, this rivalry was evident when FRETILIN refused to endorse Gusmão in the 2002 presidential election. After the candidates were announced, Alkatiri expressed his disdain, announcing that he would be casting a blank ballot or voting for both candidates (making his vote invalid) on election day. The legacy of these unreconciled differences haunts politics, with the 2006 security crisis partly attributed to "ten people, who have a shared history going back 30 years."[125] While Ramos-Horta has made efforts to reconcile Alkatiri and Gusmão, even calling for "government of national unity" to be formed after the 2007 and 2012 elections,[126] he has been unsuccessful, solidifying the breach.

However, political elites have taken steps to ameliorate tensions between them and to minimize the impact these tensions have on wider society. Before the 2012 election, political leaders and parties participated in dialogues that culminated in a February 2012 declaration to eschew violence during the elections. Despite this, some leaders still use inflammatory language, which has caused tensions, exemplified by the violence that followed comments

---

[123] Leach, "History on the Line," 233.   [124] Niner, "Martyrs, Heroes and Warriors," 117.
[125] ICG, *Resolving Timor-Leste's Crisis*, Asia Report No. 120 (Dili: International Crisis Group, 2006), 1.
[126] Quoted in A. Grigg, "Keeping the Peace in East Timor," *Australian Financial Review*, May 21, 2011.

made at the 2012 CNRT convention that were perceived as insulting to FRETILIN. Questions also remain concerning what will occur when there is a transition to a younger generation of leaders. It is unclear the extent to which CNRT in particular will remain as a consolidated political force in the absence of Gusmão's unifying presence, or whether there may be a fracturing of that party to reflect historical (and emerging) rivalries.

Are there divisions within society?

Other divisions within Timorese society have also gained salience, which suggests that the constitution-making process did not succeed in building a unified political community. While there are regional tensions and competition between the sixteen different language groups, the most significant societal division is between people from the territory's eastern region (who are referred to as Lorosa'e in Tetum)[127] and those from the western region (referred to as Loromonu).[128] These tensions are ethno-national as they combine "ethnic" regional identities with competition over the ownership of national identity. Yet, while Lorosa'e–Loromonu identities are characterized as ethnic, they do not appear to be primordial, as they do not reflect "recognised 'indigenous' or pre-colonial ethnic unities."[129] Instead, these identities emerged during Portuguese colonization, when distinctions were drawn between the Firaku from the east, who were characterized as rebellious and independent, and the Kaladi from the west, who were perceived as friendlier and more cooperative. In the period after the Second World War, Loromonu migrated to Dili and competed with resident Lorosa'e for trade at local markets, causing regional identities to harden to define competition for economic resources. These identities were perpetuated by later urban migrants.

Lorosa'e–Loromonu identities became salient in the uncertain period following the 1999 popular consultation. The "scorched earth" campaign adopted by the retreating Indonesian military and their supporting Timorese militias precipitated a major economic downturn and rise in unemployment, which prompted new political and economic competition. This competition

---

[127] Approximately 30 percent of the population from the districts of Manatuto, Baucau, Viqueque, and Lautem are Lorosa'e.

[128] Approximately 50 percent of the population from the districts of Aileu, Ainora, Liquica, Manufahi, Ermera, Bobonaro, and Covalima are Loromonu. If Oecussi, an enclave located in West Timor, is included the total increases to 55 percent of the population. A. L. Smith, *Self-Determination Conflict Profile: East Timor* (Washington: Foreign Policy in Focus, 2002).

[129] Leach, "History Teaching," 201.

solidified along Lorosa'e–Loromonu lines as thousands of displaced people migrated to Dili and settled in Lorosa'e or Loromonu "ghettos."[130] Groups claiming regional identities engaged in street fights during 2000. During this period, a historical narrative emerged to underpin the division, which claimed that Lorosa'e were "heroes" who represented the resistance fighters and the "true custodians" of independent Timor-Leste. In contrast, Loromonu were marginalized as Indonesia's "accomplices."[131] This perception was created by strategic realities that meant FALINTIL was more sustainable in the east, because it was further from the Indonesian border. As FALINTIL remained more active in the east, fewer Lorosa'e were co-opted into pro-Indonesia militias, leading to a perception that eastern regions were the source of less sustained militia action after the popular consultation.

These claims find support in the official historical narrative enshrined in the constitution, since it focuses heavily on the resistance to Indonesian occupation and FRETILIN's role in it. As FRETILIN is associated with eastern regions, it implies that Lorosa'e people played the most significant role in the resistance. Yet this is not historically accurate, as there is evidence that many Loromonu supported the independence struggle.[132] This has meant that the official historical narrative has itself "turned into a rather divisive topic in daily conversation."[133] Therefore, the Lorosa'e-Loromonu division arguably emerged to fill the vacuum created by a poorly defined national identity, as it provided a route by which groups competed for their position within the new state.

After independence, political parties and leaders instrumentally used the Lorosa'e–Loromonu division to rally support. FRETILIN is associated with Lorosa'e regions, while parties opposed to FRETILIN, including Gusmão's CNRT, are associated with Loromonu regions. It is not uncommon for political leaders to explicitly identify themselves as originating from a specific region in their speech, dress, and ceremonial behavior. Consequently, the Lorosa'e–Loromonu division has been translated into electoral results.[134] For

---

[130] D. Babo-Soares, *Branching from the Trunk: East Timorese Perceptions of Nationalism in Transition*, PhD Thesis, Australian National University, 2003, 283.

[131] J. Trindade and B. Castro, *Rethinking Timorese Identity as a Peacebuilding Strategy: The Lorosa'e–Loromonu Conflict from a Traditional Perspective*, European Union Technical Assistance to the National Dialogue Process in Timor-Leste (Dili: GTZ, 2007), 12; Babo Soares, *Branching from the Trunk*.

[132] Babo Soares, *Branching from the Trunk*.

[133] Trindade and Castro, *Rethinking Timorese Identity*, 14.

[134] M. Leach, "The 2007 Presidential and Parliamentary Elections in Timor-Leste," *Australian Journal of Politics and History* 55:2 (2009): 219–232.

example, the 2007 presidential elections saw a pattern of three regional voting blocs, with Lorosa'e regions returning majorities for Lu Olo, the central region favoring Jose Ramos-Horta, and Loromonu regions returning the strongest votes for candidates from parties that opposed FRETILIN. The results of the 2007 parliamentary election reflect a similar geographic divide, with FRETILIN doing best in the eastern districts and CNRT doing better in the western districts. As CNRT then formed the AMP government with an alliance of parties that also oppose FRETILIN, the Lorosa'e–Loromonu division was translated into state institutions. This outcome was repeated in the 2012 presidential and parliamentary elections, which saw FRETILIN's support strongest in the three easternmost districts, while CNRT generally polled well ahead in other parts of the country. However, while the regional differentiation was "noticeable" after the 2012 election, it had "moderated," as FRETILIN recovered votes in the western districts, while CNRT and PD increased their votes in the eastern districts.[135]

Political leaders have also used Lorosa'e and Loromonu identities to mobilize male youths, up to 70 percent of whom were members of "urban gangs," "martial arts clubs," and "quasi-political organizations" by 2009. Many of these youth groups are divided according to geographic lines, with Lorosa'e and Loromonu gangs affiliated with leading political figures generally being characterized as "pro-" and "anti-" FRETILIN, although these identities are fluid and can change depending on shifting alliances and perceived political goals.[136]

Most dangerously, the Lorosa'e–Loromonu division took institutional form in the security forces. On February 1, 2001, after pressure from FALINTIL leaders and on the advice of an expert study,[137] UNTAET created the F-FDTL.[138] The F-FDTL consisted of 1,500 soldiers in two battalions. Six hundred fifty FALINTIL veterans formed the first battalion, while the remaining 1,300 were demobilized. On the advice of FALINTIL commanders, 56 percent of those recruited to the first battalion were Lorosa'e. This

---

[135] M. Leach and D. Kingsbury, "Introduction: East Timorese Politics in Transition," in *The Politics of Timor-Leste: Democratic Consolidation after Intervention*, ed. M. Leach and D. Kingsbury (Ithaca: Cornell University Press, 2013), 14.

[136] AI, *Groups, Gangs, and Armed Violence in Timor-Leste*, Issue Brief No. 2 (London: Amnesty International, 2009); J. Scambary, *A Survey of Gangs and Youth Groups in Dili, Timor-Leste* (Canberra: AusAID, 2006).

[137] Centre for Defence Studies, *Independent Study on Security Force Options and Security Sector Reform for East Timor* (London: Kings College, 2000).

[138] UNTAET Regulation No. 2001/1, *On the Establishment of a Defence Force for East Timor*, UN Doc. UNTAET/REG/2001/1, January 31, 2001.

partly reflected the fact that most surviving FALINTIL commanders came from the east. To rebalance the force, when the second battalion was recruited, the selection criteria included an upper age limit of twenty-two and the requirement of a high school diploma. This excluded most remaining FALINTIL veterans, and compensating for the geographical imbalance, these new recruits were overwhelmingly Loromonu.

The 1,300 demobilized veterans were assisted by the FALINTIL Reinsertion Assistance Program. While this program was deemed to have successfully reintegrated demobilized FALINTIL,[139] many veterans had expected that their service during the resistance would be rewarded with a role in the new state. However, most missed out on positions in the public service, as selection was based on experience, expertise, and capacity,[140] which many lacked given that they had spent much of their lives as guerrilla fighters. Most also missed out on positions in the Policia Nacional de Timor-Leste (PNTL – National Police of Timor-Leste).[141] As UNTAET was operating under time pressure, it decided to recruit several former members of the Polisi Republik Indonesia (POLRI – Indonesian National Police) instead of training new police. This included the police commissioner, who set the qualifications for recruitment (with UNTAET advice) to the 1,700-member PNTL. As these qualifications were based on fitness, skills, and experience, 370 former POLRI members received places, while most FALINTIL veterans did not. In late 2001, disenchanted FALINTIL veterans formed FALINTIL veterans and antisystem "security" associations, which began to conduct parades and training, often causing disruption in Dili and other urban centers.

Although they were not necessarily from western regions, because of their past association with Indonesia, many former POLRI members who were recruited to the PNTL were characterized as Loromonu and were tainted by the POLRI's questionable human rights record.[142] While the PNTL later expanded to over 3,000 members, as former POLRI officers were more experienced, their career progression was often fast-tracked and they came to occupy higher ranks. The culture within the PNTL was therefore problematic, and allegations emerged that it was corrupt and used torture, rape, excessive

---

[139] J. McCarthy, *FALINTIL Reinsertion Assistance Program: Final Evaluation Report* (Dili: International Organisation for Migration, 2002).

[140] UNTAET Regulation No. 2000/3 *On the Establishment of a Public Service Commission*, UN Doc. UNTAET/REG/2000/3, January 20, 2000.

[141] UNTAT Regulation No. 2001/22, *On the Establishment of the East Timor Police Service*, UN Doc. UNTAET/REG/2001/22, August 10, 2001.

[142] AI, *The Democratic Republic of Timor-Leste: A New Police Service – A New Beginning*, ASA 57/002/2003 (London: Amnesty International, June 30, 2003).

detention, and other illegal methods.[143] This caused F-FDTL members to become increasingly concerned about the poor way the PNTL handled security incidents. Tensions between the two institutions culminated in a group of F-FDTL members attacking a PNTL station in Dili in December 2004.

Tensions also emerged within the F-FDTL in January 2004, when forty-two soldiers were dismissed on disciplinary grounds after alleging that they had been discriminated against in terms of promotions and living conditions because they were Loromonu. For example, older members who were FALINTIL veterans (and who tended to be Lorosa'e) were given preferential static assignments, often because of their age and health. By 2006, 35 percent of the F-FDTL were Lorosa'e and 65 percent were Loromonu, which reflected national averages. However, Lorosa'e remained overrepresented in the higher levels and constituted about half of all officers.

Allegations of discrimination came to a head in January 2006 when 159 soldiers, who were reportedly Loromonu, submitted a petition alleging that they were subject to discriminatory treatment. Dissatisfied with the F-FDTL's response, on February 17 a group of 594 soldiers (who became known as the "petitioners") left their barracks and went on strike. On March 16, the government ordered the petitioners to return to their barracks and, when they refused, dismissed them for desertion. On March 23, President Gusmão gave a speech criticizing this decision, which gave credence to the petitioners' claims that there was discrimination against Loromonu. On April 24, 2006, the petitioners began a peaceful protest in front of the Government Palace in Dili. The protest attracted a range of disaffected groups, including youths and members of veterans' and security associations. On the last day of the protest, April 28, violence erupted. As the PNTL was already suffering from numerous institutional weaknesses, it was unable to restore order. Instead, Prime Minister Alkatiri called in the F-FDTL, many of whom used disproportionate force.[144] During this time, a small group of armed military police left their barracks in support of the petitioners.

During May 2006, tensions between the F-FDTL and PNTL mounted, culminating in F-FDTL members attacking the PNTL headquarters and massacring ten unarmed PNTL officers. Gangs of youths and veterans added to the resulting violence and confusion, which expanded to include

---

[143] HRW, *Tortured Beginnings: Police Violence and the Beginning of Impunity in East Timor* (New York: Human Rights Watch, 2006); World Bank, *Strengthening the Institutions of Governance in Timor-Leste* (Washington: World Bank, 2006).

[144] UN, *United Nations Independent Special Commission of Inquiry*.

wider society. In response, the government requested the Australian-led International Stabilization Force, the F-FDTL was ordered to return to its barracks, and the PNTL collapsed. By this time, at least thirty-eight people had been killed and many more had been injured. In addition, 150,000 people were internally displaced, some because of the Lorosa'e–Loromonu tensions, others because of tensions between supporters of FRETILIN and supporters of opposition political groups, and still others who were victims of criminality, gang violence, or social jealousy. Fear of these factors was exacerbated by a lack of trust in the ability of the PNTL and F-FDTL to provide protection.[145]

The initial humanitarian response saw approximately 50,000 internally displaced persons (IDPs) return to their homes starting in July 2006. However, violence and instability continued. In October 2006, gang warfare in Dili resulted in further house destruction and displacement. More violence took place in February and March 2007, resulting in an additional 8,000 people being displaced. While the presidential elections in April and May 2007 and the parliamentary elections in June 2007 were relatively peaceful, arsonists still destroyed about 800 houses. After the formation of the new AMP government was announced on August 7, 2007, gangs burned buildings in Dili and up to 400 houses in Baucau. This caused more people to flee to IDP camps, so by the end of 2007, there were more than 100,000 IDPs. The violence reached a crescendo in February 2008, when a small group of military police who had left their barracks to support the petitioners attempted to assassinate Prime Minister Gusmão and President Ramos-Horta. During this attack, the would-be assassins were killed, captured or surrendered.

The fact that the security crisis escalated to the extent that it did signals the depth of the Lorosa'e-Loromonu tensions. This in turn suggests that the constitution had not created a unified sense of national identity capable of constituting a political community. Instead, because of its partisan nature, the official historical narrative actually supported this societal division. Lorosa'e-Loromonu tensions have diminished since the crisis, largely because the government has engaged in extensive spending, including cash payments to certain societal groups (most significantly a large scheme for FALINTIL veterans and their families), as well as smaller schemes for the elderly and disabled and female-headed households, which has alleviated some of the economic frustrations and poverty that drove the crisis.[146] The government also engaged in an extensive program of payments to return and resettle IDPs

---

[145] ICG, *Timor-Leste's Displacement Crisis, Asia Report No. 148* (Dili: International Crisis Group, 2008).
[146] Wallis, "Victors, Villains and Victims."

and introduced a disarmament, demobilization, and reintegration program for the petitioners.[147] While these payment schemes have helped to mitigate further conflict in the short term, given that oil and gas revenues provided 97 percent of the state budget in 2012 and some projections forecast that these revenues will be exhausted by 2025,[148] the question is raised of whether the peace bought by these payment programs will hold. If the Lorosa'e–Loromonu tension has been only artificially ameliorated, it may again emerge as a source of conflict.

The government also adopted a law to regulate martial arts clubs in 2008.[149] In the face of escalating violence, in December 2011 the government adopted a resolution that prohibited and criminalized the activities of martial arts clubs for one year (which was later extended).[150] In July 2013, the government resolved to dissolve all martial arts clubs.[151] The law is being observed, although given that these clubs had widespread memberships, it is unclear whether they will remain dissolved or whether they will emerge in another form, again posing a potential challenge to stability.

Does the community exhibit evidence of citizenization?

While a sense of national identity can play an important role, citizenization can also help to constitute the political community. The level of citizenization can be indicated by the presence of an ethos of constitutionalism and by the level of ongoing participation in state institutions, evidence of which includes electoral turnouts, strategic voting, and people's engagement in other opportunities for political participation provided in the constitution.

Ethos of constitutionalism

The constitution has been respected and enforced in the face of serious challenges, elections have been regularly held, changes in the executive have occurred peacefully, and no political office has been held in defiance of the expressed will of the people. The first serious challenge to the constitution

---

[147] Ibid.
[148] C. Scheiner, *How Long Will the Petroleum Fund Carry Timor-Leste?* (Dili: La'o Hamutuk, 2013).
[149] Law on the Practice of Martial Arts, No. 10/2008 (2008) (TL).
[150] Government Resolution on Measures Aimed at Ensuring Public Order and Internal Security of the Country No. 35/2011 (2011) (TL), extended by Resolution No. 24/2012; Office of the Presidency, "Press Release: Extraordinary Meeting of the Council of Ministers on 2 July 2013" (Dili: Office of the Presidency of the Council of Ministers, 2013).
[151] Government Resolution on the Extinction Martial Arts Groups No. 16/2013 (2013) (TL).

arose during the 2006 security crisis. The constitution was breached – or at least sidelined – when Prime Minister Alkatiri called out the F-FDTL, as it is not constitutionally responsible for internal security or law enforcement. In addition, Alkatiri did not consult President Gusmão, the supreme commander of the defense force.[152] However, when opposition parties called for President Gusmão to dissolve Parliament, assume extraordinary powers, and appoint a transitional government in breach of the constitution, he declined to act. Instead, after Alkatiri resigned, Gusmão appointed Ramos-Horta as his replacement, which ensured that the constitution was respected.

The second challenge arose after the 2007 parliamentary election, when President Ramos-Horta appointed Gusmão prime minister and invited his AMP coalition to form a government. This was controversial, as FRETILIN claimed that the relevant constitutional provision[153] was ambiguous and "universal democratic values" necessitated that the party that received the most votes should be given the opportunity to form a government.[154] When the relevant provision is interpreted with reference to the rest of the constitution,[155] it becomes clear that a parliamentary majority is required.[156] Despite this, Alkatiri declared that the AMP government was "illegal" and claimed that FRETILIN "will never want to cooperate with this de facto government."[157] He encouraged FRETILIN supporters to engage in a campaign of civil disobedience, and several militants with alleged ties to FRETILIN were involved in violence.[158] FRETILIN then boycotted Parliament throughout most of August 2007. However, after exploring the possibility of a legal challenge, FRETILIN eventually conceded that it would fight the constitutionality of the AMP government through political means.

---

[152] Constitution, s. 74(2).
[153] S. 106(1) states: "The Prime Minister shall be designated by the party with the most votes or the political party or alliance of political parties with a parliamentary majority and shall be appointed by the President of the Republic, after consultation with the political parties sitting in the National Parliament."
[154] Interview with a member of Parliament, May 11, 2010; S. Da Silva and J. Teixeira, "The Unconstitutional, Irrational and Damaging Decision by President Jose Ramos Horta: A Legal Opinion on the Formation of an Unconstitutional Government in Timor-Leste," *East Timor Law Journal* 5(2007).
[155] Specifically, Constitution, s. 85(d), which provides that the president has the power to appoint the prime minister "designated by the party or alliance of parties with parliamentary majority."
[156] M. Clegg, *The Constitution of Timor-Leste: Appointment of a Prime Minister*, IFES White Paper (Dili: International Foundation for Electoral Systems, 2007).
[157] Quoted in "Gusmão to be Timor-Leste's new PM," *Timor Post*, August 7, 2007.
[158] ICG, *Timor-Leste's Displacement Crisis*; personal communication from an international humanitarian worker, May 3, 2010; personal communication from an international humanitarian worker, May 6, 2010.

The constitution was challenged for a third time by the February 2008 assassination attempts against President Ramos-Horta and Prime Minister Gusmão. While Prime Minister Gusmão labeled them an attempted "coup,"[159] the government neither collapsed nor changed hands, and the constitution continued to be respected.

Despite this evidence, there are signs that political elites lack a strong ethos of constitutionalism. Most developed their understanding of constitutionalism from Indonesia or Mozambique, neither of which had a strong constitutional culture. Moreover, most were part of the resistance, which by its nature did "not generate respect for the idea of dispensing and limiting power according to a superior law."[160] As the political elites involved in making the constitution were relatively unfettered by public participation, they "see the Constitution as mouldable based on their view of the 'national interest.'"[161] For example, the constitution entrenches five-year term limits for MPs.[162] As the Constituent Assembly election had been on August 30, 2001, this implied that the first parliamentary election would be held in August 2006. However, in late 2005, Prime Minister Alkatiri announced that the election would be in 2007, as the constitution did not enter into force until 2002. Alkatiri made this decision "without any recourse to judicial review or opinion," indicating that important constitutional decisions were "made behind closed doors."[163]

Similarly, the executive is said to engage only in "weak, if not absent, reflection" concerning the constitutionality of laws.[164] Both the FRETILIN and AMP governments circumvented the Court of Appeal's power of constitutional review. For example, in 2003, the court ruled that the draft Immigration and Asylum Law was unconstitutional.[165] When it was returned for amendment, the Parliament passed it again without substantial revision.[166] The Parliament similarly passed the Law on Freedom of Assembly and Demonstration, again after it had been ruled unconstitutional and vetoed by President Gusmão.[167] Other examples include the passage of

---

[159] Quoted in "Dawn Raids – Timor-Leste," *The Economist*, February 16, 2008.
[160] L. Grenfell, "Promoting the Rule of Law in Timor-Leste," *Conflict, Security & Development* 9:2 (2009): 218.
[161] Interview with an international governance adviser (a), May 10, 2010.   [162] Constitution, s. 93.
[163] Della-Giacoma, "Ensuring the Well-Being."
[164] Interview with an international governance adviser (b), May 10, 2010.
[165] To the extent that it placed limitations on noncitizens that went beyond the scope permitted by the constitution's human rights guarantees. Court of Appeal, *Ruling of the Court in Case No. 02/2003, On the Constitutionality of the Law on Immigration and Asylum*, June 30, 2003.
[166] Law on Immigration and Asylum No. 9/2003 (2003) (TL).
[167] Law on Freedom of Assembly and Demonstration No. 1/2006 (2006) (TL).

unconstitutional state budgets and the granting of criminal amnesties and pardons, discussed in Chapter 5.

In light of this evidence, it is unsurprising that little sense of constitutionalism has developed among ordinary Timorese. The minimal opportunities for civic education or public participation during the constitution-making process did not encourage a sense of constitutionalism. In one 2004 survey, 41 percent of respondents believed that there was not genuine public participation in the process.[168] Consequently, at the time the constitution was adopted, surveys revealed that people believed there was "no law at present"[169] or had "no idea" what the constitution meant.[170] This suggests that the constitution was adopted "without a wider societal debate" and that more time and effort were required to "communicate to locals the existence and relevance of the new formal legal system."[171] Informed Timorese perceived the process to have been "Dili-based, 'elite politics'-centred" and "not represent[ative of] the full citizenry."[172] As a result, some felt that the constitution was a "FRETILIN document," which reflected "party objectives rather than more inclusive national interests."[173] Therefore, at independence popular ownership of the constitution appeared weak, with one Timorese intellectual noting that people perceive the constitution as "just pieces of paper."[174]

Public knowledge is slowly improving, and most Timorese now recognize the existence of the constitution, commonly referred to as the *lai inan* (mother law).[175] Illiteracy and a lack of civic education mean that there is little corresponding knowledge of what the constitution says,[176] with a 2004 survey revealing that 33 percent of respondents did not know what it means, while only 28 percent identified it as the source of law.[177] As the constitution is

---

[168] Asia Foundation, *Law and Justice in East Timor: A Survey of Citizen Awareness and Attitudes Regarding Law and Justice in East Timor* (Dili: Asia Foundation, 2004).

[169] D. Mearns, *Looking Both Ways: Models for Justice in East Timor* (Sydney: Australian Legal Resources International, 2002).

[170] A survey of uneducated, small-town residents and older women in 2003 found that one-third of the respondents had no idea what the constitution meant. Of the other respondents, 28 percent saw the constitution as the source of law, 8 percent believed it meant law and order, 7 percent saw it as "the rules for an independent country," and 15 percent understood it vaguely as "a way of life or guidance for citizens." Asia Foundation, *Law and Justice in East Timor*, 28, 32.

[171] Trindade and Castro, *Rethinking Timorese Identity*, 14.

[172] Quoted in Carter Centre, *East Timor Political and Election Observation*, 43.   [173] Ibid.

[174] Trindade, "Reconciling Conflicting Paradigms," 166–167.

[175] Interview with a member of Timorese civil society (a), May 14, 2010; interview with a Timorese intellectual, May 12, 2010.

[176] Interview with a member of Timorese civil society (a), May 14, 2010; interview with a member of Timorese civil society (b), May 14, 2010; interview with a Timorese intellectual, May 12, 2010.

[177] Asia Foundation, *Law and Justice in East Timor*, 4.

supposed to represent the tangible manifestation of the social contract on which the Timorese state is built, this poses serious questions about its legitimacy.

Electoral turnouts and strategic voting
However, electoral participation levels suggest that citizenization has occurred, as the opportunity for citizens to vote in elections is the main aspect of the relationship between the state and its citizens. Voter participation in the 2001 Constituent Assembly election was high, at 91.3 percent of registered voters. The 2002 presidential election saw another high turnout: 86 percent of all registered voters. Voter participation in the 2007 presidential election was also high. In the first round, on April 9, 81.79 percent of registered voters cast votes. In the second round, on May 9, there was an 81 percent participation rate. Voter participation in the June 2007 parliamentary election was also relatively high, at 80.5 percent of registered voters. Voter participation in the 2012 presidential election was slightly lower, at 78 percent for the first round and 73 percent for the second. Voter turnout for the 2012 parliamentary election was also lower, at 74.78 percent. Given that voting is voluntary, that there is a requirement that people vote in their home districts (necessitating lengthy and expensive journeys for many), and that transport and communication are difficult, these voter turnout levels suggest a high level of political participation, and consequently of citizenization. In fact, these figures might be lower than the actual levels of voter turnout because deceased and double registrants can artificially inflate the rolls.

While voter turnout is high, it has been suggested that this does not necessarily provide evidence of citizenization but could be explained by the fact that voting was compulsory during the Indonesian occupation, which may have conditioned Timorese to vote.[178] A more informative test of citizenization is whether people cast their votes strategically. The 2002 presidential election is not indicative, given that Gusmão had overwhelming support and his competitor stood primarily to give voters a democratic choice. However, strategic voting was evident in the 2007 presidential election. When Lu-Olo and Ramos-Horta progressed to the second-round run-off, Lasama announced PD's support for Ramos-Horta, as did four of the five other candidates. Only KOTA's Manuel Tilman supported Lu-Olo. In the second round, Ramos-Horta received 69.18 percent of votes, compared to Lu-Olo's 30.82 percent. These results suggest that voters were aware of which

---

[178] Federer, *The UN in East Timor*.

candidates their parties endorsed and that the majority of voters consciously made a decision to reject the FRETILIN candidate.

A pattern of strategic voting was also evident in the 2007 parliamentary election. FRETILIN's vote dropped significantly, consistent with the first round of the presidential election. The fact that a large number of voters switched their vote from FRETILIN indicates that "people did not simply choose according to historical loyalties"[179] and were capable of "distinction between political parties."[180] This pattern was also evident in the 2012 presidential election. In the second round, Matan Ruak took 61.23 percent of the vote to Lu-Olo's 38.77 percent. This result suggests that while many of Ramos-Horta and Lasama's voters switched their support to Matan Ruak, Lu-Olo managed to garner not only voters from minor parties but also other voters who may have been concerned about Matan Ruak's ambivalent history, particularly relating to the finding that, while chief of the F-FDTL, he had distributed weapons to civilians during the 2006 security crisis.[181]

Moreover, in the 2012 parliamentary elections, voters shifted support to the major parties, FRETILIN and CNRT, potentially because the AMP coalition had been relatively fractious and divided, and voters may have wished to avoid another coalition government. The election also signaled the consolidation of political parties, with the number of parties elected down to four from seven in 2007, which is generally interpreted as a positive indicator of democratic maturity. This suggests that Timorese voters are becoming increasingly sophisticated in their ability to judge the performance of political parties and to reward (or punish, in the case of smaller parties) them accordingly.

Other forms of political participation

Timorese have also signaled their citizenization by utilizing other forms of political participation provided by the constitution. First, people can submit petitions to the Parliament, which has the duty to consider them and issue recommendations to relevant state institutions.[182] In 2009, this process was utilized by a group of victims from the Indonesian occupation who (unsuccessfully) petitioned the government to seek justice for abuses they had suffered. Second, Parliament can propose referenda on "issues of relevant

---

[179] Bowles and Chopra, "East Timor: Statebuilding Revisited," 281.
[180] D. Kingsbury, "National Identity in Timor-Leste: Challenges and Opportunities," *South East Asia Research* 18:1 (2010): 156.
[181] UN, *United Nations Independent Special Commission of Inquiry*.
[182] Constitution, s. 48; Parliamentary Resolution on the Rules of Procedure of the National Parliament of the Democratic Republic of Timor-Leste, Jornal da República nr 40, November 11, 2009 (replacing Rules of Procedure of the National Parliament 2002), art. 155.

national interest."[183] Third, citizens have the "right to inform and be informed."[184] Accordingly, the FRETILIN government produced regular press releases in both Portuguese and Tetum. The AMP government made more conscious attempts to improve information dissemination, and in 2009 it prepared a "National Policy on Mass Communication"[185] and appointed a spokesperson to organize media releases and a government website. However, problems of dissemination remain, and even state actors are often unable to access information relating to draft – or even adopted – laws. For example, for at least a year after the Penal Code[186] was implemented in March 2009, many PNTL continued to apply the Indonesian Criminal Code.[187] Similarly, members of the public are unaware of many new laws, particularly those relating to criminal offences.[188] Fourth, the government is required to publish legislation and the decisions of state institutions in an official gazette.[189] Until 2008, publication of the gazette was sporadic, but it has since been published regularly.

Finally, and most significantly, "every citizen has the right to participate in the political life and in the public affairs of the country, either directly or through democratically elected representatives."[190] While the FRETILIN government was criticized as being "excessively formal and sometimes uncommunicative,"[191] it did conduct public consultations on major legislation.[192] The AMP and BGK governments have continued this approach.[193]

---

[183] A referendum may be called by the president following a proposal by one-third of the Parliament, which has been approved by a two-thirds majority of Parliament, or following a "well-founded" proposal by the government. However, issues over which the Parliament, government, or courts have exclusive jurisdiction cannot be the subject of a referendum. *Constitution*, s. 66.

[184] Ibid., s. 40(1).

[185] A. Pereira, *Draft National Policy on Mass Communication*, undated, accessed April 4, 2011, www.article19.org/pdfs/laws/timor-leste-national-policy-on-mass-communication.pdf.

[186] Decree Law Approving the Penal Code of the Democratic Republic of Timor-Leste No. 19/2009 (2009) (TL).

[187] Personal communication from an international security adviser, May 12, 2010.

[188] F. Borges, "Law and Justice: Strengthening the Rule of Law," paper presented at "Transforming Timor Leste for Sustainable Development, Human Rights and Peace: an Opportunity for Dialogue," Ministry of Foreign Affairs, Dili, July 6–7, 2009.

[189] *Constitution*, s. 73(1); Law on the Publication of Acts No. 1/2002 (2002) (TL).

[190] *Constitution*, ss. 41 and 46(1).   [191] Kingsbury, "Political Development," 26.

[192] For example, on the Petroleum Law and when developing the Office of the Provedor. Interview with a member of Parliament, May 11, 2010; World Bank, *Strengthening the Institutions*. In 2003–2004, it also participated in a constituency outreach campaign, during which MPs visited villages in every district of the country to explain the Parliament to people and discuss issues of concern. UNDP, *Strengthening Parliamentary Democracy in Timor-Leste, Project Document* (Dili: United National Development Programme, 2006).

[193] For example, on the Land Law and Law against Domestic Violence.

However, under all governments, consultation periods have often been short and generally little information is disseminated beforehand.[194] Members of the public and civil society also face difficulties because draft laws are usually produced in Portuguese, people do not understand the legislative process, and draft laws are often kept from the public until critical decisions have been made.[195] Consequently, consultations often become exercises in "socialisation."[196] At the same time, one Timorese governance adviser noted that the government is under pressure to fill the legislative vacuum and therefore imposes time limits, with the view that laws can be amended if they become problematic.[197] The high cost of public consultations has also acted as a prohibitive factor.[198] Despite these issues, a 2013 opinion poll found that 25 percent of respondents think that they have "a lot" of influence over government decision making, while 32 percent said that they have "some influence."[199]

Overall, there appears to be a developing sense of citizenization. At the same time, questions relating to the perceived relevance and legitimacy of state institutions, and indeed of liberal democracy, outlined in Chapter 5, need to be borne in mind. Moreover, a sense of citizenization has evolved almost in spite of the actions of political leaders. Indeed, while one MP noted that there is "big demand,"[200] successive governments have been slow to implement the constitutional avenues for public participation. High attendance at public consultations, strong electoral turnouts, and evidence of strategic voting indicate that many Timorese want to have a relationship with and participate in state institutions.[201] When the government does provide

---

[194] Interview with a Timorese governance adviser, May 11, 2010; interview with an international governance adviser (a), April 23, 2010; JSMP, *Overview of the Justice Sector in Timor-Leste 2009* (Dili: Judicial System Monitoring Programme, 2009); USAID, *Rule of Law in Timor-Leste* (Dili: Freedom House, USAID and the ABA Rule of Law Initiative, 2007).

[195] Interview with a member of Timorese civil society (a), May 14, 2010; interview with a Timorese governance adviser, May 11, 2010; interview with a Timorese justice adviser, May 12, 2010; interview with an international governance adviser, May 11, 2010; interview with an international governance adviser (a), May 10, 2010; La'o Hamutuk, *Democracy in Timor-Leste: Information Is Required!* (Dili: La'o Hamutuk, 2009).

[196] Interview with an international governance adviser (c), April 23, 2010.

[197] Interview with a Timorese governance adviser, April 23, 2010; interview with an international governance adviser, May 13, 2010.

[198] Representative of the Ministry of State Administration and Territorial Management, Government of Timor-Leste, speaking at "Locating Democracy: Representation, Elections and Governance in Timor-Leste," Independence Memorial Hall, Dili, April 26–27, 2010.

[199] Asia Foundation, *Timor-Leste Public Opinion Poll* (Dili: Asia Foundation, 2013), 2.

[200] Interview with a member of Parliament, May 11, 2010.

[201] Interview with an international governance adviser (b), April 23, 2010.

opportunities for participation, such as through public consultations, they often involve heated debate and criticism of the government.[202] This suggests that the more Timorese become citizenized, the more they question their state institutions. Therefore, somewhat paradoxically, citizenization may actually test the legitimacy of state institutions and the constitution that created them. While this would challenge state building, it would represent the Timorese people exercising their popular sovereignty to decide the manner in which their state is governed.

Is there a strong public sphere?

In Timor-Leste, the three institutions that make up the public sphere – the media, churches, and civil society – have faced a number of difficulties.

The media

The print media consists of three major newspapers, minor newspapers, and newsletters. These newspapers are not distributed far beyond Dili and other major towns. Consequently, weekly newspaper reach is about 21 percent nationwide,[203] and a 2013 opinion poll found that only 1 percent of respondents identified newspapers as their most-used source of news information.[204] In any event, low literacy levels undermine newspapers' utility,[205] although there are claims that they do reach "opinion leaders."[206] There is also a government-owned television station, on which most important parliamentary debates are broadcast, although there are concerns over the impartiality of its news coverage.[207] Until 2008, live television broadcasts were limited to Dili, but this has expanded through a government program of providing satellite dishes and television sets to reach 30 percent of the adult population, and television has increasingly become the preferred source of news and information.[208]

---

[202] Interview with a Timorese governance adviser, April 23, 2010; interview with an international governance adviser, May 11, 2010.
[203] E. Soares and D. Dooradi, *Timor-Leste Communication and Media Survey* (Dili: UNMIT, 2010), 3.
[204] Asia Foundation, *Timor-Leste Public Opinion Poll*, 4.
[205] Interview with an international governance adviser (a), April 23, 2010; H. von Kaltenborn-Stachau, *The Missing Link: Fostering Positive Citizen-State Relations in Post-Conflict Environments* (Washington: World Bank, 2008).
[206] UN, *Report of the Secretary-General on the United Nations Integrated Mission in Timor-Leste (for the period from 24 September 2009 to 20 January 2010)*, UN Doc. S/2010/85, February 12, 2010.
[207] Interview with a member of Timorese civil society, September 26, 2010.
[208] A 2013 opinion poll found that 35 percent of respondents identified television as the most-used source of news and information, followed by radio (18 percent), friends and family (16 percent),

Although radio has the broadest reach, with 55 percent of the population listening to the radio on a weekly basis,[209] community and commercial stations have few avenues for raising revenue, given that there is little private sector development to require advertising. The government station receives support, broadcasts important parliamentary debates, and is the most relied-upon source of information.[210] Mobile phones are also becoming a common way of conveying information, with a 2010 survey finding that 61 percent of households have at least one member who owns a mobile phone.[211] However, mobile phones have played the ambivalent role of providing a mechanism to spread "rumours or wrong information," which has resulted in conflict.[212]

The quality of the media is questionable. There are claims that journalists lack the capacity to undertake serious investigations or cover complex political issues.[213] International advisers have noted that it is common for government officials to distribute press releases that are reprinted verbatim.[214] However, the media has provided increasingly good coverage of recent legislative debates. The FRETILIN government also took a sometimes hostile approach to the media.[215] For example, in February 2005, Prime Minister Alkatiri announced a government boycott of the *Suara Timor Lorosae* newspaper after it reported alleged deaths from famine, and then (unsuccessfully) tried to have it evicted from its offices. While the AMP government instigated a number of initiatives to improve the availability and coverage of the media, it also indicated questionable regard for media freedom. For example, in December 2008, the justice minister brought a charge of criminal defamation against the editor of *Tempo Semanal* after the newspaper published reports on an investigation into corruption allegations against her.

---

and the *suco* council (15 percent). Asia Foundation, *Timor-Leste Public Opinion Poll*; Soares and Dooradi, *Timor-Leste Communication*, 45.

[209] Soares and Dooradi, *Timor-Leste Communication*, 67.
[210] Interview with an international governance adviser (a), May 10, 2010.
[211] Soares and Dooradi, *Timor-Leste Communication*, 57.
[212] Fragility Assessment Team, *Fragility Assessment in Timor-Leste: Summary Report* (Dili: Ministry of Finance, 2013), 7.
[213] Article 19/Internews, *Freedom of Expression and the Media in Timor-Leste* (London/Dili: Article 19/Internews, 2005); Trindade, "Reconciling Conflicting Paradigms"; World Bank, *Strengthening the Institutions*.
[214] Interview with an international governance adviser, May 11, 2010; interview with an international governance adviser (b), May 10, 2010.
[215] F. Crockford, "Building Demand for Better Governance: Enabling Citizen-State Engagement in Timor-Leste," in Mearns, *Democratic Governance*; interview with a Timorese governance adviser, April 23, 2010.

Churches

The Catholic Church is the strongest civil society institution and plays an active role in the public sphere. The FRETILIN government adopted a relatively hostile approach to the church. For example, in March 2005, it sought to make religious education a voluntary component of the school curriculum. This decision satisfied international human rights norms and protected the interests of minority religious groups. However, it also signaled that FRETILIN possessed "a certain level of political naivety in underestimating the popular support and affection for the Church."[216] The decision prompted church leaders to organize demonstrations that lasted for three weeks and involved tens of thousands of people. Eventually, the church and government reached a compromise involving mandatory religious education classes – but freedom of choice of religion. The church has remained vocal concerning politics and openly opposed Prime Minister Alkatiri, whom it labeled a "communist for his secular, nationalist policies." It made much of the fact that Alkatiri is Muslim and therefore implicitly "un-Timorese."[217] Consequently, the church publicly welcomed the formation of the AMP government.

The close relationship between the AMP (and now BGK) government and the church has been equally problematic, particularly as the church has been willing to interfere in politics and has shown itself intolerant of non-Catholics, particularly Muslims. Therefore, while short-term considerations of building unity and enhancing the state's legitimacy might suggest that the government should engage with the church, long-term goals of promoting democracy and human rights suggest that there may have been some merit in FRETILIN's approach.

Other civil society organizations

Other civil society organizations have played an important role via advocacy and contributions to civic education.[218] They remain centered in Dili, partly because of lack of capacity, funding, and facilities and partly to remain close to international donors.[219] These organizations generally respond enthusiastically when the government gives them the opportunity to comment on draft laws,

---

[216] Kingsbury and Leach, "Introduction," 4–5.
[217] H. Myrttinen, *Up in Smoke: Impoverishment and Instability in Post-Independence Timor-Leste* (Helsinki: KEPA, 2007), 10.
[218] J. Hunt, "Building a New Society: NGOs in East Timor," *New Community Quarterly* 2:1 (2004); World Bank, *Strengthening the Institutions*.
[219] Interview with an international governance adviser, May 11, 2010; UN Doc. S/2010/85.

and they report having a "good relationship" with the AMP (and now BGK) government, which regularly meets with them and includes civil society representatives in government working groups.[220] However, other civil society organizations have had a more ambivalent role, particularly the FALINTIL veterans and antisystem security associations and youth groups that were involved in inflaming the 2006 security crisis.

Overall, the FRETILIN government did little to encourage the development of the public sphere and actually took a hostile approach to its increasing activism. The AMP and BGK governments have done more to encourage the improvement of the media and civil society, which can play an important role in citizenization.

In 2006, a youth activist argued that "the foundations for East Timor to form a solid, national, post-independence identity have not yet been laid."[221] Based on the evidence presented in this chapter, the minimal public participation in constitution making did not generate a constituent process. The partisan nature of the official historical narrative, national symbols, national identity, and definition of a citizen enumerated in the constitution has undermined the development of a sense of unified national identity, and has in fact contributed to societal division. While there is evidence of citizenization and the development of the public sphere, this has often developed in spite of the government's efforts and the minimal opportunities for public participation during the constitution-making process.

---

[220] Interview with a member of Timorese civil society (b), May 14, 2010; interview with a member of Timorese civil society, September 26, 2010.
[221] J. Trindade, "An Open Letter to the Prime Minister and to the Timorese People," *ETAN Mailing List*, August 2006.

5

Constituted power in Timor-Leste

This chapter assesses whether the minimal public participation involved in the constitution-making process affected the role that the Timor-Leste constitution plays in creating state institutions. To do this, it considers the following five questions, which indicate whether the constitution, and the state institutions it creates, are functioning effectively and are perceived to be legitimate:

- Have state institutions been created, and are they functioning effectively?
- To what extent are the state institutions perceived to be legitimate?
- Are the state institutions delivering public goods and services?
- Are law and order enforced and is the rule of law observed?
- Are human rights and civil liberties protected?

THE ROLE OF PARTICIPATION IN CREATING STATE INSTITUTIONS

Have state institutions been created, and are they functioning effectively?

The constitution creates several state institutions, the most important of which are the "organs of sovereignty": the president, Parliament, government, and courts.[1] Relations between these institutions are guided by the principle of the "separation and interdependence of powers."[2] The constitution also requires the state to engage in political and administrative decentralization.

The Parliament
The Parliament is the legislative organ.[3] It functions and meets regularly, legislation has been adopted, and annual state budgets have been

---

[1] Constitution, s. 67.   [2] Constitution, s. 69.   [3] Ibid., ss. 92 and 95.

approved.[4] Parliamentary debates are peaceful and increasingly involve high-level policy discussions, with the Parliament willing to take an assertive oversight role, exemplified by the decision of both its opposition and government members to reject elements on the government's 2012 state budget. However, the Parliament has been relatively passive in comparison to the government, partly because its legislative capacity remains weak.[5] These difficulties are compounded by the fact that legislation is usually drafted in Portuguese, which many MPs are unable to read. While one international adviser observed that many MPs are "apathetic" and do not demand translations, this apathy was not necessarily attributed to a lack of interest, but more to the fact that many MPs feel disempowered by their lack of understanding.[6] They are unable to obtain much assistance, as the parliamentary secretariat can perform only basic administrative duties and does not employ legal advisers.[7] Consequently, the generational language division created by the constitution remains relevant, as those MPs who speak Portuguese "take over the work."[8] Given that the Parliament is the main state institution that exercises the people's constituted power, the limitation of crucial decision making to a small group of MPs raises questions over the body's legitimacy.

These questions gained urgency as a result of FRETILIN's domineering behavior in the first Parliament. As the Parliament was tasked with filling a legislative vacuum, in its first year it adopted sixteen laws, all without substantive changes resulting from legislative debate. FRETILIN appeared to have "difficulty liv[ing] with the commitment to inclusive and democratic multi-party politics" and "den[ied] the legitimacy of its parliamentary opponents," which became a source of frustration for opposition parties.[9] The situation improved when Ramos-Horta became prime minister and under the AMP government. However, while the AMP government managed to avoid legislative deadlock, it was a fragile coalition, united more by a desire to unseat

---

[4] Interview with a Timorese governance adviser, April 23, 2010; interview with an international governance adviser (b), May 10, 2010.

[5] Interview with an international governance adviser (a), May 10, 2010; UNDP, *Strengthening Parliamentary Democracy*.

[6] Interview with an international governance adviser (a), May 10, 2010; interview with a Timorese governance adviser, May 11, 2010.

[7] UNDP, *Strengthening Parliamentary Democracy*; UNOTIL, *Strengthening Accountability and Transparency in Timor-Leste: Report of the Alkatiri Initiative Review* (Dili: UN Office in Timor-Leste, January 27, 2006).

[8] Interview with an international governance adviser (a), May 10, 2010; interview with a Timorese governance adviser, May 11, 2010.

[9] D. Shoesmith, "Timor-Leste: Divided Leadership in a Semi-Presidential System," *Asian Survey* 43:2 (2003): 245.

FRETILIN than by shared policy. FRETILIN acted as a disloyal opposition, did its best to destabilize the AMP, and in May 2008, persuaded the ASDT/PSD coalition to sign an accord promising an alliance with FRETILIN in the next government. The situation has improved under the BGK government, with FRETILIN acting as a loyal opposition, partly because the constitutionality of the new government is not in question and partly because of FRETILIN's political maturity. While parliamentary decision making in liberal democracies is by its nature adversarial, given that Timor-Leste is a new state that is still building its sense of political community and state institutions, FRETILIN's behavior in opposition to the AMP government did little to assist either. The decision to create an elected constituent assembly to make the constitution may have cultivated FRETILIN's attitude, since it facilitated majoritarianism and did not emphasize consensus building.

The government
The government (or executive) is "responsible for conducting and executing the general policy of the country and is the supreme organ of Public Administration."[10] It consists of the prime minister, ministers, and secretaries of state[11] and any of their deputies.[12] The Council of Ministers, consisting of the prime minister, deputy prime ministers (if any), and ministers, sits within the government.[13] Ministers are appointed by the president on the recommendation of the prime minister.[14] The prime minister is not obliged to select ministers from the Parliament, although if MPs are selected, they are required to vacate their seat and be replaced by the next candidate on their party's list. This is contrary to the wishes of the public expressed at the Constitutional Commission hearings, where there was strong support for all members of the executive to be chosen from the Parliament.[15]

While the government is "accountable" to the president and Parliament,[16] there is no substantive mechanism to ensure this. The government is empowered to develop a "Programme of Government" in which it enumerates its policies,[17] and which must be submitted to the Parliament for "consideration."[18] The Parliament may either approve this program or reject it by an absolute majority.[19] If the program is rejected twice, the government will be dismissed.[20] The government may also be dismissed by a vote of no

---

[10] Constitution, s. 103. The government's powers are set out in Constitution, s. 115(1).
[11] Ibid., s. 104(1).   [12] Ibid., s. 104(3).   [13] Constitution, s. 105.   [14] Ibid., s. 106(2).
[15] UNTAET Constitutional Affairs Branch, *Constitutional Commission Public Hearings*.
[16] Constitution, s. 107.   [17] Constitution, s. 108.   [18] Ibid., s. 109(1).   [19] Ibid., s. 109(3).
[20] Ibid., s. 112(1).

confidence, passed by an absolute majority of the Parliament.[21] Since the Parliament is directly elected by the people and arguably is the state institution that has the best chance of representing their popular sovereignty, limiting its ability to hold the government accountable raises questions over the legitimacy of the government exercising constituted power.

Compounding these questions is the Parliament's ability to authorize the government to make laws by decree on a wide range of matters.[22] While one-fifth of MPs may petition for such laws to be submitted to the Parliament for appraisal, Parliament cannot review laws "approved under the exclusive legislative powers of the Government," which include matters relating to "its own organisation and functioning" and "the direct and indirect management of the State."[23] As this phrase is not defined, the government is arguably empowered to make decree laws – without the oversight of Parliament – in relation to a broad range of issues. However, the president does have a right of veto over government decree laws.[24]

Empowering the government to issue decree laws avoids the legislative atrophy that can occur without a unified parliamentary majority and can ensure "consistency" in law-making.[25] However, when the constitution was being made, an international adviser warned that it was "a very dangerous power to delegate," as it effectively means that "the sovereign will of the people to reflect their views democratically through their local representative will simply be transferred to the controlling party."[26] This has led to calls to strengthen the Parliament so that it can oversee the government. In this regard, the FRETILIN majority in the Constituent Assembly departed from the Portuguese constitution by failing to include provisions that give individual MPs the right to compel the government to answer questions.[27] However, such rights were later included in the Parliament's Rules of Procedure,[28] and ministers have appeared before Parliament for this purpose. In addition, while the Portuguese constitution provides that Parliament can consider

---

[21] Ibid., s. 111. [22] Ibid., ss. 96(1) and 97(1).
[23] Ibid., ss. 115(3) and 116(d); Parliament Resolution on the Rules of Procedure, art. 124.
[24] Constitution, s. 88(4).
[25] Interview with an international governance adviser (b), May 10, 2010.
[26] ICJ, *Commentary on the Draft Constitution Proposed for East Timor by the Constituent Assembly* (Dili: Australian Section, International Commission of Jurists, undated).
[27] MPs "may request" members of the government to "take part in their proceedings." Constitution, s. 101(3).
[28] Parliament Resolution on the Rules of Procedure, art. 9(h) empowers MPs to make written requests for information from the government; art. 60 grants members of the government the floor of Parliament to answer questions from MPs; arts. 143–150 provide the procedure for MPs to ask the government questions, orally or in writing.

government decree laws on a motion of ten (out of 230) MPs,[29] the Timor-Leste constitution requires such a motion to be supported by thirteen (out of sixty-five) MPs. This significantly higher threshold makes it more difficult for minor parties to garner enough votes to review the activities of the government. Consequently, "opposition parties have almost nothing to fight with."[30] As a result, one assembly member described the constitution as creating a "semi-parliamentary" system.[31]

As the literature warns, when a constitution is made by an elected body, there is a temptation for those involved – particularly political parties – to be swayed by political interests. This appears to be the case in Timor-Leste, where the FRETILIN majority in the Constituent Assembly knew that it would dominate the first government. It accordingly ensured that the constitution created a powerful government. When in office, the FRETILIN government seized the opportunity and interpreted its powers in "the broadest sense."[32] For example, while Parliament made fifty-six laws between 2002 and 2006, the government issued eighty-one decree laws in the same period. The government also made decree laws in areas with significant political consequences, including the Penal Code.[33] This is said to have created a "dominant party" system, whereby power was centered in the government and, behind this, the FRETILIN Central Committee.[34] This undermined attempts to create a multiparty system and further marginalized the opposition in Parliament.

Even though it exercised considerable power, the FRETILIN government was described as consisting of "technically ill-prepared – and in most cases inappropriately chosen – government ministers." This was partly because FRETILIN "sidelined" the few professionally qualified people and instead gave preference to party members.[35] This is despite the fact that the rationale behind an appointed executive is that it allows ministerial positions to be filled by qualified candidates in situations in which it is anticipated there are unlikely to be sufficiently qualified MPs. In addition, most FRETILIN

---

[29] Constitution of Portugal 1976, art. 156.
[30] A. Matsuno, "The UN Transitional Administration and Democracy Building in Timor-Leste," in Mearns, *Democratic Governance*, 64.
[31] Interview with a former member of the Constituent Assembly and member of Parliament, May 13, 2010.
[32] D. Shoesmith, "Remaking the State in Timor-Leste: The Case for Constitutional Reform," paper presented at the 17th Biennial Conference of the Asian Studies Association of Australia, Melbourne, July 1–3, 2008.
[33] Legislative Authorisation on Criminal Procedure Matters No. 15/2005 (2005) (TL); Legislative Authorisation on Criminal Matters No. 16/2005 (2005) (TL), amended and renewed by Law No. 13/2008.
[34] Shoesmith, "Remaking the State in Timor-Leste", 4.   [35] Federer, *The UN in East Timor*, 110.

ministers lapsed into a "form of centralised authoritarianism" based around Prime Minister Alkatiri.[36] This was reminiscent of their approach during the resistance and had been in evidence in the Constituent Assembly. As a result, the FRETILIN government was perceived as "combative, distant, and largely unaccountable,"[37] with "little tolerance for criticism."[38]

FRETILIN's approach changed when Alkatiri was replaced as prime minister by Ramos-Horta, as Ramos-Horta was a unifying and popular consensus candidate. The AMP government similarly sought to mark itself as different in style from FRETILIN. As the AMP was a coalition that had to reach consensus among its members, it "contributed to some sense of national unity," particularly as Gusmão was widely seen as the person "best placed to unite different factions, ideologies, and groups."[39] The AMP (and now BGK) government also took a less partisan approach by appointing qualified people to certain ministries, such as Ana Pessoa, who is a long-standing FRETILIN member, as prosecutor general. Yet this is not the case with all ministers, as in order to build its coalition in 2007, CNRT had to compromise on some appointments, and at least one minister was a former pro-Indonesia militia leader.

Moreover, the AMP (and now BGK) continued FRETILIN's approach of taking a robust interpretation of the government's power. In 2012, CNRT had fewer partners in the BGK coalition and was therefore able to exert more control over its government appointments. This encouraged CNRT to appoint a significantly expanded government, consisting of fifty-three members (seventeen ministers, eleven vice ministers, and twenty-five secretaries of state), up from thirty-nine members, which is only slightly smaller than the sixty-five-member Parliament. The expanded size of the government was criticized by journalists and civil society groups for being "completely unnecessary for such a small country"[40] and creating "an oligarchy" because it would be "too big and full of political interest."[41] It was defended by some commentators on the grounds that it was not excessive in comparison to the governments of other

---

[36] D. Kingsbury, "East Timor's Political Crisis: Origins and Resolution," in Mearns, *Democratic Governance*, 36; World Bank, *Strengthening the Institutions*.
[37] D. Kingsbury, *East Timor: The Price of Liberty* (New York: Palgrave MacMillan, 2009), 134.
[38] S. V. Simonsen, "The Authoritarian Temptation in East Timor: Nationbuilding and the Need for Inclusive Governance," *Asian Survey* 46:4 (2006): 584.
[39] J. C. Guterres, "Timor-Leste: A Year of Democratic Elections," *Southeast Asian Affairs* (2008): 367.
[40] FRETILIN vice president Aresenio Babo quoted in "East Timor Swears in Larger Cabinet, Critics Angry," *Agence France Presse*, August 8, 2012.
[41] Mericio Akara, Director of Luta Hamutuk, quoted in "East Timorese Fifth Government: An Oligarchy," *Tempo Semanal*, August 6, 2012.

countries and that a large government may be required to administer Timor-Leste's growing resource revenues and to advance its much-needed development.[42] The large size of the government has exacerbated the capacity challenges faced since independence, as the already limited number of qualified Timorese have had to be stretched even more thinly across the expanded ministry. This has meant that the government remains dependent on foreign advisers. Despite this, the government is "able to plan and manage its resources and deliver public services across the country, albeit with some shortcomings."[43] Although the AMP and BGK governments have taken a more inclusive approach, the fact that the constitution confers such significant powers on the government and limits opportunities to hold it accountable casts doubt on its ability to legitimately exercise the Timorese people's constituted power.

The president

The president is the head of state.[44] The president's main powers[45] include being able to exercise a right of veto over parliamentary statutes and government decree laws,[46] request constitutional review of legislation and government actions, declare a state of emergency, appoint or dismiss certain state officials, and grant pardons and commute sentences. There are claims that the constitution creates a "semi-presidential" system by dividing power between the president and government.[47] However, this characterization is disputed, as the prime minister does not share executive authority in day-to-day matters with the president.[48] In fact, the president has been described as having "virtually no substantive power."[49]

Commentators have argued that the FRETILIN majority in the Constituent Assembly created a weak presidency because it was almost inevitable that,

---

[42] M. Hardie, "Timor-Leste, the 5th Constitutional Governance and the 'Good Governance' Template," *Crikey*, August 12, 2012.

[43] Independent Evaluation Group, *Evaluation of the World Bank*, 57.   [44] Constitution, s. 74(1).

[45] As enumerated in ibid., s. 85. Later clarified by Law on the Organic Structure of the Organic Structure of the Office of the President No. 04/2006 (2006) (TL).

[46] Constitution, s. 88.

[47] D. Shoesmith, "Timor-Leste: Semi-presidentialism and the Democratic Transition in a New, Small State," in *Semi-presidentialism outside Europe: A Comparative Study*, ed. R. Elgie and S. Moestrup (London: Routledge, 2007).

[48] Interview with a former member of the Constituent Assembly and member of Parliament, May 13, 2010; interview with a member of Parliament, May 11, 2010; D. Kingsbury, "The Constitution: Clarity without Convention," in Leach and Kingsbury, *The Politics of Timor-Leste*.

[49] ICJ, *Commentary on the Draft Constitution*.

due to his prominent role in the resistance, Gusmão would become the first president.[50] Consequently, each successive draft reduced the powers of the president.[51] This was contrary to the views expressed in the Constitutional Commission hearings, in which the vast majority of Timorese favored a presidential system or a semipresidential system in which the president was allocated significant powers.[52] Consequently, the assembly's decision led one adviser to caution that Timorese "will largely not achieve in this draft Constitution a system with which they are familiar or which they have proposed."[53] This again illustrates the drawback of using an elected assembly to make the constitution, as in this case it allowed FRETILIN's political interests to hold sway. At the same time, one FRETILIN assembly member noted that a semipresidential system was included in a draft constitution that Gusmão had commissioned on behalf of The CNRT in 1998. Therefore, the member argued that the approach enshrined in the constitution was "not an attempt to sideline Xanana," who was an experienced politician and could "develop the powers of the president by convention." In addition, he noted that all drafts tabled in the assembly adopted a similar approach, indicating cross-partisan support, despite the weight of contrary public opinion.[54]

In office, Gusmão perceived himself as the "father of the nation" and interpreted his landslide electoral victory as giving him an enormous mandate.[55] He used his platform to criticize the FRETILIN government[56] and his powers to delay the implementation of legislation. For example, in 2003, the Parliament passed an Immigration and Asylum Law, which various civil society groups condemned for having an "anti-constitutional and anti-foreigner

---

[50] J. Cotton, *East Timor, Australia and Regional Order: Intervention and Its Aftermath in Southeast Asia* (London: RoutledgeCurzon, 2004); Shoesmith, "Timor-Leste: Semi-presidentialism."

[51] For example, the original FRETILIN draft gave the president the power to initiate constitutional amendments (art. 118), set dates for elections (art. 75(b)), and initiate laws and propose referenda (art. 85(1)(a)). FRETILIN draft constitution; Zifcak, *Making Timor's Constitution.*

[52] UNTAET Constitutional Affairs Branch, *Constitutional Commission Public Hearings.*

[53] ICJ, *Commentary on the Draft Constitution.*

[54] Interview with a former member of the Constituent Assembly and government official, February 2, 2010.

[55] Interview with a member of Timorese civil society, September 26, 2010; interview with a member of Timorese civil society (b), September 27, 2010.

[56] See, for example, X. Gusmão, speech twenty-three days after independence, Dili, June 12, 2002; X. Gusmão, speech after 100 days of independence, Dili, August 30, 2002; X. Gusmão, speech on the occasion of the first anniversary of independence, Dili, May 20, 2003, all reproduced in Gusmão, *Timor Lives!*

attitude."[57] Gusmão referred the bill to the Court of Appeal for review, and after the court found that two of its articles were unconstitutional, he vetoed the law in July 2003. In 2005 and 2006, Gusmão also referred the Freedom of Assembly Demonstration Law (the court agreed that it was unconstitutional) and Penal Code (the court found that this was constitutional). Similarly, after the 2006 security crisis, Gusmão invoked a state of emergency and announced that he had taken control of military and security matters. The constitutionality of this move was questionable, and Alkatiri claimed that Gusmão was attempting a "constitutional coup."[58] However, Gusmão's move was approved by the Parliament one week later.[59]

Like Gusmão, Ramos-Horta interpreted his powers as president widely and arguably exercised powers beyond those enumerated in the constitution.[60] For example, in October 2007, he created a "Fight Against Poverty Fund" to disburse $250,000 that had been approved by the AMP government's 2007 transitional budget and a further $1 million that he expected from the 2008 budget. This was later deemed unconstitutional by the Court of Appeal, on the basis that it involved the president exercising budgetary and policy powers that were reserved for the Parliament.[61] Ramos-Horta defended his decision to create this fund by arguing that "no Constitution, no Law can restrain or forbid a president to have opinions and to set up projects in favour of the poor."[62]

Matan Ruak has also taken a broad view of the president's powers. Although he received support from the CNRT during the presidential election, he has stressed his independence from the government and a willingness to be critical. He has bolstered the president's role by creating a Department of Research, Analysis, and Documentation within the Office of the Presidency to provide policy advice. He also regularly visits rural Timor-Leste, often inviting

---

[57] NGO Working Group, *Article-by-Article Commentary on the Immigration and Asylum Bill* (Dili: NGO Working Group to Study the Immigration and Asylum Bill, May 13, 2003).
[58] Quoted in M. Forbes, "Timor's Agony," *Sydney Morning Herald*, May 27, 2006.
[59] Parliamentary Resolution on the Emergency Measures Enacted by His Excellency the President of the Republic, Kay Rala Xanana Gusmão, in Order to Overcome the Crisis, No. 12/2006 (2006) (TL).
[60] Interview with a member of Parliament, September 30, 2010; personal communication from a Timorese academic, 26 April 2010.
[61] Court of Appeal, *Decision of the Court in Case No. 04/2008, On the Supervisory Process Abstract Constitutionality and Legality of Law 12/2008*, November 11, 2008; UN, *Report of the Secretary-General on the United Nations Integrated Mission in Timor-Leste (for the Period from 8 January to 8 July 2008)*, UN Doc. S/2008/501, July 29, 2008.
[62] Quoted in R. G. Feijó, "Semi-Presidentialism and the Consolidation of Democracy," in Leach and Kingsbury, *The Politics of Timor-Leste*, 56.

ministers to accompany him to answer public complaints; this move has enhanced his personal legitimacy and might signal his future intention to seek the prime ministership.

During public consultations on the constitution, most Timorese wanted a strong president, so Gusmão, Ramos-Horta, and Matan Ruak have arguably performed as the public wanted. However, their behavior indicates the wide-ranging and potentially undemocratic powers that a president can wield to frustrate the Parliament, which is the main institution that – albeit imperfectly – exercises the people's constituted power.

Decentralization

The constitution requires the state to engage in administrative decentralization so that the national government is "represented at the different administrative levels of the country"[63] and so that services are "more accessible" to the people.[64] However, this requirement is forward-looking and envisages that decentralization would not occur immediately. While this might have partly been due to concerns about a lack of capacity, it was contrary to the support for decentralization expressed by Timorese in the Constitutional Commission hearings.[65]

Decentralization was in keeping with historical experience. Portugal had adopted an administrative system in which it had direct control at the district and subdistrict (*posto*) levels but little direct presence beyond that, instead working through *liurais* in *rais*. In the 1930s, the Portuguese stripped the *liurais* of their official power and appointed village (*suco*) and hamlet (*aldeia*) chiefs, which made *sucos* the basic indigenous political unit. However, *liurais* retained their influence and the new chiefs still came from the "royal" *uma lulik*.[66] Indonesia adopted a similar administrative structure but introduced five-yearly elections for *suco* chiefs. While these elections were nominally democratic, candidate selection was decided according to traditional power structures. When there was no interference by the Indonesian authorities, a candidate from the "appropriate" *uma lulik* was selected and people voted for him or her. Even if this did not occur, the *liurai* would ceremonially appoint the elected candidate as his representative.[67] Therefore, local sociopolitical practices continued to remain influential. Indeed, the resistance relied heavily on them.[68]

---

[63] Constitution, ss. 5(1) and 71(1). [64] Ibid., s. 137(2).
[65] UNTAET Constitutional Affairs Branch, *Constitutional Commission Public Hearings*.
[66] D. Hicks, "Unachieved Syncretism: The Local-Level Political System in Portuguese Timor, 1966–1967," *Anthropos* 78(1983): 2–40.
[67] Ospina and Hohe, *Traditional Power Structures*.
[68] McWilliam, "Houses of Resistance in East Timor."

UNTAET followed the Indonesian administrative system, which was inherited by the independent state. Each of the thirteen districts and sixty-seven subdistricts is headed by a centrally appointed administrator. Below the subdistricts are 442 *sucos*, below which are 2,225 *aldeias*. At independence, *suco* and *aldeia* heads were largely selected according to local practices, with *sucos* and *aldeias* recognized merely as administrative divisions rather than as formal institutions. Reflecting the FRETILIN government's overall approach, under its tenure state administrative institutions were highly centralized. However, it was not uncommon for humanitarian donors to bypass the state and interact directly with *suco* and *aldeia* heads, as they recognized their ongoing legitimacy.[69] This highlights the fact that in times of transition, existing local structures can work as a social buffer.

The constitution also provides for political decentralization. It states that local government is to be guided by liberal principles and "constituted by corporate bodies vested with representative organs, with the objective of organising the participation by citizens in solving the problems of their own community and promoting local development."[70] The progress of political decentralization has been slow. The Local Development Programme ran from 2004 until 2006 and saw pilot "local assemblies" established in eight of the thirteen districts. That was followed in 2007 by the Local Governance Support Programme, which designed policy guidelines to manage the introduction of a single tier of local government, whereby the districts and subdistricts would be merged to form thirteen municipalities. Each municipality would have its own elected municipal assembly, which would elect a mayor who would exercise executive power and be responsible for the municipal administration.[71] It was intended that the municipalities would be delegated responsibility over certain service delivery functions and that they would coordinate with the *sucos*. While a law establishing municipalities was passed in 2009[72] and the government mooted the possibility of holding the first municipal elections in October 2010, the elections have been delayed until at least 2015, primarily due to a lack of political consensus and concern about

---

[69] Interview with a Timorese humanitarian worker, April 27, 2010.   [70] Constitution, s. 72(1).
[71] MSATM, *Decentralisation and Local Government in Timor-Leste – Policy Orientation Guidelines for Decentralization and Local Government in Timor-Leste* (Dili: Ministry of State Administration and Territorial Management, Government of Timor-Leste, March 2008); MSATM, *Timor-Leste Decentralization Strategic Framework Part 1* (Dili: Ministry of State Administration and Territorial Management, Government of Timor-Leste, March 2008).
[72] Law on Territorial Administrative Division, No. 11/2009 (2009) (TL).

the slow progress of local capacity-building.[73] Instead, the government is engaged in a program of "pre-decentralization," described as "deconcentration," whereby power and resources are to be delegated to the district level in preparation for the formation and election of the municipalities.[74]

As state institutions were highly centralized under the FRETILIN government, the Timorese state was largely absent from the lives of the more than 77 percent of the population residing in rural areas.[75] Indeed, a commonly heard phrase was *estadu seidauk mai* (the state has yet to come).[76] Instead, many Timorese continued to follow local sociopolitical practices centered on their *suco* and *aldeia*,[77] with a 2002 survey finding that *suco* chiefs were the most respected mediators for personal or property disputes and the preferred personal source of political information.[78]

In 2004, the government recognized that state institutions had only shallowly penetrated much of the country, and it introduced a program of limited administrative decentralization. This process involved liberal-local hybridity, as the decentralized system was based on local institutions in the *sucos* and *aldeias*, which the government sought to "legitimise"[79] according to liberal principles by introducing democratic elections for *aldeia* chiefs, *suco* chiefs, and *suco* councils. *Suco* chiefs were empowered to "lead activities" in a broad range of areas, including peace and social harmony; food security; education, culture, and sports; and maintenance of social infrastructure. In practice, the *suco* chief acts as the administrative contact point between the *suco* and the state and works with traditional leaders in the community. *Suco* councils were

---

[73] Representative of the Ministry of State Administration and Territorial Management, Government of Timor-Leste, speaking at "Locating Democracy: Representation, Elections and Governance in Timor-Leste."

[74] Office of the Presidency, "Press Release: Meeting of the Council of Ministers on August 13, 2013"; interview with a member of Timorese civil society (b), July 17, 2013; interview with an international governance adviser, July 18, 2013; interview with an international governance adviser, September 3, 2013.

[75] IFC, *Interim Strategy Note for the Democratic Republic of Timor-Leste FY 2010–2011* (Dili: Timor-Leste Country Management Unit, East Asia and Pacific Region, International Finance Corporation, 2009); interview with a member of Parliament, May 11, 2010; interview with an international governance adviser (c), May 10, 2010.

[76] D. Grenfell, "Governance, Violence and Crises in Timor-Leste: *Estadu Seidauk Mai*," in Mearns, *Democratic Governance*, 87; interview with a member of Timorese civil society, October 1, 2010; interview with an international academic and observer of the CAVR, January 13, 2010.

[77] McWilliam, "Houses of Resistance in East Timor"; NDI, *Government within Reach: A Report on the Views of East Timorese on Local Government* (Dili: National Democratic Institute for International Affairs, 2003).

[78] Asia Foundation, *Timor Lorosa'e National Survey*.

[79] Decree Law on Community Authorities No. 5/2004 (2004) (TL), preamble.

created that comprise the *suco* chief, *aldeia* chiefs, two women's representatives, two young people's representatives (one male, one female), and one elder (the *ansiaun*). The *suco* council was empowered to "promote debate on, and the planning, follow-up, and control of, activities to be carried out in the suco."[80] Although the *suco* councils were technically "new" bodies, they quickly became "fairly institutionalised" because they consisted of figures who possessed local sociopolitical authority.[81]

The quality of local decision making and development under this system varied, because the powers given to *suco* chiefs and councils were broad and ill-defined.[82] Many *suco* chiefs and councils were "left to govern according to their own views of rights, obligations, law and order."[83] State institutions also provided limited oversight.[84] Some *suco* chiefs were challenged by the fact that they were not *liurai* and consequently did not possess customary standing. In some cases, the *liurai* would confer legitimacy on the elected chief, but in others, the community's loyalty was divided between the elected chief and the *liurai*.[85] In addition, the government did not decentralize many resources, which meant that local leaders had little beyond what they could access locally or from donors.[86]

In 2009, the AMP government amended the law.[87] *Suco* chiefs became known as *suco* leaders,[88] although the range of activities in which the *suco* leader is entitled to exercise power remains virtually the same. The mandate of *suco* councils was also clarified and enhanced, giving the council increased power over planning, monitoring, and undertaking social infrastructure and

---

[80] Ibid., s. 6.
[81] D. Cummins, "Multiple Realities: The Need to Rethink Institutional Theory," *Local-Global: Identity, Security, Community* 11 (2012): 119.
[82] Interview with a member of Timorese civil society (a), September 4, 2013; interview with a Timorese governance adviser, July 18, 2013; interview with an international governance adviser, May 11, 2010; interview with an international governance adviser (a), April 23, 2010.
[83] J. da Costa Magno and A. Coa, "Finding a New Path between *Lisan* and Democracy at the Suku Level," *Local-Global: Identity, Security, Community* 11 (2012): 172.
[84] USAID, *The Crisis in Timor-Leste: Causes, Consequences and Options for Conflict Management and Mitigation* (Dili: USAID, 2006).
[85] D. Cummins and M. Leach, "Democracy Old and New: The Interaction of Modern and Traditional Authority in East Timorese Local Government," *Asian Politics & Policy* 4:1 (2012): 89–104; interview with a Timorese academic, September 3, 2013; interview with a Timorese public servant, September 3, 2013.
[86] S. Everett and B. Ragragio, *Decentralisation in Timor-Leste: What's at Stake?* (Dili: Asia Foundation, 2009); interview with a member of Parliament, September 30, 2010; interview with a *suco* leader, September 28, 2010; interview with a Timorese governance adviser, April 23, 2010.
[87] Law on Community Leaderships and Their Election No. 3/2009 (2009) (TL).
[88] In practice, they continue to be referred to as *suco* chiefs.

development projects. However, the 2009 law specifies that the *suco* leaders and councils are "community leaders" and that they are therefore "not included in the public administration."[89] Because this limits the influence the *sucos* can exercise over the government, it has restricted their capacity to exercise their mandate. This has led to a degree of frustration, as people do not understand why elected *suco* leaders do not have more powers or functions.[90] One Timorese public servant observed that this has also generated "confusion" concerning the status of *suco* leaders, as while the government has conferred a degree of legitimacy on them via elections, it is not involved in their everyday local activities.[91]

There are also questions about the capacity and motivation of some local leaders. Anecdotal evidence suggests that many *suco* councils fail to meet regularly or to conduct community meetings[92] and that some *suco* leaders make decisions that favor their personal interests.[93] A World Bank report even claimed that *suco* and *aldeia* leaders displayed "authoritarian characteristics."[94] These issues may be partly explained by the fact that many *sucos* are large both in terms of geographical size and population (the average size is 2,000 to 3,000 people) or are segmented and sometimes socially fractured, which means that it can be difficult and expensive for *suco* leaders and councils to generate a level of societal trust.[95] Moreover, because local leaders are often selected based on traditional power structures and ritual authority, their levels of literacy and numeracy can be low, which means that some struggle to manage the technical requirements of administrative activities and development projects.[96] However, there is evidence that as *sucos* are given increasing power and responsibility for development, the characteristics that people value in their *suco* leaders may be changing.[97]

---

[89] Ibid., art. 2(3).
[90] Interview with a member of Timorese civil society (b), September 4, 2013; interview with a Timorese governance adviser, July 18, 2013.
[91] Interview with a Timorese public servant, September 3, 2013.
[92] Interview with a member of Timorese civil society (a), September 4, 2013.
[93] D. Cummins and V. Maia, *Community Experiences of Decentralised Development in Timor-Leste* (Dili: Asia Foundation, 2012); interview with a member of Timorese civil society (a), July 17, 2013; interview with a member of Timorese civil society (c), July 17, 2013; interview with a Timorese governance adviser, July 18, 2013.
[94] D. Butterworth and P. Dale, *Local Governance and Community Development Initiatives: Contributions for Community Development Programs in Timor-Leste* (Dili: World Bank, 2011): 13.
[95] Cummins and Maia, *Community Experiences*. [96] Ibid.
[97] M. A. Brown, *Timor-Leste Report: Addressing Legitimacy Issues in Fragile Post-Conflict Situations to Advance Conflict Transformation and Peacebuilding* (Brisbane: University of Queensland, 2013).

In 2009, the government also enhanced the liberal-local hybridity of the *suco* councils by providing that they could appoint a *lia-na'in* (keeper of the words). The *lia-na'in* is responsible for maintaining *uma lisan*, the customary values, practices, and relations that guide how communities live, and for resolving conflicts within the *suco*.[98]

Reflecting their move to enhance decentralization, the AMP (and now BGK) governments have proved more willing to consult local leaders. In December 2010, the AMP government held a meeting of all 442 *suco* leaders to discuss plans for decentralization, and in September 2013, the BGK government met with all *suco* leaders to update them. *Suco* leaders also participate in decision making at the subdistrict and district levels and have opportunities to consult the government. The AMP and BGK governments have improved the oversight of *sucos* via the Directorate for *Suco* Administration in the Ministry of State Administration.[99]

The AMP and BGK governments also decentralized more resources. The 2009 law provided that *suco* leaders and council members should receive "an incentive," including an allowance and fees to attend meetings,[100] and that the government would provide *sucos* with "material and financial resources with a view to ensuring their proper functioning and development."[101] The incentive given to *suco* leaders is small, leading to claims that the position is "essentially voluntary"[102] and that the situation is "unfair," given that many leaders are very active and legitimate.[103] *Suco* leaders are not supposed to have a job, which causes additional financial strain. However, some do work or run businesses, and this in turn means that they do not have sufficient time to perform their duties.[104]

In line with the AMP government's desire to decentralize more resources, in 2009 it introduced the Pakote Referendum (Referendum Package) of

---

[98] Brown, *Timor-Leste Report*; interview with a member of Timorese civil society (c), July 17, 2013; interview with a *suco* leader, September 3, 2013; interview with a Timorese academic, September 3, 2013; interview with a Timorese governance adviser, July 18, 2013; M. Tilman, "Customary Social Order and Authority in the Contemporary East Timorese Village: Persistence and Transformation," *Local-Global: Identity, Security, Community* 11 (2012): 192–205.

[99] Interview with a Timorese governance adviser, July 18, 2013.

[100] In 2013, each *suco* leader received a motorbike, plus a monthly allowance of US$125 for transportation (repairs to the motorbike and fuel costs), US$85 for administration (usually in the form a part-time secretary), and an allowance of US$65. Interview with a *suco* leader, September 3, 2013.

[101] Law on Community Leaderships, s. 16.   [102] Magno and Coa, "Finding a New Path," 169.

[103] Interview with a member of Timorese civil society (a), July 17, 2013.

[104] Interview with a *suco* leader, September 3, 2013; interview with a Timorese academic, July 18, 2013.

infrastructure projects, such as the building of schools, roads, and health clinics, many of which were in rural areas.[105] This was followed in 2010 by the Pakote Dezenvolvimentu Desentralizasaun (Decentralized Development Package), which decentralized infrastructure projects to the district level. In 2010, the government also introduced the Planu Dezenvolvimentu Suku (*Suco* Development Plan), under which each *suco* was required to consult its members and identify development plans for their community. In 2011, the government introduced the Programa Dezenvolvimentu Dezentralizadu (Decentralized Development Programmes), which decentralized development projects to the district and subdistrict levels.[106] To harmonize the different programs and improve planning consultation and coordination, the government adopted the Planeamentu Dezenvolvimentu Integradu Distrital (Integrated District Development Plan) in 2012.[107]

These decentralized development projects have seen significant resources distributed to rural areas, prompting the creation of a flurry of new companies, which has in turn created jobs at the local level. However, the quality of these development projects has varied, primarily due to poor planning and project choice, lack of opportunities for local feedback, variable levels of local capacity, at times limited opportunities for local input, and the minimal oversight provided by the government.[108] There are also claims that a degree of patronage has been involved, with construction contracts being allocated to potential spoilers, such as veterans and those involved in the 2006 security crisis.[109]

The perceived success of these programs, combined with a recognition that development has occurred at a much slower pace in rural areas, inspired the AMP government to resolve in 2012[110] to accelerate decentralized development

---

[105] Council of Ministers, "Referendum Package to Rebuild Timor's Rural Areas," media release (Dili: Secretary of State for the Council of Ministers, Democratic Republic of Timor-Leste, October 8, 2009); interview with a member of Parliament, September 28, 2010.

[106] Decree Law on Planning of Decentralised Development Programmes I and II, No. 18/2011 (2011) (TL).

[107] Decree Law on Integrated District Development, No. 4/2012 (2012) (TL); Ministerial Decree on Organs of the Integrated District Development Planning No. 8/2012 (2012)(TL); Ministerial Decree on Elaboration of District Investment Plan No. 9/2012 (2012) (TL).

[108] Interview with a member of Timorese civil society (a), July 17, 2013; interview with a member of Timorese civil society (c), July 17, 2013; interview with a member of Timorese civil society, July 18, 2013; interview with a *suco* leader, September 3, 2013; interview with a Timorese academic, July 18, 2013; interview with a Timorese governance adviser, July 18, 2013; interview with an international governance adviser, September 3, 2013.

[109] ICG, *Timor-Leste: Stability at What Cost? Asia Report No. 246* (Brussels: International Crisis Group, 2013).

[110] Government Resolution Approving the Establishment of a National Mechanism to Accelerate Community Development No. 1/2012 (2012) (TL).

via the Programa Nasional Dezenvolvimentu Suco (National Program for Suco Development).[111] This program will see *suco* and *aldeia* leaders directly involved in the planning, construction, and management of small infrastructure development projects.[112] It implicitly involves liberal-local hybridity, as it is expected that *suco* and *aldeia* leaders will utilize local sociopolitical practices of consultation and consensus in order to garner their communities' perspectives of the development projects they require.

The AMP and BGK governments' attempts to improve the operation of local actors suggest that they recognize that many Timorese closely identity with local institutions, which might in turn encourage them to develop a sense of identification with other state institutions. This suggests that the legitimacy of the constitution, and the state institutions that it creates, may have been enhanced if the Constituent Assembly had ensured that it better reflected the role of local institutions and provided for immediate decentralization.

To what extent are the state institutions perceived to be legitimate?

The legitimacy of Timor-Leste's state institutions has been undermined by their absence from rural areas, which was complicated by their initial failure to recognize preexisting local sociopolitical institutions. As described in Chapter 3, the legitimacy was also challenged by the lack of opportunities for public participation and civic education during the constitution-making process. The decision to emphasize liberal peace methods of selecting representatives for state institutions has affected the extent to which state institutions are perceived to be legitimate, as a result of both the design of the electoral system and a gap between liberal and local sociopolitical practices.

Electoral system

As the tangible manifestation of the social contract, the constitution seeks to enumerate the relationship between the people and the state institutions that exercise their constituted power. As in all liberal democracies, this relationship is primarily manifested in the election of representatives. The adoption of a proportional electoral system calls into question whether state institutions legitimately exercise the people's constituted power. While the proportional

---

[111] Decree Law on the General Regime of the National Program for the Development of Sucos (PNDS) No. 08/2013 (2013) (TL).
[112] Initially to the value of US$50,000 per *suco*. Ibid., art. 11(1).

system does provide smaller parties with the opportunity to gain seats in Parliament, and arguably for a wider range of views to be represented,[113] the 3 percent threshold required for parties to receive seats means that very small parties do not receive one. For example, in the 2007 parliamentary election, seven political parties did not receive seats, even though Partido Nacionalista Timorense (Timorese Nationalist Party) received 10,057 votes (2.42 percent of the vote) and Partido Democratika Republika de Timor (Democratic Party of the Republic of Timor) received 7,718 votes (1.96 percent), while CNRT won eight seats at a cost of 5,564 votes each. In the 2012 election, this requirement meant that parties that received votes from one-fifth of Timorese voters did not receive representation in the Parliament. This effect was particularly controversial with respect to the Partido Kmanek Haburas Unidade Nasional Timor Oan (Enrichment of the National Unity of the Sons of Timor Party); it won 2.97 percent of the vote, which effectively meant that its 13,998 voters were deprived of representation in Parliament.

The proportional system does offer greater opportunities for women to be elected, assisted by the requirement that every third candidate on a party's list be a woman. This system also strengthens political parties; it can be compared to parliaments in other parts of the Pacific, where plurality voting results in weak parties, allowing MPs to switch political allegiance and causing frequent votes of no confidence. However, when the proportional system is combined with the nationwide electorate, there is no way to ensure that MPs will represent all regions. In addition, people cannot vote for specific candidates. This is said to have created a situation in which MPs have "little awareness...that they are elected to serve their constituents"[114] but instead focus on persuading "party leaders to place them sufficiently high on the party list to gain a seat."[115] This suggests that the proportional system may not be the best way to ensure that MPs represent the interests of the people and hence legitimately exercise their constituted power. Nevertheless, this criticism overlooks the local dynamics of kinship ties and other social networks that have given rise to a de facto form of constituency, with MPs well known in their local area.[116] In addition, MPs are allocated one day a week to visit their

---

[113] Interview with a member of Parliament, May 11, 2010.
[114] Federer, *The UN in East Timor*, 110; Della-Giacoma, "Ensuring the Well-Being"; Niner, "Martyrs, Heroes and Warriors."
[115] Shoesmith, "Remaking the State", 13; interview with a member of Parliament, September 30, 2010; NORAD, *Review of Development Cooperation in Timor Leste: Final Report* (Oslo: Norwegian Agency for Development Cooperation, 2007).
[116] Interview with a former member of the Constituent Assembly and member of Parliament, May 13, 2010; interview with a member of Parliament, May 11, 2010; interview with a member of

constituents or conduct party business.[117] While one study found that some MPs are reluctant to use this day to leave Dili,[118] others frequently visit rural areas.[119]

Even when people do access MPs, the problems with the UNATET civic education program identified in Chapter 3 combined with the lack of civic education since independence, mean that they often do not understand how Parliament works or how they should address their complaints to MPs.[120] Instead, people complain to the person they know and feel comfortable with (but who may have no capacity to respond).[121] Therefore, one MP reflected that the proportional electoral system leads "people to become frustrated."[122] Often this frustration manifests in radical ways, as occurred during the 2006 security crisis.

The gap between liberal and local sociopolitical practices

The gaps in civic education also mean that liberal democratic norms necessary to support the methods of representation created by the constitution are "very poorly understood."[123] For example, as local sociopolitical practices emphasize the need for consensus decision making, the adversarial nature of democracy is often perceived to involve opposition and violence,[124] which is widely understood as being "antagonistic to 'Timorese culture.'"[125] Indeed, a 2003 survey found that 34 percent of respondents thought that while

---

Timorese civil society (a), May 14, 2010; interview with a Timorese intellectual, May 12, 2010; interview with an international governance adviser (c), May 10, 2010.

[117] Interview with a Timorese justice adviser, May 12, 2010; Parliament Resolution on the Rules of Procedure, art. 46.

[118] NORAD, *Mid-Term Evaluation of the UNDP Timor-Leste Parliamentary Project – Strengthening Parliamentary Democracy in Timor Leste* (Oslo: Norwegian Agency for Development Cooperation, 2008).

[119] Interview with a former member of the Constituent Assembly and member of Parliament, May 13, 2010; interview with a member of Parliament, May 11, 2010; interview with a member of Parliament, September 30, 2010; interview with a member of Timorese civil society, May 12, 2010; interview with a member of Timorese civil society (b), May 14, 2010; interview with an international academic, December 22, 2009.

[120] Interview with a member of Parliament, May 11, 2010; interview with an international governance adviser (c), April 23, 2010.

[121] Interview with a Timorese governance adviser, April 23, 2010.

[122] Interview with a member of Parliament, September 30, 2010.

[123] Boege et al., *On Hybrid Political Orders*, 12; Brown and Gusmão, "Peacebuilding and Political Hybridity."

[124] T. Hohe, "Totem Polls: Indigenous Concepts and 'Free and Fair' Elections in East Timor," *International Peacekeeping* 9:4 (2002): 69–88; interview with a government official, April 27, 2010.

[125] Boege et al., *On Hybrid Political Orders*, 12.

democracy "might work in the West...it won't work" in Timor-Leste, although 84 percent were willing to give it a chance.[126] However, one government official found these claims "patronising." He noted that since 1999, Timorese have felt increasingly free to criticize and question their political leaders, and they had a sufficiently strong "opposition culture" to vote FRETILIN out of government in 2007.[127] This argument is borne out by the evidence of strategic voting outlined in Chapter 4. Focus group evidence also reveals that when questions relating to democracy are put to Timorese in a culturally resonant manner, they exhibit an understanding of the principles of representative democracy.[128]

Despite this, there is evidence that elections do not necessarily fit with local sociopolitical processes of leadership selection and representation. Indeed, local practices can "apply logic incompatible with liberal democratic principles," as MPs are often selected based on local or kin affiliations, patronage, or their membership of "royal" *uma lulik*.[129] While there is a gradual shift away from this, in many cases MPs are perceived to be legitimate only if they hold authority in the customary sphere or are endorsed by local leaders. In this regard, the majority of MPs come from *liurai* families.[130] Even when *liurai* are not elected, they often remain influential. While leaders chosen according to local customary logic might appear "arbitrary, self-serving, or parochial" to liberal thinkers, they are perceived to be "effective and legitimate" by many Timorese.[131]

Accountability institutions

Similarly, local customary practices often apply logic that is incompatible with liberal ideas when it comes to the distribution of state resources. Timorese local sociopolitical practices are based on reciprocity, according to which individual leaders dispense resources to their communities in exchange for their political support. This can be compared to the liberal idea that

---

[126] IRI, *National Opinion Poll: East Timor, November 2003* (Dili: International Republican Institute, 2003).
[127] Interview with a former member of the Constituent Assembly and government official, February 2, 2010; interview with a Timorese governance adviser, April 23, 2010.
[128] NDI, *Government within Reach*.
[129] Boege et al., "Hybrid Political Orders," 18; interview with a Timorese intellectual, May 12, 2010; interview with an international governance adviser (a), May 10, 2010.
[130] Interview with a member of Parliament, May 11, 2010; interview with an international governance adviser (a), May 10, 2010; interview with an international academic, January 7, 2010; A. McWilliam, "Customary Governance in Timor-Leste," in Mearns, *Democratic Governance*.
[131] Trindade, "Reconciling Conflicting Paradigms," 172.

individuals are abstract entities with whom state officials have no personal relationship. The practice of reciprocity has led to a culture of "corruption" seeping into the government and public service, whereby a "patronage system" has developed through the granting of government contracts, jobs, and other benefits to people with close ties to government officials.[132] For example, the former justice minister Lucia Lobato was suspended from Parliament in March 2012 after being charged for allegedly colluding with a company that was applying for a government tender. In June 2012, Lobato was found guilty of misappropriating ministry funds, fined, and imprisoned for five years. Corruption has arguably occurred under all governments since independence, as they have limited tender processes, granted sole-source supply contracts, and allegedly failed to account for revenues. Yet this may not entirely be due to corruption, as all governments have been driven by a "desire to act quickly" to produce results.[133]

To combat corruption, the AMP government approved the Anti-Corruption Commission in June 2009,[134] to assume the anticorruption functions performed by the Provedor dos Direitos Humanos e da Justiça. The commission was created in February 2010 and began forwarding cases to the Office of the Prosecutor General in 2011.[135] As it has received significant capacity-building support, the commission appears to have had more success than the *provedor* in combating corruption. The Office of the Inspector-General was created in 2000, with responsibility for internal audits and inspection of public bodies, as well as investigations in response to accusations of corruption in the execution of the public budget. In June 2009, the AMP government adopted a law specifically enumerating the office's powers and emphasizing its "technical independence and administrative autonomy."[136] The AMP government also created the Procurement Commission in early 2011 to support the office and the eProcurement Portal, which enables public monitoring of state budget execution and contracts.[137] The government has also joined the Extractive Industries Transparency Initiative to promote transparency concerning how it

---

[132] UN Doc. S/2010/85.
[133] AusAID, *Annual Program Performance Report for East Timor 2007–08* (Canberra: AusAID, 2008).
[134] Law on the Anti-Corruption Commission No. 08/2009 (2009) (TL).
[135] A. de Jesus Soares, "Combating Corruption: Avoiding 'Institutional Ritualism,'" in Leach and Kingsbury (eds.), *The Politics of Timor-Leste*.
[136] Decree Law – Statute for the Office of the Inspector-General No. 22/2009 (2009) (TL), art. 1.
[137] Decree Law Approving the Organic Law of the Procurement Follow-Up Commission and the Procurement Technical Secretariat No. 3/2010 (2010) (TL); Timor-Leste eProcurement Portal, undated, accessed November 4, 2013, www.eprocurement.gov.tl.

uses its natural resource revenues. Consequently, Timor-Leste's ranking on Transparency International's "Corruption Perception Index" improved from 143 (out of 182) in 2011 to 113 (out of 174) in 2012.[138]

While these developments appear to be positive steps towards combating corruption, one Timorese governance adviser noted that there is a "tendency to keep creating institutions to check other institutions," and that the capacity of each institution was relatively weak.[139] It is also questionable whether creating institutions to combat this behavior will be effective, given that it has deep roots in local sociopolitical practices. This suggests that it might be more effective if the state recognized and engaged with local practices to address perceived corruption.

Overall, the gap between liberal and local methods of leadership selection, representation, and accountability suggests that the constitution does not necessarily reflect the understandings of the people it seeks to govern. Indeed, during the Constitutional Commission hearings, the consensus was in favor of maintaining and recognizing local traditions and culture.[140] This suggests that had the Constituent Assembly taken account of the public's views, it might have drafted a constitution that created state institutions the people perceived to be more legitimate.

Are the state institutions delivering public goods and services?

As noted in Chapter 1, the dominant test of a government's effectiveness is whether it has the institutional capacity to deliver public goods and services. The government's delivery of the most important public good – security – is discussed below. It is possible to assess the government's delivery of certain other public goods using the indicators set out in the following table.[141]

---

[138] Transparency International, 2012 *Corruption Perception Index*, 2012, accessed October 23, 2013, cpi.transparency.org/cpi2012/results/.
[139] Interview with a Timorese governance adviser, April 23, 2010; interview with a member of Timorese civil society, September 27, 2010; Independent Evaluation Group, *Evaluation of the World Bank*.
[140] UNTAET Constitutional Affairs Branch, *Constitutional Commission Public Hearings*.
[141] Sources: DNE, *Timor-Leste in Figures*, 2008 (Dili: Direcção Nacional de Estatística, Government of Timor-Leste, 2009); DNE, *Timor-Leste in Figures 2012* (Dili: Direcção Geral de Estatística, Government of Timor-Leste, 2012); UNDP, *East Timor Human Development Report 2002*; UNDP, *International Human Development Indicators*, hdrstats.undp.org, accessed July 2, 2011; UNDP, *The Millennium Development Goals, Timor-Leste* (Dili: United National Development Programme, 2009); UNDP, *Timor-Leste Human Development Report 2006: The Path Out of Poverty, Integrated Rural Development* (Dili: United National Development Programme, 2006); UNDP, *Timor-Leste Human Development Report 2011:*

TABLE 1. *Timor-Leste development indicators*

Indicator	2001	2004	2006	2008	2010	2012
UN Human Development Index rank	N/A	158 (out of 177)	142 (out of 177)	150 (out of 177)	120 (out of 169)	134 (out of 186) (2013)
Population	794,298	923,198	1,015,000	1,081,000	1,066,000	1,140,000
Life expectancy at birth (in years)	56.7	58.8	60.2	61.1	62.1	61.62
Fertility rate (live births per woman)	7.6	6.9	6.7	6.5	6.0	5.7
Infant mortality rate (per 1,000 live births)	80	92	88	75	59	56
Children underweight for age (ages 0–5 years, as % of total)	45%	43%	46%	48.6% (2007)	49% (2009)	45%
Adult literacy rate (ages 15 and above, as % of total)	43.0%	50.1%	50.1%	50.1%	51%	58.3%
Primary education enrollment ratio (net)	76%	78%	78% (2005)	77%	85%	90%
GDP per capita (PPP $US)	$967	$732	$702	$802	$906	$1,068

The government has built many health centers, introduced mobile health centers, and rehabilitated and reconstructed several hospitals. As a result, 77 percent of the rural population now attends health clinics, more children have been immunized, and more births are supervised by health care professionals, which has increased life expectancy and reduced infant mortality rates. The government has also built and rebuilt many schools, and primary and secondary school enrollments and adult literacy have improved, although questions remain concerning the quality of the education that students receive.

Managing Natural Resources for Human Development, Developing the Non-Oil Economy to Achieve the MDGs (Dili: United National Development Programme, 2011); UNESCO, *Asia Pacific in Figures 2006* (Bangkok: United Nations Economic and Social Commission for Asia and the Pacific, 2006); UNICEF, *The State of the World's Children 2011: Adolescence, An Age of Opportunity* (New York: UNICEF, 2011); World Bank, *World Development Indicators*, undated, accessed November 2, 2013, databank.worldbank.org; World Bank/DNS, *Timor-Leste: Poverty in a Young Nation* (Dili: World Bank and Directorate of National Statistics, Timor-Leste, 2008).

However, GDP per capita dropped between 2001 and 2010. This decrease could be explained by a scaling back of the large UN presence, which was responsible for considerable internal expenditure, combined with an increase in the population, indicating that rather than shrinking, the economy simply did not grow enough to keep pace. The 2006 security crisis also affected GDP, as the non-oil economy contracted by 5.8 percent in 2007.[142] The economic growth rate did improve, and based on government figures, by the end of 2007, a 7.8 percent rate of growth was achieved, followed by a 12.8 percent rate in 2008 and a 12.2 percent rate in 2009.[143] The AMP government's decision to increase development spending has reduced the proportion of the population living under the basic needs poverty line[144] from 49.9 percent in 2007 to 41 percent in 2010.[145] Despite this, Timor-Leste's UN Human Development Index ranking fell from 2010 to 2013, and it is the third-worst place in the world for stunted growth in children, with 58 percent of children experiencing restricted growth due to malnutrition.[146] Consequently, in 2011, the UN Special Rapporteur on Extreme Poverty and Human Rights concluded that "growth and development has not translated into sustained improvements in standards of living, livelihoods and job creation. Poverty remains pervasive and widespread."[147]

Other challenges exist, as approximately 45 percent of the population is under the age of fourteen years and 62 percent is under the age of twenty-four years,[148] creating a "youth bulge" for which employment and other economic opportunities need to be created. An increasingly large population of young people have moved to Dili and other urban centers, exacerbating the negative effects of high unemployment.[149] These young people are a ready constituency that can be encouraged to join gangs and engage in criminality and violence. Indeed, many of those who inflamed the 2006 security crisis were members of youth gangs, whose experience of poverty, unemployment, and marginalization led them to

---

[142] UNDP, Timor-Leste Human Development Report 2011, 14.   [143] Ibid., 17.
[144] This was US$0.88 per day in 2008 and $1.25 in 2010.
[145] UN, *Report of the Secretary-General on the United Nations Integrated Mission in Timor-Leste (for the Period from 21 January to 20 September 2010)*, UN Doc. S/2010/522, October 13, 2010; World Bank/DNS, *Timor-Leste: Poverty in a Young Nation*.
[146] UNICEF, *The Right Ingredients: The Need to Invest in Child Nutrition* (London: UNICEF, 2013), 21.
[147] M. Sepúlveda, *Preliminary Observations and Recommendations, Mission to Timor-Leste from 13 to 18 November 2011*, 2011, accessed October 18, 2013, www.ohchr.org/EN/NewsEvents/Pages/DisplayNews.aspx?NewsID=11618&LangID=E.
[148] UNDP, *Timor-Leste Human Development Report 2011*.
[149] World Bank, *Interim Strategy Note for the Democratic Republic of Timor-Leste FY 2010–2011* (Sydney and Dili: World Bank, 2009).

feel that "they have been ignored by their leaders, by a government that did not create jobs for them and who has left them with few prospects."[150] This perception has been enhanced by the official historical narrative in the constitution, and the tendency of youth groups to coalesce around societal divisions may represent their "struggle for identity and recognition."[151]

There is also a wide disparity between urban and rural development, as while the AMP (and now BGK) government attempted to accelerate decentralization of development projects, state administrative institutions remain centralized in Dili. This means that many Timorese have not received a "peace dividend" from the state.[152] Guided by the local customary practice of reciprocity, many Timorese see the state as being "in their debt," given that they "purchased...nationhood with their blood."[153] The state has not yet repaid this debt, giving rise to a sense of frustration, which is exacerbated by the fact that many rural Timorese "paid a huge economic price for independence," as state institutions deliver fewer public services and goods than Indonesia did.[154]

The public service has faced serious capacity limitations, as many public servants possess only a "limited understanding of the role of their institutions."[155] This is partly due to the fact that young, educated Timorese have been excluded from these institutions because they lack Portuguese language skills. The AMP government did establish a civil service commission in 2009 in order to improve the effectiveness, impartiality, and professionalism of the public service,[156] and it has made good progress achieving this goal, particularly by issuing a code of ethics for all public servants in 2012. However, capacity limitations remain.[157]

In addition, for the first few years after independence, the FRETILIN government faced severe funding shortages. From 2002 to 2004, it relied on

---

[150] Plan Timor-Leste, *Like Stepping Stones in the River: Youth Perspectives on the Crisis in Timor-Leste* (Dili: Plan Timor-Leste, 2007), iv.
[151] Brown, "Security, Development and the Nation-Building Agenda," 158.
[152] Interview with an international financial adviser, September 30, 2010; Crockford, "Building Demand for Better Governance."
[153] J. J. Fox, "Repaying the Debt to Mau Kiak: Reflections on Timor's Cultural Traditions and the Obligations of Citizenship in an Independent East Timor," in Mearns, *Democratic Governance*, 125.
[154] Bowles and Chopra, "East Timor: Statebuilding Revisited," 290; D. Grenfell, "Governance, Violence and Crises in Timor-Leste."
[155] Bowles and Chopra, "East Timor: Statebuilding Revisited," 282; World Bank, *Strengthening the Institutions*.
[156] Law Approving the Statute of the Civil Service No. 8/2004 (2004) (TL), amended by Law No. 5/2009.
[157] UN Doc. S/2010/522; UN, *Report of the Secretary-General on the United Nations Integrated Mission in Timor-Leste (for the Period from 20 September 2011 to 6 January 2012)*, UN Doc. S/2012/43.

international assistance to fund 40 percent of the annual state budget, which limited its ability to make genuine economic progress.[158] In 2005, oil royalties from the Timor Gap began to flow, emerging as the state's major source of revenue. The non-oil economy is dominated by the public sector (45 percent of non-oil GDP in 2007), industry and services (28 percent), and agriculture (27 percent).[159] Public expenditure dominates the economy and reached 101 percent of the non-oil GDP in 2009.[160] Overlooked by these statistics is the fact that three-quarters of the working population are engaged in subsistence farming.[161]

The FRETILIN government introduced some social assistance programs[162] but provided little direct financial assistance to most needy people. This led to the perception that "the everyday experience of people living in poverty... [was] made secondary to institutional reform" and the government's "liberal obsessions."[163] The constitution provides little guidance concerning how to temper these obsessions, as it states that the "economic organisation" of the state is to be based on a paradoxical "combination of community forms" with the liberal principles of "free initiative and business management." It also recognizes the "coexistence of the public sector, the private sector and the cooperative and social sector of ownership of means of production."[164] This was in keeping with the views expressed in the Constitutional Commission hearings, in which the public favored the adoption of a market economy but argued that it should be tempered by subsidies to local producers and limits on foreign ownership of land.[165]

The influence of liberal economic policy has seen international development agencies encourage the government to "break" the subsistence economy.[166] Reflecting this approach, one high-ranking government official

---

[158] World Bank, *Country Assistance Strategy for the Democratic Republic of Timor-Leste, for the Period FY06–FY08* (Washington: World Bank, 2005).
[159] IMF, *Republic of Timor-Leste: Staff Report for the 2009 Article IV Consultation* (Dili: International Monetary Fund, 2009).
[160] UNDP, *Timor-Leste Human Development Report 2011*, 18.
[161] IFC, *Interim Strategy Note for the Democratic Republic of Timor-Leste*.
[162] The government increased public servant salaries, introduced free public education, and provided state-funded meals to all public school students. M. Alkatiri, *Decision Time*, speech to the Timor Leste Development Partners meeting, Hotel Timor, Dili, April 4, 2006.
[163] O. P. Richmond and J. Franks, "Liberal Peacebuilding in Timor Leste: The Emperor's New Clothes?," *International Peacekeeping* 15:2 (2008): 196–197.
[164] Constitution, s. 138.
[165] UNTAET Constitutional Affairs Branch, *Constitutional Commission Public Hearings*.
[166] Interview at a major development agency, September 27, 2006, quoted in Richmond and Franks, "Liberal Peacebuilding in Timor Leste," 194.

commented that Timor-Leste "has to change its culture and way of doing things, so that people can produce surplus products to sell."[167] However, the rapid introduction of a market economy has led to social disharmony and economic inequality, as it has disrupted local communal modes of production and intensified competition over access to economic opportunities.[168] These tensions fed into the 2006 security crisis, which would not have taken hold on such a large scale but for an environment complicated by "poverty and its associated deprivations, including high urban unemployment and the absence of any prospect of meaningful involvement and employment opportunities in the foreseeable future, especially for young people."[169]

When he became prime minister in 2006, Ramos-Horta utilized oil revenues to fund a program of public works to address entrenched poverty. In 2008, the AMP government used oil revenues to fund programs of cash payments to veterans of the resistance, internally displaced persons, the elderly and disabled, and female-headed households.[170] These programs have placated many involved in the crisis, but given that there are questions over their sustainability, it is not clear whether the peace they have bought will hold. Indeed, in 2010, the UN secretary-general reflected that "socioeconomic factors that fuelled the 2006 crisis...have improved slightly but will take many years to be fully addressed."[171]

Taking into account the level of destruction that followed the popular consultation and the difficulties of capacity and funding that the government has faced, it has had some success in the delivery of certain public goods, which indicates an increasing level of government effectiveness. However, poverty levels remain high, and when swearing in the BGK government, President Matan Ruak took the opportunity to upbraid members of the AMP government for failing to improve socioeconomic inequality, noting that "the divide in Timor is growing, and glaringly evident in the capital Dili, with villas and five-star hotels overlooking unrepaired roads."[172]

---

[167] Interview with a government official, April 29, 2010.
[168] Interview with a former member of the Constituent Assembly and member of Parliament, May 13, 2010; personal communication from an international health care worker, May 7, 2010; personal communication from an international health care worker, May 4, 2010.
[169] UN, *Report of the Secretary-General on Timor-Leste pursuant to Security Council Resolution 1690*, UN Security Council, UN Doc. S/2006/628, August 8, 2006: 9; interview with a former member of the Constituent Assembly and member of Parliament, September 30, 2010.
[170] Wallis, "Victors, Villains and Victims."   [171] UN Doc. S/2010/85, 10.
[172] Quoted in W. Fry, "Timor's Road Still Rocky Despite Peaceful Poll," *Crikey*, August 20, 2012.

Are law and order enforced and is the rule of law observed?

The most important indicator of a government's effectiveness is whether it has the institutional capacity to enforce law and order and to ensure that the rule of law is observed.

Law and order

The constitution officially sanctions two security institutions: the F-FDTL[173] and the PNTL.[174] It provides little detail concerning how they should operate, fails to delineate their authority, and does not provide clear mechanisms for civilian oversight. Until an organic law was adopted in May 2004,[175] the PNTL was under the executive authority of UNTAET. During its first few years of existence, officers were recruited and trained, but a lack of capacity and internal tensions contributed to the 2006 security crisis. After the crisis, the UN took responsibility for policing and for rebuilding the PNTL, vetting potential officers and developing capacity. Control was returned to the PNTL in March 2011, although the UN maintained a presence of over 1,200 police to support the national elections in 2012, for which the PNTL is said to have provided effective (although potentially heavy-handed) security. Full police powers were handed back to an ostensibly rebuilt PNTL in October 2012, although it has been suggested that the handover occurred "not because the PNTL had been reconstructed or because it fully met the criteria [in terms of training and vetting of officers], but due to the fact that the government of Timor-Leste was tiring of the relationship with UNMIT."[176]

The government has attempted to improve the legal regime regulating the PNTL by adopting laws on discipline, the use of force, and a new salary regime.[177] Despite these efforts, the PNTL continues to lack capacity in operations, administration and management, and there are reports that its members still engage in corruption and human rights violations.[178] Reflecting

---

[173] Constitution, s. 146; Decree Law Approving the Organic Structure of FALINTIL-FDTL No. 15/2006 (2006) (TL).

[174] Constitution, s. 147; Decree Law Approving the Organic Structure of Timor-Leste's National Police (PNTL) No. 09/2009 (2009) (TL).

[175] Organic Law of the National Police of Timor-Leste (PNTL) No. 8/2004 (2004) (TL).

[176] B. V. E. Wilson, "The Politics of Security-Sector Reform," in Leach and Kingsbury, *The Politics of Timor-Leste*, 187.

[177] Decree Law on Amendment to the Regime of Promotions Within PNTL No. 35/2011 (2011) (TL); Decree Law on the Legal Regime on the Use of Force No. 43/2011 (2011) (TL); Decree Law Amending the Salary Regime of the Timor Leste National Police No. 48/2011 (2011) (TL).

[178] Fragility Assessment Team, *Fragility Assessment*; ICG, *Handing Back Responsibility to Timor-Leste's Police*, Asia Report No. 180 (Dili: International Crisis Group, 2009); UN, *Report of the*

this, at any one time hundreds of PNTL officers face pending criminal or disciplinary issues.[179] There are also reports that Lorosa'e-Loromonu divisions continue to determine promotions and affect investigations.[180] When combined, these factors have undermined public trust in the PNTL and contributed to an emerging perception of impunity, discussed in more detail below.

The F-FDTL continued to function after the 2006 security crisis. In early 2008, the government introduced a disarmament, demobilization, and reintegration program to resolve the case of the 594 petitioners.[181] The government has since returned the F-FDTL to its pre-2006 crisis strength of 1,873 members, and in 2011 it authorized its expansion to 3,600 members by 2020.[182]

The expansion of the F-FDTL might be connected to the fact that since being called out during the 2006 crisis, the F-FDTL has demonstrated an increasing tendency to become involved in internal security issues. For example, it lobbied to be released from its barracks to deal with violence between persons displaced by the crisis. The F-FDTL's claim was bolstered after the February 2008 assassination attempts, as a "state of siege" was declared[183] and a joint command of the F-FDTL and PNTL was created to restore law and order. The command was described as a "travesty of the constitutional separation of the police and the military and a confirmation of the post-revolutionary ethos of the military as an organisation of greater prestige and authority in civilian affairs than the police."[184] It demonstrated poor discipline, committed human rights abuses, and showed little respect for

---

Secretary-General on the United Nations Integrated Mission in Timor-Leste (for the Period from 21 August 2007 to 7 January 2008), UN Doc. S/2008/26, January 17, 2008; UN Doc. S/2010/85; UN Doc. S/2010/522; UN Doc. S/2012/43.

[179] UN, *Report of the Secretary-General on the United Nations Integrated Mission in Timor-Leste (for the Period from 8 January 2011 to 20 September 2011)*, UN Doc. S/2011/641; UN Doc. S/2012/43.

[180] Personal communication from an international security adviser, April 29, 2010.

[181] M. B. Arnold, "Challenges Too Strong for the Nascent State of Timor-Leste: Petitioners and Mutineers," *Asian Survey* 49:3 (2009): 429–449; ICG, *Timor-Leste: No Time for Complacency*, Asia Briefing No. 87 (Dili and Brussels: International Crisis Group, 2009).

[182] Government Resolution on the Authorised Force Strength for Falintil-FDTL until 2020, No. 28/2011 (2011) (TL).

[183] Law Authorising the President of the Republic to Declare a State of Siege No. 1/2008 (2008) (TL), extended by Laws No. 2/2008, 4/2008, 5/2008 and 7/2008; Law on the Regulation of the State of Siege and Emergency No. 3/2008; Decree of the President of the Republic (Declaring a State of Emergency) No. 43/2008 (2008) (TL), extended by Decree Laws No. 48/2010 and 49/2010.

[184] J. Braithwaite, H. Charlesworth, and A. Soares, *Networked Governance of Freedom and Tyranny: Peace in Timor-Leste* (Canberra: ANU E-Press, 2012), 164.

the rule of law and civilian authority. Moreover, after its mandate expired on May 22, 2008, it did not wish to relinquish its power.[185] The F-FDTL claims legitimacy from the official historical narrative in the constitution and received a boost following the election of President Matan Ruak. The F-FDTL was deployed to nine districts to support the PNTL during the 2012 elections, and in response to violence that followed the announcement of the new coalition government in July 2012, Matan Ruak ordered unarmed troops to quell the violence. The F-FDTL remains deployed across Timor-Leste to improve their "familiarisation with the terrain,"[186] increasing their internal visibility.

The fact that an international intervention was required to quell the 2006 security crisis, and that UN police took control of policing between 2006 and early 2011, indicate that the Timor-Leste state has not had a monopoly over the legitimate use of physical force for much of its postindependence period, which raises questions over the government's effectiveness. The AMP and BGK governments have improved parliamentary oversight of the security sector, and the Ministry of Defence and Security has been developed for this purpose.[187] The government has also developed a package of national security laws,[188] although they do not clearly define and delineate the responsibilities of the PNTL and F-FDTL. Consequently, tensions continue to simmer between the two institutions, which has manifested in fights between their members. Lorosa'e-Loromonu tensions within and between the two also remain, highlighting the continuing legacy of the divisive official historical narrative contained in the constitution.

Reflecting their distrust of the state security forces, many Timorese communities instead rely on the local sociopolitical practice of *tarabandu* agreements to deal with antisocial behavior and crime.[189] *Tarabandu* have been likened to a "communal agreement or 'social contract' that outlines the behaviours and practices that members of the community deem to be

---

[185] ICG, *Timor-Leste: No Time for Complacency*; interview with a member of Timorese civil society (a), September 27, 2010; UN Doc. S/2008/501; UNOHCHR, *Rejecting Impunity: Accountability for Human Rights Violations Past and Present, Report on Human Rights Developments in Timor-Leste: 1 July 2008 to 30 June 2009* (Dili: UN Office of the High Commissioner for Human Rights, 2009).

[186] Interview with a F-FDTL officer, November 15, 2012, quoted in ICG, *Timor-Leste: Stability at What Cost?*, 25.

[187] UN Doc. S/2010/85.

[188] Law on Internal Security No. 4/2010 (2010) (TL); Law on National Defence No. 3/2010 (2010) (TL); Law on National Security No. 2/2010 (2010) (TL).

[189] Interview with a member of Timorese civil society (a), July 17, 2013; interview with a Timorese women's leader, July 18, 2013.

appropriate and want to enforce."[190] *Tarabandu* are generally enforced by physical sanctions, the payment of money or exchange or sacrifice of animals, and "supernatural" repercussions. Although *tarabandu* were not traditionally written down, it is becoming more common to codify them, an indication of their developing liberal-local hybridity.[191]

In another example of emerging liberal-local hybridity, and reflecting its pragmatic recognition that its law and order institutions have not fully penetrated rural areas, the government is increasingly engaging with local justice mechanisms such as the *tarabandu*. Government actors (including the PNTL) are becoming involved in creating *tarabandu*.[192] For example, the district and subdistrict administrators of Ermera worked with community and church leaders to create a districtwide *tarabandu* in 2012, which was signed by then-president Ramos-Horta.[193] Many *tarabandu* are enforced not only by *suco* or *aldeia* leaders but also by the PNTL.[194] Communities are also appointing voluntary *kablehan*, who work for the *suco* leader and essentially function as "community police."[195] In Ermera, Covalima, and Liquiça districts, the *kablehan* are trained by the PNTL and empowered to issue fines for small contraventions of the districtwide *tarabandu*. In cases of more significant transgressions, *kablehan* are required to bring the wrong-doer to the *suco* or *aldeia* leader, and if the leader fails to resolve the case, to the PNTL.[196] The appointment of *kablehan* is in line with the new "community policing" approach introduced by the government, whereby police are supposed to work with communities to resolve conflict and to mitigate potential sources of conflict and insecurity.[197] However, there are claims that community policing remains "a vague ambition rather than an immediate priority," as it is "chronically under-resourced" and there is a "lack of vision" and "an inability to see community policing as a potential solution for many problems facing the PNTL."[198]

---

[190] Belun, *Tara Bandu*, 10; interview with a Timorese academic, July 17, 2013.
[191] Interview with a member of Timorese civil society, July 18, 2013; Belun, *Tara Bandu*.
[192] Interview with a district administrator, September 1, 2013; interview with a subdistrict administrator, August 28, 2013.
[193] Interview with a Timorese women's leader, July 18, 2013.   [194] Belun, *Tara Bandu*.
[195] Interview with a member of Timorese civil society (b), September 4, 2013; interview with a *suco* leader, September 3, 2013.
[196] Belun, *Tara Bandu*; "Community Policing in Timor-Leste," *The Dili Weekly*, July 4, 2013.
[197] Organic Law of Timor-Leste's National Police (PNTL) No. 9/2009 (2009) (TL), arts. 18 and 38(1)(k).
[198] N. De Sousa, C. Belo, and M. R. Koenig, *Institutionalizing Community Policing in Timor-Leste: Exploring the Politics of Police Reform* (Dili: Asia Foundation, 2011), 1.

The rule of law

The courts are the main mechanism for ensuring that the rule of law is observed.[199] While the courts are independent,[200] because the constitution includes the proviso that judges can be held liable for their decisions "in the circumstances provided for by law," judges are not given absolute protection.[201] In addition, security of judicial tenure applies "unless otherwise provided for by law,"[202] which also limits judicial independence. The Supreme Court of Justice is the highest court[203] and has the power to review the constitutionality of "normative and legislative acts by the organs of the State."[204] As several courts provided for in the constitution have not yet been created, including the Supreme Court, the Court of Appeal is currently the highest court. The government is slowly creating courts, including the High Administrative, Taxation and Audit Court in 2011.[205] While District Courts have been established in Dili, Baucau, Suai, and Oecussi, the latter three courts operate only sporadically.[206]

The courts have faced serious constraints. In July 2003, two international judges sitting on the Court of Appeal ruled (against the dissent of the Timorese judge) that Indonesian law should not be applied. The decision gave rise to public outcry, undermined public confidence in the court, and was even ignored by lower-level courts.[207] In 2004 and 2005, the government evaluated Timorese legal practitioners. All failed and were disqualified, with their reappointment pending their completion of UNDP-run training during 2006.[208] To fill the gap, approximately 20 Portuguese-speaking international legal practitioners were recruited, although they were gradually replaced by Timorese actors. Consequently, as of March 2013, there were fifty Timorese judicial officers, up from twenty-seven in 2006.[209] There have also been

---

[199] Constitution, s. 118(1). See also UNTAET Regulation No. 2000/11, *On the Organization of Courts in East Timor* 2000/11, UN Doc. UNTAET/REG/2000/11, March 6, 2000, as amended by UNTAET Regulations 2000/14, 2001/18 and 2001/25.

[200] Constitution, s. 119.   [201] ICJ, *Commentary on the Draft Constitution*.

[202] Constitution, s. 121(3).   [203] Constitution, s. 124.   [204] Ibid., s. 126(1).

[205] Organic Law of the Chamber of Audits of the Administrative, Fiscal, Auditors High Court, Law No. 9/2011 (2011) (TL).

[206] Independent Comprehensive Needs Assessment Team, *The Justice System of Timor-Leste: An Independent Comprehensive Needs Assessment* (Dili: Independent Comprehensive Needs Assessment Team, 2009).

[207] T. Chopra, C. Ranheim, and R. Nixon, "Local-Level Justice under Transitional Administration," in *Customary Justice and the Rule of Law in War-Torn Societies*, ed. D. H. Isser (Washington: U.S. Institute of Peace, 2011), 135.

[208] JSMP, *Overview of the Justice Sector: March 2005* (Dili: Judicial System Monitoring Programme, 2005).

[209] Fragility Assessment Team, *Fragility Assessment*.

improvements in court technology, with the introduction of a database of criminal records. The BGK government has indicated that when capacity is available, it intends to decentralize judicial services by creating courts and prosecutor-generals' offices in all thirteen districts, supplemented by additional public defenders' offices. However, private lawyers also face severe capacity limitations. In 2008, the AMP government adopted a law that required all legal practitioners to complete a fifteen-month full-time course at the Legal Training Centre, followed by nine months of practice.[210] This law has reduced the number of private lawyers, as many have struggled to find the time required to complete the course or meet its Portuguese language requirements.

As a result, progress in clearing the backlog of criminal cases, estimated at 4,742 cases in August 2012, has been slow.[211] The backlog has been exacerbated by the fact that Timorese law has been published in its entirety only in Portuguese. Added to this, the Superior Council of the Judiciary ordered that from the end of 2004, all court documents had to be written in the official languages.[212] While court documents could arguably be translated into Tetum, "its usefulness as a court language is undermined by the fact that its lexicon includes few technical legal words."[213] As many judges were educated in Indonesia, they can barely understand Portuguese, and as defendants and petitioners to the court rarely speak Portuguese, "the language of rule of law separate[s] the practice of law from most people."[214] This effect is exacerbated by a lack of interpreters. As international legal practitioners leave the system, court hearings overseen by Timorese judges are increasingly being held in Tetum and the translation of laws into Tetum has begun in earnest.[215] However, a steady stream of new laws puts pressure on the courts and other

---

[210] Law on the Juridical Regime Governing the Private Legal Profession and Lawyers Training, No. 11/2008 (2008) (TL).

[211] UN, *Report of the Secretary-General on the United Nations Integrated Mission in Timor-Leste (for the Period from 7 January through 20 September 2012)*, UN Doc. S/2012/765, October 15, 2012.

[212] JSMP, *The Impact of the Language Directive on the Courts in East Timor* (Dili: Judicial System Monitoring Programme, 2004).

[213] L. Grenfell, "Legal Pluralism and the Rule of Law in Timor Leste," *Leiden Journal of International Law* 19 (2006): 311.

[214] Kingsbury, "Political Development," 23; interview with a member of Timorese civil society, May 12, 2010; JSMP, *Overview of the Justice Sector in Timor-Leste 2009*; World Bank, *Strengthening the Institutions*; Fragility Assessment Team, *Fragility Assessment*.

[215] K. Hunter, *From Timor-Leste: Citizens Finally Able to Read Laws in Own Language* (Dili: Asia Foundation, 2008); interview with an international governance adviser (a), May 10, 2010; interview with an international governance adviser (b), May 10, 2010.

justice actors. These problems demonstrate how some of the fears expressed about the choice of official languages have come to fruition.

As with other state institutions, minimal public participation during the constitution-making process and gaps in civic education mean that there is little public knowledge of the courts. For example, a 2008 survey revealed that while 59 percent of respondents had heard of a court, only 41 percent had heard of a lawyer. The survey authors concluded that "most Timorese do not understand the nature of the formal system of judicial governance or have practical access to the legal system."[216]

The enforcement of the liberal principle of the rule of law has also faced social and cultural challenges. The constitution specifies that the state will be one "based on the rule of law."[217] As Indonesia did not respect the rule of law throughout its occupation, and because much of the returning diaspora had spent the occupation in revolutionary Mozambique, many Timorese had not developed a strong understanding of the rule of law. Their understanding was not assisted during UNTAET's tenure, as the transitional administrator's extensive powers were "arguably in tension with the rule of law."[218] Moreover, as UNTAET made the pragmatic decision to rely on existing Indonesian laws in the absence of UNTAET regulations,[219] many of which are "designed to control the population," this entrenched a problematic understanding of the rule of law among young Timorese legal practitioners.[220]

The state has done little to promote the rule of law. The FRETILIN and AMP governments circumvented the Court of Appeal's power of constitutional review.[221] For example, the AMP government was accused of exhibiting "belligerence in the face of judicial criticism" after its disparaging response to the court's decision that aspects of its 2008 state budget were illegal and unconstitutional.[222] Shortly after the court's decision was issued, the contract of the Portuguese judge who had been its principal author was not renewed, leading to allegations of interference with the independence of the court.

---

[216] Asia Foundation, *Law and Justice in Timor-Leste: A Survey of Citizen Awareness and Attitudes Regarding Law and Justice 2008* (Dili: Asia Foundation, 2009), 28.
[217] Constitution, preamble, ss. 1 and 6.   [218] Grenfell, "Promoting the Rule of Law," 216.
[219] UNTAET Regulation No. 1999/1, s. 3.1.
[220] Kingsbury, *East Timor: The Price of Liberty*, 99.
[221] For example, in 2003 in relation to the draft Immigration and Asylum Law or in 2008 in relation to the state's midyear budget.
[222] Court of Appeal, *Ruling of the Court in Case No. 03/2008, On the Constitutionality of the Decree-Law no. 22/2008 of 16 July Establishing the Economic Stability Fund*, August 14, 2008; JSMP, *Legitimacy of the Court's Decision in the Case Relating to the Economic Stabilisation Fund* (Dili: Judicial System Monitoring Programme, 2009).

A specially convened panel of the court later found in the judge's favor and suspended the decision not to renew his contract.[223]

The enforcement of law and order and observation of the rule of law was challenged by the almost complete absence of the courts and PNTL from rural areas for several years after independence.[224] Even when people do have access to these institutions, they are often seen as slow and expensive.[225] Consequently, many people continue to rely on local justice mechanisms, such as *nahe biti*, *tarabandu*, and *kablehan*, which are perceived to be more sensitive to local contexts and to meet the practical considerations of accessibility, timeliness, and affordability. Indeed, a 2004 survey found that 81 percent of respondents saw customary chiefs or elders as primarily responsible for maintaining law and order in their area, while only 14 percent identified the PNTL as having this responsibility.[226] When asked the same question in 2008, 86 percent of respondents identified chiefs or elders, while only 5 percent identified the PNTL. These results were echoed in another 2008 survey, which found that 75 percent of Timorese rely primarily on local justice mechanisms, rather than the PNTL, for maintaining security.[227] This is also partly due to the type of crimes that occur, as in rural areas levels of serious crime remain low. Instead, the most common offences are theft, land grabbing, and gender violence, which community leaders have traditionally played an important role in resolving. There is an increasing preference for using state justice institutions, such as the PNTL, for handling violent crimes.[228]

---

[223] Court of Appeal, *Ruling of the Court in Proc No. 01/P.Cautelar/2008, on Judge Ivo Rosa's Petition of Temporary Injunction*, December 31, 2008.

[224] ICG, *Handing Back Responsibility*; Independent Comprehensive Needs Assessment Team, *The Justice System*.

[225] Particularly as the filing fee is $75, yet half of all Timorese people live on less than $40 per month. Asia Foundation, *Law and Justice in East Timor*; Asia Foundation, *Law and Justice in Timor-Leste*; Avocats Sans Frontieres, *Access to Legal Aid in Timor-Leste – Survey Report* (Dili: Avocats San Frontieres, 2006); JSMP, *Key Themes in Legal Development: A JSMP Retrospective, 27 April 2001 – 27 April 2008* (Dili: Judicial System Monitoring Programme, 2008).

[226] Asia Foundation, *Law and Justice in East Timor*.

[227] Asia Foundation, *Law and Justice in Timor-Leste*. See also Asia Foundation, *A Survey of Community-Police Perceptions: Timor-Leste in 2008* (Dili: Asia Foundation, 2008); T. Hohe and R. Nixon, *Reconciling Justice: "Traditional" Law and State Judiciary in East Timor* (Dili: U.S. Institute of Peace, 2003); interview with a *suco* leader, September 28, 2010.

[228] For example, when asked from whom they would seek assistance if they were threatened by a gang of men, 51 percent identified the PNTL, 21 percent the *suco* chief, 13 percent a *suco* council elder, 3 percent direct negotiation with the gang, and 13 percent other parties. Asia Foundation, *Survey of Community-Police Perceptions*. See also Avocats Sans Frontieres, *Access to Legal Aid*; interview with an international governance adviser, May 13, 2010; interview with an international governance adviser (b), April 23, 2010.

Even when serious matters are referred to state justice institutions, the PNTL often takes "an *ad hoc* and pragmatic" liberal-local hybrid approach by encouraging victims to seek recourse through local justice mechanisms.[229] The PNTL, particularly at the subdistrict level, also consults with and seeks guidance from *suco* and *aldeia* leaders, although there is no legal requirement for it to do so.[230] In addition, as Timorese judges replace international judges, there are reports that they now informally incorporate customary compensation payments into their sentences,[231] in a move described as "legal pragmatism."[232] There is also an increasing willingness to recognize out-of-court agreements reached through local justice mechanisms.[233]

Although local traditions and customs were largely overlooked during the constitution-making process, the constitution did include a provision that a law could be made to "institutionalise means and ways for the non-jurisdictional resolution of disputes."[234] This provision was not included in the original FRETILIN draft[235] and reflects changes made during the Constituent Assembly debates. Strong support was expressed during the Constitutional Commission hearings in favor of acknowledging local justice mechanisms.[236] In recognition of the weakness of both the rule of law and state justice institutions, the state has pragmatically decided to use this provision to engage with local justice mechanisms.[237] The 2004 law that sought to legitimize local political institutions also empowered *suco* leaders to "provide for the creation of grassroots structures for the resolution and settlement of minor disputes" and to "promote the creation of mechanisms for the prevention of domestic violence."[238] This law was amended in 2009, but the powers

---

[229] For example, a 2008 survey found that when combating crime and maintaining security, 94 percent of PNTL officer respondents indicated that they seek assistance from *suco* chiefs, 87 percent from elders (both elected and informal), and 81 percent from religious associations. Asia Foundation, *Survey of Community-Police Perceptions*. See also Independent Comprehensive Needs Assessment Team, *The Justice System*; interview with a Timorese governance adviser, May 11, 2010; interview with an international governance adviser, May 13, 2010; UNOHCHR, *Rejecting Impunity*.
[230] Braithwaite, Charlesworth, and Soares, *Networked Governance*.
[231] Asia Foundation, *Law and Justice in Timor-Leste*; interview with an international governance adviser (a), May 10, 2010; JSMP, *The Interaction of Traditional Dispute Resolution with the Formal Justice Sector in Timor-Leste* (Dili: Judicial System Monitoring Programme, 2005).
[232] USAID, *Rule of Law in Timor-Leste*, 24.
[233] JSMP, *The Interaction of Traditional Dispute Resolution*. [234] Constitution, s. 123(5).
[235] FRETILIN draft constitution, art. 104.
[236] UNTAET Constitutional Affairs Branch, *Constitutional Commission Public Hearings*.
[237] Interview with a member of Timorese civil society, May 12, 2010; interview with a Timorese governance adviser, May 11, 2010; interview with a Timorese intellectual, May 12, 2010.
[238] Decree Law on Community Authorities, s. 3.

given to *suco* leaders remained the same.[239] The creation of *tarabandu* and appointment of *kablehan* are examples of such grassroots structures.

However, the formal recognition of local justice mechanisms has been criticized as sending "mixed messages" that may undermine the rule of law.[240] As local justice mechanisms coexist with state justice institutions and enforce customary, rather than state, law, legal pluralism results. This could have a detrimental effect on the rule of law, as local leaders sometimes reach different decisions in similar cases or are perceived to be biased.[241] As the system currently operates, it "does not serve the rule of law because it operates without any of the checks or balances," as there are "no formal avenues of appeal and thus minimal accountability and transparency."[242] There is also inadequate oversight of local justice mechanisms.[243] This challenge is exacerbated by the fact that people can receive customary sanctions under a *tarabandu* and then face criminal punishment under the state justice system for the same crime.[244] There is also the risk that people may be sanctioned under *tarabandu* for behavior that does not contravene state law. For example, according to the Ermera district *tarabandu*, sexual relations between a married man and unmarried woman are not permitted, although there is no similar provision in state law. Enforcing this *tarabandu* may therefore violate human rights.[245]

In this regard, the constitution requires the state to "recognise and value the norms and customs of East Timor that are not contrary to the Constitution."[246] During the Constitutional Commission hearings, Timorese expressed support for the continued use of customary law as a complement to state law, particularly in relation to local matters.[247] However, the constitution merely requires the state to acknowledge custom, and in the absence of legislation clarifying its intent, this has led to confusion within the courts as to whether customary law can be utilized as a defense or applied during sentencing.[248] To this end, in October 2007, the Ministry of Justice,

---

[239] Law on Community Leaderships, art. 11.
[240] Grenfell, "Promoting the Rule of Law," 228; interview with a Timorese governance adviser, May 11, 2010.
[241] Zifcak, *Restorative Justice in East Timor*, 51.
[242] Grenfell, "Legal Pluralism and the Rule of Law in Timor Leste," 307.
[243] USAID, *Rule of Law in Timor-Leste*.   [244] Belun, *Tara Bandu*.   [245] Ibid.
[246] Constitution, s. 2(4).
[247] UNTAET Constitutional Affairs Branch, *Constitutional Commission Public Hearings*.
[248] JSMP, *Judge Applies Customary Law in a Criminal Case*, Press Release (Dili: Judicial System Monitoring Programme, May 19, 2005); JSMP, *Overview of the Justice Sector 2006–2007* (Dili: Judicial System Monitoring Programme, 2007); JSMP, *The Role, Practices and Procedure of the Court of Appeal* (Dili: Judicial System Monitoring Programme, 2005).

in cooperation with the UNDP and UNMIT, began working toward codification in a draft Customary Law.[249]

As the government has struggled to enforce law and order, questions have been raised concerning its effectiveness. As state justice institutions are weak, their ability to ensure that the rule of law is observed has been limited. However, according to liberal theory, the rule of law is essential if people are to exercise their popular sovereignty equally. Had the Constituent Assembly paid more attention to public feedback provided during the constitution-making process, local justice mechanisms and customary law might have been recognized more fully in the constitution. Instead, local justice institutions were not formally recognized until 2004, and customary law is yet to be codified, giving rise to legal pluralism.

Culture of impunity
Adding to the challenge of legal pluralism is the fact that state justice institutions are "characterised by a lack of public confidence underpinned by perceived impunity."[250] The culture of impunity is most developed with respect to crimes committed during the Indonesian occupation. During the Constitutional Commission hearings and Constituent Assembly's public consultations, Timorese insisted that the constitution provide legal certainty that the government would seek to punish these crimes.[251] This demand was unsurprising, given that nearly all Timorese experienced at least one traumatic event during the occupation.[252] While the constitution provides that such crimes will be "liable to criminal proceedings with the national or international courts,"[253] progress has been slow.

The constitution provided that the Special Panels for Serious Crimes[254] that were established under UNTAET would continue after independence.[255]

---

[249] Interview with an international justice adviser, May 14, 2010; UNMIT, *Report on Human Rights Developments in Timor-Leste (August 2006-August 2007)* (Dili: United Nations Integrated Mission in Timor-Leste, 2007).

[250] UN Doc. S/2010/85, 9; UN, *Report of the Secretary-General on the United Nations Integrated Mission in Timor-Leste (for the Period from 27 January to 20 August 2007)*, UN Doc. S/2007/513, August 28, 2007.

[251] F. Borges, "CAVR Implementation: The Key to Transforming the Country and East Timorese Society," in Mearns, *Democratic Governance*.

[252] J. Modvig et al., "Torture and Trauma in Post-Conflict East Timor (Health and Human Rights)," *The Lancet*, 356:9243 (2000): 1763–1764.

[253] Constitution, s. 160.

[254] "Serious" crimes were defined as including genocide, crimes against humanity, war crimes, and certain domestic crimes of torture, murder, and sexual offenses. These crimes must have occurred between January 1 and October 25, 1999. UNTAET Regulation No. 2000/15, *On the Establishment of Panels with Exclusive Jurisdiction over Serious Criminal Offences*, UN Doc. UNTAET/REG/2000/15, June 6, 2000.

[255] Constitution, s. 163(1).

The panels had moderate success, primarily involving plea-bargained convictions against low-level Timorese militia members, before they were terminated on May 20, 2005, at the end of the UNMISET.[256] The accompanying Ad Hoc Human Rights Court for Timor-Leste in Indonesia was "manifestly inadequate," and the Commission of Experts recommended that the UN Security Council create an international criminal tribunal.[257] While the Serious Crime Investigation Team was established under UNMIT in 2006,[258] it had the power only to investigate crimes and make recommendations to the Office of the Prosecutor General. It ceased operation without completing its investigations when UNMIT withdrew at the end of 2012, although there will be some attempt to continue prosecutions within the office.[259] As the office is vulnerable to government influence, this has affected its willingness to pursue prosecutions, which reflects the fact that the government has done little to pursue justice for these crimes. Accordingly, an alliance of civil society groups, under the umbrella of the Timor-Leste National Alliance for an International Tribunal, has called for UN support to continue the prosecution of serious crimes.[260]

Presidents Gusmão and Ramos-Horta were accused of cultivating a culture of impunity by suspending arrest warrants and releasing alleged war criminals. They also offered amnesties, passed blanket pardons for convicted criminals, and commuted sentences. For example, on May 20, 2008, Ramos-Horta remitted the sentences of the people convicted for the militia violence that followed the popular consultation.[261] He also proposed a blanket amnesty in respect to the 2006 security crisis, and although the government pursued some (although not all) convictions, Ramos-Horta either commuted the sentences of or issued pardons to those prosecuted.[262] In December 2009, Ramos-Horta

---

[256] Braithwaite, Charlesworth, and Soares, *Networked Governance*.
[257] UN, *Report to the Secretary-General of the Commission of Experts to Review the Prosecution of Serious Violations of Human Rights in Timor-Leste (then East Timor) in 1999*, May 26, 2005, Annex II to *Letter Dated 24 June 2005 from the Secretary-General Addressed to the President of the Security Council*, UN Doc. S/2005/458, July 15, 2005.
[258] S/Res/1704.
[259] Independent Comprehensive Needs Assessment Team, *The Justice System*; UN, *Report of the Security Council Mission to Timor-Leste 3 to 6 November 2012*, UN Doc. S/2012/889, November 28, 2012.
[260] S. do Santos, *Timor-Leste National Alliance for an International Tribunal Letter to UNSG*, August 14, 2012, accessed October 15, 2013, easttimorlegal.blogspot.com.au/2012/08/timor-leste-national-alliance-for.html; Timor-Leste National Alliance for an International Tribunal, *An Open Letter in Response to the CTF Report*, July 18, 2008, accessed October 15, 2013, etan.org/news/2008/07anti.htm.
[261] Decree of the President of the Republic (Presidential Pardon) No. 53/2008 (2008) (TL).
[262] Decree of the President of the Republic (Presidential Pardon) No. 31/2010 (2010) (TL); Decree of the President of the Republic (Presidential Pardon) No. 60/2010 (2010) (TL).

pardoned or commuted the sentences of those who were convicted for the 2008 assassination attempts.[263] Similarly, in August 2009, Gusmão authorized the handover to the Indonesian government of Martenus Bere, a militia leader who had been arrested on a warrant for crimes against humanity relating to the 1999 violence.

Both Ramos-Horta and Gusmão justified their actions by arguing that it was more important to achieve reconciliation than justice,[264] with Ramos-Horta arguing that "the greater justice is that we are free."[265] These arguments are at odds with the opinions of many Timorese, most of whom "have received little help to overcome the past."[266] Indeed, the UN secretary-general has argued that much of the violence that has occurred since independence traces back to "the need to address the past."[267] Ramos-Horta and Gusmão's arguments also signal their slightly paternalistic approach – Gusmão because he sees himself as the "father of the nation," Ramos-Horta because he is said to have developed an almost "messianic" complex after he survived the 2008 assassination attempt.[268] These actions have created a precedent in favor of presidents becoming involved in judicial matters,[269] undermined the rule of law, and violated the separation of powers. This is particularly the case with respect to the release of Bere, which resulted in the president of the Court of Appeal issuing a statement clarifying that the release was not ordered by a court. Gusmão's actions in relation to Bere also inspired FRETILIN to introduce a motion of "no confidence" in Parliament, although it ultimately failed after the vote divided along party lines.

The perception that the government favors reconciliation over justice was exacerbated by the establishment in August 2005 of the Indonesia-Timor Leste Truth and Friendship Commission (CTF) to "investigate the events of 1999."[270] The CTF had no powers to prosecute and emphasized "friendship" over

---

[263] Decree of the President of the Republic (Presidential Pardon) No. 34/2009 (2009) (TL).
[264] Interview with a member of Timorese civil society (a), May 14, 2010; interview with a member of Timorese civil society, May 12, 2010; interview with a Timorese intellectual, May 12, 2010; interview with an international governance adviser (a), May 10, 2010.
[265] Quoted in T. McDonnell, "No Freedom Yet for Ramos Horta," *The Australian*, February 10, 2012.
[266] Niner, *Xanana: Leader of the Struggle*, 234; CEPAD, *Timor-Leste: Voices and Paths*.
[267] UN Doc. S/2006/628.
[268] Interview with a member of Timorese civil society, September 26, 2010; interview with an international academic, January 7, 2010.
[269] Interview with a former member of the Constituent Assembly and member of Parliament, September 30, 2010; interview with a member of Timorese civil society, May 12, 2010; interview with a member of Timorese civil society, October 1, 2010.
[270] S. Yudhoyono and J. Ramos-Horta, *Joint Statement of the Heads of State of the Republic of Indonesia and the Democratic Republic of Timor-Leste*, Nusa Dua, July 15, 2008.

"truth."[271] Despite the skepticism of its critics, the CTF's report did present a balanced account of events by finding that human rights violations and crimes against humanity were committed by proautonomy militia groups, the Indonesian military, the Indonesian government, and the POLRI.[272] President Ramos-Horta presented the report to Parliament on October 9, 2008, and convened a national dialogue on justice and reconciliation in June 2009. While Parliamentary Committee A has drafted laws to implement the recommendations of the CTF and CAVR,[273] Parliament has yet to adopt them, adding to the perception of state-level impunity. That perception was enhanced in August 2011, when Prime Minister Gusmão signed a memorandum of understanding on security cooperation with Indonesia, which included military-to-military links.

Are human rights and civil liberties protected?

As the rule of law is weak, it undermines the enforcement of the liberal human rights protections entrenched in the constitution and allows the government to infringe upon civil liberties. The constitution protects a number of civil, political, economic, and social rights.[274] However, a distinction is drawn between generally applicable rights and those that can be claimed only by citizens.[275] In addition, rights can be limited by later law,[276] meaning that these rights create "an illusion of Constitutional protection

---

[271] M. Hirst, *An Unfinished Truth: An Analysis of the Commission for Truth and Friendship's Final Report on the 1999 Atrocities in East Timor* (New York: International Center for Transitional Justice, 2009).

[272] CTF, Per Memoriam ad Spem *(Through Memory to Hope): Final Report of the Commission of Truth and Friendship, Indonesia-Timor-Leste* (Bali: Commission of Truth and Friendship, 2008).

[273] Bill Establishing the Public Memory Institute No. /II (TL); Draft Law Establishing the Framework of the National Reparations Programme, No. /II (TL); interview with a member of Parliament, September 30, 2010.

[274] These include rights to equality and nondiscrimination; special protection of children, the aged, and the disabled; guaranteed access to courts; rights to life, personal freedom, and integrity; rights to privacy, free speech and information, and a free press and media; the right to work; the right to health; consumer rights; and the right to a healthy environment. Constitution, ss. 16–61.

[275] Rights of due process, freedoms of conscience, religion, and worship, and the right to housing are generally available, but the rights of freedom of speech, assembly, and association are available only to citizens.

[276] For example, later law can restrict the right to self-defense (s. 28(1)), the right to apply for *habeas corpus* (s. 33(2)), the guarantee of legal representation in criminal proceedings (s. 34(2)), and the right to freedom of speech (s. 40(3)).

only."[277] The constitution also empowers the government to ratify international treaties, and it has acceded to the majority of core international human rights instruments.

The methods for the enforcement of human rights are weak. While early drafts anticipated that citizens could seek to defend their rights in court, these provisions were removed by the Constituent Assembly.[278] Instead, the Provedor de Dereitos Humanos e Justica is mandated to perform investigations of complaints against "public bodies"[279] rather than against the "private" sphere.[280] Only citizens can complain to the *provedor*, whose ultimate sanction is merely to make recommendations to "competent organs."[281] The law for the *provedor's* office was not promulgated until April 2004,[282] the *provedor* was not elected by Parliament until early 2005, and the office did not begin operating until March 2006. This delay meant that the office was "created too late to prevent a cycle of impunity from damaging the reputation" of the PNTL.[283] This further eroded the rule of law and contributed to the lack of public confidence in state justice institutions. Recognizing this, in 2011 the government attempted to strengthen the office by adopting a new organic law establishing the organizational structure and functions of the office and providing for permanent staffing.[284]

This weak protection of rights supports the literature, which posits that the level of public participation in constitution making will affect the strength of the human rights protections included in a constitution. However, as international law is directly applicable in Timor-Leste's legal system,[285] this may be interpreted as requiring human rights claims based on international law to be justiciable in the court system.[286] As Timor-Leste has entered into a number of international human rights instruments, they theoretically apply. Yet, as the courts are weak, these provisions have had no effect.

The weak methods for the enforcement of rights protections have allowed the government to curtail civil liberties. Most controversially, in 2005, the FRETILIN government adopted a law that limited public demonstrations.[287]

---

[277] ICJ, *Commentary on the Draft Constitution*.   [278] Zifcak, *Making Timor's Constitution*.
[279] Constitution, s. 27.   [280] Charlesworth, "The Constitution of East Timor," 333.
[281] Constitution, s. 27(2).
[282] Law Approving the Statute of the Office of the Ombudsman for Human Rights and Justice No. 7/2004 (2004) (TL), as amended by Law No. 8/2009.
[283] Grenfell, "Promoting the Rule of Law," 226.
[284] Decree Law on the Organic Structure of the Office of the Provedor for Human Rights and Justice No. 25/2011 (2011) (TL).
[285] Constitution, s. 9.   [286] Charlesworth, "The Constitution of East Timor."
[287] Law on Freedom of Assembly and Demonstration No. 1/2006 (2006) (TL), art. 5.

Civil society groups criticized the law, arguing that it was aimed at insulating public officials from criticism.[288] The Court of Appeal found that two provisions were constitutionally defective, and President Gusmão vetoed the law.[289] It was then amended and passed again. The law was utilized by both the FRETILIN and AMP governments with respect to protests by students at the National University. For example, in June 2008, the AMP government purchased sixty-five new cars for MPs, which motivated student demonstrations. The PNTL utilized the law to justify using tear gas and arresting more than thirty-six protestors. While there were fears that the AMP government "was heading down the same authoritarian path as the previous FRETILIN government,"[290] the protestors were released and the government gave a public explanation of the purchase.

CONCLUSION

When reflecting on the performance of the state, a government official observed that the "National Government has only a roof but no roots."[291] Indeed, while the "roof" (the state institutions that exercise the people's constituted power) has been created, the "roots" (the foundations laid down for those institutions in the constitution) are weak, as there was minimal public participation in constitution making, and consequently, a constituent process was not generated. Public knowledge and understanding of the constitution and the state institutions that it creates appear to be generally poor, which calls into question whether these legitimately exercise the people's constituted power. Instead, local sociopolitical institutions and justice mechanisms have widespread legitimacy, which has led the government to adopt a liberal-local hybrid approach and pragmatically recognize both. That the government needed to do this suggests that state institutions were not legitimately able to exercise the people's constituted power. It also highlights the lost opportunities of the minimal public participation in constitution making. If Timorese had been given a better opportunity to exercise their popular

---

[288] HRW, *East Timor: New Law Aims to Stifle Political Dissent, Press Release* (London: Human Rights Watch, December 29, 2004); JSMP, *Draft Law 29/I/3A, Freedom of Assembly and Demonstration* (Dili: Judicial System Monitoring Programme, 2004).

[289] Court of Appeal, *Ruling of the Court in Case No. 01/2005, On the Constitutionality of the Law on Freedom of Assembly and Demonstration*, March 9, 2005.

[290] Kingsbury, *East Timor: The Price of Liberty*, 205.

[291] Quoted in T. Hohe, "Local Governance after Conflict: Community Empowerment in East Timor," *Journal of Peacebuilding & Development* 1:2 (2004): 47.

sovereignty, it is likely that they would have ensured that local practices were formally recognized and incorporated into their new state. This might have helped the constitution to create state institutions that were perceived to legitimately exercise their constituted power and that actually made sense to the people they sought to govern.

PART III
EXTENSIVE PARTICIPATION IN BOUGAINVILLE

6

State building and constitution making in Bougainville

This chapter begins by outlining a brief historical background of Bougainville, which is necessary to understand contemporary constitutional developments. It then provides a contextual description of the peace process that led to Bougainville being granted autonomy and instigated the constitution-making process. The main elements of constitution making identified in Chapter 2 are then used to examine that process.

BRIEF HISTORICAL BACKGROUND OF BOUGAINVILLE

Bougainville's precolonial population lived in a mosaic of small hamlets and nucleated villages based around landholding clan lineages, which in turn sat within wider clans. Clans were generally large, and although a person would never have known all members of the clan, he or she would have identified with them. While clans were separated by language, geography, and custom, they interacted for the purposes of trade, marriage, and ritual warfare. On Buka Island, on the atolls, and in the far south and north of Bougainville Island, leaders were selected based on a combination of heredity and achievement. Elsewhere, leaders were largely selected due to their achievement in warfare, sorcery, and feasting, often described as "big man" leadership.[1]

Although Bougainville was colonized in the late nineteenth century, most Bougainvilleans were largely untouched by colonial administration until the 1970s.[2] The main exception was in the Panguna area, about 27 kilometers inland from Kieta, on Bougainville Island, where the Australian colonial

---

[1] H. M. Griffin and A. J. Regan., "Introduction," in *Bougainville: Before the Conflict*, ed. A. J. Regan and H. M. Griffin (Canberra: Pandanus Books, 2005).

[2] D. Oliver, *Black Islanders: A Personal Perspective of Bougainville 1937–1991* (Melbourne: Hyland, 1991).

administration granted Bougainville Copper Limited (BCL) the right to build and operate a copper and gold mine in 1967. Approximately 60 percent of cash benefits from the mine went to the colonial administration (later the independent Papua New Guinea government), 35 percent to foreign shareholders, and 5 percent to Bougainville (4.27 percent to the district government and 1.36 percent to landowners).[3] To accommodate the mine, 1.5 percent of Bougainville's total land area was acquired. Local opposition to the mine met with punitive responses, which reinforced a sense of separate Bougainvillean identity and sentiment in favor of secession that had been developing since the 1950s, based on a range of grievances concerning the colonial administration.[4]

In the lead-up to Papua New Guinea's independence on September 16, 1975, Bougainvillean leaders lobbied the central government to decentralize political power and guarantee Bougainville's future right to secede. In November 1973, the central government agreed to decentralize some power to new district governments. However, it later opted against including provisions guaranteeing decentralization in Papua New Guinea's constitution. This decision brought tensions with the Bougainville district government to a head, and on May 30, 1975, the district government resolved to secede. Two Bougainvillean leaders then went to the UN in August 1975 to (unsuccessfully) present their case for independence to the Committee on Decolonisation. On September 1, 1975, Bougainvillean leaders unilaterally declared independence for the Republic of North Solomons. The central government responded by suspending the district government.[5]

Bougainvillean leaders soon recognized the practical difficulties facing Bougainville, including a lack of international recognition and the amplification of existing internal divisions.[6] As a result, when the Papua New Guinea government chose to exercise restraint, Bougainvillean leaders agreed to engage in negotiations. In August 1976, these negotiations culminated in the

---

[3] The Bougainville Copper Agreement was signed on June 6, 1967, and revised on November 21, 1974. Both agreements were approved and implemented by acts of Parliament, Mining (Bougainville Copper Agreement) Act 1967 (PNG) and Mining (Bougainville Copper Agreement) Act 1974 (PNG).

[4] D. Denoon, *Getting under the Skin: The Bougainville Copper Agreement and the Creation of the Panguna Mine* (Melbourne: Melbourne University Press, 2000).

[5] J. Griffin, "Movements towards Secession 1964–76," in Regan and Griffin, *Bougainville: Before the Conflict*; J. Griffin et al., *Papua New Guinea: A Political History* (Richmond: Heinemann Educational Australia, 1979).

[6] J. L. Momis, "Shaping Leadership through Bougainville Indigenous Values and Catholic Seminary Training – A Personal Journey," in Regan and Griffin, *Bougainville: Before the Conflict*.

Bougainville Agreement, which provided that Bougainville accept Papua New Guinea's sovereignty. In exchange, the Papua New Guinea government undertook to transfer BCL's mining royalties to the Bougainville provincial government (provinces replaced districts at independence) and to add provisions on decentralization to the Papua New Guinea constitution.[7]

The Bougainville provincial government, known as the North Solomons Provincial Government (NSPG), was one of the most effective in Papua New Guinea.[8] Consequently, Bougainville was "relatively tranquil" between 1976 and 1987.[9] However, the Papua New Guinea government was reluctant to decentralize power and resources, which undermined the NSPG's ability to deal with Bougainvilleans' grievances, many of which stemmed from the extensive environmental and social impacts of the Panguna mine. The NSPG's difficulties were compounded in 1983, when the Papua New Guinea government recentralized power. The relationship between the two governments was complicated by the central government's reliance on revenue generated by the mine, as during the mine's seventeen years of operation (from 1972 to 1989), it was responsible for 17 percent of all revenue generated within Papua New Guinea.[10] This led the then-Bougainville premier, Alexis Sarei, to comment, "Are we to be a fat cow, milked for the rest of Papua New Guinea?"[11]

Bougainvillean grievances came to a head in 1988, when a group of young landowners, led by Francis Ona, issued a number of demands to the Papua New Guinea government and BCL, most significantly for a compensation payment of 10 billion Papua New Guinea kina (K). As these demands were not met, the conflict that became known as the "Bougainville crisis" began in November 1988, when young landowners destroyed pylons carrying power lines to the mine. In April 1989, Ona reiterated the claim but added the

---

[7] Bougainville Agreement: Statements and Documents of Agreement between National Government and Provincial Government of North Solomons, August 7, 1976.

[8] J. Griffin and M. Togolo, "North Solomons Province, 1974–1990," in *Political Decentralisation in a New State: The Experience of Provincial Government in Papua New Guinea*, ed. R. J. May and A. J. Regan (Bathurst: Crawford House Press, 1997).

[9] M. Havini, "Perspectives on a Crisis," in *Bougainville: Perspectives on a Crisis*, ed. P. Polomka (Canberra: Australian National University, 1990), 24.

[10] The Panguna mine generated total revenues of K1.754 billion (at the time, the average exchange rate for the Papua New Guinea kina against the United States dollar was about US$1.1). A. J. Regan, "Development and Conflict: Self-Determination in Bougainville," in *Security and Development in the Pacific Islands: Social Resilience in Emerging States*, ed. M. A. Brown (Boulder: Lynne Rienner, 2007).

[11] Quoted in J. Connell, "Bougainville Is Legitimate Again," *Geographical Magazine* 48:11 (1976): 652.

additional demands that the mine close and that Bougainville secede from Papua New Guinea.[12]

By early 1989, groups in most areas of Bougainville actively supported Ona and mobilized militarily as the Bougainville Revolutionary Army (BRA). However, this support was not coherent and consisted of "loose coalitions of interests with diverse and sometimes contradictory goals, all seeing independence as a key to achieving them."[13] This support was also not uniform, as many leaders from Buka Island and the north and central east of Bougainville Island discouraged active support for the BRA because they identified the benefits of continued integration in Papua New Guinea or feared independence under a BRA-dominated government. As the conflict intensified, the Panguna mine was closed in May 1989. Approximately 15,000 to 20,000 non-Bougainvilleans then departed from the region in a movement described as a form of "ethnic cleansing."[14] In June 1989, the Papua New Guinea government declared a state of national emergency to justify deployment of the Papua New Guinea Defence Force (PNGDF).[15]

The NSPG attempted to negotiate a solution to the crisis, but by late 1989, the BRA had the upper hand. Consequently, in January 1990, Papua New Guinea withdrew all public servants. In February 1990, the BRA established the Bougainville Interim Government (BIG), which brought together BRA leaders (Ona became the president) with "civilian" political leaders, including Joseph Kabui, who since 1987 had been premier of the NSPG and who became vice president. The Papua New Guinea government and BIG/BRA agreed to a cease-fire in March 1990, and Papua New Guinean security forces withdrew to clear the way for political negotiations.[16] In exchange, the BRA was supposed to surrender its arms. Instead, Ona made a unilateral declaration of independence on behalf of the BIG/BRA on May 17, 1990.[17] Peace talks in

---

[12] F. Ona, "Letter to Members of the Panguna Landowners' Association, 28 April 1989," in Polomka, *Bougainville: Perspectives on a Crisis*.

[13] Y. Ghai and A. J. Regan, "Bougainville and the Dialectics of Ethnicity, Autonomy and Separation," in *Autonomy and Ethnicity: Negotiating Competing Claims in Multi-ethnic States*, ed. Y. Ghai (Cambridge: Cambridge University Press, 2000), 257.

[14] A. J. Regan, "Why a Neutral Peace Monitoring Force? The Bougainville Conflict and the Peace Process," in *Without a Gun: Australia's Experiences Monitoring Peace in Bougainville, 1997–2001*, ed. M. Wehner and D. Denoon (Canberra: Pandanus Books, 2001), 3.

[15] R. Namaliu, prime minister of Papua New Guinea, "Address to Declare a National Emergency on Bougainville, National Broadcasting Commission radio, 23 June 1989," in Polomka, *Bougainville: Perspectives on a Crisis*.

[16] Agreement to End Hostilities on Bougainville (Bougainville Ceasefire Agreement), between the Papua New Guinea government and the BRA, 1 March 1990.

[17] F. Ona, on behalf of the interim government of the Republic of Bougainville, *REQUEST FOR RECOGNITION OF BOUGAINVILLE AS AN INDEPENDENT REPUBLIC*, letter to

July 1990 failed,[18] and in August 1990, the Papua New Guinea government suspended the NSPG and implemented a blockade of Bougainville.

Once the Papua New Guinean security forces withdrew, the unifying "pan-Bougainville" opponent was removed. BRA elements became involved in localized conflict, much of which had nothing to do with secession. The nascent BIG found itself unable to effectively govern, and "anarchy" developed.[19] As a result, in September 1990, Buka Island leaders sought the return of the PNGDF to provide protection from the BRA. In February 1991, the Papua New Guinea government agreed to return services and establish interim legal authorities on Buka Island.[20] With PNGDF encouragement, armed groups on Buka Island coalesced as the Bougainville Resistance Forces (BRF). The BRF did not necessarily oppose independence but was primarily concerned with offering protection against the BRA. By December 1990, there was effectively "civil war" between the BRF and BRA on Buka Island, which later expanded to Bougainville Island.[21] Therefore, by the mid-1990s, the crisis had two dimensions: the secessionist struggle between the Papua New Guinean security forces and the BRA and the internal conflict between – and within – BRA and BRF elements, often based on localized concerns or criminal activity.[22]

A September 1994 cease-fire[23] and October 1994 peace conference[24] created space for a group of moderate Bougainvillean leaders to emerge. In November 1994, the Papua New Guinea government agreed that they could establish a Bougainville Transitional Government (BTG) in place of the NSPG.[25] The

---

diplomatic missions in Port Moresby and foreign governments, enclosing the "Declaration of Independence of the Republic of Bougainville," May 16, 1990. This declaration was later annulled by the Honiara Declaration on Peace, Reconciliation and Rehabilitation on Bougainville, between the government of Papua New Guinea and the BIG/BRA, January 23, 1991.

[18] Endeavour Accord on Dialogue and Return of Services to Bougainville, between the Papua New Guinea government and the BIG/BRA, August 5, 1990.

[19] Regan, "Why a Neutral Peace Monitoring Force?," 4.

[20] Kavieng Agreement, between the government of Papua New Guinea and chiefs from Buka Island, February 1991.

[21] M. Spriggs, "Bougainville Update: August 1990 to May 1991," in *The Bougainville Crisis: 1991 Update*, ed. M. Spriggs and D. Denoon (Bathurst: Crawford House Press, 1992), 12.

[22] Regan, "Why a Neutral Peace Monitoring Force?'

[23] Honiara Commitment to Peace on Bougainville, between the Papua New Guinea government and the BIG/BRA, September 3, 1994; Honiara Ceasefire Agreement, between the Papua New Guinea government and the BIG/BRA, September 8, 1994.

[24] Arawa Peace Conference in October 1994, at which security was provided by a multilateral South Pacific peacekeeping force. This led to the Arawa Resolution, agreed upon by the Papua New Guinea government and representatives of the BRA, October 10, 1994.

[25] Charter of Mirigini for a New Bougainville, between the Papua New Guinea government, the North Nasioi Peace Committee, and several BRA commanders, November 25, 1994; Waigani Communique, between the Papua New Guinea government and the BTG, May 18, 1995.

BTG was established in April 1995, with the BRF as its combatant force. Although the BIG opposed the BTG, over the next two years they managed to establish communications.[26] However, this intra-Bougainvillean peace process was derailed in January 1996 after the PNGDF fired on a BIG/BRA delegation, reescalating the conflict. It also motivated elements of the BRA and BRF to work together against the allegedly ill-disciplined behavior of the PNGDF, which "demonstrated the PNGDF's incapacity to defeat the BRA."[27] In response, in 1997, Papua New Guinea prime minister Julius Chan engaged mercenaries to recapture the Panguna mine.[28] This move was opposed by PNGDF commanders, who forced the mercenaries from the country. The ensuing scandal created an opportunity to advance the peace process. At the Papua New Guinea level, this was assisted by the replacement of Chan with the more moderate Bill Skate and increasing questions over the credibility of a military solution to the crisis. At the Bougainville level, the BIG/BRA leadership realized that there was a growing sense of war-weariness and that military victory would probably be achieved only at a "terrible cost in terms of divisions amongst Bougainvilleans," both over the issue of Bougainville's political future and as a result of localized conflict.[29]

THE BOUGAINVILLE PEACE PROCESS

While the peace process was often facilitated by Australia and New Zealand, it was "largely locally-initiated and controlled,"[30] and consequently, foreign intervention was "light."[31] This book considers the peace process in detail, as the resulting peace agreement outlines many of the limits on the institutional structure, power, and functions of Bougainville's autonomous government. In addition, much of the Bougainville constitution deals with mechanisms for implementing the agreement. Consequently, the process of negotiating this agreement was effectively an early stage of the constitution-making process.

The peace process can be broken into two phases. Since the crisis had resulted in deep divisions between the Bougainvillean factions, the first phase

---

[26] Joint Communiqué, agreed by BTG and the BIG/BRA, December 18, 1995.
[27] Regan, "Why a Neutral Peace Monitoring Force?," 8.
[28] Sandline Agreement for the Provision of Military Assistance, between the Independent State of Papua New Guinea and Sandline International, January 31, 1997.
[29] A. J. Regan, "The Bougainville Intervention: Political Legitimacy and Sustainable Peace-building," in *Intervention and State-Building in the Pacific: The Legitimacy of "Cooperative Intervention,"* ed. G. Fry and T. T. Kabutaulaka (Manchester: Manchester University Press, 2008), 187.
[30] Ibid., 184.   [31] Regan, *Light Intervention*.

was occupied with agreeing on a common position for the negotiations with the Papua New Guinea government. The second focused on negotiating a political settlement with the Papua New Guinea government.[32]

Phase I of the peace process

Phase I began in July 1997, with talks at the Burnham military base in New Zealand among seventy-five Bougainvillean leaders. These talks resulted in the Burnham Declaration, in which attendees committed to unity, reconciliation, a cease-fire, and peaceful negotiations with the Papua New Guinea government.[33] Further talks at Burnham in October 1997 were attended by 120 Bougainvillean leaders, local combatant commanders, and officials representing the Papua New Guinea government. These talks resulted in the Burnham Truce, in which leaders agreed to an interim cease-fire and to establish the neutral regional Truce Monitoring Group (TMG).[34] In November 1997, talks were held in Australia on arrangements for the 250-strong unarmed TMG, which deployed in December 1997.[35]

In January 1998, 300 Papua New Guinea government officials and Bougainvillean leaders met at Lincoln University in New Zealand and negotiated the Lincoln Agreement. This agreement provided for a permanent cease-fire; the establishment of the Peace Monitoring Group (PMG) to take over from the TMG and a UN political office in Bougainville (referred to as the UN Observer Mission in Bougainville [UNOMB] due to Papua New Guinea sensitivities) to monitor the peace process; the election of a Bougainville

---

[32] Regan, "The Bougainville Intervention."

[33] Burnham Declaration by Bougainville Leaders on the Re-Establishment of a Process for Lasting Peace and Justice on Bougainville, by the BIG/BRA and BTG/BRF, July 18, 1997; Joint Communique: The Bougainville Leaders Meeting, Burnham, Christchurch, New Zealand, by the BIG/BRA and BTG/BRF, July 18, 1997; Burnham Declaration – National Government Response, by the Papua New Guinea government, undated.

[34] Burnham II Preparatory Talks, Record of Understandings, between the Papua New Guinea government, BIG/BRA and BTG/BRF, 10 October 1997; Bei Isi Noken Pait, The Burnham Truce, between the Papua New Guinea government, BIG/BRA and BTG/BRF, 10 October 1997.

[35] Second Official Preparatory Talks on Bougainville – Held in Cairns, Queensland Australia November 18–23 1997 Summary of Discussions, November 1997; Cairns Commitment on Implementation of the Agreement Concerning the Neutral Regional Truce Monitoring Group (TBG) for Bougainville, between Papua New Guinea government, Australian government, Fiji government, Vanuatu government, New Zealand government, BIG/BRA, and BTG/BRF, November 24, 1997; Agreement between New Zealand, Papua New Guinea, Australia, Fiji, and Vanuatu Concerning the Neutral Truce Monitoring Group for Bougainville, between Papua New Guinea government, Australian government, Fiji government, Vanuatu government, and New Zealand government, December 5, 1997.

reconciliation government; the "phased withdrawal" of the PNGDF; and amnesty and pardons for persons involved in crisis-related offences.[36] On April 30, 1998, the cease-fire was signed in Bougainville[37] and the 300-strong unarmed PMG replaced the TMG.[38] In August 1998, the UNOMB began operating, with six international personnel and several locally employed staff. In August 1998, 5,000 leaders endorsed the Burnham Declaration at a pan-Bougainvillean conference.[39] However, divisions remained, as pro-integration leaders from Buka Island threatened to secede from Bougainville unless they were given a significant role.[40]

In December 1998, leaders from the BIG and BTG created the Bougainville Constituent Assembly to adopt a constitution for the Bougainville Reconciliation Government, with the Bougainville People's Congress (BPC) to act as its legislature.[41] Elections for the BPC were held in May 1999 and Kabui was elected president. However, John Momis, an MP in the Papua New Guinea Parliament representing the Bougainville region, challenged the formation of the BPC on the basis that Papua New Guinea had changed the law so that provincial governments were no longer separately elected but instead consisted of the MPs from that province, along with representatives of community groups, with the regional MP as provincial governor.[42] Although Bougainville had been exempted from this change between 1995 and 1998 in order to facilitate the peace process, the exemption had expired on December 31, 1998. Momis argued that this meant that a new provincial government should be formed, of which he should be governor. Momis had particularly strong support from

---

[36] Lincoln Agreement on Peace, Security and Development on Bougainville, between the Papua New Guinea government, BIG/BRA, and BTG/BRF, January 23, 1998 (acknowledged by the president of the UN Security Council, *Statement by the President of the Security Council*, UN Doc. S/PRST/1998/10, April 22, 1998).

[37] Arawa Agreement Covering Implementation of the Ceasefire, Annex 1 to the Lincoln Agreement: Agreement Covering Implementation of the Ceasefire, between the Papua New Guinea government, BIG/BRA, and BTG/BRF, April 30, 1998.

[38] Protocol Concerning the Peace Monitoring Group, Made Pursuant to the Agreement between Australia, Papua New Guinea, Fiji, New Zealand and Vanuatu Concerning the Neutral Truce Monitoring Group for Bougainville, Done at Port Moresby on 5 December 1997, between Papua New Guinea government, Australian government, Fiji government, Vanuatu government, and New Zealand government, April 29, 1998.

[39] Buin Declaration of the Pan Bougainville Leaders Congress 20–22 August 1998, between women's representatives and chiefs from north, central, and south Bougainville, August 22, 1998.

[40] Regan, "Development and Conflict."

[41] *Bougainville Peace Process Minute*, December 14, 1998, recording agreement of the officials to the attached Annex 2 to the Lincoln Agreement Basic Agreement Concerning the Bougainville Reconciliation Government (BRG), unsigned draft agreement, December 1998.

[42] Organic Law on Provincial and Local-level Governments (1995) (PNG).

groups on Buka Island, where apprehension was growing that the BRA would dominate the BPC. Momis's legal challenge "had the effect of freshening old political wounds," and tensions mounted in early 1999.[43]

New impetus to achieve a consensus between Bougainvillean leaders was provided in July 1999, when Prime Minister Bill Skate agreed that the Papua New Guinea government would consider granting a "high level of autonomy" to Bougainville.[44] Although Skate was replaced in August 1999, the process did not lose momentum as the Papua New Guinea government indicated that it might consider holding a referendum on Bougainville's future. While this announcement united most Bougainville parties, several leaders from Buka Island threatened to administer the island separately from the rest of Bougainville should that referendum decide in favor of independence. Conversely, hard-line BRA members were concerned that the proposal was designed to steer Bougainville away from independence.

On November 25, 1999, Momis's legal challenge succeeded, and he became governor of Bougainville and swore in the Bougainville Interim Provincial Government (BIPG) on March 30, 2000. However, a rapprochement had developed between Momis and his supporters and Kabui and BPC leaders, as both sides recognized the necessity of achieving a joint Bougainville position. Consequently, Momis and Kabui agreed that the BIPG would make its decisions in consultation with the BPC. This permitted the continued operation of the two institutions: the BPC as a 106-member elected body without formal powers and the BIPG as a thirty-six-member appointed body with the legal powers of a provincial government. They also agreed on a joint negotiating position, which rested on two key principles: that Bougainville would seek a high level of autonomy and that a referendum on Bougainville's political future should be held.[45]

Phase II of the peace process

Bougainvillean leaders were then able to begin negotiations with the Papua New Guinea government. By this time, opinion within the Papua New

---

[43] A. Downer, *The Bougainville Crisis: An Australian Perspective* (Canberra: Commonwealth of Australia, 2001), 25.

[44] Hutjena Minute and "Fundamental Principles for the Future of Bougainville," agreed by the Papua New Guinea government and the BPC, June 30, 1999.

[45] Greenhouse Memorandum, the Joint Bougainville Negotiating Position for Negotiations with the Government of Papua New Guinea, between the BPC, BIPG, and Leitana Council of Elders, December 14, 1999 (updated by the *Bougainville Common Negotiating Position: Expanded Details*, March 8, 2000).

Guinea government had shifted in favor of ending the crisis. It was far less anxious to reopen the Panguna mine, as the destruction of its infrastructure and poor global copper prices meant that resumption of mining was a remote possibility, and major mines and oil and gas projects had been established elsewhere in Papua New Guinea. However, there was concern that any settlement viewed as favorable to Bougainville's future independence could trigger separatist movements elsewhere. There was also concern that if Bougainville was given extensive autonomy, this could challenge the reduced autonomy of other provincial governments.

Despite this, in March 2000, the Papua New Guinea government agreed to "acknowledge...the aspirations" of Bougainvilleans for a referendum on independence.[46] From May to September 2000, Papua New Guinea and Bougainville leaders held further talks.[47] However, after the Papua New Guinea cabinet decided against any referendum that contained the option of independence, in early December 2000 the Bougainville delegation called for international assistance. Accordingly, in mid-December 2000, Australian foreign minister Alexander Downer proposed that the Bougainvillean leadership accept deferral of the referendum.[48] They agreed, if the proposal was also accepted by the Papua New Guinea government. This occurred on January 17, 2001. Papua New Guinea and Bougainville leaders then met from January 18 to 21 to agree on principles for the referendum.[49] From February to May, there were a series of talks in Australia among 180 former combatants to negotiate an accompanying program of weapons disposal.[50] The text of the Bougainville Peace Agreement was then finalized in early July, and it was signed in Bougainville on August 30, 2001.[51] A meeting of the Bougainville Joint Assemblies (the BIPG and BPC sitting together) was immediately held to brief leaders. Leaders were encouraged to engage in an awareness campaign

---

[46] Loloata Understanding, agreed by the Papua New Guinea government, BPC, BIPG, and the Leitana Council of Elders, March 23, 2000; Hutjena Record, agreed by the Papua New Guinea government, BPC, and John Momis (as governor of Bougainville), December 15, 1999.

[47] Gateway Communiqué, agreed by the Papua New Guinea government, BPC, and BIPG, June 9, 2000, attaching the *Preliminary Working Draft of Proposal for a "Special Status" Agreement between the Government of Papua New Guinea and the People of Bougainville*, June 8, 2000.

[48] Downer, *The Bougainville Crisis*.

[49] Kokopo Agreement: Agreed Principles on Referendum, agreed by the Papua New Guinea government, BPC, and BIPG, witnessed by Noel Sinclair, director, UNOMB, January 26, 2001.

[50] Rotokas Record: Joint Bougainville Ex-combatants Agreement on Weapons Disposal, between the BRA and BRF, May 3, 2001; Peace Process Consultative Committee Agreement on Weapons Disposal, between the Papua New Guinea government, BRA, and BRF, May 9, 2001.

[51] Bougainville Peace Agreement, between the Papua New Guinea government, BPC, BIPG, BRA, and BRF, August 30, 2001.

by returning to their home communities and explaining the Bougainville Peace Agreement "in as many places as possible."[52]

The Bougainville Peace Agreement awareness campaign was indicative of the transparency maintained and awareness raised throughout the peace process. The Papua New Guinea minister for Bougainville affairs made frequent public statements relating to the process, tabled important agreements in the Papua New Guinea Parliament, and communicated with the media.[53] Joint awareness teams, made up of Papua New Guinea government officials and representatives of the Bougainville parties, toured Bougainville to conduct awareness programs. Both the TMG and PMG were mandated to "spread the message of peace" by facilitating reconciliation, promoting confidence in the process, and providing information.[54] There were also numerous reports in publications and on radio programs. However, perceptions of these efforts were mixed. One former BRA leader reported that leaders spent a significant amount of time consulting people.[55] In contrast, a women's leader reported that the level of consultation at the local level was often thin, with the information gap filled by women's leaders.[56] Overall, given the difficulties of transportation and communication and the limited capacity of the BPC and BIPG, leaders made a good attempt to promote awareness and consultation. If the peace process is classified as an early stage of the constitution-making process, it therefore appears to have followed the recommendations on participation made in the literature.

Negotiations were often highly inclusive and involved large numbers of people, which also reflected the literature. This approach was adopted in response to lessons learned from peace talks during the early 1990s that had mainly involved senior leaders, who "experienced difficulties in 'selling' outcomes to combatant groups and wider communities."[57] In particular, the

---

[52] Joint Bougainville Assemblies, *Implementing the Bougainville Peace Agreement: Briefing Paper for Joint Assemblies Meeting* (Arawa: Joint Bougainville Assemblies, August 31, 2001); Bougainville Technical Team, *Bougainville Peace Agreement Analysis for Use in an Awareness Campaign* (Arawa: Bougainville Technical Team, August 2001).

[53] See, for example, Y. Hriehwazi, "Paper Gives Details of Bougainville Constitution," *The National*, August 31, 2001; "Paper Outlines Terms of Bougainville Accord," *Papua New Guinea Post-Courier*, August 31, 2001.

[54] Interview with a former member of the PMG, November 5, 2010; Agreement between New Zealand, Papua New Guinea, Australia, Fiji, and Vanuatu Concerning the Neutral Truce Monitoring Group for Bougainville.

[55] Interview with a former BRA commander and member of the ABG, November 2, 2010.

[56] Interview with a Bougainvillean women's leader, January 25, 2011.

[57] Regan, "The Bougainville Intervention," 190.

amorphous nature of both combatant factions meant that high-level agreements did not necessarily trickle down to the local level. To avoid this, starting in June 1997, talks included local BRA and BRF commanders, and some agreements were signed by leaders and local commanders as well as local traditional authorities and church leaders. Because local commanders participated in the talks, they understood and felt committed to the agreed outcomes. They also returned to their units and were able to promote awareness of and build support for the process. The participation of local traditional authorities and church leaders meant that local communities were aware of and able to monitor the implementation of the agreements. While the large scale of some of the negotiations (in one case, as many as 5,000 attendees) might suggest that the participation of individuals was relatively superficial, Bougainvillean culture requires that people participate to support decisions, even if that participation involves saying very little and instead acting as the "eyes and ears" of their communities.[58]

The high level of inclusiveness also reflected local sociopolitical practices, which emphasize extensive popular participation in decision making. In particular, since chiefs are appointed based on achievement (in some cases, combined with heredity), society is relatively egalitarian.[59] Moreover, many of the larger negotiations provided time for the customary practice of *taraut* (vomiting), which involves speakers venting their pent-up frustration and anger.[60] Customary methods of diplomacy were also utilized, as talks involved representatives of traditional authorities, churches, and women's groups. Interviewees reported that these representatives accepted responsibility for promoting awareness of the process, which linked the high-level negotiations to consensus and reconciliation at the local level and was indicative of a liberal-local hybrid approach.[61]

---

[58] Ibid.; Boege and Garasu, "Papua New Guinea: A Success Story."

[59] Interview with a former member of the PMG, November 5, 2010; personal communication from a Bougainvillean intellectual, January 24, 2011; G. White, *Indigenous Governance in Melanesia, State, Society and Governance in Melanesia Targeted Research Paper for AusAID* (Canberra: Australian National University, 2006).

[60] E. P. Wolfers, "International Peace Missions in Bougainville, Papua New Guinea, 1990–2005: Host State Perspectives," paper delivered at the Regional Forum on Reinventing Government, Exchange and Transfer of Innovations for Transparent Governance and State Capacity, Nadi, Fiji, February 20–22, 2006.

[61] Interview with a Bougainvillean women's leader, January 25, 2011; interview with a former BRA commander and member of the ABG, November 2, 2010; interview with an ABG official and member of a council of elders, January 22, 2011; A. Titus, speaking at Building Sustainable Peace in Bougainville Conference, Hutjena Secondary School, Buka, June 13, 2007.

The Bougainville Peace Agreement

An organic law and constitutional amendment were required to give effect to the Bougainville Peace Agreement.[62] These were presented to the Papua New Guinea Parliament on October 17, 2001.[63] Debate on the bills was deferred for several months due to difficulties in ensuring a sufficient number of MPs were present to meet the necessary voting thresholds and due to concerns about the Bougainville Peace Agreement setting a precedent for other provinces. Accordingly, both bills were entitled "Peace-Building on Bougainville" to emphasize that their main purpose was "to help build lasting peace by peaceful means."[64] Despite this, they have inspired other Papua New Guinea provinces to seek increased autonomy.[65] The first vote was on January 23, 2002, with eighty-six (of a total of 109) MPs voting in favor, none against. The second vote was on March 27, 2002, with eighty-five votes in favor, none against. It has been argued that this exhibits "the strength of the bipartisan commitment to lasting peace."[66]

The Bougainville Peace Agreement set out the three main elements agreed upon during phase II of the peace process. First, Bougainville was granted extensive territorial autonomy. Powers and functions were divided between the Papua New Guinea government and Autonomous Bougainville Government (ABG)[67] in accordance with two exhaustive lists.[68] The fifty-nine functions and powers available to Bougainville include culture, education, health, land and natural resources, local-level government and trade, commerce, and

---

[62] Organic Law on Peace-building in Bougainville – Autonomous Bougainville Government and Bougainville Referendum No. 29/2002 (PNG) (in force 7 August 2003); Constitutional Amendment 23 of 2002, on Peace-Building on Bougainville – Autonomous Bougainville Government and Bougainville Referendum 2002 (PNG).

[63] M. Avei, minister for Bougainville affairs, *Ministerial Statement on Presentation of the Bougainville Peace Agreement* (Port Moresby: Papua New Guinea National Parliament, October 17, 2001).

[64] M. Morauta, Papua New Guinea prime minister, quoted in "Government Agrees on Gazettal of Peace Deals," *Papua New Guinea Post-Courier*, November 14, 2001; interview with an international adviser to the Papua New Guinea government, January 24, 2010.

[65] Particularly East New Britain, West New Britain, and Morobe.

[66] E. P. Wolfers, "'Joint Creation': The *Bougainville Peace Agreement* – And Beyond," in A. Carl and L. Garasu, *Weaving Consensus: The Papua New Guinea – Bougainville Peace Process* (London: Conciliation Resources in collaboration with BICWF, 2002), 49.

[67] The abbreviation "ABG" is used as it is commonly used by the autonomous Bougainville government and Bougainvilleans.

[68] Bougainville Peace Agreement, cl. 46 and 47. Responsibility for subjects not included in either list remained with the Papua New Guinea government. Constitution of the Independent State of Papua New Guinea 1975 (Papua New Guinea Constitution), s. 292.

industry.[69] While the powers and functions provided to the ABG were extensive, they initially remained with the Papua New Guinea government. When established, the ABG had the same powers and functions as the BIPG.[70] Further powers and functions were then to be transferred after the ABG gave the Papua New Guinea government twelve months' advance notice (to allow time for necessary funding and administrative arrangements).[71] The two governments were to cooperate to draw up a joint implementation plan to affect the transfer.[72] The Papua New Guinea government does not have the power to withdraw transferred powers or to suspend the ABG.[73]

The ABG was empowered to create certain public service institutions, including a police force.[74] This was controversial, and complex arrangements were included to provide for cooperation between Bougainville institutions and their Papua New Guinea counterparts.[75] The ABG was also given the power to establish its own court system. However, Papua New Guinea's highest courts retain the power of review.[76] Connected to this, the ABG was empowered to create its own criminal laws and was given limited powers to amend the Papua New Guinea Criminal Code.[77] The Papua New Guinea government also agreed to consider giving the ABG the power to "make laws permitting courts or Councils of Elders to require clan-groups to which persons convicted of criminal offences belong to meet customary, non-custodial obligations."[78] This noncommittal approach was adopted as this issue was too controversial to resolve during the negotiations.[79] The ABG was further authorized to "provide additional guarantees of human rights" that "do not abrogate the human rights provisions" in the Papua New Guinea constitution and to "qualify human rights incidental to the exercise of its powers and functions."[80] The Bougainville delegation had originally sought to determine a separate human rights regime, with their concern being to limit

---

[69] Bougainville Peace Agreement, cl. 52; Papua New Guinea Constitution, s. 290.
[70] Bougainville Peace Agreement, cl. 102; Papua New Guinea Constitution, s. 294(2).
[71] Bougainville Peace Agreement, cl. 101 and 104; Papua New Guinea Constitution, ss. 294 and 295.
[72] Bougainville Peace Agreement, cl. 115.   [73] Ibid., cl. 268.
[74] Ibid., cl. 114; Papua New Guinea Constitution, ss. 310–318.
[75] A. J. Regan, "The Bougainville Political Settlement and the Prospects for Sustainable Peace," *Pacific Economic Bulletin* 17:1 (2002): 121.
[76] Bougainville Peace Agreement, cl. 276, 284 and 285; Papua New Guinea Constitution, ss. 306–309.
[77] Bougainville Peace Agreement, cl. 295–297; Papua New Guinea Constitution, s. 291.
[78] Bougainville Peace Agreement, cl. 128.
[79] Regan, "Resolving the Bougainville Self-Determination Dispute."
[80] Bougainville Peace Agreement, cl. 123–125; Papua New Guinea Constitution, ss. 303–304.

the right of freedom of movement of people from other parts of Papua New Guinea to Bougainville, as the internal migration of mine workers had contributed to the crisis. However, Papua New Guinea negotiators emphasized the need to protect minority rights. The Bougainville delegation eventually capitulated after its advisers warned that insisting on this claim could endanger the support of the international community if they later used such a power to develop policies that were perceived to be discriminatory. In any event, the power to "qualify" rights may still "enable Bougainville to pass laws that involve indirect limits on most rights."[81]

In order to exercise its functions and powers, the Bougainville Peace Agreement provided that the ABG would be given sufficient revenue-raising powers to enable it to become fiscally self-reliant.[82] However, Bougainville would continue to "make a fair contribution" to the Papua New Guinea government's costs.[83] To enable the ABG to achieve fiscal self-reliance, certain Papua New Guinea taxes collected in Bougainville were to go into a trust account or be paid directly to the ABG.[84] The ABG was also given the power to collect certain other taxes. While the Papua New Guinea Internal Revenue Commission would initially collect all taxes, the ABG was given the power to establish its own tax office.[85] Until the ABG achieved fiscal self-reliance, the Papua New Guinea government would provide grants to it, including a one-off establishment grant, an annual unconditional grant to cover the recurrent costs of functions for which it is responsible, an annual restoration and development grant, and conditional specific-purpose grants.[86] Intergovernmental relations between the Papua New Guinea government and ABG relating to the implementation of the autonomy and funding arrangements would be managed via the Joint Supervisory Body (JSB).[87] Disputes that cannot be resolved through the JSB are referred to mediation or arbitration, and failing that, the courts.[88]

---

[81] A. J. Regan, "Resolving the Bougainville Self-Determination Dispute: Autonomy or Complex Power-sharing?," in *Settling Self-Determination Disputes: Complex Power-Sharing in Theory and Practice*, ed. M. Weller and B. Metzger (Leiden and Boston: Martinus Nijhoff Publishers, 2008), 144.

[82] That is, when revenue from company tax, 70 per cent of value-added tax, and customs duties is equal to the value of the recurrent grant made to the ABG on a sustainable basis. Bougainville Peace Agreement, cl. 134 and 137; Papua New Guinea Constitution, s. 324(a).

[83] Bougainville Peace Agreement, cl. 135; Papua New Guinea Constitution, s. 324(b).

[84] Bougainville Peace Agreement, cl. 138, 140, 141, and 143.   [85] Ibid., cl. 145–146.

[86] Ibid., cl. 149, 151, 160, 163, and 168; Papua New Guinea Constitution, s. 326.

[87] Bougainville Peace Agreement, cl. 263–264; Papua New Guinea Constitution, s. 332–337.

[88] Bougainville Peace Agreement, cl. 265–267; Papua New Guinea Constitution, s. 334.

The Papua New Guinea government retained those powers "consistent with national sovereignty," including over defense, foreign relations, immigration, and central banking and powers required for direct implementation of the Papua New Guinea constitution.[89] However, several of its powers were limited. For example, it must seek the ABG's recommendations relating to work permits for Bougainville,[90] and it must assist Bougainville to establish a commercial bank, with the option left open for additional banking powers to be transferred to Bougainville.[91] It must also delegate control over aspects of international civil aviation, shipping, trade, and post to the ABG.[92] Most significantly, it must establish mechanisms to consult the ABG in relation to its foreign relations, and it may allow the ABG to send representatives to regional meetings.[93] Any international agreement entered into by the Papua New Guinea government intended to alter the autonomy arrangements will take effect only with the approval of both governments.[94] The ABG also has the right to seek the Papua New Guinea government's approval for it to negotiate international agreements "of particular relevance to Bougainville" and to obtain foreign aid.[95]

Second, the Bougainville Peace Agreement provided for a constitutionally guaranteed referendum on Bougainville's future political status, including the option of independence.[96] The referendum is to be held no earlier than ten years and no later than fifteen years after the election of the first ABG, after weapons disposal has been completed and once the ABG has achieved internationally accepted standards of good governance.[97] The date of the referendum will be decided after consultation between the Papua New Guinea government and the ABG, and the ABG may decide not to hold it.[98] The outcome of the referendum will be advisory only and subject to ratification by the Papua New Guinea Parliament.[99]

Third, the Bougainville Peace Agreement provided for a three-stage weapons disposal process.[100] Stage I involved containerization of BRA and BRF weapons

---

[89] Bougainville Peace Agreement, cl. 50 and 51; Papua New Guinea Constitution, s. 289(2).
[90] Bougainville Peace Agreement, cl. 81.   [91] Ibid., cl. 90 and 91.   [92] Ibid., cl. 92.
[93] Ibid., cl. 69–70.
[94] Bougainville Peace Agreement, cl. 54 and 75; Papua New Guinea Constitution, s. 293.
[95] Bougainville Peace Agreement, cl. 73 and 174; Papua New Guinea Constitution, s. 327.
[96] Bougainville Peace Agreement, cl. 309–310; Papua New Guinea Constitution, ss. 338(1) and 339.
[97] Bougainville Peace Agreement, cl. 312–313; Papua New Guinea Constitution, s. 338(2)-338(6).
[98] Bougainville Peace Agreement, cl. 312; Papua New Guinea Constitution, s. 338.
[99] Bougainville Peace Agreement, cl. 311; Papua New Guinea Constitution, s. 342.
[100] Bougainville Peace Agreement, cl. 329 and Peace Process Consultative Committee Agreement on Weapons Disposal.

and withdrawal of the Papua New Guinea security forces. Stage II provided that after amendments to the Papua New Guinea constitution to implement the Bougainville Peace Agreement were passed, containerized weapons would be put under UNOMB supervision. Stage III involved UNOMB verification of whether there was substantial compliance with the process and whether the level of security was conducive to holding elections for the ABG. Arrangements for the demilitarization of Bougainville were linked to this process. Accordingly, Papua New Guinea security forces may be deployed in Bougainville only on a "cooperative basis following consultation" between the two governments.[101] In exchange, Bougainville former combatant groups had to disband after their role in implementing the weapons disposal plan was complete. Former combatants were also required to sign a "Statement of Commitment to Unified Structures" created in accordance with the Bougainville Peace Agreement.[102] To encourage hard-line combatants to participate in the peace and weapons disposal processes, the Bougainville Peace Agreement repeated the amnesty and pardon provisions of the Lincoln Agreement.[103] There was also recognition that "no side was without guilt," so it was a "good thing to close off the conflict."[104] However, this was controversial, with women's leaders calling for amnesties to be conditional on a reconciliation process involving "public recognition of wrong done and forgiveness."[105] In this regard, there was no restriction on establishing a truth and reconciliation commission, and people could make claims in the civil courts or through the judicial human rights enforcement processes provided in the Papua New Guinea constitution.

Overall, the Bougainville Peace Agreement represented a novel way to settle Bougainville's self-determination dispute, as the combination of a constitutionally guaranteed deferred referendum and autonomy arrangements is "almost unique."[106] The level of autonomy available to Bougainville is "asymmetrical," since it is much more extensive than that given to the other provinces of Papua New Guinea.[107] Indeed, Bougainville's powers concerning foreign relations make "the quality of Bougainville's autonomy significantly

---

[101] Bougainville Peace Agreement, cl. 64 and 268.   [102] Ibid., cl. 340 and 344.
[103] Ibid., cl. 331 and 340(d); Papua New Guinea Constitution, s. 344.
[104] Interview with a former member of the PMG, November 5, 2010; interview with an international adviser to the BRA and BCC, January 18, 2010.
[105] Sr. L. Garasu, quoted in P. Howley, *Breaking Spears and Mending Hearts: Peacemakers and Restorative Justice in Bougainville* (London: Zed Books, 2002), 182.
[106] Y. Ghai and A. J. Regan, "Unitary State, Devolution, Autonomy, Secession: State Building and Nation Building in Bougainville, Papua New Guinea," *The Round Table* 95:386 (2006): 597.
[107] Ibid.

different from most autonomy agreements and blur the boundaries of sovereignty."[108] The potentially extensive nature of Bougainville's autonomy meant that the process of implementing the Bougainville Peace Agreement necessitated a process that verged on state building. Not only were new legislative, executive, and judicial institutions to be created, but administrative institutions, including a police force, were to be formed as well.

MAIN ELEMENTS OF THE CONSTITUTION-MAKING PROCESS

The Bougainville Peace Agreement and Part XIV of the Papua New Guinea constitution provided the framework for the constitution-making process. The Bougainville Peace Agreement provided that the BIPG – in consultation with the BPC – was to establish a "broadly representative" constitutional commission to "consult widely with the people of Bougainville" and prepare a draft constitution. A "broadly representative" constituent assembly would then debate and adopt the constitution. Both institutions had to "meet internationally accepted standards of good governance,"[109] which was interpreted to mean basic liberal standards. These provisions were uncontroversial and were agreed upon between the Bougainville parties and Papua New Guinea government at an early stage of the negotiations.[110] The Bougainville Peace Agreement also required that the Papua New Guinea government be "kept informed and allowed adequate opportunity to make its views known as proposals for the Bougainville Constitution are developed."[111] Before the constitution was adopted by the assembly, the Papua New Guinea government had to be consulted about its contents. After the assembly adopted the constitution, it then had to be provided to the Papua New Guinea government for endorsement before it came into effect.[112]

The Bougainville Peace Agreement and Part XIV of the Papua New Guinea constitution also outlined certain essential principles that the Bougainville constitution had to respect. It had to provide for the organization and structures of the ABG in a manner consistent with the Bougainville Peace Agreement and the names of Bougainville and the ABG. It also had to meet "internationally accepted standards of good governance,"[113] again interpreted to mean basic

---

[108] Regan, "Resolving the Bougainville Self-Determination Dispute," 142–143.
[109] Bougainville Peace Agreement, cl. 14–19; Papua New Guinea Constitution, ss. 281 and 284.
[110] Gateway Communiqué.   [111] Bougainville Peace Agreement, cl. 15.
[112] Bougainville Peace Agreement, cl. 15, 22–25; Papua New Guinea Constitution, ss. 283–285.
[113] Bougainville Peace Agreement, cl. 11, 13 and 21; Papua New Guinea Constitution, s. 282.

liberal standards. The ABG had to include a "mainly elected" legislature and an "accountable" executive body. In addition, it could include an "impartial judiciary" and "institutions responsible for public administration."[114]

The time frame given for the process

In order to provide incentives for compliance, the Bougainville Peace Agreement created linkages between the weapons disposal process and implementation of the political settlement. Accordingly, the amendments to the Papua New Guinea constitution implementing the Bougainville Peace Agreement could not come into effect until completion of stage II of the weapons disposal process.[115] By late 2002, it appeared that the UNOMB would verify that stage II was complete by mid-2003. As the constitutional amendments provided for the retrospective recognition of acts conducted prior to their coming into effect,[116] in order to avoid continued delay the Papua New Guinea government agreed that the Bougainville parties could begin the constitution-making process.[117]

From mid-2002, the BIPG and BPC consulted regarding the constitution-making process. They agreed that the mandated Bougainville Constitutional Commission (BCC)[118] should "complete its work as soon as practicable," while at the same time "ensuring that it undertakes adequate consultation with the people."[119] It was originally hoped that the BCC's work would be completed in four months, with one round of public consultation and the final draft completed by the end of January 2003.[120] However, the process was given a relatively open-ended timetable, with equal emphasis placed on producing a constitution and on ensuring that it reflected Bougainvilleans' views. This fits with the literature, which concludes that an unhurried timetable is preferable as it leaves time to build consensus and undertake public consultation.

The decision to leave the timetable relatively open-ended bore fruit, because two factors necessitated delays in the process. First, there were delays

---

[114] Bougainville Peace Agreement, cl. 28, 29, 31 and 33; Papua New Guinea Constitution, s. 282.
[115] Papua New Guinea Constitution, s. 279.   [116] Ibid., s. 281(1).
[117] Regan, *Light Intervention*.
[118] The abbreviation "BCC" is used as it was how the Bougainville Constitutional Commission commonly referred to itself.
[119] J. C. Kabui, *Making a Constitution for the Autonomous Region of Bougainville: Brief to the Bougainville Joint Assemblies Meeting, Buka, 2nd to 4th April 2003* (Arawa and Buka: Bougainville Constitutional Commission, April 2, 2003).
[120] BCC, *Report of the Bougainville Constitutional Commission: Report on the Third and Final Draft of the Bougainville Constitution* (Arawa and Buka: Bougainville Constitutional Commission, July 2004).

in the transfer of Papua New Guinea government funding. For example, while the BCC had intended to complete the first draft and undertake public consultation in early January 2003, as the funds were not transferred quickly, the completion of the first draft was delayed until late January and the consultation could not take place until February. Second, there were delays in consultations between the BCC and Papua New Guinea government, and the Papua New Guinea government delayed its approval of each successive draft provided to it. For example, the second draft was provided to the Papua New Guinea government in March 2003. However, the BCC did not receive an official response until February 2004 and formal approval in June 2004.[121]

The type of institution that was designated to draft the constitution

The BCC was an appointed body, specially convened for the purpose of drafting the constitution. While the literature argues that an elected body may be perceived as legitimate, there was "no suggestion" of holding elections to select members of the BCC.[122] Given the expense and difficulty of conducting an election in postconflict Bougainville, this decision was understandable. Moreover, the BCC was selected by the BPC (which had been elected) and the BIPG (which included the four elected Bougainville MPs in the Papua New Guinea Parliament), both of which had sufficiently strong democratic credentials. Indeed, the literature generally concludes that an appointed body is preferable, as it is more likely to negotiate compromises without the distraction of everyday politics. Appointing such a body also provides more scope to ensure that it is broadly representative and stands a better chance of drafting a constitution that satisfies all groups. This appears to be the case with respect to the BCC, as accounts indicate that "there was never any claim to do it differently," and "no one felt left out."[123]

The method by which the constitution drafters were selected, and how representative they were

The BIPG and BPC agreed that the BCC should be large enough to be "broadly representative of the people of Bougainville" but also small enough to "ensure that it could operate effectively," eventually deciding that it would have twenty-seven members.[124] The BPC and BIPG agreed on a range of

---

[121] BCC, *Report*; Kabui, *Making a Constitution*.
[122] Interview with an international adviser to the BIPG, BCC, and ABG, August 31, 2010.
[123] Ibid. [124] BCC, *Report*, 65–66.

interest groups that would be invited to nominate persons for the BCC. They also agreed that the BCC would have a chairman, Kabui (then president of the BPC), and deputy chairman, Gerard Sinato (then deputy governor of the BIPG). They then agreed on nominee selection criteria that sought to achieve representation across the different regions and political entities. They also agreed to take account of the views of the four Bougainville MPs in the Papua New Guinea Parliament. They were eager to appoint nominees who were able to understand the issues, contribute to the BCC's work, and promote teamwork and who had "integrity in the eyes of the community."[125] As a result of this process, the BCC included

- one representative of the business community;
- one trade union representative;
- one youth representative;
- one representative of Bougainvilleans living outside Bougainville;
- three women's representatives, one from each of the three main regions (North, Central, and South);
- three church representatives, one from each of the three main churches (United, Seventh Day Adventist, and Catholic);
- one representative of indigenous political and religious groups;[126]
- three BRA representatives, one from each of the three main regions;
- three BRF representatives, one from each of the three main regions; and
- five local-level government representatives, one from each of the three main regions, one from the atoll islands, and one from Buka Island.

Three positions were also set aside for representatives from the Me'ekamui government, a breakaway movement discussed in more detail in Chapter 7. However, it did not nominate representatives, and consequently, the total membership of the BCC ended up being twenty-four, which reflects the small size of the Bougainvillean population at the time (approximately 200,000) and the limited resources available.

All accounts of the BCC are that it was highly inclusive, and there are no reports of widespread discontent concerning its membership. This is in large part due to the fact that the process of agreeing to a joint Bougainville negotiating position during phase I of the peace process had "allowed a lot of issues to be resolved and anger to be dealt with." Consequently, by the time that the membership of the BCC was being selected, relations were "relatively

---

[125] Ibid., 66.
[126] These groups emerged during the Australian colonial administration and sought to promote traditional social organization.

harmonious."[127] In addition, as neither of the main Bougainville factions was perceived to have "won," they were encouraged to build consensus and achieve compromise, and care was taken to ensure that the BCC included both those who favored independence and those who favored continued integration. In this regard, the BCC appears to have been a model of the representative appointed body recommend by the literature.

The manner in which the designated institution drafted the constitution

The BIPG and BPC jointly agreed to terms of reference for the BCC. These terms clearly prioritized public consultation, as they mandated the BCC to consult Bougainvilleans to determine their views on the constitution. The BCC was required to analyze these views, propose recommendations that best reflected them, and prepare a report explaining those recommendations for the Constituent Assembly. In addition, when formulating its recommendations, the BCC had to take account of Bougainvilleans' "political aspirations," "the need to build reconciliation and unity," "the need to provide a firm institutional basis for the future governments and framework for sustainable progress and development," and the Bougainville Peace Agreement. Finally, the BCC had to draft a constitution based on the recommendations of its report.[128]

The BCC was established on September 10, 2002. It undertook ten days of induction, to which it invited five international experts with experience of constitution making. As much of the ABG's structure is contained in the Bougainville Peace Agreement, Part XIV of the Papua New Guinea constitution, and the accompanying organic law, the BCC accepted that these documents "set the main parameters" for the constitution. Despite this, they made "every effort" to find "the best ways to give effect to the wishes of the people, and to provide a basis for long-lasting reconciliation and peace."[129] Indeed, the BCC's first official act was to break into five regional teams to engage in public consultations from September 21 to October 19, 2002.

From December 9 to 20, 2002, Sir James Fraser worked with the BCC's technical officers to prepare a first working draft of the constitution based on the BCC's recommendations, which were in turn based on the feedback

---

[127] Interview with an international adviser to the BRA and BCC, January 18, 2010; interview with an international adviser to the BIPG, BCC, and ABG, August 31, 2010.
[128] BCC, *Report*, Appendix 2, 361–362.
[129] Kabui, *Making a Constitution*, 3; BCC, *Report*; interview with an international adviser to the BIPG, BCC, and ABG, August 31, 2010.

gathered during the public consultations.[130] Fraser was an expert on Papua New Guinea constitutional law and had been one of the two people who drafted the laws that implemented the Bougainville Peace Agreement. While there was some suspicion of a draftsperson closely associated with the Papua New Guinea government, it was thought that Fraser's expertise could help to ensure that the draft met the requirements of the Papua New Guinea constitution. The first working draft was considered by the chairman and deputy chairman on December 19. Some amendments were made on December 20, and then the BCC was recalled between December 21 and 23 to consider it. The BCC agreed on amendments, which Fraser made during January 2003.

The BCC met again from January 28 to 30, 2003, to consider the amended draft. Changes to this draft were made on January 31, and the official first draft was presented to the BCC chairman and released to the public on February 1.[131] There was then a second round of public consultations on the first draft, between February 2 and 16.

The BCC met from February 19 to 25 to consider the first draft in light of the second round of public consultations. As a consequence of the feedback gathered, a number of amendments were incorporated into the draft in early March 2003. A second working draft was considered by the BCC on March 18 and 19. The BCC made some minor amendments, and a second official draft was released to the public on March 25. The second draft was also presented to a meeting of the Bougainville Joint Assemblies from April 2 to 4 to enable the BCC to consult senior political leaders.[132] Meeting with the Joint Assemblies was seen as important, as their members would later constitute the Constituent Assembly that would adopt the constitution. It was hoped that giving them the opportunity to comment on the draft at this stage would reduce the likelihood of substantial revisions being made to the final draft.[133]

Additional funding was then sought for a third round of public consultations in April 2003. In August and September, the BCC met to consider the regional teams' reports on this consultation. The second draft was then amended based on issues identified in these reports.

---

[130] BCC, *Discussion of Recommendations: Minutes of Full BCC Meetings, Friday 15 November to Monday 9 December* (Buka: Bougainville Constitutional Commission, 2002).

[131] BCC, *Discussion of Constitution of the Autonomous Region of Bougainville working draft of 25/01/03: Minutes of Full BCC Meetings Tuesday 28 to Thursday 30 January* (Buka: Bougainville Constitutional Commission, 2003); UN, *Report of the Secretary-General on the United Nations Political Office in Bougainville*, UN Security Council, UN Doc. S/2003/345, March 20, 2003.

[132] BCC, *Brief on the 2nd Draft of the Bougainville Constitution for Bougainville Joint Assemblies Meeting* (Buka: Bougainville Constitutional Commission, April 2, 2003).

[133] BCC, *Report*.

From November 2003 to January 2004, there were extensive technical discussions between the BCC's advisers and officers from the Papua New Guinea Attorney General's Department. As a result, the BCC did not receive an official response on the second draft from the Papua New Guinea government until February 24, 2004. The BCC then reconvened in March and April to consider this response. Papua New Guinea government officials attended these meetings to provide clarification. The BCC made many amendments to the second draft based on issues raised by the Papua New Guinea government. However, it did not agree with the Papua New Guinea government on all issues, and for these it prepared an explanation of its reasons. BCC leaders then met with the Papua New Guinea government from May 6 to 8, 2004.

The Papua New Guinea government provided its formal position on the second draft to the BCC in early June 2004. The BCC then met from June 23 to July 8 to consider the Papua New Guinea government's position and to finalize the third – and final – draft of the constitution, as well as its accompanying report. The BCC's detailed report extended well beyond explaining the draft constitution to the Constituent Assembly, as it also contained a narrative of Bougainville's history and described the aims of the constitution to guide its later interpretation.

The literature argues that appointed drafting bodies are more likely to engage in free deliberation and to promote reason over interest, which appears to have been the case in the BCC, with its advisers reporting that its meetings were "collegial."[134] The minutes of the BCC's hearings indicate that a range of members spoke and no single member dominated the discussions.[135] However, this also meant that the BCC's meetings were often "very long," as "no one would be told to sit down – there was constant, vigorous discussion."[136] Throughout the BCC's hearings, the chairman deflected heated debate and avoided impasses by stressing that the "evolutionary" nature of Bougainville's political status meant that controversial issues (such as names) and costly proposals (such as an upper house) could be included in the draft but left open to change in the future.[137]

In this regard, the literature argues that the manner in which the drafting body makes decisions is influential. The method by which the BCC would make decisions was debated at the midway point of its first substantive

---

[134] Interview with an international adviser to the BIPG, BCC, and ABG, August 31, 2010.
[135] BCC, *Discussion of Recommendations*.
[136] Interview with an international adviser to the BRA and BCC, January 18, 2010.
[137] See, for example, on the name of the autonomous region (p. 1), on the structure of the legislature (p. 3), and on the name of the legislature (p. 5). BCC, *Discussion of Recommendations*.

hearings, from November 15 to December 9, 2002. Up to that stage, decisions had been taken by vote. However, a proposal was made that all decisions should be made by consensus, which reflected the nature of Bougainvillean customary decision making. Following this, many decisions were made by consensus; however, the BCC agreed to continue deciding difficult issues and breaking deadlocks by vote, using an open show of hands,[138] which the literature notes is the most common way drafting bodies make such decisions. Although the member representing indigenous political and religious groups requested that his cultural objection to voting be formally recorded, it was relatively uncontroversial among the other BCC members.[139]

While the literature cautions that there can be insufficient competent candidates to fill both a legislature and a constitution-drafting body, this does not appear to have been the case in Bougainville. This was assisted by the small size of the BCC. BCC members "attended everything," including BCC meetings, meetings with international advisers, and public consultations. They read documents carefully and asked for explanations when they were unsure of issues. Despite the fact that several members had not been formally educated, they were generally "engaged" and "understood key issues."[140] This understanding is reflected in the questions raised during the BCC hearings, where technical issues such as executive-legislature relations, electoral systems, and judicial independence were considered. Moreover, BCC chairman Kabui had a good understanding of the requirements of the political settlement and of constitutional issues, and he was able to guide the BCC's discussions. In addition, many BCC members had been involved in the peace process and in making constitutions for the NSPG in 1976 and the Bougainville Reconciliation Government in 1998, so they "already had a good understanding of the issues and of constitutions."[141] The BCC also had a small support staff of five people, responsible for administration and logistics, all of whom were Bougainvillean.

The levels of publicity and secrecy involved in the process

In keeping with the emphasis placed on transparency and awareness raising during the peace process, the constitution-making process was conducted in

---

[138] Interview with an international adviser to the BIPG, BCC, and ABG, August 31, 2010; interview with an international adviser to the BRA and BCC, January 18, 2010.
[139] BCC, *Discussion of Recommendations*.
[140] Interview with an international adviser to the BIPG, BCC, and ABG, August 31, 2010; interview with an international adviser to the BRA and BCC, January 18, 2010.
[141] Interview with an international adviser to the BIPG, BCC, and ABG, August 31, 2010.

public, with little secrecy. The BCC's hearings were open and were regularly reported in the media, including in broadcasts on Radio Bougainville and in the two major Papua New Guinea newspapers. The PMG also published a newsletter that covered the BCC's consultations. The second round of the BCC's public consultations was supported by a series of fifteen information programs on Radio Bougainville, which were all presented in Tok Pisin, the lingua franca. However, Radio Bougainville had poor coverage in some parts of Bougainville and faced financial difficulties, which challenged its ability to report on all aspects of the constitution-making process. In addition, newspapers were sold only in the main urban centers, although they were generally taken home to rural communities, where they were shared and read avidly.

While the process was conducted publicly, it must be acknowledged that many of the most controversial decisions concerning the referendum and level of autonomy had been conducted during the peace process, some in relative secrecy. This had occurred because the situation in Bougainville was tense, particularly at the beginning of phase I, and therefore it was difficult for the Bougainville parties to open up sensitive talks too widely.[142]

The opportunities for public participation and its role in the process

The BCC was mandated to "consult widely with the people of Bougainville." Reflecting the importance placed on public participation, the BCC conducted its first round of consultations from September 21 to October 19, 2002, only eleven days after it was formed and before any debate had taken place. On the one hand, this helped BCC members avoid making decisions before seeking Bougainvilleans' views. Consequently, members of the public were given latitude to shape the constitution via their feedback. On the other hand, it meant that the BCC did not have any preformed proposals to present to the public. As this created the risk that consultation meetings would lack structure and direction, BCC members used a questionnaire on basic choices for the constitution and the structure of the ABG to guide the discussion. This questionnaire was circulated in advance, providing time for people to go through it before consultation meetings.

To conduct the consultation, BCC members broke up into five regional teams (atolls, Buka, north, central, and south) and a small team that traveled to centers in Papua New Guinea (Rabual, Madang, Lae, and Port Moresby) to consult Bougainvilleans living outside Bougainville. The members of each

[142] Ibid.

team did not necessarily come from the region their team was consulting. The regional teams visited regional centers, important villages, and schools. The teams were mandated to inform Bougainvilleans about the BCC's work, make them "aware of their role in development a new constitution," and consult them about the contents of the constitution and the shape of the ABG.[143] Consequently, the public consultations sought to achieve the distribution of information and perform the educative role envisaged by the literature. Each team was accompanied by a technical adviser, who advised BCC members during the consultations and kept a record of the views expressed by the public. The regional teams also received approximately 150 written submissions, mainly from groups.[144]

From October 20 to November 10, 2002, the regional teams prepared reports on the issues raised during the consultations. These issues were summarized in a "Matrix of Choices," which revealed that some issues were relatively uncontroversial.[145] The BCC tried to reach compromises on controversial issues to ensure "that the concerns and interests of all groups were taken care of as much as possible."[146] The BCC then worked from November 15 to December 9 to develop its recommendations, which were used as the basis for the draft constitution. Indeed, the BCC's report and meeting minutes reveal that it took the feedback gathered from the public consultations seriously. Therefore, as recommended by the literature, extensive public participation ensured that the contents of the constitution reflected the public's understandings and views. However, it should be noted that some social issues were raised at the consultations that could not be dealt with by the BCC. For example, at some meetings, traditional leaders requested that the constitution ban women from wearing "cargo" trousers.[147] Consequently, the BCC did not adopt the feedback "wholesale."[148]

It had been anticipated that the BCC would produce only one draft of the constitution and conduct only one round of public consultations. However, during the first round of consultations, Bougainvilleans "made it clear" that

---

[143] BCC, *Report*, 71–2.
[144] These submissions came from all regions of Bougainville and were mainly submitted on behalf of women's groups, chiefs, Councils of Elders, Village Assemblies, former combatants, schools, NGOs, representatives of churches, and Bougainvilleans living outside Bougainville. BCC, *Report*.
[145] BCC Technical Team, *Matrix of Choices* (Buka: Bougainville Constitutional Commission, November 10, 2002).
[146] Kabui, *Making a Constitution*, 4; BCC, *Discussion of Constitution*.
[147] That is, of a military style, with external pockets.
[148] Interview with an international adviser to the BIPG, BCC, and ABG, August 31, 2010.

they wanted the BCC to return with the first draft and explain "what they had done with their views collected in that first round of consultations and then to get further views on the first draft."[149] As the BCC had made some savings on its budget and received additional assistance from the Australian and Papua New Guinea governments, it proceeded with a second round of consultations.

Therefore, after the official first draft was released to the public, between February 2 and 16, 2003, there was a second round of consultations. The regional teams conducted a nine-day consultation process, and the chairman, deputy chairman, and BCC's technical advisers conducted an additional five-day consultation in areas that had been identified as requiring more discussion.[150] Again, BCC members broke into five regional teams. Each team distributed copies of the first draft, a six-page information paper (in both English and Tok Pisin), and a two-page handout containing the proposed preamble (in both English and Tok Pisin).[151] While there was "quite positive" feedback about the consultation, there were complaints that the two weeks allocated were insufficient, as it meant that the teams could not hold public meetings in some areas. There were also complaints that the BCC teams had too few copies of the draft constitution to circulate, and therefore people did not have the opportunity to study it before consultation meetings.[152] This was more a consequence of limited funding than deliberate obfuscation by the BCC.

After the second draft was presented to a meeting of the Bougainville Joint Assemblies, funding was sought to enable the BCC to hold a third round of public consultations, additional regional workshops, and workshops with administrative officials. Although the BCC had not planned to conduct additional consultation, it did so in response to the high level of public interest in its work and because many Bougainvilleans had complained that the lack of access to copies of the first draft had reduced the effectiveness of the second round of consultation. Accordingly, during April 2003, the regional teams consulted on the second draft of the constitution. In advance of this consultation, 2,500 copies of the second draft were printed in the form of a small book and distributed. As the population at the time was approximately 200,000 people, there was one copy of the draft for every eighty Bougainvilleans.

---

[149] BCC, *Report*, 76.
[150] BCC, *Tentative Program for Involvement of Chairman & Deputy in Work of Regional Teams (Sunday 2 to Tuesday 11 February)* (Buka: Bougainville Constitutional Commission, January 2003).
[151] BCC, *1st Draft Bougainville Constitution – Consulting the People* (Buka: Bougainville Constitutional Commission, January 31, 2003).
[152] BCC, *Report*, 77.

The second draft was "well received," and people appreciated that a "reasonably large" number of copies of the draft were provided.[153]

Reports indicate that the conduct of meetings during each round of consultation followed a roughly similar pattern. Attendance ranged between thirty and 150 people. While there were large meetings, "it couldn't be claimed that there was a groundswell of the population." However, those who did attend tended to be the "opinion leaders," who reported back to their communities.[154] Meetings were generally held in Tok Pisin, with translators present to translate English into Tok Pisin. As Bougainvilleans are relatively well educated and there was at the time an 80 percent adult literacy rate, there was a fairly high level of understanding among those who attended the meetings. BCC members "encouraged" people to form views and to "present them forcefully." Consequently, the "material out of the consultations was very useful."[155] The BCC also conducted meetings with representatives of interest groups. In particular, during the public consultations there were security incidents involving former combatants that may have been intended to destabilize the process. Consequently, teams of BCC members met with former combatants to hear their views.

Overall, public participation in constitution making in Bougainville was extensive. It should be noted that a positive precedent of extensive public participation had been set by the widely consultative process of making the Papua New Guinea's "home-grown" constitution in the 1970s.[156] Perhaps reflecting that experience, reports indicate that during all rounds of public consultations on the ABG constitution, Bougainvilleans were "enthusiastic" in their participation.[157] They also indicate that the consultation process was highly inclusive, transparent, and participatory, managing to have a wide reach throughout Bougainville and to Bougainvilleans living elsewhere in Papua New Guinea. This approach reflects the local sociopolitical practice of decision making being inclusive, consultative, and unhurried and indicates the way in which the process reflected a hybrid of liberal and local characteristics. Consequently, one women's leader noted that the high level of participation "has really drawn people together."[158] This seems to support the prediction in the literature that constitution making can play a role in

---

[153] Ibid., 78.
[154] Interview with an international adviser to the BIPG, BCC, and ABG, August 31, 2010.
[155] Interview with an international adviser to the BRA and BCC, January 18, 2010.
[156] Papua New Guinea Constitutional Planning Committee, *Final Report* (Port Moresby: Constitutional Planning Committee, 1974), s. 15/2/2.
[157] Kabui, *Making a Constitution*, 8.
[158] Interview with a Bougainvillean women's leader, February 2, 2010.

promoting reconciliation and resolving grievances, which is discussed in more detail in Chapter 7.

The degree of international involvement

Continuing the approach adopted throughout the crisis and peace process, international involvement in the constitution-making process was light. Support primarily consisted of two legal advisers and financial and logistical support to facilitate the public consultations. While the literature cautions that legal advisers may resist technically flawed and deliberately ambiguous formulations that are necessary to achieve consensus, this was not the case in Bougainville. Both international advisers had been involved throughout the crisis and peace process and had a good understanding of the issues, strong relationships with the Bougainville parties, and an awareness of the compromises necessary to achieve consensus.[159] In addition, while these two advisers were influential, the other seven technical advisers were Bougainvillean and included people who had links to the main Bougainville parties. Therefore, there was minimal risk that the credibility of the constitution would be undermined by the perception that the two international advisers had been overly influential.

The manner in which the constitution was adopted

The BIPG and BPC decided that the Bougainville Constituent Assembly would consist of members of the Bougainville Joint Assemblies, as they would "broadly represent the people of Bougainville."[160] The BCC's final draft of the constitution, accompanied by its explanatory report, was presented to the assembly for debate in September 2004. During the assembly's debate, its members were primarily concerned with ensuring that the draft effectively reflected the Bougainville Peace Agreement.[161] After nine days of debate, the assembly gave its provisional approval to a fourth draft. This debate did not take long because the second draft had been presented to the Joint Assemblies in April 2003, so assembly members were already well acquainted with it. They had also had a chance to provide feedback at that meeting, which

---

[159] Anthony Regan, a constitutional lawyer from the Australian National University, and Ian Prentice, a lawyer and former member of the Queensland Parliament.
[160] J. Momis, governor of Bougainville, quoted in "Governor Announces New Bougainville Constituent Assembly," *Papua New Guinea Post-Courier*, January 10, 2002.
[161] Interview with an international adviser to the BRA and BCC, January 18, 2010.

had been incorporated into the draft.[162] There had further been "constant consultation" between members of the BCC, the BIPG, and BPC.[163]

In October 2004, Constituent Assembly chairman John Momis, BCC chairman Kabui, and two assembly deputy chairmen consulted the Papua New Guinea government concerning the draft. Both parties agreed to common principles to guide the assembly's amendments to the final draft. The assembly then met again on November 12. Representatives of the Papua New Guinea government also attended this meeting to present the government's views. The assembly voted to accept the common principles and then approved a slightly amended version of the draft. A traditional ceremony was then held on November 23 to present the draft and the BCC's report to the Papua New Guinea government.

Delays in Papua New Guinea government feedback and approvals had occurred throughout the process, and some voices in the Papua New Guinea government objected to the final constitution and BCC's report. However, as there was a "genuine commitment to peace" within the Papua New Guinea leadership, these objections were overruled and the draft was reviewed and ratified quickly.[164] Accordingly, on December 14, the Papua New Guinea government endorsed the draft. On December 21, the Papua New Guinea governor general signed the constitution. An official handover of the constitution by the Papua New Guinea government to the people of Bougainville occurred on January 14, 2005.

The part of the Bougainville constitution relating to the first ABG election and first meeting of the ABG Parliament came into operation on the day following the date of publication in the National Gazette (in December 2004). This was to enable the election of the ABG to take place. The remainder of the constitution came into effect on the day fixed for the return of the writs in that election.[165]

Whether the constitution was adopted on an interim basis or included a "sunset" clause

As the constitution is intended to operate while Bougainville is autonomous, with the expectation of the referendum being held, it is an interim

---

[162] Kabui, *Making a Constitution*.
[163] Interview with an international adviser to the BRA and BCC, January 18. 2010.
[164] Interview with an international adviser to the Papua New Guinea government, January 24, 2010; UN, *Report of the Secretary-General on the United Nations Observer Mission in Bougainville (Papua New Guinea)*, UN Security Council, UN Doc. S/2004/771, September 29, 2004.
[165] Constitution of the Autonomous Region of Bougainville (2002) (hereafter ABG Constitution), preamble.

constitution and specifies that the ABG will operate "until any change in the status" of Bougainville.[166] The BCC had considered two approaches to drafting the constitution. The first involved preparing a simple draft that provided for the basic institutions of the ABG but left other matters to later amendment or law. The purported advantage of this approach was that the constitution could be short, clear, and easily understood, which could minimize the likelihood of confusion and misunderstanding and reduce people's expectations of the ABG. However, the BCC opted for a second approach, which involved preparing a long constitution that provided "a detailed road-map of the full range of institutions and arrangements made possible by autonomy."[167] It was recognized that, given the financial and capacity constraints the ABG would face, many institutions would not be immediately established. Therefore, the constitution left many of the ABG's institutions and powers to evolve gradually. The BCC opted for this approach on the grounds that Bougainvilleans expressed a strong desire that the constitution "reflect the high degree of autonomy made available by the Bougainville Peace Agreement" by "paint[ing] a clear picture for the people of what was available."[168] The BCC thought that this was also the best way to satisfy those who had fought for independence and to encourage those who remained outside the peace process to join. This evolutionary approach also reflects the arrangements providing for the gradual transfer of powers and functions to the ABG in the Bougainville Peace Agreement.

Despite its purportedly evolutionary approach, the constitution is relatively difficult to amend. It can be amended only after two affirmative votes in the legislature, each supported by a two-thirds absolute majority. Amendments relating to the referendum require a three-quarter absolute majority vote.[169]

CONTEXTUAL DESCRIPTION OF POLITICAL DEVELOPMENTS
DURING THE IMPLEMENTATION OF AUTONOMY

In tandem with the constitution-making process, a number of other developments occurred that were necessary to implement the Bougainville Peace Agreement.

The amnesty and pardon provisions of the Bougainville Peace Agreement, as implemented in the Papua New Guinea constitution, came into operation

[166] ABG Constitution, s. 41(1). [167] BCC, *Report*, 100. [168] Ibid., 102.
[169] ABG Constitution, s. 219.

in July 2002.[170] From late 2002, the PMG was progressively scaled down, until in July 2003 it was replaced with the fifteen-member Bougainville Transitional Team mandated to assist in facilitating the peace process. The team withdrew in December 2003. The UNOMB remained in Bougainville until the weapons disposal process was completed in May 2005 and withdrew in June 2005. The JSB was created in February 2003.

As required by the Bougainville Peace Agreement, the Papua New Guinean security forces began to withdraw from Bougainville in late 2001. Implementation of the weapons disposal process then began. While it was hoped that stage II of the process could be completed by December 24, 2002, this did not prove possible. The process received a boost when the PNGDF withdrew on March 26, 2003. In August 2003, the UNOMB verified that stage II was complete, which brought into effect the amendments to the Papua New Guinea constitution that implemented the Bougainville Peace Agreement. However, the number of containerized weapons was only a part of the total held by former BRA and BRF members and did not include the 400 to 500 weapons held by groups not participating in the peace process.[171] Despite this, the UNOMB engaged in extensive community consultation, from which emerged a consensus in favor of verification because the situation seemed peaceful and because implementation of the political settlement was being delayed until verification. There was also a belief that pressure could be exerted later by delaying verification of stage III.[172] One former PMG member noted that "any weapons disposal would have been imperfect" and that verification came down to a political judgment concerning whether the process was "credible enough to provide psychological change."[173]

The experience of the crisis encouraged Bougainvilleans to embrace the principle of *mekim na save* (learn by doing).[174] The peace and constitution-making processes in Bougainville are an example of Bougainvilleans learning by doing, as they are almost a model of the extensive public participation advocated by the literature. Both processes were broadly representative and

---

[170] When the notice defining the period of amnesty and the offences to which it applies was published in the Papua New Guinea National Gazette. See ABG Constitution, Sch. 6.1 and 6.2.
[171] This was acknowledged by the UNOMB director in his report. N. Sinclair, *Implementation of the Bougainville Peace Agreement, Completion of Stage II of Weapons Disposal: UNOMB's Verification Report* (Buka: United Nations Observer Mission Bougainville, July 2003).
[172] Ibid.   [173] Interview with a former member of the PMG, November 5, 2010.
[174] M. T. Havini, "Women in Community During the Blockade," in ...*As Mothers of the Land: The Birth of the Bougainville Women for Peace and Freedom*, ed. J. T. Sirivi and M. T. Havini (Canberra: Pandanus Books, 2004), 69.

highly participatory and consequently managed to achieve consensus and compromise between Bougainvillean groups. Given that the Bougainville crisis was a multifaceted secessionist and civil war that resulted in thousands of deaths and the internal displacement of almost 40 percent of the population, the Bougainvillean parties' ability to negotiate a peace agreement and make the constitution in a relatively short time frame and without the resumption of conflict is evidence of the success of both processes. A particularly important contributor to this success appears to be the willingness of the Bougainvillean political leadership to compromise. In 1997, when the BRA had the military upper hand, it must have been tempting for the BIG/BRA to prolong the conflict and attempt to achieve a comprehensive victory. Instead, they recognized the terrible cost that the conflict was exacting from Bougainvilleans and opted to seek reconciliation and compromise with the BTG/BRF. That spirit of reconciliation and compromise remained throughout the constitution-making process. The next chapter considers whether it has survived in the period since.

7

Constituent power in Bougainville

This chapter begins with a brief contextual description of political developments in Bougainville since the adoption of its constitution. It then assesses whether the extensive public participation in the constitution-making process generated a constituent process by creating a political community. The following five indicators are used to assess the extent to which a unified political community is present:

- Does the constitution enumerate a unifying national identity?
- Has reconciliation been achieved?
- Are there divisions within society?
- Does the community exhibit evidence of citizenization?
- Is there a strong public sphere?

CONTEXTUAL DESCRIPTION OF POLITICAL DEVELOPMENTS SINCE THE ADOPTION OF THE CONSTITUTION

After the Papua New Guinea government ratified Bougainville's constitution, an election was required to select the members of the ABG. The election could not occur until the UNOMB had verified that stage III of the weapons disposal process was complete, which occurred in May 2005. Although only 95 percent of containerized weapons had been destroyed, the UNOMB and Bougainville parties agreed to verification as a "compromise" to keep the implementation of autonomy moving.[1]

In accordance with the Bougainville constitution, the BIPG and BPC oversaw the first ABG election, between May 20 and June 2, 2005. The BPC party, led by Joseph Kabui, won twenty-seven seats and Kabui won the

---
[1] Interview with a former BRA commander and member of the ABG, November 2, 2010.

presidency. The New Bougainville Party, led by John Momis, won five seats. The remainder of the constitution came into effect on the day fixed for the return of the writs, June 6, 2005. The BPC and BIPG then called the inaugural session of the ABG on June 15. In June 2008, President Kabui unexpectedly died and a by-election in December 2008 was won by James Tanis, one of his allies. Tanis was sworn in as president on January 6, 2009. The second ABG general election was then held, as scheduled, in May 2010. The presidency was won by Momis, and his New Bougainville Party took thirteen seats. Momis was sworn in on June 10, 2010, while the remainder of the ABG was sworn in on June 15.

THE ROLE OF PARTICIPATION IN CONSTITUTING THE POLITICAL COMMUNITY

Does the constitution enumerate a unifying national identity?

The extensive public participation during the constitution-making process resulted in a constitution that contains a detailed official historical narrative and identifies shared symbols, defines future national identity, and classifies who qualifies as "Bougainvillean."[2] Indeed, the BCC appears to have been influenced by the literature, as it noted that the constitution can play a role in reconciliation and building unity if it includes "expressions of common principles, objectives and directions."[3] To that end, the constitution sets out a number of nonjusticiable "Objectives and Directive Principles" to guide Bougainvilleans and the ABG. These principles echo and expand upon the "National Goals and Directive Principles" contained in the Papua New Guinea constitution. These principles received strong support during the BCC's public consultations, as they fulfill similar functions to customary "parables and *tok bokis*" (veiled speech)[4] used by traditional leaders to "explain principles and provide guidance to people."[5]

---

[2] Although the term "nation" is used, Bougainvilleans have differing – and possibly irreconcilable – understandings of their political future, and consequently, of their "nation-state." Therefore, the term "nation" is used to refer to a sense of collective unity that binds people together in a political community, regardless of whether that community is a sovereign state. Consequently, even if Bougainville remains autonomous within Papua New Guinea, a sense of national identity will still be required to generate political legitimacy for the ABG.
[3] BCC, *Report*, 18.   [4] That is, talking about something without mentioning it.
[5] BCC, *Report*, 137; A. J. Regan, *Notes on Preambles and on Directive Principles in Constitutions* (Buka: Bougainville Constitutional Commission, January 23, 2003).

Official historical narrative

The official historical narrative has three key elements. First, there is the importance of self-determination, understood as the "freedom and autonomy" which Bougainvilleans' ancestors "enjoyed in time immemorial."[6] The constitution states that self-determination has been achieved only after a "long struggle to free ourselves from adverse colonial and foreign influences and to renew our freedom, autonomy and customs."[7] This idea is an important unifying narrative and has played a significant role in cultivating a sense of separate Bougainvillean identity. Initially, Bougainvillean identity was based on the "bitterness" Bougainvilleans felt about being treated like "human chattels" in the territorial exchange between Germany and Britain[8] and consequently being "lumped with a people not of their choosing" in Papua New Guinea rather than incorporated into the British Solomon Islands Protectorate.[9] In this regard, Bougainville's physical remoteness from the rest of Papua New Guinea is important, as are its cultural, church, and other links to the Solomon Islands. In particular, while the rest of Papua New Guinea was dominated by Protestant churches, the strong influence of the Catholic Marist (and later Methodist) missionaries from the Solomon Islands enhanced a "sense of Solomons identity" among Bougainvilleans.[10]

The sense of a separate Bougainville identity took on a secessionist dimension in the 1950s, based on a range of grievances concerning Australian colonial neglect. Australia abandoned Bougainville during the Second World War, the severe impact of which caused the deaths of up to 25 percent of the population. There was also frustration at the lack of development following the war. Indeed, in 1962, a Bougainvillean delegation asked for the UN mandate to be transferred to the United States on the grounds that Australia had treated the Bougainvilleans "like dogs."[11] However, the colonial administration employed many Bougainvilleans in other parts of the colony, as they were regarded as reliable and as exhibiting leadership potential, which encouraged Bougainvilleans to develop a "sense of superiority."[12] This sense of superiority also had primordial roots in Bougainvilleans' "distinctive jet-black

---

[6] ABG Constitution, preamble.   [7] Ibid.   [8] Havini, "Perspectives on a Crisis," 18.
[9] M. Havini, "A Bougainvillean Perspective on the Crisis," in Spriggs and Denoon, *The Bougainville Crisis: 1991 Update*, 165.
[10] H. Laracy, "'Imperium in Imperio?' The Catholic Church in Bougainville," in Regan and Griffin, *Bougainville: Before the Conflict*, 128.
[11] J. L. Momis and E. Ogan, "Bougainville '71. Not Discovered by CRA," *New Guinea and Australia* 6:2 (1971): 32–40.
[12] A. J. Regan, "Identities among Bougainvilleans," in Regan and Griffin, *Bougainville: Before the Conflict*, 437.

skin,"[13] which was (and is) often favorably compared to that of the "red-skins" from the Papua New Guinea mainland.[14] However, this claim needs to be treated with a degree of skepticism since many Bougainvilleans do not fit the dark-skinned stereotype.[15]

In the late 1960s, grievances over the extensive environmental and social impact of the Panguna mine reinforced the sense of separate Bougainvillean identity and sentiment in favor of secession. Significantly, a large number of people from mainland Papua New Guinea were brought to Bougainville to meet the labor requirements of the mine.[16] These workers often resided in squatter settlements around the mine and, as they were outside the social control of their traditional communities, gambling, prostitution, alcohol, and vagrancy flourished. Bougainvilleans increasingly blamed the escalation of crime and social problems on these "outsiders," which enhanced the perception that there were "ethnic solidarities" among Bougainvilleans, as opposed to people from mainland Papua New Guinea.[17] During the crisis, the fact that the Papua New Guinean security forces consisted almost entirely of people from mainland Papua New Guinea assisted the conflict to acquire an "ethnic and separatist character." Therefore, the conflict hardened ethnic stereotypes of "red-skins" and "black bastards" (the pejorative term used by people from mainland Papua New Guinea to refer to Bougainvilleans).[18]

Reflecting the importance of the self-determination struggle, the constitution's directive principles oblige the ABG and all Bougainvilleans to "display and promote respect for the autonomy and territorial integrity of Bougainville."[19] This principle implicitly recognizes the aspirations of both integration and independence supporters, as it adopts a careful reading of the term "self-determination," noting that it is achieved through both autonomy and the referendum on independence. This does not explicitly imply that the referendum will result in independence, only that it will allow the "sovereignty of the People" to be recognized.[20] This approach echoes the idea of popular

---

[13] Regan, "Why a Neutral Peace Monitoring Force?," 2.
[14] J. Friedlander, "Why Do the People of Bougainville Look Unique? Some Conclusions from Biological Anthropology and Genetics," in Regan and Griffin, *Bougainville: Before the Conflict*.
[15] Interview with an international adviser to the Papua New Guinea government, January 24, 2010.
[16] As a result, by 1971, the combined workforce peaked at more than 10,000, only 27 percent of whom came from Bougainville. M. Togolo, "Torau Response to Change," in Regan and Griffin, *Bougainville: Before the Conflict*.
[17] Denoon, *Getting under the Skin*, 154.
[18] Regan, "Why a Neutral Peace Monitoring Force?," 3.   [19] ABG Constitution, s. 17.
[20] Ibid., preamble.

sovereignty by providing that the people should be given the opportunity to exercise their sovereignty to self-determine, but recognizing that they may determine to remain autonomous within Papua New Guinea. Therefore, the constitution seeks to provide a unifying narrative that does not preempt Bougainville's political future. Accordingly, all Bougainvilleans who fought for self-determination are "heroes," rather than merely those who fought for independence. This reflects the sense of identity that developed as a result of shared suffering during the crisis, and then later as a result of the reconciliation and awareness efforts that accompanied the peace and constitution-making processes.[21] However, while this approach utilizes a broad definition of self-determination in order to unite all Bougainvilleans behind a shared history, it is challenged by the fact that the question of whether Bougainvilleans will vote for independence is left open.

The second key element of the official historical narrative is the importance of reconciliation. While a shared sense of identity developed during the crisis, it also had a "devastating impact...on social capital."[22] Accordingly, the constitution stresses that Bougainvilleans are "chastened by internal conflict" and directed to "achieve and maintain peace at all times" by pursuing "mediation, reconciliation and harmony."[23] The emphasis is firmly on reconciliation as, according to local sociopolitical practices, dispute resolution and societal cohesion are provided by the principle of "balanced reciprocity," which requires reconciliation and compensation in order to restore balance within the community.[24] This reflects the BCC's recognition that reconciliation would be the best way to ensure that peace takes hold. It further reflects the views expressed during the BCC's public consultations.[25] The constitution also specifies that no Bougainvillean should "be involved in any para-military activities," and Bougainvilleans are obliged to "work towards ensuring that Bougainville is free of all firearms and of crime."[26] These provisions are directed at those who did not participate in the weapons disposal process or who stayed outside the peace process completely.[27]

---

[21] Regan, "Identities among Bougainvilleans."
[22] E. P. Wolfers, *Bougainville Autonomy – Implications for Governance and Decentralisation*, State, Society and Governance in Melanesia Discussion Paper No. 5 (Canberra: Australian National University, 2006), 5.
[23] ABG Constitution, preamble.   [24] Regan, "Identities among Bougainvilleans," 420.
[25] BCC, *Report*.   [26] ABG Constitution, s. 15.
[27] A. J. Regan, "Bougainville's New Directions: Presidential By-Election, Forming a New Ministry, and First Steps of the New Leadership," paper presented at the State, Society and Governance in Melanesian Seminar, Australian National University, Canberra, March 25, 2009.

The third key element of the official historical narrative is the recognition of the importance of Christianity. Bougainvilleans are directed to "uphold Christian and similar moral and spiritual principles." The constitution also directs the ABG to "strive to ensure partnership with…churches…in the future development and provision of services."[28] This reflects the important role that the churches have played since their arrival in the late nineteenth century. Indeed, when compared to the colonial administration, the Catholic Marist mission was "clearly the most widespread, popularly supported and coherently organised institution in Bougainville."[29] Consequently, by 1939, two-thirds of Bougainvilleans were Catholic. While Methodists and Seventh Day Adventists arrived later, neither could rival the influence of the Marists. The churches play a role in "binding people together" by forging relationships between people from different parts of Bougainville,[30] particularly by bringing secondary students from around Bougainville together in boarding schools. Although some church leaders took sides during the crisis, many remained in Bougainville and provided relief supplies, and thus "they provided an anchor for people when things were falling apart."[31] The churches also played an important role in facilitating reconciliation during the crisis and peace process and provided relief supplies that helped to mitigate the effects of the Papua New Guinean blockade. Importantly, in an echo of the liberal-local hybrid approach, the Catholic and Methodist Churches have syncretized or "interwoven" their beliefs and practices with Bougainvillean culture "so that they combine custom and Christianity."[32] Due to the syncretism, "nationalist conceptions of Bougainville tradition and identity are supported by Christian rhetoric in which the power of God as both creator of Bougainville and facilitator of the crisis are central."[33]

National symbols

The most important national symbol identified in the constitution is the name of the autonomous territory. The constitution declares the formal name to be "The Autonomous Region of Bougainville" but directs that otherwise the territory will be known as "Bougainville."[34] Although the majority view during

---

[28] ABG Constitution, s. 35(1). [29] Laracy, "'Imperium in Imperio?,'" 127.
[30] Interview with a Bougainvillean women's leader, February 2, 2010.
[31] C. Baria, Oxfam Bougainville, quoted in Howley, *Breaking Spears and Mending Hearts*, 166; R. V. Saovana-Spriggs, "Christianity and Women in Bougainville," *Development Bulletin* 51 (2000): 58–60.
[32] Boege and Garasu, "Papua New Guinea: A Success Story," 573.
[33] A. Hermkens, "Religion in War and Peace," *Culture and Religion* 8:3 (2007): 284.
[34] ABG Constitution, s. 1(2).

the BCC's consultations was in favor of "Bougainville,"[35] this issue was hotly debated in the BCC. Suggested names were "Morahe"[36] and "Toromon";[37] however, other BCC members argued against using such *tok ples* (local language) names from particular regions of Bougainville on the grounds that it would be "divisive."[38] The BCC also considered using "North Solomons," which had been chosen at the time of the first declaration of independence in 1975 to reflect Bougainville's cultural and historic links to the Solomon Islands. It was also chosen in 1977 for the provincial government. Indeed, during the crisis there was talk of Bougainville (re)unifying with the Solomon Islands, although this met with little enthusiasm from that country's government, as it was grappling with its own challenges. The BCC noted that the name "North Solomons" lost favor during the crisis, when new political institutions (such as the BIG, BTG, BPC, and BIPG) used the name "Bougainville" to "mark a difference from the pre-conflict situation."[39] The BCC also noted that there was significant international recognition of the name "Bougainville" as a result of the crisis.

The constitution states that the government will be known as the "Autonomous Bougainville Government."[40] The BCC's decision to prominently include the word "autonomous" emphasizes Bougainville's "unique status, distinct from the provinces elsewhere in Papua New Guinea."[41] The constitution leaves it to later laws to create other symbols of Bougainville or the ABG,[42] and in 2013, the ABG accordingly declared that May 17 would be known as "Bougainville Day" to remember those who died during the crisis. Most other symbols had already largely been agreed upon in preparation for the 1975 declaration of independence and were inherited by the ABG. Bougainvillean symbols tend to adopt an ethno-symbolist approach, as they utilize long-standing symbols that resonate widely with the population. For example, the flag has a blue background, and in the center a *upei* sits on a white star cut out of a green background. The blue represents the sea, the green Bougainville's "rich resources," and the white star the badge worn by paramount chiefs, while the *upei* is a hat worn by teenage boys during initiation ceremonies.[43] However, the choice of a *upei* as the national symbol

---

[35] BCC Technical Team, *Matrix of Choices*.
[36] Meaning "motherland" or "main island" in the Motuna language.
[37] Meaning "island of beauty" or "island of women" in the Suir language.
[38] BCC, *Discussion of Recommendations*: 1–2.   [39] BCC, *Report*, 125.
[40] ABG Constitution, s. 2. Colloquially, the government is referred to within Bougainville as the "ABG."
[41] Ghai and Regan, "Unitary State," 600.   [42] ABG Constitution, s. 4(1).
[43] M. Havini, "Perspectives on a Crisis," in Polomka, *Bougainville: Perspectives on a Crisis*, 23.

is problematic, as it is associated with male ceremonies, which means that women are prohibited from wearing the flag[44] and are thereby implicitly excluded from the main symbol of Bougainvillean national identity.

During the crisis, there was "a real worry that Bougainvillean identity was being threatened." Consequently, "no side ever took a proprietary hold on Bougainvillean identity" and the symbols retained their unifying nature.[45] A similar approach has been taken with respect to the capital. Before the crisis, the capital was Arawa, on Bougainville Island. Since the crisis, the interim capital has been at Buka Town, on Buka Island. The constitution leaves the permanent capital to later law, noting that the law should ensure that the capital does not contribute to development problems and is "as accessible as possible to the People."[46]

Defining national identity

The two major ways in which the constitution seeks to define future national identity are via the definition of a "Bougainvillean" and by provisions that seek to promote the recognition of custom and tradition. Significantly, the constitution does not recognize an official language. Instead, in keeping with Papua New Guinea practice, English is the official language for government documents. Primary education is generally conducted in English, Tok Pisin, and *tok ples*, with secondary and tertiary education in English. Overall, there are approximately twenty-one distinct languages and many more sublanguages and dialects in Bougainville.[47] Almost all Bougainvilleans are fluent in Tok Pisin and their *tok ples*, and many are also fluent in English.

The definition of a Bougainvillean was one of the most controversial issues addressed by the BCC. In keeping with the emphasis on Bougainvilleans having black skin, during the public consultations people raised concerns about "half caste" and "quarter caste" people being formally recognized as Bougainvilleans and proposed that chiefs should screen people of "mixed parentage." However, the BCC was reluctant to include requirements that could be perceived as overly discriminatory and instead agreed that "the issue is not so much whether blood is mixed as to whether people belong to the

---

[44] A. Hermkens, "Mary, Motherhood and Nation: Religion and Gender Ideology in Bougainville's Secessionist Warfare," *Intersections: Gender and Sexuality in Asia and the Pacific* 25 (2011).
[45] Interview with an international adviser to the BIPG, BCC, and ABG, August 31, 2010.
[46] ABG Constitution, s. 5.
[47] D. Tryon, "The Languages of Bougainville," in Regan and Griffin, *Bougainville: Before the Conflict*.

culture."[48] Therefore, a person qualifies as a Bougainvillean if he or she is a member (whether by birth or by adoption into a clan lineage) of a clan lineage that owns customary land in Bougainville or if he or she is married to or the child of a Bougainvillean. The constitution does provide that where this definition would lead to "injustice or hardship or disadvantage," a later law can provide exceptions.[49] By emphasizing clan membership, the definition acknowledges that each of Bougainville's "different communities has developed its own strong sense of identity."[50] This reflects Bougainvilleans' possession of levels of identity, with their primary identity being as a member of a particular family hamlet or village, which is based around a single landholding clan lineage, which in turn sits within a wider clan. The constitutional definition provides space for these identities but recognizes that "although there are many differences between [Bougainville's] many language and cultural groups, there are also many similarities."[51]

The definition also highlights the important relationship of Bougainvilleans with their *graun* (land) by anchoring Bougainvillean identity in its ownership. *Graun* not only has a material value as a source of subsistence agriculture and cash crop production, but, Bougainvilleans believe, "it is our *graun* that is the fountain and centre of our lives."[52] *Graun* is communally owned by a clan according to (mostly) matrilineal land lineages and distributed to its members based on seniority and need. Land ownership includes "all resources both upon and below the land," and "outsiders" are not able to enter land without the clan leaders' permission.[53] The emphasis placed on customary land ownership in the definition of a Bougainvillean "does not sit well with the modern concept of citizenship," which is anchored to territorial jurisdiction rather than to specific land.[54] The Papua New Guinea government was particularly concerned that this emphasis would cause people from other parts of Papua New Guinea who reside in Bougainville to be denied the right to equality guaranteed by the Papua New Guinea constitution. However, when read closely, the definition actually provides a "liberal interpretation" of who

---

[48] BCC, *Discussion of Recommendations*, 74–76.   [49] ABG Constitution, s. 7.
[50] BCC, *Report*, 27.
[51] Ibid.; interview with a Bougainvillean women's leader, February 2, 2010; Regan, "Identities among Bougainvilleans."
[52] BCC, *Report*, 132.
[53] P. Polomka, "Land as 'Life,' Security and Impediment to Unity," in Polomka, *Bougainville: Perspectives on a Crisis*, 2.
[54] V. Boege, *Bougainville and the Discovery of Slowness: An Unhurried Approach to State-Building in the Pacific*, The Australian Centre for Peace and Conflict Studies, Occasional Paper Number 3 (Brisbane: University of Queensland, 2006), 32.

qualifies as a Bougainvillean by making it clear that it is "not just a matter of race or appearance," but that anyone can become a member of a landowning clan by marriage, adoption, or otherwise according to custom (and this is not uncommon in practice).[55] At the same time, this mechanism is heavily tied to local sociopolitical practices and therefore militates against an individual being considered Bougainvillean unless he or she engages with – and is accepted by – that sphere.

Although the BCC noted that it was not appropriate to have Bougainvillean citizenship unless Bougainville becomes independent, BCC members were keen to ensure that the rights and obligations of Bougainvilleans were enumerated in the constitution.[56] The idea that rights are accompanied by obligations was not new and is contained in the Papua New Guinea constitution. The inclusion of rights and obligations in the constitution means that the definition of who is a Bougainvillean has important implications. First, only Bougainvilleans can own *graun*,[57] which "logical[ly]" flows from the definition of a Bougainvillean as a member of a landowning clan.[58] However, the BCC did acknowledge that there are increasing pressures on customary landownership and that the ABG will need to formulate a land policy. Second, only Bougainvilleans can vote or stand in ABG elections.[59] This created problems for the BCC, as the Papua New Guinea constitution provides that only Papua New Guinea citizens may vote or stand in elections,[60] but there were people who could meet the definition of "Bougainvillean" without being citizens of Papua New Guinea, some of whom had political grounds for not taking Papua New Guinea citizenship. Eventually, the BCC decided that as Bougainville remained part of Papua New Guinea, the Bougainville constitution had to comply. Consequently, the requirement that Bougainvilleans who vote or stand in elections must also be Papua New Guinea citizens was included. While the Papua New Guinea government expressed concern that limiting these rights only to Bougainvilleans might be discriminatory, the BCC was satisfied that the definition of a Bougainvillean was sufficiently wide to include most long-term residents of Bougainville. Third, Bougainvilleans owe obligations to promote the goals and directive principles set down in the constitution.[61] The BCC justified inclusion of these

---

[55] Interview with an international adviser to the Papua New Guinea government, January 24, 2010.
[56] BCC, *Discussion of Recommendations*.   [57] ABG Constitution, s. 8(1).
[58] BCC, *Report*, 133.   [59] ABG Constitution, ss. 8(1) and 110.
[60] Papua New Guinea Constitution, s. 56.
[61] ABG Constitution, s. 9. These are nonjusticiable, but the constitution and all other Bougainville laws shall be read and applied so as to give effect to the preamble. ABG Constitution, s. 211.

obligations on the basis that "members of our *kastomary* [customary] communities in Bougainville have always enjoyed rights, but at the same time have owed significant obligations to their communities."[62]

The second way the constitution seeks to define future national identity is by emphasizing the central role of custom and tradition. Reflecting an ethnosymbolist approach, it requires that "customary values and practices which enhance the dignity and well-being of Bougainvilleans," historical ancestral sites, artifacts, and Bougainville languages should be "recognized, promoted and preserved."[63] These provisions echo the BCC's public consultations, in which Bougainvilleans expressed an "absolute commitment" to custom and tradition[64] and said that they wanted the constitution to recognize "the rightful place" of customary authority and ways.[65]

Most significantly, the constitution seeks to ensure that customary practices are taken into account during land and resource development.[66] It requires the ABG to develop a land policy that recognizes the roles of traditional leaders in relation to "customary land matters" and incorporates customary practices into "the development and implementation of land law."[67] This reflects feedback received at the BCC's public consultations, at which Bougainvilleans expressed their desire that customary ownership of *graun* be respected. It also reflects the fact that customary landownership includes "all resources both upon and below the land."[68] The failure of the colonial administration and Papua New Guinea government to recognize this fact in respect to the Panguna mine was a major grievance, and during the BCC's public consultations, there was a widespread commitment to clarifying the ownership of natural resources to better reflect Bougainvillean understandings.

The constitution also seeks to recognize and strengthen the clan structure and customary leadership, along with the role of traditional chiefs and other traditional leaders. Accordingly, it recognizes the importance of local customary practices and traditional leaders in respect to governance, alternative dispute resolution, and the administration of justice and protection of human rights, which are discussed in Chapter 8. Overall, the strong recognition of custom and tradition in the constitution reflects the extensive public participation in the constitution-making process, as this meant that Bougainvilleans were given the chance to exercise their constituent power at

---

[62] BCC, *Report*, 136. [63] ABG Constitution, s. 37.
[64] Interview with an international adviser to the BRA and BCC, January 18, 2010.
[65] BCC, *Report*, 51. [66] ABG Constitution, s. 23(1). [67] Ibid., s. 44.
[68] Polomka, "Land as 'Life,'" 2.

the grassroots level and consequently to make sense of the constitution in their village contexts.[69]

Has reconciliation been achieved?

The crisis resulted in "widespread death, injury, trauma and destruction."[70] Government services, infrastructure, and economic activity in most parts of Bougainville were destroyed. There were also less obvious – although no less destructive – consequences. By 1997, when the conflict formally ended, Bougainvilleans were deeply divided, as the crisis had not been just a war of secession between Bougainville and Papua New Guinea but was also a multifaceted conflict within Bougainville – and among Bougainvilleans.[71] Since neither the BRA nor BRF were cohesive, unitary actors, the conflict was essentially a "multiparty" one in which "the adversaries were often nothing more than loose coalitions."[72] In addition, there were "intercommunal customary sub- or mini-wars between traditional societal entities," rooted in preexisting tensions related to economic inequality, access to land, criminality, and traditional disputes.[73] Consequently, the crisis divided families, communities, and clans. The BCC recognized that multifaceted reconciliation was required. It appeared to be aware of the literature, particularly of the notion that a participatory constitution-making process can provide a forum in which grievances can be addressed, compromises reached, and reconciliation achieved. Indeed, the BCC noted that if constitution making is "consultative and inclusive," and if the constitution provides mechanisms to encourage "previously opposed groups to cooperate," this can promote reconciliation.[74] The emphasis on participation, reconciliation, and unification is also explicable by Bougainvillean customary sociopolitical practices, which emphasize all three goals.

Prior to constitution making, the peace process had already achieved significant reconciliation, facilitated by the fact that it was "at times painfully slow."[75] This slow approach "reflected the Melanesian tendency to take time,"

---

[69] Interview with an international academic, January 18, 2010.
[70] UNDP, *Bougainville Rehabilitation, Reconstruction and Development Project*, Project Document Papua New Guinea/98/002 (Port Moresby: United National Development Programme, 2002).
[71] V. Boege, "Peacebuilding and State Formation in Post-Conflict Bougainville," *Peace Review*, 21 (2009): 32.
[72] Regan, *Light Intervention*, 2.
[73] Boege, "Peacebuilding and State Formation," 32; Regan, "Development and Conflict."
[74] BCC, *Report*, 18.   [75] Regan, "The Bougainville Political Settlement," 118.

which contributed to stabilizing the peace.[76] While this led to some concern that the BRA – or at least elements of it – might lose confidence in the process, there was "generally enough progress being made...to assure the Bougainville factions that the National government was in good faith."[77] The peace process was also assisted by the continued operation of both the BPC and BIPG. While this arrangement was "unwieldy and costly," it did mean that a wide range of leaders were involved in decision making, which "probably helped in building understanding of and support for the compromises that the leaders have had to make."[78] The effectiveness of this reconciliation is illustrated by the ability of the members of the different Bougainvillean factions to cooperate in negotiating the Bougainville Peace Agreement and in forming the BCC to make the constitution. This meant that no Bougainville party felt that it had "won."

The peace and constitution-making processes were also accompanied by extensive "informal" reconciliation at the local level, which was "of at least similar importance."[79] This informal process involved liberal-local hybridity, as it drew upon traditional practices dictated by the principle of balanced reciprocity, Christian principles, and more modern liberal practices such as local "peace committees" and "peace treaties."[80] Reconciliation was particularly important as the cultural concept of "collective responsibility" means that clan lineages are held responsible for the acts of their individual members. If wrongdoings are not reconciled, they will be passed down the clan lineage and remain a source of tension even after the wrongdoer has died. While customary reconciliations had been ongoing since the beginning of the crisis, they picked up pace after the Burnham Truce was made in October 1997, with hundreds – and possibly thousands – of reconciliations being held in the time since to "weave...together" formerly opposing parties.[81] One adviser to the Bougainvillean parties argued that these reconciliation efforts "have done more to consolidate popular commitment to peace than any other aspect of the process."[82] This is evidenced by the fact that former combatants

---

[76] Boege, *Discovery of Slowness*, 12.   [77] Regan, "The Bougainville Political Settlement," 118.
[78] Regan, "Why a Neutral Peace Monitoring Force?," 13–14.
[79] Boege, "Peacebuilding and State Formation," 32.
[80] V. Boege, "Hybrid Forms of Peace and Order on a South Sea Island: Experiences from Bougainville (Papua New Guinea)," in *Hybrid Forms of Peace: From Everyday Agency to Post-Liberalism*, ed. O. P. Richmond and A. Mitchell (Houndmills: Palgrave Macmillan, 2012), 94–95.
[81] J. T. Sirivi, "Reconciliation and Renewing the Vision," in Sirivi and Havini, *...As Mothers of the Land*, 176.
[82] Regan, "Why a Neutral Peace Monitoring Force?," 15.

participated in the weapons disposal process, disbanded the BRA and BRF in late 2002, and formed the united Bougainville Ex-Combatants Association in June 2005. Despite this, reconciliation remains incomplete, particularly in the local context, which could pose challenges as the deferred referendum draws nearer.

As the peace and constitution-making processes facilitated reconciliation between much of the political leadership and many combatant leaders, they have worked together more successfully "than might have been expected."[83] Reconciliation ceremonies have also continued, facilitated by the ABG's Division of Peace and Reconciliation.[84] Lurking behind this reconciliation is the referendum on independence, to be held sometime between 2015 and 2020 (unless the ABG decides not to hold it). It was envisaged that the deferred referendum would play a nation-building role when it was combined with the weapons disposal process and the ABG's ability to operate relatively free of the dominance of one particular region (facilitated by the consociational mechanisms discussed below), as it would give Bougainvilleans time to continue reconciliation and learn to work together. However, the knowledge that the referendum will probably be held may provide an incentive to some groups to keep their differences alive. For the time being, both pro-integration and pro-independence leaders appear to want Bougainvilleans to be given a real choice at the referendum so that it constitutes a genuine exercise of self-determination.

Despite this, when the ABG took office in June 2005, societal tensions and unresolved conflicts remained. The most significant societal tension related to Francis Ona and the people of his "Republic of Me'ekamui," who had remained outside the peace and constitution-making processes. This tension was exacerbated by the arrival of Noah Musingku, who acted as a spoiler during the later stages of the constitution-making process and has inflamed tensions in the south of Bougainville Island.

Francis Ona and the Me'ekamui no-go zone

Ona declared his opposition from the early stages of the peace process, claiming that his May 1990 declaration of independence stood. Consequently, he opposed the deployment of the TMG and set up armed roadblocks around

---

[83] A. J. Regan, "Bougainville," paper presented at the Diminishing Conflict Seminar Series, College of Asia and the Pacific, Australian National University, July 29, 2008.

[84] BHRC, *Universal Periodic Review: Bougainville Civil Society Stakeholder Shadow Report to OHCHR* (Buka: Bougainville Human Rights Committee and Civil Society Bougainvilleans, 2011).

a large part of Bougainville Island near the Panguna mine, which he declared a "no-go zone" that included between 5 and 10 percent of the total population of Bougainville. Ona later declared that this no-go zone was the independent "Republic of Me'ekamui,"[85] and the 10 to 15 percent of the BRA who remained loyal to him became known as the Me'ekamui Defence Force (MDF). Ona criticized the peace and constitution-making processes, which created an "air of uncertainty about the survival of peace."[86] However, Ona and his supporters did not actively try to derail either process and largely remained inside the no-go zone, with small pockets of support elsewhere. The main exception was the roadblocks, the most important of which was at Morgan Junction on Bougainville Island, where the east coast trunk road and the only road to the no-go zone intersect. This roadblock constituted a serious limitation on freedom of movement, particularly for those in the south.[87]

The decision by the parties to allow the peace and constitution-making processes to proceed without Ona and his supporters prevented them acting as spoilers. But, it also meant that the processes of making both the Bougainville Peace Agreement and the constitution did not include all Bougainvilleans. Consequently, the peace process was arguably "incomplete" as it "[did] not cover all people in all areas of Bougainville."[88] In addition, the constitution was not the product of the constituent power of all Bougainvilleans. In this regard, several people living within the no-go zone expressed frustration at being kept out of the peace and constitution-making process and submitted a petition to the Papua New Guinea inter-governmental relations minister calling for its removal, which was not achieved. However, Bougainvillean leaders frequently tried to include Ona and his supporters, and Me'ekamui representatives did attend some of the peace talks. During the constitution-making process, the Me'ekamui government was invited to nominate a technical officer to the BCC. Although it did nominate someone, that person never took up the position. In addition, while three positions were set aside on the BCC for representatives from the Me'ekamui government, it did not nominate anyone. Teams of BCC members also sought contact with Ona and his supporters.

---

[85] *Me'ekamui* is similar to "sacred land" in the Nasioi language of central Bougainville. Regan, "Development and Conflict."

[86] J. Kabui, "Peacebuilding & Consolidation," in *Weaving Consensus: The Papua New Guinea – Bougainville Peace Process*, ed. A. Carl and L. Garasu (London: Conciliation Resources in collaboration with BICWF, 2002), 64.

[87] Personal communication from a former BRA supporter, January 25, 2011; Regan, "The Bougainville Intervention."

[88] P. Barter, former Bougainville affairs minister, speaking at "Building Sustainable Peace."

After the constitution was adopted, Ona perceived the ABG as a threat to the viability of his "republic" and staged demonstrations in protest. However, by this time his supporters had begun to question his leadership, particularly after he transformed his republic into the "Kingdom of Me'ekamui" and was crowned its "king" in May 2004. Consequently, more Me'ekamui people began to engage with the peace and constitution-making processes, including eleven Me'ekamui candidates who contested the 2005 ABG election and Me'ekamui people who voted in that election.

After the ABG was formed, MDF members continued to man armed roadblocks, which meant that the ABG did not exercise authority over the entire territory of Bougainville. Indeed, in 2005, the Me'ekamui no-go zone was running as a rival to the ABG, as it had its own institutions of government and dispute resolution and security force. To an extent, this threat was diffused in July 2005 when Ona died, as this created space for increasingly open discussion among the Me'ekamui people about the need to restore formal government services and freedom of movement. Two factions then emerged within the Me'ekamui leadership: the Original Me'ekamui Government (OMG) led by Ona "loyalist" Chris Uma and the Me'ekamui Government of Unity (MGU) led by "dissidents" such as Philip Miriori. In 2006, the MGU opened a dialogue with President Kabui. In August 2007, these talks culminated in the Panguna Communiqué, in which the MGU agreed that an administration would be established under the joint authority of the ABG and the MGU. This saw the MGU leadership, and much of the population of the no-go zone, "effectively agree to join the peace process."[89] A Panguna district administration office was then opened in late 2007. The MGU then formed a political party and fielded two candidates in the 2008 presidential by-election. More people from the no-go zone were able to participate in the 2008 election, with the Morgan Junction roadblock opened to allow electoral officers to reach more of the area.

Efforts to open up the Me'ekamui no-go zone received a boost in December 2008 when Tanis was elected president. Tanis had been a BRA commander and had maintained communication with key MDF leaders. His reconciliation efforts culminated in the February 2009 Panguna Meeting Resolution between the ABG, MGU, Panguna landowners, chiefs, women's and youth leaders, and former combatants. The resolution recorded their agreement to advance reconciliation and to form new landowners' associations to negotiate reopening the Panguna mine. MDF elements associated

---

[89] Regan, *Light Intervention*, 115.

with the MGU and the OMG also began developing a weapons disposal program in late 2009.[90] In March 2010, detailed discussions occurred among the OMG, the MGU, and the ABG and culminated in a memorandum of understanding in which all three entities agreed to continue discussions regarding reopening the mine, establish local government in the no-go zone, and advance reconciliation and weapons disposal. While the memorandum involved "little more than a commitment to continue talking," it was the first time that the three groups had met and, most significantly, the first time that Uma and the OMG "effectively appeared to be entering into the peace process, even if only tentatively."[91] Indeed, many followers of the OMG participated in the 2010 ABG election.

However, hardline Ona loyalists continue to man the Morgan Junction roadblock, hampering the ABG's ability to penetrate some parts of the no-go zone. Despite these efforts, the return of formal government services has received such widespread support within the no-go zone that it has become untenable to prevent ABG officers from entering. The men running the roadblock are also under increased pressure from MGU and OMG leaders, who held a reconciliation ceremony in April 2011 that was witnessed by ABG representatives, after which they pledged to work together to advance weapons disposal and the return of ABG services to the no-go zone. In July 2011, officers conducting the Papua New Guinea census were then permitted into the Me'ekamui area, as was the Australian high commissioner in August 2011, the first time that an Australian government official had entered the no-go zone since the beginning of the crisis. In February 2013, the OMG reiterated its agreement to work with the ABG and MGU in accordance with the ABG's 2011 Panguna Peace Building Strategy, which is intended to promote reconciliation and weapons disposal.

While Ona and the Me'ekamui people remained outside the peace and constitution-making processes, the inclusive nature of those processes enhanced the legitimacy of the Bougainville Peace Agreement, the constitution, and the ABG. This provided an incentive for the Me'ekamui people to reconcile with other Bougainvilleans and to engage with the ABG. Therefore, while reconciliation was not achieved during the constitution-making process, arguably the consensus building and awareness raising achieved during the process cultivated an environment in which later reconciliation could take place. Consequently, although some groups of the Me'ekamui people continue to

---

[90] Personal communication from a village chief and prominent traditional peacemaker, January 27, 2011.
[91] Regan, *Light Intervention*, 117.

maintain their autonomy from the ABG, within the span of ten years significant parts of the Me'ekamui no-gone zone have gradually been incorporated into the ABG, or have at least come to acknowledge its legitimacy.[92]

Noah Musingku and tensions in the south
Tensions arising from the presence of the Me'ekamui no-go zone were exacerbated in 2003 with the arrival of Musingku.[93] Musingku had operated a "failed Ponzi scheme" in Papua New Guinea and had fled to the no-go zone to evade arrest by the Papua New Guinea police.[94] He won Ona's support by promising that he had developed a "new world economic system" that would provide financial support for the Me'ekamui government. Musingku also used Christianity to bolster his legitimacy, by drawing on Pentecostal "prosperity theology" to support his claim that he could "finance the end-time harvest" for his investors.[95]

It was Musingku who encouraged Ona to be crowned king of the "Kingdom of Me'ekamui," at which time Musingku declared himself "prince" of the associated "Kingdom of Papala." However, as it became increasingly clear that Musingku was unable to deliver his promised financial windfall, he fell out of Ona's favor in late 2004. Consequently, he retreated to an area near his home village in the south of Bougainville Island, accompanied by several MDF members who formed the basis of his "royal guard." He then used this guard to attempt to establish roadblocks, with the aim of creating a no-go zone around his "kingdom."

Local communities perceived Musingku as a serious threat to peace and stability, and in 2006, a group of former BRA and BRF combatants formed the Bougainville Freedom Fighters (BFF) to counterbalance him. There were several reported incidents of violence between the BFF and Musingku's guard. The ABG did attempt to reconcile with Musingku and held peace talks with him in September 2006, which resulted in a memorandum of understanding that provided for government services to be returned to the

---

[92] A. J. Regan, "Bougainville Update," paper presented at the State, Society and Governance in Melanesia Seminar Series, College of Asia and the Pacific, Australian National University, November 27, 2012.
[93] For Musingku's perspective, see *The Real Story of the Sovereign Nation of Bougainville Islands & the Twin Kingdoms of Papa'ala and Me'ekamui*, June 2012, accessed September 23, 2013, www.ourbougainville.org/.
[94] Regan, *Light Intervention*, 117.
[95] J. Cox, *Financing the End-Time Harvest: Pyramid Schemes and Prosperity Gospels in Papua New Guinea*, State, Society and Governance in Melanesia Discussion Paper 2009/5 (Canberra: Australian National University, 2009), 7.

Papala no-go zone. Despite this, Musingku and his guard continue to operate. While he is generally regarded as a fraud by educated Bougainvilleans, his clever utilization of modern technology, local custom, and Christian principles has attracted support among some villagers.

The presence of the Me'ekamui and Papala no-go zones also fed ongoing tensions in the south of Bougainville Island throughout the constitution-making process. In response, many former combatants in the south did not participate in the weapons disposal process. Approximately ten different armed groups (such as the BFF) also emerged, purporting to offer local protection. This led to local tensions, many of which arose from unresolved conflict, land disputes, and the scarcity of economic opportunities.[96] These tensions were exacerbated by the ABG's limited role in the south, largely as a result of the Morgan Junction roadblock.[97] From 2005 to 2008, these tensions boiled over into other armed roadblocks and open conflict, resulting in up to sixty deaths. Out of frustration, in October 2006, chiefs from the south demanded that the ABG request an international intervention to restore law and order and remove weapons, with one chief claiming that "Bougainville is a failed state."[98] Due to concern about the dangers of the escalating conflict, increased efforts at promoting reconciliation began in late 2007. In 2008, the ABG developed a task force to support local reconciliation; in 2009, it created the Ministry of Peace, Reconciliation and Weapons Disposal; and in 2012, it adopted the Peace, Security and Weapons Disposal Strategy. These efforts delivered results from mid-2008, and leaders of several armed groups began to exercise restraint and explore ways to end the conflict.[99] While other armed groups remain outside these efforts and continue to inflame tensions in the region, as reconciliation efforts with the MGU, OMG, and other armed groups advance, the ABG should be able to gain better access to the region, which may help mitigate tensions.

Overall, in keeping with the emphasis on inclusiveness and reconciliation that resulted from the extensive public participation during the constitution-making

---

[96] R. Masono, acting chief administrator, Bougainville administration, speaking at "Building Sustainable Peace"; R. Pihei, Fr. J. Bosco, and J. Misang, speaking at "South Bougainville 2005–2008: Local Conflict, Reconciliation, Weapons Disposal and Peace-building," State, Society and Governance in Melanesia seminar, Australian National University, Canberra, November 25, 2008.

[97] Regan, *Light Intervention*, 124.

[98] Quoted in R. Masiu, "Chiefs Demand Arms Clean-up," *Papua New Guinea Post-Courier*, October 17, 2006.

[99] Interview with a former BRA commander and member of the ABG, November 2, 2010; personal communication from an international academic, January 24, 2011.

process, the ABG has attempted to engage with Musingku and other armed groups in the south. Therefore, while their continued presence challenges the ability of the ABG to penetrate those areas and to deliver public goods and services to the people living there, they do not fundamentally challenge the ongoing existence of the ABG.

Are there divisions within society?

While there are divisions between clans and language groups, the most important division is a regional one, which became salient during the crisis and the peace and constitution-making processes. Buka Island, the atoll islands, and the northern parts of Bougainville Island are referred to as the "North," the central part of Bougainville Island as "Central," and the southern part of Bougainville Island as the "South."[100] These labels are roughly based on the boundaries used for Papua New Guinea electorates. While artificial, these boundaries "reflect existing differences, rather than create them."[101] In general, people in the North speak Austronesian languages, follow a matrilineal land tenure system, and select chiefs primarily by heredity. People in the South speak Papuan languages and follow a patrilineal land tenure system, and their chiefs adopt "big man" leadership techniques. People in Central speak Papuan languages but adopt a matrilineal land tenure system and have chiefs that are selected based on a mixture of heredity and "big manship."[102]

The regional division has its roots in the colonial period, during which contact was largely restricted to Buka Island because of its relative geographic proximity to the rest of Papua New Guinea. This led people from Buka to develop "a strong sense of superiority" (in terms of qualities such as intelligence and perceptiveness) related to their "role in bringing 'civilization' to the rest of Bougainville."[103] This perception has been aided by the North's better access to the colonial – later independent – administration and to the educational opportunities and economic development it brought, which means that a high proportion of Buka people are employed in senior positions in Bougainville and other parts of Papua New Guinea. Indeed, a favored stereotype in Buka Island is of Bougainville as a human body, with the brains located

---

[100] M. T. Havini, "The Women's Voices at Burnham: Burnham I Negotiations, 5–18 July 1997," in Sirivi and Havini, ... As Mothers of the Land.
[101] Interview with an international adviser to the BIPG, BCC, and ABG, August 31, 2010.
[102] Ibid.; Griffin et al., Papua New Guinea.
[103] Regan, "Identities among Bougainvilleans," 437.

in Buka Island. In contrast, the South had the least colonial contact and is characterized as a less flattering body part.[104]

Regional identities emerged as a political factor in the late 1960s during the debate about Bougainville's future political status. Leaders from the North tended to favor continued integration with Papua New Guinea, while those from the South, and to a lesser extent Central, favored secession.[105] As momentum for independence built, in 1973 leaders from the North threatened to secede from the rest of Bougainville if leaders from Central and the South passed a resolution in favor of secession. In addition, in the early 1970s, Central (which was home to the Panguna mine) was seen to receive unfair advantages, including compensation payments to landowners.[106]

The regional division was institutionalized in the NSPG. The NSPG constitution utilized consociational techniques to achieve balanced regional representation in the provincial executive, by requiring committees made up of members from constituencies in each region to nominate regional representatives.[107] In addition, a convention developed that the premier, deputy premier, and speaker of the legislature should all be from different regions. The provincial budget also ensured that revenue was distributed fairly between regions.[108]

Once the crisis developed, there was less support for independence in the North. The PNGDF "exploited" this sentiment by co-opting people from the North to form the BRF and support the PNGDF.[109] This has contributed to the emergence of a "long-term ethnic divide between elements of the Buka population and the Bougainville mainland."[110] However, it should be noted that this ethnic division is not the same as those that occur in many other internal conflicts, as it does not involve two or three distinctive ethnic groups. Instead, while the regional division is significant, each region is home to numerous clan and language groups, with none large enough to dominate.

---

[104] A. J. Regan, *Conflict among Bougainvilleans 1988–1998: Implications for the Peace Process*, State, Society and Governance in Melanesia Working Paper 1999 (Canberra: Australian National University, 1999).

[105] A. Mamack and R. Bedford, "Bougainville Copper Mineworkers Strike, 1975," in *Race Class and Rebellion in the South Pacific*, ed. A. Mamack and A. Ali (Sydney: George Allen and Unwin, 1974).

[106] Regan, "Identities among Bougainvilleans."

[107] *Constitution of North Solomons Provincial government 1976*, s. 49.

[108] Regan, "Identities among Bougainvilleans."

[109] Ghai and Regan, "Bougainville and the Dialectics of Ethnicity," 258.

[110] Regan, "Development and Conflict," 101.

Therefore, division between groups, including those identified as ethnic, is not the main basis on which political leaders seek to mobilize support.[111]

During the peace process, Bougainvillean leaders were at pains to achieve reconciliation between the three regions, particularly between pro-independence and pro-integration supporters. These efforts shifted to achieving "equitable geographical representation in the structures of government" during the constitution-making process.[112] The BCC sought to achieve this via a number of consociational mechanisms in the constitution. First, constituencies are evenly distributed across the three regions.[113] Second, the president and vice president must come from different regions.[114] Third, within the legislature, members from each region must form regional committees. Fourth, to ensure even representation in the executive, its members must be evenly selected from lists nominated by the regional committees.[115] Fifth, seats reserved for representatives of women and former combatants in the legislature are elected on a regional basis.

When these efforts are combined with the nation-building work done by the constitution, threats that Buka Island might secede if Bougainville becomes independent have diminished. In particular, many Buka people recognize that Buka Island relies on the rest of Bougainville for funding.[116] However, the South is more politically active and more militant, and the Morgan Junction roadblock means there continues to be some disparity between the level of public services and economic development delivered in the North compared to that in the South.[117] While the level of service delivery in the South is improving as the ABG gains access to more areas, there is a strong impression that the North "seems to be enjoying everything in post-conflict Bougainville."[118] Despite this, the salience of the regional division seems to have lessened since autonomy, evidenced by the fact that Bougainvilleans have not pressured the ABG to create the regional governments foreseen in the constitution. Moreover, in July 2011, the first interdistrict reconciliation, between districts in Central and South Bougainville, was held. This suggests that nation-building and reconciliation efforts throughout the

---

[111] A. J. Regan, *Bougainville: The Peace Process and Beyond, Submission to the Foreign Affairs Sub-Committee of the Joint Standing Committee on Foreign Affairs, Defence and Trade Inquiry*, June 1999.

[112] BCC, *Report*, 214. [113] ABG Constitution, s. 105. [114] Ibid., s. 96(1). [115] Ibid., s. 71.

[116] Interview with an international adviser to the BIPG, BCC, and ABG, August 31, 2010.

[117] Interview with a Bougainvillean intellectual, October 16, 2010; I. Scales, R. Craemer, and I. Thappa, *Market Chain Development in Peace Building: Australia's Roads, Wharves and Agriculture Projects in Post-Conflict Bougainville* (Canberra: AusAID, 2008).

[118] J. Misang, speaking at "South Bougainville 2005–2008."

peace and constitution-making processes, as well as the mechanisms to achieve even regional representation in the ABG incorporated into the constitution, have had some effect.

The reduced salience of the regional division is reflected in the results of the 2010 ABG general election. Momis, the leader of the pro-integration New Bougainville Party, comprehensively won the presidential election, taking 43,047 votes overall (52.35 percent). His closest competitor, Tanis, the leader of the pro-independence Bougainville Independence Movement, took only 17,205 votes (20.93 percent). Momis not only took a comprehensive lead in the North (with 19,341 votes, or 54.09 percent) compared to Tanis (who had 5,834 votes, or 16.32 percent), but he also achieved an overwhelming majority in the South (with 17,771 votes, or 61.63 percent) compared to Tanis (who had 6,217 votes, or 21.56 percent). Given that Momis's supporter base is generally in the more pro-integration North and the South is generally considered to be pro-independence, it appears that the regional division did not influence voters' decision making. The results in Central were closer, with Momis taking 5,935 votes (or 33.66 percent) compared to Tanis's 5,154 votes (29.23 percent), which can be explained by the fact that Tanis is from Central and has a significant support base there.[119]

Does the community exhibit evidence of citizenization?

The level of citizenization in Bougainville can be indicated by the presence of an ethos of constitutionalism and the level of ongoing participation in government institutions, evidence of which includes electoral turnouts, strategic voting, and people's engagement in other opportunities for political participation provided in the constitution.

Ethos of constitutionalism

There appears to be a relatively strong ethos of constitutionalism among political elites, who have worked through the ABG and other institutions created by the constitution since its adoption in 2005. This ethos was challenged almost immediately after the ABG came into existence, when Momis attempted to mount a legal challenge to the 2005 ABG election results, claiming that there were irregularities in the poll and that voters had been intimidated. However, he garnered little sympathy; instead, there were calls

---

[119] N. Kelly, *Electoral Democracy in Post-Conflict Melanesia: The 2010 Bougainville and Solomon Island Elections*, Centre for Democratic Institutions Policy Paper on Political Governance 2010/20 (Canberra: Australian National University, 2010).

for him to accept the outcome and not jeopardize the implementation of the political settlement. After two weeks, Momis dropped his challenge, apparently in order to avoid destabilizing the ABG, which ensured that the constitution remained in place.

There was some indication that President Kabui developed a level of disregard for the constitution. For example, after reports that then–vice president Joseph Watawi was drunk in public, Kabui dismissed him from the vice presidency in May 2007. However, Watawi remained in the executive, which gave rise to claims that Kabui had breached the constitutional requirement that a person dismissed from the vice presidency ceases to be a member of the executive.[120] Kabui acknowledged that he had technically breached the constitution by letting Watawi remain in the executive, but he justified his decision as being in "the best interest of Bougainville and its people."[121]

Political elites demonstrated their commitment to constitutionalism following President Kabui's death in June 2008. As Kabui had taken a leading role in the BPC, BCC, and ABG, his sudden absence created a "palpable sense of drift," aided by the fact that it took six months to organize a by-election due to the challenges of building capacity and obtaining funding from the Papua New Guinea government.[122] This period of uncertainty offered "strong men" who had emerged in the legislature an opportunity to destabilize the ABG, and there were proposals to amend the constitution to allow the selection of a new president from within the legislature. When this proposal was made public, "there was a strong sense on the street that that just was not possible," as people wanted to see a new president elected.[123] Consequently, none of the emergent strong men felt that they had the credibility to assume the presidency, and a by-election was called. Therefore, the constitution continued to be obeyed and the new president was elected in accordance with its provisions.

The extensive public participation that occurred during the constitution-making process assisted the inculcation of an ethos of constitutionalism among ordinary Bougainvilleans, who already had a sense that constitutions are something that will – and should – be adhered to from Papua New Guinea's good record of observing its constitution (albeit with exceptions during the crisis).[124] While the high level of participation meant that Bougainvilleans

---

[120] ABG Constitution, s. 96(2).
[121] Quoted in "Kabui Breached Law: Rabanz," *Papua New Guinea Post-Courier*, May 24, 2007.
[122] Regan, "Bougainville's New Directions."   [123] Ibid.
[124] A. J. Regan, "Introduction," in *Twenty Years of the Papua New Guinea Constitution*, ed. A. J. Regan, O. Jessep, and E. L. Kwa (Sydney: Lawbook Co., 2001).

were aware that their new constitution was being drafted and that it would create the ABG, it is questionable how widely the constitution has been distributed to the predominantly rural population, and there is consequently little knowledge among the rural population of its technical aspects, including the actual powers held by the ABG. This has led to some disappointment among Bougainvilleans concerning the performance of the ABG, as they had "high expectations" that it would have the powers and functions to immediately deal with the issues that precipitated the crisis.[125] Instead, the process for the transfer of powers in the Bougainville Peace Agreement meant that the ABG was immediately able to exercise only the same powers as the BIPG.

Electoral turnouts and strategic voting

High levels of electoral participation are a quantifiable indicator of citizenization. Voter turnout for the 2005 ABG general election was strong, at 58 percent of registered voters. While this was lower than expected, it can be partly explained by the fact that there were problems with the completeness of the electoral roll, which prevented people from casting votes and inflated the number of registered voters through duplication and deceased voters remaining on the list. Challenges of transport and communication, which are even more extreme in Bougainville than in Timor-Leste, also made traveling to polling booths difficult. In addition, while the two-week electoral period meant that polling teams could travel around to access voters, some of these visits clashed with local religious and customary ceremonies. Problems also arose when people were outside their constituencies, as Bougainville does not allow absentee voting. In light of these challenges, many voters may have been simply unable – as opposed to unwilling – to cast their vote. Indeed, since the election was the "culmination for many people of the peace process," mobilizing voters was "a relatively easy matter."[126]

Electoral participation in the 2008 presidential by-election was much lower, at 28.5 percent of registered voters. There were again problems with the electoral roll. In addition, the by-election was held only eighteen months

---

[125] Interview with a former BRA commander and member of the ABG, November 2, 2010; R. Masono, *Government Capacity and Citizen Expectations in Bougainville: The Impact of Political Autonomy*, Crawford School of Economics and Government Discussion Paper 06–08 (Canberra: Australian National University, August 2006); personal communication from a member of the ABG, November 4, 2010.
[126] Regan, "Bougainville's New Directions"; Commonwealth Secretariat/PIF, *General Election for the Autonomous Bougainville Government: Report of the Commonwealth-Pacific Islands Forum Expert Team* (Suva: Pacific Islands Forum/Commonwealth Secretariat, June 4, 2005).

before the "real" ABG general election, so many leading figures did not stand as candidates but opted to conserve their campaign finances and energies for the general election. Therefore, the election involved fourteen candidates who were not clearly differentiated and engaged in little campaigning. Consequently, there was no sense that the election was important to Bougainville's political future and there was little enthusiasm for any one candidate.[127]

The 2010 ABG election saw the highest electoral turnout to date, at 63.6 percent of registered voters. This rate of turnout would probably have been higher but for continuing inaccuracies in voter registration rolls, lack of provision for absentee votes,[128] and serious challenges of transport and communication.

The voting strategies utilized by Bougainvilleans illustrate a growing sense of citizenization. The 2005 ABG election was an obvious contest between Kabui and Momis, each with strong party support, money, mobilization, and "clear ideological differences," as Kabui was pro-independence and Momis favored continued integration with Papua New Guinea. Since Momis had been governor of the BIPG for five years and Kabui had been president of the BPC for six years, "effectively there was a very long campaign period" and people "knew what these two people stood for, or thought they did."[129] In addition, the BIPG had established an awareness program relating to the ABG and the elections, although there were questions over the effectiveness of this program, with claims that some leaders used the funding provided to support their election campaigns.[130] Churches and civil society groups also undertook an awareness campaign about the ABG. The election campaign was further covered on Radio Bougainville and in the two Papua New Guinea newspapers.

There was evidence of a shift in the issues people considered when making their electoral choice in the 2008 presidential by-election. Voters began to move their focus away from the issues of the crisis and toward the performance of the ABG, appearing to prioritize immediate concerns of local conflict and economic development, which seems to indicate growing political sophistication.[131]

---

[127] Regan, "Bougainville's New Directions."
[128] Except for limited provision for eligible Bougainvilleans to vote at polling stations in major Papua New Guinea cities.
[129] Regan, "Bougainville's New Directions."
[130] "Leadership Fails to Turn Up," *Papua New Guinea Post*-Courier, May 2, 2005; R. Masiu, "Call for Proper Poll Awareness," May 4, 2005.
[131] A. J. Regan, speaking at "Elections in Bougainville and Solomon Islands," State, Society and Governance in Melanesia Conference, Australian National University, Canberra, November 3, 2010.

Significantly, the MGU fielded three candidates in the election, which signaled a growing sense of citizenization among the Me'ekamui people.

Voters continued to exhibit a developing sophistication when making their electoral choices in the 2010 ABG election. The question of Bougainville's future political status had little influence as there was a "sense that autonomy is going ahead and that the referendum will happen."[132] Significantly, candidates who campaigned as former combatants did not do well; they were met with claims that "people want to move on."[133] Instead, voters took an interest in the performance of the ABG, progress in the implementation of the Bougainville Peace Agreement, and improvements in Bougainville's development. As a result of dissatisfaction with the way members of the ABG had performed, 75 percent of sitting members lost their seats, which suggests that Bougainvilleans are aware that they are entitled to public goods and services from the ABG, expect them to be provided, and are willing to punish their elected representatives if they are not. Importantly, many Bougainvilleans appear to have been interested in these issues and cast their votes accordingly.

However, while the New Bougainville Party took thirteen seats in the 2010 election, the BPC party two seats, and the Labour Party one seat, independent candidates took the remaining twenty-three seats. These results suggest that political parties are relatively weak. Indeed, during the election campaign, the two leading presidential candidates, Momis and Tanis, did not refer to their party affiliation on their campaign posters. While parties did endorse candidates for all seats, "no party displayed an identifiable slogan, logo or colour to connect voters with the party 'brand.'"[134] The apparent weakness of political parties may challenge the claim that there is strong citizenization, since political parties are seen as constituting avenues by which people exercise their citizenship, as they can organize people to pursue policy-making agendas and make demands of the ABG. Yet, even if Bougainvilleans make their electoral decisions based on the individual personalities of candidates rather than on their party affiliations, there is no reason to assume that they are not (at least in part) making these decisions based on those candidates' policies and performance. The weakness of political parties may simply reflect the views expressed during the BCC's public consultation, in which the majority of Bougainvilleans did not favor having political parties.[135]

Evidence of growing citizenization is also provided by the lack of any significant violence during or after the three elections. Independent electoral

---

[132] Ibid.
[133] P. Nisira and J. Tanis, speaking at "Elections in Bougainville and Solomon Islands."
[134] Kelly, *Electoral Democracy*, 10.   [135] BCC, *Report*.

observers have concluded that the elections were "democratic, transparent, inclusive and credible."[136] In preparation for the 2010 election, the MGU allowed the ABG's electoral commission, police, and international observers unfettered access to the no-go zone. Importantly, in the Me'ekamui and Papala no-go zones and in the conflict-ridden South, there was no interference in the 2010 election by roadblocks or armed groups. One member of the ABG argued that this demonstrates the "maturity" of Bougainvilleans in accepting the democratic process and moving away from conflict.[137]

Other forms of political participation

As predicted in the literature, the extensive public participation in the constitution-making process resulted in a constitution that provides several innovative ways in which Bougainvilleans can participate in government. Indeed, the BCC noted that during public consultations, Bougainvilleans made "strong demands" that the ABG be "highly democratic and accountable to the people."[138] The first way the constitution seeks to achieve this is via citizen-initiated legislation. Based on its public consultations, the BCC determined that Bougainvilleans wanted a participatory approach to political decision making, in accordance with the consultative nature of local sociopolitical practices.[139] With this aim in mind, the constitution provides scope for a later law to establish a procedure whereby Bougainvilleans can initiate proposals for making laws, and those proposed laws can to be subjected to a poll in which Bougainvilleans can vote on whether they become law.[140] With the goal of achieving "participatory democracy" in mind, the BCC also agreed that the ABG should be empowered to conduct plebiscites to consult people on "issues of major importance."[141] Therefore, the constitution provides scope for a later law to establish a procedure allowing for the conduct of plebiscites. There is also a mechanism allowing for the recall of members of the legislature, which is discussed in Chapter 8.

In addition to these mechanisms, Bougainvilleans have conducted marches and organized petitions to protest the perceived poor performance of ABG members. For example, in May 2007, after reports that then–vice president Watawi was drunk in public, more than 500 people held a protest march in Buka to demand his dismissal. Former combatants also submitted a petition calling for his dismissal and for that of any ABG member perceived to

---

[136] Commonwealth Secretariat/PIF, *General Election*; PIF, *Report of the Pacific Islands Form Secretariat's Election Observer Team to the 2010 Elections for the Office of President and Members of the House of Representatives of the Autonomous Region of Bougainville*, Suva, Pacific Islands Forum, 2010.

[137] Nisira, speaking at "Elections in Bougainville and Solomon Islands."   [138] BCC, *Report*, 213.

[139] Ibid.   [140] ABG Constitution, s. 196.   [141] Ibid., s. 195.

disregard the constitution. They lodged another petition in December 2007 calling for international intervention to end conflict in the South. Similarly, in September 2009, youth groups held a march in Buka to call for the ABG to eradicate corruption and comply with the constitution. In September 2012, ex-combatants marched in Buka to present a petition to the ABG to voice their frustrations about the lack of progress being made on the implementation of the Bougainville Peace Agreement. However, on occasion, Bougainvilleans have let their frustration become violent. For example, in January 2008, the ABG District Office in Arawa was burned down by local people who felt that they were not getting enough public services.

As the ABG has become more established, there are now strong indications that Bougainvilleans are "highly politicised" and feel free to scrutinize – and criticize – the ABG.[142] Bougainvillean interlocutors commented that "you have to be really ready to be a Member of Parliament"[143] because "everybody wants to know what happens and be included in decision-making."[144] There have been community demands for more information about the ABG. In response, in June 2006, all public servants stopped work for three days to undertake an education campaign. In addition, in 2008, the role of parliamentary education officer was established within the Office of the Clerk of Parliament. This officer is tasked with "taking Parliament to the people" via a "Parliament Today" radio program, community outreach to provide education and awareness about the ABG, a simulated youth parliament, and an education group, which aims to promote the UN Millennium Development Goal of achieving sustainable development.[145] The officer reported that each of these initiatives has met with an "enthusiastic" response, with people requesting additional workshops and awareness sessions relating to the ABG in their villages. In particular, after the high turnover of members of the legislature in the 2010 election, several members of the ABG requested that educational sessions be held in their constituencies in the hope that if people better understand the functions and powers of the ABG, they might be more forgiving of their representatives at the next election.[146] Most recently, the ABG has embarked on education and awareness campaigns in which

---

[142] Interview with an ABG official and member of a council of elders, January 22, 2011; Regan, speaking at "Elections in Bougainville and Solomon Islands."
[143] Interview with a Bougainvillean intellectual, October 16, 2010.
[144] Interview with an ABG official and member of a council of elders, January 22, 2011.
[145] E. Kenehata, ABG parliamentary education officer, speaking at "Elections in Bougainville and Solomon Islands"; personal communication from a former member of the ABG, November 9, 2010.
[146] Personal communication from E. Kenehata, November 4, 2010; personal communication from a former member of the ABG, November 9, 2010.

members of the ABG toured the region with the aim of "instilling democratic values, [and the] rule of law"[147] as well as updating people on the progress being made on implementing the Bougainville Peace Agreement. In 2012, the ABG also created its own website, on which it publishes the "Bougainville Bulletin" to provide information about its work.[148]

A number of factors help to explain the high level of citizenization in Bougainville. The extensive public participation that occurred during the constitution-making process, and the peace process before it, empowered Bougainvilleans through the experience of seeing that their views and activities "really do count and can make a difference."[149] The emphasis placed on political participation reflects local sociopolitical practices of consultation and consensus in political decision making. In this regard, Volker Boege draws parallels between local sociopolitical decision making and deliberative democracy.[150] Indeed, the BCC recognized that because Bougainvilleans are used to a participatory and inclusive system, they did not want "just indirect democracy, where the only direct role for the people is selecting representatives who would make all key decisions on their behalf. They wanted a direct role."[151] Overall, the high level of citizenization appears to support the arguments presented in the literature regarding the benefits of extensive public participation in constitution making.

Is there a strong public sphere?

The three main elements of the public sphere in Bougainville are the media, churches, and civil society.

The media

The print media consists of two daily newspapers, which are published out of Port Moresby. They are available in Buka and are brought back to villages by people who commute to work there. Both newspapers provide coverage of the work of the ABG. The most widely circulated paper, the *Post-Courier*, has a dedicated Bougainville page in each edition. As literacy levels are high, newspapers are well read and understood when they reach people.

Radio is the main way that people – particularly in rural areas – receive news. Bougainville has two radio stations, the government-funded Radio

---

[147] J. Momis, speaking in "President Reflects on Progress in Bougainville Peace Process," *Radio Australia*, February 21, 2011.
[148] www.bougainvillebulletin.com/, accessed October 20, 2013.
[149] Boege, *Discovery of Slowness*, 14. [150] Ibid. [151] BCC, *Report*, 213.

Bougainville and the privately owned New Dawn Bougainville. In 2005, sessions of the Bougainville legislature were broadcast live on Radio Bougainville, although this later ceased due to lack of funding.[152] In its place, there is a weekly "Parliament Today" program run by the ABG's parliamentary education officer, which features stories explaining parliamentary procedures and interviews with ministers, members of the legislature, and the chairs of the different parliamentary committees.[153] The "Parliament Today" program has a wide audience and receives "very good feedback,"[154] indicating that Bougainvilleans are interested in hearing how their legislature works and what it is doing. In 2011, the ABG also began a weekly radio program, "Know Your Government," on New Dawn FM, on which the ABG president also has a weekly information program, although New Dawn is presently broadcast only on Buka Island. It is also common to use songs to portray political messages. For example, in the lead-up to the 2010 ABG election, a song explaining the importance of voting was regularly broadcast on Radio Bougainville. As song and dance play an important role in Bougainville custom, the use of a song to communicate this message had particular resonance.

While many Bougainvilleans do own televisions and can receive both Papua New Guinea and Australian television broadcasts, the low level of electrification and expense of running diesel generators mean that they are rarely watched. However, an increasingly important communications tool is mobile telephones. The two mobile phone networks collectively cover nearly 100 percent of the North and 70 percent of Central, though they have less reach in the South.[155] A popular way of circulating political messages and critiques is via text message "phone trees." During fieldwork in 2011, a popular text message being circulated used a clever adaptation of the Lord's Prayer to critique the performance of the ABG.

Churches

The churches continue to play the most prominent role in the public sphere. In particular, during the crisis and peace process, church groups were involved in conflict resolution and facilitating reconciliation. Accordingly, President Kabui sought counsel from the heads of the churches in relation to ABG policy. President Momis is a former Catholic priest who retains strong ties to the church. Church leaders play an important role in shaping public

---

[152] Interview with an ABG official and member of a council of elders, January 22, 2011.
[153] Kenehata, speaking at "Elections in Bougainville and Solomon Islands."
[154] Personal communication from E. Kenehata, November 4, 2010.
[155] UNDP, *UNDP Bougainville Programme: End of Year Report* (Buka: United National Development Programme, 2008).

opinion via their sermons and, increasingly, by their ties to (or at least endorsements of) political candidates.[156] Because the three main churches remain the largest providers of education and health care, they also have considerable political weight. This weight has been enhanced by the churches' growing engagement in commercial projects such as real estate, hotels, shipping, agriculture, and plantations.

Other civil society organizations

There is an increasingly active civil society, with women's organizations the most prominent. Many of these groups date back to the crisis period, when they were formed to promote reconciliation.[157] They then played an important role in promoting awareness of the peace and constitution-making process, and since autonomy, they have campaigned aggressively to promote women's rights and development. At the same time, only a small proportion of Bougainvilleans, mostly from educated, urban backgrounds, belong to these groups. In addition, the individuals involved are often traditional or church leaders or members of the ABG (or, before that, the BIPG or BPC) and local governments. Therefore, it is unclear whether these groups attract support because of this or because of the legitimacy of their message.[158]

CONCLUSION

In its report, the BCC described how "the many identities of our communities within Bougainville combine to shape our Bougainville identity, just like many small streams combining to form a river."[159] In 1997, when the peace process began, these small streams were turbulent and seemed destined to run in opposite directions. While challenges remain, the Bougainville case in many ways constitutes an ideal-type participatory (peace- and) constitution-making process, as there was extensive participation, which generated a constituent process. As a result, extensive reconciliation has been achieved and the many conflicting small streams of society have been funneled together to form a relatively united Bougainvillean identity.

---

[156] Interview with an ABG official and member of a council of elders, January 22, 2011.
[157] Sirivi and Havini, ... As Mothers of the Land.
[158] A. J. Regan, "An Outcomes Perspective on Civil Society in Melanesia: Reflections on Experience from Bougainville," paper presented at the Fourth Plenary: Governance and Civil Society, State, Society and Governance in Melanesia Project, Australian National University, Canberra, October 1, 2003.
[159] BCC, Report, 59.

8

Constituted power in Bougainville

This chapter assesses whether the extensive public participation in the constitution-making process affected the role that the Bougainville constitution plays in creating state institutions. To do this, it considers the following five indicators of whether the constitution and the state institutions it creates are functioning effectively and are perceived to be legitimate:

- Have state institutions been created, and are they functioning effectively?
- To what extent are the state institutions perceived to be legitimate?
- Are the state institutions delivering public goods and services?
- Are law and order enforced and is the rule of law observed?
- Are human rights and civil liberties protected?

This chapter concludes by considering the implications of Bougainville's uncertain political future.

THE ROLE OF PARTICIPATION IN CREATING STATE INSTITUTIONS

Have state institutions been created, and are they functioning effectively?

As in all liberal democracies, the constitution creates institutions to exercise the Bougainvillean people's political power. These institutions consist of the ABG, the levels of formal government below it, and the traditional system of government.[1] The ABG consists of three organs: the House of Representatives, the Bougainville Executive Council, and the Bougainville courts. The BCC considered the liberal concept of the separation of powers. It noted that the small scale of customary sociopolitical institutions meant that "there has never

---

[1] ABG Constitution, s. 40.

been the same need for the degree of specialisation in the functions of government as there is in larger societies."[2] However, it concluded that the separation of powers should be enshrined in the constitution, given the larger scale of the ABG. Accordingly, the constitution specifies that "in principle, the respective powers and functions of the three principal arms shall be kept separate from each other."[3]

The House of Representatives and Executive Council

The House of Representatives is the primary organ that exercises legislative power.[4] It is a liberal institution with thirty-nine democratically elected members (MHRs):[5]

- thirty-three MHRs representing single-member constituencies;[6]
- three MHRs representing the interests of the women, one from each region of Bougainville; and
- three MHRs representing the interests of former combatants, one from each region.[7]

The Speaker, who is appointed from outside the House by a vote of the MHRs,[8] and the directly elected Bougainville president, who heads the Bougainville Executive Council,[9] also sit in the House. The BCC considered different models of executive-legislative relations and decided that apart from the president, all members of the council must be MHRs.[10] It was hoped that a directly elected president would remove the threat of votes of "no-confidence" that regularly destabilize Papua New Guinea's Westminster system. There was a broad consensus in favor of this in the BCC's public consultations.[11] The "parliamentary executive" model is "regarded in many ways as having the worst features" of both the Westminster and presidential systems, as it can see a president elected from a different party from the one dominating the House.[12] This occurred after Momis won the presidency in 2010, as only thirteen of his New Bougainville Party members were elected. While he appointed as many as possible to the council, he has no control over the House to ensure that his

---

[2] BCC, *Report*, 227.   [3] ABG Constitution, s. 41.   [4] Ibid., ss. 53–54.   [5] Ibid., s. 55(2).
[6] Ibid., s. 105.   [7] Ibid., s. 55(5)-(8).
[8] Ibid., s. 60. The Speaker will not vote unless it is to break a tie or where one vote is needed to constitute a majority greater than a simple majority vote. ABG Constitution, s. 64. A deputy Speaker is also appointed from within the House to exercise the Speaker's powers when the Speaker is absent. Ibid., ss. 62–63(3).
[9] Ibid., ss. 88, 89 and 93.
[10] Ibid., ss. 79–80; BCC, *Discussion of Recommendations*; BCC, *Report*.
[11] BCC, *Discussion of Recommendations*.   [12] Regan, "Bougainville's New Directions."

legislative program is passed. In addition, if the president is in serious conflict with the majority of the House, he or she cannot be easily removed, even if this leads to legislative deadlock. This occurred when James Tanis was elected president in 2008, as he was the only member of the Bougainville Independence Party and the House blocked several of his proposed bills.

The House of Representatives and Executive Council function as intended, and "as well as any others in the region."[13] The House has passed many procedural laws, including a detailed Bougainville Elections Act, Transport Infrastructure Act, and Parliamentary Service Act.[14] While parliamentary committees meet monthly, the legislature generally sits for only three to four days every three months, which has meant that it has not yet passed many laws relating to the wide range of functions and powers that are available to the ABG.[15] In the absence of Bougainville laws, Papua New Guinea laws continue to apply.[16] This rate of legislative development can be largely attributed to the slow transfer of powers and functions from the Papua New Guinea government.[17] The ABG was immediately given the same powers and functions as the BIPG,[18] as the Papua New Guinea government already had staff in Bougainville exercising them, so there was capacity and funding in place. Until 2010, this remained the extent of the functions and powers exercised by the ABG, with the exception of policing powers, which were transferred to the BIPG in December 2003. More recently, legislative development has been hampered by the fact that four MHRs either stepped down from their positions or died, and by-elections for their replacements were delayed by almost a year due to a lack of funding.

In November 2006, the ABG applied for the transfer of mining, oil, and gas functions and powers, as well as twenty-seven related powers. It became clear that while the provisions of the Bougainville Peace Agreement and Part XIV of the Papua New Guinea constitution dealt with the internal procedures to be followed by the ABG when considering whether to apply for a transfer, the Bougainville Peace Agreement and Papua New Guinea constitution were unclear about the formal procedures that would govern interactions between

---

[13] Interview with an ABG official and member of a council of elders, January 22, 2011.
[14] Bougainville Elections Act (2007) (ABG); Transport Infrastructure Act (2013) (ABG); Parliamentary Service Act (2009) (ABG).
[15] Interview with an ABG official and member of a council of elders, January 22, 2011.
[16] Papua New Guinea Constitution, s. 296(1).
[17] J. Momis, "Challenges of Implementing the Bougainville Peace Agreement," State, Society and Governance in Melanesia Seminar, Australian National University, March 1, 2011; Regan, *Light Intervention*.
[18] Bougainville Peace Agreement, cl. 52(a); Papua New Guinea Constitution, s. 294(2).

the ABG and Papua New Guinea government. Accordingly, at the November 2006 JSB meeting, the two governments signed an Agreed Understanding that provided a six-step process of transfer. As the transfer of mining, oil, and gas powers was particularly complex, the two governments agreed to a specific fifteen-step process for that transfer.

There are several reasons why the transfer of powers and functions to the ABG has been slow. The process has created coordination challenges for the Papua New Guinea government, as numerous departments and agencies are responsible for different powers and functions.[19] To address these, the government has created a Central Agencies Coordination Committee and a National Coordination Office for Bougainville Affairs. The ABG also has little capacity, staff, facilities, or funding, which has generated reluctance within the Papua New Guinea government to transfer powers.[20] In addition, many Papua New Guinea government officials do not understand their government's obligation to make transfers, partly because people involved in negotiating the Bougainville Peace Agreement have left the government. Instead, Bougainville is often seen as just "another province."[21] The process has also been complicated by tensions between the two governments, particularly during Kabui's tenure as president. There was a "marked decrease" in tensions during Tanis's term, as he worked to develop better links with the Papua New Guinea government.[22] As a result, the process of transferring mining powers began in earnest in late 2008 and is now nearing completion. In February 2009, Tanis also requested the transfer of five basic functions: women's and youth affairs, time zones, public holidays, sports and recreation, and licensing the sale of alcoholic beverages. He achieved the transfer in March 2010. While these powers were largely "symbolic," they did allow the ABG to "save face."[23]

There is some suggestion that one of the reasons Bougainvilleans voted for Momis as president in 2010 is because they expected that his long tenure as a member of the Papua New Guinea Parliament would facilitate the transfer of powers.[24] This was not initially the case. During the first six months of Momis's term, tensions rose, with the Papua New Guinea government

---

[19] Wolfers, "Bougainville Seeks Transfer of Powers."
[20] P. Barter, speaking at "Building Sustainable Peace"; interview with an international adviser to the BIPG, BCC, and ABG, August 31, 2010.
[21] Personal communication from a member of the ABG, November 4, 2010; Momis, "Challenges of Implementing."
[22] Regan, "Bougainville's New Directions."
[23] Interview with a former BRA commander and member of the ABG, November 2, 2010; interview with an international adviser to the BIPG, BCC, and ABG, August 31, 2010.
[24] Personal communication from a member of the ABG, November 4, 2010.

canceling a special meeting of the JSB in August 2010 without notifying the ABG. When the meeting was rescheduled to October 2010, Papua New Guinean ministers did not attend, leading to the meeting being postponed. However, when the meeting was eventually held in February 2011, a breakthrough was achieved when key divisions of the Bougainville administration signed memoranda of understanding with their Papua New Guinea government counterparts relating to the transfer of functions and powers. Accordingly, in March 2011, a transfer of twenty-five health-related functions was made to the ABG Health Department. In June 2011, about one-third of the powers and functions relating to education were transferred to the ABG's Education Department. However, tensions resurfaced when the March 2012 JSB meeting was cancelled because members of the Papua New Guinea government failed to attend, leading President Momis to observe that the Papua New Guinea government "is not taking its commitments seriously."[25]

The situation improved after a change of the Papua New Guinea government in July 2012, and by August, 140 powers and functions had been transferred or delegated to the ABG relating to education, health, land and physical planning, forestry, primary industry, and community development. The new Papua New Guinea government has also been more willing to meet with ABG officials, transfer funding, and take concrete steps to prepare for the referendum. Accordingly, the JSB was held in October 2012, at which the ABG and Papua New Guinea government signed the Kokopo Communique, in which the Papua New Guinea government agreed to increase funding to Bougainville in order to support the development of its autonomy. In March 2013, the ABG and Papua New Guinea government also convened a panel of experts to conduct a "Joint Review of Autonomy Arrangements" to report on the implementation of the Bougainville Peace Agreement.

Despite this recent progress, the relatively slow transfer of powers has caused frustration within the ABG. In addition, one ABG member observed that ordinary Bougainvilleans have "become frustrated" as many do not understand that the ABG does not already have all the powers available to it under the Bougainville Peace Agreement. This frustration may be partly a result of the extensive public participation in the constitution-making process, which meant that "people had high expectations of the ABG."[26] Therefore, somewhat ironically, participation successfully generated a sense of expectation

---

[25] Quoted in "Referendum Delay Irks Momis," *Papua New Guinea Post Courier*, June 21, 2012.
[26] Personal communication from a member of the ABG, November 4, 2010; personal communication from an international adviser to the ABG, November 5, 2010.

among Bougainvilleans concerning the institutions that would exercise their constituted power. This has been undercut by the limited number of functions and powers the ABG has been able to exercise. The ABG has recognized this issue, and in early 2011 it launched an awareness campaign in which ABG officials and MHRs toured the country to talk to people regarding the challenges faced by the ABG.[27]

The work of the House of Representatives, and of the ABG more generally, has also been complicated by the presence of four Bougainvillean MPs in the Papua New Guinea Parliament. The BCC debated whether these MPs should play a role in the ABG, noting that during the public consultations people had expressed concern about them sitting in the House, as it could create the perception that Bougainville was no different from Papua New Guinea provinces.[28] BCC members decided to make these MPs ex-officio MHRs, who can attend meetings of the House and take part in debates and proceedings. However, they may not introduce motions, vote, or be counted toward a quorum.[29] In practice, these MPs generally do not "put a lot of effort into attending the ABG," which might partly be explained by the fact that most favor continued integration with Papua New Guinea.[30] The regional MP elected in 2012, Joe Lera, has attempted to attend more ABG sittings. These MPs have also been criticized for failing to advocate on behalf of Bougainville in the Papua New Guinea Parliament, particularly over the (non)payment of funds to Bougainville. Indeed, several have attempted to undermine the ABG.[31] For example, in September 2005, one MP, James Togel, called for a review to determine whether the Bougainville constitution breaches the Papua New Guinea constitution. Another former MP, Fidelis Semoso (who was replaced by Lera at the 2012 election), was a particularly harsh critic – and sometimes allegedly a saboteur – of the ABG. Semoso claimed that as the regional member, he was governor of Bougainville, since this is what occurs in provincial governments. Semoso was also known to invite the Bougainville president to events at which he was distributing Papua New Guinea government funding and then ask what the ABG was going to give.[32] As Semoso was minister for Bougainville affairs in the Papua New

---

[27] Momis, "Challenges of Implementing."
[28] BCC, *Discussion of Recommendations*; BCC, *Report*.   [29] ABG Constitution, s. 55(3).
[30] Interview with an international adviser to the Papua New Guinea government, January 24, 2010.
[31] Momis, "Challenges of Implementing."
[32] Interview with a former BRA commander and member of the ABG, November 2, 2010; interview with an international adviser to the BIPG, BCC, and ABG, August 31, 2010; Momis, "Challenges of Implementing."

Guinea government, he was able act as a constant stumbling block for the ABG in its relations with the Papua New Guinea government.

The Bougainville Advisory Body

Opinion in the public consultations and the BCC was divided over whether to have one or two legislative houses. Those who favored one house were concerned about cost. Those who favored two houses noted that an upper house could provide a check on the lower house, which was seen as particularly important given the high levels of corruption known to occur in Papua New Guinea's unitary system. In addition, an upper house could act as a forum for chiefs and other traditional leaders to play a role in government.[33] As the weight of public opinion favored an upper house, the constitution provides scope for the ABG to create an advisory body "consisting of representatives of traditional chiefs and other traditional leaders" when it is financially sustainable to do so. This body will advise the Executive Council and House of Representatives on matters they have referred to it, proposed constitutional amendments, and the role of custom.[34] Concerns have since emerged regarding whether to establish the body. More "modern" Bougainvilleans are concerned about giving traditional leaders a role in the ABG, while "traditionalists" are concerned that becoming involved in the ABG may taint the authority and legitimacy of traditional leaders. There is also some concern about how to identify "genuine" traditional leaders, as there is "confusion and competition" in some areas concerning who qualifies.[35] Despite this, although sufficient funding is not yet available, the responsible minister is interested in establishing the body and has been studying similar bodies in Fiji and Vanuatu.[36]

Decentralization

The question of how many levels of government to have below the ABG was one of the most controversial of the constitution-making process, with public feedback recommending between two and four levels.[37] On the basis of

---

[33] BCC; *Discussion of Recommendations*; BCC Technical Team, *Matrix of Choices*.
[34] ABG Constitution, s. 52.
[35] V. Boege, *Bougainville Report, Project: Addressing Legitimacy Issues in Fragile Post-Conflict Situations to Advance Conflict Transformation and Peacebuilding* (Brisbane: University of Queensland, 2013), 26.
[36] Interview with an ABG official and member of a council of elders, January 22, 2011.
[37] Bougainvilleans in Papua New Guinea and from the atoll islands favored three levels (ABG, regional, and district); the South also favored three (ABG, local level, and village level); North and Central wanted two levels (ABG and village); and Buka Island wanted four (ABG, regional, district, and village). BCC Technical Team, *Matrix of Choices*.

concerns about costs, the constitution provides that the ABG will develop regional governments when it is financially practicable to do so. In 2008, the ABG created regional commissioners to administer the regions, below which sit twelve district administrations, run by district managers. Councils of Elders sit below the district managers. However, the regional and district administrations are "weak"[38] and are said to merely create "administrative bottlenecks" between the ABG and the councils.[39]

During the BCC's consultations, Bougainvilleans expressed their desire for chiefs and local sociopolitical institutions to be recognized as the basis of formal government at the village level. People expressed the perception that liberal institutions were "remote" and hard to "understand or obey," as they seemed "so different to the *kastomary* [customary] forms of government."[40] In contrast, village chiefs were seen as the "custodians of land and culture," so if they were formally recognized, local government could be "firmly rooted down to the basics of culture."[41] The BCC therefore concluded that recognizing the authority of chiefs and local institutions would provide a "basis for people to feel that government belongs to them, is not something put on top of them from outside."[42] Consequently, the constitution makes a "serious attempt to come to grips with the local level."[43]

There was historical precedent for the formal recognition of chiefs and local sociopolitical institutions. The Australian colonial administration had established Native Village Councils, led by traditional chiefs, to which it gave some responsibility for maintaining public order.[44] These councils were superseded in 1963 by elected Local Government Councils, which were complemented by Village Courts in 1973.[45] However, both sought to sidestep traditional leaders, as the councils were elected and young, educated people were appointed to the courts, which diminished their local legitimacy.[46] Both were also "alien" institutions, as they were "based on the Australian local government system which was inappropriate to Papua New Guinea conditions and

---

[38] V. Boege, *A Promising Liaison: Kastom and State in Bougainville*, The Australian Centre for Peace and Conflict Studies, Occasional Paper Number 12 (Brisbane: University of Queensland, 2008), 28.
[39] Interview with an ABG official and member of a council of elders, January 22, 2011.
[40] BCC, *Report*, 201, 55.   [41] BCC, *Discussion of Recommendations*: 34.   [42] Ibid., 34.
[43] Interview with an international adviser to the Papua New Guinea government, January 24, 2010.
[44] Papua New Guinea Act (1949) (Aust); Native Village Government Councils Ordinance (1949) (Aust) (later renamed Native Local Government Councils Ordinance [1954] [Aust]).
[45] Village Courts Act (1973) (PNG).
[46] R. J. May, *State and Society in Papua New Guinea: The First Twenty-Five Years* (Canberra: ANU E-Press, 2004).

meant little to the average villager."[47] After Papua New Guinea's independence, the NSPG aimed to create a local government system based on a combination of traditional authority and democratic elections.[48]

During the crisis, the BIG tried to fill the political and administrative vacuum created by the Papua New Guinea government's withdrawal, but it was ill prepared to do so. Instead, communities fell back on local sociopolitical institutions, with traditional leaders taking responsibility for public goods provision, social organization, and dispute resolution.[49] Consequently, local sociopolitical institutions "experienced a renaissance."[50] The BIG recognized this and based its local administration on a system of Councils of Chiefs, which were established in most of Bougainville Island during 1991. Similarly, the BTG (later BIPG) established a two-tiered system in which each village had a Village Assembly responsible for local security, dispute resolution, and reconciliation. A number of assemblies then combined to form a Council of Elders, which was vested with legislative and executive powers and operated as a village court.[51]

As both the Councils of Chiefs and Councils of Elders were relatively successful, there was an "absolute" commitment during the BCC's consultations in favor of recognizing a similar system of local government in the constitution.[52] Two main models emerged from the discussion: the first was based on the Council of Elders system, and the second provided for recognition of existing indigenous village governments. To reconcile the two, it was agreed that the constitution would recognize the role of chiefs and that indigenous village governments would continue to exist and would feed up into the councils.[53] Therefore, the council system is two-tiered. Each of the approximately 600 census villages[54] has a Village Assembly based on existing

---

[47] J. Connell, "Introduction" in *Local Government Councils in Bougainville*, ed. J. Connell (Christchurch: Bougainville Special Publications, University of Canterbury, 1977), 2.
[48] Community Government Act (1978) (NSPG).
[49] A. J. Regan, "'Traditional' Leaders and Conflict Resolution in Bougainville: Reforming the Present by Re-writing the Past?," in *Reflections on Violence in Melanesia*, ed. S. Dinnen and A. Ley (Canberra: Asia Pacific Press, 2000).
[50] Boege, "Peacebuilding and State Formation," 33; Havini, "Women in Community"; Togolo, "Torau Response to Change."
[51] Council of Elders Act (1996) (BTG); A. J. Regan, *The Bougainville Council of Elders System*, paper prepared for the Bougainville Transitional Government, September 22, 1998.
[52] Interview with an international adviser to the BRA and BCC, January 18, 2010; BCC, *Report*.
[53] BCC, *Discussion of Recommendations*. Accordingly, after its creation, the ABG adopted the Council of Elders Act.
[54] Census villages were originally the large villages into which the colonial administration organized people for administrative purposes. They were retained after independence as units for census purposes. Although people actually live in small hamlets and homesteads, people

indigenous village governance arrangements, comprising all the people who reside in the village and the land associated with it.[55] A number of census villages then form a council, of which there are currently eighty-nine.[56] Each council is headed by a chairman, who is paid, as are their clerks.

The Councils of Elders are liberal-local hybrid institutions, as to achieve balance between the liberal emphasis on democratic elections and local emphasis on customary authority, councils (and other formal levels of government established below the ABG) must be "mainly elective," but must also "recognize the traditional role in governance of traditional chiefs and other traditional leaders."[57] In practice, these elections are more like "selections," as there is no competition of candidates, with council members chosen in a consensual manner, reflecting local practices.[58] Council members usually have five-year terms in office. The councils include "elders" rather than "chiefs," to create room for leaders who are not traditional chiefs,[59] and most councils include representatives of women, churches, and youth. Councils also often include the local MHR and MP as ex-officio members.[60] The councils are vested with legislative, executive, and judicial powers in the council area and must incorporate "traditional systems of governance" where practicable.[61] In the performance of their executive powers, the councils implement projects and public services, such as primary education and small community development projects.[62] Councils are funded by a combination of ABG grants, head taxes, and fines.[63]

The Councils of Elders have been the "most effective governance institutions below the ABG,"[64] as they connect the "modern, formal" ABG with

---

know what census village they belong to, so it is a convenient unit of jurisdiction for the council of elders. Regan, *Bougainville Council of Elders System*.

[55] Council of Elders Act, ss. 9–10.
[56] The decision concerning which census villages will group together is made according to a consultative process. Regan, *Bougainville Council of Elders System*.
[57] ABG Constitution, s. 49.   [58] Boege, *Bougainville Report*, 19.
[59] "Elder" is defined as a person who "by custom or tradition is regarded by a clan or sub-clan as a hereditary leader of that clan or sub-clan; or by virtue of education, wealth, business acumen or political involvement is considered by a clan or sub-clan or by person resident in the area as suitable for selection to the Council of Elders." Council of Elders Act, Part 1.2.
[60] Interview with an ABG official and member of a council of elders, January 22, 2011.
[61] ABG Constitution, s. 49; Council of Elders Act, ss. 24, 32, 38–47.
[62] C. L. Sasa, *Local Government Accountability in Bougainville*, Masters of Philosophy, Massy University, 2013.
[63] Council of Elders Act, ss. 52–53; Head Tax Act (2007) (ABG). Each of the councils of elders is granted K55,000 annually. The general amount of the head tax is K20 per person, per annum. Some councils of elders exempt the elderly (those over sixty years of age) from the tax.
[64] Boege, *A Promising Liaison*, 28.

the traditional Village Assemblies[65] that continue to regulate the lives of the over 90 percent of Bougainvilleans who live in rural areas.[66] While many councils are relatively well established, have adopted constitutions and development plans, and have the capacity to collect head taxes and fines and to implement projects, others are still being established. The Bougainville Division of Local Level Government provides training and advice for the councils, assists with financial management and the establishment of services, and functions as the auditing and supervisory body. The division has assigned an officer to each district administration, who is responsible for providing advice and support to councils. Councils also report to these officers, who in turn pass these reports on to the division.[67] In 2013, to enhance the standing of the councils, the division traveled around Bougainville for five months to conduct "swearing in ceremonies" for the members of the councils, who in turn made a "declaration of loyalty" to the ABG and took an oath of office. This process also allowed the minister of local level government and division staff to talk to councils and their community about the operation of the councils. While the division had also intended to conduct orientation for council members, this has been delayed due to a lack of funding.

The ABG recently reviewed the Council of Elders structure and has undertaken study tours of customary governance systems in Fiji and Tonga. In October 2011, the Executive Council approved a "white paper" that was generated by this review. In 2012, the Division of Local Level Government conducted a series of consultative workshops on the paper throughout Bougainville. While funding constraints have limited the completion of these consultations, the ABG has approved a number of changes to the council system based on the paper, including aligning councils with the ABG constituencies; realigning the Village Assemblies to reflect the new alignment of the councils; clarifying the role of the councils (including whether they are legislative, executive, or judicial); legislating to provide greater access for women, religious, and youth representatives to participate in councils; clarifying the distinction between the councils, assemblies, and other forms of traditional governance; strengthening and supporting councils by linking them to district administrations and managers; developing salaries and other remuneration determinations for council members and incorporating them

---

[65] Interview with a former BRA commander and member of the ABG, November 2, 2010.
[66] Finnroad, *Papua New Guinea – Australia Transport Sector Support Program (TSSP) Supported by the Australian Government – AusAID: Socio-Economic Study – TSSP Provinces, Baseline Report* (Helsinki: Finnroad, 2008).
[67] Sasa, *Local Government Accountability*.

into the ABG salaries and wage structure; and transforming the division into a department in order to improve its capacity.[68]

While the ABG has been committed to improving the operation of the Councils of Elders, it has very few resources, so its grants to the councils cover only administrative costs[69] and are not enough to fund the implementation of substantial projects. The local tax base is also small, which means that the councils have insufficient funding to implement substantial projects. Given that councils are the primary institution through which people have contact with the ABG, there is a proposal to distribute additional funding to them so that development "can come from the bottom up."[70]

The Councils of Elders are currently the only elected level of government below the ABG, but traditional systems of government also continue to play an important role. Indeed, the BCC pragmatically recognized that "the majority of our people in rural communities live under traditional rather than the formal systems of government."[71] The term "Village Assembly" is used to describe these traditional systems of government, which are the (often loosely organized) methods by which traditional chiefs consult their people and perform their traditional administrative and dispute resolution role.[72] The assemblies are also said to provide a "pivotal link between the Council of Elders and the communities – and vice versa."[73] There are questions concerning whether these traditional systems are fixed and primordial or relatively recent inventions. Despite this, they remain highly relevant. For example, in the village in which I conducted fieldwork, the assembly met every Thursday morning in the *tsuhana* (traditional meeting house). The chief led a discussion in which those present considered issues arising in the village, made plans for village life, and agreed on "community service" tasks.

There can be some separation (and even competition) between the Village Assemblies and Councils of Elders, as some chiefs abstain from becoming members of councils, which they view as "talk shops," in comparison to the assemblies, where it is perceived that "real work" is done.[74] However, due to its

---

[68] "An Update from the Division of LLG and Traditional Authority on Bougainville's Councils of Elders," *Bougainville Bulletin*, August 12, 2012, accessed October 2, 2013, www.bougainvillebulletin.com/past-editions/12-aug-2012-edition/18-an-update-from-the-division-of-llg-and-traditional-authority-on-bougainville-s-council-of-elders.

[69] K40,000 in 2010, which was equivalent to approximately US$16,000.

[70] Interview with an ABG official and member of a council of elders, January 22, 2011; Momis, "Challenges of Implementing."

[71] BCC, *Report*, 206.

[72] Council of Elders Act, ss. 9–10; interview with an ABG official and member of a council of elders, January 22, 2011; Regan, *Bougainville Council of Elders System*.

[73] Sasa, *Local Government Accountability*, 53.   [74] Boege, *Bougainville Report*, 24.

financial challenges, the ABG's funding stops at the councils, which means that the chiefs who sit in assemblies receive only a small monthly allowance,[75] although many spend considerable time attending to village matters. This has led to some concern that traditional chiefs and the assemblies may "die out, because they cannot survive in the modern system," despite the fact that "chiefs are the ones who are keeping the peace together."[76] The lack of funding has also had perverse effects, with an increase in chiefs applying excessive fines to offenders in disputes they have been called to resolve.

To what extent are the state institutions perceived to be legitimate?

Based on its public consultations, the BCC identified creating a government "that we Bougainvilleans can identify with" and that is "truly responsive to the needs of our people" as the key challenge for the constitution.[77] While the liberal idea that popular sovereignty can legitimately be exercised only by state institutions through democratic means has become almost universal at the international level and has guided liberal peace state building, the BCC recognized that democratically electing the members of the ABG would not be sufficient to ensure that it is perceived as legitimate by Bougainvilleans. Instead, legitimacy was partly to be achieved by recognizing the Council of Elders, so that a level of formal government is close to the people. It was also partly to be achieved by ensuring that ABG members represent and are responsive and accountable to the people. The BCC utilized a combination of liberal and local practices to achieve this goal. To ensure that specific groups are represented in the House of Representatives, seats are reserved for representatives of women and former combatants. To enhance the responsiveness of the ABG, the BCC sought to incorporate elements of local sociopolitical practices. The BCC also created several mechanisms to ensure the accountability of members of the ABG.

Electoral system
As in all liberal democracies, members of the ABG are elected, with elections occurring at least every five years,[78] and Bougainvilleans are said to believe in the "rightfulness of democratic process," as "democratic rights and freedoms

---

[75] K26 in 2010, equivalent to approximately US$10.
[76] Interview with a former BRA commander and member of the ABG, November 2, 2010.
[77] BCC, *Report*, 116.
[78] ABG Constitution, s. 107. The maximum term of office for all members of the ABG is five years. ABG Constitution, s. 57.

have taken root."[79] Bougainvilleans cast four votes: for the president, for their constituency member, for their regional women's representative, and for their regional former combatants' representative.[80] Therefore, although the women's and former combatants' members represent these special interests, they are elected by all voters. The Papua New Guinea government decided to change to a limited preferential vote (LPV) electoral system in 2007.[81] To avoid confusing voters, the BCC decided that Bougainville would retain Papua New Guinea's simple plurality system for the 2005 ABG election and then follow Papua New Guinea's conversion to the LPV system.[82] There was strong support during the public consultations for a preferential voting system.[83] Although the BCC considered a proportional system, it was thought that it would be too difficult to have a different system from that of Papua New Guinea, and the BCC's consultations had revealed strong support for an electoral system that provided individual and accountable local representation.[84]

As in the rest of Papua New Guinea,[85] the use of the simple plurality system for the 2005 election encouraged candidates to "focus on their own camp" (their home area, clan, and churches) and to use money to buy votes.[86] The LPV system was introduced for the 2008 presidential by-election. Both former president Tanis and current vice president Patrick Nisira have argued that in the 2008 and 2010 elections, the LPV system encouraged candidates to network, collaborate, and campaign beyond their home area in order to secure preferences. It also discouraged vote-buying, as most candidates could not afford to buy enough votes and preferences to win.[87]

Reserved seats

The second way in which the BCC sought to ensure the representativeness of the ABG was by reserving seats in the House for women and former combatants. There was heated debate during the public consultations and within the BCC concerning whether there should be reserved seats for special interest

---

[79] Boege, *Bougainville Report*, 57.   [80] ABG Constitution, s. 55(9).
[81] Organic Law on National and Local-Level government Elections No. 3/1997 (1997) (PNG), as amended.
[82] ABG Constitution, s. 109.
[83] BCC, *Discussion of Recommendations*; BCC Technical Team, *Matrix of Choices*.
[84] BCC, *Report*.
[85] See, for example, F. Fukuyama, *Governance Reform in Papua New Guinea*, September 2007, accessed January 24, 2009, www.sais-jhu.edu/faculty/fukuyama/publications.html; H. Nelson, *Governments, States and Labels, State Society and Governance in Melanesia Discussion Paper* 2006/1 (Canberra: Australian National University, 2006).
[86] Nisira, speaking at "Elections in Bougainville and Solomon Islands."
[87] Ibid.; Tanis, speaking at "Elections in Bougainville and Solomon Islands."

groups. The BCC considered reserved seats for representatives of the three main churches, on the basis that they had played an important role as partners in development. However, the representatives of the churches sitting in the BCC did not favor direct representation in the legislature, and instead preferred an administrative partnership with the ABG. Therefore, churches are represented by a ministry in the ABG. The BCC also considered seats for youth representatives. As with the churches, it was agreed that their interests could be dealt with administratively. Similarly, the BCC considered creating a reserved seat for Bougainvilleans living outside Bougainville, which could encourage them to maintain links with and possibly return to Bougainville, bringing their education and experience with them. It could also reconcile Bougainvilleans who had remained outside during the crisis with those who had stayed behind. Ultimately, the BCC decided that this was not required.[88]

The most contentious proposal was to reserve seats for former combatants from the BRA and BRF.[89] Several BCC members argued that former combatants had been some of the first to engage with the peace process and that they had "special problems" that warranted their specific representation. Others were concerned that not including these seats might undermine the weapons disposal process, and there was apprehension that former combatants posed a potential threat to future stability if they were "alienat[ed]" from the process.[90] Therefore, it was thought that reserved seats could "domesticate" them by "introducing them into the democratic system."[91] The BCC initially accepted a proposal by the former combatants' representatives for six reserved seats, one each for the BRA and BRF from the three regions. This proposal gave rise to heated debate both in the BCC and its public consultations, particularly over questions of its fairness and concerns that if former combatants also won constituency seats, they could dominate the legislature and result in Bougainville being perceived to have a "military government."[92] Eventually, in response to the strong skepticism expressed in the public consultations, the BCC agreed that there should be only one reserved seat for each region, representing both former BRA and BRF combatants. This compromise contributed to relatively widespread public acceptance of these reserved seats and was in accordance with the Bougainville Peace Agreement requirement that the BRA and BRF disband at the end of the weapons disposal process. Indeed, providing that a single former combatant would represent all former combatants in each region was seen as a way to "encourage the groups of former

---

[88] BCC, *Discussion of Recommendations*; BCC, *Report*. [89] BCC, *Report*.
[90] BCC, *Discussion of Recommendations*: 64. [91] BCC, *Report*, 163.
[92] BCC, *Discussion of Recommendations*: 11.

combatants to dissolve distinctions and to work together."[93] To diffuse concerns over the risk that these seats could entrench the position of former combatants, the BCC decided that they would remain only until the referendum is held (or until it is agreed that it will not be held), or until the ABG passes a motion removing them.[94] In addition, while former combatant groups requested that these seats be voted for only by former combatants, the BCC concluded that they should be elected by all voters in each region to ensure that they represent a wider range of interests.[95]

The less contentious proposal was to include reserved seats for women's representatives, as it was generally seen as important to recognize women as a vulnerable group. While it was initially proposed to reserve only one seat for women, the BCC's women's representatives and other women's leaders argued that this number should be increased to be on par with the number for former combatants. This proposal met with strong opposition from certain BCC members, who argued that it would lead other groups to demand representation. Despite this, after the public consultations, the number of seats was increased to three. This reflected the significant pressure applied by women's groups, as well as recognition of the role that women played in achieving reconciliation.[96] The requirement that at least one of the three women's representatives is appointed to the Council provides further assurance that women's views will be heard within the ABG.[97] These reserved seats have ensured that women have their views represented in the House, which is important given that there are indications that women have been increasingly "marginalised" since the peace process concluded.[98] These seats may also socialize men to the idea of voting for women, which might affect their voting decisions in regard to the constituency seats.[99] The women's representatives may also act as role models for other women and encourage them to become politically active. There is evidence that the experience and confidence gained through occupying these seats have encouraged the women's representatives to stand for other seats.[100] However, there have been claims that the

---

[93] BCC, *Report*, 166; ibid.   [94] ABG Constitution, s. 55(5)-(8).
[95] BCC, *Discussion of Recommendations*.
[96] Interview with a Bougainvillean women's leader, January 25, 2011; interview with a Bougainvillean women's leader, February 2, 2010.
[97] ABG Constitution, s. 80(1)(c).
[98] Titus, speaking at "Building Sustainable Peace"; Kenehata, speaking at "Elections in Bougainville and Solomon Islands."
[99] R. Pihei, speaking at "Elections in Bougainville and Solomon Islands."
[100] While twenty-five women contested the three reserved seats in 2005, women did not contest any of the constituency seats. In contrast, in 2010, seventeen women contested the three women's seats, five women contested constituency seats, and one former women's

reserved seats have created a perception that constituency seats and the presidency are for men.[101] Yet, a similar effect has not occurred with respect to the seats reserved for former combatants, with many former combatants contesting constituency seats and the presidency.

Incorporating local sociopolitical practices
During the BCC's public consultations, many Bougainvilleans questioned why it was necessary to incorporate competitive liberal democratic decision making in the constitution, and why the local sociopolitical practice of seeking consensus was not sufficient.[102] In particular, many argued that having political parties and an opposition in the legislature would be divisive and contrary to custom, and instead MHRs should be encouraged to work together.[103] This conclusion was also based on a fear that such a system of government might be "dangerous," as it could disrupt the unity generated during the peace process.[104] When the BCC considered banning political parties and legislative opposition, their technical advisers raised concerns that this could infringe upon the right to freedom of association protected in the Papua New Guinea constitution. Advisers also cautioned that political parties were a principle of modern democracy and should be provided for in the constitution, particularly given that the Bougainville Peace Agreement required the ABG to comply with "internationally accepted standards of good governance." Eventually, the BCC agreed that the constitution would remain silent on the issue of a legislative opposition and provide that a later law would regulate and register parties.[105]

In practice, the House operates in "traditional Melanesian style," according to which "interjection is regarded as a breach of traditional protocol and diplomacy."[106] In June 2005, the first ABG formed a "grand coalition" unity government without an opposition. However, in June 2007, MHRs Thomas Lugabai and Marceline Getsi moved to create a formal opposition bench, on the grounds that it would facilitate debate and accountability. This move was

representative contested the presidency. R. Saovanna Spriggs, speaking at "Elections in Bougainville and Solomon Islands."
[101] Commonwealth Secretariat/PIF, *General Election*; Kelly, *Electoral Democracy*.
[102] BCC, *Report*.
[103] BCC Technical Team, *Matrix of Choices*; interview with an international adviser to the BRA and BCC, January 18, 2010.
[104] Interview with a former BRA commander and member of the ABG, November 2, 2010; Nisira, speaking at "Elections in Bougainville and Solomon Islands."
[105] BCC, *Discussion of Recommendations*; BCC, *Report*.
[106] Personal communication from a former member of the ABG, November 9, 2010.

welcomed in some quarters, with then Speaker Nick Penai approving arrangements that facilitated members of the opposition sitting together. He did so on the basis that, while the constitution does not mention having a formal opposition, it could act as a check and balance on the House's law making. Yet the idea was met with some resistance, and two members of the New Bougainville Party resigned from their party in protest at their party colleagues' support of the decision.[107] Similarly, when the women's representative in the Executive Council, Magdalene Toroansi, criticized some of the Kabui government's business dealings, she was dismissed for breaching government solidarity. Toroansi's sacking precipitated a serious threat to the unity of the grand coalition government, with indications that a majority in the House shared her concerns about the business deals and would vote to overturn them. Her sacking also indicated Kabui's increasingly authoritarian tendency to take unilateral decisions. This controversy was short-circuited by Kabui's death in June 2008, after which the ABG changed its approach and organized a public forum to discuss concerns about its business dealings in July 2008.

The constitution also seeks to recognize local sociopolitical practices through allowing for the recall of MHRs, if at least one-third of the enrolled voters in their constituency sign a petition stating the reasons for the recall. A poll is then to be held in which voters are asked whether or not their member should be recalled. The recalled member is not allowed to stand in a simultaneous by-election. If more than one-half of enrolled voters vote in favor, that member is recalled and the new member is determined based on the result of the by-election.[108] This provision received strong support during the BCC's consultations, as people thought it would enhance the accountability of the legislature and provide a degree of "direct democracy."[109] This procedure echoes local sociopolitical practices as, while there are hereditary chiefs in some areas, leaders generally have to prove their capabilities, with their role accepted only if they provide genuine leadership.[110]

However, although the constitution attempted to increase the responsiveness of MHRs by utilizing local sociopolitical practices, some MHRs have been relatively distant and unresponsive to their electorates. There are claims that several MHRs do not regularly visit their electorates, which led the ABG Speaker, Andrew Miriki, to call on MHRs to operate constituency offices in their electorates from 2013. President Momis has echoed these calls and visits different areas of Bougainville on weekends to promote awareness of the

---

[107] Police Minister E. Massat and Works Minister P. Nisira.   [108] ABG Constitution, s. 58.
[109] BCC Technical Team, *Matrix of Choices*, 6.
[110] Boege, *Discovery of Slowness*; interview with a Bougainvillean intellectual, January 24, 2011.

progress of the ABG and the implementation of the Bougainville Peace Agreement. There has also been concern about a lack of transparency concerning how MHRs use the support funds that they are allocated to spend on development in their constituencies.[111]

Accountability institutions
In this regard, the BCC noted that "there was probably no issue on which people felt more strongly than...the need for accountability of leadership."[112] In particular, the public wanted to make sure that the "corruption and mismanagement" experienced in Papua New Guinea were not repeated in Bougainville.[113] One of the objectives and directive principles in the constitution states that the ABG will "take all lawful measures to ensure accountability in government and to expose and eradicate corruption and abuse or misuse of power."[114] The constitution also provides that several liberal institutions can be created to ensure the accountability of political leaders. The Office of Bougainville Auditor-General will be responsible for inspecting and auditing Bougainville's public accounts.[115] Due to limited funding, the office has not yet been established, and the Papua New Guinea auditor-general continues to oversee Bougainville. The Office of Bougainville Ombudsman will seek to ensure that all governmental bodies are "responsive to the needs and aspirations of the People," eliminate "unfairness and discrimination" by those bodies, and enforce the Bougainville Leadership Code.[116] Again, due to funding limitations, the ombudsman has not yet been created. In the meantime, the Papua New Guinea Ombudsman Commission continues to have jurisdiction. When the Bougainville ombudsman is created, the Bougainville Leadership Code will apply.[117] Until then, the Papua New Guinea Leadership Code continues to apply. Reflecting the views expressed during the BCC's consultations, the Bougainville code draws on local sociopolitical practices by requiring that leaders comply with "long-established standards of customary leadership."[118]

As Bougainville-based accountability institutions have not been created, there was a fairly wide acknowledgment during fieldwork in 2011 that corruption exists in the ABG. Rumors of corruption were particularly vociferous during the latter period of Kabui's presidency, as the government accepted a

---

[111] In 2012, these funds were K100,000.
[112] BCC, *Report*, 218; BCC Technical Team, *Matrix of Choices*; BCC, *Discussion of Recommendations*.
[113] BCC, *Report*, 213.   [114] ABG Constitution, s. 38(3).   [115] Ibid., s. 159.
[116] Ibid., ss. 166–168.   [117] Ibid., s. 169.   [118] Ibid., s. 170.

large payment in exchange for granting a Canadian company the right to export alluvial gold from Bougainville. The ABG then became partners with that company in the Bogenvil Resources Development Corporation, to which it granted an exclusive right to explore and exploit Bougainville's resources (excluding Panguna) for three years, which led to accusations that Kabui had sold "the island to outside investors."[119] The deal was controversial, as it was signed before the formal transfer of mining powers and potentially in breach of the constitutional requirement that the ABG recognize customary rights to natural resources.[120] This controversy was magnified after an audit revealed that much of the money paid to the ABG was used for cash payments to unspecified individuals.[121] These allegations were diffused by Kabui's death, and when Tanis assumed office as president, he ensured that members of the council signed a "very tight" Code of Conduct before they were sworn in.[122] Despite good intentions, enforcement of this code was said to have been "weak," with corruption continuing to "seep" into the ABG during Tanis's tenure and in the period since.[123] More recently, there have been proposals to create an independent commission to investigate corruption, similar to the Anti-Corruption Commission in Timor-Leste.[124]

Therefore, while the ABG is democratic, there are questions over its legitimacy. However, a distinction must be drawn between the legitimacy of the ABG as an institution and the legitimacy of its individual members. While questions have been raised concerning the conduct of certain MHRs, for many Bougainvilleans the ABG is seen as the legitimate "prelude to political independence,"[125] enhanced by the liberal-local hybrid approach taken in the constitution.

Are the state institutions delivering public goods and services?

As noted in Chapter 1, the dominant test of a government's effectiveness is whether it has the institutional capacity to deliver public goods and services. The ABG's delivery of the most important public good – security – is discussed

---

[119] MHRs quoted in R. Masiu, "New Body to Control Bougainville Mineral Rights," *The National*, May 4, 2008; G. Binin, "Call for Kabui to Resign," *Papua New Guinea Post-Courier*, May 5, 2008.
[120] ABG Constitution, s. 23(1).
[121] S. Marshall, prod., *Bougainville – The Killer Deal*, Foreign Correspondent, ABC Television, June 17, 2008.
[122] Regan, "Bougainville's New Directions."
[123] Interview with an ABG official and member of a council of elders, January 22, 2011.
[124] Ibid.   [125] Masono, speaking at "Building Sustainable Peace."

TABLE 2. *Bougainville development indicators*

Indicator[126]	Bougainville (2007)	Papua New Guinea (2007)
Population	200,000	6,732,159
Average life expectancy	59.6 years	60.7 years
Adult (15+ years) literacy rate	79.72%	57.8.1%
Gross primary school enrollment ratio	40.23%	40.7%

below. Its delivery of other goods and services can be assessed using data relating to development indicators. As Bougainville remains part of Papua New Guinea, very little data specifically relating to its human development performance is available. However, in 2007, the UNDP prepared a Human Development Report about Bougainville,[127] the most significant data from which is summarized in the above table.

There is evidence that the Bougainville public service is managing to deliver some services at a higher level than in the rest of Papua New Guinea. While life expectancy levels and primary school enrollment levels are similar, Bougainville's adult literacy rates are much higher than the Papua New Guinea average and those of most provinces of Papua New Guinea, as is the average level of formal education that has been achieved.[128] In addition, in 2006, Bougainville was awarded a prize for the best medical services in the country,[129] although this is perhaps reflective of the comparatively low level of health care across Papua New Guinea. Indeed, Bougainville's health sector faces severe funding limitations, and while the ABG has worked to reopen aid posts and health centers, many remain closed or unstaffed and lack medicines. Primary (grades 1–8) and secondary (grades 9–12) schools, training centers, and technical schools are reopening across the region. However, there are shortages of teachers and funding remains limited. Those wanting to access secondary or technical training have to move away from their village, which has created a population of "disaffected and disillusioned youth who cannot

---

[126] UNDP, *Bougainville Human Development Report 2007, Developing Education from Within: Communities as Critical Agents of Change* (Port Moresby: United Nations Development Programme, 2009); UNDP, International Human Development Indicators.

[127] UNDP, *Bougainville Human Development Report 2007*.

[128] Finnroad, *The Socio Economic Impact of AusAID Funded Road Maintenance and Rehabilitation of National Priority Roads in Ten Provinces of Papua New Guinea 2010* (Helsinki: Finnroad, 2010).

[129] B. Gomez, (ed.), *2006 Papua New Guinea Yearbook* (Noumea: The National & Cassowary Books, 2006).

proceed beyond grades 6 & 8."[130] Despite this, there are now as many functioning schools in Bougainville as there were before the crisis, and enrollments are increasing, although a 2011 survey revealed that one in every three children living in urban areas was still not in school.[131] The ABG has also embarked on an electrification project, with hydroelectric projects established in Central and the North, which has seen twenty-four-hour electricity supply restored to Arawa, in addition to Buka.

The constitution provides that the ABG may establish a Bougainville public service.[132] The Papua New Guinea public service officers in Bougainville who perform the functions and powers transferred to the ABG have been absorbed into the Bougainville administration.[133] The capacity of the administration is generally "weak," although there are "some impressive officials at all levels, working extremely hard."[134] In particular, there have been concerns about the administration's capacity to manage financial issues and to execute the ABG budget, which in 2013 led the ABG to approve a motion to conduct an independent audit of the ABG's funds. Opinions differ concerning the practical effect of the administration being funded by the Papua New Guinea government and its officers remaining employees of the Papua New Guinea public service. One MHR observed that it has made it difficult for the ABG to direct the administration, because "they have two masters," and drew the analogy of a wife who has two husbands and is not sure which one to listen to.[135] However, an administration official claimed that there is no interference by Papua New Guinea officials in its work, which is helped by the fact that the administration reports to the Bougainville administrator, who acts as the link to the Papua New Guinea administration.[136] In order to improve the performance of the administration, in 2012 steps were taken to create a Bougainville public service, with the conversion of divisions to departments within the existing Bougainville administration. In July 2012, public service powers were transferred to the Bougainville administration, paving the way for the creation of the Bougainville public service in 2014.

[130] BHRC, *Universal Periodic Review*.
[131] S. Chand, *Data Collection in Difficult Environments: Measuring Economic Recovery in Post-Conflict Bougainville*, 2011, accessed October 10, 2013, www.slideshare.net/CivMilCouncil of Elders/satish-chand.
[132] ABG Constitution, ss. 138, 146 and 147.
[133] Personal communication from an officer of the Bougainville administration, March 1, 2011.
[134] Regan, "Bougainville's New Directions."
[135] Personal communication from a member of the ABG, November 4, 2010.
[136] Personal communication from a Bougainville administration official, March 1, 2011.

In addition, Bougainville's comparatively good development indicators may not be entirely due to the performance of the Bougainville administration and could also be a product of the extensive network of churches that provide services. Many schools and health facilities are run by churches, and some are jointly funded by the church and the administration.[137] Indeed, one public servant noted that the churches are "traditionally seen as the right hand of government in terms of development." Accordingly, the ABG pays "tithes" to the churches.[138]

The Bougainville administration has been hampered by funding limitations faced by the ABG. The constitution notes that the ABG will "aim to achieve fiscal self-reliance as soon as possible."[139] Achieving this goal is difficult for Bougainville, which relies on a limited range of agricultural products (mostly cocoa and copra), has no significant industrialization, and has poor infrastructure, largely due to the damage done during the crisis.[140] Consequently, in 2007, the UNDP found that only 14 percent of the surveyed population received cash income.[141] Indeed, a 2010 livelihoods study found that 80 percent of men and 86 percent of women identified as subsistence farmers[142] who grow their own food and produce a surplus for exchange and barter based on the customary principle of reciprocity.

While the relative affluence of the subsistence economy means there is little chronic hunger, malnutrition, and homelessness, because it does not produce a surplus capable of being taxed, it is difficult to see how it can provide a sufficient economic base to fund the ABG. However, incomes are rising, with a 2010 livelihoods survey finding that the share of households with an income of less than K500 per annum dropped from 48 percent in 2008 to 27 percent in 2010, primarily due to increased cocoa and copra production, better prices, and better access to markets due to improved roads.[143] The communal nature of Bougainvillean land tenure and economic activity also challenges a liberal peace approach to developing a market economy. Efforts to develop the private sector have been hampered by the destruction of plant and infrastructure during the crisis. Consequently, economic reconstruction has primarily been based on the restoration of small-holder cash cropping. Yet cash crops can absorb land that is otherwise used for subsistence food

---

[137] Interview with an international academic, January 8, 2010; Masono, *Government Capacity*.
[138] Interview with an ABG official and member of a council of elders, January 22, 2011.
[139] ABG Constitution, s. 153(1).
[140] J. Connell, "Bougainville: The Future of an Island Microstate," *The Journal of Pacific Studies* 28:2 (2005): 192–217.
[141] UNDP, *Bougainville Human Development Report 2007*.
[142] Finnroad, *The Socio Economic Impact*.   [143] Ibid.

production, leading to food shortages, and they are difficult to tax at the point of production and sale because of their small-scale, cash-in-hand nature. Capacity limitations also undermine the ABG's tax collection efforts,[144] with the most effective tax the one placed on liquor and cigarettes in 2012.[145] There are also claims that the Papua New Guinea government does not collect (or pass on) sufficient tax, including income tax, stamp duty, company tax, customs duties, and goods and services tax, which led the ABG to propose creating its own tax system.

To advance development, the ABG has created the Bougainville Restoration and Development Authority, which is part of the ABG Division of Technical Services. This authority will implement infrastructure development projects, such as a palm oil plantation, a limestone project, and a commercial fishery. The ABG has also created a Bougainville-China Cooperation Committee to facilitate Chinese investment in joint enterprises in Bougainville and the Bougainville Import and Export Wholesale Company to facilitate trade with China. Finally, the ABG has formed a Division of Culture, Tourism, Environment and Conservation, although due to a lack of funding for office space, this division initially operated from a hotel and in parks under shady trees. However, many of these projects are likely to generate significant revenues only in the medium to long term and are therefore unlikely to be of much utility in funding the creation of an independent Bougainville if the referendum is held between 2015 and 2020.

These difficulties have generated increasing pressure to reopen the Panguna mine and to engage in additional mining activities, which partly explains the Kabui government's decision to enter into the Canadian gold deal.[146] Given the low level of economic development, it is difficult to see how Bougainville could achieve "fiscal self-reliance" without mining. To that end, the ABG has taken steps to review arrangements relating to the Panguna mine with the Papua New Guinea government and to adopt a mining policy and law. This mining law regulates not only large-scale mining (such as at Panguna) but also the extensive small-scale mining that is conducted in areas around the Panguna mine.

The ABG's move to reopen the Panguna mine is supported by many Bougainvilleans, who see the mine as a source of potential employment,

---

[144] The ABG did establish a customs agency in February 2006. However, due to lack of funding and accommodation, the agency closed in October 2008, before reopening in April 2009. In March 2010, the ABG and Papua New Guinea government signed an agreement to develop the capacity of Bougainville's tax administration.

[145] Liquor Control Act (2011) (ABG) and Sales Tax (Beer and Cigarettes) Act (2011) (ABG).

[146] Interview with an international adviser to the BIPG, BCC, and ABG, August 31, 2010; Momis, "Challenges of Implementing."

income, and economic opportunity. There are also groups who argue that people from the Panguna area owe the rest of Bougainville a "blood debt" for instigating the crisis.[147] The ABG is attempting to mitigate the likelihood of renewed conflict by making efforts to reconcile with Panguna landowners and involve them in negotiations about the future of the mine. Six Panguna landowner associations have been created under an umbrella association to negotiate the future of the mine. A Panguna stakeholders meeting was held in July 2011 involving all interested parties (including the MGU and OMG), at which they agreed to the Panguna Stakeholders' Hahela Understanding, which included an undertaking to work with the ABG to resolve the conflict and the future of the mine. The ABG then held forums in each of the three regions in 2012 and 2013 to inform and consult people about the possible reopening of the mine, and in July 2012, it facilitated a meeting between the landowners' associations and BCL.[148] While there is an "emerging consensus" on the need to reopen the mine, a small number of hardline members of the MDF remain outside these efforts.[149] Moreover, the Bougainville Peace Agreement deferred the decision on how mining revenue would be shared between the ABG (or an independent Bougainville) and the Papua New Guinea government. The Bougainville constitution recognizes customary rights in relation to mineral and oil resources.[150] This clashes with the Papua New Guinea constitution, which provides that natural resources should be "conserved and used for the collective benefit of us all."[151] It is unclear how this clash will be resolved should the mine again begin operating, which might put pressure on the Bougainville Peace Agreement.

In the meantime, the ABG remains dependent on the Papua New Guinea government and international donor funding. While the Papua New Guinea government honored its financial commitments until 2010, it provided a "bare minimum."[152] This has been less than some Bougainvilleans expected, as they assumed that delaying the referendum would give the Papua New Guinea government an incentive to provide generous funding to encourage Bougainvilleans to favor integration.[153] In contrast, voices within the Papua New Guinea government have increasingly questioned the logic of investing resources in Bougainville, given that it is expected to vote for independence

---

[147] Regan, "The Bougainville Conflict: Political and Economic Agendas," 153; Momis, "Challenges of Implementing."
[148] R. Masono, speaking at "Bougainville Mining Seminar," Canberra, Australian National University, February 14, 2013.
[149] Regan, "Bougainville Update." [150] Bougainville Constitution, s. 23.
[151] Papua New Guinea Constitution, s. 4. [152] Momis, "Challenges of Implementing."
[153] Regan, Light Intervention.

and that providing funding may just assist its progress towards this.[154] However, it should be acknowledged that the Papua New Guinea government has faced significant financial difficulties.

There have also been serious disputes over funding. For example, the Papua New Guinea government's 2010 budget did not include provision for the K15 million restoration and development grant payable under the Bougainville Peace Agreement. When the ABG raised the issue at the JSB meeting in December 2009, the Papua New Guinea government claimed that it regarded other kinds of funding as compensating for the grant, although it did accept that the grant should have been paid and made an initial allocation of K5 million in early 2010. However, the remaining K10 million was not paid, and a further expected K15 million grant was omitted from the 2011 Budget. As the ABG regarded this as a breach of the Bougainville Peace Agreement, it considered a Supreme Court challenge. In February 2011, the Papua New Guinea government agreed to pay the grant (which it did in November 2011) and promised the ABG K500 million for "high impact" infrastructure development projects over the following five years (the first payment of K100 million was made in November 2012). Yet even when the Papua New Guinea government provides funding, it often delays its transfer. For example, in 2003, delays in funding transfers undermined the delivery of public services and almost led to the BIPG taking court action against the Papua New Guinea government. Delays in transfers also held up the 2008 presidential by-election and 2010 ABG general election.[155] The Papua New Guinea government consistently delays the payment of the annual K15 million restoration and development grant and the K500 million high-impact grant. While it defends these delays based on claims that the ABG has not adequately acquitted its past expenditure or costed its future projects, these delays have undermined the delivery of public services in Bougainville and consequently caused significant hardship.

The apparent reluctance of the Papua New Guinea government to transfer funding and powers to the ABG has generated concern about interference. These concerns have been enhanced by the fact that some development projects funded under the "high impact" grant are said to have been planned and conducted by the Papua New Guinea government without consultation with the ABG. Accordingly, President Momis has been careful to stress the independence of the ABG legislature. He has observed that it is "authorised under the Constitution of Papua New Guinea and its actions are constitutionally and legally binding and cannot be determined or undermined by any

---

[154] Regan, "Bougainville's New Directions."
[155] Personal communication from an international adviser to the ABG, November 5, 2010.

external bodies."[156] Overall, there is an emerging pattern of behavior that suggests that elements of the Papua New Guinea government may be seeking to roll back some of the autonomy granted to Bougainville, which has undermined the ability of the ABG to deliver public goods and services.

Are law and order enforced and is the rule of law observed?

The most important public good that indicates government effectiveness is the institutional capacity to enforce law and order and ensure that the rule of law is observed. Reflecting the BCC's general approach, the constitution adopts a liberal-local hybrid approach. Indeed, during the BCC's consultations, Bougainvilleans stated that they "want[ed] to see *kastom* [custom] built into, and recognised as part of, the justice system."[157]

Law and order

The main institution to enforce law and order is the Bougainville Police Service (BPS).[158] Powers over policing were transferred to the BIPG in December 2003 and were inherited by the ABG. While the BPS is relatively autonomous, it still remains under the "functional control" of the Royal Papua New Guinea Constabulary (RPNGC) and is strongly associated with that organization.[159] In accordance with the attempt to achieve liberal-local hybridity, the BPS is mandated to "preserve peace and good order," strengthen customary authority, respect human rights, and develop "rehabilitatory and reconciliatory concepts of policing." It is also required to "work in harmony and partnership" with Councils of Elders, Village Assemblies, and other traditional leaders "to resolve disputes and maintain law and order in communities."[160] Accordingly, the BPS incorporates the Bougainville Community Auxiliary Police Service (CAPS), mandated to conduct community policing.

In early 2004, concern was expressed about the deteriorating law and order situation in Bougainville.[161] However, during 2004, the situation improved as

---

[156] J. L. Momis, *Bougainville High Impact Projects Remain Top Priority: Media Release* (Buka: Autonomous Bougainville Government, September 4, 2013).
[157] BCC, *Report*, 55.   [158] ABG Constitution, ss. 148–150.
[159] NRI, *Bougainville Community Crime Trends: A Survey of Crime in Arawa and Buka* (Port Moresby: National Research Institute, 2005): 16; S. Dinnen and G. Peake, "More Than Just Policing: Police Reform in Post-Conflict Bougainville," *International Peacekeeping* (2013), accessed November 20, 2013, DOI: 10.1080/13533312.2013.853961.
[160] ABG Constitution, s. 148(2).
[161] UN, *Report of the Secretary-General on the United Nations Observer Mission in Bougainville (Papua New Guinea)*, UN Security Council, UN Doc. S/2005/204, March 28, 2005;

the BPS deployed 100 officers and 400 CAPS officers were trained and deployed. The situation continued to improve during 2005,[162] and BPS and CAPS officers were able to provide security for the 2005 ABG general election in "a professional and non-threatening manner."[163] A 2005 survey found that crime victimization was lower in Bougainville than in the Papua New Guinea capital, Port Moresby, and that the crimes reported "appear to be less serious." However, the survey's authors did note that the situation is "complex," particularly as the crisis saw the withdrawal of policing services, which meant that "many of the younger respondents did not have much in the way of knowledge about, or expectations of the police." Despite this, "virtually all respondents stated that they knew where the local police station was" and more than two-thirds thought the police were "doing a good job."[164] In addition, a 2006 survey revealed that the frequency of household crime victimization had dropped between 2004 and 2006 and that such crimes occurred less frequently in Bougainville than in certain other areas of Papua New Guinea. That survey also revealed that firearms were used in crimes in Bougainville less than half as often as in certain other parts of Papua New Guinea.[165] This positive trend continued in 2007, when a survey found that Bougainville reported lower levels of firearm use in crime compared with certain other parts of Papua New Guinea.[166]

Despite this, the BPS is perceived to be "a weak institution, suffering poor morale, bad discipline and low effectiveness."[167] The weak capacity of the BPS is primarily due to funding shortfalls, which meant that in 2013 there were only 179 regular police personnel, who are based primarily in urban areas. Consequently, the BPS's investigative capacity is weak, and it is common for police not to make arrests.[168] This has allowed a rise in crimes such as domestic violence, rape, and drug and alcohol abuse.[169] Weaknesses

UNIFEM, *Getting It Right, Doing It Right: Gender and Disarmament, Demobilization and Reintegration* (New York: United Nations Development Fund for Women, 2004).

[162] UN Doc. S/2004/771.   [163] Commonwealth Secretariat/PIF, *General Election*.
[164] NRI, *Bougainville Community Crime Trends*, 39.
[165] Law & Justice Sector Secretariat, *Law and Justice Sector: Annual Performance Report 2006* (Port Moresby: Law & Justice Sector Secretariat, 2007).
[166] Law & Justice Sector Secretariat, *Law and Justice Sector: Annual Performance Report 2007* (Port Moresby: Law & Justice Sector Secretariat, 2008).
[167] J. McGovern and M. Taga, *Review of the Bougainville Community Police Project (Phase 4): BCCP Review Report*, 2009, accessed October 10, 2013, www.aid.govt.nz/about-aid-programme/measuring-results/evaluation/activity-reports/2010-review-and-evaluation-reports/bougainville-com, 10; A. Regan "Bougainville Update."
[168] Regan, "Bougainville's New Directions"; BHRC, *Universal Periodic Review*.
[169] For example, a 2013 UNDP survey found that 80 percent of respondents reported having perpetrated physical and/or sexual partner violence and 62 percent reported having perpetrated

in the BPS also mean that there have been disciplinary issues and officers have been accused of brutality.[170] As a result, in 2011 a telephone line was created for people to report abuses by members of the BPS. The BPS's capacity to deal with violence has been complicated by the fact that its officers do not carry weapons, so they are said to "feel powerless" to confront armed groups,[171] and there have been a number of escapes from poorly guarded police station cells. To bolster the BPS's capacity, the ABG has engaged ex-combatants as "special constables" to assist the BPS during its operations, most notably over the 2012 Christmas season.[172] President Momis has also proposed that ex-combatants form "private security firms" that could work alongside the BPS. However, this would raise serious constitutional questions and has led to concerns that this might undermine the BPS, particularly as some of the existing security firms are said to be "breeding grounds for violence."[173]

There is some confusion concerning the transfer of policing powers to the ABG and consequently about which agency has oversight of the BPS.[174] The BIPG (later inherited by the ABG) was delegated the power to direct and control the RPNGC assistant commissioner in Bougainville, and through him the members of the BPS. The Bougainville Peace Agreement specifies that the BPS will be subject to the control of the ABG only.[175] Despite this, the RPNGC appears to consider that it retains control over the BPS, as was evident in early 2013, when the RPNGC decided to transfer the assistant commissioner in Bougainville and appoint a replacement without consulting the ABG. After ABG protests, the decision was rescinded.

Although there are only approximately 350 CAPS officers, their performance has been described as "fantastic," and they are seen as "more effective" than the BPS,[176] as they are involved in "community dispute resolution and peace building practices" as well as "law and order and conflict prevention."[177] The CAPS are said to have "developed into a highly functional culturally and situationally appropriate community policing system that

---

a form of rape against a woman or girl. E. Fulu et al., *Why Do Some Men Use Violence Against Women and How Can We Prevent it?* (Bangkok: UNDP, UNFPA, UN Women and UNV, 2013); Interview with a Bougainvillean women's leader, January 25, 2011.

[170] McGovern and Taga, *Review of the Bougainville Community Police Project*.
[171] BHRC, *Universal Periodic Review*.
[172] J. Momis, speaking at "Bougainville Mining Seminar."
[173] BHRC, *Universal Periodic Review*.
[174] McGovern and Taga, *Review of the Bougainville Community Police Project*.
[175] Bougainville Peace Agreement, cl. 210.
[176] Personal communication from an international adviser to the ABG, November 5, 2010.
[177] McGovern and Taga, *Review of the Bougainville Community Police Project*, 9; S. Dinnen and Peake, "More Than Just Policing."

complements and supports formal law and justice sector processes."[178] CAPS officers operate in all areas of Bougainville and have been accepted in some areas where regular police cannot operate, including the no-go zone. They also provide security to Village Courts, which allows the courts to function safely.[179] The success of the CAPS is partly due to the fact that CAPS officers utilize a "community based approach" to policing and work closely with the Council of Elders and traditional leaders to mediate local disputes, encourage reconciliation, and prevent the escalation of conflict.[180] People selected to be CAPS officers are endorsed by their community representatives, including their local council, which has enhanced their acceptability at the local level. As a result, the approach they take, and the solutions they reach, are often more "culturally relevant" than those of the BPS, which follows a more formal policing methodology.[181] The success of CAPS is also partly due to the fact that it receives support, uniforms, and training under the New Zealand Community Policing Project. However, this support is limited, as CAPS officers are paid for only two to three hours maximum per day, even though they are often required to work much longer hours, which has led to some tension between the CAPS and the better-paid BPS. In recognition of this fact, the ABG decided to double the allowances paid to CAPS officers in 2013. There is also tension arising from the lack of clarity about the relationship between the CAPS and BPS.[182] As a consequence of this rivalry, there have been cases where the two police services have refused to refer cases to each other or to pass on evidence, which has undermined the effectiveness of both,[183] although this might also be explained by a lack of capacity within both services.

As a result of weaknesses in the policing services, the ABG has not achieved a monopoly over the legitimate use of physical force in all parts of Bougainville, which raises questions over its effectiveness when measured by a Weberian standard. This is particularly the case in the South, where the police have struggled to establish a presence due to the large number of weapons that

---

[178] NZAID, "Bougainville Community Policing Project Mid Term Review," July 1, 2006, accessed October 9, 2013, www.aid.govt.nz/about-aid-programme/measuring-results/evaluation/activity-reports/2006-reveiw-and-evaluation-reports/bougainville-com.
[179] Ibid.
[180] Interview with an international adviser to the BIPG, BCC, and ABG, August 31, 2010; NRI, *Bougainville Community Crime Trends*; Dinnen and Peake, "More Than Just Policing."
[181] Personal communication from an international adviser to the ABG, November 5, 2010; McGovern and Taga, *Review of the Bougainville Community Police Project*.
[182] McGovern and Taga, *Review of the Bougainville Community Police Project*.
[183] Interview with a women's leader, January 25, 2011.

continue to circulate in the hands of localized groups and in the Me'ekamui and Papala no-go zones. The most notorious group was led by Damien Koike, who claimed to be the MDF commander in the South. In response, numerous groups of ex-combatants organized and took up arms to combat the threat, most notably the Wisai Liberation Movement (WILMO). Yet, the atmosphere of reconciliation created by the peace and constitution-making processes encouraged Koike, WILMO leaders, and other parties to the conflict to sign the Konnou Agreement, according to which they agreed to a truce, in November 2011. Moreover, in early 2011, the BPS opened a police post in Wisai. More than 2,000 people attended the opening ceremony, indicating their support for a BPS presence. The CAPS and BPS are also increasingly active in the two no-go zones, and elsewhere in Bougainville there is a growing tendency for people to refer crimes to the BPS, which indicates developing faith in it.[184] Despite this, problems remain in the South, and the BPS has been reluctant to confront armed groups for fear of the situation escalating into an armed confrontation. Yet the perverse effect of the BPS's reluctance is that other groups take up arms to provide "defence" against these groups.[185]

The rule of law

The main institutions that seek to ensure that the liberal principle of the rule of law is observed are the Bougainville Courts, which consist of the Bougainville High Court (although this has not yet been established),[186] the Papua New Guinea Supreme Court (which is the final court of appeal), the Papua New Guinea National Court (which has the power to review decisions of Bougainville courts other than the High Court), and other courts established under the Papua New Guinea constitution.[187]

The loss of a significant amount of court infrastructure and the destruction of many court files during the crisis has hampered the establishment of the Bougainville courts and the ability of Papua New Guinea courts to finalize cases. When the Papua New Guinea National Court began sitting again in the North in late 2004, it had a backlog of cases dating as far back as 1997.[188] The Papua New Guinea District Court began sitting again in the North in 2006 and in the South in April 2010, after a break of more than twenty years and facing serious backlogs. As new court infrastructure has developed, the courts have been circuiting more regularly and have made progress clearing the backlog, particularly of serious criminal cases. The Office of the Public

---

[184] Ibid.; Momis, "Challenges of Implementing." [185] Momis, "Challenges of Implementing."
[186] ABG Constitution, s. 116–117. [187] Ibid., ss. 112 and 114. [188] UN Doc. S/2005/204.

Solicitor also opened a new office in Buka in November 2012 to provide legal advice to Bougainvilleans. Illustrating increasing awareness of the courts, there has been a rise in people seeking interim protection orders in cases of violence against women and children. However, the development of the courts has been complicated by the lack of funding provided to the ABG and a lack of capacity in the BPS, which regularly fails to serve bench warrants.

The most established courts are the Village Courts created by Papua New Guinea law, which operate in most areas.[189] Village Court magistrates are appointed by the District Court magistrate in consultation with the Council of Elders and generally consist of recognized local dispute settlers.[190] A Village Court has jurisdiction over any civil dispute arising in its area and over specified criminal matters.[191] A Village Court is mandated to "ensure peace and harmony in the area for which it is established by mediating in and endeavouring to obtain just and amicable settlements of disputes."[192] A Village Court may impose fines, orders to carry out useful community work, or imprisonment if its order has been ignored and a District Court magistrate ratifies the decision.[193] Appeals from Village Courts are to a District Court magistrate, who sits with two Village Court magistrates to hear the appeal.[194] As of 2006, Bougainville had the second-best Village Court access ratio compared to other provinces of Papua New Guinea, with one Village Court per 1,690 people, compared to the Papua New Guinea average of one court per 5,399.[195]

Village Courts constitute an example of liberal-local hybridity; they are formal institutions, but since magistrates are untrained and lawyers do not appear in Village Courts, it is usual for magistrates to utilize a "creative" mix of formal and customary law.[196] While Village Courts are intended to operate as

---

[189] Village Courts Act.
[190] Ibid., ss. 6 and 7; interview with a former BRA commander and member of the ABG, November 2, 2010.
[191] Including motor vehicle offences, minor assaults, drinking, property damage, and disturbing the peace. Village Courts Act, ss. 15, 23 and 25.
[192] Ibid., s. 19. See also A. Paliwala, "Law and Order in the Village: The Village Courts," in *Law and Social Change in Papua New Guinea*, ed. D. Weisbrot, A. Paliwala, and A. Sawyerr (Sydney: Butterworths, 1982).
[193] Village Courts Act, s. 26, 33–36.   [194] Ibid., ss. 49–51.
[195] Law & Justice Sector Secretariat, *Law and Justice Sector: Annual Performance Report 2007*.
[196] M. Goddard, "Three Urban Village Courts in Papua New Guinea: Comparative Observations on Dispute Settlement," in Dinnen and Ley, *Reflections on Violence*, 242; Boege, *A Promising Liaison*; interview with a former BRA commander and member of the ABG, November 2, 2010.

a link between the formal and local justice systems, their customary credentials have been undermined by the fact that they are governed by rules that decide what matters they can hear and what penalties they can impose.[197] Despite this, Village Courts are said to perform a valuable role, as they are "readily accessible" and "relatively unbiased" and offer a forum in which the local community "can witness the righting of wrongs and the reasonable settlement of disputes."[198] Village Courts are also able to provide outcomes that are "highly contextualised and consequently of considerable local credibility and legitimacy."[199] However, they are said to be overworked and under-resourced,[200] as until the formal justice system becomes well established, the Village Courts are being asked to deal with cases that extend well beyond their powers.[201]

In addition to the Village Courts, the constitution provides scope for further liberal-local hybridity, as it empowers the ABG to create alternative dispute resolution mechanisms. These mechanisms may include "traditional chiefs and other traditional leaders" and would "deal with matters primarily with reference to custom, or in accordance with customary procedures."[202] However, these bodies would not be able to "impose a sentence of death or imprisonment, or to impose any other penalty as for a criminal offence."[203] The constitution also seeks to strengthen local authority with respect to criminal law by requiring the ABG to incorporate "customary practices and norms" when developing criminal law.[204] These provisions reflect the BCC's public consultations, in which "people expressed a desire for recognition of the long established role that *kastom* [custom] and traditional authority have in dealing with crime or anti-social behaviour," which became particularly prominent during the conflict, when there were no police or courts.[205] In addition, the constitution notes that the ABG and Papua New Guinea government will establish a joint commission to consider giving the ABG the power to permit courts or Councils of Elders to require clan groups to which persons convicted of criminal offences belong to meet customary noncustodial obligations,[206] in accordance with the local practice of communal responsibility for wrongdoings.

Therefore, legal pluralism is evident in Bougainville, as customary and formal (Papua New Guinea and ABG) law, and formal justice institutions that operate according to liberal principles and local institutions that operate

---

[197] Goddard, "Three Urban Village Courts." [198] Ibid., 243.
[199] D. Hegarty, "Governance at the Local Level in Melanesia – Absent the State," *Commonwealth Journal of Local Governance* 3 (2009): 1–19, 3.
[200] In 2011, village court magistrates were paid K2 per week (less than US$1).
[201] BHRC, *Universal Periodic Review.* [202] ABG Constitution, s. 126. [203] Ibid., s. 115.
[204] Ibid., s. 148(2)(c) and (d). [205] BCC, *Report*, 194. [206] ABG Constitution, s. 45.

according to a mixture of liberal and local principles, coexist. This could have a detrimental effect on the rule of law, since it may result in inconsistent decision making if different customary laws are applied across different justice institutions. However, because the BCC recognized the ongoing relevance of local justice mechanisms and because strong support for the recognition of customary law was expressed during its public consultations, local justice mechanisms have been partially recognized and incorporated into formal justice institutions. This means that the Village Courts can be supervised by the ABG Division of Local Level Government, the Papua New Guinea District Courts, and the Papua New Guinea Village Court secretariat.

Culture of impunity
In addition to the challenge of legal pluralism, there is evidence that the rule of law has been undermined by the provision of amnesties and pardons for certain crimes that occurred during the crisis, which has cultivated a culture of impunity, as it has "given the impression to the general population that there is [sic] no consequences for abusing the rights of others."[207] During the BCC's consultations, Bougainvilleans were "generally supportive" of the amnesty and pardon provisions of the Bougainville Peace Agreement, but there was no consensus on how to deal with crimes that occurred during the crisis.[208] Some people called for a truth and reconciliation commission to tell "the story of what happened"; others favored traditional reconciliation initiatives that are "truly grounded in Bougainvillean culture."[209] There was less support within the BCC for a truth and reconciliation commission, with some BCC members claiming that it would be "contrary to custom" and could inhibit the weapons disposal process.[210] Instead, the constitution recognizes that human rights "issues" occurred during the crisis and requires the Executive Council to formulate a policy for dealing with them and for effecting reconciliation that utilizes Bougainville "customs and practices...so far as is possible."[211] The constitution also reiterates the amnesty and pardon provisions of the Bougainville Peace Agreement.[212]

Guided by the constitution, reconciliation in accordance with customary practices has been the focus of the ABG's efforts to deal with human rights abuses committed during the crisis.[213] Reconciliation is prioritized because it

---

[207] BHRC, *Universal Periodic Review*.   [208] BCC, *Report*, 251.   [209] Ibid., 252.
[210] BCC, *Discussion of Recommendations*: 114–115.   [211] ABG Constitution, s. 187.
[212] Ibid., s. 187 and Sch. 6.1 and 6.2.
[213] During the crisis, women's leader Marilyn Havini kept a record of human rights abuses that had been committed. M. T. Havini, *A Compilation of Human Rights Abuses against the People of Bougainville 1989–1995*, Vol. 1 (Sydney: Bougainville Freedom Movement, 1995);

is seen by Bougainvilleans as offering a way to "reunite us to be one people again" and ensure that "whatever happened during the war is not passed on to the next generation."[214] Utilizing customary practices to effect these reconciliations means that they are "irrevocable. Whatever we decide by these traditional means, will be guaranteed by society."[215] While crimes and other human rights have been "hardly talked about and hardly discussed" during the reconciliation process,[216] a recent push by women's leaders has seen proposals to create a truth and reconciliation commission gain momentum.[217] Questions have been raised concerning such proposals, with one ABG adviser noting that a distinction needs to be drawn between the views of educated women who are involved in civil society groups, for whom international donors have created political space to advocate for such a commission, and those of women who are embedded within communities, who have had to "reconcile in order to survive."[218] However, while many reconciliations have been "inclusive affairs" that have "brought entire communities together," they have often "failed...to address the need for truth telling and justice for deeper healing," instead encouraging a "forgive and forget" approach to past wrongs.[219] There has also been "no mechanism to ensure compliance" with reparation agreements and other reciprocal arrangements agreed upon during reconciliation ceremonies.[220]

As formal justice institutions have not dealt with crimes committed during the crisis and there are questions over the conduct of many customary reconciliations, there is some evidence that a culture of impunity has developed with respect to crimes committed since autonomy. As a result, Bougainvilleans are said to be "confused as to their rights to pursue justice in individual cases of severe abuse."[221] In the face of this perceived impunity, the families of victims are engaging in increasingly violent forms of "local justice," including "horrific tortures and executions" as "payback,"[222] which is also having a detrimental effect on law and order and the rule of law.

M. T. Havini, *A Compilation of Human Rights Abuses against the People of Bougainville 1989–1996*, Vol. 2 (Sydney: Bougainville Freedom Movement, 1996). Amnesty International also recorded abuses that occurred during the early stages of the crisis. AI, *Papua New Guinea: Human Rights Violations on Bougainville, 1989–1990* (London: Amnesty International, 1990).

[214] Sr L. Garrasu, speaking in L. Thompson (prod.), *Breaking Bows and Arrows: Bougainville*, television broadcast, SBS Television Australia, March 22, 2002.
[215] J. Boboso, speaking in Thompson, *Breaking Bows and Arrows*.
[216] Garrasu, speaking in Thompson, *Breaking Bows and Arrows*.
[217] Interview with a Bougainvillean women's leader, January 25, 2011; BHRC, *Universal Periodic Review*.
[218] Interview with an international adviser to the BIPG, BCC, and ABG, August 31, 2010.
[219] BHRC, *Universal Periodic Review*. [220] Ibid. [221] Ibid. [222] Ibid.

Bougainvilleans expressed a clear desire during the BCC's public consultation for local justice practices to be recognized in the constitution. As a constitution enumerates the way in which the people's constituted power is to be exercised, it rightly reflects the people's views by recognizing the role of the Village Courts and traditional alternative dispute resolution mechanisms. However, the decision to prioritize local customary reconciliation over prosecution in formal justice institutions for crimes committed during the crisis, and the resulting developing culture of impunity, highlights the challenge of achieving a balance between liberal and local customary practices.

Are human rights and civil liberties protected?

Legal pluralism and challenges facing the establishment of the rule of law have affected the protection of human rights and civil liberties in Bougainville. During the BCC's public consultations, people stated that they wanted the ABG "to show the strongest possible commitment to the protection of human rights."[223] Accordingly, the constitution notes that the basic rights protections provided by the Papua New Guinea constitution continue to apply[224] and that additional rights may be protected in the future.[225] In addition, in some circumstances Bougainville laws may qualify certain of the basic rights provided by the Papua New Guinea constitution, "to the extent that the law is reasonably justifiable in a democratic society having a proper regard for the rights and dignity of mankind."[226] This provision is largely directed at addressing problems of internal migration that gave rise to the crisis and that people expressed concern about during the BCC's consultations.[227] In line with the principle of strengthening customary authority, the constitution also requires that when enforcing human rights protections, the courts should utilize "the customary methods of dealing with such abuses…wherever possible,"[228] although this has yet to be tested.

Human rights protections are enforceable by the High Court, the Supreme Court, or the National Court "either on the initiative of the Court itself or on application by any person who has an interest in its protection or enforcement."[229] In addition, reflecting views expressed during the BCC's consultations, a specialist human rights enforcement body may be created at a later date.[230] One adviser to the BCC noted that it was recognized that there was not – and was unlikely to be for some time – sufficient capacity to enforce

---

[223] BCC, *Report*, 251. [224] ABG Constitution, s. 178. [225] Ibid., s. 179.
[226] Ibid., ss. 180–181. [227] BCC, *Report*. [228] ABG Constitution, s. 186. [229] Ibid., s. 183.
[230] Ibid., s. 185; BCC, *Report*.

human rights protections in Bougainville. Instead, he foresaw that human rights recognition "will develop over time," with local sociopolitical practices based on clan responsibility ensuring that egregious human rights abuses are dealt with in the meantime.[231]

Therefore, the extensive participation evidence during the constitution-making process (and the peace process that preceded it) means that a constituent process emerged in Bougainville. The BCC appears to have been heavily influenced by the views expressed during its public consultations. Consequently, the resulting constitution appears to reflect the people's views and understandings and to have created liberal-local hybrid governance and justice institutions that make sense to the people whose constituted power they exercise.

BOUGAINVILLE'S UNCERTAIN POLITICAL FUTURE

For the purpose of comparison, this book has treated the Bougainville constitution-making process as part of a state-building operation, in light of the extensive powers and functions available to Bougainville. Extensive autonomy was granted to Bougainville in the hope that it would "strengthen national unity by producing a better balance" between the Papua New Guinea government and the ABG.[232] The Papua New Guinea government assumed that combining autonomy with a deferred referendum on Bougainville's political future would reduce support for independence, as this theoretically provided time for it to encourage Bougainvilleans to recognize the advantages of integration in Papua New Guinea.[233] The fact that the referendum was nonbinding allowed the Papua New Guinea government to argue that it did not undermine Papua New Guinea's sovereignty. The promise of a constitutionally guaranteed referendum was also necessary to sell autonomy and deferral to hard-line secessionists, who believed that a high vote for independence (perhaps comparable to the 98.8 percent achieved in South Sudan) would be difficult for the Papua New Guinea government to ignore and could secure international pressure in their favor.[234] Many pro-integration supporters backed the referendum on the grounds that it would give Bougainvilleans the chance to exercise their self-determination concerning Bougainville's political future.[235]

---

[231] Interview with an international adviser to the BRA and BCC, January 18, 2010.
[232] Ghai and Regan, "Unitary State," 602.
[233] Momis, "Challenges of Implementing"; Regan, *Light Intervention*.
[234] Ghai and Regan, "Unitary State."
[235] Interview with a former BRA commander and member of the ABG, November 2, 2010; Momis, "Challenges of Implementing."

Although the referendum is scheduled to be held between 2015 and 2020, the slow transfer of funding, powers, and functions to the ABG led one former government member to observe in 2010 that it would take a "miracle" for Bougainville to achieve full autonomy and be ready for independence by then.[236] This has caused significant frustration among Bougainvilleans, as they perceive the Papua New Guinea government to be "reneging on the public commitment" it made in the Bougainville Peace Agreement.[237] Somewhat paradoxically, by appearing to make it difficult for Bougainville to develop its autonomy, the Papua New Guinea government may actually reinforce a sense of Bougainvillean resentment, distinctiveness, and sentiment in favor of secession. Therefore, the Bougainville case suggests that states should make sincere attempts to transfer substantive powers and funding to their autonomous regions so that autonomy is perceived to be genuine and the central government to be committed to the peace process.[238] Such perceptions may increase the likelihood that the result of a referendum is accepted by the parties to the self-determination dispute and decrease the likelihood that conflict will recur. Consequently, President Momis is keen to advance Bougainville's autonomy and improve the ABG's effectiveness so that Bougainvilleans have a "real choice" at the referendum.[239]

The referendum is also conditional on weapons disposal and the ABG achieving internationally accepted standards of good governance. While the latter condition does not appear problematic, weapons continue to circulate in Bougainville. The Papua New Guinea government could rely on this fact to block or delay the referendum. This is not unforeseeable, given that there are voices within the Papua New Guinea government that oppose Bougainville's independence on the grounds that it could set a precedent for other provinces and precipitate the breakup of the Papua New Guinea state. These voices have grown louder as memories of the PNGDF's near-defeat during the Bougainville conflict have begun to fade.

The prospects for an independent Bougainville are not necessarily negative. Bougainville has roughly the same population as its neighboring states Samoa and Vanuatu and a substantially larger population than Kiribati and

---

[236] Interview with a former BRA commander and member of the ABG, November 2, 2010; interview with an ABG official and member of a council of elders, January 22, 2011.
[237] Momis, speaking in "President Reflects on Progress in Bougainville Peace Process."
[238] J. Wallis, "Nation-Building, Autonomy Arrangements and Deferred Referendums: Unresolved Questions from Bougainville, Papua New Guinea," *Nationalism and Ethnic Politics* 19:3 (2013): 310–332.
[239] Ibid.; Momis, speaking at "Bougainville Mining Seminar"; Regan, *Light Intervention*.

Tonga. Bougainville also has a much larger land mass and many more natural resources than those states. Bougainville is not remote from metropolitan powers, making trade easier and providing some potential for tourism. Therefore, Bougainville is "reasonably well placed for some degree of success within conventional development strategies."[240] The similarities between Bougainville and Timor-Leste also suggest that it could learn from Timor-Leste's experience.

A factor complicating Bougainville's independence is the Panguna mine, which most Bougainvilleans acknowledge will be a necessary source of revenue for an independent state. As the mine was closed at the beginning of the war, it was sidelined as a factor in the peace process. Consequently, grievances relating to the mine have not been fully resolved but instead effectively suspended until serious moves are made to reopen the mine. As these moves are now being made, questions remain concerning whether Bougainvilleans are sufficiently united to negotiate reopening the mine.

Even if the referendum is held, it is not clear what the outcome will be or how the Bougainville parties will react. The general consensus among Bougainvilleans (even those who support integration) is that voters will opt for independence. If this occurs, the Papua New Guinea government may not accept the outcome and ratify it as required by the Bougainville Peace Agreement. It is not uncommon for governments to agree to a referendum without any intention of honoring it, and while the Papua New Guinea government agreed to the Bougainville Peace Agreement, this was not the same as it agreeing to Bougainville's independence.[241] There is a fairly strong consensus among Bougainvilleans that they want to avoid a recurrence of the horrors of the crisis, and President Momis has argued that the differences between Bougainvilleans are now "far less significant."[242] However, one adviser to the Papua New Guinea government cautioned that just because the different Bougainville factions cooperated during the peace and constitution-making processes, this "does not mean that previous preferred positions, alliances and differences have necessarily been left behind, or resolved."[243] This could place serious pressure on the Bougainville Peace Agreement, particularly on the cease-fire and the reconciliation achieved since.

---

[240] Connell, "Bougainville: The Future," 196.
[241] Interview with an international adviser to the Papua New Guinea government, January 24, 2010.
[242] Momis, "Challenges of Implementing."
[243] Interview with an international adviser to the Papua New Guinea government, January 24, 2010.

It is also not clear how pro-integration supporters would react to a vote for independence. During the crisis, there was talk on Buka Island, where pro-integration sentiment is strongest, of seceding from the rest of Bougainville if this occurred. However, this would appear practically unfeasible. Pro-integration sentiment is not uniform on Buka Island, which is separated from Bougainville Island only by a very narrow sea passage that is traversed thousands of times per day. In addition, the temporary regional capital is on Buka, and most public institutions and private enterprises are located there. Yet this question could be moot, as the K500 million to conduct "high impact" development projects that the Papua New Guinea government is supposed to be transferring to Bougainville between 2012 and 2017 may encourage many Bougainvilleans to perceive benefits to continued integration in Papua New Guinea. In this regard, one member of the Bougainville administration noted that he did not want to see the Bougainvillean leadership "put identity above being able to provide services to the people." Instead, he proposed that Bougainvilleans remain autonomous in Papua New Guinea and think of themselves as a "state within a state."[244] Bougainvilleans are also aware of practical considerations, such as whether they would hold dual Papua New Guinea–Bougainville citizenship, how Bougainvilleans living in Papua New Guinea would be treated (and how Papua New Guineans living in Bougainville would be treated), and how the links of education, marriage, employment, and investment between Papua New Guinea and Bougainville would be managed. Even if the referendum is held and Bougainvilleans do choose independence, the extensive links between Papua New Guinea and Bougainville suggest that they are likely to remain in some form of relationship, perhaps along the lines of the "free association" between the Cook Islands and New Zealand.

Therefore, Bougainville's self-determination question has been put on hold rather than resolved. While extensive public participation in constitution making appears to have generated a constituent process that has played a positive role in state building in Bougainville, this success may be temporary. However, this does not necessarily diminish the findings in relation to the role of a constituent process in state building. Indeed, the fact that Bougainvilleans were able to put the question of their political future on hold may be because the generation of a constituent process has created a relatively unified political community and an environment conducive to reconciliation.

---

[244] Personal communication from a member of the Bougainville administration, January 24, 2011.

PART IV
COMPARING THE TWO CASES
AND CONCLUSIONS

9

Comparing the constitution-making processes

Timor-Leste and Bougainville are in many ways paradigmatic examples of the different roles that constitution making can play in state building. In both cases, the constitution-making processes were working toward the clear political endpoint of building a state, without a substantial external threat. At least when constitution making commenced, both populations were relatively supportive of this goal. And, while there were prominent political actors and organizations, their state-level political landscapes were free of formal institutions. Consequently, in both cases, a constituent process was required to unite fragmented societies with little experience of centralized statehood and to build institutions capable of legitimately and effectively governing them.

In Timor-Leste, public participation in constitution making was minimal, which meant that a constituent process did not emerge, while in Bougainville it was extensive, which meant that one did. Therefore, a comparison of these two cases offers a good illustration of the consequences of these differing approaches to public participation for the emergence of a constituent process, and subsequently for state building. As described in Parts II and III, minimal public participation in Timor-Leste resulted in state institutions that were (at least initially) neither effective nor legitimate and a society that was riven by divisions that almost caused the collapse of the state. In contrast, in Bougainville, extensive public participation helped the ABG's institutions to become widely viewed as legitimate, and deep divisions that had challenged society were largely reconciled. Therefore, the Timor-Leste and Bougainville cases suggest that the higher the level of public participation involved in a constitution-making process, the more likely it is to generate a constituent process that can play a positive role in state building.

This chapter compares the constitution-making processes in Timor-Leste and Bougainville, with a particular focus on their levels of public participation, since this determines whether a constituent process will emerge. It identifies the main points of difference between the two processes as being their time frames, the type of body that drafted their constitutions, the method by which constitution drafters where selected, the manner in which their constitutions were drafted, the levels of publicity and secrecy involved, the opportunities for and role of public participation, the degree of international involvement, and the manner in which their constitutions were adopted. The next chapter compares the effect that these differences have had on whether a constituent process emerged, and consequently on state building in each case. Both chapters draw generalizable insights based on the Timor-Leste and Bougainville cases for future constitution-making processes.

THE TIME FRAME GIVEN FOR THE PROCESS

The first point of distinction between the Timor-Leste and Bougainville constitution-making processes is their time frames. In Timor-Leste, the time frame was initially just under nine months, although it was later extended to one year. While this short time frame was supported by many local elites, as predicted in the literature it was also heavily influenced by the UN, which was eager to scale back its presence. In contrast, in Bougainville, the time frame was left relatively open-ended and ultimately took over two years. The time frame was even longer if the four-year peace process is taken into account. While this time frame was to an extent a result of delays in Bougainville's autonomy negotiations with the Papua New Guinea government, there was little external pressure to rush the process, given that international involvement was light. The relatively open-ended timetable was also influenced by local sociopolitical practices, which emphasize taking time in order to build consensus and allow all those affected by a decision to be involved. Consequently, the Bougainville process appears to fit the recommendations made in the literature, which generally concludes that an unhurried timetable is preferable, as it provides opportunities for public participation, allows the draft constitution to reflect lessons learned, and leaves time to build consensus, resulting in a constituent process. These benefits appear to have been realized in Bougainville, while the costs of a rushed process have been borne out in Timor-Leste, which suggests that future constitution-making processes should adopt a similarly unhurried approach.

THE TYPE OF INSTITUTION THAT WAS DESIGNATED TO DRAFT THE CONSTITUTION

The second point of distinction between the two constitution-making processes is the type of institution that was designated to draft the constitution.

In Timor-Leste, the constitution was drafted by the elected Constituent Assembly, while in Bougainville it was drafted by the appointed Constitutional Commission. The literature argues that an elected constitution-making body can encourage political leaders to buy in, provide the public with opportunities to communicate their interests to candidates during the election campaign, and enhance the legitimacy of the body. However, these benefits do not appear to have been realized in Timor-Leste, due to questions over the Constituent Assembly election campaign. Although the FRETILIN party, which led Timor-Leste's independence struggle, was always going to play a prominent role in the assembly, the decision to designate an elected drafting body meant that FRETILIN was able to win a majority of seats in the assembly and control the process, and it had little incentive to build consensus with other political parties or to invite public participation. In contrast, the Bougainville process followed the recommendation in the literature that constitution-making bodies should be appointed, since elections may induce political parties to succumb to majoritarian interests. However, it should be acknowledged that FRETILIN was a well-organized liberation movement that, partly due to the approach adopted by UNTAET, was able to monopolize the constitution-making process in Timor-Leste. In contrast, the Bougainville parties were more disparate, and no single one was able to dominate the constitution-making process, so an environment of consensus and reconciliation developed.

The literature also generally concludes that it is preferable for constitutions to be drafted by specially convened conventions, as occurred in Bougainville. Such institutions are thought to be less likely to succumb to institutional self-interest when dividing institutional power in the constitution, and more likely to negotiate compromises and resist the temptation of politicking. These predictions were borne out in Bougainville, where the BCC was perceived as broadly representative and inclusive of all societal groups, which helped to achieve a constituent process. This suggests that future constitution-making processes should consider adopting a similar approach.

THE METHOD BY WHICH CONSTITUTION DRAFTERS WERE SELECTED, AND HOW REPRESENTATIVE THEY WERE

In Timor-Leste, there was a focus on the liberal principle of democratically electing (ostensibly) representative constitution drafters. As predicted in the literature, UNTAET pushed for early elections, which allowed FRETILIN to capitalize on its comparatively strong reputation, organization, and financing to seize control of the Constituent Assembly. Timor-Leste adopted a proportional voting system, which the literature argues stands the best chance of delivering results that are broadly representative, as it provides an opportunity for minor parties to secure seats. Despite this, the fact that FRETILIN won enough seats to control the assembly created the perception that the election was "winner-takes-all." In contrast, the BCC was appointed by (mostly) elected political organizations, which enhanced its democratic credentials. Bougainville also allocated seats to include representatives of all major social groups, which was important, since the literature argues that the perceived representativeness of the drafting body can affect the legitimacy of the constitution.

The Timor-Leste case challenges the liberal peace assumption that democracy is crucial to state building, as it suggests that emphasizing the importance of democratically electing constitution drafters may do more harm than good. In Timor-Leste, UNTAET focused on holding "free and fair" elections before parties had time to consolidate, formulate political platforms, and present them to the voters, and before the broader cultural, political, and institutional evolution involved in a process of democratization had taken place. In contrast, as it was subject to only light international intervention, the BCC had more space to avoid a potentially disruptive election by appointing constitution drafters who broadly reflected society.

THE MANNER IN WHICH THE DESIGNATED INSTITUTION DRAFTED THE CONSTITUTION

In both Timor-Leste and Bougainville, constitution-making institutions made difficult decisions by majority vote, which the literature notes is the most common method. The point of distinction between the two is the fact that the Timor-Leste Constituent Assembly was elected, which undermined the representativeness of the constitution, as FRETILIN was able to dictate all decisions. Consequently, the Timor-Leste constitution is frequently referred to as a "FRETILIN document." In contrast, the appointed BCC was broadly representative, and decisions taken by vote did not follow a consistent pattern. Instead, BCC members appear to have been free to vote (at least ostensibly) according to the views of the groups they were appointed to represent. The literature also advocates consensus decision making for difficult decisions, which, it notes, can be deferred to be addressed by later law or decided by referendum. While the Timor-Leste process followed the liberal peace emphasis on democratic decision making, the BCC made a number of decisions by consensus, which also reflected local sociopolitical practices. However, it should be noted that both constitutions do defer certain difficult issues.

Overall, both cases suggest that while it is common for constitution drafters to make decisions by majority vote, the manner in which those drafters are selected will have important implications for the design – and perceived legitimacy – of the resulting constitution. The Bougainville case also highlights the important role that achieving consensus can play in diffusing conflict and achieving widespread support for the constitution, by avoiding the perception of "winner takes all" created by majoritarian decision making.

THE LEVELS OF PUBLICITY AND SECRECY INVOLVED IN THE PROCESS

There was a high degree of publicity in both processes. The literature argues that publicity can minimize opportunities for partisan interests and logrolling to influence constitution drafters. However, these positive effects were not evident in Timor-Leste, where the FRETILIN majority in the Constituent Assembly appeared to have been guided by partisan interests, rather than seeking to offer impartial arguments framed in terms of the common good. These positive effects were evident in Bougainville, where the minutes of the BCC's debates provide little evidence that partisan – or pro-secession or pro-integration – interests held sway.

The literature also cautions that publicity can result in negative consequences, as it can increase the likelihood that constitution drafters will engage in strategic precommitments and create a vanity-induced reluctance to compromise. Both consequences occurred in Timor-Leste, where FRETILIN precommitted to its draft and was reluctant to change it during the Constituent Assembly's debates. This also occurred in Bougainville, where many of the negotiations on the Bougainville Peace Agreement were conducted in secret and acted as precommitments that bound constitution drafters. However, perhaps because the members of the BCC were mostly not politicians, they exhibited a willingness to compromise.

To an extent, the high level of publicity in both processes was a result of many significant decisions concerning the future constitutions having already been made. In Timor-Leste, the FRETILIN diaspora had prepared a draft of the constitution during the Indonesian occupation, and in Bougainville, many of the most controversial decisions concerning the referendum and level of autonomy had been made during the peace process. Since the literature argues that secrecy may facilitate bargaining and provide space for clear thinking and careful drafting, there is some merit to these significant decisions having been made in relative secrecy before the processes began. At the same time, deciding too many issues in secret affects the ability of the constitutions to legitimately represent the exercise of the Timorese and Bougainvillean peoples' constituent power. This question is particularly resonant in Timor-Leste, where FRETILIN did not publicize its draft constitution during the Constituent Assembly election, which might have allowed the Timorese people to exercise their popular sovereignty to approve it by voting for – or against – FRETILIN. In contrast, in Bougainville, political and military leaders engaged in constant public consultation and awareness activities throughout their negotiations on the Bougainville Peace Agreement, which also fits with the emphasis placed on inclusiveness and consultation by local sociopolitical practices. Therefore, the evidence from the two cases concerning the role of publicity and secrecy is mixed, and suggests that secrecy may play a role in facilitating early compromises when the constitution-making process is being created, while publicity may play a role later in the process, when decisions regarding the shape of the future state are being made.

THE OPPORTUNITIES FOR PUBLIC PARTICIPATION AND ITS ROLE IN THE PROCESS

In this regard, the most significant distinction between the Timor-Leste and Bougainville constitution-making processes relates to the opportunities for public participation and the role that it played. In Timor-Leste, there were few opportunities for participation, beyond the UNTAET civic education program, the month-long Constitutional Commission hearings, the election of Constituent Assembly members, and the week-long assembly consultations. This was partly due to the short time frame given for the process and partly because many Timorese political leaders appear to have had little interest in it. In contrast, the BCC undertook three rounds of public consultation, the first lasting one month, the second two weeks, and the third one month. Indeed, the time frame was extended partly to allow for additional participation.

The quality of the consultations also differed. In Timor-Leste, the Constitutional Commission consultations were undertaken by UNTAET appointees, which posed the challenge of how their outcomes would be communicated to constitution drafters. In contrast, in Bougainville, all consultations were undertaken by constitution drafters, which ensured that the feedback received fed directly into the drafting process. Moreover, in Timor-Leste, there was no set procedure to ensure that the same material was covered or to organize and record the views expressed by the public in the consultation hearings. Conversely, the BCC adopted a questionnaire to guide its first round of consultation and structured the second and third rounds of consultation around drafts of the constitution. Technical advisers were appointed to record the views expressed.

The distribution of information and drafts prior to the consultations also differed. In Timor-Leste, little information was provided to the public in the lead-up to the Constitutional Commission hearings, which meant that the benefits of information distribution identified in the literature were missed, and people were underprepared to participate in the hearings. The effects of this were exacerbated by delays in establishing the civic education program, which meant that it ran concurrently with, rather than in preparation for, the commission hearings. In addition, while thousands of copies of the draft constitution and explanatory magazine were distributed in preparation for the Constituent Assembly's public consultation, they were often not in languages that people could understand and did not account for low levels of adult literacy (43 percent). Consequently, most Timorese were unable to properly digest the draft constitution, which undermined their ability to comment on it during the assembly's consultation hearings. In contrast, in Bougainville, the questionnaire used during the first round of consultation hearings was distributed in advance. Copies of the first draft of the constitution and explanatory materials were also distributed before the second round of consultation in languages most Bougainvilleans could understand. High levels of adult literacy (80 percent) meant that many Bougainvilleans were able to digest these materials. As there were still concerns about the availability of the materials, thousands of copies of the second draft of the constitution were distributed in advance of the third round of consultations. The extensive distribution of information helped Bougainvilleans to garner the educative benefits of information distribution identified in the literature and appears to have placed them in a good position to provide informed feedback during the consultation hearings.

The timing of the public consultations in both processes also differed. In Timor-Leste, the Constitutional Commission hearings occurred before the Constituent Assembly was elected and before there had been much public debate concerning the contents of the constitution or the identity of constitution drafters. Therefore, the hearings were arguably held too soon to allow Timorese the chance to develop their views. The assembly's public consultations were then held late in the process, after the draft of the constitution had largely been agreed upon. While Timorese could have been in a good position to comment on the contents of the draft, low levels of adult literacy, the inadequate distribution of the draft, and problems in the conduct of the consultation hearings meant that this opportunity was lost. In contrast, in Bougainville, the first round of consultations were held after the BCC had been chosen but before it had conducted any substantive drafting debates. Thus, the feedback gathered during the first round shaped the BCC's debates from the outset. The second and third rounds of consultation were timed so that they provided the public with an opportunity to comment on the first and second drafts and allowed time for the BCC to incorporate these comments.

The opportunities for public participation and the way in which public feedback was utilized in Timor-Leste and Bougainville largely reflect the respective mandates of the two constitution-making bodies and the attitudes of constitution drafters. The mandate for the Timor-Leste Constituent Assembly to engage in public consultation was weak, while it was central to the BCC. In Timor-Leste, the FRETILIN majority in the assembly had not only won the election but also felt that they had won Timor-Leste's independence. Consequently, they assumed that they had a mandate to draft the constitution with little input from other political parties or the public. This attitude also affected the role that public participation played. While the Constitutional Commission hearings were relatively good examples of public participation, the assembly ignored the feedback they gathered. Similarly, the assembly largely treated its consultations as an opportunity to socialize its draft rather than to gather substantive public feedback that could generate amendments. In contrast, the BCC based its drafting process around public consultations. As outlined in the substantive chapters, the influence of these consultations during the debates and on the Bougainville constitution is clear.

The extensive participation that occurred in Bougainville resulted in almost the ideal type of public participation in constitution making. Bougainvillean constitution drafters allowed ample time for public consultations, distributed information to enable people to participate in them, and ensured that they generated useable feedback that was reflected in their drafting debates. This can be contrasted to the minimal opportunities for participation offered in Timor-Leste. The positive role that extensive participation played in generating a constituent process, and consequently in state building, in Bougainville is illustrated in Chapter 10, and suggests that future constitution-making processes should adopt a similar approach.

THE DEGREE OF INTERNATIONAL INVOLVEMENT

There was significantly more international involvement in Timor-Leste than in Bougainville because Timor-Leste was subject to a large UN state-building operation, while international intervention in Bougainville was relatively light. The literature notes that international actors can play an influential role in the constitution-making process, most commonly through the provision of expert advisers. In Timor-Leste, there were five official international advisers to the Constituent Assembly and numerous advisers provided by international organizations. However, while the literature notes that these external advisers can play a valuable role in providing technical support, in Timor-Leste none of the official advisers had experience in constitution making or strong knowledge of Timor-Leste. In contrast, in Bougainville, the two international advisers had deep knowledge of the local situation, and one had advised several other constitution-making processes.

The literature cautions that international involvement can veer into interference if international actors seek to influence the process or the constitution. There was little risk of interference in Bougainville, given that international involvement was largely confined to a facilitating role. At the same time, it must be acknowledged that the Papua New Guinea government was able to influence the process, as the Bougainville Peace Agreement required that it be consulted on, and ultimately ratify, the constitution. However, local constitution drafters were left to design their process and opted to incorporate substantial public participation, which reflected local sociopolitical practices.

In Timor-Leste, the evidence relating to international involvement is mixed. While UNTAET purported to take a hands-off approach to the constitution-making process, it exerted extensive influence over state building. Most significantly, it empowered the Timorese political elites and groups with whom it chose to interact, which allowed FRETILIN to take a leading role and removed the pressure for it to compromise and reconcile. UNTAET also influenced the design of the constitution-making process as, while the Constituent Assembly was all Timorese, it was created and operated in a UN-influenced liberal peace framework. This partly explains why so much emphasis was placed on electing constitution drafters and making decisions by vote in the assembly. At the same time, given that FRETILIN assumed that it would dominate elections, the FRETILIN members who drafted the mandate for the constitution-making process also favored elections. The time pressure UNTAET put on the process also limited the constitution-making options available, most significantly the opportunities for public participation. However, the evidence in Part II suggests that many Timorese elites supported the short time frame and limited public participation. UNTAET sought to influence the constitution, although as it did so in order to ensure that it reflected international human rights norms, it is questionable whether this interference could be characterized as malign. There are also claims that UNTAET did not interfere enough, as it provided little guidance concerning the framework for the process and did not do much to promote the interests of minority parties. On the one hand, UNTAET claimed that it stood back so that the constitution could be seen as the product of a truly Timorese process. On the other hand, if UNTAET had sought to exert its influence, this might have resulted in a process that was more representative and provided greater opportunities for public participation.

The Timor-Leste and Bougainville cases suggest that international involvement can play a positive role in constitution making if it facilitates a locally led process and provides technical and logistical support to constitution drafters, who are often operating in postconflict environments where capacity is weak, infrastructure has been destroyed, and transport and communication are difficult. However, the (often unintentional) influence that UNTAET had over the Timor-Leste process suggests that caution should be exercised to ensure that international actors do not distort the process, which may have consequences for the legitimacy of the resulting constitution.

THE MANNER IN WHICH THE CONSTITUTION WAS ADOPTED

The constitution-making literature notes that the manner in which a constitution is adopted is significant, since it determines the extent to which the constitution is perceived to be an exercise of the people's constituent power. While a popular referendum is the most straightforward way of ensuring that the people have agreed to a constitution, the literature raises concerns over the mechanics of referendums. Instead, it generally concludes that adoption by an elected assembly sufficiently represents an exercise of the people's constituent power. In both Timor-Leste and Bougainville, the constitutions were adopted by constituent assemblies; the Timor-Leste assembly was directly elected, while the Bougainville assembly consisted of the (mostly) elected members of existing political organizations. Therefore, the adoption of both constitutions arguably involved a legitimate exercise of the respective people's constituent power.

However, as the Timor-Leste Constituent Assembly both drafted and adopted the constitution, and as the vote to adopt the constitution followed the same party divisions that had dictated every vote during its debates, this raises questions over whether the constitution reflects the Timorese people's constituent power or merely that of FRETILIN supporters. In contrast, while the vote to adopt the constitution in the Bougainville Constituent Assembly was not unanimous, as the constitution was made by a separate institution, this minimized the opportunity for a particular political party or group to influence its contents. Consequently, the Bougainville constitution arguably provides a better reflection of the people's constituent power. Therefore, the two cases highlight that constitutions should be drafted and adopted by separate institutions, so that the institution that adopts the constitution can provide a check, and some balance, on the activities of drafters. Both cases also suggest that constitutions should be adopted by elected bodies, since this will increase their democratic credentials.

Another aspect of the adoption of constitutions concerns whether they are adopted on an interim basis or include a sunset clause that mandates their later review. These measures are advocated in the literature, on the basis that they allow opportunities for the people to exercise their constituent power to revise the constitution. For this reason, in Timor-Leste, the minority parties in the Constituent Assembly unsuccessfully lobbied for the constitution to be adopted on an interim basis. In contrast, the Bougainville constitution is by necessity an interim one, because Bougainville is an autonomous region and a referendum on its political future is likely to be held between 2015 and 2020. In addition, the BCC was careful to stress the evolutionary nature of the constitution by including provisions that allow for further institutions to be developed and powers and functions to be exercised. Therefore, the constitution provides more opportunities for the Bougainvillean people to continue to exercise their constituent power.

CONCLUSION

Overall, a comparison of the Timor-Leste and Bougainville cases suggests that the constitution-making process in Bougainville better reflects the recommendations made in the literature. In many ways, the Bougainville process was an ideal type of participatory constitution making that helped to generate a constituent process. It was inclusive and unhurried, which allowed time for Bougainvilleans to deliberate and build consensus about both the common identity that united their constituent power and the design of the institutions that would exercise their constituted power. It was accompanied by reconciliation, which allowed many Bougainvilleans to resolve their grievances. It involved the extensive distribution of information, which educated Bougainvilleans about the constitution and about the institutions of their new autonomous region. It also represented an attempt to garner the public's views and to reflect these in the constitution. In contrast, while there were some opportunities for public participation in Timor-Leste, the feedback received had almost no influence over the resulting constitution. This minimal public participation meant that in many ways the Timor-Leste process resembled an elite-led constitution-making process.

As the Bougainville constitution-making process involved extensive participation, it also managed to strike a balance between the liberal practices of democratic decision making by constitution drafters and the adoption of the constitution by (mostly) democratically elected representatives with the local sociopolitical practices of inclusiveness, consultation, and consensus building, which enhanced its legitimacy. Therefore, the Bougainville process was arguably a relatively good example of the Bougainvillean people exercising their constituent power to create their constitution in a manner that resonated with their local practices. However, it must be acknowledged that it might have been easier to incorporate local practices during the Bougainville process because it was locally led. Local constitution drafters were probably more sensitive to local sociopolitical practices and institutions because they were intimately aware of them. In contrast, the process in Timor-Leste was subject to extensive international involvement, and there was a subsequent focus on the liberal peace principle of democratically elected constitution drafters, but little emphasis on the local practices of consultation and consensus building. The consequences of these differing approaches for state building are outlined in the next chapter.

10

The role of a constituent process in state building

This book has argued that the higher the level of public participation involved in a constitution-making process, the more likely it is to generate a constituent process, and consequently to play a positive role in state building. Participation in constitution making may assist in building a sense of political community, so that the people unite to exercise their constituent power. Participation may affect the contents of the constitution, so that it better reflects public views, which can legitimize the institutions it creates to exercise the people's constituted power. This chapter compares the findings outlined in Parts II and III in order to illustrate that these claims are largely correct. The minimal participation in Timor-Leste meant that a constituent process did not emerge, which undermined the creation of a political community and the legitimacy and effectiveness of the state institutions created to exercise the people's constituted power. In contrast, the extensive participation in Bougainville helped to ensure that a constituent process emerged and, subsequently, that a relatively unified political community has been formed and that state institutions are relatively legitimate and functioning.

As described in Part I, the extent to which a unified political community is present can be assessed by considering the following indicators: whether the constitution enumerates a unifying national identity, whether reconciliation has been achieved, whether there are divisions within society, whether the community exhibits evidence of citizenization, and whether there is a strong public sphere. The extent to which a constitution and the state institutions it creates are functioning effectively and are perceived to be legitimate can be assessed by considering whether state institutions have been created and are functioning as intended, to what extent state institutions are perceived to be legitimate, whether state institutions are delivering public goods and services, whether law and order are enforced and the rule of law is observed, and whether human rights and civil liberties are protected.

CONSTITUENT POWER

Does the constitution enumerate a unifying national identity?

Both the Timor-Leste and Bougainville constitutions enumerate common societal values, aspirations, and shared symbols that seek to build a national identity. They differ concerning the extent to which these identities resonate with their respective populations. As there were minimal opportunities for public participation in Timor-Leste, Timorese were not given the chance to negotiate on and agree to values and symbols that were capable of generating a unifying sense of national identity. Given the strong commonalities among Timorese traditions and customs, there was ample material that constitution drafters could have used to adopt an ethno-symbolist approach to nation building. Indeed, there was strong support in favor of drawing on local traditions and customs in the public consultations during constitution making. Instead, within the Constituent Assembly, the FRETILIN majority strongly emphasized FRETILIN's role in the official historical narrative and national symbols. This excluded other actors in the resistance, as well as those who favored integration with Indonesia, and arguably fed into the societal divisions that drove the 2006 security crisis. The choice of Portuguese as an official language has also alienated much of the population. In contrast, as Bougainvillean constitution drafters used the feedback received from the public to guide their drafting, they utilized an ethno-symbolist approach to ground the sense of Bougainville identity enumerated in the constitution in local custom and tradition.

An ethno-symbolist approach to nation building that draws on locally resonant tradition and custom appears to offer the best prospects for constructing a unified national identity in postconflict societies like Timor-Leste and Bougainville, given the divisiveness of their recent histories and the commonalities among their traditions and customs. However, this will not always be the case, particularly in states whose populations share few – if any – common traditions and customs. In such cases, the modernist approaches to nation building outlined in Chapter 1 may offer more utility.

Moreover, while an ethno-symbolist approach to nation building appears to have the most potential for Timor-Leste and Bougainville, it must be acknowledged that much tradition and custom is highly localized and specific. This poses the risk that placing too much emphasis on it as a tool of nation building might prove divisive, as it may encourage people to identify with their local village or region at the expense of national identity. Indeed, the BCC acknowledged that there can be "tensions between local identity and our Bougainville identity."[1] While the BCC's solution was to attempt to weave clan identities into Bougainvillean identity, as these other identities are deeply held, it may prove difficult to "gloss over" the frictions between them and a wider Bougainvillean identity.[2] Despite this, the Bougainville constitution at least attempted to grapple with this challenge, in contrast to the Timor-Leste constitution. Consequently, there is evidence that Timorese national identity is "re-read into the narrative of local communities,"[3] and survey evidence reveals an increase in respondents identifying with local or regional identities.[4] This may be partly attributable to the emergence of politicized regional identities, the 2006 security crisis, and "the reconsolidation of forms of traditional authority and community."[5] However, there are a number of longstanding commonalities in both Timorese and Bougainvillean traditions and customs, which suggests that an ethno-nationalist approach offers the best prospects of constructing a unified national identity. Consequently, the Bougainville case suggests that extensive public participation in constitution making helps to generate a constituent process, one aspect of which is that the resulting constitution will enumerate a national narrative capable of binding its population together as a political community.

Has reconciliation been achieved?

As constitution making in both Timor-Leste and Bougainville took place in environments that had been riven by conflict, significant reconciliation was required. In Timor-Leste, reconciliation was not achieved during the constitution-making process, in large part due to the minimal opportunities for public participation and the relatively short time frame. Instead, much reconciliation occurred after the constitution was adopted, under the auspices of the CAVR. This meant that the constitution was made before the Timorese people had reconciled, which raises questions concerning whether the constitution is an exercise of their unified constituent power.

In contrast, multifaceted reconciliation occurred during the highly participatory Bougainville process, and if the peace process that preceded constitution making is taken into account, there were more than six years of reconciliatory activities. These activities included the lengthy and inclusive

---

[1] BCC, *Report*, 56.   [2] Boege, *Discovery of Slowness*, 32.
[3] Grenfell, "Governance, Violence and Crises," 93; E. G. Traube, "Unpaid Wages: Local Narratives and the Imagination of the Nation," *The Asia Pacific Journal of Anthropology* 8:1 (2007): 9–25.
[4] Leach, "East Timorese Tertiary Student Attitudes."   [5] Ibid., 428.

negotiations involved in the peace process and thousands of informal customary reconciliation activities at the local level. As a result, much reconciliation had occurred before constitution making began. Bougainvillean leaders had cooperated with Timorese leaders throughout their respective self-determination campaigns and observed the state-building efforts in Timor-Leste (and were invited to participate in some aspects of them). From this observation, they concluded that achieving "healing" and "reconciling" was important before an attempt at state building was made, noting that in Timor-Leste it was "back to front."[6]

However, in Bougainville, there were unreconciled differences between localized groups in its "no-go zone" and the South during the constitution-making process. Consequently, many Bougainvilleans were not involved in the process, calling into question whether it was a true exercise of the Bougainvillean people's constituent power. Yet, the environment of inclusiveness and reconciliation created during the peace and constitution-making processes meant that much progress in reconciling these differences has taken place since the constitution was adopted. Therefore, many Bougainvilleans who did not participate in the constitution-making process subsequently recognized the constitution and engaged with the institutions it created. Although challenges remain, the evidence indicates that the momentum in favor of this recognition and engagement is likely to continue. As a result, the Bougainville case suggests that extensive participation in constitution making can play a role in generating a constituent process by resolving grievances and creating an environment conducive to continued reconciliation, which can in turn play a valuable role in unifying a political community.

Are there divisions within society?

The extent to which a constitution-making process has built a unified political community can also be indicated by the divisions that exist within society. In Timor-Leste and Bougainville, regional divisions became increasingly salient during their constitution-making processes. After the Timor-Leste constitution was adopted, regional divisions became severe and manifested in a major security crisis in 2006. The salience of this division was enhanced by the official historical narrative in the constitution. In contrast, while a regional division hardened during the Bougainville crisis, it appears to have diminished since the constitution was adopted. During the constitution-making

---

[6] J. Kabui, speaking at "Building Sustainable Peace."

process, Bougainvillean leaders sought to achieve broad representation and participation across the regions in all negotiations and decisions. Care was taken to provide even regional representation in the BCC, to see that constitution drafters were sent to consult the public in areas that were not necessarily in their region of origin, and to ensure that the feedback received at the public consultations was organized and considered in a way that sought to achieve equity between the different regions. In addition, the constitution utilized consociational methods to achieve even regional representation in government institutions. Consequently, the Bougainville case illustrates that extensive public participation in constitution making can generate a constituent process by assisting parties to mediate societal differences. Again, the Timor-Leste case illustrates the dangers of minimal participation and a consequent failure to generate a constituent process for the future security and stability of society.

Does the community exhibit evidence of citizenization?

The literature argues that public participation in constitution making can educate citizens and increase demand for information about their constitution and the institutions it creates, which can facilitate their citizenization and political participation. On the surface, there is evidence of citizenization in both Timor-Leste and Bougainville. Political elites in both cases have exhibited an ethos of constitutionalism, as both constitutions have been observed in the face of serious challenges and governments have changed only in accordance with the respective constitutions. However, a creeping disrespect for constitutionalism has emerged in Timor-Leste, influenced in part by the fact that the political elites who made the constitution were relatively unfettered by public participation and therefore see the constitution as something they can shape. Despite this, a broad sense of constitutionalism has developed among ordinary people in both cases, with people generally aware that their constitutions exist.

Election turnouts are very high in Timor-Leste and relatively high in Bougainville, and there is evidence of strategic voting in both, with voters exhibiting a developing level of sophistication when making their electoral choices. Most significantly, in both cases electors have chosen to remove parties and representatives from office if they are perceived to have underperformed. This behavior could be evidence of citizenization, since it suggests that voters are aware that their governments and government members are supposed to meet certain leadership requirements and deliver public goods and services, and are willing to punish them if they are perceived not to be.

Both constitutions include several mechanisms that allow for political participation outside elections. As predicted in the literature, the extensive public participation in Bougainville resulted in the constitution including more of these provisions. Timorese and Bougainvilleans have proved themselves willing to utilize these mechanisms. The responsiveness of the two governments has varied, with the Timor-Leste government apparently less committed to public participation for the first few years after independence, as it was slow to disseminate information. In contrast, the Bougainville government has made concerted attempts to encourage political participation and information dissemination, most significantly through the creation of the parliamentary education officer, education tours, and radio broadcasts.

Overall, there appears to be a relatively strong sense of citizenization in both cases. While the literature would expect this to occur in Bougainville, which had extensive public participation in its constitution-making process, the fact that citizenization has developed in Timor-Leste may call the literature into question. However, in light of evidence that citizenization has developed since independence in Timor-Leste, it appears that it can also be generated by later events.

Is there a strong public sphere?

Evidence of a strong public sphere, including media and civil society, is the final indicator of whether a sense of political community has developed, since it can assist in citizenization and is suggestive of whether a democratic environment has been cultivated. Given that both Timor-Leste and Bougainville are postconflict societies, their media are still developing. However, in both there is evidence of a strong societal demand for information about political developments. While this would be expected in Bougainville, as the literature predicts this will occur as a result of extensive participation, it could be expected that Timorese would also want information about the institutions they fought to create, given that they experienced a long struggle to achieve independence.

Both case studies illustrate that the inherent challenges present in developing country contexts make establishing civil society extremely difficult. Consequently, civil society is primarily manifest in churches, which are also the main providers of many public goods. Moreover, when secular civil society groups emerge, the activities of veterans and youth groups during the 2006 security crisis in Timor-Leste illustrates that they are often destabilizing forces.

In summary, the relatively strong sense of unified political community evident in Bougainville, compared to Timor-Leste, appears to support the argument in the literature that extensive participation in constitution making will assist in generating a constituent process, and consequently in building a sense of political community. The Bougainville case supports the argument that extensive public participation can help the people agree to common societal values and shared symbols, which can constitute the basis of a unifying national identity. It also appears to support the argument that an unhurried, inclusive, and highly participatory process can play a role in promoting reconciliation and reaching compromises, particularly if it seeks to ensure even representation and does not favor one particular region or group. The minimal participation in Timor-Leste has generated contrary results.

CONSTITUTED POWER

Have state institutions been created, and are they functioning effectively?

In addition to helping to build a political community, when public participation in constitution making generates a constituent process, it can play a role in legitimizing the institutions the constitution creates to exercise the people's constituted power. The constitutions of both Timor-Leste and Bougainville create the institutions of government that typically exist in liberal democracies (the legislature, executive, and judiciary). These institutions function largely (although imperfectly) as intended. The main point of distinction concerns the relationship between the legislature and the executive. In Timor-Leste, there is the potential for competition between the comparatively weak president and the strong prime minister. In addition, the institutionalization of a separate executive and legislature restricts the ability of the legislature to hold the executive accountable, the effect of which is exacerbated by the executive's ability to make laws by decree. In contrast, in Bougainville, the president is the head of the executive and sits within the legislature, and all other members of the executive are members of the legislature, which improves the capacity of the legislature to hold them accountable. The design of institutions might be partly attributable to the role of public participation in the respective constitution-making processes. While Timorese expressed a preference for a strong presidency, the FRETILIN majority in the Constituent Assembly took little account of the feedback generated during public consultations and opted for a weak presidency, as they expected the position would initially be filled by their political rival, Gusmão. In contrast, in Bougainville, the BCC took account of feedback received during its consultations, which favored an executive within the legislature.

However, given that the majority of the populations of both Timor-Leste and Bougainville are subsistence agriculturalists who live relatively untouched by the state, state-level institutions are in many ways secondary to local sociopolitical institutions. This can challenge the legitimacy of state institutions, which become one of only many "alternative" sites of institutional and legitimate power.[7] Reflecting this, during both constitution-making processes, people expressed a clear preference for the recognition of local sociopolitical institutions and the decentralization of political and administrative functions to them.

Decentralization refers to "the assignment of powers to governing bodies located at different jurisdictional tiers in governmental systems."[8] The literature identifies three types of decentralization. Administrative decentralization refers to a central government dispersing its agents, resources, and responsibility for the delivery of selected public services to lower tiers of government. Fiscal decentralization involves a central government transferring influence over budgets, financial decisions, and taxation. Political decentralization (often referred to as devolution) involves the transfer of power and decision-making authority. The literature on decentralization has parallels with the literature on liberal-local hybridity, as it implies that the role of already functioning, locally legitimate sociopolitical institutions should be recognized.[9] However, neither strand of literature calls for blanket decentralization, which would effectively lead to the collapse of the state. Central governments can also perform an important role in the equitable redistribution of resources and in inducing cooperative behavior by citizens in response to challenges and for the provision of public goods. Some service provision requires a level of technical input, such as medical or engineering expertise, that is unlikely to be generally available at the local level. Consequently, a balance in power and functions between tiers of government is recommended. The literature on liberal-local hybridity similarly recognizes that often no clear delineation exists between the central government and local institutions.

As a constituent process did not emerge in Timor-Leste, the FRETILIN majority in the Constituent Assembly largely ignored calls for decentralization,

---

[7] Nelson, *Governments, States and Labels*; P. Dauvergne, "Weak States, Strong States: A State-in-Society Perspective," in *Weak and Strong States in Asia-Pacific Societies*, ed. P. Dauvergne (St. Leonards: Allen & Unwin, 1998).

[8] A. Breton, A. Cassone, and A. Fraschini, "Decentralization and Subsidiarity: Toward a Theoretical Reconciliation," *University of Pennsylvania Journal of International Economic Law* 21:1 (1998): 23.

[9] J. Wallis, "What Role Can Decentralisation Play in State-Building? Lessons from Timor-Leste and Bougainville," *Commonwealth & Comparative Politics* 51:4 (2013): 424–446.

and consequently the constitution included only short provisions envisaging future political and administrative decentralization. In contrast, reflecting public feedback, the Bougainville constitution provided for immediate political, administrative, and (limited) fiscal decentralization by recognizing existing Councils of Elders and traditional systems of government and by providing space for the later recognition of other levels of government. It should be acknowledged that the Indonesian occupation of Timor-Leste lasted for twenty-four years and saw the Indonesian government make concerted attempts to dismantle – or at least displace – Timorese sociopolitical practices. In contrast, the Bougainville crisis lasted for only eight years and, because Papua New Guinea did not gain a comprehensive foothold in the territory, it was never capable (and never had aspirations) of dismantling local sociopolitical institutions. While there was a resurgence of Timorese local sociopolitical practices after Indonesia withdrew, the BCC was able to build upon much more established local practices when making the Bougainville constitution.

The differing approaches to decentralization adopted in Timor-Leste and Bougainville have had consequences for the legitimacy and effectiveness of state institutions and their subsequent ability to exercise the people's constituted power. As state power and functions were highly centralized in Timor-Leste at independence, the state was largely absent from the lives of most rural Timorese, who instead continued to follow local sociopolitical practices. This situation continued until the government made the pragmatic decision to formally engage with local sociopolitical institutions in 2004. The fact that the government needed to do this raises questions concerning whether state institutions were legitimately exercising the Timorese people's constituted power. It also suggests that the Timor-Leste constitution might have better reflected Timorese views had the Constituent Assembly provided more opportunities for public participation and taken the public feedback it received into account. In contrast, the BCC took public feedback seriously and provided for the decentralization of powers and functions in the constitution, which meant that the government was immediately present at the village level via already functioning local institutions, and was arguably better able to exercise Bougainvilleans' constituted power.

Therefore, the Bougainville case suggests that extensive public participation can facilitate the emergence of a constituent process, an aspect of which is the recognition of local sociopolitical institutions, and a form of power sharing that mediates state institutions through local institutions, which can in turn enhance the legitimacy of state institutions.[10] This approach recognizes that

---

[10] V. Boege et al., "Building Peace and Political Community in Hybrid Political Orders," *International Peacekeeping* 16: 5 (2009): 599–615.

while local institutions have their faults, they are often the "only mechanisms available to dispense any kind of justice or administration in the places where they exist."[11] In this regard, the Bougainville case – and later the Timor-Leste case – demonstrates that political, administrative, and fiscal decentralization can bridge the gap between the state and society. People tend to participate in local institutions that they can identify closely with, which in turn may encourage them to identify with state-level institutions to which they are connected. In this way, the state can "buil[d] on existing social entities rather than supplanting them."[12] Therefore, decentralization to liberal-local hybrid institutions may play an important role in building new and postconflict states. The cost of failing to utilize local institutions when engaging in decentralization is evident from the case of Sierra Leone, where the state effectively sought to sideline local traditional leaders, which has led to competition between chiefs and the new local governments.[13]

Importantly, decentralization to liberal-local hybrid institutions appears to have played a role in extending democracy to the local level in Timor-Leste and Bougainville, which can be crucial in new and postconflict states. While Timorese and Bougainvilleans tend to appreciate the opportunity to vote, elections alone do not necessarily confer legitimacy on local leaders, who also have to possess (or have conferred upon them) customary or traditional legitimacy.[14] However, in Timor-Leste, there is an emerging concern that elections might actually have reduced participation,[15] as elections occur only once every four years and *suco* leaders and councils do not necessarily consult their communities in between.[16] This highlights the need for decentralization to liberal-local hybrid institutions to be designed to avoid undermining local sociopolitical practices, which favor community consultation and consensus decision making in both Timor-Leste and Bougainville.

---

[11] R. Nixon, "The Crisis of Governance in a New Subsistence State," *Journal of Contemporary Asia* 36:1 (2006): 91.

[12] L. S. Meitzner Yoder, "Hybridising Justice: State-Customary Interactions over Forest Crime and Punishment in Oecusse, East Timor," *The Asia Pacific Journal of Anthropology* 8:1 (2007): 52.

[13] P. Jackson, "Reshuffling an Old Deck of Cards? The Politics of Local Government Reform in Sierra Leone," *African Affairs* 106:422 (2006): 95–111.

[14] Cummins and Leach, "Democracy Old and New"; A. B. dos Santos and E. da Silva, "Introduction of a Modern Democratic System and Its Impact on Societies in East Timorese Traditional Culture," *Local-Global: Identity, Security, Community* 11 (2012): 206–220.

[15] M. Pereira and M. M. Lete Koten, "Dynamics of Democracy at the *Suku* Level," *Local-Global: Identity, Security, Community* 11 (2012): 222–232.

[16] M. A. Brown, "Entangled Worlds: Villages and Political Community in Timor-Leste," *Local-Global: Identity, Security, Community* 11 (2012): 54–71.

In this regard, decentralization can "draw powerful figures at local levels into official positions of power, so that the central government can cultivate them as allies,"[17] as occurred in Somaliland, where selected clan leaders have been co-opted by the government via patronage relationships.[18] This effect is particularly evident when political parties become involved in local elections.[19] In Timor-Leste, the first round of *suco* elections in 2005 and 2006 was highly politicized, which was perceived as "divisive, with the polarisation of politics at the national level now penetrating to the local level."[20] The introduction of political party politics at the local level contributed to friction, hampered the ability of many *suco* leaders and councils to operate, affected their perceived legitimacy, and undermined local sociopolitical practices."[21] As a result, political parties were prevented from running in the 2009 *suco* elections[22] (although anecdotal evidence suggests that they were still active). In Bougainville, most Bougainvilleans expressed the view during public consultations on their future constitution that having political parties would be divisive and contrary to custom.[23] This suggests that there may be some merit to depoliticizing local governments, at least until reconciliation has occurred.

If decentralization encourages local political participation, this can assist local governments to draw on local knowledge and preferences in order to improve the legitimacy and effectiveness of government.[24] In Timor-Leste, the introduction of decentralized development programs has progressively provided communities with the opportunity to participate in the prioritization and implementation of development projects. There is evidence from other cases that this participation may contribute to improvements in the delivery of public services, and correspondingly to government effectiveness.[25] Increased participation at the local level may also improve the accountability and responsiveness of governments by providing routes for people to engage in

---

[17] J. Manor, *The Political Economy of Democratic Decentralization* (Washington: World Bank, 1999), 39.
[18] Renders and Terlinden, "Negotiating Statehood."
[19] Jackson, "Reshuffling an Old Deck of Cards?"
[20] Brown, "Security, Development and the Nation-Building Agenda," 151.
[21] Interview with a Timorese governance adviser, July 18, 2013; interview with a member of Timorese civil society, July 18, 2013.
[22] Law on Community Leaderships, s.21.   [23] BCC Technical Team, *Matrix of Choices*.
[24] G. Lutz and W. Linder, *Traditional Structures in Local Governance for Local Development* (Bern: Institute of Political Science, University of Berne, 2004); M. Turner, *Issues in the Design of Decentralisation, State, Society and Governance in Melanesia Discussion Paper 2003/7* (Canberra: Australian National University, 2003).
[25] R. Work, *The Role of Participation and Partnership in Decentralized Governance* (New York: UNDP, undated); World Bank, *World Development Report 2004: Making Services Work for Poor People* (Washington: World Bank, 2004).

"monitoring, evaluation and planning from below,"[26] particularly if it involves liberal-local hybridity and utilizes local methods of oversight and accountability, as increasingly occurs in Timor-Leste and Bougainville. Moreover, if enhanced local participation leads to the distribution of information and improved transparency, it can also make populations more aware and understanding of government policies and more realistic in their expectations.[27] Studies have found that this can improve satisfaction with government performance,[28] which can help to establish the legitimacy of state institutions.

Decentralization may also ameliorate tensions between geographically concentrated groups by providing them with a degree of political, administrative, and fiscal autonomy.[29] This can play an important role in state building in both Timor-Leste and Bougainville, where there are regional tensions. However, the example of the Dayton Agreement in Bosnia suggests that in these circumstances, excessive decentralization can leave the central government with insufficient power and resources to function and lacking an identity capable of motivating people's support.[30] Moreover, in situations where natural resources are geographically dispersed, too much resource autonomy may exacerbate tensions if groups in resource-rich areas are perceived to receive disproportionate benefits, which was a factor that contributed to the Bougainville crisis. This suggests that the central government retains an important role in equitably distributing resources.

Thus, while decentralization can play a positive role in state building, it also raises challenges. Most importantly, there is a danger that unless there is genuine partnership, the central government might be perceived to be using local sociopolitical institutions instrumentally in order to extend its dominance over society, which would echo the colonial practice of indirect rule.[31] However, the increasing assertiveness of local leaders toward the central government in Timor-Leste and Bougainville illustrates that they are not just passive subjects and can instrumentalize custom to take back control. For example, in Timor-Leste, *suco* leaders meet with members of the subdistrict

---

[26] Manor, *Democratic Decentralization*, 38; S. J. Burki, G. E. Perry, and W. R. Dillinger, *Beyond the Center: Decentralizing the State* (Washington: World Bank, 1999).
[27] Ibid.
[28] R. C. Crook and J. Manor, *Democracy and Decentralization in South Asia and West Africa: Participation, Accountability and Performance* (Cambridge: Cambridge University Press, 1998); World Bank, *Colombia Local Government Capacity: Beyond Technical Assistance* (Washington: World Bank, 1995)xs.
[29] Fleiner et al., "Federalism, Decentralisation."
[30] M. Cox, *State Building and Post-Conflict Reconstruction: Lessons from Bosnia* (Geneva: Centre for Applied Studies in International Negotiations, 2001).
[31] Boege et al., *On Hybrid Political Orders*; Jackson, "Reshuffling an Old Deck of Cards?"

and district administrations and the central government,[32] although it is often very difficult for *suco* leaders to exert significant influence during these meetings.[33] Formal engagement with local sociopolitical institutions might also undermine their authenticity,[34] particularly as many evolved to manage small-scale decision making, and their effectiveness may diminish if they are expanded beyond the local level.[35] Local governments might also be unable to manage disputes between their community and others or between their community and the state.[36] However, examples of the way in which hybrid models that combine local and state practices have effectively managed natural resources in Timor-Leste, based around the local practice of *tarabandu*, illustrate how such disputes can be resolved.[37]

Moreover, local governments can be captured by elites and manipulated "as an instrument of social and political control."[38] This highlights the risk that ordinary people may suffer most from romanticizing local practices and institutions, since "it is the privileged who can afford to tell the poor to preserve their traditions."[39] Indeed, the recognition of local institutions can lead to malevolent forms of hybridity if they are "historically oppressive by nature" or have "been brutalised by conditions of conflict,"[40] exemplified by the co-option of "warlords" in Afghanistan and Iraq. This saw deeply ambivalent actors provided with political legitimacy and resources, often resulting in corruption, dysfunctional political economies, human rights abuses, or further conflict.[41] In these cases, local institutions can lose their legitimacy, and there

---

[32] Interview with a *suco* leader, September 28, 2010.
[33] Interview with a member of Timorese civil society, July 17, 2013; interview with a Timorese governance adviser, July 18, 2013.
[34] R. MacGinty, "Gilding the Lily? International Support for Indigenous and Traditional Peacemaking," in *Palgrave Advances in Peacebuilding: Critical Developments and Approaches*, ed. O. P. Richmond (Basingstoke: Palgrave, 2010).
[35] J. Fraenkel and B. Grofman, "Introduction: Political Culture, Representation and Electoral Systems in the Pacific Islands," *Commonwealth & Comparative Politics* 43:3 (2005): 261–275.
[36] D. Butterworth and P. Dale, *Articulations of Local Governance in Timor-Leste: Lessons for Development under Decentralization*, Justice for the Poor Policy Note 56931 (Dili: World Bank, 2010).
[37] Meitzner-Yoder, "Hybridising Justice": Palmer and do Amaral de Carvalho, "Nation Building and Resource Management."
[38] S. Lawson, *Tradition Versus Democracy in the South Pacific: Fiji, Tonga and Western Samoa* (Cambridge: Cambridge University Press, 1996), 4.
[39] E. Hau'ofa, "The New South Pacific Society: Integration and Independence," in *Class and Culture in the South Pacific*, ed. A. Hooper et al. (Auckland and Suva: University of Auckland and University of the South Pacific, 1987), 7.
[40] J. Chopra and T. Hohe, "Participatory Intervention," *Global Governance* 10:3 (2004): 299.
[41] S. Lister, *Understanding State-Building and Local Government in Afghanistan* (London: Crisis States Research Centre, LSE, 2007); J. C. O'Brien, "Lawyers, Guns, and Money:

is a "strong desire for centralised authority."[42] This has not yet occurred in Timor-Leste and Bougainville, as in both cases local sociopolitical practices tend to be "participatory and consultative," as local leaders rely on the support of their community for power.[43]

Local institutions may also be inherently incompatible with liberal practices, which concerns liberal peace state builders. In Timor-Leste and Bougainville, local sociopolitical practices can discriminate against women and young people, since it is generally elder males who have authority in local contexts (although there are women chiefs in parts of Bougainville).[44] However, both the *suco* councils in Timor-Leste and the Councils of Elders in Bougainville reserve seats for women and young people in order to ensure their participation. The Bougainville councils use the gender-neutral term "elders" rather than "chiefs," and Timor-Leste has similarly changed its local government law to refer to *suco* "leaders" rather than "chiefs." In Timor-Leste, women are emerging as local leaders, with the number of female *suco* leaders rising from seven in 2004 to eleven after the 2009 election and the number of female *aldeia* leaders rising from twenty-two in 2004 to thirty-seven in 2009. Although this is only a fraction of the 442 *suco* leaders and 2,225 *aldeia* leaders elected, it does suggest that society is gradually shifting away from patriarchy. It must be acknowledged that there are structural barriers to women taking leadership positions at the local level. In both cases, local leaders receive only a small allowance, which can be economically prohibitive for women, as they usually do not have an independent source of income and are required to complete significant domestic and agricultural work.[45] Even when women do take on a leadership role, evidence from Timor-Leste indicates that it is

---

Warlords and Reconstruction After Iraq," *UC Davis Journal of International Law & Policy* 11:1 (2004–2005): 99–122; S. Schmeidl and M. Karokhail, "'Prêt-à-Porter States': How the McDonaldization of State-Building Misses the Mark in Afghanistan," in *Peace in the Absence of States: Challenging the Discourse of State Failure*, ed. in M. Fischer and B. Schmelzle (Berlin: Berghof Research Center, 2009).

[42] S. Lister and A. Wilder, "Strengthening Subnational Administration in Afghanistan: Technical Reform or State-Building?," *Public Administration and Development* 25 (2005): 42.

[43] Boege et al., "Hybrid Political Orders," 18; Boege, *A Promising Liaison*; interview with a *suco* leader, September 28, 2010; interview with a Timorese intellectual, May 12, 2010.

[44] D. Hicks, "*Adat* and the Nation-State: Opposition and Synthesis in Two Political Cultures," in Leach and Kingsbury, *The Politics of Timor-Leste*; interview with a Bougainvillean women's leader, February 2, 2010; interview with a Timorese women's leader, April 29, 2010; interview with an ABG official and member of a council of elders, January 22, 2011.

[45] D. Cummins, "The Problem of Gender Quotas: Women's Representatives on Timor-Leste's Suku Councils," *Development in Practice* 21:1 (2001): 85–95; interview with a Timorese women's leader, July 18, 2013.

difficult for them to influence decision making,[46] partly because *uma lisan* often perpetuates a patriarchal approach to political decision making.[47] This suggests that training and support might be required to ensure that liberal-local hybrid institutions are not overly discriminatory and that disadvantaged groups are able to participate in them.

There are often limited administrative resources and technical capacity at the local level, which can undermine the effectiveness of local governments and, by extension, challenge the legitimacy and effectiveness of new and postconflict states.[48] The perceived legitimacy of liberal-local hybrid institutions in Timor-Leste has also been challenged by their performance, as the capacity of *suco* leaders to plan and implement projects has varied.[49] Similar issues arise in Bougainville, although many Councils of Elders have adopted development plans and have the capacity to implement projects. In both cases, the reluctance of the central government to engage in fiscal decentralization has affected the capacity of local governments. Methods of collecting taxation and other revenue are often an important determinant of the success of decentralization. When decentralized governments have minimal powers of taxation, or if the taxation base is low, they are likely to be disempowered relative to the central government and can be encouraged to engage in corruption.[50] Conversely, where decentralized governments collect the bulk of revenue, this is likely to empower them at the expense of the central government[51] and can also facilitate corruption and patronage.[52] As few resources have been decentralized to local leaders in Timor-Leste and Bougainville and they have few ways to generate revenues locally, incentives for manipulation and opportunities for corruption have been minimal. With more resources and development projects being decentralized to *sucos* in

---

[46] Interview with a member of Timorese civil society (a), September 4, 2013; interview with a member of Timorese civil society (c), July 17, 2013; interview with a Timorese governance adviser, July 18, 2013; interview with a Timorese women's leader, July 18, 2013.

[47] Cummins and Maia, *Community Experiences*; interview with a member of Timorese civil society (a), July 17, 2013; interview with a member of Timorese civil society (c), July 17, 2013; interview with a Timorese governance adviser, July 18, 2013.

[48] J. Litvack, J. Ahmad, and R. Bird, *Rethinking Decentralization in Developing Countries* (Washington: The World Bank, 1998); Lutz and Linder, *Traditional Structures*.

[49] Everett and Ragragio, *Decentralisation in Timor-Leste*; interview with a member of Parliament, September 30, 2010; interview with a *suco* leader, September 28, 2010; interview with a Timorese governance adviser, April 23, 2010.

[50] Jackson, "Reshuffling an Old Deck of Cards?"; Lister and Wilder, "Strengthening Subnational Administration."

[51] Cox, *State Building and Post-Conflict Reconstruction*.

[52] D. Watt, R. Flanary, and R. Theobald, "Democratisation or the Democratisation of Corruption? The Case of Uganda," *Commonwealth & Comparative Politics* 37:3 (1999): 37–64.

Timor-Leste, instances of corruption might increase. This suggests that decentralization should be governed by an unambiguous legal framework that specifies the distribution of power and resources and provides mechanisms for accountability and oversight.[53]

The relationship between central and local governments can also be too large for meaningful interactions, which can undermine central government oversight. This challenge is exacerbated in new and postconflict states like Timor-Leste and Bougainville, where transport and communication infrastructure is often underdeveloped. A partial solution might be to create midlevel regional governments to link the central and local tiers.[54] Due to capacity and funding limitations, substantive regional decentralization has not occurred in Timor-Leste or Bougainville. In Timor-Leste, district administrators are said to lack power or resources to implement programs, and the allocation of power between the central and district governments is unclear.[55] Similarly, in Bougainville, regional and district administrators are relatively weak and merely create "administrative bottlenecks" between the central government and the councils.[56] This suggests that while regional governments can play a role in linking the central and local levels, they may initially be of little utility in new and postconflict states, where resources and capacity are often limited.

Conversely, if substantial power and resources are decentralized, this may legitimize local governments at the expense of state-level institutions. This is evident in Bosnia and Herzegovina, where excessive decentralization has weakened the state,[57] and in Afghanistan, where local institutions have undermined the central government.[58] To an extent, this effect is already evident in Timor-Leste, where a 2008 survey found that there was confusion over who is "primarily responsible for making the rules that govern people's lives," with 48 percent of respondents identifying community leaders and only 33 percent identifying state institutions.[59] The Bosnia and Herzegovina case suggests that a balance has to be struck that gives central and decentralized governments sufficient power and resources to function effectively and legitimately, as well as mechanisms to encourage cooperation – rather than

---

[53] Burki, Perry, and Dillinger, *Beyond the Centre*; Litvack, Ahmad, and Bird, *Rethinking Decentralization*.
[54] Manor, *Democratic Decentralization*.
[55] Interview with a member of Timorese civil society, July 17, 2013; interview with a Timorese governance adviser, July 18, 2013.
[56] Interview with an ABG official and member of a council of elders, January 22, 2011.
[57] Cox, *State Building and Post-Conflict Reconstruction*.
[58] Lister, *Understanding State-Building*. [59] Asia Foundation, *Law and Justice in Timor-Leste*.

competition – between them. Connected to this, in situations where the central government is weak, there is a temptation for humanitarian agencies to bypass it and deal directly with functioning local sociopolitical practices, as occurred in Timor-Leste. While this highlights that existing local structures can work as a social buffer in times of transition, care must be taken not to disproportionately empower local institutions at the expense of building the state.

To what extent are the state institutions perceived to be legitimate?

The extent to which state institutions are perceived to be legitimate in Timor-Leste and Bougainville has been affected by the differing approaches to public participation during the two constitution-making processes and the consequent effect on the emergence of a constituent process. This has in turn affected the way in which the two cases have approached decentralization and the way in which they have achieved an engagement between liberal and local political practices. Both opted to select representatives for state institutions by election, as occurs in all liberal democracies. As outlined in Parts II and III, the design of their respective electoral systems has implications for the representativeness of the people selected.

The more important question concerns the extent to which the liberal principle of democracy resonates in the local context. This question is generally raised by external observers, who argue that democratic elections "are not really held in high esteem as they are based on alien principles"[60] of "disputation, discord, dissensus and individualism"[61] rather than on the local sociopolitical practices of consultation and consensus. This suggests that elected leaders will not be perceived to be legitimate. Again, external observers argue that representatives in state institutions often "can only enjoy authority if they also hold status in the customary sphere or are endorsed by traditional authorities."[62] However, most Timorese and Bougainvilleans interlocutors did not perceive the legitimacy of their representatives to be affected by the fact that many are elected based on a combination of their capacity, qualifications, and customary standing. Therefore, while elected representatives chosen partly according to customary logic might appear parochial or arbitrary to liberal observers, given that they exercise the people's constituted power,

---

[60] Boege, *A Promising Liaison*, 34.
[61] Lawson, *Tradition Versus Democracy*, 165–166; Boege et al., "Hybrid Political Orders"; P. Larmour, *Foreign Flowers: Institutional Transfer and Good Governance in the Pacific Islands* (Honolulu: University of Hawai'i Press, 2005).
[62] Boege et al., "Hybrid Political Orders," 18.

their perceived legitimacy in the local context is what matters.[63] Indeed, in Bougainville, elected representatives also acquire customary standing, with, for example, the president generally referred to as "President Chief."[64] In another example, the new regional MP for Bougainville in the Papua New Guinea Parliament, Joe Lera, was initiated as a paramount chief following his election in July 2012.

The two cases vary in how they dealt with the potential for elected leaders to have customary obligations. The BCC recognized the possibility that leaders might be influenced by their customary obligations or relationships, as did Bougainvilleans, who expressed a desire during the constitution-making process that the constitution ensure their responsiveness and accountability. Consequently, the constitution included several innovative mechanisms to achieve this, which involve a combination of liberal and local sociopolitical practices. In contrast, despite public calls during the constitution-making process and public consultations to the contrary, in Timor-Leste the responsiveness and accountability of representatives can be achieved only via the liberal practices of democratic elections and relatively weak accountability institutions.

The two cases also vary in the extent to which they have achieved liberal-local hybridity by incorporating traditional and customary leaders in state-level institutions. Reflecting the emergence of a constituent process, the Bougainville constitution incorporates feedback received during the public consultations and provides that an advisory body consisting of traditional leaders can be created to act as an "upper" parliamentary house. In recognition of the ongoing legitimacy of local sociopolitical practices in Timor-Leste and the questionable legitimacy of state institutions, there are suggestions for ways in which traditional and customary leaders might be included in state-level institutions to enhance the latter's legitimacy. For example, certain members of the Constituent Assembly attempted to have a Council of *Liurais* enshrined in the constitution, which would have performed a similar role to that of the Bougainville Advisory Body.[65] Indeed, several other constitutions across the Pacific give a degree of recognition to local sociopolitical authorities, either as an advisory body or as having the power to appoint offices or veto parliamentary bills.[66] This has similarly occurred in parts of Africa, where

---

[63] Lutz and Linder, *Traditional Structures*, 27; Chopra and Hohe, "Participatory Intervention."
[64] Interview with an ABG official and member of a council of elders, January 22, 2011.
[65] R. Nixon, "Indonesian West Timor: The Political-Economy of Emerging Ethno-Nationalism," *Journal of Contemporary Asia* 34:2 (2004): 163–185.
[66] For example: American Samoa, Cook Islands, Federated States of Micronesia, Marshall Islands, Palau, Tonga, Vanuatu, Wallis and Futuna, and Western Samoa. Hassall and Saunders, *Asia-Pacific Constitutional Systems*.

"re-traditionalisation" has seen traditional elders officially incorporated into state hierarchies.[67] The idea of establishing such a council was mooted in the Timor-Leste Constituent Assembly but was rejected because of concerns that it could enshrine patriarchal leadership structures.[68] There was also the concern that formally recognizing the power of *liurais* might entrench unequal social structures and "keep people in slavery."[69] In this regard, traditional society was highly stratified, and even today, Timorese are "acutely aware...who was a commoner and who was a slave."[70] Indeed, rumors that *liurais* in Dili (including some with positions in the Parliament and public service) continue to keep people of lower social status as slaves are widespread.[71] However, if such a council included "elders" rather than "*liurais*," it might be better able to reflect changing social structures.

Are the state institutions delivering public goods and services?

A government's effectiveness can be assessed based on its institutional capacity to deliver public goods and services. Taking into account the low level of development in Timor-Leste and Bougainville, exacerbated by the extensive destruction caused during their self-determination conflicts, both governments have managed to achieve improvements in the delivery of public goods and services, which indicates a level of government effectiveness. However, the geographic distribution of these services in both cases is uneven. In Timor-Leste, services were highly centralized and slow to trickle out from Dili to rural areas. In Bougainville, the government was slow to access certain regions, which undermined its ability to deliver services, although improvements have been made.

In both cases, the delivery of public goods and services has been challenged by funding limitations, which is complicated in Bougainville because as an autonomous region, it is reliant on the Papua New Guinea government, which has been reticent to make funding available. Indeed, the former

---

[67] For example, in Namibia, South Africa, Ghana, Mozambique, Uganda, Zambia, and Cameroon. H. M. Kyed and L. Buur, *Recognition and Democratisation: "New Roles" for Traditional Leaders in Sub-Saharan Africa*, Working Paper 2006/11 (Copenhagen: Danish Institute for International Studies, 2006).
[68] Interview with a former member of the Constituent Assembly and government official, February 2, 2010.
[69] Interview with a member of Parliament, May 11, 2010.
[70] Kammen, "Master-Slave, Traitor-Nationalist," 75.
[71] Personal communication from an international security adviser in Timor-Leste, May 11, 2010; ibid.

Bougainvillean president Joseph Kabui declared that "funding has been our biggest enemy,"[72] as it has challenged the ABG's ability to exercise the functions and powers to which it is entitled. As both cases are primarily subsistence barter economies, it is difficult for the governments to raise tax revenue, as the bulk of the population is able to maintain a high degree of economic autonomy.[73] Because taxation is one of the main aspects of the relationship between the state and its citizens, rural people who do not – or cannot – pay them "are much less inclined to develop a sense of citizenship and a demand for effective central governance and accountability."[74] As both governments struggle to collect taxation, they look elsewhere for revenue. In Timor-Leste, funding pressures have been relieved by the significant oil revenues it began to receive starting in 2005. There is considerable pressure on Bougainville to similarly access resource revenues via the resumption of copper and gold mining. However, large-scale resource extraction can challenge government accountability, as when the main source of taxation revenue comes from resource producers, it encourages the government to see those corporations as its primary constituency. Indeed, this was a factor in the grievances over the Panguna mine that helped to instigate the Bougainville conflict. Large-scale resource extraction can also generate conflict, as scholars have identified that "the greater the *competition and inequalities* among groups in heterogeneous societies, the greater the salience of ethnic identities and the greater likelihood of open conflict."[75] In Timor-Leste, the introduction of cash payment schemes for certain societal groups and the granting of large contracts under the decentralized development programs, funded by oil revenues, have created the potential for conflict over the distribution of these resources. Similar potential for conflict is evident in Bougainville if mining resumes and the distribution of resources is perceived to favor certain groups.

If the liberal peace assumption that the introduction of a market economy is the best way to promote development is followed, it is difficult to see how other aspects of the private sector in either case could be developed in the short to medium term. While many local construction companies have been created in Timor-Leste, they largely rely on government contracts and are

---

[72] J. Kabui, speaking in S. Marshall, prod., *Bougainville – The Killer Deal*, Foreign Correspondent, ABC Television, June 17, 2008.
[73] Calhoun, *Nations Matter*; Foster, *Nation Making*.
[74] Boege et al., *On Hybrid Political Orders*, 25.
[75] T. R. Gurr, "Peoples Against States: Ethnopolitical Conflict and the Changing World System," *International Studies Quarterly* 38 (1994): 347; W. Easterly and R. Levine, "Africa's Growth Tragedy: Policies and Ethnic Divisions," *Quarterly Journal of Economics* 112:4 (1997): 1203–1250.

therefore not representative of a true private sector. Even if a market economy is cultivated, liberal economic reforms can "aggravate the vulnerability of sectors of populations to poverty" and encourage conflict.[76] To moderate the market and diffuse the likelihood of conflict arising from private sector development, Western states relied on welfare policies and economic development.[77] This leads Oliver Richmond to suggest implementing welfare policies that might stabilize everyday life and lead to democratic politics in new and postconflict states.[78] To an extent, this advice has been heeded in Timor-Leste, where the government has introduced several cash payment schemes. However, as these schemes favor certain societal groups, they may have the perverse consequence of fostering societal conflict rather than diminishing it.[79]

Overall, given that their populations are primarily subsistence agriculturalists who understand ownership communally, it appears that in Timor-Leste and Bougainville, the governments should consider mechanisms that seek to achieve liberal-local hybridity in economic development. Achieving such hybridity is not unheard of elsewhere in the Pacific, where cooperatives and land trusts provide mechanisms for local communal practices to interact with the market. This approach is already evident in Bougainville with respect to efforts to reopen the Panguna mine, as the government has facilitated the creation of landowners' associations to consult local communities.

Are law and order enforced and is the rule of law observed?

The most important indicator of a government's effectiveness is whether it has the institutional capacity to enforce law and order and ensure that the rule of law is observed. Reflecting their general approach to public participation and local sociopolitical practices, Timorese constitution drafters opted to emphasize the role of formal justice institutions by creating a police force and army as the state's security institutions and a court system to observe the rule of law. In contrast, because a constituent process was generated in Bougainville, constitution drafters heeded the preference of many Bougainvilleans for recognizing the local justice mechanisms that had been operating throughout the conflict. In this context, the term "local justice mechanisms" refers to

---

[76] Pugh, "The Political Economy of Peacebuilding," 25; A. Chua, *World on Fire: How Exporting Free Market Democracy Breeds Ethnic Hatred and Global Instability* (New York: Anchor, 2004).

[77] C. Offe, "Some Contradictions of the Modern Welfare State," *Critical Social Policy* 2:2 (1982): 7–14.

[78] Richmond, "The Romanticisation of the Local."   [79] Wallis, "Victors, Villains and Victims."

practices that vary across the community but have in common their "origins in long-standing localized social structures, which informs their notions of justice."[80] Accordingly, the Bougainville constitution created both formal and community auxiliary police services. It also provided that Village Courts would continue to operate, with provision for later law to empower traditional leaders and create alternative dispute resolution mechanisms that utilize customary practices. In Timor-Leste, the formal justice institutions, the PNTL and courts, were largely absent from the lives of most rural people for the first few years after independence and faced severe capacity limitations. Instead, many rural Timorese relied on local justice mechanisms. Consequently, in 2004, the government pragmatically adopted a liberal-local hybrid approach and recognized these local mechanisms by empowering village leaders to resolve disputes. In 2009, the government also introduced a clear mandate for the PNTL to engage in community policing, and the government and PNTL are increasingly involved with customary *nahe biti* mediation practices, *tarabandu* agreements, and working with *kablehan* community police.

The fact that customary and state law – local justice mechanisms that operate according to a mixture of liberal and local principles and state justice institutions that operate according to liberal principles – coexist means that legal pluralism is evident in both Timor-Leste and Bougainville. Paul Berman has identified the potential for a normative "jurisprudence of hybridity"[81] and three mechanisms to accommodate the legal pluralism generated by the coexistence of state and local justice mechanisms. First, there is the "margin of appreciation doctrine" used by the European Court of Human Rights to strike a balance between deference to national courts and legislators on the one hand, and European requirements and supervision on the other. Second, there are "limited autonomy regimes," whereby territorially concentrated groups are given limited autonomy within the state, power-sharing arrangements are implemented between different groups, or personal law is accommodated via parallel civil and religious legal systems. Third, there is the principle of "conflict of laws," according to which nonstate legal practices that are largely internal and primarily reflect an individual's affiliation with a nonstate community are "given more leeway than when the state itself is part of the relevant affiliation."[82] There are positive examples of these mechanisms being implemented in Australia, where local justice actors are involved in

---

[80] D. H. Isser, "Shifting Assumptions from Abstract Ideals to Messy Realities," in Isser, *Customary Justice*, 7.
[81] P. Schiff Berman, "Towards a Jurisprudence of Hybridity," *Utah Law Review* 1 (2010): 12.
[82] Ibid., 26.

state court decision making in cases involving indigenous persons and local justice sanctions are taken into account by the state courts.[83]

All three mechanisms are also evident in Timor-Leste and Bougainville, although they have been implemented to differing degrees, as Timorese constitution makers were reluctant to formally recognize legal pluralism, whereas Bougainvillean constitution makers took seriously public feedback relating to the continued importance of local justice mechanisms. The margin of appreciation is evident via the recognition that *suco* leaders in Timor-Leste and Village Courts and other local justice mechanisms in Bougainville are the preferred forum for many local disputes. In both Timor-Leste and Bougainville, formal justice institutions increasingly respect the decisions of local justice mechanisms, such as by recognizing customary compensation payments. Limited power regimes are also evident in both cases, as communities have been given limited autonomy over many local law and order issues and local justice mechanisms apply localized customary law, often in combination with state law. The application of localized customary law by local justice mechanisms also means that the conflict-of-laws principle is evident in both cases.

However, these mechanisms raise the challenge of "forum-shopping,"[84] which may undermine the uniformity of justice institutions and consequently, the rule of law. Increasing internal migration toward urban areas also raises questions concerning which customary law should be applied to persons living outside their traditional local area.[85] As there was less engagement with legal pluralism in Timor-Leste, the implementation of all three mechanisms is unofficial and therefore neither uniform nor subject to oversight and review. However, in Timor-Leste, the draft Customary Law provides for appeals from local mechanisms to state justice institutions, which gives people the opportunity to access uniform state law if they are dissatisfied with the decision of the local justice institution.[86] In Bougainville, because local justice mechanisms have been recognized, Bougainvilleans may appeal from their Village

---

[83] E. Marchetti and K. Daly, "Indigenous Sentencing Courts: Towards a Theoretical and Jurisprudential Model," *Sydney Law Review* 29:3 (2007): 415–444; B. McAsey, "A Critical Evaluation of the Koori Court Division of the Victorian Magistrates' Court" *Deakin Law Review*, 10:2 (2005): 654–685.

[84] L. Grenfell, "Promoting the Rule of Law in Timor-Leste," *Conflict, Security & Development* 9:2 (2009): 213–238; interview with a member of Timorese civil society, May 12, 2010; interview with an international governance adviser, May 13, 2010.

[85] A. Marriot, "Justice in the Community, Justice in the Courts: Bridging East Timor's Legal Divide," in Mearns, *Democratic Governance*; Mearns, *Looking Both Ways*.

[86] Interview with an international justice adviser, May 14, 2010.

Courts to the Papua New Guinea District Courts. The Village Courts can be supervised by the ABG, Papua New Guinea District Courts and the Papua New Guinea Village Court secretariat. As these bodies perform this role jointly, there is no single body monitoring these courts and collecting data relating to how they operate. Capacity limitations also mean that this supervision is rarely exercised. Despite this, the fact that such supervision is possible is an example of the way in which legal pluralism can be managed in order to strengthen the rule of law.

Legal pluralism can also be managed by formally recognizing customary law, in order to provide some certainty concerning the content and hierarchy of laws. Such recognition might "give the local population some feeling of ownership over, and connection with, the applicable law and its values."[87] In both Timor-Leste and Bougainville, there are a number of difficulties when seeking to identify elements of customary law that are sufficiently common and certain to be codified, since it is generally oral, constantly evolving, and highly localized between groups.[88] As it can be difficult to identify what constitutes "law," particularly in non-Western societies, it is useful to utilize the conception of law as a "folk concept," that is, "law is what people within social groups have come to see and label as 'law.'"[89] Although not all societies will necessarily understand the term or idea "law," all will be governed by sociopolitical norms, rules, and practices that are perceived to be legitimate and enforced by local institutions and are therefore equivalent to law. Indeed, in Timor-Leste, consultations on the draft Customary Law found that while local practices were diverse in terms of language and dialects, most handled things in the same way,[90] although this finding has been criticized as being based on "flawed assumptions."[91] While codifying customary law is difficult, it at least provides a degree of the consistency and uniformity required to help

---

[87] Grenfell, "Legal Pluralism and the Rule of Law," 324.
[88] Interview with a Bougainvillean intellectual, October 16, 2010; interview with a Timorese governance adviser, May 11, 2010; interview with a Timorese justice adviser, May 12, 2010; interview with an international governance adviser (b), April 23, 2010; interview with an international adviser to the BIPG, BCC, and ABG, August 31, 2010.
[89] B. Z. Tamanaha, "Understanding Legal Pluralism: Past to Present, Local to Global," *Sydney Law Review* 30 (2008): 396.
[90] Interview with an international justice adviser, May 14, 2010. See also C. Graydon, "Local Justice Systems in Timor-Leste: Washed Up, or Watch This Space?," *Development Bulletin* 68 (2005): 66–70; E. Harper, *Re-constructing a Legal System in East Timor: Challenges to Introducing International Legal Norms and Principles into Post-Conflict States under UN Administration*, PhD Thesis, University of Melbourne, 2007.
[91] A. Marriott, "The Justice Sector: Achievements, Challenges, and Comparisons," in Leach and Kingsbury, *The Politics of Timor-Leste*, 102.

entrench the rule of law. However, recognizing and enumerating customary law can prove problematic. In Guatemala, the state has sought to incorporate a form of Mayan law into court proceedings, but it has been accused of usurping and assimilating that law while failing to deliver its benefits.[92] In Tanzania and South Africa, efforts to incorporate customary law have made it even more rigid and oppressive.[93] This highlights the fact that efforts to recognize and incorporate customary law can alter it to such an extent that they reduce its legitimacy. Moreover, what is identified as "customary law" may in fact be "inventions or selective interpretations by...sophisticated indigenous elites who created customary law to advance their interests or agendas."[94] This suggests that efforts to codify customary law in Timor-Leste and Bougainville need to be conducted utilizing extensive consultation with Timorese and Bougainvilleans to ensure that they reflect how people at the local, rather than just the elite, level understand their customary law.

The formal recognition of local justice mechanisms and customary law is also challenged by the fact that they may not necessarily comply with liberal human rights standards. In both Timor-Leste and Bougainville, there are concerns over the neutrality of local justice decision makers, the consistency of their decision making, and their treatment of women, particularly in cases of sexual assault and domestic violence.[95] For example, in Timor-Leste, a 2008 survey revealed that 58 percent of respondents disapprove of women being able to speak for themselves in local justice mechanisms.[96] More disturbingly, at least from a liberal perspective, in both cases, when an unmarried woman is raped, the customary solution is for the perpetrator to either marry her or pay compensation to her family to "cover the parents' shame."[97] This highlights the fact that local justice mechanisms should not be

---

[92] J. Hessbruegge and C. F. Ochoa Garcia, "Mayan Law in Post-Conflict Guatemala," in Isser, *Customary Justice*.

[93] T. W. Bennett and A. Pillay, "The Natal and KwaZulu Codes: The Case for Repeal," *South African Journal on Human Rights* 19:2 (2003): 217–238; I. Yngstrom, "Women, Wives and Land Rights in Africa: Situating Gender Beyond the Household in the Debate over Land Policy and Changing Tenure Systems," *Oxford Development Studies* 30:1 (2002): 21–40.

[94] Tamanaha, "Understanding Legal Pluralism," 384.

[95] Hohe and Nixon, *Reconciling Justice*; interview with an international governance adviser, May 13, 2010; interview with an international adviser to the BIPG, BCC, and ABG, August 31, 2010; interview with an international adviser to the BRA and BCC, January 18, 2010; UNOHCHR/UNMIT, *Facing the Future: Periodic Report on Human Rights Developments in Timor-Leste, 1 July 2009–30 June 2010* (Dili: UN Office of the High Commissioner for Human Rights and UNMIT, 2010).

[96] Asia Foundation, *Law and Justice in Timor-Leste*.

[97] Hohe and Nixon, *Reconciling Justice*, 19. Note that many reported cases of rape involve situations where there has been consensual sex, but the man has reneged on his promise to

romanticized, nor should state justice institutions be "automatically disregarded as imposed, harmful and culturally inappropriate."[98] Therefore, it has been argued that local justice mechanisms can provide a "check on the inability of state law to grapple with contextual injustices in a local language in which citizens can understand the proceedings, and state justice is a check on the failure of traditional justice to guarantee" liberal human rights.[99] Conversely, the liberal state system can mitigate the potential for local justice mechanisms to breach rights. In Bougainville, parties can seek the judicial enforcement of the basic rights laid down in the Papua New Guinea constitution (and incorporated into the Bougainville constitution) in order to mitigate the effects of customary law practices that clearly breach these protections. Although the reality of subsistence life means that many Bougainvilleans are unable to pursue this route, it does represent a way in which concerns about the human rights compatibility of customary laws could be dealt with in the future. Similarly, the Timor-Leste constitution specifies that local "norms and customs" must be taken into account to the extent that they are not "contrary to the Constitution."[100] Consequently, they are subject to the human rights protections enshrined in the constitution, although these mechanisms are admittedly weak.

In this regard, there is potential in both cases for formal justice institutions to supervise local justice mechanisms, such as through reviewing whether the penalties imposed in local mechanisms are proportionate and comply with the human rights protections enshrined in the two constitutions. In Bougainville, sentences involving imprisonment that are handed down by Village Courts must be ratified by a Papua New Guinea District Court magistrate. In Timor-Leste, there are proposals to mandate the *provedor* to monitor local justice institutions to ensure that human rights are being respected.[101] In addition, educational programs could be adopted to assist communities to adapt to reflect the human rights protections contained in the constitutions.[102] In Timor-Leste, the consultation process on the draft Customary Law indicated that once it was explained how local practices conflict with liberal human rights standards, communities were prepared to alter their local practices accordingly.[103] Educational and training programs could also be implemented

---

marry the woman. Chopra, Ranheim, and Nixon, "Local-Level Justice"; Howley, *Breaking Spears and Mending Hearts.*

[98] Mac Ginty, "Indigenous Peace-Making," 150.
[99] Braithwaite, Charlesworth, and Soares, *Networked Governance*, 218.
[100] Timor-Leste Constitution, s. 2(4). [101] Grenfell, "Promoting the Rule of Law."
[102] Grenfell, "Legal Pluralism and the Rule of Law."
[103] Interview with an international justice adviser, May 14, 2010.

for those involved in local justice mechanisms, on topics such as human rights protections, state legal requirements, and improving mediation and conflict-resolution skills.[104]

The establishment of the rule of law has also been challenged in both cases by the provision of amnesties and pardons for certain crimes that occurred during their respective conflicts, which has contributed to a developing culture of impunity. The literature predicts that the generation of a constituent process can be facilitated by the utilization of methods of reconciliation, including criminal trials, a truth and reconciliation process, or a locally designed restorative justice mechanism. During UNTAET's tenure in Timor-Leste, there was an effort to deal with serious crimes relating to the Indonesian occupation via formal criminal prosecutions. This approach influenced the Constituent Assembly, which included provisions requiring the prosecution of people who committed such serious crimes in the constitution. As described in Part II, most prosecutions were unsuccessful, and successive presidents have granted amnesties and pardons in relation to serious crimes. These have contributed to the development of a culture of impunity, since offenders are perceived to have been excused of their crimes without having to undergo customary reconciliation. Instead, formal prosecutions crowded out customary reconciliation practices with respect to serious crimes.

In Bougainville, amnesties and pardons were agreed upon during the peace process and incorporated into the final constitution. There is some suggestion that a culture of impunity has developed in Bougainville because major crimes committed during the crisis were reconciled without prosecution. However, because these amnesties and pardons were accompanied by customary reconciliation, the sense that justice has been denied is not as strong (or as destructive) as in Timor-Leste. In any event, it is difficult to see how a transitional justice procedure could have occurred in Bougainville without significant international involvement, given the lack of capacity. The difficulties faced by transitional justice efforts in Timor-Leste, which had significant international support, illustrate this. Instead, local sociopolitical practices were utilized that were partly retributive, but as they operated with the aim of achieving reconciliation, they were also restorative, and any punishments were usually aimed at restoring the status quo and repaying the community for the wrongdoing. However, as the Bougainville case reveals, these local practices are not unproblematic, particularly as they deny the perpetrator the right to a fair trial in accordance with the rule of law, and the punishments

---

[104] B. Baker, "Linking State and Non-State Security and Justice," *Development Policy Review* 28:5 (2010): 597–616.

they mete out can breach liberal human rights standards. This highlights the importance of adopting a liberal-local hybrid approach, whereby the local practices work in conjunction with liberal standards to ameliorate the most extreme consequences of both and to achieve a balance between them.

The evidence from Timor-Leste and Bougainville suggests that amnesties and pardons can play a pragmatic role during a constitution-making process. However, the Bougainville case highlights the importance of accompanying them with locally recognized reconciliation and restorative justice procedures if they are to be perceived as legitimate and to play a role in generating a constituent process and reuniting postconflict societies. Indeed, the CAVR process for minor crimes in Timor-Leste is evidence that Timorese understand justice as punishment and as involving compensation, accountability, and other forms of reciprocity.[105]

Overall, the Bougainville case again suggests that extensive public participation in constitution making generates a constituent process and leads to the recognition of local sociopolitical practices in the constitution, including local justice mechanisms. While this can challenge the establishment of the rule of law, the Bougainville case suggests that the rule of law is better served by recognizing legal pluralism than by ignoring it, as occurred in the Timor-Leste case, where minimal public participation meant that opportunities to generate a constituent process were missed and the constitution consequently overlooked the role of local justice mechanisms.

Are human rights and civil liberties protected?

Liberal human rights and civil liberties protections are included in both constitutions. While the Timor-Leste constitution includes a range of human rights protections, many are available only to Timorese citizens and the methods for their enforcement are weak, which has created space for the government to encroach on citizens' civil liberties. In contrast, in Bougainville, the constitution incorporates the extensive human rights protections available in the Papua New Guinea constitution and provides that the Bougainville government may protect additional rights. Bougainville's courts are developing their capacity and are therefore unlikely to be able to enforce human rights protections in the short term, but Bougainvilleans have the option of going to Papua New Guinea courts to seek protection of their rights. This evidence appears to bear out the prediction in the literature that the

---

[105] P. Pigou, *The Community Reconciliation Process of the Commission for Reception, Truth and Reconciliation* (Dili: United National Development Programme, 2004).

higher the level of participation in a constitution-making process, the more likely the resulting constitution is to protect human rights.

Yet, while liberal human rights protections are included in both constitutions, there are questions over the extent to which the concept of human rights is understood. In both cases, the concept appears to be widely known, and people are frequently heard referring to their "right" to perform an act or receive a service.[106] However, there are questions concerning whether many Timorese and Bougainvilleans have developed a substantive understanding of the rights to which they are entitled, the way in which these rights are protected, and the parties against which these rights can be enforced. For example, in Timor-Leste, it is now common for people to claim that they have the "right" to commit crimes.[107] Similarly, in Bougainville, the phrase *i lail bilong wan wan* (the wish of an individual to do as he or she pleases) is now frequently used, particularly by young people, to argue that "he/she has the right to behave how he/she wishes to...regardless of wider community interests."[108] It is also unclear whether breaches of liberal human rights standards are necessarily perceived negatively, particularly as these breaches often have social logic and may be seen by the victim as the best approach in the absence of better alternatives. The victim may also choose to prioritize reconciliation over retribution. For example, when referring to the customary solution to rape, one Bougainville woman commented: "People were usually happy to forego some of their rights if it is for the good of the community. She [the victim] would not see this as a big thing."[109]

There is evidence of a developing interest in ensuring human rights are protected, which suggests that local practices may be evolving to accommodate this liberal concept. In Timor-Leste, the government has attempted to

---

[106] Interview with a member of Parliament, September 27, 2010; interview with a member of Timorese civil society, May 12, 2010; interview with a member of Timorese civil society, May 14, 2010; interview with a Timorese intellectual, May 12, 2010; interview with an international academic, January 18, 2010; interview with an international adviser to the BIPG, BCC, and ABG, August 31, 2010; interview with an international adviser to the BRA and BCC, January 18, 2010; interview with an international governance adviser (a), May 10, 2010; interview with an international human rights adviser, July 28, 2010.

[107] Interview with a member of Timorese civil society, May 14, 2010; interview with a Timorese justice adviser, May 12, 2010; Trindade, "Reconciling Conflicting Paradigms." A 2004 survey revealed that 22 percent of respondents interpreted "human rights" to mean "the right to do things" and "freedom." Asia Foundation, *Law and Justice in East Timor*, 29.

[108] N. G. Ahai, "Grassroots Development Visions for a New Bougainville," in *Building Peace in Bougainville, National Research Institute Special Publication No. 27*, ed. G. Harris et al. (Armidale: University of New England and the National Research Institute, Papua New Guinea, 1999), 120.

[109] Quoted in Howley, *Breaking Spears and Mending Hearts*, 141–142.

enhance rights protections, as removing the mandate for investigating corruption from the *provedor* enables that office to focus on human rights. It has also created a National Commission on the Rights of the Child to enforce a Children's Code.[110] But, problems remain, including in respect to the behavior of the F-FDTL and PNTL and in the decisions of local justice mechanisms. Similarly, in 2008, the ABG established the Bougainville Human Rights Committee, which has subcommittees in each of the three regions, comprising representatives of the ABG, NGOs, and the media. These committees work with the ABG's Division of Community Development to promote the observance of human rights protections in each region. The ABG has also created an Office of *Lukautim Pikinini* (Child Protection) intended to protect children's rights.

CONCLUSION

In conclusion, a comparison of the Timor-Leste and Bougainville cases illustrates the way in which differing levels of participation in constitution making have affected the generation of a constituent process, which has had implications for the creation of state institutions. In Timor-Leste, minimal public participation saw the creation of state institutions heavily influenced by the liberal peace approach. As the gap between the constitution and the society it sought to govern became obvious, a liberal-local hybrid approach has slowly emerged. In contrast, in Bougainville, extensive public participation saw immediate engagement between the liberal and the local, so that liberal-local hybridity was achieved. Given that Bougainvilleans appear to perceive their institutions as legitimate, this suggests that the higher the level of participation involved in constitution making, the more likely it is to generate a constituent process and consequently that the resulting constitution will make sense to the society it seeks to govern.

---

[110] *Draft Children's Code*, released for public comment in May 2011, accessed June 16, 2011, www.mj.gov.tl/files/TC_EN_CHILDS_CODE_MAY_2011_versao_para_distribui%C3%A7%C3%A30.pdf.

Conclusion

This book has demonstrated that public participation in constitution making can help fragmented and divided societies, which are not immediately compatible with centralized statehood, be accommodated and adjust to state structures during state building. If constitution making involves extensive public participation, it is likely to generate a constituent process, which can help to foster a sense of political community and to produce a constitution that enhances the legitimacy and effectiveness of the state institutions it creates by achieving liberal-local hybridity. This book builds on the increasing challenge that the literature on public participation is making to widespread assumptions relating to the utility of elite-led constitution making and liberal peace state building.

The case studies of Timor-Leste and Bougainville support arguments in favor of generating a constituent process and show that it can play a positive role in state building. The extensive public participation in constitution making in Bougainville produced a constituent process that built a relatively strong sense of political community by creating a sense of common identity and by reconciling many of the most severe divisions between societal groups. In contrast, the minimal participation in Timor-Leste did not generate a constituent process, and consequently did not create a unifying national identity, so certain societal divisions remain unreconciled, while others have become salient. The Bougainville process also produced a constitution and state institutions that make sense to Bougainvilleans, as it achieved liberal-local hybridity. In contrast, the Timor-Leste process produced a largely liberal peace constitution and state institutions that did not recognize the local sociopolitical practices that regulated most Timorese people's lives, which challenged their legitimacy.

LESSONS FROM THIS BOOK

As this book has constructed and applied a strong normative framework, it is possible to draw generalizable inferences from the two case studies for both the literature and for ongoing and future constitution-making processes and state-building operations in fragmented and divided new and postconflict states, such as Fiji, Nepal, Tunisia, and Egypt.

The first lesson is that future constitution-making processes should encourage extensive public participation in constitution making if the constitution-making process is to truly represent an exercise of the people's popular sovereignty and the constitution their social contract. This book has demonstrated that public participation in constitution making can generate a constituent process by several means: first, assisting people to unite to exercise their constituent power; second, encouraging reconciliation and the resolution of grievances; third, encouraging individuals to become citizens who recognize the legitimacy of their constitution and the state institutions it creates to exercise their constituted power; and fourth, creating a liberal-local hybrid constitution and state institutions that better reflect public understandings and views.

The level of international involvement in a constitution-making process may influence the level of public participation. The Timor-Leste case suggests that extensive international involvement can place time pressures on the process, which can limit opportunities for public participation, as international actors are rarely willing to bear the expense of a sustained state-building operation. The Timor-Leste case also indicates that international actors can empower (whether by accident or design) certain political elites and groups, which can limit opportunities for public participation. As has been illustrated in Afghanistan and Iraq, the international community can put too much emphasis on holding early democratic elections, which in Timor-Leste affected the representativeness of constitution makers and their attitude to public participation. Therefore, it appears that international involvement in constitution-making processes should focus on facilitating a locally led process by providing technical and logistical support. International actors should also avoid placing time pressures on the process to provide space for broader political, cultural, and institutional development to occur, in order to enhance the likelihood that the constitution-making process will be representative and that extensive opportunities for public participation are offered.

The second lesson is that a liberal-local hybrid approach to state building can build a relatively legitimate and effective state in societies in which liberal state institutions are not embedded and in which local sociopolitical practices and institutions remain resilient. Local sociopolitical institutions are often the most legitimate and effective level of government in new and postconflict states, and therefore, a liberal-local hybrid approach that decentralizes power and resources to local institutions should be adopted early during state building. Given that liberal democracy is usually the result of struggle and evolution, local sociopolitical institutions can act as a buffer in the short to medium term while society adjusts to and accommodates statehood.

The liberal-local hybrid approach is not unproblematic and can lapse into cultural relativism if it romanticizes local sociopolitical practices.[1] Cultural relativism is not inherently negative and can play a valuable role in countering racist ideas.[2] However, it can also inhibit the evaluation – and critique – of local practices and institutions. Therefore, while relativism is not rejected in favor of universalism, some value judgments do need to be made. Yet, the adoption of a liberal-local hybrid approach need not necessarily "imply that the local must be the source or depository of all things that are great."[3] In this regard, liberalism should also not be romanticized, since liberal peace state building often resorts to illiberal or "uncivil" methods.[4] Indeed, the process of building many liberal democracies was inherently violent.[5]

Moreover, the Bougainville case illustrates that societies often choose to draw upon liberal principles during constitution making as part of their liberal-local hybrid approach to state building. To argue that Bougainvilleans did so only as a result of international pressure denies them agency. A better explanation is that they valued aspects of liberalism, which they did not necessarily view as antithetical to local practices, especially as they had lived under the relatively liberal Papua New Guinea constitution since 1975. There are also indications from both cases that local sociopolitical practices are "evolving" – rather than "fixed" – as they can adapt to new realities and demands for the greater accommodation of liberal norms.[6] Indeed, one former member of the ABG cautioned that "custom will not work if it is left

---

[1] G. A. Almond and J. Coleman, *The Politics of Developing Areas* (Princeton: Princeton University Press, 1960); O. P. Richmond, "De-romanticising the Local, De-mystifying the International: Hybridity in Timor Leste and Solomon Islands," *The Pacific Review* 24:1 (2011): 115–136.

[2] A. Montagu, *Man's Most Dangerous Myth: The Fallacy of Race* (Cleveland: World Publishing Company, 1964).

[3] Richmond, "Becoming Liberal, Unbecoming Liberalism," 334.   [4] Ibid.

[5] C. Tilly, *Coercion, Capital, and European States, AD 990–1992* (Oxford: Blackwell, 1992).

[6] Brown, "Security, Development and the Nation-Building Agenda," 155; Boege, *Discovery of Slowness*; Mearns, *Looking Both Ways*.

alone. It will not survive in the modern world. It has to be supported and integrated with modern ways."[7] In this regard, in Timor-Leste, the consultation process associated with the Domestic Violence Law[8] was praised by women's groups because it provided the opportunity to socialize liberal human rights standards into local practices.[9] Even before the law was formally adopted, an awareness program had led to a noticeable increase in reporting of domestic violence to the PNTL.[10] There are several other examples of communities altering their local practices when they became aware that they clashed with liberal human rights standards.[11] This illustrates that the liberal and local are not inextricably opposed and that a process of engagement can facilitate accommodation and adjustment between them.

Therefore, in order to generate a constituent process, future constitution-making processes should encourage public participation regarding the extent to which local sociopolitical practices and institutions are recognized in the constitution, and constitution drafters should take seriously the feedback they receive in this regard. It might have been easier to adopt this approach from the outset in Bougainville, because the peace and state-building processes were locally led. In Timor-Leste and other cases where greater concentrations of international actors are involved in state building, awareness of local practices is likely to be limited. Yet this is not an excuse for international state builders to overlook the local. Instead, it is a reason why they should engage with local people in their everyday settings, with public participation in constitution making one of the best ways to achieve this engagement. In this regard, the Bougainville case again suggests that, where possible, state building should be conducted by local actors, with the international community intervening only to the extent necessary to provide support. Constitution makers should also remain alive to the challenges that certain local practices may pose and use public participation in constitution making to conduct agonistic encounters that seek to achieve engagement between the liberal and the local.

---

[7] Interview with a former BRA commander and member of the ABG, November 2, 2010.
[8] Law Against Domestic Violence No. 7/2010 (2010) (TL).
[9] Interview with a Timorese governance adviser, May 11, 2010; interview with a Timorese women's leader, April 29, 2010.
[10] Interview with a member of Timorese civil society, April 28, 2010; personal communication from an international security adviser in Timor-Leste, April 28, 2010.
[11] For example, when negotiating a *tarabandu*, one community became aware that their local treatment of rape victims did not reflect the state penal code and changed their agreement accordingly. Interview with an international governance adviser, May 13, 2010; Belun, *Tara Bandu*.

FURTHER RESEARCH

This book represents an attempt to undertake a sustained empirical study in order to demonstrate that public participation in constitution making can play a positive role in state building by generating a constituent process. Further research on this issue, using a larger number of comparative case studies or studies of cases from different regions and with larger populations, will be required to determine whether the social and cultural background or small size of Timor-Leste and Bougainville was influential and to confirm that the findings hold in different contexts.

Moreover, emerging evidence from both cases suggests that this positive role may be limited temporally or may become dependent on other factors. The Bougainville case suggests that if the state does not have the power and resources to operate effectively, then generating a constituent process might not be enough to ensure the state survives in the long term. Somewhat ironically, extensive participation in constitution making achieved almost precisely what it was intended to in Bougainville by creating a relatively unified political community and cultivating a sense of citizenization among Bougainvilleans, who then had high expectations of their new government.[12] However, the resource constraints experienced by the ABG have disappointed their expectations. One ABG member commented that he felt as though the government's "hands are tied" in relation to Bougainville's future, because as an autonomous region, it is hamstrung by its reliance on the Papua New Guinea government for funding.[13]

In contrast, the Timor-Leste case indicates that while minimal public participation and a failure to generate a constituent process can undermine a new state in the short to medium term, once it is able to access substantial resources and deliver services more effectively, its legitimacy may increase. Timor-Leste has been greatly assisted by the large oil revenues it began to access in 2005. Yet, some projections forecast that these resources will be exhausted by 2025, particularly as the cost of overcoming the disadvantage of the failure to generate a constituent process has been high. It remains to be seen whether the legitimacy and effectiveness that these resources have bought the government endure once these resources run out. The fact that the UN and the International Stabilization Force remained in Timor-Leste

---

[12] Regan, "The Bougainville Political Settlement."
[13] Personal communication from a member of the ABG, November 4, 2010; interview with an international adviser to the BRA and BCC, January 18, 2010; Momis, "Challenges of Implementing."

until the end of 2012 suggests that societal divisions and questions over the legitimacy of state institutions remain, which indicates that Timor-Leste has only a small window to achieve reconciliation, resolve grievances, and build a sense of political community if the state is to survive. Otherwise, the failure to generate a constituent process in Timor-Leste might have long-term consequences.

This emerging evidence is not meant to offer a pessimistic conclusion to this book, but merely to provide a note of caution that public participation in constitution making is not a panacea that, if adopted, will ensure the stability and survival of all new and postconflict states. The Timor-Leste and Bougainville cases suggest that public participation in constitution making plays an important role in helping to legitimize new and postconflict states, which can buy them time to develop government effectiveness and increases the likelihood of their success and survival.

Bibliography

Ackerman, B. "The Rise of World Constitutionalism." *Virginia Law Review* 83 (1997): 771–802.
  We the People: Foundations. Cambridge: Belknap Press of Harvard University Press, 1991.
Ackerman, B., and J. Fishkin. *Deliberation Day*. New Haven: Yale University Press, 2004.
Ahai, N. G. "Grassroots Development Visions for a New Bougainville." In *Building Peace in Bougainville, National Research Institute Special Publication No. 27*, edited by G. Harris et al. Armidale: University of New England and the National Research Institute, Papua New Guinea, 1999.
AI. *The Democratic Republic of Timor-Leste: A New Police Service – A New Beginning*, ASA 57/002/2003. London: Amnesty International, June 30, 2003.
  Groups, Gangs, and Armed Violence in Timor-Leste, Issue Brief No. 2. London: Amnesty International, 2009.
  Papua New Guinea: Human Rights Violations on Bougainville, 1989–1990. London: Amnesty International, 1990.
Al-Ali, Z. "Constitutional Drafting and External Influence." In Ginsburg and Dixon, *Comparative Constitutional Law*.
Almond, G. A. and J. Coleman. *The Politics of Developing Areas*. Princeton: Princeton University Press, 1960.
Almond, G. A. and S. Verba. *The Civic Culture: Political Attitudes and Democracy in Five Nations*. Princeton: Princeton University Press, 1963.
Anderson, B. *Imagined Communities: Reflections on the Origins and Spread of Nationalism*. London: Verso, 1991.
  "Imagining East Timor." *Arena Magazine* 4 (1993): 23–27.
Arato, A. *Constitution Making Under Occupation: The Politics of Imposed Revolution Iraq*. New York: Columbia University Press, 2009.
  "Iraq and its Aftermath." *Dissent* 51:2 (2004): 21–28.
  "Redeeming the Still Redeemable: Post Sovereign Constitution Making." *International Journal of Politics, Culture, and Society* 22 (2009): 427–443.
Arato A. and Z. Miklósi. "Constitution Making and Transitional Politics in Hungary." In Miller, *Framing the State*.

Arjomand, S. A. "Constitutional Development and Political Reconstruction from Nation-Building to New Constitutionalism." In Arjomand, *Constitutionalism and Political Reconstruction.*

Arjomand, S. A., editor. *Constitutionalism and Political Reconstruction.* Leiden: Brill, 2007.

Armstrong, J. *Nations before Nationalism.* Chapel Hill: University of North Carolina Press, 1982.

Arnold, M. B. "Challenges Too Strong for the Nascent State of Timor-Leste: Petitioners and Mutineers." *Asian Survey* 49:3 (2009): 429–449.

Article 19/Internews. *Freedom of Expression and the Media in Timor-Leste.* London/Dili: Article 19/Internews, 2005.

Asia Foundation. *East Timor National Survey of Voters' Knowledge (Preliminary Findings).* Dili: Asia Foundation, 2001.

  Law and Justice in East Timor: A Survey of Citizen Awareness and Attitudes Regarding Law and Justice in East Timor. Dili: Asia Foundation, 2004.

  Law and Justice in Timor-Leste: A Survey of Citizen Awareness and Attitudes Regarding Law and Justice 2008. Dili: Asia Foundation, 2009.

  A Survey of Community-Police Perceptions: Timor-Leste in 2008. Dili: Asia Foundation, 2008.

  Timor Lorosa'e National Survey of Citizen Knowledge. Dili: Asia Foundation, 2002.

  Timor-Leste Public Opinion Poll. Dili: Asia Foundation, 2013.

Aucion, L. and M. Brandt. "East Timor's Constitutional Passage to Independence." In Miller, *Framing the State.*

AusAID. *Annual Program Performance Report for East Timor 2007–08.* Canberra: AusAID, 2008.

Avei, M. *Ministerial Statement on Presentation of the Bougainville Peace Agreement.* Port Moresby: Papua New Guinea National Parliament, October 17, 2001.

Avocats Sans Frontieres. *Access to Legal Aid in Timor-Leste – Survey Report.* Dili: Avocats San Frontieres, 2006.

Babo-Soares, D. *Branching from the Trunk: East Timorese Perceptions of Nationalism in Transition.* PhD Thesis, Australian National University, 2003.

  "Challenges for the Future." In *Out of the Ashes: Destruction and Reconstruction of East Timor*, edited by J. J. Fox and D. Babo Soares. Canberra: ANU E-Press, 2003.

  "Nahe Biti: The Philosophy and Process of Grassroots Reconciliation and Justice in East Timor." *The Asia Pacific Journal of Anthropology* 5:1 (2004): 15–33.

Baker, B. "Justice and Security Architecture in Africa: The Plans, the Bricks, the Purse and the Builder." *Journal of Legal Pluralism* 63 (2011): 25–47.

  "Linking State and Non-State Security and Justice." *Development Policy Review* 28:5 (2010): 597–616.

Balkin, J. M. "Respect-worthy: Frank Michelman and the Legitimate Constitution." *Tulsa Law Review* 39 (2003–2004): 485–510.

Baltazar, A. "An Overview of the Constitution Drafting Process in East Timor." *East Timor Law Journal* 9 (2004).

Banks, A. M. "Expanding Participation in Constitution Making: Challenges and Opportunities." *William and Mary Law Review* 49:4 (2008): 1043–1069.

Bannon, A. L. "Designing a Constitution-Drafting Process: Lessons from Kenya." *Yale Law Journal* 116 (2007): 1824–1872.

Banting, K. G., and R. Simeon, editors. *Redesigning the State: The Politics of Constitutional Change*. Toronto: University of Toronto Press, 1985.
"Introduction: The Politics of Constitutional Change." In Banting and Simeon, *Redesigning the State*.
Barcham, M. *Conflict, Violence and Development in the Southwest Pacific: Taking the Indigenous Context Seriously, Centre for Indigenous Governance and Development Working Paper Series, Working Paper Number 4/2005*. Palmerston North: Massey University, 2005.
Bater, R. "Hope from Below: Composing the Commons in Iceland," December 1, 2011. Accessed August 14, 2013. www.opendemocracy.net/richard-bater/hope-from-below-composing-commons-in-iceland.
Bauman, R. W., and T. Kahana, editors. *The Least Examined Branch: The Role of Legislatures in the Constitutional State*. New York: Cambridge University Press, 2006
BCC. *1st Draft Bougainville Constitution – Consulting the People*. Buka: Bougainville Constitutional Commission, January 31, 2003.
Brief on the 2nd Draft of the Bougainville Constitution for Bougainville Joint Assemblies Meeting. Buka: Bougainville Constitutional Commission, April 2, 2003.
Discussion of Constitution of the Autonomous Region of Bougainville Working Draft of 25/01/03: Minutes of Full BCC Meetings Tuesday 28 to Thursday 30 January. Buka: Bougainville Constitutional Commission, 2003.
Discussion of Recommendations: Minutes of Full BCC Meetings, Friday 15 November to Monday 9 December. Buka: Bougainville Constitutional Commission, 2002.
Report of the Bougainville Constitutional Commission: Report on the Third and Final Draft of the Bougainville Constitution. Arawa and Buka: Bougainville Constitutional Commission, July 2004.
Tentative Program for Involvement of Chairman & Deputy in Work of Regional Teams (Sunday 2 to Tuesday 11 February). Buka: Bougainville Constitutional Commission, January 2003.
BCC Technical Team. *Matrix of Choices*. Buka: Bougainville Constitutional Commission, November 10, 2002.
Bellamy, R. *Political Constitutionalism: A Republican Defence of the Constitutionality of Democracy*. Cambridge: Cambridge University Press, 2007.
Belo, C. X. *The Road to Freedom: A Collection of Speeches, Pastoral Letters, and Articles from 1997–2001*. Sydney: Caritas Australia, 2001.
Belun. *Tara Bandu: Its Role and Use in Community Conflict Prevention in Timor-Leste*. Dili: Belun and Asia Foundation, 2013.
Benhabib, S. "Toward a Deliberative Model of Democratic Legitimacy." In Benhabib, *Democracy and Difference*.
Benhabib, S., editor. *Democracy and Difference: Contesting the Boundaries of the Political*. Princeton: Princeton University Press, 1996.
Bennett, T. W. and A. Pillay. "The Natal and KwaZulu Codes: The Case for Repeal." *South African Journal on Human Rights* 19:2 (2003): 217–238.
Benomar, J. "Constitution-Making After Conflict: Lessons for Iraq." *Journal of Democracy* 15:2 (2004): 81–95.
Benton, L. *Law and Colonial Cultures 1400–1900*. Cambridge: Cambridge University Press, 2001.

Berlin, I. *Four Essays on Liberty.* Oxford: Oxford University Press, 1969.
Bermeo, N. *Ordinary People in Extraordinary Times: The Citizenry and the Breakdown of Democracy.* Princeton: Princeton University Press, 2003.
Bhabha, H. *The Location of Culture.* London: Routledge, 1994.
BHRC. *Universal Periodic Review: Bougainville Civil Society Stakeholder Shadow Report to OHCHR.* Buka: Bougainville Human Rights Committee and Civil Society Bougainvilleans, 2011.
Biggar, N. "Making Peace or Doing Justice: Must We Choose?" In *Burying the Past: Making Peace and Doing Justice After Civil Conflict,* edited by N. Biggar. Washington: Georgetown University Press, 2003.
Billig, M. *Banal Nationalism.* London: Sage, 1997.
Binin, G. "Call for Kabui to Resign." *Papua New Guinea Post-Courier,* 5 May 2008.
Blindenbacher, R., and A. Koller, editors. *Federalism in a Changing World – Learning from Each Other.* Montreal: McGill-Queen's University Press, 2003
Blount, J. "Participation in Constitutional Design." In Ginsburg and Dixon, *Comparative Constitutional Law.*
Blount, J., Z. Elkins, and T. Ginsburg. "Does the Process of Constitution-Making Matter?" In Ginsburg, *Comparative Constitutional Design.*
Boege, V. *Bougainville and the Discovery of Slowness: An Unhurried Approach to State-Building in the Pacific, the Australian Centre for Peace and Conflict Studies, Occasional Paper Number 3.* Brisbane: University of Queensland, 2006.
  Bougainville Report, Project: Addressing Legitimacy Issues in Fragile Post-Conflict Situations to Advance Conflict Transformation and Peacebuilding. Brisbane: University of Queensland, 2013.
  "Hybrid Forms of Peace and Order on a South Sea Island: Experiences from Bougainville (Papua New Guinea)." In *Hybrid Forms of Peace: from Everyday Agency to Post-Liberalism,* edited by O. P. Richmond and A. Mitchell. Houndmills: Palgrave Macmillan, 2012.
  "Peacebuilding and State Formation in Post-Conflict Bougainville." *Peace Review* 21 (2009): 29–37.
  A Promising Liaison: Kastom and State in Bougainville, the Australian Centre for Peace and Conflict Studies, Occasional Paper Number 12. Brisbane: University of Queensland, 2008.
Boege, V., et al. "Building Peace and Political Community in Hybrid Political Orders." *International Peacekeeping* 16: 5 (2009): 599–615.
  "Hybrid Political Orders, Not Fragile States." *Peace Review* 21 (2009): 13–21.
  On Hybrid Political Orders and Emerging States: State Formation in the Context of "Fragility." Berlin: Berghof Research Center for Constructive Conflict Management, 2008.
  "On Hybrid Political Orders and Emerging States: What Is Failing? States in the Global South or Research and Politics in the West?" In *Building Peace in the Absence of States: Challenging the Discourse of State Failure,* edited by M. Fisher and B. Schmelzle. Berlin: Berghof Research Centre, 2009.
Boege, V. and L. Garasu, "Papua New Guinea: A Success Story of Postconflict Peacebuilding in Bougainville." In *Searching for Peace in Asia Pacific: An Overview of Conflict Prevention and Peacebuilding Activities,* edited by A. Heijmans, N. Simmonds, and H. va de Veen. Boulder: Lynne Rienner, 2004.

Borges, F. "CAVR Implementation: The Key to Transforming the Country and East Timorese Society." In Mearns, *Democratic Governance in Timor-Leste.*
"Law and Justice: Strengthening the Rule of Law." Paper presented at "Transforming Timor Leste for Sustainable Development, Human Rights and Peace: an Opportunity for Dialogue," Ministry of Foreign Affairs, Dili, July 6–7, 2009.
Bougainville Technical Team. *Bougainville Peace Agreement Analysis for Use in an Awareness Campaign.* Arawa: Bougainville Technical Team, August 2001.
Bouckaert, P. N. "Shutting Down the Death Factory: The Abolition of Capital Punishment in South Africa." *Stanford Journal of International Law* 32 (1996): 287–326.
"Bougainville Mining Seminar," Canberra, Australian National University, February 14, 2013.
Bowles E. and T. Chopra. "East Timor: Statebuilding Revisited." In *Building States to Build Peace*, edited by C. T. Call. Boulder: Lynne Rienner, 2008.
Braithwaite, J., H. Charlesworth, and A. Soares. *Networked Governance of Freedom and Tyranny: Peace in Timor-Leste.* Canberra: ANU E-Press, 2012.
Brandt, M. *Constitutional Assistance in Post-Conflict Countries: The UN Experience: Cambodia, East Timor & Afghanistan.* New York: United National Development Programme, 2005.
Brandt, M., et al. *Constitution-Making and Reform: Options for the Process.* Switzerland: Interpeace, 2011.
Brass, P. *Ethnicity and Nationalism.* London: Sage, 1991.
Breslin, B. *The Communitarian Constitution.* Baltimore: Johns Hopkins University Press, 2004.
From Words to Worlds: Exploring Constitutional Functionality. Baltimore: Johns Hopkins University Press, 2009.
Breton, A., A. Cassone, and A. Fraschini. "Decentralization and Subsidiarity: Toward a Theoretical Reconciliation." *University of Pennsylvania Journal of International Economic Law* 21:1 (1998): 21–51.
Breuilly, J. *Nationalism and the State.* Manchester: Manchester University Press, 1993.
Brown, M. A. "Entangled Worlds: Villages and Political Community in Timor-Leste." *Local-Global: Identity, Security, Community* 11 (2012): 54–71.
"Security, Development and the Nation-Building Agenda – East Timor." *Conflict, Security and Development* 9:2 (2009): 141–164.
Timor-Leste Report: Addressing Legitimacy Issues in Fragile Post-Conflict Situations to Advance Conflict Transformation and Peacebuilding. Brisbane: University of Queensland, 2013.
Brown M. A. and A. F. Gusmao. "Peacebuilding and Political Hybridity in East Timor." *Peace Review* 21 (2009): 61–69.
Brown, N. J. "Reason, Interest, Rationality, and Passion in Constitution Drafting." *Perspectives on Politics* 6:4 (2008): 675–689.
"Building Sustainable Peace in Bougainville Conference." Hutjena Secondary School, Buka, June 13, 2007.
Burki, S. J., G. E. Perry, and W. R. Dillinger. *Beyond the Center: Decentralizing the State.* Washington: World Bank, 1999.
Butterworth D. and P. Dale. *Articulations of Local Governance in Timor-Leste: Lessons for Development under Decentralization, Justice for the Poor Policy Note 56931.* Dili: World Bank, 2010.

Local Governance and Community Development Initiatives: Contributions for Community Development Programs in Timor-Leste. Dili: World Bank, 2011.

Calhoun, C. "Constitutional Patriotism and the Public Sphere: Interests, Identity, and Solidarity in the Integration of Europe." In *Global Justice and Transnational Politics*, edited by P. de Greiff and C. Cronin. Cambridge: MIT Press, 2002.

——— "Imagining Solidarity: Cosmopolitanism, Constitutional Patriotism, and the Public Sphere." *Public Culture* 14:1 (2002): 147–171.

——— *Nations Matter: Culture, History, and the Cosmopolitan Dream*. London: Routledge, 2007.

Canovan, M. *Nationhood and Political Theory*. Cheltenham: Edward Elgar, 1996.

——— "Patriotism Is Not Enough." *British Journal of Political Science* 30:3 (2000): 413–432.

——— "The People." In Dryzek, Honig, and Phillips, *The Oxford Handbook of Political Theory*.

——— "Sleeping Dogs, Prowling Cats, and Soaring Doves: Three Paradoxes in the Political Theory of Nationhood." *Political Studies* 49 (2001): 203–215.

Carey, J. "Does It Matter How a Constitution Is Created?" In *Is Democracy Exportable?*, edited by Z. Barany and R. G. Moser. New York: Cambridge University Press, 2009.

Carl, A., and L. Garasu, editors. *Weaving Consensus: The Papua New Guinea–Bougainville Peace Process*. London: Conciliation Resources in collaboration with BICWF, 2002.

Carter Center. *The East Timor Political and Election Observation Project: Final Project Report*. Atlanta: Carter Center, April 2004.

——— *Timor-Leste Election Democratic and Peaceful: Carter Center Preliminary Statement*. Dili: Carter Center, July 3, 2007.

CAVR. *Chega! The Report of the Commission for Reception, Truth and Reconciliation in Timor-Leste: Executive Summary*. Dili: Commission for Reception, Truth, and Reconciliation Timor-Leste, 2005.

Centre for Defence Studies. *Independent Study on Security Force Options and Security Sector Reform for East Timor*. London: Kings College, 2000.

CEPAD. *Timor-Leste: Voices and Paths to Peace*. Dili: Centre of Studies for Peace and Development and Interpeace, 2010.

Certeau, M. de. *The Practice of Everyday Life*. Berkeley: University of California Press, 1984.

Chambers, S. "Contract or Conversation? Theoretical Lessons from the Canadian Constitutional Crisis." *Politics & Society* 26:1 (1998): 143–172.

——— "Democracy, Popular Sovereignty, and Constitutional Legitimacy." *Constellations* 11:2 (2004): 153–173.

——— *Reasonable Democracy*. Ithaca: Cornell University Press, 1996.

Chand, S. *Data Collection in Difficult Environments: Measuring Economic Recovery in Post-Conflict Bougainville*, 2011. Accessed October 10, 2013. www.slideshare.net/CivMilCouncil of Elders/satish-chand.

Chandler, D. *Empire in Denial: The Politics of State-Building*. London: Pluto Press, 2006.

——— "Introduction: Peace without Politics?" *International Peacekeeping* 12:3 (2005): 307–321.

——— "Peacebuilding and the Politics of Non-linearity: Rethinking "Hidden" Agency and 'Resistance.'" *Peacebuilding* 1:1 (2013): 17–32.

"The Uncritical Critique of 'Liberal Peace.'" *Review of International Studies* 36:1 (2010): 137–155.
Charlesworth, H. "The Constitution of East Timor, May 20, 2002." *International Journal of Constitutional Law* 1:2 (2003): 325–344.
Chesterman, S. "East Timor." In *United Nations Interventionism, 1991–2004*, edited by M. Berdal and S. Economides. Cambridge: Cambridge University Press, 2007.
Chopra, J., and T. Hohe. "Participatory Intervention." *Global Governance* 10:3 (2004): 289–305.
Chopra, T., C. Ranheim, and R. Nixon. "Local-Level Justice under Transitional Administration." In Isser, *Customary Justice and the Rule of Law in War-Torn Societies*.
Choudhry, S. "Civil War, Ceasefire, Constitution: Some Preliminary Notes." *Cardozo Law Review* 33 (2011–2012): 1907–1921.
——— editor. *Constitutional Design for Divided Societies: Integration or Accommodation?* New York: Oxford University Press, 2008.
CHRI. "Background Paper to Accompany CHRI's Recommendations to CHOGM '99" and "Recommendations to Commonwealth Heads of Government." In *Promoting a Culture of Constitutionalism and Democracy in Commonwealth Africa*, edited by H. Ebrahim, K. Fayemi, and S. Loomis. Pretoria: Commonwealth Human Rights Initiative, 1999.
CHRI/M. Daruwala. *Civil Society Involvement in Constitutional Review: A Letter from Maja Daruwala, Director of Commonwealth Human Rights Initiative (CHRI) to Justice M.N. Venkatachelliah, Chairman of the National Commission for Reviewing the Constitution and Chief Justice of India*, 2001.
Chua, A. *World on Fire: How Exporting Free Market Democracy Breeds Ethnic Hatred and Global Instability*. New York: Anchor, 2004.
Citizen's Forum for Constitutional Reform. *Background*, 1999. Accessed March 6, 2010. www.cdd.org.uk/cfcf/bkg.htm.
Clegg, M. *The Constitution of Timor-Leste: Appointment of a Prime Minister, IFES White Paper*. Dili: International Foundation for Electoral Systems, 2007.
CNRT (The). *Broad Timeline for the Process Leading to East Timor's Declaration of Independence*, presented to the National Council by CNRT/National Council President Xanana Gusmão, December 12, 2000. Dili: CNRT, 2000.
——— *Outcomes of the CNRT National Congress 21–30 August 2000*. Dili: CNRT, August 2000.
——— *Reconstructing East Timor: Analysis of the Past and Perspectives for the Future Conference, Final Report (Tibar Document)* (Tibar: CNRT May 29–June 2, 2000.)
Cohen, J. "Deliberation and Democratic Legitimacy." In *The Good Polity: Normative Analysis of the State*, edited by A. Hamlin and P. Pettit. Oxford: Basil Blackwell, 1989.
——— "Democracy and Liberty." In Elster, *Deliberative Democracy*.
Collier, P. and A. Hoeffler. "Greed and Grievance in Civil War." *Oxford Economic Papers* 56 (2004): 563–595.
Colon-Rios, J. I. "Notes on Democracy and Constitution-Making." *New Zealand Journal of Public and International Law* 9 (2011): 17–41.
Committee on Political Affairs. *Report on the Political Transitional Calendar*. Dili: National Council, February 22, 2001.

Commonwealth Secretariat/PIF. *General Election for the Autonomous Bougainville Government: Report of the Commonwealth-Pacific Islands Forum Expert Team.* Suva: Pacific Islands Forum/Commonwealth Secretariat, June 4, 2005.

Conflict, Security and Development Group. *A Review of Peace Operations: A Case for Change East Timor Study.* London: Kings College London, 2003.

Connell, J. "Bougainville Is Legitimate Again." *Geographical Magazine* 48:11 (1976): 650–654.

——— "Bougainville: The Future of an Island Microstate." *The Journal of Pacific Studies* 28:2 (2005): 192–217.

——— "Introduction." In *Local Government Councils in Bougainville*, edited by J. Connell. Christchurch: Bougainville Special Publications, University of Canterbury, 1977.

Connolly, W. *The Ethos of Pluralization.* Minneapolis: University of Minnesota Press, 1995.

Connor, W. *Ethno-Nationalism: The Quest for Understanding.* Princeton: Princeton University Press, 1994.

Constituent Assembly. *Handout on Constitution of East Timor* (as approved by the Constituent Assembly up to December 24, 2001). Dili: Constituent Assembly, 2001.

Constituent Assembly Secretariat. *Press Releases.* Dili: Constituent Assembly Secretariat, January 10, 2002; January 11, 2002; and January 14, 2002.

Constituent Assembly Systemization and Harmonization Commission. *Matrix of Recommendations by the Thematic Committees and the Chair of the Systemization and Harmonization Commission.* Dili: Constituent Assembly, December 7, 2001.

Constituent Assembly Thematic Commission IV: Fundamental Principles/Guarantee, Monitoring and Revision of the Constitution/Final and Transitional Provisions. *Report to the Systematization and Harmonization Commission.* Dili: Constituent Assembly, undated.

Cooke, B. "The Social Psychological Limits of Participation." In Cooke and Kothari, *Participation: The New Tyranny?*

Cooke B., and U. Kothari. "The Case for Participation as Tyranny." In Cooke and Kothari, *Participation: The New Tyranny?*

——— editors. *Participation: The New Tyranny?* London: Zed Books, 2001.

Cotton, J. *East Timor, Australia and Regional Order: Intervention and Its Aftermath in Southeast Asia.* London: RoutledgeCurzon, 2004.

Council of Ministers. *Referendum Package to Rebuild Timor's Rural Areas, Media Release.* Dili: Secretary of State for the Council of Ministers, Democratic Republic of Timor-Leste, 8 October 2009.

Cox, J. *Financing the End-Time Harvest: Pyramid Schemes and Prosperity Gospels in Papua New Guinea, State, Society and Governance in Melanesia Discussion Paper 2009/5.* Canberra: Australian National University, 2009.

Cox, M. *State Building and Post-Conflict Reconstruction: Lessons from Bosnia.* Geneva: Centre for Applied Studies in International Negotiations, 2001.

Crockford, F. "Building Demand for Better Governance: Enabling Citizen-State Engagement in Timor-Leste." In Mearns, *Democratic Governance in Timor–Leste.*

Crook, R. C. and J. Manor. *Democracy and Decentralization in South Asia and West Africa: Participation, Accountability and Performance.* Cambridge: Cambridge University Press, 1998.

Crowder, G. "From Value Pluralism to Liberalism." In *Pluralism and Liberal Neutrality*, edited by R. Bellamy and M. Hollis. London: Frank Cass, 1999.
CTF. *Per Memoriam ad Spem (through Memory to Hope): Final Report of the Commission of Truth and Friendship, Indonesia-Timor-Leste*. Bali: Commission of Truth and Friendship, 2008.
Cummins, D. "Multiple Realities: The Need to Rethink Institutional Theory." *Local-Global: Identity, Security, Community* 11 (2012): 110–122.
——— "The Problem of Gender Quotas: Women's Representatives on Timor-Leste's Suku Councils." *Development in Practice* 21:1 (2001): 85–95.
Cummins, D. and M. Leach. "Democracy Old and New: The Interaction of Modern and Traditional Authority in East Timorese Local Government." *Asian Politics & Policy* 4:1 (2012): 89–104.
Cummins, D. and V. Maia. *Community Experiences of Decentralised Development in Timor-Leste*. Dili: Asia Foundation, 2012.
da Costa Guterres, F. *Elites and Prospects of Democracy in East Timor*. PhD Thesis, Griffith University, January 2006.
da Costa Magno, J. and A. Coa. "Finding a New Path between *Lisan* and Democracy at the *Suku* Level." *Local-Global: Identity, Security, Community* 11 (2012): 166–178.
da Silva, S., and J. Teixeira. "The Unconstitutional, Irrational and Damaging Decision by President Jose Ramos Horta: A Legal Opinion on the Formation of an Unconstitutional Government in Timor-Leste." *East Timor Law Journal* 5 (2007).
Dahl, R. A. "The City in the Future of Democracy." *American Political Science Review* 61 (1967): 953–969.
——— *Democracy and Its Critics*. New Haven: Yale University Press, 1989.
——— "Further Reflections on the Elitist Theory of Democracy." *American Political Science Review* 60:2 (1966): 296–305.
Dauvergne, P. "Weak States, Strong States: A State-in-Society Perspective." In *Weak and Strong States in Asia-Pacific Societies*, edited by P. Dauvergne. St. Leonards: Allen & Unwin, 1998.
"Dawn Raids – Timor-Leste," *The Economist*, February 16, 2008.
de Jesus Soares, A. "Combating Corruption: Avoiding 'Institutional Ritualism.'" In Leach and Kingsbury, *The Politics of Timor-Leste*.
——— "For an Interim Constitution." *La'o Hamutuk Bulletin* 2:5 (2001).
——— *Speaking My Language – The Rise and Fall of Linguistic Empires*, New Internationalist Radio, July 8, 2008.
de Jesus Soares, A., and dos Reis, F. B. Letter to Peter Galbraith, Department of Political Affairs and Timor Sea, UNTAET, April 18, 2001. Accessed March 7, 2011. www.etan.org/et2001b/may/13-19/14ngo.htm.
de Maistre, J. *Against Rousseau: "On the State of Nature" and "On the Sovereignty of the People"*, translated and edited by R. A. Lebrun. Montreal: McGill-Queen's University Press, 1996.
De Sousa Santos, B. *Toward a New Legal Common Sense*. Cambridge: Cambridge University Press, 2004.
——— *The World Social Forum: A User's Manual*, 2005. Accessed February 14, 2011. www.ces.uc.pt/bss/documentos/fsm_eng.pdf.
De Sousa, N., C. Belo, and M. R. Koenig. *Institutionalizing Community Policing in Timor-Leste: Exploring the Politics of Police Reform*. Dili: Asia Foundation, 2011.

Deegan, H. "A Critical Examination of the Democratic Transition in South Africa: The Question of Public Participation." *Commonwealth and Comparative Politics* 40:1 (2002): 43–60.
Deleuze, G. and F. Guattari. *Anti-Oedipus: Capitalism and Schizophrenia*. Minneapolis: University of Minnesota Press, 1983.
Della-Giacoma, J. "Ensuring the Well-being of a Nation: Developing a Democratic Culture through Constitution Making in East Timor." Paper presented at the Fletcher Conference on Innovative Approaches, Boston, 1 April 2005.
  "Results Over Process, Analysis of the Creation of the East Timor Constituent Assembly." Unpublished paper, undated.
Delli Carpini, M. X., et al. "Public Deliberation, Discursive Participation, and Citizen Engagement: A Review of the Empirical Literature." *American Review of Political Science* 7 (2004): 315–344.
Denoon, D. *Getting under the Skin: The Bougainville Copper Agreement and the Creation of the Panguna Mine*. Melbourne: Melbourne University Press, 2000.
Deutsch, K. W., and W. Foltz, editors. *Nation-Building*. New York: Atherton Press, 1966.
Deveaux, M. "Agonism and Pluralism." *Philosophy and Social Criticism* 25:4 (1999): 1–22.
  Cultural Pluralism and Dilemmas of Justice. Ithaca: Cornell University Press, 2000.
Diamond, L. J. "Lessons from Iraq." *Journal of Democracy* 16:1 (2005): 9–23.
Dinnen, S. *The Twin Processes of Nation-Building and State-Building, State, Society and Governance in Melanesia Briefing Note, No. 1/2007*. Canberra: Australian National University, 2007.
Dinnen, S., and A. Ley, editors. *Reflections on Violence in Melanesia*. Canberra: Asia Pacific Press, 2000
Dinnen S., and G. Peake. "More Than Just Policing: Police Reform in Post-Conflict Bougainville." *International Peacekeeping* (2013). Accessed November 20, 2013, DOI: 10.1080/13533312.2013.853961
DNE. *Timor-Leste in Figures, 2008*. Dili: Direcção Nacional de Estatistica, Government of Timor-Leste, 2009.
  Timor-Leste in Figures 2012. Dili: Direcção Geral de Estatística, Government of Timor-Leste, 2012.
do Santos, S. *Timor-Leste National Alliance for an International Tribunal Letter to UNSG, 14 August 2012*. Accessed October 15, 2013. easttimorlegal.blogspot.com.au/2012/08/timor-leste-national-alliance-for.html.
Dodd, M. "FRETILIN Accused of Threatening Poll Tactics," *Sydney Morning Herald*, 24 August 2001.
dos Santos A. B. and E. da Silva. "Introduction of a Modern Democratic System and Its Impact on Societies in East Timorese Traditional Culture." *Local-Global: Identity, Security, Community* 11 (2012): 206–220.
Downer, A. *The Bougainville Crisis: An Australian Perspective*. Canberra: Commonwealth of Australia, 2001.
Doyle, M. "Three Pillars of the Liberal Peace," *American Political Science Review* 99:3 (2005): 463–466.
Duffield, M. *Development, Security and Unending War*. London: Polity, 2007.
Dunn, J. *Crimes against Humanity in East Timor, January to October 1999: Their Nature and Causes*. Dili: UNTAET, 14 February 2001.

East Timor: A Rough Passage to Independence. Double Bay: Longueville Books, 2003.
Dryzek, J. S. *Discursive Democracy: Politics, Policy, and Political Science.* New York: Cambridge University Press, 1990.
Dryzek, J. S., B. Honig, and A. Phillips, editors. *The Oxford Handbook of Political Theory.* Oxford: Oxford University Press, 2006
Dyzenhaus, D. "The Politics of the Question of Constituent Power." In Loughlin and Walker, *The Paradox of Constitutionalism.*
East Timor International Support Center. *A Gradual Path to full Sovereignty in East Timor.* Dili: East Timor International Support Center, 2001.
"East Timor Leader Says FRETILIN Confident of Winning Presidential [sic] Election," *Xinhua News Agency,* June 26, 2001.
"East Timor Swears in Larger Cabinet, Critics Angry," *Agence France Presse,* August 8, 2012.
"East Timorese Constituent Assembly to Become First National Parliament," *Associated Press Newswires,* January 13, 2002.
"East Timorese Fifth Government: An Oligarchy," *Tempo Semanal,* August 6, 2012.
Easterly, W. and R. Levine. "Africa's Growth Tragedy: Policies and Ethnic Divisions." *Quarterly Journal of Economics* 112:4 (1997): 1203–1250.
Eckersley, R. "From Cosmopolitan Nationalism to Cosmopolitan Democracy." *Review of International Studies* 33 (2007): 675–692.
Elazar, D. J. "Constitution-Making: The Pre-eminently Political Act." In Banting and Simeon, *Redesigning the State.*
"Elections in Bougainville and Solomon Islands," State, Society and Governance in Melanesia Conference, *Australian National University,* November 3, 2010.
Elkins, Z., T. Ginsburg, and J. Melton. *The Endurance of National Constitutions.* New York: Cambridge University Press, 2009.
Elster, J. "Clearing and Strengthening the Channels of Constitution Making." In Ginsburg, *Comparative Constitutional Design.*
  "Constitution-Making in Eastern Europe: Rebuilding the Boat in the Open Sea." *Public Administration* 71:1–2 (1993): 169–217.
  "Deliberation and Constitution-Making." In Elster, *Deliberative Democracy.*
  "Forces and Mechanisms in the Constitution-Making Process." *Duke Law Journal* 45:2 (1995): 364–396.
  "Introduction." In Elster, *Deliberative Democracy.*
  "Legislatures as Constituent Assemblies." In Bauman and Kahana, *The Least Examined Branch.*
  "The Optimal Design of a Constituent Assembly." In *Collective Wisdom: Principles and Mechanisms,* edited by H. Landemore and J. Elster. New York: Cambridge University Press, 2012.
  "Ways of Constitution-Making." In Hadenius, *Democracy's Victory and Crisis.*
Elster, J., editor. *Deliberative Democracy.* Cambridge: Cambridge University Press, 1998.
Elster, J., C. Offe, and U. K. Preuss. *Institutional Design in Post-communist Societies: Rebuilding the Ship at Sea.* Cambridge: Cambridge University Press, 1998.
EU. *EU Election Observer Mission, Presidential Elections 9 April 2007, Preliminary Statement.* Dili: Delegation of the European Union to East Timor, April 11, 2007.

Euben, R. *Enemy in the Mirror: Islamic Fundamentalism and the Limits of Modern Rationalism.* Princeton: Princeton University Press, 1999.
Everett, S. and B. Ragragio. *Decentralisation in Timor-Leste: What's at Stake?* Dili: Asia Foundation, 2009.
Eyben, R. and S. Ladbury. *Building Effective States: Taking a Citizen's Perspective.* Brighton: Centre for Citizenship, Participation and Accountability, 2006.
Fearon, J. D. "Deliberation as Discussion." In Elster, *Deliberative Democracy.*
Fearon, J. D. and D. Laitin. "Violence and the Social Construction of Ethnic Identity." *International Organization* 54:4 (2000): 845–877.
Federer, J. *The UN in East Timor: Building Timor Leste, a Fragile State.* Darwin: Charles Darwin University Press, 2005.
Feijó, R. G. "Semi-Presidentialism and the Consolidation of Democracy." In Leach and Kingsbury, *The Politics of Timor-Leste.*
Field, A. "Acknowledging the Past, Shaping the Future: How the Churches and Other Religious Communities Are Contributing to Timor-Leste's Development." In Mearns, *Democratic Governance in Timor-Leste.*
Finnroad. *Papua New Guinea – Australia Transport Sector Support Program (TSSP) Supported by the Australian Government – AusAID: Socio-Economic Study – TSSP Provinces, Baseline Report.* Helsinki: Finnroad, 2008.
The Socio Economic Impact of AusAID Funded Road Maintenance and Rehabilitation of National Priority Roads in Ten Provinces of Papua New Guinea 2010. Helsinki: Finnroad, 2010.
Fishkin, J. S. "Deliberative Democracy and Constitutions." In *What Should Constitutions Do?*, edited by E. Frankel Paul, F. D. Miller, and J. Pail. New York: Cambridge University Press, 2011.
Fishkin, J. and C. Farrar. "Deliberative Polling: From Experiment to Community Resource." In *The Deliberative Democracy Handbook: Strategies for Effective Civic Engagement in the Twenty-First Century*, edited by J. Gastil and P. Levine. San Francisco: Jossey-Bass, 2005.
Fitzpatrick, D. "Land Claims in East Timor: A Preliminary Assessment." *Australian Journal of Asian Law* 3:2 (2001): 135–166.
Fleiner, T., et al. "Federalism, Decentralisation and Conflict Management in Multicultural Societies." In Blindenbacher and Koller, *Federalism in a Changing World.*
Forbes, M. "Timor's Agony," *Sydney Morning Herald,* 27 May 2006.
Forsyth, M. "Hobbe's Contractarianism: A Comparative Analysis." In *The Social Contract from Hobbes to Rawls*, edited by D. Boucher and P. Kelly. London: Routledge, 1994.
"Forum: East Timor's Jose Ramos Horta," *BBC News,* 12 June 2002.
Foster, R. J., editor. *Nation Making: Emergent Identities in Postcolonial Melanesia.* Ann Arbor: University of Michigan Press, 1995.
Fox, J. J. "Repaying the Debt to Mau Kiak: Reflections on Timor's Cultural Traditions and the Obligations of Citizenship in an Independent East Timor." In Mearns, *Democratic Governance in Timor-Leste.*
Fraenkel, J. and B. Grofman. "Introduction – Political Culture, Representation and Electoral Systems in the Pacific Islands." *Commonwealth & Comparative Politics* 43:3 (2005): 261–275.

Fragility Assessment Team. *Fragility Assessment in Timor-Leste: Summary Report*. Dili: Ministry of Finance, 2013.
Franck, T. M. "The Emerging Right to Democratic Governance." *The American Journal of International Law* 86 (1992): 46–91.
Franck, T. M. and A. K. Thiruvengadam. "Norms of International Law Relating to the Constitution-Making Process." In Miller, *Framing the State*.
Franklin, D. P. and M. J. Baun. "Introduction: Political Culture and Constitutionalism." In *Political Culture and Constitutionalism: A Comparative Approach*, edited by D. P. Franklin and M. J. Baun. New York: M.E. Sharpe, 1995.
FRETILIN, Frente Revolucionaria Do Timor-Leste Independente (FRETILIN): Projecto De Constituição (Draft Constitution), adopted at the Extraordinary National Conference of FRETILIN. Sydney: FRETILIN, 14–20 August 1998.
Friedlander, J. "Why Do the People of Bougainville Look Unique? Some Conclusions from Biological Anthropology and Genetics." In Regan and Griffin, *Bougainville: Before the Conflict*.
Fry, W. "Timor's Road Still Rocky Despite Peaceful Poll," *Crikey*, 20 August 2012.
Fukuyama, F. *Governance Reform in Papua New Guinea*. September 2007. Accessed January 24, 2009. www.sais-jhu.edu/faculty/fukuyama/publications.html.
Fulu, E., et al. *Why Do Some Men Use Violence against Women and How Can We Prevent it?* Bangkok: UNDP, UNFPA, UN Women and UNV, 2013.
Galbraith, P. Paper at the "Conference on Reconstructing East Timor: Analysis of the Past and Perspectives for the Future," Tibar, May 29, 2000.
  The Shape of Things to Come: Thoughts on the Post-Election Government of East Timor. Unpublished paper, June 7, 2001.
Galston, W. *Liberal Pluralism: The Implications of Value Pluralism for Political Theory and Practice*. Cambridge: Cambridge University Press, 2002.
Galtung, J. "Cultural Violence." *Journal of Peace Research* 27:3 (1990): 291–305.
Gambetta, D. "'Claro!': An Essay on Deliberative Machismo." In Elster, *Deliberative Democracy*.
Garlicki, L. and Z. A. Garlicka. "Constitution Making, Peace Building, and National Reconciliation: The Experience of Poland." In Miller, *Framing the State*.
Garrison, R. *The Role of Constitution-Building Processes in Democratisation: Case Study, East Timor*. Stockholm: International IDEA, 2005.
Gaventa, J. "Towards Participatory Governance: Assessing the Transformative Possibilities." In Hickey and Mohan, *Participation: From Tyranny to Transformation?*
Gavison, R. "Legislatures and the Phases and Components of Constitutionalism." In Bauman and Kahana, *The Least Examined Branch*.
Geertz, C. *The Interpretation of Cultures*. London: Fontana, 1973.
Gellner, E. *Nations and Nationalism*. Oxford: Basil Blackwell, 1983.
Ghai, Y. P. *The Role of Constituent Assemblies in Constitution Making, Institute for Democracy and Electoral Assistance Research Paper*. Unpublished paper, 2006.
Ghai, Y. and A. J. Regan. "Bougainville and the Dialectics of Ethnicity, Autonomy and Separation." In *Autonomy and Ethnicity: Negotiating Competing Claims in Multi-ethnic States*, edited by Y. Ghai. Cambridge: Cambridge University Press, 2000.
  "Unitary State, Devolution, Autonomy, Secession: State Building and Nation Building in Bougainville, Papua New Guinea." *The Round Table* 95:386 (2006): 589–608.

Ghai, Y. and G. Galli. *Constitution Building Processes and Democratization*. Stockholm: International Institute for Democracy and Electoral Assistance, 2006.

Giddens, A. *The Nation-State and Violence*. Cambridge: Polity Press, 1985.

Ginsburg, T., editor. *Comparative Constitutional Design*. New York: Cambridge University Press, 2012.

Ginsburg, T. and R. Dixon, editors. *Comparative Constitutional Law*. Cheltenham: Edward Elgar, 2011.

Ginsburg, T., S. Chernykh, and Z. Elkins. "Commitment and Diffusion: How and Why National Constitution Incorporate International Law." *University of Illinois Law Review* (2008): 201–237.

Ginsburg, T., Z. Elkins, and J. Blount. "Does the Process of Constitution Making Matter?" *Annual Review of Law and Social Science*, 5 (2009): 201–223.

Gloppen, S. *South Africa: The Battle over the Constitution*. Brookfield: Ashgate, 1997.

Go, J. "A Globalizing Constitutionalism? Views from the Postcolony, 1945–2000." In Arjomand, *Constitutionalism and Political Reconstruction*.

Goddard, M. "Three Urban Village Courts in Papua New Guinea: Comparative Observations on Dispute Settlement." In Dinnen and Ley, *Reflections on Violence in Melanesia*.

Goldstone, A. "UNTAET with Hindsight: The Peculiarities of Politics in an Incomplete State." *Global Governance* 10:1 (2004): 83–98.

Gomez, B., editor. *2006 Papua New Guinea Yearbook*. Noumea: The National & Cassowary Books, 2006.

Gordon, R. "Growing Constitutions." *University of Pennsylvania Journal of Constitutional Law* 1:3 (1999): 528–582.

"Government Agrees on Gazettal of Peace Deals," *Papua New Guinea Post-Courier*, November 14, 2001.

"Governor Announces New Bougainville Constituent Assembly," *Papua New Guinea Post-Courier*, January 10, 2002.

Graydon, C. "Local Justice Systems in Timor-Leste: Washed Up, or Watch This Space?" *Development Bulletin*, 68 (2005): 66–70.

Grenfell, D. "Governance, Violence and Crises in Timor-Leste: *Estadu Seidauk Mai*." In Mearns, *Democratic Governance in Timor-Leste*.

Reconstituting the Nation: Reconciliation and National Consciousness in Timor-Leste. Melbourne: RMIT Publishing, 2006.

Grenfell, L. "Legal Pluralism and the Rule of Law in Timor Leste." *Leiden Journal of International Law* 19 (2006): 305–337.

"Promoting the Rule of Law in Timor-Leste." *Conflict, Security & Development* 9:2 (2009): 213–238.

Griffin, H. M. and A. J. Regan. "Introduction." In Regan and Griffin, *Bougainville: Before the Conflict*.

Griffin, J. "Movements towards Secession 1964–76." In Regan and Griffin, *Bougainville: Before the Conflict*.

Griffin, J., et al. *Papua New Guinea: A Political History*. Richmond: Heinemann Educational Australia, 1979.

Griffin J. and M. Togolo. "North Solomons Province, 1974–1990." In *Political Decentralisation in a New State: The Experience of Provincial Government in Papua New Guinea*, edited by R. J. May and A. J. Regan. Bathurst: Crawford House Press, 1997.

Griffiths, J. "What Is Legal Pluralism?" *Journal of Legal Pluralism and Unofficial Law* 24 (1986): 1–55.
Grigg, A. "Keeping the Peace in East Timor," *Australian Financial Review*, 21 May 2011.
Grosby, S. "Religion and Nationality in Antiquity." *European Journal of Sociology* 32:2 (1991): 229–265.
Gurr, T. R. "Peoples against States: Ethnopolitical Conflict and the Changing World System." *International Studies Quarterly* 38 (1994): 347–377.
"Gusmão to be Timor-Leste's new PM," *Timor Post*, August 7, 2007.
Gusmão, X. *Timor Lives! Speeches of Freedom and Independence.* Alexandria: Longueville Media, 2005.
  To Resist Is to Win! The Autobiography of Xanana Gusmão, edited by S. Niner. Richmond: Aurora Books, 2000.
Guterres, J. C. "Timor-Leste: A Year of Democratic Elections." *Southeast Asian Affairs* (2008): 359–372.
Gutierrez, A. *Proposed UNTAET Regulation.* Presented to the National Council in January 2001.
Gutmann, A. and D. Thompson. *Democracy and Disagreement.* Cambridge, MA: Belknap Press of Harvard University Press, 1996.
Habermas, J. *Between Facts and Norms: Contributions to a Discourse Theory of Law and Democracy*, translated by W. Rehg. Cambridge: MIT Press, 1996.
  "The European Nation State: On the Past and Future of Sovereignty and Citizenship." In *The Inclusion of the Other: Studies in Political Theory*, edited by C. Cronin and P. De Greiff. Cambridge: Polity Press, 1999.
  The New Conservatism: Cultural Criticism and the Historians' Debate, edited and translated by S. Weber Nicholsen. Cambridge: MIT Press, 1989.
  The Structural Transformation of the Public Sphere. Cambridge: MIT Press, 1989.
Hadenius, A., editor. *Democracy's Victory and Crisis: Nobel Symposium No. 93.* Cambridge: Cambridge University Press, 1997.
Hamber, B. and G. Kelly. *A Working Definition of Reconciliation.* Belfast: Democratic Dialogue, 2004.
Hardie, M. "Timor-Leste, the 5th Constitutional Governance and the "Good Governance" Template," *Crikey*, August 12, 2012.
Harper, E. *Re-constructing a Legal System in East Timor: Challenges to Introducing International Legal Norms and Principles into Post-Conflict States under UN Administration.* PhD Thesis, University of Melbourne, Faculty of Law, 2007.
Hart, V. "Constitution Making and the Right to Take Part in a Public Affair." In Miller, *Framing the State.*
  "Constitution-Making and the Transformation of Conflict." *Peace & Change* 26:2 (2001): 153–176.
  Democratic Constitution Making, U.S. Institute of Peace Special Report 107. Washington: U.S. Institute of Peace, 2003.
Hart, V. and S. C. Stimson. "Introduction." In *Writing a National Identity: Political, Economic, and Cultural Perspectives on the Written Constitution*, edited by V. Hart and S. C. Stimson. Manchester: Manchester University Press, 1993.

Hassall, G. and C. Saunders. *Asia-Pacific Constitutional Systems*. Cambridge: Cambridge University Press, 2002.

Hastings, A. *The Construction of Nationhood: Ethnicity, Religion and Nationalism*. Cambridge: Cambridge University Press, 1997.

Hatchard, J., M. Ndulo, and P. Slinn. *Comparative Constitutionalism and Good Governance in the Commonwealth: An Eastern and Southern African Perspective*. Cambridge: Cambridge University Press, 2004.

Hatchard, J. and P. Slinn. "The Path towards a New Order in South Africa." *International Relations* 12:4 (1995): 1–26.

Hau'ofa, E. "The New South Pacific Society: Integration and Independence." In *Class and Culture in the South Pacific*, edited by A. Hooper et al. Auckland and Suva: University of Auckland and University of the South Pacific, 1987.

Havini, M. "A Bougainvillean Perspective on the Crisis." In Spriggs and Denoon, *The Bougainville Crisis: 1991 Update*.

"Perspectives on a Crisis," In Polomka, *Bougainville: Perspectives on a Crisis*.

Havini, M. T. *A Compilation of Human Rights Abuses against the People of Bougainville 1989–1995, Vol. 1*. Sydney: Bougainville Freedom Movement, 1995.

A Compilation of Human Rights Abuses against the People of Bougainville 1989–1996, Vol. 2. Sydney: Bougainville Freedom Movement, 1996.

"Women in Community During the Blockade." In Sirivi and Havini, *...As Mothers of the Land*.

"The Women's Voices at Burnham: Burnham I Negotiations, 5–18 July 1997." In Sirivi and Havini, *...As Mothers of the Land*.

Haysom, N. R. L. "Constitution Making and Nation Building." In Blindenbacher and Koller, *Federalism in a Changing World*.

Heathershaw, J. "Towards Better Theories of Peacebuilding: Beyond the Liberal Peace Debate." *Peacebuilding* 1:2 (2013): 275–282.

Hechter, M. *Internal Colonialism: The Celtic Fringe in British National Development, 1536–1966*. London: Routledge and Kegan Paul, 1975.

Hegarty, D. "Governance at the Local Level in Melanesia – Absent the State." *Commonwealth Journal of Local Governance* 3 (2009): 1–19.

Hermkens, A. "Mary, Motherhood, and Nation: Religion and Gender Ideology in Bougainville's Secessionist Warfare." *Intersections: Gender and Sexuality in Asia and the Pacific*, 25 (2011).

"Religion in War and Peace." *Culture and Religion* 8:3 (2007): 271–289.

Hessbruegge, J. and C. F. Ochoa Garcia. "Mayan Law in Post-Conflict Guatemala." In Isser, *Customary Justice and the Rule of Law in War-Torn Societies*.

Hickey, S. and G. Mohan, editors. *Participation: From Tyranny to Transformation?* London: Zed Books, 2004

"Towards Participation as Transformation: Critical Themes and Challenges." In Hickey and Mohan, *Participation: From Tyranny to Transformation?*

Hicks, D. "*Adat* and the Nation-State: Opposition and Synthesis in Two Political Cultures." In Leach and Kingsbury, *The Politics of Timor-Leste*.

"Unachieved Syncretism: The Local-level Political System in Portuguese Timor, 1966–1967." *Anthropos* 78 (1983): 2–40.

Higgins, R. *Problems and Process: International Law and How We Use It*. Oxford: Clarendon Press, 1994.

High Level Panel on Threats, Challenges and Change. *Report of the Secretary-General's High Level Panel on Threats, Challenges and Change*, UN Doc. A/59/565, December 1, 2004.

Hill, H. *Stirrings of Nationalism in East Timor: FRETILIN 1974–1978*. Otford: Otford Press, 2002).

Hirst, M. *An Unfinished Truth: An Analysis of the Commission for Truth and Friendship's Final Report on the 1999 Atrocities in East Timor*. New York: International Center for Transitional Justice, 2009.

Hobsbawm, E. and T. Ranger, editors. *The Invention of Tradition*. Cambridge: Cambridge University Press, 1983.

Hohe, T. "The Clash of Paradigms: International Administration and Local Political Legitimacy in East Timor." *Contemporary Southeast Asia* 24:3 (2002): 569–589.

―――. "Local Governance After Conflict: Community Empowerment in East Timor." *Journal of Peacebuilding & Development* 1:2 (2004): 45–56.

―――. "Totem Polls: Indigenous Concepts and 'Free and Fair' Elections in East Timor." *International Peacekeeping* 9:4 (2002): 69–88.

Hohe, T. and R. Nixon. *Reconciling Justice: "Traditional" Law and State Judiciary in East Timor*. Dili: U.S. Institute of Peace, 2003.

Honig, B. *Democracy and the Foreigner*. Princeton: Princeton University Press, 2001.

―――. *Political Theory and the Displacement of Politics*. Ithaca: Cornell University Press, 1993.

Horowitz, D. "Conciliatory Institutions and Constitutional Processes in Post-Conflict States." *William and Mary Law Review* 49:4 (2008): 1213–1248.

―――. *Ethnic Groups in Conflict*. Berkeley: University of California Press, 1985.

Howard, A. E. D., editor. *Constitution Making in Eastern Europe*. Washington: Woodrow Wilson Centre Press, 1993.

Howard, M. "Ethnic Conflict and International Security." In *Nationalism: Critical Concepts in Political Science, Vol. V.*, edited by J. Hutchinson and A. D. Smith. London: Routledge, 2000.

Howley, P. *Breaking Spears and Mending Hearts: Peacemakers and Restorative Justice in Bougainville*. London: Zed Books, 2002.

Hriehwazi, Y. "Paper Gives Details of Bougainville Constitution," *The National*, 31 August 2001.

HRW. *East Timor: New Law Aims to Stifle Political Dissent, Press Release*. London: Human Rights Watch, 29 December 2004.

―――. *Tortured Beginnings: Police Violence and the Beginning of Impunity in East Timor*. New York: Human Rights Watch, 2006.

Hunt, J. "Building a New Society: NGOs in East Timor." *New Community Quarterly* 2:1 (2004).

Hunter, K. *From Timor-Leste: Citizens Finally Able to Read Laws in Own Language*. Dili: Asia Foundation, 2008.

Huntington, S. P. *Political Order in Changing Societies*. New Haven: Yale University Press, 1968.

Hurd, I. "Legitimacy and Authority in International Relations." *International Organization* 53:2 (1999): 379–408.

Hutchinson, J. *Modern Nationalism*. London: Fontana, 1994.

Hyden, G. and D. Venter. *Constitution-Making and Democratization in Africa*. Pretoria: Institute of South Africa, 2001.

ICG. *Handing Back Responsibility to Timor-Leste's Police*, Asia Report No. 180. Dili: International Crisis Group, 2009.
  Resolving Timor-Leste's Crisis, Asia Report No. 120. Dili: International Crisis Group, 2006.
  Timor-Leste: No Time for Complacency, Asia Briefing No. 87. Dili and Brussels: International Crisis Group, 2009.
  Timor-Leste: Reconciliation and Return from Indonesia, Asia Briefing No. 122. Dili: International Crisis Group, 2011.
  Timor-Leste: Stability at What Cost? Asia Report No. 246. Brussels: International Crisis Group, 2013.
ICISS. *The Responsibility to Protect: Report of the International Commission on Intervention and State Sovereignty*. Ottawa: International Development Research Centre, 2001.
ICJ. *Commentary on the Draft Constitution Proposed for East Timor by the Constituent Assembly*. Dili: Australian Section, International Commission of Jurists, undated.
IDEA. *Constitution Building after Conflict: External Support to a Sovereign Process*. Stockholm: International Institute for Democracy and Electoral Assistance, 2011.
IFC. *Interim Strategy Note for the Democratic Republic of Timor-Leste FY 2010–2011*. Dili: Timor-Leste Country Management Unit, East Asia and Pacific Region, International Finance Corporation, 2009.
IMF. *Republic of Timor-Leste: Staff Report for the 2009 Article IV Consultation*. Dili: International Monetary Fund, 2009.
Inbal, A. B. and H. Lerner. "Constitutional Design, Identity, and Legitimacy in Post-Conflict Reconstruction." In *Governance in Post-Conflict Societies: Rebuilding Fragile States*, edited by D. W. Brinkerhoff. London: Routledge, 2007.
Independent Comprehensive Needs Assessment Team. *The Justice System of Timor-Leste: An Independent Comprehensive Needs Assessment*. Dili: Independent Comprehensive Needs Assessment Team, 2009.
Independent Electoral Commission. *Statement of Reasons in Relation to Decision Number 2001-79 of 9 September 2001*. Dili: Independent Electoral Commission, September 9, 2001.
Independent Evaluation Group. *Evaluation of the World Bank Group Program, Timor-Leste Country Program Evaluation, 2000–2010*. Washington: The World Bank, 2011.
IRI. *National Opinion Poll: East Timor, November 2003*. Dili: International Republican Institute, 2003.
Irving, H. "Drafting, Design, and Gender." In Ginsburg and Dixon, *Comparative Constitutional Law*.
Isser, D. H., editor. *Customary Justice and the Rule of Law in War-Torn Societies*. Washington: U.S. Institute of Peace, 2011.
  "Shifting Assumptions from Abstract Ideals to Messy Realities." In Isser, *Customary Justice and the Rule of Law in War-Torn Societies*.
Jackson, P. "Reshuffling an Old Deck of Cards? The Politics of Local Government Reform in Sierra Leone." *African Affairs* 106:422 (2006): 95–111.
Jackson, R. *Quasi-States: Sovereignty, International Relations, and the Third World*. Cambridge: Cambridge University Press, 1990.
  Sovereignty: Evolution of an Idea. Cambridge: Polity Press, 2007.

Jackson, V. C. "What's in a Name? Reflections on Timing, Naming, and Constitution-Making." *William and Mary Law Review* 49:4 (2008): 1249–1305.

Jacobsohn, G. *Constitutional Identity*, Cambridge: Harvard University Press, 2010.

"Constitutional Values and Principles." In Rosenfeld and Sajó, *The Oxford Handbook of Comparative Constitutional Law*.

"The Formation of Constitutional Identities." In Ginsburg and Dixon, *Comparative Constitutional Law*.

James, M. R. *Deliberative Democracy and the Plural Polity*. Lawrence: University of Kansas, 2004.

Jennings, I. *The Approach to Self-Government*. Cambridge: Cambridge University Press, 1956.

Joint Bougainville Assemblies. *Implementing the Bougainville Peace Agreement: Briefing Paper for Joint Assemblies Meeting*. Arawa: Joint Bougainville Assemblies, August 31, 2001.

Jolly, M. and N. Thomas, editors. *Oceania Special Issue: The Politics of Tradition in the Pacific* 62 (1992).

Johnson, J. "Arguing for Deliberation: Some Skeptical Considerations." In Elster, *Deliberative Democracy*.

JSMP. *Draft Law 29/I/3A, Freedom of Assembly and Demonstration*. Dili: Judicial System Monitoring Programme, 2004.

The Impact of the Language Directive on the Courts in East Timor. Dili: Judicial System Monitoring Programme, 2004.

Judge Applies Customary Law in a Criminal Case, Press Release. Dili: Judicial System Monitoring Programme, May 19, 2005.

Key Themes in Legal Development: A JSMP Retrospective, 27 April 2001 – 27 April 2008. Dili: Judicial System Monitoring Programme, 2008.

Legitimacy of the Court's Decision in the Case Relating to the Economic Stabilisation Fund. Dili: Judicial System Monitoring Programme, 2009.

Overview of the Justice Sector: March 2005. Dili: Judicial System Monitoring Programme, 2005.

Overview of the Justice Sector 2006–2007. Dili: Judicial System Monitoring Programme, 2007.

Overview of the Justice Sector in Timor-Leste 2009. Dili: Judicial System Monitoring Programme, 2009.

The Role, Practices and Procedure of the Court of Appeal. Dili: Judicial System Monitoring Programme, 2005.

Unfulfilled Expectations: Community Views on Constituent Assembly's Community Reconciliation Process. Dili: Judicial System Monitoring Programme, 2004.

"Kabui Breached Law: Rabanz," *Papua New Guinea Post-Courier*, 24 May 2007.

Kabui, J. C. *Making a Constitution for the Autonomous Region of Bougainville: Brief to the Bougainville Joint Assemblies Meeting, Buka, 2nd to 4th April 2003*. Arawa and Buka: Bougainville Constitutional Commission, 2 April 2003.

"Peacebuilding & Consolidation." In Carl and Garasu, *Weaving Consensus*.

Kammen, D. "Master-Slave, Traitor-Nationalist, Opportunist-Oppressed: Political Metaphors in East Timor." *Indonesia* 76 (2003): 69–85.

Kedourie, E. *Nationalism*. London: Hutchinson, 1960.

Keesing R. M. and R. Tonkinson, editors. *Mankind Special Issue, Reinventing Traditional Culture: The Politics of Kastom in Island Melanesia* 13:4 (1982).
Kelly, N. *Electoral Democracy in Post-Conflict Melanesia: The 2010 Bougainville and Solomon Island Elections, Centre for Democratic Institutions Policy Paper on Political Governance 2010/20*. Canberra: Australian National University, 2010.
King, D. Y. "East Timor's Founding Elections and Emerging Party System." *Asian Survey* 43:5 (2003): 745–757.
Kingsbury, D. "The Constitution: Clarity without Convention." In Leach and Kingsbury, *The Politics of Timor-Leste*.
  "East Timor's Political Crisis: Origins and Resolution." In Mearns, *Democratic Governance in Timor-Leste*.
  East Timor: The Price of Liberty. New York: Palgrave MacMillan, 2009.
  "National Identity in Timor-Leste: Challenges and Opportunities." *South East Asia Research* 18:1 (2010): 133–159.
  "Political Development." In Kingsbury and Leach, *East Timor: Beyond Independence*.
Kingsbury, D. and M. Leach, editors. *East Timor: Beyond Independence*. Clayton: Monash University Press, 2007
  "Introduction." In Kingsbury and Leach, *East Timor: Beyond Independence*.
Kissane, B. and N. Sitter. "National Identity and Constitutionalism in Europe: Introduction." *Nations and Nationalism* 16:1 (2010): 1–5.
Klein, C. and A. Sajó. "Constitution-Making: Process and Substance." In Rosenfeld and Sajó, *The Oxford Handbook of Comparative Constitutional Law*.
Kohen, A. "The Catholic Church and the Independence of East Timor." In Tanter, Selden, and Shalom, *Bitter Flowers, Sweet Flowers*.
Kornblith, M. "The Politics of Constitution-Making: Constitutions and Democracy in Venezuela." *Journal of Latin American Studies* 23:1 (1991): 61–89.
Kreimer, S.F. "Invidious cComparisons: Some Cautionary Remarks on the Process of Constitutional Borrowing." *University of Pennsylvania Journal of Constitutional Law* 1 (1999): 640–650.
Kritz, N. "Constitution-Making Process: Lessons for Iraq," testimony before a joint hearing of the Senate Committee on the Judiciary, Subcommittee on the Constitution, Civil Rights, and Property Rights, and the Senate Committee on Foreign Relations, *Subcommittee on Near Eastern and South Asian Affairs*, June 25, 2003.
Kucinich, D. J., et al. *Letter to Mr. Francisco "Lú-olo" Guterres, Speaker, Constituent Assembly*, Dili, January 10, 2002. Accessed February 25, 2011. members.pcug.org.au/~wildwood/02jancongress.htm.
Kyed, H. M. and L. Buur. *Recognition and Democratisation: "New Roles" for Traditional Leaders in Sub-Saharan Africa, Working Paper 2006/11*. Copenhagen: Danish Institute for International Studies, 2006.
Kymlicka, W. *Multicultural Citizenship: A Liberal Theory of Minority Rights*. Oxford: Oxford University Press, 1995.
Laffey, M. and S. Nadarajah. "The Hybridity of Liberal Peace: States, Diasporas and Insecurity." *Security Dialogue* 43:5 (2012): 403–420.
Landau, D. "Constitution-Making Gone Wrong." *Alabama Law Review*, forthcoming.
  "The Importance of Constitution-Making." *Denver University Law Review* 89:3 (2012): 611–633.

La'o Hamutuk. *Democracy in Timor-Leste: Information Is Required!* Dili: La'o Hamutuk, 2009.

Laracy, H. "'Imperium in Imperio?' The Catholic Church in Bougainville." In Regan and Griffin, *Bougainville: Before the Conflict*.

Larke, B. "'...And the Truth Shall Set You Free': Confessional Trade-Offs and Community Reconciliation in East Timor." *Asian Journal of Social Science* 37 (2009): 646–676.

Larmour, P. *Foreign Flowers: Institutional Transfer and Good Governance in the Pacific Islands*. Honolulu: University of Hawai'i Press, 2005.

"Political institutions." In *Tides of History: The Pacific Islands in the Twentieth Century*, edited by K. R. Howe et al. Honolulu: University of Hawaii Press, 1994.

Law & Justice Sector Secretariat. *Law and Justice Sector: Annual Performance Report 2006*. Port Moresby: Law & Justice Sector Secretariat, 2007.

Law and Justice Sector: Annual Performance Report 2007. Port Moresby: Law & Justice Sector Secretariat, 2008.

Lawson, S. *Tradition Versus Democracy in the South Pacific: Fiji, Tonga and Western Samoa*. Cambridge: Cambridge University Press, 1996.

Leach, M. "The 2007 Presidential and Parliamentary Elections in Timor-Leste." *Australian Journal of Politics and History* 55:2 (2009): 219–232.

"History on the Line: East Timorese History after Independence." *History Workshop Journal* 61:1 (2006): 223–237.

"History Teaching: Challenges and Alternatives." In Kingsbury and Leach, *East Timor: Beyond Independence*.

"Surveying East Timorese Tertiary Student Attitudes to National Identity: 2002–2007." *South East Asia Research* 16:3 (2008): 405–431.

"Talking Portuguese: China and East Timor." *Arena Magazine*, December 2007.

"Valorising the Resistance: National Identity and Collective Memory in East Timor's Constitution." *Social Alternatives* 21:3 (2002): 43–47.

Leach, M. and D. Kingsbury. "Introduction: East Timorese Politics in Transition." In Leach and Kingsbury, *The Politics of Timor-Leste*.

editors. *The Politics of Timor-Leste: Democratic Consolidation after Intervention*. Ithaca: Cornell University Press, 2013.

"Leadership Fails to Turn Up," *Papua New Guinea Post-Courier*, 2 May 2005.

Lederach, J. P. *Building Peace: Sustainable Reconciliation in Divided Societies*. Washington: U.S. Institute of Peace Press, 1997.

Lemay-Hébert, N. "Statebuilding without Nation-Building? Legitimacy, State Failure, and the Limits of the Institutionalist Approach." *Journal of Intervention and Statebuilding* 3:1 (2009): 21–45.

Lerner, H. *Making Constitutions in Deeply Divided Societies*. Cambridge: Cambridge University Press, 2011.

Lessnoff, M. "Introduction: Social Contract." In *Social Contract Theory*, edited by M. Lessnoff. Oxford: Basil Blackwell Ltd, 1990.

Lidén, K., R. Mac Ginty, and O. P. Richmond. "Introduction: Beyond Northern Epistemologies of Peace: Peacebuilding Reconstructed?" *International Peacekeeping* 16:5 (2009): 587–598.

Lijphart, A. *Thinking About Democracy: Power Sharing and Majority Rule in Theory and Practice*. London: Routledge, 2007.

Lind, M. "In Defence of Liberal Nationalism." *Foreign Affairs* 1:23 (1994): 87–99.
Linnekin, J., and L. Poyer, editors. *Cultural Identity and Ethnicity in the Pacific*. Honolulu: University of Hawaii Press, 1990.
Linz, J. J. and A. C. Stepan. *The Breakdown of Democratic Regimes: Crisis, Breakdown, and Reequilibration, Vol. I*. Baltimore: Johns Hopkins University Press, 1978.
Lipset, S. M. "Some Social Requisites of Democracy: Economic Development and Political Legitimacy." *American Political Science Review* 53:1 (1959): 69–105.
Lister, S. *Understanding State-Building and Local Government in Afghanistan*. London: Crisis States Research Centre, LSE, 2007.
Lister, S., and A. Wilder. "Strengthening Subnational Administration in Afghanistan: Technical Reform or State-Building?" *Public Administration and Development* 25 (2005): 39–48.
Litvack, J., J. Ahmad, and R. Bird. *Rethinking Decentralization in Developing Countries*. Washington: The World Bank, 1998.
Long, W. and P. Brecke. *War and Reconciliation: Reason and Emotion in Conflict Resolution*. Cambridge: MIT Press, 2003.
Loughlin, M. and N. Walker. "Introduction." In Loughlin and Walker, *The Paradox of Constitutionalism*.
 editors. *The Paradox of Constitutionalism: Constituent Power and Constitutional Form*. Oxford: Oxford University Press, 2007.
Lutz, D. S. *Principles of Constitutional Design*. New York: Cambridge University Press, 2006.
Lutz, G. and W. Linder. *Traditional Structures in Local Governance for Local Development*. Bern: Institute of Political Science, University of Berne, 2004.
Lutz, N. M. "Constitutionalism as Public Culture in East Timor." *Paper presented at the Law and Society Association meeting, Pittsburgh*, 7 June 2003.
Mac Ginty, R. "Between Resistance and Compliance: Non-participation and the Liberal Peace." *Journal of Intervention and Statebuilding* 6:2 (2012): 167–187.
 "Gilding the Lily? International Support for Indigenous and Traditional Peacemaking." In *Palgrave Advances in Peacebuilding: Critical Developments and Approaches*, edited by O. P. Richmond. Basingstoke: Palgrave, 2010.
 "Hybrid Peace: The Interaction Between Top-Down and Bottom-Up Peace." *Security Dialogue* 41:4 (2010): 391–412.
 "Indigenous Peace-Making Versus the Liberal Peace." *Cooperation and Conflict* 43:2 (2008): 139–163.
 International Peacebuilding and Local Resistance: Hybrid Forms of Peace. Basingstoke: Palgrave Macmillan, 2012.
Mac Ginty R. and O. P. Richmond. "Myth or Reality: The Liberal Peace and Post-Conflict Reconstruction." *Global Society* 21:4 (2007): 491–497.
Mamack A. and R. Bedford. "Bougainville Copper Mineworkers Strike, 1975." In *Race, Class and Rebellion in the South Pacific*, edited by A. Mamack and A. Ali. Sydney: George Allen and Unwin, 1974.
Mancini, S. "Secession and Self-Determination." In Rosenfeld and Sajó, *The Oxford Handbook of Comparative Constitutional Law*.
Mann, M. "The Autonomous Power of the State: Its Origins, Mechanisms and Results." In *States in History*, edited by J. A. Hall. Oxford: Basil Blackwell, 1986.
Manor, J. *The Political Economy of Democratic Decentralization*. Washington: World Bank, 1999.

Bibliography

Mansbridge, J. *Does Participation Make Better Citizens?*, 1995. Accessed March 6, 2010. www.cpn.org/sections/new_citizenship/theory/mansbridgeI.html.

Mansfield, E. D. and J. Snyder. "Democratization and the Danger of War." *International Security* 20:1 (1995): 5–38.

Marchetti, E. and K. Daly. "Indigenous Sentencing Courts: Towards a Theoretical and Jurisprudential Model." *Sydney Law Review* 29:3 (2007): 415–444.

Marks, S. P. "The Process of Creating a New Constitution in Cambodia." In Miller, *Framing the State*.

Marriot, A. "Justice in the Community, Justice in the Courts: Bridging East Timor's Legal Divide." In Mearns, *Democratic Governance in Timor-Leste*.

——— "The Justice Sector: Achievements, Challenges, and Comparisons." In Leach and Kingsbury, *The Politics of Timor-Leste*.

Marshall, S., producer. *Bougainville – The Killer Deal*, Foreign Correspondent, ABC Television, 17 June 2008.

Masiu, R. "Call for Proper Poll Awareness," 4 May 2005.

——— "Chiefs Demand Arms Clean-up," *Papua New Guinea Post-Courier*, 17 October 2006.

——— "New Body to Control Bougainville Mineral Rights," *The National*, 4 May 2008.

Masono, R. *Government Capacity and Citizen Expectations in Bougainville: The Impact of Political Autonomy*, Crawford School of Economics and Government Discussion Paper 2006–2008. Canberra: Australian National University, August 2006.

Matsuno, A. "The UN Transitional Administration and Democracy Building in Timor-Leste." In Mearns, *Democratic Governance in Timor-Leste*.

May, R. J. *State and Society in Papua New Guinea: The First Twenty-Five Years*. Canberra: ANU E-Press, 2004.

McAsey, B. "A Critical Evaluation of the Koori Court Division of the Victorian Magistrates' Court." *Deakin Law Review* 10:2 (2005): 654–685.

McCarthy, J. *FALINTIL Reinsertion Assistance Program: Final Evaluation Report*. Dili: International Organisation for Migration, 2002.

McCarthy, T. "Legitimacy and Diversity: Dialectical Reflections on Analytical Distinctions." In *Habermas on Law and Democracy: Critical Exchanges*, edited by M. Rosenfeld and A. Arato. Berkeley: University of California Press, 1998.

McDonnell, T. "No Freedom Yet for Ramos Horta," *The Australian*, February 10, 2012.

McGovern, J., and M. Taga. *Review of the Bougainville Community Police Project (Phase 4): BCCP Review Report*, 2009. Accessed October 10, 2013. www.aid.govt.nz/about-aid-programme/measuring-results/evaluation/activity-reports/2010-review-and-evaluation-reports/bougainville-com.

McGurik, R. "Fretilin Majority Could Be Bad," *Australian Associated Press*, 1 September 2001.

McWilliam, A. "Customary Governance in Timor-Leste." In Mearns, *Democratic Governance in Timor-Leste*.

——— "Houses of Resistance in East Timor: Structuring Sociality in the New Nation." *Anthropological Forum* 15:1 (2005): 27–44.

Mearns, D., editor. *Democratic Governance in Timor-Leste: Reconciling the Local and the National*. Darwin: Charles Darwin University Press, 2008

——— "Introduction: Imagining East Timor Again: The Ideas of a 'National Identity' and 'Democratic Governance' in Timor-Leste." In Mearns, *Democratic Governance in Timor-Leste*.

Looking Both Ways: Models for Justice in East Timor. Sydney: Australian Legal Resources International, 2002.
Meitzner Yoder, L. S. "Hybridising Justice: State-Customary Interactions over Forest Crime and Punishment in Oecusse, East Timor." *The Asia Pacific Journal of Anthropology* 8:1 (2007): 43–57.
Menkhaus, K. "Governance without Government in Somalia." *International Security* 31: 3 (2006/07): 74–106.
  "State Failure and Ungoverned Space." *Adelphi Series* 50:412–413 (2010): 171–188.
Merry, S. E. "Legal Pluralism: Review Essay." *Law and Society Review* 22:5 (1988): 869–898.
Michelman, F. "Is the Constitution a Contract for Legitimacy?" *Review of Constitutional Studies* 8 (2003): 101–128.
Mill, J. S. *"On Liberty" and Other Writings*, edited by S. Collini. Cambridge: Cambridge University Press, 1989.
Miller, D. *On Nationality*. Oxford: Oxford University Press, 1995.
Miller, L. E. "Designing Constitution-Making Processes: Lessons from the Past, Questions for the Future." In Miller, *Framing the State*.
  editor. *Framing the State in Times of Transition: Case Studies in Constitution Making*. Washington: U.S. Institute of Peace Press, 2010
Modvig, J. et al. "Torture and Trauma in Post-Conflict East Timor (Health and Human Rights)." *The Lancet* 356:9243 (2000): 1763–1764.
Moehler, D. C. *Distrusting Democrats: Outcomes of Participatory Constitution Making*. Ann Arbor: University of Michigan Press, 2008.
Molnar, A. K. "The First Democratic Elections in East Timor, Asia's Newest Nation: Factors of Social and Political Conditions Surrounding the Election of the First Constitutional Assembly." Paper presented at the Brown Bag Lecture series of the Center for Southeast Asian Studies, Northern Illinois University, November 9, 2001.
  Timor Leste: Politics, History, and Culture. Abingdon: Routledge, 2009.
Momis, J. L. *Bougainville High Impact Projects Remain Top Priority: Media Release*. Buka: Autonomous Bougainville Government, September 4, 2013.
  "Challenges of Implementing the Bougainville Peace Agreement," State, Society and Governance in Melanesia Seminar, Australian National University, March 1, 2011.
  "Shaping Leadership Through Bougainville Indigenous Values and Catholic Seminary Training – A Personal Journey." In Regan and Griffin, *Bougainville: Before the Conflict*.
Momis, J. L. and E. Ogan. "Bougainville '71. Not Discovered by CRA." *New Guinea and Australia* 6:2 (1971): 32–40.
Montagu, A. *Man's Most Dangerous Myth: The Fallacy of Race*. Cleveland: World Publishing Company, 1964.
Moore, M. "Normative Justifications for Liberal Nationalism: Justice, Democracy and National Identity." *Nations and Nationalism* 7:1 (2001): 1–20.
Morrow, J. "Deconstituting Mesopotamia: Cutting a Deal on the Regionalization of Iraq." In Miller, *Framing the State*.
  Iraq's Constitutional Process II: An Opportunity Lost, Special Report 155. Washington: U.S. Institute of Peace, 2005.

Morrow J. and R. White. "The United Nations in Transitional East Timor: International Standards and the Reality of Governance." *Australian Year Book of International Law* 22 (2002): 1–45.
Mouffe, C. *The Deliberative Paradox*. London: Verso, 2000.
——— "Democracy, Power, and the 'Political.'" In Benhabib, *Democracy and Difference*.
MSATM. *Decentralisation and Local Government in Timor-Leste – Policy Orientation Guidelines for Decentralization and Local Government in Timor-Leste*. Dili: Ministry of State Administration and Territorial Management, Government of Timor-Leste, March 2008.
——— *Timor-Leste Decentralization Strategic Framework Part 1*. Dili: Ministry of State Administration and Territorial Management, Government of Timor-Leste, March 2008.
Murphy, W. F. "Constitutions, Constitutionalism, and Democracy." In *Constitutionalism and Democracy: Transitions in the Contemporary World*, edited by D. Greenberg et al. New York: Oxford University Press, 1993.
Murray, C. and R. Simeon. "Recognition without Empowerment: Minorities in a Democratic South Africa," in Choudhry, *Constitutional Design for Divided Societies*.
Myrttinen, H. *Up in Smoke: Impoverishment and Instability in Post-Independence Timor-Leste*. Helsinki: KEPA, 2007.
Nairn, T. *The Break-up of Britain: Crisis and Neo-Nationalism*. London: Verso, 1977.
Namaliu, R. "Address to Declare a National Emergency on Bougainville, National Broadcasting Commission Radio, 23 June 1989." In Polomka, *Bougainville: Perspectives on a Crisis*.
Narayan, D. *Voices of the Poor: Can Anyone Hear Us?* New York: Oxford University Press, 2000.
NDI. *Carrying the People's Aspirations: A Report on Focus Group Discussions in East Timor*. Dili: National Democratic Institute for International Affairs and Faculty of Social and Political Sciences, University of East Timor, 2002.
——— *Government Within Reach: A Report on the Views of East Timorese on Local Government*. Dili: National Democratic Institute for International Affairs, 2003.
——— *"Timor Loro Sa'e is our nation": A Report on Focus Group Discussions in East Timor*. Dili: The National Democratic Institute for International Affairs, 2001.
Ndulo, M. "The Democratic State in Africa: The Challenges for Institution Building." *National Black Law Journal* 16:1 (1998–2000): 70–101.
——— "Zimbabwe's Unfulfilled Struggle for a Legitimate Constitutional Order." In Miller, *Framing the State*.
Nelson, H. *Governments, States and Labels, State Society and Governance in Melanesia Discussion Paper 2006/1*. Canberra: Australian National University, 2006.
Newman, E. "A Human Security Peace-Building Agenda." *Third World Quarterly* 32:10 (2011): 1737–1756.
NGO Forum. *Letter from East Timor NGO Forum to Members of the Security Council United Nations*, March 17, 2001. Accessed January 15, 2010. www.etan.org/news/2001a/03ngoconst.htm.
NGO Working Group. *Article-by-article Commentary on the Immigration and Asylum Bill*. Dili: NGO Working Group to Study the Immigration and Asylum Bill, 13 May 2003.

Nixon, R. "Indonesian West Timor: The Political-Economy of Emerging Ethno-Nationalism." *Journal of Contemporary Asia* 34:2 (2004): 163–185.

Niner, S. "Martyrs, Heroes, and Warriors: The Leadership of East Timor." In Kingsbury and Leach, *East Timor: Beyond Independence*.

Xanana: Leader of the Struggle for Independent Timor-Leste. North Melbourne: Australian Scholarly Publishing Pty Ltd, 2009.

Nixon, R. "The Crisis of Governance in a New Subsistence State." *Journal of Contemporary Asia* 36:1 (2006): 75–101.

"Indonesian West Timor: The Political-Economy of Emerging Ethno-Nationalism." *Journal of Contemporary Asia* 34:2 (2004): 163–185.

NORAD. *Mid-Term Evaluation of the UNDP Timor-Leste Parliamentary Project – Strengthening Parliamentary Democracy in Timor Leste*. Oslo: Norwegian Agency for Development Cooperation, 2008.

Review of Development Cooperation in Timor Leste: Final Report. Oslo: Norwegian Agency for Development Cooperation, 2007.

NRI. *Bougainville Community Crime Trends: A Survey of Crime in Arawa and Buka*. Port Moresby: National Research Institute, 2005.

NSD. *Population and Housing Census of Timor-Leste, 2010: Social and Economic Characteristics*. Dili: National Statistics Directorate, 2011.

NZAID. "Bougainville Community Policing Project Mid Term Review," July 1, 2006. Accessed October 9, 2013. www.aid.govt.nz/about-aid-programme/measuring-results/evaluation/activity-reports/2006-reveiw-and-evaluation-reports/bougainville-com.

O'Brien, J. C. "The Dayton Constitution of Bosnia and Herzegovina." In Miller, *Framing the State*.

"Lawyers, Guns, and Money: Warlords and Reconstruction After Iraq." *UC Davis Journal of International Law & Policy* 11:1 (2004–2005): 99–122.

Offe, C. "Micro-aspects of Democratic Theory: What Makes for the Deliberative Competence of Citizens?" In Hadenius, *Democracy's Victory and Crisis*.

"Some Contradictions of the Modern Welfare State." *Critical Social Policy* 2:2 (1982): 7–14.

Office of the Presidency. *Press Releases*. Dili: Office of the Presidency of the Council of Ministers, July 2 and August 13, 2013.

O'Flynn, I. *Deliberative Democracy and Divided Societies*. Edinburgh: Edinburgh University Press, 2006.

Oliver, D. *Black Islanders: A Personal Perspective of Bougainville 1937–1991*. Melbourne: Hyland, 1991.

Oliver, Q. "Developing Public Capacities for Participation in Peacemaking." In *Owning the Process: Public Participation in Peacemaking*, edited by C. Barnes. London: Conciliation Resources, 2002.

Ona, F. "Letter to Members of the Panguna Landowners' Association, 28 April 1989." In Polomka, *Bougainville: Perspectives on a Crisis*.

Ospina, S. and T. Hohe. *Traditional Power Structures and Local Governance in East Timor, Études Courtes no. 5*. Geneva: Graduate Institute of Development Studies, 2002.

Otto, T. and N. Thomas, editors. *Narratives of Nation in the South Pacific*. Amsterdam: Harwood Academic Publishers, 1997.

Pact of National Unity, Dili, July 8, 2001. Accessed February 24, 2011. members.pcug.org.au/~wildwood/01augnup.htm.

Paine, T. *Common Sense and the Rights of Man*, edited by T. Benn. London: Phoenix Press, 2000.

Paliwala, A. "Law and Order in the Village: the Village Courts." In *Law and Social Change in Papua New Guinea*, edited by D. Weisbrot, A. Paliwala, and A. Sawyerr. Sydney: Butterworths, 1982.

Palmer, L. and D. do Amaral de Carvalho. "Nation Building and Resource Management: The Politics of 'Nature' in Timor Leste." *Geoforum* 39:3 (2008): 1321–1332.

Papagianni, K. "Participation and Legitimation." In *Building States to Build Peace*, edited by C. T. Call and V. Wyeth. Boulder: Lynne Rienner, 2008.

"Paper Outlines Terms of Bougainville Accord," *Papua New Guinea Post-Courier*, August 31, 2001.

Papua New Guinea Constitutional Planning Committee. *Final Report*. Port Moresby: Constitutional Planning Committee, 1974.

Parekh, B. *Rethinking Multiculturalism: Cultural Diversity and Political Theory*. London: Palgrave, 2000.

Paris, R. *At War's End: Building Peace after Civil Conflict*. Cambridge: Cambridge University Press, 2004.

Partlett, W. "The Dangers of Popular Constitution-Making." *Brooklyn Journal of International Law* 38:1 (2012): 193–238.

Pateman, C. *Participation and Democratic Theory*. Cambridge: Cambridge University Press, 1970.

Patten, A. "Beyond the Dichotomy of Universalism and Difference: Four Responses to Cultural Diversity." In Choudhry, *Constitutional Design for Divided Societies*.

Pattie, C. J., P. Seyd, and P. Whiteley. *Citizenship in Britain: Values, Participation and Democracy*. Cambridge: Cambridge University Press, 2001.

Pereira, A. *National Policy on Mass Communication (draft)*, undated. Accessed April 4, 2011. Draft available from: www.article19.org/pdfs/laws/timor-leste-national-policy-on-mass-communication.pdf.

Pereira, M. and M. M. Lete Koten. "Dynamics of Democracy at the *Suku* Level." *Local-Global: Identity, Security, Community* 11 (2012): 222–232.

Peterson, J. H. "A Conceptual Unpacking of Hybridity: Accounting for Notions of Power, Politics and Progress in Analyses of Aid-Driven Interfaces." *Journal of Peacebuilding & Development* 7:2 (2012): 9–22.

Pettit, P. *Republicanism: A Theory of Freedom and Government*. Oxford: Oxford University Press, 1997.

Philpott, D. *The Politics of Past Evil: Religion, Reconciliation, and Transitional Justice*. Notre Dame: University of Notre Dame Press, 2006.

PIF. *Report of the Pacific Islands Form Secretariat's Election Observer Team to the 2010 Elections for the Office of President and Members of the House of Representatives of the Autonomous Region of Bougainville*. Suva, Pacific Islands Forum, 2010.

Pigou, P. *The Community Reconciliation Process of the Commission for Reception, Truth and Reconciliation*. Dili: United National Development Programme, 2004.

—— *Crying without Tears, in Pursuit of Justice and Reconciliation in Timor-Leste: Community Perspectives and Expectations*. Dili: International Center for Transitional Justice, 2003.

Pires, M. "East Timor and the Debate on Quotas," 2000. Accessed February 25, 2010. www.quotaproject.org/fr/CS/CS_East_Timor.pdf.
Plan Timor-Leste. *Like Stepping Stones in the River: Youth Perspectives on the Crisis in Timor-Leste*. Dili: Plan Timor-Leste, 2007.
Polomka, P., editor. *Bougainville: Perspectives on a Crisis*. Canberra: Australian National University, 1990
  "Land as 'Life,' Security and Impediment to Unity." In Polomka, *Bougainville: Perspectives on a Crisis*.
"President Reflects on Progress in Bougainville Peace Process," *Radio Australia*, February 21, 2011.
Preuss, U. K. "Constitution-Making and Nation-Building: Reflections on Political Transformations in East and Western Europe." *European Journal of Philosophy* 1:1 (1993): 81–92.
  "Constitutional Powermaking for the New Polity: Some Deliberations on the Relations between Constituent Power and the Constitution." *Cardozo Law Review* 14 (1992): 639–660.
Proceedings, Workshop on Constitution Building Processes., Bobst Center for Peace & Justice, Princeton University, in conjunction with Interpeace and International IDEA, 17–20 May 2007.
Przeworski, A. M., and H. Teune. *The Logic of Comparative Social Inquiry*. New York: John Wiley, 1970.
Pugh, M. "The Political Economy of Peacebuilding: A Critical Theory Perspective." *International Journal of Peace Studies* 10:2 (2005): 23–42.
Pugh, M., et al. "Conclusion: The Political Economy of Peacebuilding – Whose Peace? Where Next?" In *Whose peace? Critical Perspectives on the Political Economy of Peacebuilding*, edited by M. Pugh et al. London: Palgrave, 2008.
Radan, P. "Secession: A Word in Search of a Meaning." In *On the Way to Statehood: Secession and Globalisation*, edited by A. Pavkovic and P. Radan. Aldershot: Ashgate, 2008.
Radcliff, B. and E. Wingenbach. "Preference Aggregation, Functional Pathologies, and Democracy: A Social Choice Defence of Participatory Democracy." *Journal of Politics* 62:4 (2000): 977–998.
Ramos-Horta, J. *Funu: The Unfinished Saga of East Timor*. Trenton, NJ: The Red Sea Press, Inc, 1987.
Ramsbotham, O., T. Woodhouse, and H. Miall. *Contemporary Conflict Resolution*. Cambridge: Polity Press, 2011.
Ratner, S. R. "Drawing a Better Line: *Uti Possidetis* and the Borders of New States." *American Journal of International Law* 90:4 (1996): 590–624.
Rawls, J. A. *A Theory of Justice*. Cambridge: The Bellnap Press of Harvard University Press, 1971.
"Referendum Delay Irks Momis," *Papua New Guinea Post Courier*, June 21, 2012.
Regan, A. J. "Bougainville," Diminishing Conflict Seminar Series, College of Asia and the Pacific, Australian National University, July 29, 2008.
  The Bougainville Council of Elders System. Paper prepared for the Bougainville Transitional Government, September 22, 1998.
  "The Bougainville Intervention: Political Legitimacy and Sustainable Peace-Building." In *Intervention and State-Building in the Pacific: The Legitimacy of*

"Cooperative Intervention," edited by G. Fry and T. T. Kabutaulaka. Manchester: Manchester University Press, 2008.

Bougainville: The Peace Process and Beyond, Submission to the Foreign Affairs Sub-Committee of the Joint Standing Committee on Foreign Affairs, Defence and Trade Inquiry, June 1999.

"The Bougainville Political Settlement and the Prospects for Sustainable Peace." *Pacific Economic Bulletin* 17:1 (2002): 114–129.

"Bougainville Update," State, Society and Governance in Melanesia Seminar Series, College of Asia and the Pacific, Australian National University, November 27, 2012.

"Bougainville's New Directions: Presidential By-Election, Forming a New Ministry, and First Steps of the New Leadership," State, Society and Governance in Melanesian Seminar, Australian National University, Canberra, March 25, 2009.

Conflict Among Bougainvilleans 1988–1998: Implications for the Peace Process, State, Society and Governance in Melanesia Working Paper 1999. Canberra: Australian National University, 1999.

"Constitution Making in East Timor: Missed Opportunities?" In *Elections and Constitution Making in East Timor*, edited by D. de Costa Babo Soares et al. Canberra: Australian National University, 2003.

"Development and Conflict: Self-Determination in Bougainville." In *Security and Development in the Pacific Islands: Social Resilience in Emerging States*, edited by M.A. Brown. Boulder: Lynne Rienner, 2007.

"Identities among Bougainvilleans." In Regan and Griffin, *Bougainville: Before the Conflict*.

"Introduction." In *Twenty Years of the Papua New Guinea Constitution*, edited by A. J. Regan, O. Jessep, and E. L. Kwa. Sydney: Lawbook Co., 2001.

Light Intervention: Lessons from Bougainville. Washington: U.S. Institute of Peace Press, 2010.

Notes on Preambles and on Directive Principles in Constitutions. Buka: Bougainville Constitutional Commission, January 23, 2003.

"An Outcomes Perspective on Civil Society in Melanesia: Reflections on Experience from Bougainville," paper presented at the Fourth Plenary: Governance and Civil Society, State, Society and Governance in Melanesia Project, Australian National University, Canberra, October 1, 2003.

"Resolving the Bougainville Self-determination Dispute: Autonomy or Complex Power-sharing?" In *Settling Self-determination Disputes: Complex Power-sharing in Theory and Practice*, edited by M. Weller and B. Metzger. Leiden and Boston: Martinus Nijhoff Publishers, 2008.

"'Traditional' Leaders and Conflict Resolution in Bougainville: Reforming the Present by Re-writing the Past?" In Dinnen and Ley, *Reflections on Violence in Melanesia*.

"Why a Neutral Peace Monitoring Force? The Bougainville Conflict and the Peace Process." In *Without a Gun: Australia's Experiences Monitoring Peace in Bougainville, 1997–2001*, edited by M. Wehner and D. Denoon. Canberra: Pandanus Books, 2001.

Regan, A. J. and H. M. Griffin, editors. *Bougainville: Before the Conflict*. Canberra: Pandanus Books, 2005.

Renders, M. and U. Terlinden. "Negotiating Statehood in a Hybrid Political Order: The Case of Somaliland." *Development and Change* 41:4 (2010): 723–746.

Requejo, F. "Democratic Legitimacy and National Pluralism." In Requejo, *Democracy and National Pluralism*.

"Introduction." In Requejo, *Democracy and National Pluralism*.

Requejo, F., editor. *Democracy and National Pluralism*. London: Routledge, 2001.

Richmond, O.P. "Becoming Liberal, Unbecoming Liberalism: Liberal-Local Hybridity via the Everyday as a Response to the Paradoxes of Liberal Peacebuilding." *Journal of Intervention and Statebuilding* 3:3 (2009): 324–344.

"Beyond Local Ownership in the Architecture of International Peacebuilding." *Ethnopolitics* 11:4 (2012): 354–375.

"De-romanticising the Local, De-mystifying the International: Hybridity in Timor Leste and Solomon Islands." *The Pacific Review* 24:1 (2011): 115–136.

"A Post-liberal Peace: Eirenism and the Everyday." *Review of International Studies* 35:3 (2009): 557–580.

"The Problem of Peace: Understanding the 'Liberal Peace.'" *Conflict, Security & Development* 6:3 (2006): 291–314.

"Resistance and the Post-liberal Peace." *Millennium* 38:3 (2010): 665–692.

"The Romanticisation of the Local: Welfare, Culture and Peacebuilding." *The International Spectator* 44:1 (2009): 149–169.

Richmond, O. P. and J. Franks, "Liberal Peacebuilding in Timor Leste: The Emperor's New Clothes?" *International Peacekeeping* 15:2 (2008): 185–200.

Riker, W. H. "The Experience of Creating Institutions: The Framing of the United States Constitution." In *Explaining Social Institutions*, edited by J. Knight and I. Sened. Ann Arbor: University of Michigan Press, 1995.

Robinson, G. "With UNAMET in East Timor: A Historian's Personal View." In Tanter, Selden, and Shalom, *Bitter Flowers, Sweet Flowers*.

Rosenfeld, M. "Constitutional Identity." In Rosenfeld and Sajó, *The Oxford Handbook of Comparative Constitutional Law*.

Constitutionalism, Identity, Difference, and Legitimacy: Theoretical Perspectives. Durham: Duke University Press, 1994.

The Identity of the Constitutional Subject: Selfhood, Citizenship, Culture, and Community. Abingdon: Routledge, 2010.

Rosenfeld, M. and A. Sajó., editors. *The Oxford Handbook of Comparative Constitutional Law*. Oxford: Oxford University Press, 2012.

Rosenn, K. S. "Conflict Resolution and Constitutionalism: The Making of the Brazilian Constitution of 1988." In Miller, *Framing the State*.

Rotberg, R. I. "Failed States, Collapsed States, Weak States: Causes and Indicators." In *State Failure and State Weakness in a Time of Terror*, edited by R. I. Rotberg. Cambridge: Brookings Institution Press, 2003.

Rousseau, J. J. *The Social Contract and Other Later Political Writings*, edited by V. Gourevitch. Cambridge: Cambridge University Press, 1997.

Rumsey, A. "The Articulation of Indigenous and Exogenous Orders in Highland New Guinea and Beyond." *The Australian Journal of Anthropology* 17:1 (2006): 47–69.

Said, E. *Orientalism*. New York: Vintage Books, 1978.

Samuels, K. *Constitution Building Processes and Democratization: A Discussion of Twelve Case Studies*. Stockholm: International Institute for Democracy and Electoral Assistance, 2006.

"Post-Conflict Peace-Building and Constitution-Making." *Chicago Journal of International Law* 6:2 (2006): 663–682.

State-Building and Constitutional Design after Conflict. New York: International Peace Academy, 2006.

Sandel, M. *Liberalism and the Limits of Justice.* Cambridge: Cambridge University Press, 1982.

Sanders, L. "Against Deliberation." *Political Theory* 25:3 (1997): 347–376.

Saovana-Spriggs, R. V. "Christianity and Women in Bougainville." *Development Bulletin* 51 (2000): 58–60.

Sasa, C. L. *Local Government Accountability in Bougainville.* Masters of Philosophy Thesis, Massy University, 2013.

Saunders, C. "Constitution Making in the 21st Century." *Melbourne Legal Studies Research Paper No. 630.* Melbourne: University of Melbourne, 2012.

Scales, I., R. Craemer, and I. Thappa. *Market Chain Development in Peace Building: Australia's Roads, Wharves and Agriculture Projects in Post-Conflict Bougainville.* Canberra: AusAID, 2008.

Scambary, J. *A Survey of Gangs and Youth Groups in Dili, Timor-Leste.* Canberra: AusAID, 2006.

Scheeringa, S. "Enhancing the Local Legitimacy of Transnational Justice Institutions: Local Embeddedness and Customary Law in Constituent Assembly." In Kingsbury and Leach, *East Timor: Beyond Independence.*

Scheiner, C. *How Long Will the Petroleum Fund Carry Timor-Leste?* Dili: La'o Hamutuk, 2013.

Scheuerman, W. E. "Critical Theory Beyond Habermas." In Dryzek, Honig, and Phillips, *The Oxford Handbook of Political Theory.*

Schiff Berman, P. "Towards a Jurisprudence of Hybridity." *Utah Law Review* 1 (2010): 11–29.

Schlosberg, D. "The Pluralist Imagination." In Dryzek, Honig, and Phillips, *The Oxford Handbook of Political Theory.*

Schmeidl, S. and M. Karokhail. "'Prêt-à-Porter States': How the McDonaldization of State-Building Misses the Mark in Afghanistan." In *Peace in the Absence of States: Challenging the Discourse of State Failure,* edited by M. Fischer and B. Schmelzle. Berlin: Berghof Research Center, 2009.

Segura, R. and A. M. Bejarano. "*Ni una asamblea más sin nosotros!* Exclusion, Inclusion, and the Politics of Constitution-Making in the Andes." *Constellations* 11:2 (2004): 217–236.

Selassie, B. H. "Constitution Making in Eritrea: A Process-Driven Approach." In Miller, *Framing the State.*

Sepúlveda, M. *Preliminary Observations and Recommendations, Mission to Timor-Leste from 13 to 18 November 2011.* Accessed October 18, 2013. www.ohchr.org/EN/NewsEvents/Pages/DisplayNews.aspx?NewsID=11618&LangID=E.

Seton-Watson, H. *Nations and States.* London: Methuen, 1977.

Shils, E. "Primordial, Personal, Sacred and Civil Ties." *British Journal of Sociology* 8:2 (1957): 130–147.

Shoesmith, D. "Remaking the State in Timor-Leste: The Case for Constitutional Reform." Paper presented at the 17th Biennial Conference of the Asian Studies Association of Australia, Melbourne, July 1–3, 2008.

"Timor-Leste: Divided Leadership in a Semi-Presidential System." *Asian Survey* 43:2 (2003): 231–252.

"Timor-Leste: Semi-presidentialism and the Democratic Transition in a New, Small State." In *Semi-presidentialism outside Europe: A Comparative Study*, edited by R. Elgie and S. Moestrup. London: Routledge, 2007.

Sieyès, E. J. *What Is the Third Estate?*, edited by S. E. Finer and translated by M. Blondel. New York: Praeger, 1963.

Simonsen, S. V. "The Authoritarian Temptation in East Timor: Nationbuilding and the Need for Inclusive Governance." *Asian Survey* 46:4 (2006): 575–596.

Sinclair, N. *Implementation of the Bougainville Peace Agreement, Completion of Stage II of Weapons Disposal: UNOMB's Verification Report*. Buka: United Nations Observer Mission Bougainville, July 2003.

Sirivi, J. T. "Reconciliation and Renewing the Vision." In Sirivi and Havini, *...As Mothers of the Land*.

Sirivi, J. T. and M. T. Havini, editors. *...As Mothers of the Land: The Birth of the Bougainville Women for Peace and Freedom*. Canberra: Pandanus Books, 2004.

Sisk, T. *Power Sharing and International Mediation in Ethnic Conflict*. Washington: United States Institute of Peace Press, 1996.

Smith, A.D. *Nationalism: Theory, Ideology, History*. Cambridge: Polity Press, 2001.

"State-Making and Nation-Building." In *The State: Critical Concepts Vol. II*, edited by J. A. Hall. London: Routledge, 1994.

The Antiquity of Nations. Cambridge: Polity Press, 2004.

Smith, A. L. "East Timor: Elections in the World's Newest Nation." *Journal of Democracy* 15:2 (2004): 145–159.

Self-Determination Conflict Profile: East Timor. Washington: Foreign Policy in Focus, 2002.

Snyder, J. *Transitions to Democracy and the Rise of Nationalist Conflict*. Israel: Leonard Davis Institute, 2000.

Snyder J., and K. Ballentine. "Nationalism and the Marketplace of Ideas." *International Security* 21:2 (1996): 5–40.

Soares, E., and D. Dooradi. *Timor-Leste Communication and Media Survey*. Dili: UNMIT, 2010.

"South Bougainville 2005–2008: Local Conflict, Reconciliation, Weapons Disposal and Peace-building," State, Society and Governance in Melanesia seminar, Australian National University, Canberra, November 25, 2008.

Spinner-Halev, J. "Democracy, Solidarity and Post-nationalism." *Political Studies* 56 (2008): 604–628.

Spriggs, M. "Bougainville Update: August 1990 to May 1991." In Spriggs and Denoon, *The Bougainville Crisis: 1991 Update*.

Spriggs, M. and D. Denoon, editors. *The Bougainville Crisis: 1991 Update*. Bathurst: Crawford House Press, 1992.

Starr, P. *Freedom's Power: The History and Promise of Liberalism*. New York: Basic Books, 2007.

Steiner, H. J. "Political Participation as a Human Right." *Harvard Human Rights Yearbook* 1 (1988): 77–134, 77–78.

Stokes, S. C. "Pathologies of Deliberation." In Elster, *Deliberative Democracy*.

Sunstein, C. R. *Designing Democracy: What Constitutions Do*. New York: Oxford University Press, 2001.

Tamanaha, B. Z. *On the Rule of Law: History, Politics, Theory.* Cambridge: Cambridge University Press, 2004.
  "Understanding Legal Pluralism: Past to Present, Local to Global." *Sydney Law Review* 30 (2008): 375–411.
Tamir, Y. *Liberal Nationalism*. Princeton: Princeton University Press, 1995.
Tanter, R., M. Selden, and S. Shalom, editors. *Bitter Flowers, Sweet Flowers: East Timor, Indonesia and the World Economy*. Oxford: Rowman and Littlefield, 2000
Taylor, C. "Democratic Exclusion (and Its Remedies?)." In *Multiculturalism, Liberalism and Democracy*, edited by A. K. B. Rajeev Bhargava and R. Sudarshan. New Delhi: Oxford University Press, 1999.
  Sources of the Self. Cambridge: Cambridge University Press, 1989.
Taylor, J. *Indonesia's Forgotten War: The Hidden History of East Timor*. New York: Zed Books, 1994.
Teitel, R. "Transitional Justice and the Transformation of Constitutionalism." In Ginsburg and Dixon, *Comparative Constitutional Law*.
  The Real Story of the Sovereign Nation of Bougainville Islands & the Twin Kingdoms of Papa'ala and Me'ekamui, June 2012. Accessed September 23, 2013. www.ourbougainville.org/.
Therik, T. *Wehali: The Female Land, Traditions of a Timorese Ritual Centre*. Canberra: Pandanus Books, 2004.
Thier, J. A. "Big Tent, Small Tent: The Making of a Constitution in Afghanistan." In Miller, *Framing the State*.
Thomas, N. *In Oceania: Visions, Artefacts, Histories*. Durham: Duke University Press, 1997.
Thompson, L., producer. *Breaking Bows and Arrows: Bougainville*, SBS Television Australia, 22 March 2002.
Tierney, S. *Constitutional Law and National Pluralism*. Oxford: Oxford University Press, 2004.
Tilly, C. *Coercion, Capital, and European States, AD 990–1992*. Oxford: Blackwell, 1992.
  Democracy. Cambridge: Cambridge University Press, 2007.
Tilman, M. "Customary Social Order and Authority in the Contemporary East Timorese Village: Persistence and Transformation." *Local-Global: Identity, Security, Community* 11 (2012): 192–205.
Timor-Leste National Alliance for an International Tribunal. *An Open Letter in Response to the CTF Report*, July 18, 2008. Accessed October 15, 2013. etan.org/news/2008/07anti.htm.
Togolo, M. "Torau Response to Change." In Regan and Griffin, *Bougainville: Before the Conflict*.
Transparency International. *2012 Corruption Perception Index*, 2012. Accessed October 23, 2013. cpi.transparency.org/cpi2012/results/.
Traube, E.G. "Unpaid Wages: Local Narratives and the Imagination of the Nation." *The Asia Pacific Journal of Anthropology* 8:1 (2007): 9–25.
Trindade, J. "An Open Letter to the Prime Minister and to the Timorese People," *ETAN Mailing List*, August 2006.
  "Reconciling Conflicting Paradigms: An East Timorese Vision of the Ideal State." In Mearns, *Democratic Governance in Timor-Leste*.

Trindade, J. and B. Castro. *Rethinking Timorese Identity as a Peacebuilding Strategy: The Lorosa'e–Loromonu Conflict from a Traditional Perspective, European Union Technical Assistance to the National Dialogue Process in Timor-Leste*. Dili: GTZ, 2007.

Tripp, A. M. "The Politics of Constitution Making in Uganda." In Miller, *Framing the State*.

Tully, J. "The Imperialism of Modern Constitutional Democracy." In Loughlin and Walker, *The Paradox of Constitutionalism*.

Strange Multiplicity: Constitutionalism in an Age of Diversity. Cambridge: Cambridge University Press, 1995.

"The Unfreedom of the Moderns in Relation to their Ideals of Constitutionalism and Democracy." *Modern Law Review* 65 (2002): 204–228.

Tully, J. and A. G. Gagnon, editors. *Multinational Democracies*. Cambridge: Cambridge University Press, 2001.

Turner, M. *Issues in the Design of Decentralisation, State, Society and Governance in Melanesia Discussion Paper 2003/7*. Canberra: Australian National University, 2003.

Tushnet, M. "Constitution-Making: An Introduction." *Texas Law Review* 91 (2013): 1983–2013.

"How Do Constitutions Constitute Constitutional Identity?" *International Journal of Constitutional Law* 8:3 (2010): 671–676.

"Some Skepticism about Normative Constitutional Advice," *William and Mary Law Review* 49:4 (2008): 1473–1495.

"Two East Timorese Party Activists Arrested over Campaign Threats," *Agence France-Presse*, August 24, 2001.

UN. *Interim Report of the Secretary-General on the United Nations Transitional Administration in East Timor*, UN Security Council, UN Doc. S/2001/436, May 2, 2001.

Progress Report of the Secretary-General on the United Nations Transitional Administration in East Timor, UN Security Council, UN Doc. S/2001/719, July 24, 2001.

Report of the Secretary-General on the United Nations Integrated Mission in Timor-Leste (for the Period from 27 January to 20 August 2007), UN Doc. S/2007/513, August 28, 2007.

Report of the Secretary-General on the United Nations Integrated Mission in Timor-Leste (for the Period from 21 August 2007 to 7 January 2008), UN Doc. S/2008/26, January 17, 2008.

Report of the Secretary-General on the United Nations Integrated Mission in Timor-Leste (for the Period from 8 January to 8 July 2008), UN Doc. S/2008/501, July 29, 2008.

Report of the Secretary-General on the United Nations Integrated Mission in Timor-Leste (for the Period from 24 September 2009 to 20 January 2010), UN Doc. S/2010/85, February 12, 2010.

Report of the Secretary-General on the United Nations Integrated Mission in Timor-Leste (for the Period from 21 January to 20 September 2010), UN Doc. S/2010/522, October 13, 2010.

Report of the Secretary-General on the United Nations Integrated Mission in Timor-Leste (for the Period from 8 January 2011 to 20 September 2011), UN Doc. S/2011/641, October 14, 2011.

Report of the Secretary-General on the United Nations Integrated Mission in Timor-Leste (for the Period from 20 September 2011 to 6 January 2012), UN Doc. S/2012/43, January 18, 2012.

Report of the Secretary-General on the United Nations Integrated Mission in Timor-Leste (for the Period from 7 January through 20 September 2012), UN Doc. S/2012/765, October 15, 2012.

Report of the Secretary-General on the United Nations Observer Mission in Bougainville (Papua New Guinea), UN Security Council, UN Doc. S/2004/771, September 29, 2004.

Report of the Secretary-General on the United Nations Observer Mission in Bougainville (Papua New Guinea), UN Security Council, UN Doc. S/2005/204, March 28, 2005.

Report of the Secretary-General on the United Nations Political Office in Bougainville, UN Security Council, UN Doc. S/2003/345, March 20, 2003.

Report of the Secretary-General on the United Nations Transitional Administration in East Timor, UN Security Council, UN Doc. S/2002/432, April 17, 2002.

Report of the Secretary-General on Timor-Leste pursuant to Security Council resolution 1690, UN Security Council, UN Doc. S/2006/628, August 8, 2006.

Report of the Secretary-General: Question of East Timor, UN Doc. A/53/951-S/1999/513, May 5, 1999.

Report of the Security Council Mission to Jakarta and Dili, 8 To 12 September 1999, UN Doc. S/1999/976, September 14, 1999.

Report of the Security Council Mission to Timor-Leste 3 to 6 November 2012, UN Doc. S/2012/889, November 28, 2012.

Report of the United Nations Independent Special Commission of Inquiry for Timor-Leste, UN Doc. S/2006/822, October 2, 2006.

Report to the Secretary-General of the Commission of Experts to review the Prosecution of Serious Violations of Human Rights in Timor-Leste (then East Timor) in 1999, 26 May 2005, Annex II to *Letter dated 24 June 2005 from the Secretary-General addressed to the President of the Security Council*, UN Doc. S/2005/458, July 15, 2005.

UNDP. *Bougainville Human Development Report 2007, Developing Education from Within: Communities as Critical Agents of Change*. Port Moresby: United National Development Programme, 2009.

Bougainville Rehabilitation, Reconstruction and Development Project, Project Document Papua New Guinea/98/002. Port Moresby: United National Development Programme, 2002.

East Timor Human Development Report 2002: Ukun Rasik A'as, The Way Ahead. Dili: United National Development Programme, 2002.

International Human Development Indicators. Accessed July 2, 2011. hdrstats.undp.org.

The Millennium Development Goals, Timor-Leste. Dili: United National Development Programme, 2009.

Strengthening Parliamentary Democracy in Timor-Leste, Project Document. Dili: United National Development Programme, 2006.

Timor-Leste Human Development Report 2006: The Path Out of Poverty, Integrated Rural Development. Dili: United National Development Programme, 2006.

Timor-Leste Human Development Report 2011: Managing Natural Resources for Human Development, Developing the Non-Oil Economy to Achieve the MDGs. Dili: United National Development Programme, 2011.

UNDP Bougainville Programme: End of Year Report. Buka: United National Development Programme, 2008.

UNESCO. *Asia Pacific in Figures 2006*. Bangkok: United Nations Economic and Social Commission for Asia and the Pacific, 2006.

UNHCHR. *Report of the High Commissioner for Human Rights on the Situation of Human Rights in East Timor*, February 6, 2001, UN Doc. E/CN.42001/37.

UNICEF. *The Right Ingredients: The Need to Invest in Child Nutrition*. London: UNICEF, 2013.

The State of the World's Children 2011: Adolescence, An Age of Opportunity. New York: UNICEF, 2011.

UNIFEM. *Getting It Right, Doing It Right: Gender and Disarmament, Demobilization and Reintegration*. New York: United Nations Development Fund for Women, 2004.

United Nations Security Council, *Resolutions on the Situation in East Timor (Timor-Leste)*, S/Res/1236, May 7, 1999; S/Res/1264, September 15, 1999; S/Res/1272, October 25, 1999; S/Res/1319, September 20, 2000; S/Res/1338, January 31, 2001; S/Res/1392, January 31, 2002; S/Res/1410, May 17, 2002; S/Res/1480, May 19, 2003; S/Res/1543, May 14, 2004; S/Res/1573, November 16, 2004; S/Res/1599, April 28, 2005; S/Res/1677, May 12, 2006; S/Res/1690, June 20, 2006; S/Res/1703, August 18, 2006; S/Res/1704, August 25, 2006; S/Res/1745, February 22, 2007; S/Res/1802, February 25, 2008; S/Res/1867, February 26, 2009; S/Res/1912, February 26, 2010; S/Res/1969, February 24, 2011; S/Res/2037, February 23, 2012.

UNMIT. *Report on Human Rights Developments in Timor-Leste (August 2006–August 2007)*. Dili: United Nations Integrated Mission in Timor-Leste, 2007.

UNOHCHR. *Rejecting Impunity: Accountability for Human Rights Violations Past and Present, Report on Human Rights Developments in Timor-Leste: 1 July 2008 to 30 June 2009*. Dili: UN Office of the High Commissioner for Human Rights, 2009.

Report of the International Commission of Inquiry on East Timor to the Secretary-General, January 31, 2000, UN Doc. A/54/726, S/2000/59.

UNOHCHR/UNMIT. *Facing the Future: Periodic Report on Human Rights Developments in Timor-Leste, 1 July 2009–30 June 2010*. Dili: UN Office of the High Commissioner for Human Rights and UNMIT, 2010.

UNOTIL. *Strengthening Accountability and Transparency in Timor-Leste: Report of the Alkatiri Initiative Review*. Dili: UN Office in Timor-Leste, January 27, 2006.

UNTAET. *Political Activity, a Fundamental Right, Public Statement*. Dili: UNTAET, November 1, 2000.

press briefing media notes, March 16, 2001; March 27, 2001; March 29, 2001; March 30, 2001; August 20, 2001; August 21, 2000; January 31, 2002; February 20, 2002; March 1, 2002.

Proceedings of the Constituent Assembly Week 6, 22–27 October 2001: Report for the Human Rights Unit. Dili: UNTAET, 2001.

Proceedings of the Constituent Assembly Week 7, 29 October–2 November 2001: Report to the Human Rights Unit. Dili: UNTAET, 2001.

UNTAET Constitutional Affairs Branch. *Civic Education Material*. Dili: UNTAET, undated.
Constitutional Commission Public Hearings, Executive Summary. Dili: UNTAET, September 2001.
Constitutional Consultation: Fact Sheet No. 4. Dili: UNTAET, July 3, 2001.
Draft Constitutional Introduction, Themes and Narratives. Dili: UNTAET, April 19, 2001, and May 18, 2001.
A Report of the National Constitutional Consultation in East Timor, June–July 2001. Dili: UNTAET, 2001.
Training of Trainers Workshop: Constitutional Commissions. Dili: UNTAET, May 2001.
UNTAET Human Rights Unit. *UNTAET Human Rights Unit Report*. Dili: UNTAET, March 2001.
"An Update from the Division of LLG and Traditional Authority on Bougainville's Councils of Elders," *Bougainville Bulletin*, August 12, 2012. Accessed October 2, 2013. www.bougainvillebulletin.com/past-editions/12-aug-2012-edition/18-an-update-from-the-division-of-llg-and-traditional-authority-on-bougainville-s-council-of-elders.
USAID. *The Crisis in Timor-Leste: Causes, Consequences and Options for Conflict Management and Mitigation*. Dili: USAID, 2006.
Rule of Law in Timor-Leste. Dili: Freedom House, USAID, and the ABA Rule of Law Initiative, 2007.
USIP. *Iraq's Constitutional Process: Shaping a Vision for the Country's Future, Special Report 132*. Washington: U.S. Institute of Peace, 2005.
van den Berghe, P. "Does Race Matter?" *Nations and Nationalism* 1:3 (1995): 357–368.
Viroli, M. *For Love of Country: An Essay on Patriotism and Nationalism*. New York: Clarendon Press, 1995.
Voigt, S. "The Consequences of Popular Participation in Constitutional Choice – Toward a Comparative Analysis." In *Deliberation and Decision*, edited by A. van Aaken et al. Aldershot: Ashgate, 2003.
von Kaltenborn-Stachau, H. *The Missing Link: Fostering Positive Citizen-State Relations in Post-Conflict Environments*. Washington: World Bank, 2008.
Waki, A. and W. Gituro. "The New Constitution of Kenya: The Process of Implementation," undated. Accessed August 14, 2013. www.coulsonharney.com/News-Blog/Blog/The-new-constitution-Implementation.
Walker, J. L. "A Critique of the Elitist Theory of Democracy." *American Political Science Review* 15:3 (1966): 285–295.
Wallis, J. "Building a Liberal-local Hybrid Peace and State in Bougainville." *Pacific Review* 25:5 (2012): 613–635.
"A Local-liberal Peace Project in Action? The Increasing Engagement between the Local and Liberal in East Timor." *Review of International Studies* 38:4 (2012): 735–761.
"Nation-building, Autonomy Arrangements and Deferred Referendums: Unresolved Questions from Bougainville, Papua New Guinea," *Nationalism and Ethnic Politics* 19:3 (2013): 310–332
"Ten Years of Peace: Assessing Bougainville's Progress and Prospects." *The Round Table* 101:1 (2012): 29–40.

"Victors, Villains and Victims: Capitalizing on Memory in Timor-Leste." *Ethnopolitics* 12:2 (2013): 133–160.

"What Role Can Decentralisation Play in State-Building? Lessons from Timor-Leste and Bougainville," *Commonwealth & Comparative Politics* 51:4 (2013): 424–446

Walzer, M. *Spheres of Justice*. Oxford: Basil Blackwell, 1983.

Watt, D., R. Flanary, and R. Theobald. "Democratisation or the Democratization of Corruption? The Case of Uganda." *Commonwealth & Comparative Politics* 37:3 (1999): 37–64.

Weber, M. "Science as a Vocation." In *From Max Weber: Essays in Sociology*, edited by H. H. Gerth and C. Wright Mills. New York: Oxford University Press, 1958.

Weiner, A. S. "Constitutions as Peace Treaties: A Cautionary Tale for the Arab Spring." *Stanford Law Review Online* 64:8 (2011): 8–15.

Weller, M. *Escaping the Self-determination Trap*. Dordrecht: Martinus Nijhoff, 2008.

White, G. *Indigenous Governance in Melanesia, State, Society and Governance in Melanesia Targeted Research Paper for AusAID*. Canberra: Australian National University, 2006.

Widner, J. A. "Constitution Writing and Conflict Resolution." *The Round Table* 94:381 (2005): 503–518.

"Constitution Writing and Conflict Resolution Project," undated. Accessed March 6, 2010. www.princeton.edu/~pcwcr/.

"Constitution Writing in Post-Conflict Settings: An Overview." *William and Mary Law Review* 49 (2007): 1513–1537.

Wigglesworth, A. *Becoming Citizens: Civil Society Activism and Social Change in Timor Leste*. PhD Thesis, Victoria University, 2010.

Wilson, B. V. E. "The Politics of Security-Sector Reform." In Leach and Kingsbury, *The Politics of Timor-Leste*.

W. Wilson, "Address on War Aims," delivered at a Joint Session of the Two Houses of Congress, Washington, February 18, 1918.

Wiuff Moe, L. "Hybrid and 'Everyday' Political Ordering: Constructing and Contesting Legitimacy in Somaliland." *Journal of Legal Pluralism and Unofficial Law* 63 (2011): 143–177.

Wolfers, E. P. *Bougainville Autonomy – Implications for Governance and Decentralisation, State, Society and Governance in Melanesia Discussion Paper No. 5*. Canberra: Australian National University, 2006.

"International Peace Missions in Bougainville, Papua New Guinea, 1990–2005: Host State Perspectives." Paper delivered at the Regional Forum on Reinventing Government, Exchange and Transfer of Innovations for Transparent Governance and State Capacity, Nadi, Fiji, February 20–22, 2006.

"'Joint Creation': The Bougainville Peace Agreement – And Beyond." In Carl and Garasu, *Weaving Consensus*.

Woodley, B. "The Countdown to Democracy," *The Australian*, August 11, 2001.

Work, R. *The Role of Participation and Partnership in Decentralized Governance*. New York: UNDP, undated.

World Bank. *Colombia Local Government Capacity: Beyond Technical Assistance*. Washington: World Bank, 1995.

Country Assistance Strategy for the Democratic Republic of Timor-Leste, for the Period FY06-FY08. Washington: World Bank, 2005.

Interim Strategy Note for the Democratic Republic of Timor-Leste FY 2010–2011. Sydney and Dili: World Bank, 2009.
Report of the Joint Assessment Mission to East Timor. Washington: World Bank, 1999.
Strengthening the Institutions of Governance in Timor-Leste. Washington: World Bank, 2006.
World Development Indicators, undated. Accessed July 5, 2011. databank.worldbank.org.
World Development Report 2004: Making Services Work for Poor People. Washington: World Bank, 2004.
World Bank/DNS. *Timor-Leste: Poverty in a Young Nation.* Dili: World Bank and Directorate of National Statistics, Timor-Leste, 2008.
"Xanana Resigns as National Council President," *Suara Timor Lorosae*, March 30, 2001.
Yack, B. "Popular Sovereignty and Nationalism." *Political Theory* 29:4 (2001): 517–536.
Yngstrom, I. "Women, Wives and Land Rights in Africa: Situating Gender Beyond the Household in the Debate over Land Policy and Changing Tenure Systems." *Oxford Development Studies* 30:1 (2002): 21–40.
Young, I. M. "Communication and the Other: Beyond Deliberative Democracy." In Benhabib, *Democracy and Difference*.
Yudhoyono, S., and J. Ramos-Horta. *Joint Statement of the Heads of State of the Republic of Indonesia and the Democratic Republic of Timor-Leste.* Nusa Dua, July 15, 2008.
Zifcak, S. *Making Timor's Constitution.* Undated memorandum.
——— *Restorative Justice in East Timor: An Evaluation of the Community Reconciliation Process of the Constituent Assembly.* New York: Asia Foundation, 2004.
Zubrycki, T., director, and S. Browning, producer. *The Diplomat.* Lindfield: Film Australia, 2000.

LEGISLATION

Bill Establishing the Public Memory Institute No. /II (TL).
Bougainville Elections Act (2007) (ABG).
Community Government Act (1978) (NSPG).
Constitution of the Autonomous Region of Bougainville (2005).
Constitution of the Democratic Republic of Timor-Leste (2002).
Constitutional Amendment 23 of 2002, on Peace-Building on Bougainville – Autonomous Bougainville Government and Bougainville Referendum (2002) (PNG).
Council of Elders Act (1996) (BTG).
Decree Law Approving the Organic Law of the Procurement Follow-Up Commission and the Procurement Technical Secretariat No. 3/2010 (2010) (TL).
Decree Law Approving the Organic Structure of FALINTIL-FDTL No. 15/2006 (2006) (TL).
Decree Law Approving the Organic Structure of Timor-Leste's National Police (PNTL) No. 09/2009 (2009) (TL).
Decree Law Approving the Penal Code of the Democratic Republic of Timor-Leste No. 19/2009 (2009) (TL).

Decree Law Amending the Salary Regime of the Timor Leste National Police No. 48/2011 (2011) (TL).
Decree of the President of the Republic (Declaring a State of Emergency) No. 43/2008 (2008) (TL).
Decree of the President of the Republic (Presidential Pardon) No. 53/2008 (2008) (TL).
Decree of the President of the Republic (Presidential Pardon) No. 34/2009 (2009) (TL).
Decree of the President of the Republic (Presidential Pardon) No. 31/2010 (2010) (TL).
Decree of the President of the Republic (Presidential Pardon) No. 60/2010 (2010) (TL).
Decree Law on Amendment to the Regime of Promotions Within PNTL No. 35/2011 (2011) (TL).
Decree Law on the Legal Regime on the Use of Force No. 43/2011 (2011) (TL).
Decree Law on Community Authorities No. 5/2004 (2004) (TL).
Decree Law on Integrated District Development No. 4/2012 (2012) (TL).
Decree Law on Planning of Decentralised Development Programmes I and II No. 18/2011 (2011) (TL).
Decree Law on the General Regime of the National Program for the Development of Sucos (PNDS) No. 08/2013 (2013) (TL).
Decree Law on the Organic Structure of the Office of the Provedor for Human Rights and Justice No. 25/2011 (2011) (TL).
Decree Law – Statute for the Office of the Inspector-General No. 22/2009 (2009) (TL).
Draft law Establishing the Framework of the National Reparations Programme No. /II (TL).
Government Resolution Approving the Establishment of a National Mechanism to Accelerate Community Development No. 1/2012 (2012) (TL).
Government Resolution on Measures Aimed at Ensuring Public Order and Internal Security of the Country No. 35/2011 (2011) (TL).
Government Resolution on the Authorised Force Strength for Falintil-FDTL until 2020, No. 28/2011 (2011) (TL).
Government Resolution on the Extinction Martial Arts Groups No. 16/2013 (2013) (TL).
Head Tax Act (2007) (ABG).
Law Approving the Statute of the Civil Service No. 8/2004 (2004) (TL).
Law Approving the Statute of the Office of the Ombudsman for Human Rights and Justice No. 7/2004 (2004) (TL).
Law Authorising the President of the Republic to Declare a State of Siege No. 1/2008 (2008) (TL).
Law on Citizenship No. 9/2002 (2002) (TL).
Law on Community Leaderships and Their Election No. 3/2009 (2009) (TL).
Law on Immigration and Asylum No. 9/2003 (2003) (TL).
Law on Freedom of Assembly and Demonstration No. 1/2006 (2006) (TL).
Law on Internal Security No. 4/2010 (2010) (TL).
Law on National Defence No. 3/2010 (2010) (TL).
Law on National Security No. 2/2010 (2010) (TL).
Law on Territorial Administrative Division No. 11/2009 (2009) (TL).
Law on the Anti-Corruption Commission No. 08/2009 (2009) (TL).
Law on the Election of the National Parliament No. 6/2006 (2006) (TL).

Law on the Election of the President of the Republic No. 07/2006 (2006) (TL).
Law on the Juridical Regime Governing the Private Legal Profession and Lawyers Training No. 11/2008 (2008) (TL).
Law on the Organic Structure of the Organic Structure of the Office of the President No. 04/2006 (2006) (TL).
Law on the Practice of Martial Arts No. 10/2008 (2008) (TL).
Law on the Publication of Acts No. 1/2002 (2002) (TL).
Law on the Regulation of the State of Siege and Emergency No. 3/2008 (2008) (TL).
Legislative Authorisation on Criminal Procedure Matters No. 15/2005 (2005) (TL).
Legislative Authorisation on Criminal Matters No. 16/2005 (2005) (TL).
Liquor Control Act (2011) (ABG).
Mining (Bougainville Copper Agreement) Act (1967) (PNG).
Mining (Bougainville Copper Agreement) Act (1974) (PNG).
Ministerial Decree on Organs of the Integrated District Development Planning No. 8/2012 (2012) (TL).
Ministerial Decree on Elaboration of District Investment Plan No. 9/2012 (2012) (TL).
Native Village Government Councils Ordinance (1949) (Aust).
Native Local Government Councils Ordinance (1954) (Aust).
Organic Law of the Chamber of Audits of the Administrative, Fiscal, Auditors High Court, Law No. 9/2011 (2011) (TL).
Organic Law of the National Police of Timor-Leste (PNTL) No. 8/2004 (2004) (TL).
Organic Law of Timor-Leste's National Police (PNTL) No. 9/2009 (2009) (TL).
Organic Law on National and Local-Level Government Elections No. 3/1997 (1997) (PNG).
Organic Law on Peace-building in Bougainville – Autonomous Bougainville Government and Bougainville Referendum No. 29/2002 (2002) (PNG).
Organic Law on Provincial and Local-level Governments (1995) (PNG).
Papua New Guinea Act (1949) (Aust).
Papua New Guinea Constitution (1975) (PNG).
Parliamentary Resolution on the Rules of Procedure of the National Parliament of the Democratic Republic of Timor-Leste, Jornal da República nr 40, November 11, 2009.
Parliamentary Resolution on the emergency measures enacted by His Excellency the President of the Republic, Kay Rala Xanana Gusmão, in order to overcome the crisis, No. 12/2006 (2006) (TL).
Parliamentary Service Act (2009) (ABG).
Sales Tax (Beer and Cigarettes) Act (2011) (ABG).
Transport Infrastructure Act (2013) (ABG).
Village Courts Act (1973) (PNG).
UNTAET Directive No. 2001/3, *On the Establishment of Constitutional Commissions for East Timor*, UN Doc. UNTAET/DIR/2001/3, March 31, 2001.
UNTAET Regulation No. 1999/1, *On the Authority of the Transitional Administration in East Timor*, UN Doc. UNTAET/REG/1991/1, November 27, 1999.
UNTAET Regulation No. 1999/2, *On the Establishment of a National Consultative Council*, UN Doc. UNTAET/REG/1992/2, December 2, 1999.
UNTAET Regulation No. 2000/3 *On the Establishment of a Public Service Commission*, UN Doc. UNTAET/REG/2000/3, January 20, 2000.

UNTAET Regulation No. 2000/11, *On the Organization of Courts in East Timor* 2000/11, UN Doc. UNTAET/REG/2000/11, March 6, 2000.
UNTAET Regulation No. 2000/15, *On the Establishment of Panels with Exclusive Jurisdiction over Serious Criminal Offences*, UN Doc. UNTAET/REG/2000/15, June 6, 2000.
UNTAET Regulation No. 2000/23, *On the Establishment of the Cabinet of the Transitional Government in East Timor*, UN Doc. UNTAET/REG/2000/23, July 14, 2000.
UNTAET Regulation No. 2000/24, *On the Establishment of a National Council*, UN Doc. UNTAET/REG/2000/24, July 14, 2000.
UNTAET Regulation No. 2001/1, *On the Establishment of a Defence Force for East Timor*, UN Doc. UNTAET/REG/2001/1, January 31, 2001.
UNTAET Regulation No. 2001/2, *On the Election of a Constituent Assembly to Prepare a Constitution for an Independent and Democratic East Timor*, UN Doc. UNTAET/REG/2001/2, March 16, 2001.
UNTAET Regulation No. 2001/10, *On the Establishment of a Commission for Reception, Truth and Reconciliation in East Timor*, UN Doc. UNTAET/REG/2001/10, July 13, 2001.
UNTAET Regulation No. 2001/28, *On the Establishment of the Council of Ministers*, UN Doc. UNTAET/REG/2001/28, September 19, 2001.
UNTAT Regulation No. 2001/22, *On the Establishment of the East Timor Police Service*, UN Doc. UNTAET/REG/2001/22, August 10, 2001.

CASE LAW

Court of Appeal, *Ruling of the Court in Case No. 02/2003, On the Constitutionality of the Law on Immigration and Asylum*, June 30, 2003.
Court of Appeal, *Decision of the Court in Case No. 04/2008, On the Supervisory Process Abstract Constitutionality and Legality of Law 12/2008*, November 11, 2008.
Court of Appeal, *Ruling of the Court in Case No. 03/2008, On the Constitutionality of the Decree-Law no. 22/2008 of 16 July Establishing the Economic Stability Fund*, August 14, 2008.
Court of Appeal, *Ruling of the Court in Proc No. 01/P.Cautelar/2008, on Judge Ivo Rosa's Petition of Temporary Injunction*, December 31, 2008.
Court of Appeal, *Ruling of the Court in Case No. 01/2005, On the Constitutionality of the Law on Freedom of Assembly and Demonstration*, March 9, 2005.

BOUGAINVILLE PEACE PROCESS AGREEMENTS
(IN CHRONOLOGICAL ORDER)

Bougainville Agreement: Statements and Documents of Agreement between National Government and Provincial Government of North Solomons, August 7, 1976.
Agreement to End Hostilities on Bougainville (Bougainville Ceasefire Agreement), between the PNG government and the BRA, March 1, 1990.
Ona, F., on behalf of the Interim Government of the Republic of Bougainville, REQUEST FOR RECOGNITION OF BOUGAINVILLE AS AN INDEPENDENT REPUBLIC, letter to diplomatic missions in Port Moresby and

Bibliography

foreign governments, enclosing the "Declaration of Independence of the Republic of Bougainville," May 16, 1990.

Endeavour Accord on Dialogue and Return of Services to Bougainville, between the PNG government and the BIG/BRA, August 5, 1990.

Honiara Declaration on Peace, Reconciliation and Rehabilitation on Bougainville, between the PNG government and the BIG/BRA, January 23, 1991.

Kavieng Agreement, between the PNG government and chiefs from Buka Island, February 1991.

Honiara Commitment to Peace on Bougainville, between the PNG government and the BIG/BRA, September 3, 1994.

Honiara Ceasefire Agreement, between the PNG government and the BIG/BRA, September 8, 1994.

Arawa Resolution, agreed by the PNG government and representatives of the BRA, October 10, 1994.

Charter of Mirigini for a New Bougainville, between the PNG government, the North Nasioi Peace Committee, and several BRA commanders, November 25, 1994.

Waigani Communique, between the PNG government and the BTG, May 18, 1995.

Joint Communiqué, agreed upon by BTG and the BIG/BRA, December 18, 1995.

Sandline Agreement for the Provision of Military Assistance, between the Independent State of Papua New Guinea and Sandline International, January 31, 1997.

Burnham Declaration by Bougainville Leaders on the Re-Establishment of a Process for Lasting Peace and Justice on Bougainville, by the BIG/BRA and BTG/BRF, July 18, 1997.

Joint Communiqué: The Bougainville Leaders Meeting, Burnham, Christchurch, New Zealand, by the BIG/BRA and BTG/BRF, July 18, 1997.

Burnham Declaration – National Government Response, by the PNG government, undated.

Burnham II Preparatory Talks, Record of Understandings, between the PNG government, BIG/BRA, and BTG/BRF, October 10, 1997.

Bei isi noken pait, The Burnham Truce, between the PNG government, BIG/BRA, and BTG/BRF, October 10, 1997.

Second Official Preparatory Talks on Bougainville – Held In Cairns, Queensland Australia November 18–23 1997 Summary of Discussions, November 1997.

Cairns Commitment on Implementation of the Agreement Concerning the Neutral Regional Truce Monitoring Group (TBG) for Bougainville, between PNG government, Australian government, Fiji government, Vanuatu government, New Zealand government, BIG/BRA, and BTG/BRF, November 24, 1997.

Agreement between New Zealand, Papua New Guinea, Australia, Fiji, and Vanuatu Concerning the Neutral Truce Monitoring Group for Bougainville, between PNG government, Australian government, Fiji government, Vanuatu government, New Zealand government, December 5, 1997.

Lincoln Agreement on Peace, Security and Development on Bougainville, between the PNG government, BIG/BRA, and BTG/BRF, January 23, 1998 (acknowledged by the president of the UN Security Council, Statement by the President of the Security Council, UN Doc. S/PRST/1998/10, April 22, 1998).

Protocol Concerning the Peace Monitoring Group, Made Pursuant to the Agreement between Australia, Papua New Guinea, Fiji, New Zealand and Vanuatu

Concerning the Neutral Truce Monitoring Group for Bougainville, Done at Port Moresby on 5 December 1997, between PNG government, Australian government, Fiji government, Vanuatu government, New Zealand government, April 29, 1998.

Arawa Agreement Covering Implementation of the Ceasefire, Annex 1 to the Lincoln Agreement: Agreement Covering Implementation of the Ceasefire, between the PNG government, BIG/BRA, and BTG/BRF, April 30, 1998.

Buin Declaration of the Pan Bougainville Leaders Congress 20–22 August 1998, between women's representatives and chiefs from North, Central and South Bougainville, August 22, 1998.

Bougainville Peace Process Minute, December 14, 1998, recording agreement of the officials to the attached Annex 2 to the Lincoln Agreement Basic Agreement concerning the Bougainville Reconciliation Government (BRG), unsigned draft agreement, December 1998.

Hutjena Minute and "Fundamental Principles for the Future of Bougainville," agreed upon by the PNG government and the BPC, June 30, 1999.

Hutjena Record, agreed by the PNG government, BPC, and John Momis (as governor of Bougainville), December 15, 1999.

Greenhouse Memorandum, the Joint Bougainville Negotiating Position for Negotiations with the Government of Papua New Guinea, between the BPC, BIPG, and Leitana Council of Elders, December 14, 1999 (updated by the Bougainville Common Negotiating Position: Expanded Details, March 8, 2000).

Loloata Understanding, agreed by the PNG government, BPC, BIPG, and the Leitana Council of Elders, March 23, 2000.

Gateway Communiqué, agreed upon by the PNG government, BPC, and BIPG, June 9, 2000, attaching the Preliminary Working Draft of Proposal for a "Special Status" Agreement Between the Government of Papua New Guinea and the People of Bougainville, June 8, 2000.

Kokopo Agreement: Agreed Principles on Referendum, agreed by the PNG government, BPC, and BIPG, witnessed by Noel Sinclair, director, UNOMB, January 26, 2001.

Rotokas Record: Joint Bougainville Ex-combatants Agreement on Weapons Disposal, between the BRA and BRF, May 3, 2001.

Peace Process Consultative Committee Agreement on Weapons Disposal, between the PNG government, BRA, and BRA, May 9, 2001.

Bougainville Peace Agreement, between the PNG government, BPC, BIPG, BRA, and BRF, August 30, 2001.

Index

agonism – 39, 67, 348
Aliança da Maioria Parlamentar (AMP) – 112, 124, 132, 135, 137–8, 141–2, 145–7, 149, 150, 153–4, 156, 160, 162–4, 168, 171–2, 174, 177, 180–1, 190
Mari Alkatiri – 77, 80, 91–2, 97, 110–11, 120, 128–9, 134, 137–8, 145–6, 153, 156
Associacão Popular Democratica Timorense (APODETI) – 76, 81, 116
Associacão Social Democrata Timorense (ASDT) – 76, 91–2, 104, 107, 109–12, 118, 150
Australia – 6, 9–10, 64, 77, 111, 135, 195, 200–1, 204, 222, 231, 245, 259, 268, 336–7

Bahasa – 95, 105, 117, 120–1
Balibo Declaration – 76, 128
Banks, Angela – 70
Belo, Carlos – 102, 105, 110
Bere, Martenus – 187
Berman, Paul – 336
Bloku Governu Koligasaun (BGK) – 113, 124, 142, 146–7, 150, 153–4, 162, 164, 172, 174, 177, 180
Boege, Volker – 258
Bogenvil Resources Development Corporation – 280
Bougainville – 6
  Bougainville Agreement – 197
  churches – 206, 215, 231, 234, 254, 259–60, 270, 274–5, 283
  European colonization – 9–10, 195–6, 231, 234, 239, 248–9, 268
  constituent power
    citizenization – 251–8, 319–20
      ethos of constitutionalism – 251–3, 319
      electoral turnouts and strategic voting – 253–6
    other forms of political participation – 256–8
    public sphere – 258–60, 320–1
  national identity – 230, 236–40, 316–17
    citizenship – 238
    role of custom and tradition – 239–40
    national symbols – 234–6
    official historical narrative – 231–4
  constituted power
    Autonomous Bougainville Government (ABG) – 207, 261–73, 321–31
    accountability institutions – 279–80, 332
      Bougainville Leadership Code – 279
      Office of Bougainville Auditor-General – 279
      Office of Bougainville Ombudsman – 279
    Bougainville administration – 282–3
      delivery of public services – 280–7, 333–5
      transition to Bougainville public service – 282
    Bougainville Advisory Body – 267, 332
    decentralization – 267–73, 322–31
      Australian colonial system – 268
      Councils of Elders – 208, 268–73, 287, 290, 292–3, 323, 329
      district managers – 268
      Division of Local Level Government – 271, 294
      during the crisis – 269
      regional commissioners – 268
      Village Assemblies – 269–73, 287
    economic development – 283–7, 334–5
    elections – 229, 230, 251, 253–6, 273
      perception of democracy – 331–2
      reserved seats – 274–7
    Executive Council – 262–3, 267
    House of Representatives – 262–3, 266–7

396   Index

Bougainville – (cont.)
    law and order
        Bougainville Police Service (BPS) –
            287–92
        Community Auxiliary Police (CAPS) –
            287–91
    president – 262–3
    rule of law
        courts – 291–4
        alternative dispute resolution
            mechanisms – 293
        Bougainville High Court – 291, 296
        culture of impunity – 294–6, 341
        legal pluralism – 293–4, 336–9
        local justice mechanisms – 293, 335–6
            concerns over human rights –
                339–40
            supervision by formal justice
                institutions – 340
        Papua New Guinea Supreme Court –
            291, 296
        Papua New Guinea National Court –
            291, 296
        Papua New Guinea District Court –
            291–2, 294, 338, 340
        Village Courts – 268, 290, 292–4,
            336–8, 340
    transfer of powers – 263–6
constitution making – 9, 212–26
    adoption of constitution – 224–5, 312–13
    framework – 212–13, 216
    time frame – 213–14, 304
    Bougainville Constitutional Commission
        (BCC) – 212–24, 305
        selection of members – 214–16, 305–6
        drafting process – 216–19
        international involvement – 216, 224,
            310–12
        method of decision making – 218–19,
            306–7
        public participation/consultation – 7,
            216–17, 220–4, 308–10
        publicity and secrecy – 219–20, 307–8
    Bougainville Constituent Assembly – 212,
        217, 224–5
    interim nature of constitution – 225–6, 313
crisis – 6, 197–8
human rights – 296–7, 342–4
incorporation into Papua New Guinea – 10,
    196–7, 231
languages – 235–7, 239, 248
local sociopolitical practices – 206, 223, 233,
    238, 240, 256, 258, 261, 268–9, 273,
    277–9, 297, 304, 306, 308, 311, 314,
    322–3, 328, 331–2, 341–2
North Solomons Provincial Government –
    197–9, 249, 269

Panguna mine – 195, 197–8, 200, 204, 232,
    239, 243, 244, 249, 284–5, 299,
    334, 335
    Bougainville Copper Limited (BCL) –
        196–7
    Panguna Stakeholders' Hahela
        Understanding – 285
peace process – 200–4
    phase I – 201–3
        Burnham Declaration – 201–2
        Burnham Truce – 201, 241
        Lincoln Agreement – 201
    phase II – 203, 204
        Bougainville Peace Agreement – 204,
            205, 207–13, 216–17, 224, 226–7,
            241, 243, 245, 253, 255, 257–8,
            263–5, 275, 277, 279, 285–6, 289,
            294, 298–9, 307–8, 311
        amnesties and pardons – 202, 211,
            226, 294, 341–2
        autonomy – 6, 203–4, 207–12, 226,
            229, 232, 250, 255, 265, 287, 295,
            297–8
        referendum – 203–4, 210–11, 220,
            225–6, 232, 242, 255, 265, 276,
            284–5, 297–300
        weapons disposal process – 210–11,
            213, 227, 229, 275, 298
    public participation – 205–6
pre-colonization – 195
reconciliation – 233, 240–8, 250, 294–5,
    317–18
    during the peace and constitution making
        processes – 240–2, 318–19
    with the Me'ekamui people – 242–6
        Panguna Communiqué – 244
        Panguna Meeting Resolution – 244
    with Noah Musingku – 246–8
    since the crisis – 294–5
Republic of North Solomons – 196
self-determination – 10, 211, 231–3, 297–8,
    300
societal divisions – 248–51, 318–19
state building – 7, 10, 212, 297
uncertain political future – 297–300
unilateral declaration of independence –
    198
Bougainville Freedom Fighters (BFF) – 246–7
Bougainville Independence Party – 263
Bougainville interim government (BIG) –
    198–200, 202, 228, 235, 269
Bougainville interim provincial government
    (BIPG) – 203–5, 208, 212–14, 216,
    224–5, 229–30, 235, 241, 253–4, 260,
    263, 269, 286–7, 289
Bougainville Joint Assemblies – 204, 217, 222,
    224

Index

Bougainville People's Congress (BPC) – 202–5, 212–16, 224–5, 229–30, 235, 241, 254, 260
Bougainville People's Congress (BPC) party – 229, 255
Bougainville Reconciliation Government – 202, 219
Bougainville Resistance Forces (BRF) – 199–200, 206, 211, 215, 227–8, 240, 242, 246, 249, 275
Bougainville Revolutionary Army (BRA) – 198–200, 203, 205–6, 210, 215, 227–8, 240–4, 246, 275
Bougainville transitional government (BTG) – 199–200, 202, 228, 235, 269
Bougainville Transitional Team – 227

Calhoun, Craig – 27
Chambers, Simone – 53
Chan, Julius – 200
Cohen, Joshua – 56
Comissão de Acolhimento, Verdade e Reconciliacao (CAVR – Commission for Reception, Truth and Reconciliation) – 127–8, 188, 317, 342
Communitarianism – 33–4
Congresso Nacional de Reconstrução de Timor-Leste (CNRT) – 111–13, 130–2, 141, 153, 155–6, 165
Conselho Nacional da Resistencia Timorense (The CNRT) – 77, 80, 82, 88, 118
Consociationalism – 25, 249–50, 319
constitution making – 2, 40
  constituent legislature – 45
  collection and analysis of public feedback – 50
  in Afghanistan – 44, 46–7, 50–1
  in Australia – 64
  in Bolivia – 45, 66
  in Bosnia-Herzegovina – 42, 60
  in Brazil, 70–1
  in Cambodia – 42, 52
  in Canada – 64
  in Chad – 66
  in Colombia – 44
  in Ecuador – 49
  in Eritrea – 48–9, 64
  in Ethiopia – 64
  in Fiji – 64
  in Hungary – 43
  in Iceland – 49
  in Iraq – 42, 44, 50–1, 61, 66
  in Kenya – 47, 50, 54
  in Kosovo – 25, 51
  in Mali – 49
  in Namibia – 42
  in Nepal – 47
  in Poland – 43
  in Rwanda – 48, 50, 53
  in South Africa – 43, 47–9, 54, 58, 70
  in Thailand – 64
  in Uganda – 49–50, 61, 70
  in the United States – 64
  in Venezuela – 42, 45–6, 66
  in Zimbabwe – 58
  interim constitutions – 53–4, 313
  implementation of constitution – 54
  international involvement – 50–2, 310–12
  manner in which constitution adopted – 52–3, 312–13
  method of decision making – 46–7, 306–7
  importance of a framework – 41–2
  legal mandate for public participation – 50
  methods of public participation – 48, 308–10
  nature of the body – 43–6, 304–5
  publicity and secrecy – 47–8, 307–8
  timing of public participation – 49, 308–10
  role of public participation (see constituent process)
  time frame – 42–3, 304
  timing and method of elections – 44–5, 305–6
constitutional patriotism – 23
constitutional identity – 31–2
constitutionalism – 4, 20, 24–5
  ethos of – 54, 61, 319
constitutions
  as social contract – 19
  definition – 2
  foundational role – 2
  role in nation building – 30
  technical role – 2
constituent power – 20, 21–32, 312–14, 316–21
constituent process – 5, 38–40, 54–63, 303, 313, 345, 349–50
  addresses grievances and promotes reconciliation – 59–61, 317–18
  builds a sense of political community – 58–9, 315, 317–18, 320–1, 345, 349–50
  builds a sense of national identity – 59, 316–17
  criticisms of, – 63
    challenge meaning of participation – 68
    conceals power relations and biases – 64–5
    elitist – 63–4
    expense and institutional capacity – 67–8
    instrumentalist – 66–7
    nonparticipation – 68–9
    reduces political trust – 65
    unclear how take feedback into account – 69–70

constituent process – (cont.)
  unrealistic expectations – 68–9
  effect on constitution-making process – 57
  effect on contents of constitution – 62–3
  extensive participation – 63
  minimal participation – 63
  moderate participation – 63
  role in citizenization – 61–2, 319–20
  role of, – 54, 55, 57
  roots in deliberative democracy – 56
constituted power – 20, 26, 32–3, 315, 321–44
Council for the Popular Defence of the Democratic Republic of Timor-Leste (CPD-RDTL) – 90

decentralization – 322–31
  challenges – 326–8
  of development projects – 325
  divisive effects – 325
  participation by women – 328–9
  regional governments – 330
  role in ameliorating tensions – 326
  role in extending democracy – 324
deliberative democracy – 56–7
discursive participation – 57
de Mello, Sergio Vieira – 78–9, 85
do Amaral, Francisco Xavier – 76, 109
do Araujo, Fernando "Lasama" – 112, 128, 140–1
Downer, Alexander – 204

East Timor Public Administration (ETPA) – 97, 101
East Timor Transitional Administration (ETTA) – 79, 80, 94, 97
Elazar, Daniel – 20
Elkins, Zachary – 61
Elster, Jon – 41, 43, 48
ethnies – 29
everyday (the) – 36

Forças Armadas de Libertação Nacional de Timor-Leste (FALINTIL) – 76–7, 115, 118–19, 127, 131–5, 147
Fraser, James – 216–17
Franck, Thomas – 55–6
Frente de Libertação de Moçambique (FRELIMO) – 77
Frente Revolucionaria de Timor Leste Independente (FRETILIN) – 76–7, 80–1, 83–4, 88–98, 101–2, 104, 106–8, 110–15, 117–25, 127–32, 135, 137–8, 141–2, 145–7, 149–55, 158–9, 167, 172–3, 181, 183, 187, 189–90, 305–8, 310–12, 316, 321–2
Frente-Mudança – 113, 129

Galtung, Jospeh – 59
Gambetta, Diego – 56
Getsi, Marceline – 277
Ginsburg, Tom – 63
Gusmão, Kay Rala Xanana – 77, 80–1, 83, 88–9, 91, 98, 102, 109–13, 123–4, 128–31, 134–5, 137–8, 140, 153, 155–7, 186–8, 190, 321
Guterres, Francisco "Lu-Olo" – 92, 111–12, 140–1

Hart, Vivien – 55
human rights – 33, 342–4

Indonesia – 6, 10, 76–8, 81, 87, 90, 95, 114–17, 119–31, 133, 138, 140–1, 157–8, 172, 180–1, 185–7
Indonesia-Timor Leste Truth and Friendship Commission – 187–8
integrative power-sharing – 25
International Force for East Timor (InterFET) – 78
International Institute for Democracy and Electoral Assistance – 55, 63
International Stabilization Force (Timor-Leste) – 6, 111, 113, 135, 349

Jackson, Vicky – 64
Jacobsen, Gary – 32
Joint Supervisory Body (JSB) (Bougainville) – 209, 227, 264–5, 286
Jennings, Ivor – 21
judiciary – 32

Kabui, Joseph – 198, 202–3, 215, 219, 225, 229–30, 244, 252, 254, 259, 264, 278–80, 284, 334
Klibur Oan Timor Aswain (KOTA) – 76, 92, 107, 140
Koike, Damien – 291
Kokopo Communique – 265
Konnou Agreement – 291

Labour Party – 255
legal pluralism – 36, 336–9
  recognition of customary law – 338–9
legislature – 32
Lera, Joe – 266, 332
liberal-local hybrid approach – 4–5, 35–6
  criticisms of – 37, 38
  relationship with decentralization – 322–4
  to state building – 7, 35–6, 345–8
liberal peace – 1, 33
liberalism – 22–4, 32–3
  role of democracy – 32
  reconciliation with pluralism – 34
local – 36–7

Lorosa'e – 130
Loromonu – 130
Lugabai, Thomas – 277

de Maistre, Joseph – 20
Me'ekamui – 215, 242–6
    Me'ekamui Defence Force (MDF) – 243–6, 285, 291
    Me'ekamui Government of Unity (MGU) – 244–5, 247, 255–6, 285
    Original Me'ekamui Government (OMG) – 244–5, 247, 285
Melanesia – 9
Miriki, Andrew – 278
Miriori, Philip – 244
Moehler, Devra – 61
Momis, John – 202–3, 225, 230, 251–2, 254–5, 259, 262, 264–5, 278, 286, 289, 298–9
Musingku, Noah – 242, 246–8

nation – 27
nation building – 11, 27–31
nation making – 30
National Consultative Council (Timor-Leste) – 79
National Council (Timor-Leste) – 79–85, 97–8, 106, 128
nationalism – 26–7
    ethno-symbolism – 29–30
    modernism – 27–8
    perennialism – 29
    primordialism – 29
national identity – 26–7
Negara Timor Raya – 116
New Bougainville Party – 230, 251, 255, 262, 278
New Zealand – 200–1, 290, 300
NGO Forum – 99
Nisira, Patrick – 274

Ona, Francis – 197, 198, 242–4, 246

Paine, Thomas – 19–20
Papua New Guinea – 6, 9–10
    constitution – 197, 208, 210–13, 216–17, 226–7, 230, 237–8, 263, 266, 277, 285, 291, 296, 340, 342, 347
    electoral system – 274
    independence – 196
    Papua New Guinea Defence Force (PNGDF) – 198–200, 202, 227, 249, 298
    relationship with the Autonomous Bougainville Government – 252, 263–7, 279, 282, 284–7, 291–4, 297–300, 333, 338, 340, 349

    role in the Bougainville constitution-making process – 212–26, 237–8, 311
    role in the Bougainville crisis – 197–200, 232, 323
    role in the Bougainville peace process – 200–12
Royal Papua New Guinea Constabulary (RPNGC) – 287, 289
Partido Democratica (PD) – 89, 91, 104, 111–13, 128, 132, 140
Partido do Povo de Timor (PPT) – 90
Partido Nacionalista Timorense – 165
Partido Democratika Rpublika de Timor – 165
Partido Kmanek Haburas Unidade Nasional Timor Oan – 165
Partido Socialista Democratica (PSD) – 85, 91, 104, 111–12, 150
Partido Socialista de Timor (PST) – 88, 92, 107
Peace Monitoring Group (PMG) (Bougainville) – 201–2, 205, 220, 227
Penai, Nick – 278
pluralism – 34, 39
Polisi Republik Indonesia (POLRI) – 133, 188
political community – 5, 8, 19, 23–4, 26–8, 30, 39, 58–9, 61–2, 64, 71, 315, 317–21
popular sovereignty – 3–5, 11, 17–22, 27, 30, 32–3, 38–9, 53, 108, 144, 151, 185, 273, 308, 346

Ramos-Horta, José – 77, 89, 111–13, 124, 128–9, 132, 135, 137–8, 140–1, 149, 153, 156–7, 174, 178, 186–8
reconciliation – 55, 59–60, 305, 313, 317–18
republicanism – 23–4
Richmond, Oliver P. – 335
Rosenfeld, Michel – 31
rule of law – 20, 32, 36, 315, 335–42

Sarei, Alexis – 197
Saunders, Cheryl – 51–2
secession – 24–5
secretary-general (United Nations) – 80, 174, 187
self-determination – 21–5
Semoso, Fidelis – 266–7
Sieyès, Abbé de – 20, 24
Skate, Bill – 200, 203
Sinato, Gerard – 215
Smith, Anthony – 27
social contract – 2, 17–21
Solomon Islands – 9, 231, 235
state (the) – 18
state building (n.) 1–9, 17, 23, 32,
    liberal peace – 7, 32
    liberal-local hybrid – 33–28
Stokes, Susan – 56

Tanis, James – 230, 244, 251, 255, 263–4, 274, 280
Taylor, Charles – 27
Timor-Leste – 6
  1974 civil war – 76, 87, 105, 128
  attempted assassination of president and prime minister – 6, 112, 135, 138, 176, 187
  cash payment schemes – 135, 136, 174, 334
  Catholic Church – 81, 83, 101–2, 105, 116, 117, 120, 146
  citizenization – 136–44, 319–20
    electoral turnouts and strategic voting – 140–1
    ethos of constitutionalism – 136–40, 319
    other forms of political participation – 141–3
    public sphere – 144–7, 320–1
  constituent power
    citizenship – 125–6
    national identity – 113, 119–26, 316–17
    official historical narrative – 113–17, 177, 316, 318
    national symbols – 117–19
  constituted power – 148–64, 321–31
    accountability institutions – 167–9, 332
      Anti-Corruption Commission – 168
      Office of the Inspector-General – 168
      Procurement Commission – 168
      Provedor does Direitos Humanos e da Justiça – 168, 189, 340, 344
    Council of Liurais (proposals for) – 332–3
    decentralization – 157–64, 322–31
      administrative decentralization – 159–62
      aldeias – 157–64, 178, 183, 328
      developmental decentralization – 162–4, 325
      Indonesian system – 157
      political decentralization – 158–9
      Portuguese system – 157
      sucos – 157–64, 178, 183–4, 324–9, 337
      UNTAET system – 158
    FALINTIL-Forças de Defesa de Timor Leste (F-FDTL – FALINTIL-Defence Force of Timor-Leste) – 118, 132, 133, 134, 135, 175, 176, 177,
    electoral system – 164–6
      perception of democracy – 331–2
    government (executive) – 150–4
      delivery of public services – 170–4, 333–5
    law and order – 175–9
      Policia Nacional de Timor-Leste (PNTL) – 133–5, 142, 175–8, 182–3, 189–90, 336, 344, 348
    Local justice mechanisms – 178, 182–5, 336
      concerns over human rights – 339, 340
      draft Customary Law – 185, 337–8, 340
      kablehan – 178, 182, 184, 336
      nahe biti – 86–7, 123–4, 127–8, 182, 336
      tarabandu – 123–4, 177–8, 182, 184, 327, 336
      supervision by formal justice institutions – 340
    Parliament – 148–52
    president – 154–7
    rule of law – 179–85
      Ad Hoc Human Rights Court for Timor-Leste – 186
      amnesties – 186, 341–2
      commuted sentences – 186–7
      Court of Appeal – 156, 179–82, 187, 190
      courts – 179–82
      culture of impunity – 185–6, 341
      District Courts – 179
      High Administrative, Taxation and Audit Court – 179
      legal pluralism – 184, 336, 337, 338, 339
      Office of the Prosecutor General – 168, 180, 186
      Supreme Court of Justice – 179
  constitution-making – 9, 80
    civic education program – 85–7, 309
    Constituent Assembly – 82–107, 305
      adoption of constitution – 107, 312–13
      drafting process – 92–7
      election – 83–91, 305, 306
      international involvement – 105–7, 310–12
      legislative council – 97
      method of decision-making – 95–6, 306–7
      proposals for interim constitution – 108, 313
      public participation – 98–105, 308–10
      publicity and secrecy – 97–8, 307–8
      Systematization and Harmonization Committee – 93–4, 104–6
    Constitutional Commission – 98–101
    time frame – 80–2, 304
    type of body – 82–3
  economic development – 171–4, 334, 335
  elections – 111–13, 132, 135, 137
  human rights – 188–90, 342–4
  independence – 6, 109
  Indonesian occupation – 6, 10, 76–7, 87, 95, 114–18, 120–3, 127, 131, 140, 181, 185, 323, 341

languages – 95, 105, 117, 120–2, 130, 149, 172, 180–1, 309, 316
local sociopolitical practices – 79, 123, 124, 127, 157, 159–60, 164, 166–7, 169, 177, 183–4, 190, 322–5, 328, 331–2, 338, 341, 345
Portuguese colonization – 9–10, 75–6, 87, 114, 117–21, 130, 157
popular consultation – 77–8, 84–5, 88, 118, 126, 130–1, 186
pre-colonization – 75
reconciliation – 126–30, 317–18
   between pro-independence and pro-integration supporters – 126–7
   between political elites – 128–30
security crisis (2006) – 6, 110–11, 124, 129, 134–7, 141, 147, 156, 163, 166, 171, 174–7, 186, 316–18, 320
self-determination attempts – 10
societal divisions – 130–6, 176–7, 318–19
state building – 10, 78–80
unilateral declaration of independence – 76
Togel, James – 266
Toroansi, Magdalene – 278
Transitional Government (Timor-Leste) – 79
Truce Monitoring Group (TMG) – 201–2, 205, 242

Uma, Chris – 244
United Nations (UN) – 6–7, 9–10, 21, 50, 77–8, 80, 83, 108, 171, 175, 177, 186, 196, 231, 304, 310–11, 349
United Nations Development Programme (UNDP) – 55, 179, 185, 281, 283

United Nations Integrated Mission in Timor-Leste (UNMIT) – 110, 113, 175, 185–6
   Serious Crime Investigation Team – 186
United Nations Mission of Support in East Timor (UNMISET) – 109–10, 186,
United Nations Observer Mission on Bougainville (UNOMB) – 201–2, 211, 213, 227, 229
United Nations Office in Timor-Leste – 110
United Nations Security Council – 78, 80, 81, 186
United Nations Transitional Administration in East Timor (UNTAET) – 78–110, 126, 132–3, 158, 175, 181, 185, 305–6, 308, 311–12, 341
   Special Panels for Serious Crimes – 185–6
   Transitional Administrator – 78–9, 82, 85, 89, 97, 99, 100, 106, 127, 181
União Democratica Timorense (UDT) – 76–7, 81, 90–1, 104, 111, 115, 128
Unidade Nacional Democrátia da Resistência Timorense – 115
United States Institute of Peace – 55
uti possidetis juris – 22

Vasconcelos, Jose Maria ("Taur Matan Ruak") – 112, 141, 156–7, 174, 177

Watawi, Joseph – 252, 256
Weber, Max – 18
Widner, Jennifer – 41, 55, 60, 63
Wisai Liberation Movement (WILMO) – 291
Wilson, Woodrow – 21

Yack, Bernard – 27

For EU product safety concerns, contact us at Calle de José Abascal, 56–1°,
28003 Madrid, Spain or eugpsr@cambridge.org.

www.ingramcontent.com/pod-product-compliance
Ingram Content Group UK Ltd.
Pitfield, Milton Keynes, MK11 3LW, UK
UKHW011328060825
461487UK00005B/416